- This text also features *a chapter about various differences in speaking ability* that limit students' literacy, such as communication apprehension and language delays.
- With chapters on how to diagnose and remediate writing, spelling, grammar, speaking, and listening difficulties, readers can *instantly implement the research and content within their classrooms.*

▪ End-of-Chapter Features WITHDRAWN

Chapter Problems and Discussion Questions

End-of-chapter problems and discussion questions enable students to apply what they have learned, while professors can use them in their classes and practicing teachers can use them in a book study.

Chapter Summaries and Key Terminology

Each chapter ends with a summary, as well as a *practical list of key terms* that allows readers to assess their immediate recall of the definitions by checking those they know. Page numbers are cited so that readers may readily look up definitions and see the words in context, refreshing their memories before moving on.

Case Studies with Questions and Answer Key

A vivid case study at the end of each chapter tells the story of a real life classroom situation. In doing so, it also reflects and demonstrates the issues presented in the preceding chapter. Provoking questions follow each case study and readers can check their responses against those in the Answer Key provided at the end of the text.

Thinking and Writing about What You Have Learned

At the end of each chapter is a section containing questions and activities designed to carry concepts into the classroom. Thoughtful questions inspire readers to make connections and apply what they've read, stimulating them to stretch their minds and go one step beyond simple recall of the text. *Activities are taken from real-life experiences* and include answers from teachers who have actually made the decision or confronted the issues being questioned. Readers can thus compare their ideas and solutions to those of other professionals.

Web Resources: Onto the Information Superhighway

This new feature will bring both you and your students out of the classroom and directly onto the Information Superhighway of the World Wide Web. Most chapters conclude with these sections, which *list a variety of useful websites and/or include valuable literacy activities that use materials found on the web.* The websites relate to topics within the chapter, giving readers both direction and easy access to additional material that is only a click away. In some cases, the author even provides quick summaries of the sites.

second edition

LITERACY DIFFICULTIES

Diagnosis and Instruction for Reading Specialists and Classroom Teachers

Cathy Collins Block
Texas Christian University

Boston I New York I San Francisco
Mexico City I Montreal I Toronto I London I Madrid I Munich I Paris
Hong Kong I Singapore I Tokyo I Cape Town I Sydney

Series Editor: Aurora Martínez Ramos
Editorial Assistant: Beth Slater
Senior Marketing Manager: Elizabeth Fogarty
Editorial-Production Service: Omegatype Typography, Inc.
Manufacturing Buyer: JoAnne Sweeney
Composition and Prepress Buyer: Linda Cox
Cover Administrator: Linda Knowles
Electronic Composition: Omegatype Typography, Inc.

Library of Congress Cataloging-in-Publication Data

Block, Cathy Collins.
    Literacy difficulties : diagnosis and instruction for reading specialists and classroom teachers/ Cathy Collins Block—2nd ed.
        p. cm.
    Includes bibliographical references and indexes.
    ISBN 0-205-34385-6
    1. Reading disability.   2. Reading—Remedial teaching.   3. Reading—Ability testing.   I. Title.

LB1050.5 .B56 2003
371.91'44—dc21

2002023069

Printed in the United States of America
10 9 8 7 6 5 4 3 2 1   07 06 05 04 03 02

Photo credits
p. 1: Spencer Grant/PhotoEdit; pp. 17, 31, 263, 393: Will Hart; p. 54: Frank Siteman/PhotoEdit; p. 80: Mary Kate Denny/PhotoEdit; pp. 103, 318, 454: David Young-Wolff/PhotoEdit; p. 141: Jim Cummins/Getty Images, Inc.; p. 199: Will Hart/PhotoEdit; p. 228: Myrleen Ferguson Cate/PhotoEdit; pp. 358, 416: Tony Freeman/PhotoEdit

This book is dedicated to my loving and supportive husband, Stan Block, who shares and contributes to every goal I reach; my wonderful mother, Jo Ann Zinke, my sister, Wanda Zinke, and my graduate assistant, Rebecca Johnson, who worked by my side at every stage of this book's creation; my strong family, Michael Donegan, Michelle, Reggie, Paige, and Reid Goldsmith, Randy Block, Maury and Rosalyn Wolfson, and Donna, Jordan, Connor, and Douglas Cowman, who add joy to my life.

BRIEF CONTENTS

CONTENTS

part 2   Conditions That Can Impede Literacy Development   54

part 3   Instructional Adaptations in Reading   141

10. ENHANCING COMPREHENSION 318

11. ASSISTING RELUCTANT WRITERS 358

part 5   Specialized Adaptations   454

14. SUPPORT FOR SPECIAL PROBLEMS   454

PREFACE

The purpose of *Literacy Difficulties: Diagnosis and Instruction for Reading Specialists and Classroom Teachers,* Second Edition, is to serve as a primary textbook for undergraduate and graduate courses concerning remedial reading instruction. The book is designed to prepare teachers to meet the reading and writing needs of students whose progress is not moving as rapidly as their peers'.

This second edition has several unique features. First, it introduces a continuum of development that eliminates the tendency to assign negative labels to students with literacy difficulties. This developmental continuum replaces connotations that students are "remedial" with descriptions of methods that use the strengths those students demonstrate to overcome problems. Special boxes of information for reading specialists, classroom teachers, reading recovery teachers, and tutors have been added throughout the book.

Second, this second edition presents instructional strategies to build reading, writing, and speaking abilities. Because many of today's developmental reading and writing programs are integrated, new strategies are needed to advance students' literacy abilities in an integrated fashion. This book provides such instructional assistance. These strategies have been shown to advance students' literacy, and students have reported that they also "made us want to learn." Thus, the information in this textbook can be used in integrated language arts programs, self-contained classrooms, small group settings, tutorial conferences, pull-out programs, and clinical programs.

Third, the instruction in this book addresses literacy differences using a literature-based approach to instruction. It contains authentic assessment instruments followed by guided practice activities that mirror the realities of the classroom. These assessments emphasize the need to precede instruction for special students with careful observations. These observations enable us to understand each student's speaking, reading, and writing strengths and needs. At least 12 new assessment methods not present in other textbooks concerning literacy challenges can be found in this second edition of *Literacy Difficulties.*

Another special feature of the second edition is an increased focus on cognitive, affective, social, and cultural factors that create differences in literacy abilities. Included are two chapters on writing development for students who have difficulty with composing, revising, spelling, and handwriting. The book also contains a chapter that describes various differences in speaking ability, such as communication apprehension and language delays, that limit students' literacy. Middle and high school applications are also new to this edition.

Last, the text has several features that encourage readers to learn the information it contains. Each chapter begins with an overview and list of key points. The overview allows preservice/in-service teachers to pose questions that will be answered in the chapter and to read key points before they begin the chapter text. Several chapters also contain Resource Cards of recommended selections of children's literature that can be used to diagnose and instruct the topics described in those chapters.

Each chapter ends with a summary and a list of vocabulary terms. Readers can assess their immediate recall of the definitions by checking those they know. Page numbers are cited so that readers may refresh their memories if they are not clear about a term's meaning before moving on to the next chapter. Each chapter also includes at least one Case Study. Most chapters have a feature, "Onto the Information Superhighway," that either lists useful websites or includes literacy activities that use materials found on the Internet.

Also at the end of each chapter is a section entitled "Thinking and Writing about What You Have Learned." This section contains activities designed to carry concepts into the classroom. These activities are taken from real-life experiences and include answers from teachers who actually made the decision or confronted the issues being questioned. In this way, readers can compare their ideas and solutions to those of other professionals. [An Instructor's Manual with Test Bank (ISBN: 0-205-37881-1) accompanies the text with concept outlines as well as test items.]

■ Acknowledgments

I want to express my appreciation to all my students who contributed to this book by challenging my thinking, reviewing the final draft, and supplying real-world tests of the activities. I also extend my deepest gratitude to Tom Caron, Marshall University, Graduate College; Sharon Y. Cowan, East Central University; and Margaret Bell Davis, Eastern Kentucky University. The insights they gave in their reviews shaped this book to become more comprehensive and valuable for educators. I appreciate the friendship, professionalism, and wisdom of Aurora Martínez and Beth Slater, acquisitions editor and editorial assistant for this book. They made working on this edition a pleasure.

c h a p t e r 1

These third graders are learning to comprehend material written at their grade level. Their teacher is using the activities and principles in Chapter 1.

Teaching to Remove the Remedial Reader Label

Dear Dr. Block,

I now realize that the diagnostic process is not solely the understanding of the reading/writing process, the reading/writing developmental continuum, and the context variables of instruction, but is my willingness to deal with these complexities as they interact for every student. Teaching has become much more than designing lessons. For me, it involves the combining and recombining of information about individual students in order to solve the complex challenges that confront each child's literacy in a constantly changing environment.

Could you send me more information about how I can assist readers and writers to become more able meaning-makers?

Thank you,
Bill Fuller, fourth grade teacher

■ Chapter Overview: Key Points

The purpose of this chapter is to describe the importance of teachers for students who face literacy challenges. As educators, we have only recently begun to understand how much teachers can do to disentangle the intermingled needs of students who do not read, write, or speak as well as they desire. By the end of this chapter, you will know the following:

- Stages of reading and writing development and programs that enhance students' literacy

- How to deploy successful teacher actions such as removing physical and psychological space between you and your students

- How to hold discovery discussions that address individual students' literacy needs

- How to adapt curriculum based on literacy-challenged students' interests and needs

- How to model and scaffold effectively for less accomplished literacy users

- How to reflect questions back to students

- Three beliefs of exemplary teachers—teachers meeting the literacy needs of students whose developmental pace is different from that of the majority of their classmates

◼ Who Are Students with Special Literacy Needs?

This book does not discuss the needs of highly successful readers and writers. Nor does it describe instruction for those who already guide their reading/writing/speaking effectively, who value the knowledge they gain through literacy, and who are progressing along the developmental continuum at a pace that is not interfering with their comprehension or enjoyment of literacy. Those students can usually depend on their own literacy strategies to obtain meaning without additional external supports.

Instead, this book discusses the special needs of **average readers/writers**—those who gain meaning from text and engage in written and oral assignments without aid, but who need special support to realize ultimate value from, and joy in, their literacy. It also discusses the special needs of **externally prompted and externally supported readers/writers**—those previously labeled as "remedial readers." Any student who has fallen, is falling, or is likely to fall between the cracks in the traditional developmental reading program will benefit from the special support, observation, diagnosis, assessment, and instruction described in this book. These students experience difficulties that have not been removed by previous instructional strategies. Many children will seem withdrawn because of frustrations inherent in most of their reading, writing, and speaking encounters. Without your support (and the special instruction described in this book), these students may not have access to the information necessary to read and write proficiently (Baker, 2001; Kintgen, Kroll, & Rose, 1988). Such students are not self-initiating literacy for pleasure or information, and they often sit on the fringe of reading and writing groups.

Stages of Literacy Achievement

The literacy continuum that follows is based on research conducted at the Northeast Regional Laboratory (Lazear, 1994), the Kentucky Department of Education (KIRIS Descriptors, 1994), the Standards and Assessment Development and Implementation Council of the State of Colorado (1995); and the Texas Center for Reading and Language Arts (Osborn & Chard, 2001). Each of these groups identified the following sets of behavior that characterize students at different stages of literacy achievement.

STAGE 1: EMERGENT READING AND WRITING. Students at this point on the literacy continuum are beginning to realize that print has meaning. They are becoming aware

Literacy Continuum*

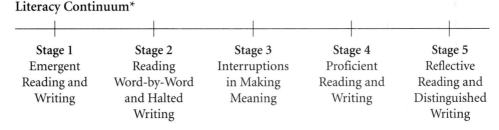

Stage 1	Stage 2	Stage 3	Stage 4	Stage 5
Emergent Reading and Writing	Reading Word-by-Word and Halted Writing	Interruptions in Making Meaning	Proficient Reading and Writing	Reflective Reading and Distinguished Writing

*When confronted with new material, even proficient readers/writers can move backward along the continuum.

of the sound-to-symbol relationship in English words. Students pass to Stage 2 as soon as they realize that letters are different from numbers, print words represent their spoken counterparts, printed text is read from left to right, and English follows syntactical principles. Students who don't reach Stage 2 by age 7 are likely *not* to experience grade-appropriate, pleasure-filled comprehension.

STAGE 2: READING AND WRITING WORD-BY-WORD. At this level, readers and writers demonstrate a limited awareness of audience, purpose, and literal meaning. Ideas are comprehended only occasionally, and written expressions either ramble or are weakly organized. These readers/writers recall or write limited or unrelated details and show only rudimentary understanding of correct sentence structure and wording. Mechanical errors usually are disproportionate to the length and complexity of written pieces. The amount of meaning gained from reading is dwarfed by the amount of time and effort needed to construct it. Readers at this point on the literacy continuum usually relegate the majority of attention to decoding and encoding single words. This effort often limits the energy available to organize writings and comprehend while reading. Although all readers/writers pass through this stage, students who have not moved beyond it before third grade will profit from the special supports and activities in this textbook. (It is important to remember that readers/writers of any age often revert to this level of ability when the material contains many unfamiliar vocabulary terms. The difference is, however, that they return to higher levels of ability unaided when the challenging reading or writing is completed.)

STAGE 3: READING AND WRITING WITH INTERRUPTED MEANING-MAKING. At this stage, readers/writers are able to establish but have trouble maintaining meaning and purpose through clear communication with an audience. These readers/writers demonstrate a logical focus of thoughts. The ideas they develop may include some personal reflection. Details supporting main points, however, are unelaborated or repetitious. Simplistic sentence structure and language also characterize this performance level. While decoding or written convention errors may be present, they usually do not interfere with making meaning. Students unable to move beyond this level of literacy ability through their regular reading program will profit from the activities in this book.

STAGE 4: READING AND WRITING PROFICIENCY. Proficient readers/writers can produce fully developed, focused responses to a reading and complete a focused piece of writing. In addition, their ideas contain elaborations and analyses. These readers/writers include relevant details, support main points, understand sentence structure, and choose words that contribute to the effectiveness of the communication. Few decoding and written convention errors are evident relative to the length and complexity of the material.

STAGE 5: REFLECTIVE, EXPERT READING AND DISTINGUISHED WRITING. At this performance level, readers/writers develop ideas with insight and perception. They organize thoughts with care and precision and support their theme with elaborated, pertinent details. Both complex sentence structures and sophisticated word choices enhance the overall effectiveness of their readings and writings. At the distinguished level, readers/writers have mastered control of decoding, literal/inferential/applied comprehension, and writing mechanics.

Programs That Address Literacy Needs

To better understand readers/writers at the five literacy stages, envision how students learn to ride a bike. Before they sit on their first tricycle, they will likely have seen many models of people enjoying bicycle riding. They will have expressed a desire to learn to do so themselves (emergent reading and writing, Stage 1). However, most students need modeling and support as they learn each movement to propel a bicycle (reading and writing single words, Stage 2). Once students can ride without training wheels, they no longer want parents running beside them as they ride (reading and writing with interrupted meaning-making, Stage 3), even if they fall occasionally. Only when bike riding becomes a pleasurable and valuable self-selected pursuit in their lives do they become internally guided riders (and proficient or distinguished readers, Stages 4 and 5).

The purpose of this book is to provide effective teaching actions and instructional activities for less accomplished students at all stages of literacy achievement. One key to the success of these activities is that they eliminate the student humiliation of having a teacher telling them the words in front of their peers. Another reason this book was written was to remove the negative connotations associated with students whose literacy developmental pace is different from that of the majority of their peers. This book is based on the premise that with proper support all pupils can become proficient, even expert, readers and writers.

In like manner, this text is not specifically designed to describe traditional approaches to reading instruction, or programs that would be identified as developmental. **Developmental reading/writing instruction** refers to broad, comprehensive reading programs designed for the majority of students in a school. The name is derived from the fact that activities are designed to meet the average literacy and developmental needs of students at a specific age. When this instruction is not effective for all students, it is necessary to move beyond the basic developmental program. This additional instruction was traditionally called a **remedial reading program.** To remove the remedial reading label, throughout this book we will refer to such instruction as Tier 1 supports, Tier 2 supports, Tier 3 supports, and Tier 4 supports, or alternative, adapted instruction.

Adapted instruction, defined as special teaching, instructional, and curriculum approaches (Tier 1) designed to modify the pace (for students who learn with less speed than the majority of their peers), focuses on different learning strengths. As shown in Figure 1.1, these personalized approaches begin as Tier 1 supports, so as to become the least intrusive. They occur in self-contained heterogeneous groups in which all students are fully participating, respected members. Tier 1 supports usually occur in the presence of other students and are performed by masterful teachers who adapt instruction as soon as they observe that a student needs an alternative strategy to learn a new literacy concept.

Tier 2 supports are the second least intrusive types. They also occur in small groups. In these groups, however, special student needs are addressed through personalized, teacher interventions. Tier 2 supports usually occur in a self-contained classroom setting involving heterogeneously grouped students, or in special resource rooms where students of similar needs meet for adapted instruction. Several forms of Tier 2 supports

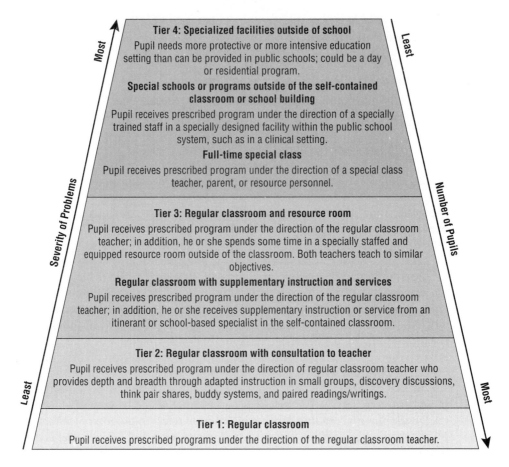

FIGURE 1.1 Support Tiers

exist, including one-to-one conferences between a student and teacher (as described in Chapter 4), needs-based groups with a teacher (as described in Chapter 8), carefully planned peer interactions (as described in Chapter 8), individualized instruction, team teaching, and cross-age tutoring. The benefit of Tier 1 and 2 supports is that students in these groups are less likely to be identified as "different" by peers than if they are placed in Tier 3 or 4 supports, as illustrated in Figure 1.1.

Tier 3 supports take students out of their regular classroom to meet with specialists. These specialists can be reading consultants, reading diagnosticians, directors of special programs, psychiatrists, psychologists, physicians, speech therapists, Chapter 1/ Title 1 teachers (federally funded program for students who read at least two grade levels below their grade placement), early prevention program personnel (as described in Chapter 14), resource teachers (usually paid through special education funding), or community agency staff members. In Tier 3 supports, an adjunct adapted program is added to the developmental reading program. To be most effective, educators should plan the adapted program in conjunction with the teacher who is delivering the developmental program for each pupil.

Tier 4 supports occur outside of school and school hours. Recently, Tier 4 supports have utilized parents, older schoolmates, mentors, senior citizens, and volunteers, as well as independent studies and special summer classes. Other forms occur through implementing basic learning principles (Chapter 2) that were absent in the student's prior educational experiences and through special physical/cognitive (Chapter 3), motivational (Chapter 4), or sociocultural instructional aids (Chapter 5). In essence, an adapted instructional program in either Tier 3 or Tier 4 begins whenever a student is not benefiting as much as the teacher and he or she desire from a developmental program.

Unfortunately, in the past a common mistake in instruction for students who read at the single word or interrupted meaning levels was to jump quickly from no support to a Tier 3 support. These actions become known as pull-out programs and have been criticized for lack of efficiency and effectiveness (see Block & Pressley, 2002 for a review of these critiques). Also, some students in these Tier 3 programs did not receive instruction that specifically addressed the literacy difficulty they faced or that used the literacy strengths they possessed. Rather, readers at Stages 2 and 3 of achievement received only a slightly altered version of the types of instruction that they had already received in the developmental program that had not worked for them in the first place.

Therefore, the goal of this book is to increase a teacher's ability to implement Tier 1 through Tier 4 supports effectively—through individualized, diagnostic, and prescriptive programs in combination with basic developmental programs.

Successful Teacher Actions for Less Accomplished Readers and Writers

Do you think the most successful teachers of less accomplished readers/writers are no different from other good teachers? While it is true that all good reading teachers share common traits, teachers who incorporate the actions and hold the beliefs presented in this chapter are distinct. They are the group of educators who are most effective for readers with special needs (Block, 2002a; Brophy, 1994; Ruddell & Ruddell, 1995).

To better understand why special teaching qualities are necessary, pause for a moment to identify the biggest problem that you face in your life right now. As you reflect, recall all you have done to cope with and to solve this problem. Realizing that you have not yet solved this problem unaided, go to a teacher who could help you and whom you trusted. What would this teacher be like? What would this teacher do to help you through your difficulty?

Having recalled a challenge that you have not yet overcome without outside assistance, you can better understand the desires and feelings of frustrated readers/writers. Literacy is likely to be among the greatest difficulties in their lives. They are likely to have (a) tried to avoid reading and writing experiences, (b) camouflaged their differences so others would not discover them, (c) asked friends for help, (d) become depressed, (e) felt stupid, (f) thought that there must be something terribly wrong with them, and

(g) occasionally felt sorry for themselves because it seemed as if everyone else in the world was doing well except them.

Further, when readers/writers are not as successful as they desire, they tend to respond with one or more of the following behaviors:

- Limiting the number of difficult texts that they read and using only a few decoding and comprehension strategies
- Continuing to use ineffective attending skills that interfere with their ability to reason through literacy obstacles
- Avoiding commitments to perform in public, as they become increasingly anxious about making mistakes before peers
- Accepting less and less precision in their literacy efforts

The specific instructional activities in this textbook enable such students to move to greater levels of proficiency and expertise.

Two things must change before these students can overcome their literacy barriers: There must be a *change in themselves,* and there must be a *variation in the instruction they receive.* Because they have already tried many things to attain literacy through traditional means, they need special strategies before their differences can disappear. Equally important, they have to *believe* that these new strategies will work for them. Therefore, these strategies must be sensitive to each student's learning strengths and must capitalize on the levels of literacy the students have already attained.

To accomplish this, such readers/writers need teachers who provide extra physical, cognitive, affective, motivational, social, and cultural supports. These teachers become more than the "facilitators of learning" that existed in the 1980s. They become enablers, explorers, inventors, and self-knowledge builders. They are not "sages on the stage" or "guides at the side." Rather, they become "sages of wisdom at every struggling reader's side." They do so by employing the following strategies.

Remove Physical and Psychological Distance

Some less effective teachers unknowingly distance themselves from readers/writers who are functioning at the lower end of the literacy continuum. They pay less attention to them, call on them less during class discussions, seat them at the back of the room, and in general demand less from them (Allington, 1995; Block, 1996; Willinsky, 1990). Furthermore, in lessons for lower achievement groups, less effective teachers often allow more interruptions by those outside the instructional group than in lessons for higher achieving students. For example, in one study, during instruction of less accomplished readers, interruptions were 20 times more frequent than during instruction of proficient readers (Willinsky, 1990). Moreover, much time is often lost to the "negotiations of embarrassment" as struggling readers read out loud. One researcher has noted that "[such] children are living with what is in effect a caste system in which it is all too apparent that learning to read does not offer adequate compensation for the humiliation it can cause" (Willinsky, 1990, p. 82).

More effective reading specialists and classroom teachers, on the other hand, seat readers who need special supports near them, smile more frequently, and maintain more eye contact. They provide at least 3 seconds of wait time after asking questions. They elaborate and give specific feedback concerning their students' literacy strengths and differences. They use **think alouds**—instructional tools introduced by Meichenbaum (1985)—to model the cognitive processes that occur as they read or write.

Students who view reading or writing as a challenge are wise to the distance concept and use it to their advantage. Such students know that less effective teachers are hesitant to call on someone who is likely to disrupt the class. Therefore, they have learned to avoid the humiliation of not knowing a literacy answer by creating disciplinary problems when called on. Some feign complete helplessness. Others try to elicit sympathetic treatment from teachers and peers, hoping that someone will supply the answers for them.

Thus, a first strategy you can employ for less successful students is to remove physical distance by placing them as close to you as possible during instruction, as often as possible. In this way, you can identify their specific needs immediately and introduce strategies to address them as soon as possible.

Another effective strategy is to remove psychological distance by avoiding the "low group" or "remedial reading" labels that others may have given to these students. Without the psychological limitations that such labels impose, you and your students can more clearly perceive the breadth and depth of each reader's capabilities. As Graves (1994) suggests: "I try to carry the uniqueness of each child in my head. Each child possesses unique capabilities that are worthy of attention" (p. 123). Focusing on students' strengths enhances their self-confidence, which many will need before they can blossom as readers.

Hold Discovery Discussions

Encourage students to engage in conversations with you and with one another in which all students are respected partners. The opportunity such conversations afford for presenting one's own ideas and reflecting on others' ideas enables readers/writers at lower levels of literacy development to alter their conceptions of themselves and of literacy. In such interactions, students have full power in deriving relevance. These engaging conversations are a stark departure from traditional teacher–student–teacher response chains in which students acquiesce to the teacher to differentiate between "good" and "bad" ideas, and where students speak only in minuscule sound bytes when they are almost certain that they are "correct." The assessment tool on page 11 can be used to diagnose individual needs during discovery discussions.

To have successful full-class conversations, you will likely need to help struggling readers become respected and fully participating leaders in the conversations. You may do so by moving conversations forward with the following tactics:

- Asking them to associate characters and themes to their own lives
- Prompting them to share their own literary voices and life stories
- Constructing chains of reasoning between their and classmates' comments
- Asking questions
- Having them justify or expound on personal positions

1.1 DIAGNOSIS AND ASSESSMENT

Discovery Discussions: Teaching Students the Process of Asking Others for Help

1. Create a chart on which you and students can sign up for discovery discussions.

2. Create a folder in which you can record the information discussed in discovery discussions. A form for record keeping appears on the facing page.

3. Explain to students how to sign up for a discovery discussion. Specify that they can sign up for as many as one every week if they want to discuss new discoveries that they are making about heir reading abilities.

4. Hold no more than three discovery discussions a day so you are not depleted of the energy to stay intensely focused on each student's story about his or her reading abilities.

5. Allow students to make the first comment to open the discovery discussion. If they do not, begin with a question. Among the best are:

   • "What have you discovered about your reading (or writing) abilities?"

   • "What are you learning about comprehension?"

   • "What do you want to learn to comprehend more?"

   • "What is bothering you about your reading abilities?"

   • "What would you like to learn next time we have reading, and why?"

   • "What is your next goal in reading, what do you want me to do to reach it, and how can I or others help you the most?"

6. When students share an insight, paraphrase and ask if you heard them accurately. If you have observed that a student has increased comprehension in a specific way, ask if your observation is accurate. Then the student can demonstrate the new process.

7. To become a trusted mentor, you cannot rush from one student to another. Rather, provide your undivided attention. The most important section of discovery discussions often occurs at the end. It is at this latter point when many students gain the confidence to risk asking a very important question and sharing an insight about their reading weaknesses. Without discovery discussions, many students will not have the opportunity to describe their weaknesses from their perspective.

In your room, conversations about literacy are not inquisitions or lectures but *discovery discussions.* Such teaching is not easy. Full-class conversations revolve around honesty and openness. For example, you might say, "I'm puzzled about this part of the book. Can you help me understand what the author meant, or tell me what it meant to you?" With this degree of two-way openness, less accomplished readers/writers can participate without fear of being put down by classmates. They will not be made to feel foolish *again* by giving an "incorrect" answer. You can also reduce fears by teaching all students the characteristics of good listening, as shown in Figure 1.2. Through such instruction, students have been shown to probe more deeply to understand one another's responses to reading (Collins, 1992c).

Discovery Discussion Diagnostic Record Form

Name: _____

Teacher: _____

Date	Book or story read or discussed	Grade level	Has previously read story	Predicting characters/events	Pointing at words	Fluency/phrasing	Reading with accuracy	Using initial visual cues	Using medial visual cues	Using ending visual cues	Using meaning cues	Self-correcting	Reread for comprehension	Goal for next week	Comments (e.g., specific errors, specific teaching points, comprehension strengths/weaknesses student suggested)

Villaume (1994) illustrates a conversation or discovery discussion that occurred during a Tier 2 small group discussion of *James and the Giant Peach* (Dahl, 1961). The teacher abandoned her initial intent to lecture. Instead, she sought to understand issues that were important to her less accomplished students, helping them to become equal partners in the conversation and attending instantly to interruptions in their meaning-making:

[I] tended to gloss over the first page where James' parents were eaten by an angry rhinoceros. [I] also failed to react strongly to the cruel treatment James suffered under the guardianship of his two aunts. [My struggling readers], however, responded strongly to

Directions to Students: To practice using good listening skills, find a picture in your textbook and describe it to your partner. Your partner will do the same for you.

We are going to learn six steps to improve your listening ability. When we are finished you will draw a second picture to see if it looks more like the intended object. If it does, your listening skills have improved.

Six Steps to Improving Listening Skills
In the future you can improve your listening ability by doing the following six things:

1. As soon as you begin to listen, try to hear the sentence that tells what the subject is. Ask yourself what the main idea of the person's talk is. Pick the most important details the person mentions.
2. Pay close attention to all words that tell directions, such as *north, south, east, west, up, down, here, there, over, under,* or *above.* As soon as you hear such a word, picture it in your mind.
3. Listen for the words that signal order, such as *first, second, last, after, before,* and *also.* Try to put yourself in the place of the person speaking and, in your mind, perform the order of the activities he/she is describing.
4. As you listen, picture what is described. This mental picture will help you distinguish the most important details and how they relate to one another. As you hear each detail, tie it to the detail immediately preceding it. The person talking had a very important reason for putting these details together, and you have to be thinking what that reason is.
5. Pay special attention to words such as *and, or, but, yet,* and *because.* These words tell you how two ideas are related to each other.
6. Ask questions of the person talking to clarify the points being made.

FIGURE 1.2 Learning Skills

Source: Adapted from C. Block (1992), *Teaching the Language Arts,* p. 119. Boston: Allyn & Bacon. Copyright © 1992 by Allyn & Bacon. Reprinted by permission of Allyn & Bacon.

the book's setting. They did not want to talk about the adventure of the giant peach. They wanted to talk about guardianship, if their parents were to die; they wanted to talk about child abuse and what children can do. As [I] began sharing the discussion agendas with students, [I] became more aware of the issues that mattered to [my less accomplished] fourth grade [readers]. If [I] truly want [these readers/writers] to share personal responses, [I] must encourage and value the transactions that [they] made with text based on their own world experiences and personal concerns. (p. 468)

It is exciting to watch the evolution that occurs in reluctant literacy users when such full-class conversations become dependable events in the classroom schedule. Students' contributions will move beyond direct recall, retelling parts of stories they've read, or merely relaying experiences they've had. Fewer of their statements will begin with "I liked [or I hated] the part where. . . ." However, some students will need extra Tier 1 support to engage in full-class discussions. Such students benefit from your asking them to share the responsibility for maintaining the conversation, rather than requiring them to give ideas from material read or written. For example, you could say, "John, what did you think about LaCretia's comment?" or "Marty, ask anyone in our class what they thought about Susan's idea" or "I've told you what I think and believe. What do you think that is different?" If any reader/writer has not contributed to the first round of a full-class conversation, you can include that student by asking if he or she judged a previous comment to be an accurate reflection of his or her own feelings, and why.

Another example of the power of full-class conversation was reported by Isidor I. Rabi, a nuclear physicist who won the Nobel Prize in 1944 for his work on atomic nuclei. Someone asked him what were the most important things that enabled him to rise from humble beginnings in Brooklyn to international scientific acclaim. Rabi responded that when all his friends were growing up and came home from school, their

1.2 CLASSROOM TEACHERS

Special Tier 1 and 2 Strategies for Reluctant Readers in Class Discussions

You can encourage effective full-class conversations for less accomplished readers and writers by drawing these students' attention to the aspect of the reading/writing material that pleased them most. You do this by asking the students to do one or all of the following:

- Associate feelings evoked during the reading of the story with events that recently occurred at school or home (e.g., ask "What was important to you about this story?" or "Has something like this ever happened to you?")
- Empathize with story characters by telling what they would have done
- Predict possible outcomes not in book
- Describe mental images evoked by the story (e.g., say "Tell us more about _____.")
- Tie together past knowledge with new information (do this by asking a question that begins with the word why) (Menke & Pressley, 1994)

In addition, you can extend invitations to students so as to reduce the one-sidedness that can occur when more accomplished readers/writers carry too much of the discussion. Invitations can include statements like these:

"I see that this is important to you. Can you tell us more?"

"That's something I haven't studied very much. What else do you know?"

"You've convinced me! Thank you for telling us about your thought."

"Your idea makes sense to me."

"I never thought about it that way. Can you say more about it?"

"That's a creative way of looking at the issue. How did you arrive at that answer?"

"Can you tell me how you put these ideas in order?"

"What I don't understand is . . ."

"What did you notice?"

"What puzzled you?"

"Did you notice any patterns in this story?"

mothers asked them, "What did you learn today?" Rabi's mother, however, was different. She asked, "Izzy, did you ask a good question today?" (Bransford & Stein, 1993). By asking your students to ask questions of their peers during conversations, you are helping them to engage in higher-level thinking than if they are only required to give answers to others' questions.

By sharing Rabi's story with your students, you can also institute the habit of ending your full-class conversations by having students ask questions that still puzzle them. In such a climate, students at the lower ends of literacy ability often become less inhibited about exploring a complexity of literacy that still eludes them.

Another effective strategy is to encourage all students in the class to write about ideas they want to share before full-class conversations begin. You can say, "I want all of you to take a few minutes to jot down anything you were thinking about this story. I'd like to begin our conversation by having a few of you read what you wrote." Some students may respond by writing, "I don't know. I didn't think anything about it. I don't understand what you want me to write." Others may write something they think you want to hear. After a few experiences, however, even the most reluctant readers/writers will begin to write statements such as "I like it because . . ." or "I don't think that _____, but I'm not going to _____ like Virginia said."

A good indication that quality conversations include students at all points on the literacy continuum in your classroom or reading specialist session is that people who enter the classroom notice that all students can "get the floor" simply by starting to talk. Second and third measures are that less accomplished students know more about a book at the end of the conversation than when it started, and that neither they nor you can tell who the group leader was. With these supports all readers/writers will have their best opportunities to attain high levels of competence in literacy.

Adapt Curriculum to Meet the Needs of Struggling Readers

Harste (1986) made this observation: "Children must become the curriculum informants if we are ever to move from a paper curriculum to a real curriculum" (p. 45). Thus, the first criterion in selecting a book or activity for struggling readers/writers is the degree to which it will give them a lot to think about, will enable multiple interpretations, and will elicit their aesthetic and efferent responses to literature. Also bear in mind that most readers/writers at these levels of ability enjoy stories that describe how life is or that show how life could be (Block, 1993b, 2002b). Whenever possible, it is also advantageous to allow these readers/writers to read more than one book about the same subject, as it enables them to develop a broader **schema**—a framework consisting of all the experiences, emotions, and readings that students have encountered concerning that topic. Students then recall these stored images to better comprehend the topic, deepen background knowledge, and provide more advanced vocabulary. Box 1.3 demonstrates how books are used by reading specialists to diagnose and instruct to eliminate specific reading difficulties.

When reading specialists and classroom teachers select appropriate material, readers/writers who have less achievement than their peers have been demonstrated to develop more commitment, persistence, and involvement in reading or writing (Brock, 2002a). Such quality literature has been identified as having reliable, vivid characters;

1.3 READING SPECIALISTS

Eliminating Difficulties in Comprehension

Directions: Select two books from the same series. Read one book orally as a struggling reader follows the text with you. Ask the student to read the second book orally alone. List words missed. Go back and ask questions over texts to assess comprehension. Because students should be familiar with content, errors can be interpreted as weaknesses in tying new experiences to background knowledge and lack of adequate decoding and comprehension strengths. Older students read both books silently.

Reading Level	Series with Same Characters	Author
First and Second Grades	Clifford the Big Red Dog	N. Bridewell
	Arthur books	L. Hoban
	Frog and Toad	A. Lobel
	George and Martha	J. Marshall
	Little Critters	M. Mayer
	Little Bear	E. Minarik
	Amelia Bedelia	P. Parish
	Curious George	H. A. Rey
	Henry and Mudge	C. Rylant
	Mr. Putter and Tabby	C. Rylant
	Marvin Redpost	L. Sachar
	Harry (The Dirty Dog) Books	G. Zion
	Nonfiction books	E. Carle
Second and Third Grades	Amber Brown	P. Danziger
	Pee Wee Scouts	J. Delton
	Kids of Polk Street School	P. R. Giff
	Horrible Harry	S. Kline
	Kids on Bus 5	M. Leonard
	Junie B. Jones	B. Park
	Nate the Great	M. Sharmat
	Boxcar Children	G. Warner
	Peter Rabbit	B. Potter
	Magic School Bus	J. Cole
	Encyclopedia Brown	D. Sobol
	Nonfiction All about _____	Scholastic
	Ask a Question about Nature	Scholastic
Fourth and Fifth Grades	Harry Potter	J. K. Rowling
	Nancy Drew	C. Keene
	The True Confessions of Charlotte Doyle	Avi
	Nothing but the Truth: A Documentary Novel	Avi

continued

1.3   READING SPECIALISTS

Eliminating Difficulties in Comprehension *(continued)*

Reading Level	Series with Same Characters	Author
Fourth and Fifth Grades *(continued)*	What Do Fish Have to Do with Anything	Avi
	The Summer of the Swans	B. Byars
	The Pinballs	B. Byars
	Cracker Jackson	B. Byars
	The Wretched Stone	C. Van Allsburg
	Just a Dream	C. Van Allsburg
	Sleeping Ugly	J. Yolen
	Julie of the Wolves	J. C. George
	Sounder	W. H. Armstrong
Sixth Grade	Maniac Magee	J. Spinelli
	Roll of Thunder, Hear My Cry	M. Taylor
	Hey, Al	A. Yorinks
	Shiloh	P. R. Naylor
	Mrs. Frisby and the Rats of NIMH	R. C. O'Brien
	Hatchet	G. Paulsen

demonstrating some virtue and/or reality about humankind, such as integrity or self-discipline; generating passion in readers; and displaying memorable craftsmanship (Huck, 1994; Norton, 1995).

Model Literacy Processes Effectively

Modeling is demonstrating how to perform a process or strategy before asking students to do so. When reading specialists and classroom teachers model for struggling readers, they demonstrate each step in the process of comprehending, decoding, or writing. For example, if students are to set their own purposes for reading/writing, you first model how you set purposes. You also could invite respected older schoolmates, adults, and community leaders to model how they read and write (Block, 1993a, 2002b). Such actions convince reluctant readers/writers that they have the authority and ability to think and to initiate their imagination before they begin literary pursuits.

Modeling is distinguished from think alouds in that the former balances direct instruction and discovery learning, whereas the latter is fully direct instruction. Specifically, when you and reluctant readers and writers engage in a modeling activity, you

Modeling both visually and verbally enables readers/writers at Levels 2 and 3 to create literacy solutions for themselves. Many need both oral and written exemplars before they feel safe enough to try to read or write a new word.

provide enough expanded explanation so students can achieve an initial success at their first attempt, but you do not provide so much instruction that students lose their enthusiasm for attempting literacy challenges unaided.

Moreover, to be more effective, you do not offer help when it isn't solicited. Rather, you capture teachable moments when struggling students request your help. For example, Jody Stapleton, a masterful reading specialist working with less accomplished first graders in an inner-city school, once faced a difficult request from one of his students. He possessed the expertise to meet this request and the wisdom to capture a teachable moment. These exemplary teaching abilities culminated in a struggling student's first public display of literacy competence. Jody had prepared to make dinosaur nests with his Tier 3 first graders one morning. He arrived an hour early and made sure all the exciting "make-believe" dinosaur eggs were ready and placed at each student's desk. The bell rang, and students were so excited they could hardly wait to begin. Then Roberto, a Mexican American student who had been in the room for only a week and who had never read a book aloud, handed Jody a book about dinosaurs that his father had bought him the night before. Roberto asked, "Could you teach me to read this so I can read it to my regular class after lunch?"

What would you have done, if you had been the teacher? Many options lay before Jody. After all, he had planned a different activity for that morning, and the other students were eager to start. But Jody recognized this as a teachable moment for Roberto. Jody went to the back of his room and unveiled a box of dinosaur books that he had not intended to show to the children until the nests were built. Then he asked each child to read and write alone or with a partner until he asked them to come together and share what they learned. Students were so eager to choose their books that they momentarily forgot about making nests. As the rest of the class engaged in silent and partner reading, Jody spent 45 minutes teaching Roberto to read *Danny, the Dinosaur.* Roberto became one of the highest readers in Jody's group by the end of the year.

Capturing these teachable moments is very important because students who view literacy as a large challenge often do not believe they are able to improve their abilities (Aaron, Joshi, & Williams, 1999; Kang, 1993). Because of this, and to avoid humiliation, such readers/writers actually improve *more* when the average amount of unrequested help you provide is *low*. Similarly, if the spread of ability levels in the classroom is large, less accomplished readers/writers do not profit as much from individual oral praise before the group as they do in homogeneously grouped settings. In classrooms where the ability range is large, such readers/writers will become more **efficacious** (capable of improving themselves) when you do not praise them before the Tier 3 or 4 group or classroom peers for tasks completed correctly immediately after you modeled them. In summary, some modeling and praise actions that appear on the surface to be positive instead imply that the students who receive them are lower in ability than their peers (Graham & Barker, 1990; Joshi & Aaron, 2000; Kang, 1993).

Scaffold Effectively

Scaffolding can be defined as enabling learners to handle complex tasks by assisting them with parts of the task the first time they attempt it (Means & Knapp, 1991). Like the physical scaffolding that enables construction workers to climb high buildings, when you scaffold you will perform part of a reading/writing process for students who cannot do so themselves without assistance. When left alone, less accomplished readers/ writers tend to engage in literacy tasks they already know how to do. With your scaffolding, however, these students more frequently attempt new tasks, soon discover how clever they are, and begin to believe they can increase their literacy abilities (Svotlovskaya, 1992).

Vygotsky (1978) first discussed the value of scaffolding. His theory is based on the concept of instructing in a student's **zone of proximal development.** He defined this zone as "the distance between the actual developmental level as determined by independent problem solving and the level of potential development as determined through problem solving under adult guidance or in collaboration with more capable peers" (Vygotsky, 1978, p. 6). In essence, students learn literacy fastest when they select something they want to read and ask you or a peer to help them learn it.

The most extensive form of scaffolding is to read the text aloud as less accomplished readers who have not yet mastered decoding skills read along. Through such a scaffold, these students can execute comprehension processes because you and they unlock phonetic codes together. A second example of extensive scaffolding, used by a reading specialist with a slightly older child, follows:

> One teacher was working with a child who could sound out words, but using this strategy alone caused him to read slowly and impaired his comprehension. As he stumbled over an unfamiliar word in a passage he was reading aloud, the teacher began by asking, "What would make sense and sounds like what you're saying?" This prompt [scaffold] allowed him to use his facility in sounding out words at the same time as he thought about what made sense in the context of the passage. (Walker, 1992, p. 23)

Such scaffolds are particularly valid when reading specialists and classroom teachers ask a reader/writer, "What makes sense?" By doing so, they remind students in both Tier 1/2 and Tier 3/4 settings to use the overall meanings of passages as clues each time they read. Similarly, when they ask, "What word would make sense that begins with the letter *s*?" they are reminding readers to use meaning and initial consonant sounds to decode new words. Notice that neither of these hints tells the answer or provides such obvious clues that students don't have to engage their own thinking.

A second type of scaffolding involves reducing the complexity of comprehension required. One way to do this might be to diagram an author's writing pattern before students read, and then show them how you identified that pattern. For others, telling the "final" goal (comprehension) you derived from a reading before they begin will reduce the enormity of the task because the end goal is in sight.

In summary, by scaffolding successfully you can establish a classroom environment that (1) presents learning challenges with your academic and emotional support, (2) provides security through successful risk taking *on a daily basis,* and (3) includes appropriate opportunities for students to assume responsibilities for instruction that they select and that are important to them. Of equal importance is assisting students to develop their own ability to extract knowledge from information and to recognize patterns and linkages that on the surface appear unrelated. Given that the world's store of knowledge doubles approximately every 7 years, the simple recall of facts and information is becoming inadequate as an end product of reading. Therefore, the lessons throughout the remainder of this text are designed to enable readers/writers to (a) analyze and synthesize information as they read, (b) practice flexing and reporting their thoughts and attitudes, (c) create novel approaches to the problems they encounter in the content and literacy processes, (d) integrate information from a variety of media sources, and (e) develop "a sense of 'empowerment' to shape rather than merely react to the future" (Walker, 1992, p. 7).

Reflect Questions Back to the Class

By answering students' questions with a question, you demonstrate that no question is ever "dumb." As shown in the list of questions in Table 1.1, you reflect questions back to students by asking them (a) to elaborate, (b) to think **metacognitively** (to think about their own thinking—e.g., "What were you thinking when . . ."), (c) to solve problems (e.g., "Can you think of another way to . . ."), and (d) to support their answers (e.g., "What led you to feel that way?"). For instance, if a student asks why Sounder had to die in William Armstrong's award-winning book, you reflect the question back: "Class, why do you think the author ended the book with Sounder's death? Why do you think Charlotte died at the end of *Charlotte's Web*?" (White, 1952). Back-to-back questions like these will help struggling

TABLE 1.1 Reflecting Questions Back to Students

Elaboration

Does this make you think of anything else you read?

Would you like to be one of the people in this? Who? Why?

Did you like this more or less than the last thing you read? Why?

What parts of this have you especially liked or disliked?

What did you mean by _____? Can you give me an example?

If _____ happened, what else could happen?

Does this story remind you of any other one? Why? What specific characteristics do they have in common?

Did the author make you feel any specific emotion?

Can you describe the _____?

How could you advertise this book?

If you had a chance to talk to this author, what would you speak to him or her about?

Why do you suppose the author gave this title? Can you think of another appropriate title?

Why is this an important story to share?

Metacognition (Thinking about Thinking)

How would you feel if _____ happened?

What were your thoughts when you decided whether to _____ or _____? How did you decide?

Why did you choose this selection to read?

Do you think this story could really happen? Explain.

After reading this story, has your perception or view of _____ changed? Explain.

Can you describe your thinking? I need to hear more details.

What makes you think he or she _____? How do you know this?

What do you know that you did not know before reading this?

Did your thoughts and feelings change as you were reading? How and why?

Did you have to remember what you already knew?

Problem Solving

What do you need to do next?

Can you think of another way we could do this?

How did you solve this problem?

What did you do when you came to these difficult words?

What do you do when you get stuck?

What do you do when you do not understand the content or context?

How did you come up with this, and what helped you the most?

How could we go about finding if this is true?

Supporting Answers

Why is this one better than that one?

Yes, that's right—but how did you know?

What are your reasons for saying that?

What do you (or author) mean by _____?

Why does this go here instead of there?

Do you have good evidence for believing that?

How did you know that?

readers to make connections from text context and to their own lives—and will teach them to use questioning to make connections in the future, when you are not with them. Relevance is established through such question reflection, and readers at lower levels on the literacy continuum can realize deeper meaning through their readings and writings.

MIDDLE SCHOOL and HIGH SCHOOL

1.4

Using Graduated Books with Middle School, High School, and Second-Language Learners

Graduated books can be used to focus students' attention on getting "the big things" in reading and writing (Fitzgerald, 1993). Moving from pictures to books increases students' interactions with the holistic features common to all language, such as keeping audience interest, getting and giving main ideas, and tailoring messages to the audience. With these global goals and thinking processes in mind, the issues that vary by content—such as phrasings, decodings, word choices, and literal comprehension—become easier for secondary struggling readers.

Graduated books are defined as moving from picture, to concept, to predictable, to question-and-answer, to beginning chapter, to full chapter books about one theme. Whenever possible include several cultural and economic perspectives in the graduated books curriculum. Books with cultural themes are becoming easier to find in social studies, and many trade books at low readability levels are now available. For a list of concept books, see Resource Card 1. Various versions of fairy tales (see Resource Card 2) also assist second-

language learners. To illustrate, there are more than 900 culturally distinct versions of the Cinderella story, including the traditional German, French, and English versions as well as the Vietnamese *In the Land of the Small Dragon,* the Native American *The Algonquin Cinderella,* the modern American *Cinderella,* and the lower socioeconomic spoof *The Paper Bag Princess.* When dialectically distinct and second-language learners (especially at the secondary school level) select a book and read about the wishes and goals of the main character, how the literary character's wishes are granted, what determines heroic actions, and how the conditions in the main character's culture impact his or her life, many come to understand and appreciate their own culture and unique speaking traits. Many of these books contain beautiful photos and diagrams of difficult concepts as well as sentence structures and vocabulary from the student's background experiences, which increase comprehension. Carr, Buchanan, Wentz, Weiss, and Brant (2002) list 91 exceptionally valuable titles of student favorite graduated book selections.

Three Desirable Teacher Beliefs

> It was one of the most radical discoveries Gandhi was to make in a lifetime of experimentation: In order to transform others, you have first to transform yourself.
>
> Aknath Eawaran, *Gandhi the Man*

In addition to the instructional actions you can take to assist readers/writers (i.e., removing the physical and psychological distance between yourself and students, conducting full-class conversations and discovery discussions, adapting curriculum to meet student needs, modeling, scaffolding, and reflecting questions back to students, a positive attitude is essential. Teachers who accept the three beliefs presented next assist greater numbers of readers/writers to attain their full literacy potential (Block, 2002a).

In recent decades, many researchers have explored how reading specialists' and teachers' beliefs about themselves and their students affect instruction (Allington, 1995;

Concept Books for Struggling Readers

Alphabet

Burningham, J. (1967). *John Burningham's ABC.* New York: Bobbs-Merrill.

Crowther, R. (1978). *The most amazing hide and seek alphabet book.* New York: Viking.

Fletcher, H. J. (1978). *Picture book ABC.* New York: Platt & Munk.

Isadora, R. (1983). *City seen from A to Z.* New York: Greenwillow.

Johnson, L. (1982). *The teddy bear ABC.* New York: Green Tiger.

Merriam, E. (1980). *Good night to Annie.* New York: Four Winds.

Piers, H. (1987). *Puppy's ABC.* New York: University.

Pragoff, F. (1987). *Alphabet.* New York: Doubleday.

Counting

Bang, M. (1983). *Ten, nine, eight.* New York: Greenwillow.

Bridgeman, E. (1977). *All the little bunnies: A counting book.* New York: Atheneum.

Carle, E. (1968, 1987). *1, 2, 3, to the zoo: A counting book.* New York: Philomel.

Carle, E. (1969). *The very hungry caterpillar.* New York: Collins.

Gardner, B. (1987). *Can you imagine . . . ? A counting book.* New York: Dodd, Mead.

Hoban, T. (1987). *26 letters and 99 cents.* New York: Greenwillow.

Lindbergh, R. (1987). *The midnight farm.* New York: Dial.

Pragoff, F. (1987). *How many?* New York: Doubleday.

Miscellaneous

Hoban, T. (1978). *Is it red? Is it yellow? Is it blue?* New York: Greenwillow.

Macmillan, B. (1988). *Dry or wet.* New York: Lothrop.

Macmillan, B. (1988). *Step by step.* New York: Lothrop.

Martin, B., Jr., & Archambault, J. (1985, 1987). *Here are my hands.* New York: Holt.

Messenger, J. (Illus.). (1986). *Twinkle, twinkle little star.* New York: Macmillan.

Potter, B. (1904, 1986). *The two bad mice.* New York: Warner.

Pragoff, F. (1987). *Growing.* New York: Doubleday.

Pragoff, F. (1987). *What color.* New York: Doubleday.

Rockwell, A. (1986). *Things that go.* New York: Dutton.

Wallner, J. (Illus.). (1987). *The three little pigs.* New York: Viking.

Poetry and Rhymes

Allen, S., & Meadows, J. (1987). *Shakin' loose with Mother Goose.* New York: Kids Matter.

Conover, C. (1987). *The adventures of Simple Simon.* New York: Farrar, Straus & Giroux.

Emberley, B. (1967). *Drummer Hoff.* New York: Treehouse.

Fujikawa, G. (1968, 1987). *Mother Goose.* New York: Grosset & Dunlap.

Hayes, S. (1988). *Clap your hands: Finger rhymes.* New York: Lothrop.

Hughes, S. (1988). *Out and about.* New York: Lothrop.

Josefowitz, N. (1988). *A hundred scoops of ice cream.* New York: St. Martin's.

Marshall, J. (Illus.). (1979). *James Marshall's Mother Goose.* New York: Farrar, Straus & Giroux.

Tarant, M. (Illus.). (1978). *Nursery rhymes.* New York: Crowell.

Zolotow, C. (1987). *Everything glistens and everything sings.* San Diego: Harcourt Brace Jovanovich.

Zolotow, C. (1958, 1988). *Sleepy book.* New York: Harper & Row.

Source: Compiled and modified from discussions in M. F. Heller (1995), *Reading-Writing Connections: From Theory to Practice,* 2nd ed. Copyright © 1995, 1991 by Longman Publishers USA. Reprinted by permission of Addison-Wesley Educational Publishers Inc.

RESOURCE CARD 2

Different Versions of Fairy Tales for Secondary School Readers

The Three Little Pigs

The three little Hawaiian pigs and the magic shark, by Laird & Laird
The three little pigs, by E. Blegvad
The three little pigs, by P. Galdone
The three little pigs, by M. Zemach
The true story of the three little pigs, by J. Scieszka
Walt Disney's the three little pigs, by B. Brenner

Little Red Riding Hood

Little Red Cap, by J. Grimm
Little Red Riding Hood, by P. Galdone
Little Red Riding Hood, by J. Goodall
Little Red Riding Hood, by J. Marshall
Lon Po Po: A Red Riding Hood story from China, translated by E. Young

Jack and the Beanstalk

Jack and the beanstalk, by L. Cauley
Jack and the beanstalk, by W. de la Mare
Jack and the beanstalk, by B. deRegniers
Jack and the beanstalk, by J. Jacobs
Jack and the beanstalk, by D. W. Johnson
Jack and the bean tree, by G. Haley
Jack and the wonder beans, by J. Still
Jim and the beanstalk, by R. Briggs

The Old Lady Who Swallowed a Fly

I know an old lady who swallowed a fly, by E. Adams
I know an old lady who swallowed a fly, by N. B. Westcott
There was an old woman, by S. Kellogg

The Gingerbread Boy

The bun: A tale from Russia, by M. Brown
The gingerbread boy, by P. Galdone
The gingerbread rabbit, by R. Jarrell
Johnny-Cake, by J. Jacob
Journey cake, ho! by R. Sawyer
The pancake, by A. Lobel
The runaway pancake, by A. Asogojornsen & J. Moe

The Hare and the Tortoise

The hare and the tortoise, by C. Castle
The hare and the tortoise, by P. Galdone
The hare and the tortoise, by J. Stevens
The hare and the tortoise, by B. Wildsmith

Cinderella

Cinderella, by M. Brown
Cinderella, by A. Ehrlich
Cinderella, by P. Galdone
Cinderella, by J. Grimm
Cinderella, by C. Perrault
The Egyptian Cinderella, by S. Climo
Korean Cinderella, by E. Adams
Moss grown, by W. Hooks
The paper bag princess, by R. Munson
Princess Furball, by C. Huck
The rough-face girl, by R. Martin
Sydneyrella and the glass slipper, by B. Myers
Tatterhood and other tales, by E. J. Phelps
Yeh-Shen, by A. Louie
Princess Smartypants, by J. Scieszka

Block, 2002a; Ruddell, 1995). These studies demonstrate that beliefs impact the decisions teachers make, students' self-esteem, students' beliefs about their own abilities to learn, and students' level of achievement. (For reviews of these studies see Block, 1993a, 2002a; Hiebert, 1991.)

In this section of the chapter, you can compare your beliefs to those that distinguish the most successful educators of struggling readers. Before the discussion begins, list (mentally or on paper) three beliefs that you think differentiate more effective teachers from less effective teachers of readers/writers who perform at the lower ends of the literacy continuum. Also bear in mind that *you* are the most important variable in your students' success. Your students can become only as literate as your teaching enables them to become; in other words, the most powerful determinant of success for these readers/writers is the quality of your teaching. Now, after pausing to reflect on the beliefs you deem most desirable, compare your thoughts to those beliefs identified by research.

BELIEF 1: *All students, with support, can experience the joy, growth, and fulfillment that comes from expert literacy abilities.* This belief is strong even though the number of students who avoid literary activities is increasing (Adams, 1993; Ostosis, 2000; Ruddell & Ruddell, 1995). As Hartle-Schutte (1993) points out:

> Either we continue the status quo, blaming the students for what we perceive as their deficits and lack of readiness for performing according to the school expectations, or we actively restructure the school curriculum so that the literacy knowledge and experiences that each child brings to school are valued and built upon. We need to recognize that there is no single, but multiple paths to literacy. No single set of materials, no single scope and sequence is adequate to capture the interests and needs of all of the children, particularly children of different ethnic and sociocultural backgrounds. If schools can only meet the needs of children who have had "school-valued" experiences at home and in their communities, then schools have failed. (p. 652)

Reading specialists and teachers who believe in children's potential as learners and who accept responsibility for children's learning are more likely to offer these children more and better instruction (Allington, 1993; Pool, 2001). Such teachers are very committed to the educational success of their students, perceiving themselves as instructional innovators who use new theories and instructional practices. They exercise their autonomy to create instruction that is adapted to their students. They also reject the notion that any of their students might leave their care intellectually or academically disadvantaged.

When teachers believe in their students, a dependable result occurs. It is an interesting human phenomenon that people tend to live up to others' expectations of them. When children realize their teachers see the best in students, children at lower levels of literacy development tend to turn their best selves toward their teachers. They will engage in significantly more literacy tasks because they want to share more of their best selves with their teachers. In addition to believing in these learners' potential, such teachers are enthusiastic about their job and the content they teach. They have energy, commitment, passion, warmth, caring, flexibility, and high expectations. They nurture students' aptitudes and create an intellectual excitement in the classroom for all readers/writers (Block et al., 2002; Ruddell, 1995).

Most effective **diagnosticians** (reading specialists who have credentials to assess reading difficulties) and teachers do not think about changing the student to fit the reading/writing program. Rather, they change the program to meet individual children's needs. They also give less accomplished readers/writers a choice of materials. Such choices are crucial for these students because materials of high personal interest are easier for them to relate to. Offering choices can be even more effective when you assist in their selection by providing several books concerning a student's specific interest. This approach is illustrated by Kirsten Borchert, a dynamic second grade teacher of readers/writers at low levels of literacy development. She has witnessed that a lifelong love for reading and writing begins through the practice of *choice*. Borchert describes how she supports this choice:

> Roberta picked Johanna Hurwitz's *Class President* from a variety of books I brought for her choice. She always chooses below her level if I let her choose from the library, so I let her choose from five books I bring to her.

BELIEF 2: *Effective reading specialists and teachers listen to their students every day.* Listening to students helps to evaluate their beliefs about literacy and enables the students to realize the effects of these beliefs on their own achievement. As students complete their conversations, expert teachers reflect and evaluate, then alter the instructional program each student will receive that week.

Unfortunately, some teachers make the mistake of focusing so much on what they have to *do* for their students that they don't actively *listen* to them. Consider this example from teacher Patricia Guitterez:

> One of my greatest strengths is my tenacity. I was not going to give up on Marisa! She was very uncooperative and almost belligerent much of the time. She gave me reasons to want to throw in the towel—but I was not going to, because I knew there was a way to reach her and I would continue to try to find that way. I wanted to give her a strategy that would help her become a better reader. I tried Compare/Contrast, Repeated Readings, Context Clues, and a Word Bank, only to be met with complete refusal. [See Chapter 9 for a description of these methods.] I was doing everything I had learned in school. I read an additional article about these new strategies from the Benchmark School to see if I was doing something wrong. How could I be failing so miserably when I was doing what I had been told to do at college?
>
> From this question came one of my best lessons. I suddenly realized that all this time I was too busy focusing on the mechanics of what I was doing and trying to do everything just right. I forgot to be flexible and modify the strategies to fit Marisa. Once I remembered that, the remainder of our work was better. . . . I used reciprocal teaching—she accepted this because we both were reading—and writing about stories that we were reading or sometimes about whatever we wanted, and she was even beginning to use her Word Bank.
>
> Her reading had improved a lot, her spelling was doing better, and her vocabulary had increased. Marisa was doing better than her previous teacher had ever anticipated. This teacher had expressed that Marisa was mentally retarded and was where she was, and would never do much better. . . . I have no miracles or huge revelations to report. I am a person who sees that there is potential, great and small, in everyone. The more familiar I become with literacy processes, the more I can take ownership over it and enhance it for every reader.

One of the values of sincere, active listening is that when readers/writers who labor intensively with literacy voice an idea about their reading or writing, they are usually unsure if their ideas are worthy of anyone else's attention. When their idea is judged meritorious by their teacher, they perceive it to be more accurate than they originally believed. This change strengthens their self-monitoring abilities during literary pursuits.

To build listening time into the schedule, some teachers begin instruction once a week in a 10- to 20-minute discovery discussion with individuals or a small group. On the next day, they tie the ideas that students expressed to the ideas to be discussed in class on that day. They make this connection not only by mentioning ideas so as to make a student feel good, but by demonstrating how others can expand their literacy abilities based on ideas expressed by students at the initial levels of literacy achievement.

Unless you listen, many readers/writers who do not sustain uninterrupted meaning-making will hide their literacy differences in various ways. Some will be shy to the extent that they will avoid reading aloud for fear of making mistakes. Others will become extremely talkative, trying to disguise their literacy weaknesses. Others mask frustration by convincing others that they are "above it all" and could read and write well if they wanted to. Even though these defense mechanisms may be firmly in place, you can be sure that all readers/writers want to be heard, to learn, and to be judged as valuable. However, as Gordon and MacGinnis (1993) discovered, if students' comments about what might help them learn more do not result in instructional changes, or at the very least in an explanation of why instructional modifications are not possible, the students' self-esteem and confidence in their literacy abilities decrease even more.

BELIEF 3: *Effective diagnosticians, reading specialists, and teachers intervene on behalf of their students and take direct action to help them overcome individual physical, cognitive, social, cultural, and affective barriers to maximum reading achievement.* Such teachers become genuinely excited about the subjects and skills that their struggling readers/writers want to learn. They let their students know they are there for them because they truly care about them—not simply because it's their job (Short, Kane, & Peeling, 2000). They know that their students are concerned about being placed in situations in which their literacy abilities will be compared to the abilities of students whose literacy is more fully developed. These students are also reluctant to engage in discussions in which teachers or peers do not listen to them. As one fourth grade teacher paraphrased the feelings of a student in her class: "I'm concerned about talking to teachers and people in my class because my ideas sometimes go unnoticed. I know my ideas will not bring results."

Effective teachers intervene on their students' behalf by helping them become more well liked and respected by peers. Studies show, for instance, that long-term improvements in student popularity can be enhanced through coaching (Leibert, 1991). **Coaching** involves giving positive reinforcement to peer behaviors that assist students' learning. For example: "Martin and LaCretia, we know that Martin's goal is to learn to read faster orally, and sometimes it is difficult for him. You are helping him, LaCretia, by waiting and answering his questions about words. I know this takes extra effort on your part and I know Martin appreciates it, as do I. Because of your help he is reaching his goal. Thank you."

Many struggling readers/writers try to hide who they are. With you as their advocate, they are able to discover their full potential. To do so, you will not unintentionally reward students for squelching their ideas or their emotional selves, and you will not mistake a broken, downtrodden spirit as merely a quiet, cooperative, unopinionated one. You will seek such readers' involvement in many shared life experiences in class, so that these can become memorable episodes to relate to in their writings and readings.

In summary, effective teachers are caring, listening, devoted, and actively involved in advancing their students' lives and literacy. One indicator that you are succeeding is that a stranger who walks into your classroom cannot distinguish readers/writers whose reading and writing are pleasure-filled from those whose literacy activities are labor intensive. The quality of both groups' engagement and participation in class interactions is equal.

Chapter Summary

As we discard the remedial reader label, we enable more students to discover their full literacy potential. This chapter identified five stages of literacy abilities and four types of programs (tiers of support) that can be developed to improve literacy. It also offered instructional actions and beliefs that research has identified as being valuable for assisting less accomplished readers/writers. Six instructional actions that improve students' reading/writing are (1) to remove physical and psychological distance between yourself and students, (2) to use full-class conversations and discovery discussions to identify student strengths, (3) to adapt the curriculum to meet student needs, (4) to model, (5) to scaffold, and (6) to reflect questions back to students. Beliefs that increase literacy for less accomplished students are: (1) all students, through your support, can experience literacy proficiency; (2) active listening to students is important; and (3) intervention on their behalf is necessary. Now that the principles for effective instruction have been identified, Chapter 2 will describe the historical and contemporary theories on which these principles are based.

Key Terminology

The following terms were introduced in this chapter. If you know the meaning of a term, place a check mark in the blank that precedes it. If you are not certain of a meaning, you can quickly turn back to the page number that follows the term to review its meaning. If you learned at least five of these terms in your initial reading of the chapter, you are learning well and comprehending the chapter's intent.

_____ **average readers/writers** (page 3)
_____ **externally prompted and externally supported readers/writers** (page 3)
_____ **developmental reading/writing instruction** (page 5)
_____ **remedial reading program** (page 5)
_____ **adapted instruction** (page 5)
_____ **think alouds** (page 9)
_____ **schema** (page 14)

_____ **modeling** (page 16)
_____ **efficacious** (page 18)
_____ **scaffolding** (page 18)
_____ **zone of proximal development** (page 18)
_____ **metacognitively** (page 19)
_____ **diagnosticians** (page 24)
_____ **coaching** (page 26)

Case Study

Making Professional Decisions

In the following real-life example of a class-room episode, pretend you are the teacher. Identify what principles in this chapter were used. Then list which ones you would add to improve the value of this lesson for less accomplished readers/writers. Explain the reasoning behind your decision.

The day begins with a 10-minute journal writing activity. Three readers who are at an early stage of literacy ability are assisting you by writing the absentee names, date, and one question they have for the class to answer on the board. This question will open the day's discussion period. Then the class writes about the upcoming Valentine's Day.

Immediately after the 10-minute writing period has ended, students organize themselves in small groups to read their work. During the 10-minute writing you notice that Marco had difficulty getting only three sentences on his paper and that he did not share his writing in his small group. Also, Tiffany looked away from her book constantly until at last she closed its covers and placed her head on her desk.

What would you do next? What would you add to this lesson? (If you want to compare your answer to the actual response of the reading specialist who was directing this class, write your answer and then turn to the Answer Key at the end of the book.)

Thinking and Writing about What You Have Learned

1. What did you learn about your abilities and convictions as they relate to teaching readers/writers who have not yet reached literacy proficiency?

2. Which effective instructional actions will be easiest for you? Why?

3. Which of these actions will be most difficult for you? Why?

4. Which of the three beliefs is strongest for you? Why?

5. Which of the three beliefs is weakest? How can you strengthen it for students' welfare?

6. It may be easier to relate the information in this chapter to your life if you think of a specific struggling reader/writer that you know. As you recall this student, write specific actions you would take with that student to implement the instructional actions and the beliefs described in this chapter.

Onto the Information Superhighway

Favorite author websites engage struggling readers. They build Internet usage skills. For each of the following authors, have students read a book by the author, then research some historical information about the author. Provide students with a boxed study matrix for them to complete. Each row of the box will be labeled with the title of one of the author's books, and the columns will be labeled *Characters, Setting, Problems, Solutions,* and *Author's Craft,* or with other labels.

Author Study: Eric Carle

Book	Characters	Setting	Problems	Solutions	Author's Craft
The Very Hungry Caterpillar					
[List other Carle books read]					

Author Studies: Early Elementary School

Eric Carle

www.eric-carle.com

Have the students read one of Eric Carle's books and do research on him. The students should then write a story in the same format as Eric Carle or a story that correlates with his content and/or characters. When the students are done, they should have three things to present: (1) a book review, (2) background information on the author, and (3) a completed book.

Norman Bridwell

www.scholastic.com/clifford/kids/welcome.htm

Complete a guided reading of Clifford the Big Red Dog *with the students. Students in a group can talk about the author (Norman Bridwell) and, as a class, discuss how Norman Bridwell writes his books. In groups, younger students can write a short story about an animal that has personification. (Include a discussion of personification for younger students.)*

Gene Zion: Harry and the Dirty Dog books

http://my.linkbaton.com/bibliography/zion/gene

Author Studies: Elementary School

Stan and Jan Berenstain

http://villa.lakes.com/mariska/bears/bio.html

Have students read one of the Berenstain Bears books. The students should complete an author study about Stan and Jan Berenstain. After the completion of these two activities, have the students draw a cartoon. The cartoon should include characters with a problem; there should be problem-solving tactics, and so on. Length and content should be teacher specific.

Joanna Cole and Bruce Degen

www.scholastic.com/magicschoolbus/books/index.htm

Students should read one of the Magic School Bus books and do an author study of Joanna Cole and Bruce Degen. Prepare any lesson that correlates to the book that has been read. Have the students create another "magic object" and write a short story about it. When the stories are completed, have the students read their stories in the authors' chair.

Tomie dePaola

www.bingley.com/Biography.html

Chris Van Allsburg

www.remc8.k12.mi.us/eastgr/rapr/htmls/new/
people/ewfam.html

www.eduplace.com/rdg/author/cva/classroom.html

Dr. Seuss

www.randomhouse.com/seussville

Author Studies: Older Elementary School–Middle School

Jan Brett

www.janbrett.com

Have students write a short chapter book. Introduction of lesson should focus on chapter books and how they are for advanced readers. If having the students read a chapter book by themselves is too difficult, set some extra time at the end of the day to have a shared reading. Read the book aloud and have students follow along with their own books.

Judy Blume

www.judyblume.com

Have students read one of Judy Blume's books and do research on her. The students should then write a story in the same format as the book they read or a story that resembles typical Judy Blume content and/or characters.

R. L. Stein

http://scholastic.com/goosebumps/high/index.htm

Have the students read one of the Goosebumps books, following the same general guidelines as in the other author studies. Have the students write a mystery book that has some frightening elements. Class discussion should involve creating a mystery and how to add frightening elements. Discuss with the students the appropriate level of horror for their mysteries.

Arnold Lobel: Frog and Toad books

www.sdcoe.k12.ca.us/score/frog/frogtg.html

E. B. White: Stuart Little

www.harperchildrens.com/hch/author/author/white

Roald Dahl: Matilda *and* James and the Giant Peach

www.geocities.com/Hollywood/Academy/4613/
dahl.html

Lynne Reid Banks: The Indian in the Cupboard *and other books*

www.friend.ly.net/scoop/biographies/bankslynne/
index.htm

www.lynnereidbanks.com

Madeleine L'Engle: A Wrinkle in Time

http://the-casteels.com/~castiron/lengle.html

L. M. Montgomery: Anne of Green Gables books

www.dd.chalmers.se/~f95lean/authors/lmmlink.html

J. K. Rowling: Harry Potter books

www.sffworld.com/authors/r/rowling_jk

William Steig: Abel's Island

www.williamsteig.com

Author Studies: Middle School

Sherry Garland

www.scholastic.com/dearamerica/index.htm

According to its publishers, the Dear America books invite you "into the personal experience of girls from different times in American history. The books and television shows are inspired by real letters and diaries from girls who lived in extraordinary circumstances. You will experience firsthand what it was like to grow and live in another time and place." Have students write a letter about what is currently happening in the world. Create a time capsule and have each student contribute to the time capsule. Bury the time capsule in the schoolyard and have a reunion set for the following year, or ever later, when students can rediscover their letters.

Ann M. Martin

www.scholastic.com/annmartin/bsc/index.htm

Have a class perform the same activities for a Baby-Sitters Club book as in the rest of the author studies. The students should then write a lesson about responsibility. Lead a discussion of responsibility and how to become a responsible student. Use everyday examples and examples that can be applied in the classroom.

In the 1800s, students who had difficulty reading had to remain after school, stand, and read orally for the teacher. Today, struggling readers use their learning strengths to build literacy.

History and Theories of Literacy Instruction

Dear Dr. Block,

So far, I think I have learned that every time I sit with my students I discover something about their abilities and difficulties that I did not previously realize. I can't use just one test or technique and think, "That's it, that's his problem and here's how we fix it." For example, how come I did not see Gene move his finger under his words while he read orally last week? Was I unobservant? Was the work easier then? Is this a new problem he developed because of something I did? I know that you taught me to be aware of the changes in our students' strategies for reading, writing, and speaking. Until I actually observed, listened, and monitored all the time I did not realize how many clues I had let slip by! I will improve with practice. I will make my future experiences lead to greater insights. I will never say "Now I have seen it all. I can just pigeonhole all my students from now on."

Sincerely,
Judith Sear, elementary teacher

■ Chapter Overview: Key Points

This chapter is designed to assist you in envisioning instruction that enables less accomplished readers/writers to attain their full literacy potential. There are many effective methods that enable students to overcome literacy challenges. In this chapter you will learn about the following:

- The history of literacy instruction, including methods for less accomplished readers that have been used since the Middle Ages
- Reading instruction for struggling readers today
- Pulling historical and theoretical threads together

The chapter begins with a gleam into the history of instruction. The purposes are (1) to understand the roots of the theories and methods that exist today; (2) to determine the reasons why students whose literacy activities are labor intensive responded to earlier instructional approaches as they did; (3) to use the knowledge gained from history so that we will not repeat its mistakes, and (4) to increase our abilities to distinguish genuine progress in literacy research/practice from mere "pendulum swings."

Later in the chapter, current theories of reading instruction are described. Projections are made for improving instruction and assessment in the twenty-first century. By chapter's end, you will also have answers for the following questions:

1. How have the practices of earlier reading specialists and teachers established a new understanding of the literacy needs of less accomplished readers?
2. What changes are likely to occur in the future for students who do not use reading/writing for pleasure and personal growth?
3. What are the changing societal needs that literacy has addressed throughout history?
4. What methods have been used and are being developed for students who struggle to comprehend and/or compose?

■ The History of Literacy Instruction

In this section, you will discover that some literacy methods have been in use for a long time. A description of their origins will help you understand their intent. For some practices, tradition alone, rather than effectiveness, sustains their use today. For others, the needs that they addressed in the past are still being addressed effectively today.

From the Middle Ages to the Seventeenth Century

The first record of reading instruction appeared in 813 A.D. At this time students were taught to read the religious creeds of the Catholic Church, the Lord's Prayer, the Ten Commandments, and psalms. The textbook was (and still is) called a **basal reader.** Monks named the first basal reader *The Primer,* not because it was the *first* book of reading instruction, but because it was considered the *primary,* fundamental printed word—the minimum essentials necessary for a person's spiritual existence. From 1607 until 1777, the primer was the standard book for instruction in England and the United States. During this period, family and school were at one in their beliefs about the purposes and high value of reading instruction. In fact, until the dawn of the eighteenth century it was unanimously agreed throughout the Western world that religious content should be the subject matter and purpose for reading instruction.

Students in these early days were expected to learn to "read" by age 10. "Reading" was defined as being able to "word-call" (pronounce words in the primer and the Bible correctly); knowing the meanings of words was not an important instructional goal. By word-calling, children could read the Bible aloud in church (their illiterate parents echoed the words immediately after their children's reading to show that they were reading as well). Bible verses intended for the next Sunday's church service formed the basis of that week's reading instruction. Such verses were memorized through word-calling from Monday through Friday on the week preceding each service (Smith, 1989).

It is significant that during this period, because most adults were illiterate, children's word-calling served an important family and community function. Moreover, because there usually was only one copy of documents and other information in a community, children could word-call from these single copies to members of the community. At the family level, the Bible was the only book in most home libraries. Often families without a Bible would meet before the fireplace of neighbors to share in religious readings performed by a child who had mastered the art of reading.

Early American Colonial Period

During the early colonial period, all readers received the same lessons at the same pace as all others at their grade level. Those who could not keep up had to stay after school to echo words read by their instructor, as illustrated in the line drawing that opened this chapter.

Because parents viewed their children's learning to read as a necessary step toward spiritual salvation, youngsters who did not work hard at reading were viewed as "sinful," destined to anger God and to disgrace their families (Ford, 1897). For this reason, unsuccessful readers did their best to memorize as many words as they could and to hide their reading problems. These readers also endured the drudgery of recitation: "Boys and girls were obliged to spend many weary hours naming the letters in syllables and words before reading sentences in a contextual context" (Smith, 1989, p. 67).

From 1800 to 1840

The American Revolution changed the purpose of literacy instruction. With independence from England, reading instruction was designed to develop students' perfect use of "the American version of English, to build students' character, and to make students morally good" (Cobb, 1840, p. 1). The fathers of democracy viewed a national reading curriculum as the key to national unity among the colonies. In addition, the founding fathers believed that unity would occur more rapidly if dialectical differences among the colonies were eliminated. Instruction in proper diction was to become the means. As a result, for about 100 years, a large proportion of time in America was spent teaching students to enunciate each letter of every word. Most instruction consisted of individual students taking turns in the oral reading of one sentence after another from the basal reader, and in the completion of enunciation drills on single letter sounds.

Moreover, to establish a national curriculum, the first multipaged textbooks were published, including *First Book, Spelling Book, Juvenile Reader, McGuffey Reader,* and *The North American Reader.* Approximately 350 of the more than 500 pages in these readers would contain selections about America by American authors. The content was equally divided between historical essays (designed to instill patriotism in students) and moral treatises, short stories, and poems (chosen for their character-building qualities). Such instruction, and the concern with effective oral recitation of text, seemed eminently suited for a new nation wanting to safeguard both the freedoms of the pulpit and the democratic ideals of the public forum that its citizens had fought so hard to gain (Robinson, Faraone, Hittleman, & Unruh, 1990).

The instructional approach of the time utilized phonics, the ancient spelling method of the Greeks. As Marrou (1948) recounts:

> The first thing to be learned was the alphabet, then syllables, then words, then sentences, and finally continuous passages. One stage was not tackled until all the problems in the preceding stage had been fully dealt with—which meant spending a long time on each [level of word analysis]. (p. 150)

It is important to note that until the 1840s unsuccessful readers received no instruction designed specifically for them. Students who had difficulty reading might drop out of school; or they might learn to word-call just enough of the basic words to get the gist of stories in the primer and bulletins posted in stores, banks, and town halls, in an attempt to hide their illiteracies.

The Nineteenth and Early Twentieth Centuries

In the 1840s a universal call was made to promote a more law-abiding, intelligent citizenry through literacy. In an attempt to entice everyone to learn to read, publishers began to place pictures in books. It was believed that such illustrations would make the reading more interesting and that people or students could associate the meanings of words to the pictures. (See Figure 2.1, a sample from one of the first books to contain pictures—an 1849 basal reader.) In addition, during the 20 years between 1840 and 1860, schools changed from using the same textbook for students of all ages to the use of several graded books (one per grade level). With this change the first instructional adaptation was made for students who had difficulties reading. Such students read and reread the same primer-level books, while others advanced to readers for grade 2 and then the higher sequential levels.

62   SANDERS' SERIES.

pie ces   crouch es   grow ing
an gry   mo ment   mount ain
lash es   yon der   be yond

THE LION.

Is this a lion? No; it is only the picture of a lion. The lion lives in his den. He is very strong.

He has a great deal of thick, yellow hair about his neck. That is his mane.

FIGURE 2.1 1879 Basal Reader, with Illustrations

Source: McGuffey's Sixth Eclectic Reader, Revised Edition. (1879). Cincinatti, New York: Van Antwerp, Bragg & Co.

Subject matter and instructional strategies in these books were also transformed. While moral selections retained their prominence, intensely patriotic materials all but disappeared. In North America the new interest was to offer a broad range of topics so as to create an educated citizenry, and the content of reading textbooks reflected this goal. Upper-division readers included treatises in science, history, art, philosophy, economics, and politics; nature and scientific topics dominated in basal readers for grades 1 through 3. Moreover, with an increased need to learn content area words and their meanings, the ancient Greek phonics approach fell into disrepute and the whole-word method appeared:

> It is not, perhaps, very important that a child should know the letters before he begins to read. He may learn first to read words by seeing them, hearing them pronounced, having their meanings illustrated, and afterwards—he may learn to analyze them or name the letters of which they are composed. (Worcester, 1828, p. 3)

It was also during this period that instruction shifted from an emphasis on oral to silent reading and began to include the development of comprehension. For example, a typical lesson between 1890 and 1920 would have followed this scenario taken from a teacher's manual of that era:

> The children are in their usual seats. Print on the blackboard COME TO CLASS. (This is the *first step* in teaching a child to *receive an idea*—in this case, the idea of following directions.)
>
> Pointing to the words, talk informally to the pupils. Waste no words. Say something like this: "What I have printed here (indicating) means that all of you are to rise whenever you see this and come to this place where the little chairs are. I call this place 'the class.' "
>
> Before the children can comply with the request and COME TO CLASS, the teacher erases the request, saying nothing more. She then prints it again, still saying nothing, and looks at the class. Those pupils less timid than others will do as the words indicate. Tell the timid pupils just what it means.
>
> When all the pupils are seated "in class," turn to the board and print GO TO YOUR SEATS. Tell the pupils that when that is printed it means: go and sit in your own seat.
>
> The children return to their original seats. The teacher erases all words from the board. Again print COME TO CLASS. Say nothing, but look at the children. They rise, come to the class, and seat themselves. Now erase the words and re-print GO TO YOUR SEATS, and if necessary explain again. Repeat the exercise of coming to the class and returning to the seats as many times as necessary. (Watkins, 1922, p. 31)

RECOGNIZING READING "DISABILITIES." In 1920, when instruction began to focus on comprehension, students' inability to understand what they read became apparent. As a result, tests were created to diagnose why such inabilities existed. These tests were designed to detect what was termed at that time to be "reading disabilities." At the time, causes for literacy difficulties were attributed to inadequate mental ability, heredity, conditions related to cerebral balance, abnormal emotional tendencies, visual/auditory deficiencies, and faulty reading habits. Among the most prominent theories was one that explained reading problems as **strephosymbolia** (meaning "twisted symbols" and later to be called *dyslexia*), developed by Samuel Orton, a physician (Orton, 1928). This theory proposed that "reading deficiencies" occurred because students were forced to read before they had outgrown "laterality." **Laterality** was defined as the inability to process print accurately because the left hemisphere of the brain was not sufficiently developed to perform this function.

To address various reading needs, educators began to use ability grouping. All students who had "reading disabilities," "inadequate mental ability," "laterality," and/or "strephosymbolia" were grouped together for reading instruction. Teachers usually created three to five groups: (1) a fast-moving group (pupils who were judged to be naturally more resourceful, self-reliant, and capable of covering large amounts of reading work), (2) an average-moving group (pupils who were judged capable of covering the required amount of reading work for their age level with reasonable amounts of study and effort), and (3) one to three slow-moving groups grouped by labeled cause of difficulties (pupils who were to confine their energies to the minimum essentials, with seatwork and books that were simple enough to be within their ability so they would not be faced with failure and discouragement) (Smith, 1989, p. 185).

Also during this period, a division began between educators as to the proper philosophy to guide instruction for these separate groups. Elements of this debate continue today. One group believed that readers who read only single words or who could not sustain understanding should practice sequential, separate skills that were presented carefully by their teacher; others believed that such students should set their own purposes and engage in literacy activities designed to fulfill those purposes. The latter group was known as the Activity Movement, which is similar to the whole language movement of today (discussed later in this section, under "The 1970s and 1980s"). Those who adhered to the skills philosophy belonged to what became known as the Basic Skills Movement and continued to use basal readers exclusively for the instruction of all readers. Members of the Activity Movement, on the other hand, used materials written by children, adult reference materials, and books children chose to read as a result of their own interests.

During the 1930s the first widely accepted alternative pull-out or Tier 4 instructional program—still in use today—was created. This program, called the Fernald Kinesthetic Method, was created and practiced in the reading clinic at the University of California at Los Angeles by Dr. Grace M. Fernald. As explained in Fernald's first book, *Remedial Techniques in Basic School Subjects* (1943), readers at Stages 2 and 3 of literacy ability were asked to trace words written for them. As they traced each word in parts, they also said the word aloud until they could reproduce it in its entirety without looking at the copy. Then students wrote the word as a label or in a story.

From 1940 to 1970

During the 1940s reading instruction suffered its first dethronement as the major method of infusing new goals into society. This dethronement came from more widespread mass communication. As the radio replaced the lamp on living room tables in homes across the United States, and as movies became increasingly popular, reading decreased in prominence as a recreational pursuit. In an attempt to make reading more appealing, educators adopted strategies designed to capture readers' attention—such as providing more age-appropriate content in basals, conducting individual conferences, extending silent reading periods, making more long-range assignments, writing workbooks to accompany the basals so students had more varied materials to read, using self-guided materials such as programmed instruction, conducting instruction in smaller groups of only five or six students, and allowing students to give book reports (Durrell, 1937; Russell, Ousby, Wolfing, & Haynes, 1948–1951).

You may be surprised that it was only 50 years ago that colleges and school districts first offered courses to address "the urgent need for increased understanding of reading problems" (National Society for the Study of Education, 1948, p. 291). These courses were first offered through summer sessions, extension and home-study courses, workshops, reading conferences, and consultant services.

In the 1950s, context clues and structural analysis were created as instructional techniques to help students read the expanding number of words being added to the **lexicon** (the dictionary of words in our language). Moreover, in an effort to export democratic principles to other countries and remain the world leader, U.S. publishers produced more children's **trade books** (books sold in bookstores; non-textbooks) in content areas such as science, math, social studies, and world geography; periodicals for children also were published (e.g., *Weekly Reader*).

In 1957, when the former USSR sent the first satellite, *Sputnik,* into space, the supremacy of the United States was challenged for the first time in post–World War II history. A "thundering demand for public education" resulted (Carr, 1960, p. 7). Reading, once again, was commonly acknowledged as the foundation upon which U.S. supremacy was to be regained. Pressure to produce greater numbers of more competent readers—faster and faster—led to a search for quick-fix panaceas and new methods of instruction for readers at all levels on the literacy continuum.

In addition, during the 1960s, President Lyndon Johnson announced his intention to use education, and particularly reading instruction, to "make war on joblessness, and on poverty, and to provide 'Civil Rights' for all citizens" (*Elementary and Secondary Educational Act,* 1965). Government appropriations, under Chapter 1 of the *Elementary and Secondary Education Act,* established reading centers to teach unemployed, illiterate adults and youth. Equality in civil rights was also to be advanced through $1.3 million in state grants to purchase books for school libraries. In this way, reading materials of interest to students from many cultural backgrounds would be readily available. (Amazingly, before the enactment of this legislation, 70 percent of all the elementary schools in the United States *did not even have a school library.*) President Johnson further stated that "remedial reading courses would open up new vistas for slow learners" and that the number of separate classes for remedial reading instruction should increase (Johnson, 1965).

Despite these efforts, however, problems still existed. For instance, one of the most frequent educational options for readers who were not progressing at the same pace as their peers was retention—repeating a grade. Because of the stigma attached to "flunking," many students learned to hide their reading problems so that they could at least remain in the "low group" with their peers, doing just enough to avoid being held back. In this way they passed from grade to grade—but they also moved into ever more difficult reading material without improving their decoding and comprehension strategies or increasing their enjoyment of reading and writing (Smith, 1989).

To compound this problem, basal reader stories became increasingly more dense, using text and textual features that were less reader-friendly than in the past (Allington, 1995). Also, because students remained in school until the high school years, reading classes were extended into high school. Publishers provided **high-interest, low-vocabulary books** (books written about topics of interest to students in grades 3 and above, but on reading levels that were no higher than grade 3). The rationale was that these carefully selected readings of easy content would help less accomplished readers/writers to increase their literacy abilities because they would enjoy reading more.

The 1970s and 1980s

A fundamental assumption governed much of the new reading curricula developed in the 1970s: Certain skills are *basic* (such as decoding) and must be mastered before students receive instruction on more advanced skills such as reading comprehension and writing composition (Means & Knapp, 1991). Following this assumption, students who remained in the lower levels of literacy ability received intensive instruction that focused on the "basics"—such as completing separate phonics worksheets for each phonetic rule. **Phonics** can be defined as a method of teaching reading whereby students analyze words, matching individual letters or word parts to the sounds they represent in spoken language—an approach similar to that in vogue during the period from 1800 to 1840. Because many students who were at the lower levels of literacy ability were also among those who learned slowly at the outset, these students continued to receive more and more practice in the basics without opportunities to see that the purpose of the written word is to create meaning. Similarly, instruction in composition taught penmanship, grammar, and spelling as prerequisites to be mastered before students could script their own ideas. Thus, students who were slower in mastering these basic skills received extensive practice in completing fill-in-the-blank worksheets in lieu of an opportunity to write meaningful expressions of their own ideas.

Furthermore, as a result of the federal legislation described earlier, these students were placed in pull-out "remedial" programs and no longer received reading instruction in their regular classroom. Most special reading teachers and classroom teachers did not coordinate their instruction, so the content and objectives covered in the self-contained classroom were not the same as those used in the instruction of "remedial readers." Another shortcoming of the pull-out programs was that, because they had to spend time gathering their materials and walking down the hall to another room and teacher, less advanced readers actually spent *less* time in reading instruction than classmates at higher levels of literacy achievement. It was not until 1991 that a federal law decreed that such compensatory reading instruction must not occur in place of regular reading instruction.

During the 1970s and 1980s, education's focus on the fundamentals seemed reasonable. Thus, limiting "remedial reading" instruction to repetition of only the most basic skills was believed to be the most effective approach to developing higher levels of literacy (Allington, 1980; Brophy, 1986; Brophy & Good, 1974).

THE TECHNOLOGICAL REVOLUTION. Another factor that shaped reading instruction during the 1970s and 1980s was the explosion of knowledge as a result of the technological revolution. First, because technology replaced the need for thousands of unskilled, illiterate laborers, the choice of just going to work instead of staying in school became less attractive and less feasible. As a result, for the first time in history, high school students could not freely choose the option of *not* learning to read without tremendous financial ramifications. Moreover, the necessity to read and understand complicated operating instructions for newly created technological devices concomitantly raised the level of functional literacy people needed to survive. For example, in the 1930s most students could survive successfully throughout their lives with only a second grade level of literacy (Smith, 1989). Beginning in the 1970s (and continuing today), a literacy ability at the eighth grade level was required, because directions for personal and professional products are written at this level (e.g., instructions for using calling cards to dial long distance, manuals for Nintendo games and word processing, and employee training manuals for human resource development programs). Furthermore, beginning in the 1980s many high school students were taught biotechnology, laser technology, microelectronics, robotics, and multimedia computer-driven design applications for professions such as architecture, engineering, ranching, medicine, physics, biology, ecology, art, and music. Thus, if students had reading difficulties, they had fewer career opportunities than their peers.

NEW APPROACHES TO INSTRUCTION. In the 1980s, educators began to shift away from a *deficit model* (something is missing in or wrong with the child) to a *difference model* (children learn to read in different ways and at different rates) to describe literacy levels. This change prompted a reexamination of instructional issues, placed greater emphasis on the teaching of reading and writing as processes that use strategies, and encouraged the redesign of assessments used to measure levels of literacy achievement. Also at this time, educators worked to coordinate instruction between classroom teachers and Tier 3 and 4 support personnel. School-day scheduling was adjusted so that these educators could plan together, discuss lessons, and share materials (Johnston, Allington, & Afferbach, 1985; Oakes, 1986). As a result, more readers had more time to reflect on and discuss what they read, and so to join the **"literacy club"**—a term coined by Smith (1987) to refer to students who choose reading and writing to achieve personal goals and to receive pleasure.

Although the **whole language movement** began much earlier in Canada, Australia, New Zealand, and England, the 1980s were the first period in U.S. history that this movement gained momentum and nationwide support. Whole language is a philosophy of literacy development with instructional approaches embedded within it. This philosophy includes the use of children's literature and children's writing to develop students' motivation, abilities, and interests in literacy. Advocates within the whole language movement also promote instructional innovations for readers in regular as well as compensatory programs. Students are encouraged to pursue meaningful interests and to use literacy abilities to solve problems and improve their lives.

Another reform of this period was to use extended reading passages to assess comprehension strategies and to use students' writings to assess reading/writing processes. Portfolios, journals, response groups, and children's literature gained prominence (rather than basal readers) as materials for literacy instruction and assessment. This was also the most prolific period in history for the refining, redefining, and creation of theories to explain the wide spectrum of literate behaviors and differences on the literacy continuum (Ruddell & Ruddell, 1994).

Reading Instruction for Struggling Readers Today

In 1992 Walmsley reported that readers at beginning stages of literacy ability are less likely to be exposed to full-length selections of children's literature in their adapted instructional programs than are more accomplished readers. Without frequent engagement with full-length literature, it is hard for these readers to learn strategies for untangling and enjoying complex plots and boldly drawn characters. Moreover, most are also still being taught in homogeneous reading groups similar to those in use in the 1920s and not as equal members in a larger community of learners. Such readers are also taken through books with more structure, more teacher direction, and less speed. They are expected to concentrate more on literal comprehension than personal appreciation of what they read.

In addition, criticism of traditional pull-out programs is mounting because these programs have been shown to (1) fragment readers' instruction, (2) stigmatize students, and (3) diminish the consistency in instruction that could occur if Tier 1 through 3 supports from both teachers and specialists were provided in the same room and involved the same instructional objectives. Moreover, research suggests that students tend to become more like the average reader in their most intimate community grouping. Therefore, if readers at the beginning levels of independent comprehension abilities are placed in groups with more accomplished peers, they will gravitate to higher mean performances than if they remain in homogeneous groups (Shepard, 1992).

In 1992 the U.S. government amended the Chapter 1 program to require that compensatory instruction be coordinated with classroom instruction (Allington, 1993). As a result, three new approaches to instruction for readers emerged: in-class instructional support, extended schooling, and schoolwide restructuring (Bean, Cooley, Eichelberger, Lazar, & Zigmond, 1991). **In-class instructional support** refers to Tier 1 and 2 supports provided for readers in their regular classroom. If Tier 3 instructional supports could be moved into the self-contained classroom, eliminating the amount of instructional time lost traveling down the hall and providing as much as an hour of increased instructional time each week. Moreover, when the reading specialist and classroom teacher work as a team in the same room, potential stigmatization is also reduced as both teachers work with all students.

Another new program is the extended school alternative. In this approach, struggling readers arrive early, stay after school, and/or come on Saturday mornings for extra instructional sessions. The extended year option is also increasing in popularity, with some districts offering many readers/writers the opportunity to receive instruction beyond the required days for 6 weeks in the summer. The assumption common to these approaches is that readers/writers who have not reached pleasure-filled comprehension benefit from more time and support to break the reading code and to learn how to enjoy and profit from literacy. As with all new approaches, however, only time can prove their effectiveness:

> The full impact of these recent approaches has yet to be realized. For example, some of the successful whole-language practices may need to be reexamined to explore better why they work. We suspect, for example, that predictable books are useful primarily

because (a) they help to ensure early success, and (b) they provide for the repetition of words, and *not* because they prepare children to be predictors and context users. Other practices, such as those concerned with the role of direct decoding instruction, will need to be reconsidered with care if recent results are to be accommodated. Until more is known, our own advice to practitioners can be summarized in two words: caution and self-reliance. Through even-handed consideration of what has been written, and through careful reflection on their own classroom experiences, teachers appear to be arriving at approaches that work for them, regardless of how those approaches may be labeled by others. (McKenna, Robinson, & Miller, 1993, p. 149)

You and the Future

In 1890 public education first assumed the responsibility of teaching *all* students to read. This responsibility becomes increasingly complex every year. For example, until about 1940 students could be self-sufficient as adults with only a minimal literacy level—they could read labels, sign their names, and comprehend less complex sentences. By 1940, functional literacy had risen to about a sixth grade level.

From 1940 to the present, because of the increased sophistication of industrial equipment, the demand for a more highly literate citizenry has continued to accelerate (Giorgis & Johnson, 2001). Specialization also demands higher levels of vocabulary development. The complexity in our legal system increases the need for abstract comprehension abilities to deal effectively with contract law and disputes related to failed communication efforts. In the twenty-first century the need continues for higher levels of literacy to enable people to reach maximum personal and professional fulfillment. Moreover, the student population of the future will continue to become more diverse socioculturally and linguistically. Already the Department of Labor is projecting incomes not on the basis of completing high school, as it did until 1965, but on whether students have obtained a college degree. Therefore, the responsibility of reading teachers is to provide students with grade 16 (college-level) literacy abilities—and this responsibility has substantial ramifications for students' economic well-being. For example, in 1980 a person graduating from college could expect to earn twice as much as a person with a high school education. Today a college education (and college-level reading ability) has increased in value: Students who complete a college degree will earn 4 times as much as students who are unable to handle the reading/writing responsibilities that accompany college-level work or who do not desire to attend college (U.S. Labor Department, 1994). The Department of Labor also estimates that by the year 2005, graduate college-level reading ability will be worth *17 times more* than non-college-level reading ability.

As reading instruction has moved away from the 1970s skills hierarchy, curriculum objectives for struggling readers have become more global. Students can learn the purposes and pleasures of reading/writing/speaking/listening (e.g., using self-selected books for reading activities, checking the bulletin board to see who will go first to lunch or which books are available at 10:00, and finishing a book they "love" so they can find out what the main character "ended up doing"). The new assumption is that decoding instruction is more effective if words are used to form messages that a student values.

Present and future programs for readers/writers at all levels of literacy development will be more effective if they include all that we have learned from the history of reading instruction. Specifically, such instruction should:

- Appreciate and build on the literacy accomplishments that every learner brings to school
- Use students' strengths to overcome weaknesses
- Understand students' cultural, social, and linguistic strengths to avoid misinterpreting differences as deficits
- Develop a curriculum that focuses on complex, meaningful problems
- Help students master basic skills in the context of more global tasks they will have to do in the real world
- Assist students to connect literacy with out-of-school experiences
- Increase higher-level thinking during literacy instruction
- Encourage multiple instructional approaches
- Move from didactic to conversational instructional formats, with students acting as informants, researchers, teachers, and learners
- Design curricula and instructional methods for students who are linguistically and educationally different that build on their prior learning rather than contradicting their experiences outside of school

Pulling Historical and Theoretical Threads Together

There are several theories and philosophies that today's educators advocate to prevent and diagnose reading difficulties and to instruct and assess readers. A **philosophy** can be defined as a set of criteria used to choose actions and resolve dilemmas when equally attractive instructional alternatives compete for attention. To more clearly identify and articulate your own instructional philosophy, it is helpful to (1) reflect on what you want your students to do as readers and writers, (2) analyze actions that other teachers have employed to help students become readers and writers who reach their fullest potentials, and (3) understand the theories and philosophies that other professionals advocate.

Therefore, before you study a few widely accepted contemporary theories, consider the questions that follow. Write down your own answers. If you have not yet taught, try to imagine what you would do, think, and expect from students who have not reached their potential the literacy continuum.

1. What do you expect all students to be able to do as readers/writers by the time they leave your room?
2. What indicators will clearly demonstrate that you have succeeded in providing the supports the students needed to reach this goal?

3. What types of instruction and assessment were most profitable to you when you were learning to read and write? How could these be adapted for students in your classroom who are decoding single words and whose meaning-making is frequently interrupted?
4. What do you want your students to be able to do as readers, writers, speakers, and listeners for the rest of their lives?

At the end of this chapter, you can return to your answers and compare them to the six widely referenced contemporary philosophies discussed on the following pages. In this way you can more accurately identify the instructional and assessment principles you most value, particularly as they apply to the readers who have special needs. Moreover, in the future, when new theories are proposed, you can determine the aspects of each that you think are most likely to truly advance literacy for students. You can avoid being led astray by misassumptions about literacy development or by trends that mostly replicate past, less successful instructional approaches.

The Bottom-Up or Additive Model

In the bottom-up or additive model, students begin with specific skills instruction and then add to these abilities as they "work their way up." Students are provided with as much specific instruction in decoding, comprehension, and affective responses to reading as possible. The instructional content comprises facts, skills, concepts, and principles that govern the order of words, sentences, and paragraphs in reading, writing, and speaking. Teachers provide direct instruction and practice on individual word analyses and comprehension processes so that students can interpret and apply what they read to their lives. The difference between what learners know, on the one hand, and what is available to be known about literacy, on the other, defines the instructional task. Literacy is taught through expanded explanations and practice; individual literacy skills are explained during instruction. These lessons are not taught at point of need, within the context of material students select to read. Rather, they are presented in a predetermined order, similar to the sequence created in 1840. According to this model, in the purest interpretation, today's less accomplished readers would be taught all the sounds of the letters in the alphabet; major English word parts such as *-at, -en, -oy,* and *-ut;* and compound words before they would be asked to read a passage silently with a peer, or aloud.

Similarly, instructional material is selected not by what students already know about literacy, but rather by what they do not know. Essentially, according to this model, the best method of moving readers/writers to higher levels of literacy development is to reduce the discrepancy between what they can do and what they should be able to do by teaching them content that they do know.

The Top-Down or Meaning Emphasis Model

The top-down or meaning emphasis model is also referred to as the **psycholinguistic model** (Goodman, 1967) and the **information-processing model** (Smith, 1971). According to this model, readers learn facts, processes, concepts, and principles more indirectly than in the bottom-up model: They learn to use the redundancy in written messages (spelling pattern cues, sentence pattern cues, and meaning cues) to derive meaning. Thus, the task of learning to read is to develop skill through an inquiry process in which readers communicate all that they know and want to learn.

Students engage in many processes while they are interacting with reading/writing/ speaking through material they select. Teachers must guide learners to interact with these reading materials in such a way that important principles relative to individual texts are learned. For example, a struggling reader who chooses to read *Arthur's Thanksgiving* by Marc Brown—and who also has trouble decoding longer words—would receive instruction on how structural analysis (breaking words into base words, prefixes, and suffixes) can become a very effective decoding strategy for words like *Thanksgiving*. Alternatively, another struggling reader who chose the same book would not be taught about structural analysis but might be asked to read *Arthur's Halloween* just as soon as she finished reading *Arthur's Thanksgiving*. To help the student better understand the second book, the reading specialist or teacher would tell her to think about all she had learned about Arthur in the first book before reading the next one. After the second book was completed, the teacher would show how to apply prior knowledge so that the student will comprehend more in the future.

Essentially, according to this model, teachers and reading specialists help students add new processes and methods of questioning to their literacy repertoires. They support and guide students' use of these processes so they more closely approximate the way expert readers/writers conduct their literacy pursuits. Words students need are displayed around the room; there is greater use of children's literature, rather than separate worksheets about individual decoding skills; and drama becomes another way to teach reading.

Proponents of top-down models follow the general instructional guidelines labeled as *whole language.* The goal of instruction is to create a literate environment that provides many opportunities for students to learn to read as they are drawn into it through their natural inclinations. Students use language, read, write, and grapple with meaning in the varied forms in which language presents itself in the books they choose to read. The key instructional feature of this approach is that it provides instruction according to each individual's need rather than in a curriculum-driven, sequential way (as in the bottom-up model). However, teachers and reading specialists must pay careful attention to ensure that all struggling readers receive all the decoding and comprehension strategies they need for literacy proficiency and that gaps of knowledge are closed for students as needs arise. A balanced approach that incorporates bottom-up and top-down learning experiences has been demonstrated to significantly increase struggling readers' decoding and comprehension abilities (Block & Pressley, 2002; Pressley, Allington, Wharton-McDonald, Block, & Morrow, 2001).

The Interactive Model

The interactive model (Rumelhart, 1976) describes literacy as the ability of a reader/ writer to select meaning by combining different information sources. These sources include the following:

- Meaning carried from past life experiences and literary material
- Semantic symbol systems in our language, known as *semantics*
- Sentence structure and grammatical features of our language, known as *syntax*
- Phonetic features of letters and morphemic features of words

In this model students are taught to identify words by combining sounds or word parts that they recognize with context clues. The reader then ties this new word to past experiences to seek meaning by using the context in which the word appears. Because the student is problem-solving while reading, promoting higher-order thinking during reading (and writing) is important. Teachers should stress that any "reading *of* the lines" is greatly aided by "reading *between* the lines" and "reading *beyond* the lines"—and that students should learn to use all three processes simultaneously.

The interactive model emphasizes interdisciplinary content as well as reading skills. It strives to boost comprehension when it appears to be faltering. Therefore, according to this model, students with word recognition weaknesses are taught to use context clues, pictures, prior knowledge, and predictions simultaneously to compensate. On the other hand, if readers have weak comprehension abilities, they can be taught to increase their stronger word recognition skills and to put the individual word meaning-making together—thereby reducing comprehension inabilities, limiting the problem to readings outside their personal vocabularies. According to this theory, readers are encouraged to rely on their perceived strengths to tackle their weaknesses. Extending this concept, Stanovich (1980) proposes that in an **interactive–compensatory model,** when readers have weaknesses in one aspect of literacy they can compensate by using other knowledge sources. For example, if readers' letter-to-sound knowledge is weak, they should be taught to rely more heavily on lexical knowledge of words (such as the position words hold in a particular sentence) to derive meaning. Thus, in classrooms that adhere to an interactive model, teachers would engage in many think alouds. These would be more dominant in the curriculum than expanded explanations (bottom-up model) or asking students about what they want to learn (top-down model). However, these think alouds (and other demonstrations of expert readers' strategic thinking processes) would vary according to students' needs, as in the top-down model, rather than following a sequential, prescribed order, as in the bottom-up model.

Whereas the bottom-up model begins instruction with the smallest unit of print (letters and sounds) and the top-down model begins with the largest unit of print (a whole book), interactive instruction focuses on process. It identifies what students could do relative to particular reading materials so as to help them learn the types of processes that distinguished readers utilize. This model is less intense than the balanced approach.

The Constructivist Model

In the constructivist model, meaning in texts is believed to exist only in the interactions of printed materials with individual reader's minds. As students exert effort to read, they invest feelings and emotions that influence the interpretation of that text as well as the cognitive processes used to derive meaning.

According to this model, reading comprehension is a selective process under readers' control; it requires interpreting, retelling the story to oneself, and rereading when a thread of meaning is lost (McKenna, Robinson, & Miller, 1993; Shepard, 1992). When readers do not see the relevance or meaningfulness of aspects of reading/writing instruction, they should learn to interpret the concepts in the material as relevant and meaningful in their own lives. The teacher's task is to draw analogies and metaphors based on what readers know to help them connect to what they do not understand. For example, according to the constructivist model, when readers at lower stages of accomplishment have difficulties interpreting a novel, the teacher should ask them to compare the dilemmas faced by the main characters to those the students face in their own lives. In this way, social, emotional, motivational, and personal aspects of readers' lives are called on to strengthen understanding. Academic content is thereby transformed into something that is meaningful and relevant to diverse learners.

Success in a reading/writing program is measured by the extent to which students are transformed into people with an active, self-initiated interest in reading; people who seek further knowledge without prompting; and people who utilize reading, writing, and speaking to interpret events around them (Gergen, 1985; Platt, 1994). For example, in a classroom that adheres to the constructivist theory, students are taught that many meanings are possible. If readers/writers have difficulty comprehending, they meet with their teachers or a peer partner to discuss what they don't understand. During this conversation, the meanings students have attached to individual words, sentences, and paragraphs are explored to determine if decoding errors or improper syntactical or semantical clues interfered with students' meaning-making. If this is the case, several connotations (synonyms) of a word's meaning are discussed so students can select the one they prefer for this context.

The Social Constructivist or Learning Community Model

The social constructivist or learning community model emphasizes the formation of a strong learning community to increase literacy. According to this model, social factors in reading materials and social context variables within the classroom influence literacy (Gee, 1992; Green & Weade, 1987). Reading lessons are viewed as containing well-established procedures and social structures (such as who can speak first and for how long), academic structures (content themes), and activity structures (what is going on with the story). In this theory, participation increases readers' knowledge of reading processes, written language conventions, and literary interpretative possibilities because students become more aware of multiple perspectives on literary themes (Eeds & Wells, 1989; Rogers, 1991; Snow & Ninio, 1986). Such social exchanges often also lead to the development of critical judgments about literary works (Golden, 1986; Guthrie, Schafer, Wang, & Afflerbach, 1995).

Prevalent in this model are the norms concerning reading/writing that the specific community of learners values or shuns. The teacher's task is to become a member of this community of learners while simultaneously developing ways to improve the norms of reading/writing to which the community subscribes. These standards are determined, in part, by cultural patterns and the social settings in which reading/writing occurs. Students derive multiple interpretations of their readings/writings/speeches through ideas created by classroom discussions.

According to this model students (1) are immersed in a classroom environment that is print-rich and filled with meaningful literary experiences adapted to accommodate the cultural and social needs of this particular learning community, (2) are aware that the teacher and classmates hold high standards and expectations of them to meet their learning responsibilities even though this may be difficult for them, and (3) know that they must take risks and use approximations of reading/writing skills until the conventional form can be created independently. Essentially, the reading specialist's and teacher's job is to advance students' levels of literacy independence by creating a classroom community or clinical setting that draws on the norms of literacy, the norms of collegiality, and equal participation—so all students will want to build literacy competencies (Shannon, 1991).

The Transactional Model

According to transactional theory, students bring all their personal experiences, along with the influence of their sociocultural milieu, to material they read (Rosenblatt, 1985, 1988). To make a meaning, a transaction must occur between all that students are, all that they bring with them—cognitively, affectively, and socially—and all the meaning that appears in the text. As depicted in Figure 2.2, reading and meaning are likely to be different for each reader. When an interaction between text and reader ignites, knowledge expands or collides—and this experience changes a reader's understanding in some way.

Rosenblatt distinguishes between types of reading interactions as being *aesthetic* or *efferent*. **Aesthetic reading** occurs when students receive pleasure from and can connect emotionally to a text, applying what was read, identifying with information, and/or exhibiting empathy for characters. When reading aesthetically, readers focus on the thoughts, feelings, images, and associations that the story evokes for them. In effect, they live through the reading experiences, pausing to reflect on how similar things have affected or could influence their own lives. On the other hand, **efferent reading** occurs when students interact with text to gain information, to do tasks, or to learn something new. In these interactions the most important emotional response is the satisfaction of having learned and understood something.

Which Model to Use?

Each of the contemporary theories presented in this section contributes to the creation of a strong philosophy of effective instruction for students who are not functioning at the highest stages of literacy competence. The bottom-up model provides a description of distinct meaning-bearing units of language that can assist readers/writers to learn and depend on the regularities and redundancies that exist in their language. The top-down model teaches students to value reading and writing as important tools to help answer their questions about life. It also urges these students to seek answers to their questions about literacy and to continue expanding their own repertoire of literacy competencies. The interactive model assists students to overcome obstacles to meaning-making through the interaction between the decoding and comprehension strengths that exist within themselves and the clues to be found in a given passage. The constructivist model enables students to value the meaning that they make through reading, even if this meaning differs from that of their peers. The social constructivist model enables students to understand how important their voices are in class discussions and why their meanings can help others. The transactional model helps students to understand how their cultural values and past experiences contribute to the meanings they create.

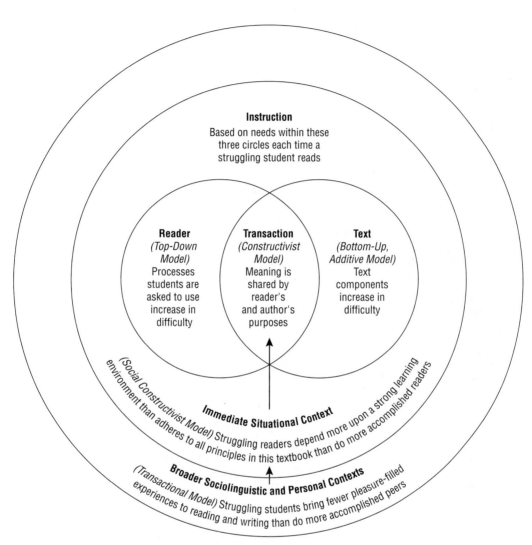

FIGURE 2.2 Interactive–Compensatory Model Surrounded by Conditions That Contribute to Each Struggling Reader's Literacy Success

Source: Adapted and expanded from model of C. Weaver (1988), *Reading process and practice: From Socio-Psycholinguistic to Whole Language,* p. 50. Portsmouth, NH: Heinemann.

Because each model has merit, many of the most successful reading specialists and teachers follow a combined model, as shown in Figure 2.2, and teach it to older less accomplished readers. By better understanding what literacy involves, these readers/writers can more clearly recognize specific dimensions of their literacy processing that they can strengthen.

Taken together, these models demonstrate the interplay between reading, writing, and speaking processes, showing why the job of advancing all readers/writers' abilities requires a masterful orchestration of many interdependent variables. To be successful, teachers and reading specialists working with readers/writers who have less literacy proficiency must have a sophisticated, multifaceted understanding not just of literacy processes and not just of their students (and the relationships between the two), but of themselves as well. As Shepard (1992) states:

> It follows from these principles that effective instruction should engage children in meaningful, contextually situated tasks where the goal is to practice and develop strategic thinking/literacy about important subject matter. The progress of instruction should be designed to help students use what they already know to arrive at new understandings. And prior knowledge is defined not just as vocabulary and information mastery but includes all of the images, language patterns, social relations, and personal experiences that a student relies on to make sense of something new. (p. 295)

Through much of the twentieth century, students who obtained reading scores on standardized tests that were at least two grade levels below their grade placements were labeled as remedial readers. Today, however, we need to remove the label from these students. Literacy demands on all readers/writers have increased in scope due to the increased functional literacy demands of our complex society. People can function at any of the five stages of literacy ability and can exhibit one or more of the following characteristics at different times: (1) lack of reflection on and application of material they read and write; (2) negative attitude toward reading and writing; (3) absence of persistence, self-monitoring, self-correction, and independence in reading/writing/speaking; (4) inability to actively construct meaning; (5) limited strategies for decoding and comprehending; and, (6) restricted repertoire of literary tastes and writing/speaking styles.

In the future, we must continue to search for new ways to expand our teaching repertoires and stretch beyond our present knowledge. We need to create and validate new and more appropriate instructional and assessment materials for readers and writers who do not develop high levels of literacy without special supports (Leu, 2001). These materials need to be tested, new methods discovered, and additional philosophies validated so that everyone can enjoy the new reading and writing challenges and pleasures that will accompany the innovative, technologically driven communication advancements that are sure to come in the twenty-first century.

Chapter Summary

The purpose of this chapter was to describe the history of instructional approaches and to survey theories of literacy development. Through this knowledge, teachers may avoid instructional beliefs and practices that limit reading success. The chapter also discussed the disadvantages of labeling students, separating them from their peers on a consistent basis, and lowering our expectations of their capabilities. By reviewing the history of literacy instruction and employing principles from contemporary theory, instructors can provide struggling students with increased instructional time, and a richer, interactive–compensatory approach that leads to higher levels of literacy competence. Moreover, by learning about the bottom-up, top-down, interactive, constructivist, social constructivist, and transactional theories of instruction, older struggling readers/writers can become more active partners with their teachers to advance their own literacy abilities.

Another major purpose of this chapter was to remind us all that the professional decisions we make, and the depth and breadth of our teaching repertoire, will be the most critical factors in determining our students' success as readers and writers. Further, if we remove the negative connotations and define literacy difficulties in a more comprehensive way, it becomes clear that all of us—when we are reading or writing difficult texts—can sometimes profit from the instructional strategies and supports described in the remainder of this book. All of us drop to lower stages of literacy proficiency at times. The only difference between us and less accomplished readers is that those in the latter group more frequently face challenges with reading and writing.

Realizing this may enable us—and all readers/writers—to eliminate any stigma attached to the adapted instruction that will be described in the remainder of this book. There are no longer people who are less able, but rather only one group of readers/writers, alike in that all *sometimes* experience situations in which literacy challenges emerge. Those readers/writers who cannot *sustain* understandings at the level they desire will profit most from the activities in this book. In Chapter 3, physical and cognitive differences in literacy abilities are described, as well as strategies that can be used to overcome difficulties relative to them.

Key Terminology

Many readers of this textbook enjoy writing their own definitions of the terms in the chapter. You can improve your retention of their meanings if you write the definitions in the margins or next to each term. If you already know the meaning of a term, place a check mark in the blank that precedes it. If you are not certain, review its meaning by turning to the page number that follows the term. If you have learned the meanings of 10 or more of these terms after your initial reading of the chapter, it is a good indication that your efferent comprehension was strong.

____ **basal reader** (page 33)
____ *The Primer* (page 33)
____ **strephosymbolia** (page 36)
____ **laterality** (page 37)
____ **lexicon** (page 38)
____ **trade books** (page 38)
____ **high-interest, low-vocabulary books** (page 39)
____ **phonics** (page 39)

____ **"literacy club"** (page 40)
____ **whole language movement** (page 40)
____ **in-class instructional support** (page 41)
____ **philosophy** (page 43)
____ **psycholinguistic model** (page 44)
____ **information-processing model** (page 44)

_____ interactive–compensatory model (page 46)

_____ aesthetic reading (page 48)
_____ efferent reading (page 48)

 Case Study

Making Professional Decisions

Caroline was 11 years old and had just completed the sixth grade when she was brought to the Reading Center. She had been referred by her sixth grade teacher, who was concerned about both her poor reading performance and her social adjustment.

According to her school reports, Caroline was reading at the third grade level. Initial testing at the Reading Center also indicated that her reading was about third grade level.

Caroline's mother came to the interview session, but her father was unable to attend because he and Caroline's stepmother lived out-of-state. During the interview, Caroline's mother stated that because of Caroline's father's work in the building construction business, the family had lived in four different cities since Caroline's birth. As a result, she went to different schools for grades 1, 2, and 3, and to her present school for grade 4.

According to her mother, she had always been a rather shy child. Her mother thought that she withdrew even more after her older sister married and moved away. In fact, during the last year, Caroline withdrew from the few friends she had. Her mother noted that she had not received any invitations to parties given by her classmates, even for Halloween.

Caroline's cumulative school records showed that she entered first grade at the age of 5 years, 9 months. The first school Caroline attended did not provide a full-day kindergarten. Before she entered school, Caroline was given a readiness test. Because of her age and her poor performance on the test, the teachers advised Caroline's parents to wait a year before enrolling her in school. However, her parents decided that it was best for the total family to have Caroline begin school immediately. Reading problems were noted continuously from the time that Caroline entered school. Problems in other academic subjects became apparent in the third grade.

The interview with Caroline's mother and the examination of school records showed that each of the three schools she had attended adhered to a different theoretical model to teaching reading. Moreover, Caroline's first school, in which she was in grade 1, had used a sight word approach. The second school, where she was in grade 2, used a phonics approach, and grade 3 used a whole language, language experience approach. Her present school used a balanced model.

In interviews Caroline's fourth grade teacher described her as "lazy." She said that Caroline "did not try hard enough." The only positive comments were made by her music teacher.

The Tier 3 support Clinic teacher said Caroline had difficulty discussing her reading problems. Also, she refused to read orally. During an informal conversation, Caroline described school as "terrible." She expressed a strong desire to have more friends, and she called herself "dumb."

Caroline was very enthusiastic about playing the piano. She had been taking lessons in school for 2 years, and she was making excellent progress.

Respond to the following questions, then check your responses against the Answer Key at the end of the book.

1. What environmental factors or individual factors could be associated with Caroline's reading problems? Which theoretical approach might best address her needs?
2. What suggestions could you make for ways that Caroline's mother could help her with reading and social difficulties?
3. Does Caroline have any interests that could be used to lead into a reading program? How could these interests be used?

Thinking and Writing about What You Have Learned

1. In your opinion, what is the most important topic that we should explore in the twenty-first century concerning the instruction and assessment of readers/writers who are not as proficient as they desire? Why? What can you see yourself doing to contribute to new discoveries relative to this topic?

2. List the five most important learning principles and teacher actions on which your instruction will be based by combining what you have learned in Chapters 1 and 2.

3. Summarize the key points you have learned thus far in the text concerning effective reading and writing instruction for less accomplished readers.

4. First, write out a definition of *reading*. Then, if you wish, compare your definition to mine. Don't read the definition that follows until after you have written your own.

   In my opinion, *reading* can be defined as the act of understanding an author's printed message, assigning purposes of one's own as well as deducing the author's intentions, and using the information gained to increase one's knowledge in a personally meaningful way. In the process of making inferences, readers utilize decoding processes, internal logic, facts, concepts, connotations, figurative language, personal experience, and the application of new information to other areas of one's knowledge, expertise, and experience. I believe Francis Bacon, who said: "Reading maketh a full person; conference a ready person; and writing an exact person."

5. Return to your previous answers concerning how you want to teach. Which of the six contemporary theories are reflected in your answers? Now, in approximately one paragraph, write a concise description of your philosophy for instructing and assessing less accomplished readers/writers. This description will help you verbalize to students, colleagues, students' parents, and administrators how you make your instructional and assessment decisions.

 Onto the Information Superhighway

Websites That Provide Ready-to-Use Lessons and Activities for Thematic Units

The American Library Association (ALA)
www.ala.org/parents/index.html

The Children's Book Council
www.cbcbooks.org

"On-Lion" for Kids (New York Public Library)
www.nypl.org/branch/kids

The Youth Division of the Internet Public Library
www.ipl.org/youth

Fairrosa Cyber Library
www.dalton.org/libraries/fairrosa

chapter 3

Physical and Cognitive Conditions That Create Differences in Literacy Achievement

Tiana used to be labeled with a physical condition. Now she is an active member of a self-contained classroom to which her resource teacher comes on a regular basis. Tiana enjoys leading peers each day in a Teacher Reader Group. In this role, she teaches using books she has read the day before.

Dear Dr. Block,

Tiana was so cooperative! Something happened during our time together today. It enabled me to relate to Tiana better than ever before. I brought a tape recorder to use in our lesson and it was not working. I apologized and explained to her that I had even tried it the night before. The tape recorder worked fine then. Suddenly, she leaned across the table, gently touched my arm, and tenderly replied, "I understand. Sometimes things don't work out for me, either. I have no idea why, because I always do just what I'm supposed to do."

—Doug Cowman,
second grade teacher and reading specialist

Chapter Overview: Key Points

The purpose of this chapter is to examine the physical and cognitive barriers that impede students' literacy progress. In Chapters 4 and 5, the affective, cultural, and societal variables that also impinge upon students' success will be discussed. Taken together, these chapters can develop (1) an appreciation for the complexity of the literacy process, (2) a comprehensive perspective on the distinctions between readers/writers at different stages of development, (3) a commitment to avoid labeling, and (4) a teaching repertoire so that preinstructional conditions do not lower your expectations for any student's capabilities.

By the end of this chapter you will know the following:

- Actions you can take to diagnose and instruct students with physical challenges that limit reading abilities
- Actions we can take to diagnose and instruct students who face mental, visual, or auditory challenges
- Cognitive variables that limit literacy competence

Diagnosis and Instruction of Students Who Face Physical Challenges

Even though each is discussed separately, the effects of physical, social, affective, and cultural differences on individual students' literacy are multiplicative and interactive. For example, myopia (a vision difficulty) left undetected at an early age can lead to inadequate exposures to print, so a child may not develop emergent reading abilities on a par with peers, which in turn may create a poor self-image and emotional maladjustment.

In the 1980s as many as 25 percent of all students labeled "remedial readers" were diagnosed with one or more of the inalterable physical or cognitive differences described in this chapter, while only 2 percent of the general population had such differences (Chall, 1993). This means that today, in contrast to the misdiagnoses of earlier decades, you will probably have only one child every 2 years who needs to be placed in an entirely different program and environment at a Tier 4 level because of his or her physical or cognitive differences. The special programs for this population are described in Chapter 14. This chapter will assist you to diagnose, instruct, and assess other students who have less limiting physical conditions. Instruction of these students can occur within the regular classroom setting, through Tier 2 small group support both within and outside the self-contained classroom, and through Tier 3 one-to-one tutorial sessions with peers, teachers, trained instructional aides, and parents.

Neurological Differences

Although scientists have made progress in understanding brain differences that affect literacy, curative actions are not yet available for many of them (Jensen, 2000). A single category of dysfunction can be caused by brain damage, by atypical maturation of the brain (one area may develop more slowly than others), or by a **congenital brain defect** (underdevelopment of an area of the brain at birth). Such slowly developing and neurologically delayed functioning often exhibits itself in in-appropriate physical and emotional outbursts. Unfortunately, because of these behaviors many students with neurological differences have been misdiagnosed, labeled "emotionally disturbed," and placed in ineffective Tier 4 programs. This program placement is incorrect for these students because it does not address their neurological process needs.

To differentiate between a reader who has one of these neurological differences and one with an emotional difference, consider the type of perceptual–motor problems that exist. If they are general coordination problems and include difficulties performing many types of learning tasks, a neurological difference is likely to be the cause. On the other hand, if inappropriate behaviors are not directly tied (or solely tied) to perceptual–motor tasks, the cause of difficulty is less likely to stem from neurological differences. Also, speaking difficulty is often present in neurologically different readers; these severe articulation differences interfere with these readers' word discrimination capabilities.

A second category of neurological difference occurs because of physical disorders outside of the brain. The major causes of neurologically based reading differences in this category are glandular dysfunction, virus disease or bleeding during pregnancy, false labor, Rh factor complications, kidney and liver malfunctions, infections such as PKU and jaundice, severe inner ear or middle ear infections, and infections of the nervous system such as encephalitis and meningitis. A lack of oxygen to the brain (due to prolonged convulsions), certain medical conditions (such as severe dehydration or inadequate blood circulation), and prolonged fevers above 104 degrees can also create neurologically based difficulties. In addition, many students with these differences also have weak general health. Thus, these students may be tired from lack of sleep, chronically ill, or inattentive for prolonged periods of time, which exacerbates literacy difficulties. The instruction they miss further impedes their literacy progress (Schlozman & Schlozman, 2000).

A third category of neurological differences can be more ambiguous in its manifestations and more difficult to diagnose. **Attention deficit disorder** (ADD) has recently been reclassified into two types of neurological differences. ADD is a neurological condition in which students exhibit behaviors such as distractibility, inattentiveness, short attention spans, and quick frustration with reading/writing tasks. **Attention deficit disorder with hyperactivity** (ADHD) is a neurological difference with the above symptoms, but students with this difficulty also have unjustified and unusual amounts of motor activity during reading and other more sedentary tasks. To obtain the most accurate diagnosis of the presence of either ADD or ADHD requires a medical professional. Moreover, many question whether ADD or ADHD can be the proper diagnosis for a student who does not have specific neurological damage (Bohline, 1985; Ingersol & Goldstein, 1993; Sawyer, 1989).

BRAIN PROCESSES. To better understand how neurological differences occur, it will be helpful to consider how the brain normally processes text. At any step of this process, a student could have a physical condition that would impede literacy development.

As shown in Figure 3.1, the brain is made up of neurons. A **neuron** is a brain cell and consists of a cell body, dendrites, and an axon. **Dendrites** are wispy fingerlike parts

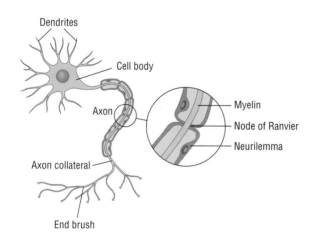

Schematic of a Neuron   **Cross-Section of a Brain**

FIGURE 3.1 Brain Components

Source: Adapted from L. A. Harris, P. D. Pearson, & G. Garcia (1995). *Reading Difficulties: Instruction and Assessment,* 2nd ed., p. 23. New York: McGraw Hill.

3.1 READING SPECIALISTS

Resources for Alternative Programs to Improve Reading Ability

COMMUNITY RESOURCES

Scottish Rite Hospital Child Development Department	214-559-7815
Child Study Center Patient Services Department	817-390-2900
Key School	817-446-3738
Hill School & Learning Center—Brenda Worley	817-923-9482

WEBSITES

Recording for the Blind and Dyslexic	www.rfbd.org
International Dyslexic Association	www.interdys.org
Levinson Medical Center for Learning Disabilities	www.dyslexiaonline.com
SofDesign International (with Scottish Rite Hospital)	www.sofdesign.com/dyslexia

surrounding the neuron cell body. An **axon** is a single, tail-like stem that is attached to each cell body. **Neurotransmitters** are chemicals that carry messages from one neuron to another. **Synapses** are gaps between neurons in which the electrical impulses emitted by neurotransmitters ignite.

Harris, Pearson, and Garcia (1995) provide a simplified version of what we presently know about how the brain works when we speak, listen, read, or write:

1. Sensory receptors all over the body (e.g., in the eyes, ears, and so on) send messages to the brain.
2. When the initial message reaches the brain, neurons further process it in the following way:
   a. Dendrites receive the message and expel an electrical impulse.
   b. This impulse is moved to the axon, which releases a chemical called a neurotransmitter.
   c. The neurotransmitter moves across a synapse to the dendrite of the next neuron.
   d. This process is repeated over and over through many of the 5 to 25 billion neurons in the brain, each of which is as complicated as a computer.

The brain comprises many areas, including the cerebral cortex, limbic cortex, corpus callosum, thalamus, hypothalamus, hippocampus, amygdala, and cerebellum, plus the lower brain stem, which is connected to the spinal cord. Specific sections specialize in specific activities, but often more than one brain area is involved in functions and behaviors. Scientists still do not understand all the neural codes that translate sensory perceptions into the processing performed in the brain.

Vision Differences

Some challenges to students' abilities to perceive print are explained in Table 3.1. Because the eye is such a complex organ, diagnosis of visual difficulties requires varied assessments.

Vision is the physical ability to see clearly and accurately. When we refer to visual **acuity,** we are referring to clarity in the reception of stimuli. If we wish to include mental interpretation of images, we refer to **visual perception/discrimination.** For reasons not yet known, the 1990s witnessed a growing population of students with vision problems. Approximately 50 percent of reading disabilities are now related to vision differences, difficulties, or defects (Bond, Wasson, Tiakes, & Wasson, 1994). Therefore, all students should be required to have eye examinations at least once a year. It is also

TABLE 3.1 Vision Problems, How to Detect Them, and Their Relationship to Reading Difficulties

Condition	Effects	Symptoms	Instructional Actions
Nearsightedness (myopia)	Clear vision at near point; blurring of distant images	Squinting at the board; holding print close to face; inattention to board work	Glasses; use action 1 of Box 3.2
Farsightedness (hyperopia)	Clear vision at far point; blurring of close objects	Holding print well away from face; disinterest in close work; eye fatigue during reading	Glasses; use action 2 of Box 3.2
Astigmatism	Distortion and/or blurring of part (or all) of visual field, far and near	Eye fatigue; headache; squinting; tilting or turning head; nausea during reading	Glasses; use action 3 of Box 3.2
Lazy eye (amblyopia)	Suppression of vision in one eye; dimming of vision without structural cause	Tilting or turning head to read; eye fatigue on one side; headache	Glasses; use action 4 of Box 3.2
Cross-eye (strabismus)	Difficulty converging and focusing both eyes on the same object	Squinting; closing or covering one eye to focus; eyes misaligned	Use actions 1–4 of Box 3.2
Binocular incoordination	Imbalance of ocular muscles; difficulty converging and focusing both eyes equally	Squinting; closing or covering one eye	Use resources in Box 3.1

Source: Adapted from G. Bond, B. Wasson, M. Tinker, & J. Wasson (1994), *Reading Difficulties,* p. 397. Boston: Allyn & Bacon.

important to remember that children will assume that how they see is how everyone else sees—so they cannot recognize that their blurred or impaired vision is causing difficulties. Children with vision problems have a behavioral tendency to daydream, which can be a clue to their vision problems. They develop rich fantasy lives to escape from endless hours of being out of touch with classmates and classroom activities. Many reading obstacles can be overcome instantly when vision problems are corrected.

The most common vision problem affecting elementary school children is **near-sightedness,** or *myopia.* With this condition, eyes focus properly on objects that are close but not on objects at a distance. Many nearsighted students hold reading materials close and have trouble reading words on a distant chalkboard. Although corrective lenses can fix the problem, too often the students do not wear their glasses. (Laser surgery and radial keratotomy are two surgical procedures that can correct nearsightedness. They are, however, usually reserved for extreme cases—and it should also be pointed out that eye muscles must be fully developed before these surgeries are performed.) The usual period of onset for nearsightedness is between the ages of 6 and 18. Because myopia develops rapidly during this period, teachers should be alert to notice children who begin to hold their reading material very close to their eyes.

With **farsightedness,** or *hyperopia,* eyes can focus on objects at a distance but not those that are close. Farsightedness is more common in adults than children and is easily corrected with reading glasses. This condition can be detected in students when teachers notice that they hold reading material farther away from their eyes than their peers.

Astigmatism is usually accompanied by nearsightedness or farsightedness and is caused by a misshapen lens. With astigmatism, objects and letters blur—which creates eye fatigue and reduced concentration while reading. Corrective lenses can remedy this problem.

Although most of children's vision difficulties involve the eye lens, two involve afflictions in the eye muscles. **Strabismus** is incoordination of the muscles that control the eyes and results in the condition commonly called *cross-eye.* Letters do not align properly when students with strabismus try to read: Two separate images of each letter are received by the brain. Its effect on reading progress is obvious. Eventually one eye will become nonfunctional if the lack of muscular fusion is not corrected. **Nystagmus** also involves optical muscle coordination and is characterized by rapid, involuntary eye movements that interfere with bringing words into focus. Eye exercises and corrective lenses that refract light in a different manner correct this condition.

Other types of ocular differences that interfere with reading progress (refer again to Table 3.1) include amblyopia ("lazy eye"), binocular incoordination (eyes fail to form a single vision), fusion difficulties (blurred and double images occur), and aniseikonia (differences of image in each eye).

Once vision difficulties are detected, you can make several adjustments to assist your students. Among these are repeating orally the information you write on the chalkboard; enlarging print on handouts and overhead projections; using closed-circuit television (described in Chapter 14); using Big Books, whose enlarged print enables students to see the words as someone else says them; and providing large-print books from the sources listed on Resource Card 3. You can then match the instructional actions described in Box 3.2 to address specific visual challenges.

RESOURCE CARD 3

Sources for Large-Print Books for Instruction of Students Who Face Visual Challenges

ABC-Clio and ISIS Large Print Books
2040 Alameda Padra Serra
Box 4397
Santa Barbara, CA 93140-4397
   200 titles in print
   805-963-4221
   800-422-2546
   800-824-2103 (CA)

American Printing House for the Blind
Box 6085
Louisville, KY 40206
   1,400 titles in print
   502-895-2405

A-R Editions
315 W. Gorham St.
Madison, WI 53703
   225 titles in print
   608-251-2114

John Curley & Associates
Box 37
South Yarmouth, MA 02664
   1,700 titles in print
   617-394-1280
   800-621-0182

Grey Castle Press
Pocket Knife Square
Lakeville, CT 06039
   50 titles in print
   203-435-0868
   800-458-7664

G. K. Hall & Co.
70 Lincoln St.
Boston, MA 02111
   3,500 titles in print
   617-423-3990
   800-343-2806

Jewish Braille Institute of America
110 E. 30th St.
New York, NY 10016
   10,000 titles in print
   212-889-2525

Linch Publishing
Box 75
Orlando, FL 32802
   30 titles in print
   305-647-3025
   800-327-7055

John Milton Society for the Blind
475 Riverside Dr., Rm. 455
New York, NY 10115
   45 titles in print; Spanish cassettes;
     free for visually handicapped only
   212-870-3335

Fleming H. Revell Co.
184 Central Ave.
Old Tappan, NJ 07675
   700 titles in print
   201-768-8060

Thorndike Press
295 Kennedy Dr.
Waterville, ME 04901
   700 titles in print
   207-948-2962
   800-223-6121

Walker & Co.
720 Fifth Ave.
New York, NY 10019
   1,400 titles in print
   212-265-3632
   800-AT-WALKER

Source: Adapted from L. M. Clary (1989), "Reading for Teenage Parents," in *Journal of Reading* (November), p. 146.

3.2 READING SPECIALISTS

Tier 1–4 Supports to Address Specific Visual Challenges

TEACHING LEFT-TO-RIGHT
EYE MOVEMENTS

1. **Using markers.** The marker should be moved from left to right so that one letter of the confused word is shown at a time. (You can make a marker by cutting a piece of tagboard into a narrow strip.)
2. **Underlining.** Underline the first letter of the word with green (go) and the last letter with red (stop).

3. **Developing chart stories.** Encourage your students to dictate stories to you. As you are writing their stories, emphasize the left-to-right direction of reading, using a pointer as you and your students orally read the story.
4. **Tracing.** Help the student trace the unknown word and write it in the sand. The student should say the confused word, then say each letter as it is traced. Repeat the word when tracing is complete.

To assess vision difficulties that affect literacy, reading specialists and classroom teachers can complete the evaluations in Box 3.3. This checklist was developed by the Optometric Extension Program Foundation in Santa Ana, California, and it describes specific problems so that a student may be referred for further vision screening by school nurses and physicians.

TESTING FOR VISUAL PROBLEMS. The Snellen chart that you had to read from the wall when you were in school is not adequate for detecting vision difficulties that affect reading performance; it does not test farsightedness or the muscular fusion of children's eyes. Rather, the Snellen chart tests nearsightedness, which is less common in children than in adults and does not greatly affect reading performance.

There are, however, many widely accepted school-administered screening tests for detecting students' vision problems. Among them are the following:

Ortho-Rater and *School Vision Tester* (published by Bausch & Lomb Optical Company, Rochester, New York)

Titmus II Vision Tester—Pediatric Model—Preschool and Primary (published by Titmus Ophthalmic Products, Petersburg, Virginia)

If a student has normal vision but appears to have difficulty discriminating between letters, the problem may involve not just eyesight but his or her visual perception/discrimination. Tests to help identify visual perception difficulties include these:

Bender Visual Motor Gestalt Test (published by the American Orthopsychiatric Association)

Minnesota Percepto-Diagnostic Test (published in the *American Educational Research Journal,* No. 6, pp. 207–226)

3.3 DIAGNOSIS AND ASSESSMENT

Diagnosing Vision Difficulties: A Checklist

Student's Name: _____ Date: _____

1. **Appearance of eyes:**
   One eye turns in or out at any time ____
   Reddened eyes or lids ____
   Eyes tear excessively ____
   Encrusted eyelids ____
   Frequent sties on lids ____
2. **Complaints when using eyes at desk:**
   Headaches in forehead or temples ____
   Burning or itching after reading or
     desk work ____
   Nausea or dizziness ____
   Print blurs after reading a short time ____
3. **Behavioral signs of visual problems:**
   A. *Eye movement abilities (ocular motility)*
      Head turns as reads across page ____
      Loses place often during reading ____
      Needs finger or marker to keep
        place ____
      Displays short attention span in
        reading or copying ____
      Too frequently omits words ____
      Repeatedly omits "small" words ____
      Writes up- or downhill on paper ____
      Rereads or skips lines unknowingly ____
      Orients drawings poorly on page ____
   B. *Eye teaming abilities (binocularity)*
      Complains of seeing double
        (diplopia) ____
      Repeats letters within words ____
      Omits letters, numbers, or phrases ____
      Misaligns digits in number
        columns ____
      Squints or closes or covers one eye ____
      Tilts head extremely while working
        at desk ____
      Consistently shows gross postural
        deviations at all desk activities ____
   C. *Eye–hand coordination abilities*
      Must feel things to assist in any in-
        terpretation required ____

Eyes not used to "steer" hand
  movements (extreme lack of
  orientation, placement of
  words or drawings on page) ____
Writes crookedly, poorly spaced;
  cannot stay on ruled lines ____
Misaligns both horizontal and vertical series of numbers ____
Uses hand or fingers to keep place
  on the page ____
Uses other hand as "spacer" to
  control spacing and alignment
  on page ____
Repeatedly confuses left–right
  directions ____
   D. *Visual form perception (visual comparison,
      visual imagery, visualization)*
      Mistakes words with same or simi-
        lar beginnings ____
      Fails to recognize same word in
        next sentence ____
      Reverses letters and/or words in
        writing and copying ____
      Confuses likenesses and minor
        differences ____
      Confuses same word in same
        sentence ____
      Repeatedly confuses similar begin-
        nings and endings of words ____
      Fails to visualize what is read
        either silently or orally ____
      Whispers to self for reinforcement
        while reading silently ____
      Returns to "drawing with fingers"
        to decide likes and differences ____
   E. *Refractive status (nearsightedness,
      farsightedness, focus problems, etc.)*
      Comprehension reduces as reading
        continues; loses interest too
        quickly ____

continued

3.3 · DIAGNOSIS AND ASSESSMENT

Diagnosing Vision Difficulties: A Checklist *(continued)*

Mispronounces similar words as continues reading ____

Blinks excessively at desk tasks and/or reading; not elsewhere ____

Holds book too closely; face too close to desk surface ____

Avoids all possible near-centered tasks ____

Complains of discomfort in tasks that demand visual interpretation ____

Closes or covers one eye when reading or doing desk work ____

Makes errors in copying from chalkboard to paper on desk ____

Makes errors in copying from reference book to notebook ____

Squints to see chalkboard, or requests to move nearer ____

Rubs eyes during or after short periods of visual activity ____

Fatigues easily; blinks to make chalkboard clear up after desk task ____

Source: Reprinted with permission from the *Educator's Guide and Checklist* [pamphlet], Optometric Extension Program Foundation, Inc. (OEP), Santa Ana, California.

Another very useful device for detecting differences in visual perception/discrimination is shown in Box 3.4. The student is asked to reproduce each of several shapes such as the three shown in the box (as used by Manzo & Manzo, 1993). If the child is properly orienting images, his or her figures will be close representations of the original forms. If the child does not reproduce the shapes fairly accurately, the test administrator would suspect a visual perception problem—the cause of which might be neurologically, developmentally, or emotionally based. Thus, if the student's copy is at least one-third larger or smaller than the model (as shown in the first two images in Box 3.4) or if it rotates by at least 35 degrees in any direction (as shown in the third image), then there is evidence of a visual perception problem, and a physician should be consulted for corrective treatment.

If a student has erratic or unusual eye movements, a test of his or her **peripheral vision**—what is seen at the outer part of the field of vision (in the "corner of the eye")—would be valuable. This test consists of placing a pencil dot in the center of a sheet of paper and cutting an opening starting ¼ inch to the right of the dot, as shown in Box 3.5. This "window" should be about ⅞ inch long—long enough so that, as the reader moves the sheet across a normal line of print in a book, he or she can see eight or nine letters at a time. Next, ask the reader to focus his or her eyes on the dot to the left of the hole. If the student is not able to read perfectly, referral to an ophthalmologist for further assessment is important for the student's subsequent improvements in literacy.

Visual–Perceptual Copy Tasks Used to Diagnose Neurological Organization

Model	Student's Version	Interpretation
		too small; poor reproduction
		oversized; poor reproduction
		35 degree rotation; error in reproduction (upsweep on opposite side)

Source: Literacy Disorders: Holistic Diagnosis and Remediation by Anthony V. Manzo and Ula Casale Manzo. Copyright © 1993 by Holt, Rinehart and Winston, Inc. Reproduced by permission of the publisher.

Auditory Differences

Auditory differences can be caused by hearing loss at birth, by lowered cognitive processing due to other physical differences or illnesses, or by prolonged exposure to high-pitched or loud sounds. If students are exposed to an environment in which sounds are sustained in decibels above 60 or at pitches of more than 28:4,000–8,000 vibrations per second, the auditory damage can cause hearing loss and an inability to discern distinctions between letter sounds. These students cannot discriminate consonants or ending sounds auditorily; nor can these students discriminate medial, long, and short vowel sounds. Other students cannot hear certain pitches.

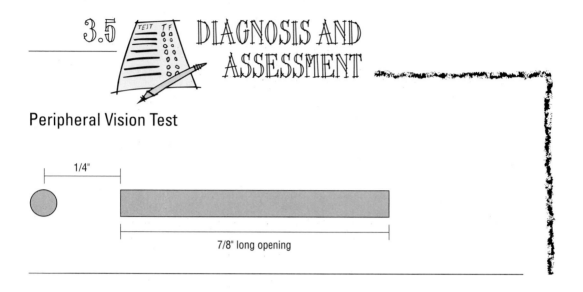

3.5 DIAGNOSIS AND ASSESSMENT

Peripheral Vision Test

Because 95 percent of the learning we achieve in life occurs through, or in cooperation with, auditory perception, hearing losses can have a devastating effect on reading and writing (Manzo & Manzo, 1993). Approximately 4.5 students in every 100 have a hearing loss that affects their reading/writing abilities, so there will probably be at least one child in your room each year who will need your assistance with this problem (Schloss, Smith, & Schloss, 1995). Two obvious student behaviors that indicate possible hearing difficulty are standing very close to people when talking and overly loud speech. Sometimes a child with hearing loss develops unusual and annoying habits to compensate for not receiving orally presented information. For instance, the student might closely watch classmates to see what they do after classroom directions are given. Other more subtle indicators can hint at auditory difficulty. Suspect possible hearing loss if a student exhibits any of the following:

- Inappropriate repeating of individual letter sounds or blending of sounds within single words
- Limited participation in class discussions
- Poor listening and speaking vocabulary
- Weak general knowledge of experiences that rely on auditory input
- Complaints of ringing or buzzing in ears, or drainage from ears
- Inattention when others speak
- Tilting of head while listening
- Unusual enunciation of familiar words
- Struggling to think about the words needed to express ideas

To diagnose a student's auditory difficulties unobtrusively, stand behind the child and whisper four directions for him or her to follow. The first is whispered directly behind the right ear—for example, whisper the student's name, and if he or she doesn't turn around, repeat the name with a command such as "Raise your right hand." Then, issue a similar direction while whispering behind the center of the head, and then behind the left ear. Last, when all other students are out of the room, walk across the room from this student, turn your back to him or her, and issue a command. If the child doesn't complete the command, move closer to the child and repeat the same command. Continue with this procedure until you have moved close enough to the child so that the command is heard. Evaluate if this volume and distance are what you would expect in normal children. You can also use one of the more extensive tests that appear in the "For Further Reference" list at the end of the chapter. These tests also assess students' auditory comprehension, auditory recall, and auditory memory. In addition, other standardized tests for auditory acuity and discrimination can be administered by a physician or a school nurse.

Students with another category of auditory need are those who have normal hearing but have difficulty processing language. While we know the least about this group, you can assume that students who pass all of the auditory screening instruments but who still demonstrate auditory differences have language processing difficulties.

For these students (and others with auditory-based difficulties), the following actions assist learning:

- Provide the student with preferential seating, close to you and the chalkboard, to limit distractions and help him or her maintain easier focus on words that you say and write.

- When giving important directions and reminders (such as at the end of the day), ensure that all students are sitting still and not talking, and that there are no distracting noises. Then have students list key points to take home and show you their lists as they walk out the door. This strategy inconspicuously enables you to check for accuracy in auditory processing each day.

- Ask auditorily weak students to repeat back to you instructions that you give the class, so you can be sure they heard them properly before assignments begin.

- Discuss with students the information received from their auditory screening assessments so that you can involve them in plans for an adaptive instructional program.

Teachers must always be alert to the auditory abilities of their students, because the heavy emphasis on literacy instruction during the first years of school places sophisticated demands on students' auditory systems. Once diagnoses are complete, there are several adaptations you can make in instruction to assist students who have difficulties in this area. Most fundamental is to remember that children with poor auditory discrimination should not be taught with a predominantly phonic approach or with a basal reader that highlights phonics as the predominant decoding strategy. Such students profit more from literacy instruction that involves language–experience activities (see Chapter 9 for sample lessons). Big Books, which were mentioned as helpful for students with vision difficulty, are also beneficial for auditory problems. Other excellent aids are predictable books (see Resource Card 4), which help students learn the sounds of letters and words through repetition.

Kinesthetic–Tactile Differences

Some literacy differences are caused by lack of stimulation, inadequate muscular development, or nerve damage through injury. They are classified as kinesthetic–tactile differences and can create an inability to hold images stable in space and on the page; weak auditory perception; lack of integration of auditory–visual stimuli; and poor orientation or perception in space, which can make letter orientation difficult.

Some of these physical problems are so severe that they are labeled as learning disabilities; in the past they were sometimes referred to as **minimal brain dysfunction.** The direct causes of these difficulties are unknown but are claimed by some to be the result of brain degeneration or nervous system dysfunction.

You can limit difficulties for students with kinesthetic–tactile differences by making provisions for students who have frequent or lengthy absences, minimizing traumas and disruptions in educational programming, and using nonfragmented instruction. Most common for these students is a general level of fatigue, which can often be improved when parents are advised that late night television viewing or activities limit performance at school. Similarly, you can assist students and their parents to understand that frequent absences due to colds, asthma, allergies, headaches, and upset stomachs can lead to literacy difficulties because of missed instruction. This is especially crucial in kindergarten through second grade. It is also important to make referrals for any of these physical differences, because additional tests can determine what actions to take to advance the students' literacy. A referral form and description of the process is described in Chapter 14. Sample lessons geared to a kinesthetic–tactile approach appear in Chapters 6 and 14.

RESOURCE CARD 4

Top 10 Favorite Predictable Books Selected by Struggling Readers

Brown, M. W. (1947). *Good night moon.* New York: Harper & Row.

Carle, E. (1970). *The very hungry caterpillar.* New York: Hamion Hamilton.

Christelow, E. (1989). *Five little monkeys jumping on the bed.* New York: Clarion.

Crews, D. (1978). *School bus.* New York: Greenwillow.

Fox, M. (1986). *Hattie and the fox.* New York: Bradbury.

Hutchins, P. (1968). *Rosie's walk.* New York: Macmillan.

Martin, B., Jr. (1967). *Brown bear, brown bear, what do you see?* New York: Holt.

Shaw, C. (1947). *It looked like spilt milk.* New York: Harper & Row.

Tolstoy, A. (1968). *The great big enormous turnip.* New York: Franklin Watts.

Zemach, M. (1965). *The teeny tiny woman.* New York: Scholastic.

Source: C. C. Block (2002), "Teaching Non-Fiction: What We Do Well, What We Need to Do, & What We Need to Learn in the Future," in *California Reader, 35*(2), 3–11.

One Tier 4 support that is especially beneficial for readers with kinesthetic–tactile differences is to develop a mentor relationship for them. These mentors can be older schoolmates, senior citizens, or parent volunteers who provide support and expanded explanations about specific reading or writing difficulties.

These students also profit from knowing that others have overcome literacy challenges. For example, at one time Albert Einstein was labeled as a low achiever with learning difficulties with literacy, as were Leonardo da Vinci, Woodrow Wilson, George Patton, Winston Churchill, and Nelson Rockefeller. Some teachers have noticed that by reading biographies of these people to the class, they can help many students increase their fortitude.

In fact, readers with any of the differences in this chapter—neurological, visual, auditory, or kinesthetic–tactile—benefit from learning about how people they respect had to overcome difficulties in order to succeed. They can read about Abraham Lincoln, Babe Ruth, or Marie Curie: Each failed at some aspect of life but overcame these setbacks to contribute to society. Through the many available high-interest, low-vocabulary biographies, students will discover that Abraham Lincoln was defeated seven times when he ran for political office, that Babe Ruth struck out 1,330 times, and that Marie Curie constructed 487 experiments that failed before her work with radioactivity earned Nobel prizes in physics and in chemistry.

Cognitive Variables

There are three categories of cognitive variables that interact with literary success: cognitive differences relative to gender, schema, and cognitive style.

Gender Differences

A student's gender relates to literacy success in several ways. For example, 60 to 90 percent of students referred for special reading classes in the 1980s in the United States, Canada, France, and Japan were boys. However, German boys normally are better readers than German girls, and Israeli students of both genders are about equal in achievement. Whether the tendency for males in some cultures to experience greater literacy difficulties is culturally based or a result of the types of instruction and teacher interactions is not known (U.S. Department of Labor, 1994).

Such differences could stem from gender-related brain maturational delays or from socialization patterns in certain cultures. There is evidence, however, that teachers relate differently to boys and girls. For example, Banks and McGee (1993) recorded the following classroom responses to a boy and a girl that were based on cultural patterning rather than to any inherent physical difference between genders:

Peter: [hollers out without raising his hand] A cello.

Mrs. Howe: You're all close. It's another string instrument, but it's not another violin or a cello.

Ruth: [hollers out without raising her hand] What about a viola?

Mrs. Howe: Ruth, you know I don't allow shouting out. Raise your hand next time.

Peter: [hollers out again without raising his hand] A viola.

Mrs. Howe: Very good. This is a special kind of concerto Mozart wrote for both the violin and viola called *Symphony Concertante*. (p. 116)

As this scenario demonstrates, Mrs. Howe acknowledged Peter favorably although he twice violated her rule for gaining the floor. Ruth, on the other hand, was reprimanded for committing the same offense only once, even though her answer was as correct as Peter's.

In addition, research demonstrates that male students in the United States, Canada, France, and Japan can gain attention through nonliterary pursuits more often than females. They are also praised more frequently for answers that can be given whether or not they have read the text under discussion, and they have developed more ways to avoid being called on when they did not read or comprehend a text (Cazden, 1994; U.S. Department of Labor, 1994). While some explain these differences as culturally based rather than as the result of innate cognitive differences, in a large study of fourth, sixth, and eighth graders in more than 100 U.S. classrooms, teachers gave boys more attention during reading lessons than girls. They asked boys more questions and gave them more precise and clear feedback concerning the quality of their reading responses (Banks & McGee, 1993). It seems that one reason boys get more teacher attention is that they demand it. They are approximately eight times as likely to shout out questions and answers and to dominate full-class conversations. Lower-achieving males are also more likely to receive the most negative attention from their teachers. Female students, on the other hand, are more likely to be ignored (Morrow, 1993).

There is evidence, however, that a physical explanation exists for differences in rate of literacy growth experienced by females and males:

> One mental difference between men and women that experts can agree upon is that women are generally superior at verbal tasks and men are superior at spatial abilities. It appears that this is a biological difference caused by the faster maturation and reduced lateralization of the female. (Phinney, 1988, p. 99)

The word **lateralization** refers to the development of independent operation by the two hemispheres of the brain. Each hemisphere at first specializes in the operation of its own functions. Then, the two mature enough to operate together. Because males have a slower maturational process, they have more time to build a strong, well-organized visual–spatial right hemisphere separately from their left hemisphere's more literacy-dominant functions. Alternatively, because the female brain matures faster, a girl's left hemisphere, which dominates in language functions, is less independent. Thus, girls have less time for their right hemisphere to develop its separate strength before it unites with left-brain function. In essence, girls are able to use all their mental abilities at a younger age than boys to translate letters into distinct phonic sounds. Further evidence for this theory comes from findings that slow-maturing girls follow the same developmental pattern as boys and mature with stronger spatial abilities (Phinney, 1988). This maturation difference is compounded for boys. Because male hemispheres develop less rapidly than females', the opportunities are greater for nerve fiber damages to occur, which would also effect later literacy success.

Gender also appears to be related to continued motivation and persistence while reading and writing. Girls tend to hold unduly low expectations, to avoid challenge, to focus on ability attributions to explain their failures, and to exhibit debilitation under failure. Girls also tend to prefer tasks at which they can succeed, whereas boys prefer tasks they have to sustain continuous hard work to master (Smey-Richman, 1988). These and other gender differences in literacy can be corrected when teachers' differential treatment of boys and girls is eradicated. Boys should be given larger literacy challenges and praise for increasing their literacy abilities. Girls should be given explanations as to why they did not reach their goals and should experience several literacy successes each week that are acknowledged by their teacher and peers.

Schema Differences

The term **schema,** as mentioned in Chapter 1, refers to the pictures and associations that the brain creates whenever a person hears or reads words and sentences. The way that these pictures, emotions, and associations are stored in the brain is analogous to the way information is stored in a filing cabinet. Schemas, "file folders" containing similar information, are bundled together as units. Therefore, if a student's exposures to a concept have been extensive, his or her schema will contain more exemplars; it will be a "thicker folder." For example, if a student enjoys computer work at home, his or her schema for computers will include the ability to attach meaning to terms such as *bits, disks, CD-ROM, delete, function keys, macros, sorts,* and *spellcheck.* This student has a broader schema than peers who have never used a computer—and broader schemas enhance comprehension.

Students who have weaker schema fail to connect their thinking with the content they read or write. According to recent surveys, four or five students in your room may have such a cognitive processing difficulty (Chall, 1993). Most theorists agree that successful readers can initiate purpose, recognize meaning, sample details, connect facts, select sentences based on importance relative to the main idea of the paragraph, predict, infer so that they go beyond available information, engage their schema effectively, become absorbed in ideas as they read and write, correct their thinking, terminate search behaviors, and retain what is read or written (O'Neil, 1991; Ruddell & Ruddell, 1994). Many struggling readers appear to have "short circuits" that interrupt these processes. Thus, meaning cannot be created (Jensen, 2000; Shapiro, Odgen, & Lind-Blad, 1990).

Studies also show that some of these readers lack a concern for accuracy in reading, have not developed an active approach to problem solving while reading/writing, guess more frequently than peers, and have difficulty breaking down complex sentences and words into simpler ones (Chance, 1986). Others spend little time considering a question and choose answers based on only a few clues (Whimbey, 1984). Similarly, when Anderson, Brubaker, Alleman-Brooks, and Duffy (1984) interviewed first graders working on seat work assignments, many students with cognitive processing difficulties were satisfied by responding randomly to literacy tasks or by picking any word to fill in a blank without first reading the sentence. Such readers were also often less inclined to pay attention to the teacher's explanation and more likely to provide general or imprecise reasons for why they did not comprehend a text (Brown & Campione, 1986; Brown, Palinscar, & Purcell, 1986). And there is considerable evidence that such readers have difficulty monitoring their mental processes. They do not make appropriate adjustments when literacy obstacles occur (Kimmel & MacGinitie, 1985).

Many such readers begin each new reading task as if it is the first time they have ever read. Each word is viewed as a challenge; each sentence as a consecutive collection of new words (Brown, 1980; Lipson, 1986). Such readers need to be taught how to draw on their schemas and experiences to interpret *as they read* and *how to connect single word meanings.*

Also, the more frequently students retrieve individual schema "folders," the more rapidly they can apply their knowledge to the situation at hand, the more frequently they can employ several folders collectively to understand something read, and the more reflective and metacognitive they can become. Therefore, you can assist a student's prereading retrieval of relevant schemas by asking questions like "Why did you select your favorite book? Why was it one you wanted to read?" The most frequent answer you will receive is that the book's subject matches the student's prior experiences or interests. This is a good time to teach the student that recalling and applying related knowledge he or she has to the new reading will make that reading more enjoyable and easier to understand.

Think alouds, also mentioned in Chapter 1, are used to tell students what you are thinking about as you perform a literacy task, and are a second way to help them expand their schema "folders." The purpose is to reveal the thinking processes that go into successful decoding and comprehension. You can tell students what you are thinking at any time, but among the most difficult processes for less accomplished readers/writers are predicting, imaging, and correcting confusions. The basic procedure for constructing a think aloud would go like this:

First, select a passage to read aloud that contains points of difficulty, contradictions, ambiguities, or words that would challenge the readers for whom the think aloud is to be performed. Then demonstrate predictive thinking as you read by stopping to make statements such as, "When I see subtitles, I know this is the main idea, so I think about what could be described relative to that main idea." To demonstrate imagery as you read, stop to make statements like "I have a picture of this countryside in my mind. I made it by taking the information from this sentence: [read sentence] . . . and tying it to the new things I learned in this sentence: [read sentence]." Then describe your mental image and ask students how theirs is different because of their schema of concepts depicted in these sentences. To demonstrate how to use strategies to overcome confusion you can say, "When I come to something like this that I don't understand, I stop reading and tell myself this doesn't make sense. Then I think: Should I read ahead to see if it becomes clear? Is there a word I misread or overlooked? Should I reread? Is there a new word that I gave a wrong meaning? I look for context clues or check the dictionary—or sometimes I ask someone to help me with a word."

A valuable instructional intervention to build schema and background experiences is to use serial books. Call readers who have limited background experiences to a small, needs-based grouping and read one of the serial books together. Then demonstrate how readers can apply what they learned from the first in this series of books to a second book in that same series. Next, ask students to apply their knowledge independently and to share their results in a conference with you. Because main character names, story settings, and authorial writing style will become a part of the students' prior experiences, subsequent readings in the series will be easier. Once readers have read two books from the same series, ask them to describe how they activated their prior knowledge before and during the reading of the second book. Additional instructional interventions that strengthen schema will be described in Chapter 10.

INNATE INTELLIGENCE AND SCHEMA. Many parents believe the cause of their child's literacy difficulties is genetically related. Most difficulties, however, relate more to limited experiences with concepts read (limited schemas and prior knowledge) and to ineffective interpretative strategies than to inborn mental deficits (Snow & Ninio, 1986). Most students with literacy difficulties do not have below-average mental abilities. Innate intellectual capacity is not the major cognitive influence on literacy failure.

Rather, difficulties in cognitive processes are often a product of the depth, breadth, and quality of students' prior experiences. As you may already know, children who have been exposed to a print-rich environment prior to school will likely move faster and more flexibly along the literacy continuum than students who have not been read to regularly (Cazden, 1995; Morrow, 1993). When children are exposed to letter names, see extensive uses of literacy in their home, test their initial letter-to-sound relationships with parents or day care providers, or respond to environmental print, the cognitive processing of literary symbols strengthens.

In addition, research demonstrates that intelligence is enhanced through learning (Farnham-Diggery, 1986). As students learn, both intelligence and potential enlarge. Further, intelligence is not one-dimensional but multidimensional. Several researchers have identified the components of students' intelligence with different names, but Howard Gardner's (1993) components are the most widely used. The following descriptions of these components are provided as an introduction to this concept, and a more complete explanation of these dimensions of intelligence is provided in Chapter 14, in the subsection titled "Using Multiple Intelligence Theory to Overcome Literacy Barriers." All students possess various levels of each of these intelligences; the first is the most influential in literacy development.

The components are as follows:

1. **Verbal–linguistic intelligence** is the ability to process printed and spoken words and symbols.
2. **Logical–mathematical intelligence** is the ability to manipulate quantities through numerical reasoning or objective, quantifiable analyses.
3. **Visual–spatial intelligence** is the ability to manipulate visual shapes mentally and to create images.
4. **Musical–rhythmical intelligence** is the ability to perceive pitch and rhythm and to learn through nuances of sound.
5. **Kinesthetic intelligence** is the ability to use movement and physical sensations to learn.

6. **Interpersonal intelligence** is the ability to relate well with others and to learn through verbal interactions and group experiences.
7. **Intrapersonal intelligence** is the ability to reflect and understand aspects of one's own abilities.

By fourth grade, intelligence becomes more influential in literacy progress, because reading material above the third grade level often requires a high degree of abstract reasoning. Thus, fourth graders and above whose innate verbal–linguistic intelligence is below average for their age will likely have more difficulty with reading and interpreting implicit material. Middle and high school students who face these challenges profit from materials ordered by reading specialists and teachers that correlate reading assignments to high-interest television programs (see Box 3.6). In Chapter 7, however, you will learn other methods to assist such students so they can make educational adaptations that maximize their innate intellectual strengths.

Remember, readers with cognitive limitations in verbal–linguistic intelligence, difficulties activating their prior knowledge, and/or problems creating schemas need your assistance (1) to engage their prior experiences before and during reading, and (2) to enlarge and reorganize their schemas as a result of reading. Readers and writers who frequently display partial recall and gaps in knowledge (while word calling accurately) are likely to have one of these cognitive differences. Once you assist these students to

MIDDLE SCHOOL and HIGH SCHOOL

3.6

Television Teaching Aids

Reading specialists and teachers can order materials from the following sources that can be used in many ways to enrich literacy instruction for secondary students with verbal–linguistic weaknesses.

Action for Children's Television
46 Austin Street
Newton, MA 02160

Children's Advertising Review Unit
Council of Better Business Bureaus
845 3rd Avenue
New York, NY 10022

ABC
1330 Ave. of the Americas
New York, NY 10019

Capital Cities Communication
4100 City Line Ave.
Philadelphia, PA 19131

Teachers Guide to TV
699 Madison Ave.
New York, NY 10021

CBS TV Network
51 West 52nd St.
New York, NY 10019

Zillion Ad Complaints
256 Washington St.
Mt. Vernon, NY 10553

Agency for Instructional TV
Box A
Bloomington, IN 47401

recognize and use their intellectual strengths to increase their literacy abilities, you will see the following indicators of growth:

- Students will become more flexible and determined in their cognitive processes. They will ask questions when they misunderstand, paraphrase another person's point of view, and change their minds in light of new evidence.
- Students will become aware of their metacognition by being able to describe what they know and need to know.
- Students will reflect on the accuracy of their written work and take pride in their comprehension and compositions.
- Students will use more precise language instead of vague nouns like *things* when they write and fewer expressions like *ya know* as they speak.

By pointing out these growths to your students each time they occur, you can help metacognitions increase more rapidly.

Cognitive Style Differences

Cognitive styles are individual preferences based on differences in cognition, personality, perception, and/or a students' preferred modalities, or methods, of learning. Separate features of cognitive style include *field dependence* versus *field independence*. **Field dependence** means difficulty in focusing on individual words and individual elements in an array such as a landscape or page of print. **Field independence** is ease in discerning differences between words on a page. Cognitive style also has to do with a person's tendency toward either complexity or simplicity in classifying tasks and objects. Complex classifiers, for instance, are more likely to see similarities between words that end in -*tion* (and will group them together for more instant recognition of other words in this family) than are more specific classifiers, who view each word as distinct. Cognitive style also involves a student's global view of causation. For example, some students tend to blame a decoding failure on their *total* inadequacy as a reader, rather than analyzing more specifically which part of a word they did not recognize.

Teachers can assist readers/writers with special cognitive needs by identifying their modality preferences. Modalities are conditions within a learning environment that encourage students to focus intently on the literacy task at hand. The following classroom adaptations, developed by many researchers (Dunn, 1993; Thomas, 1993), provide some helpful strategies:

1. Create a quiet space for these students to read. This may mean providing a headset that blocks out noise; providing a headset that makes a humming sound called "white noise"; or allowing students to read in the library, the lunchroom, or a vacant classroom for 15 minutes alone regularly.
2. Allow them to eat dry cereal or sip from a glass of water in the space they use to read and write silently.
3. Ask how many movement options readers need to improve their learning. For example, one boy with a strong kinesthetic learning style found that if he walked in his bedroom from one side to the other as he read, he learned more. Therefore, as

his teacher you could assign the readings that the class would do in the coming week on the preceding Friday so that this reader could read at home, using kinesthetic movements, before the readings in class. Then, during the time that the rest of the class is reading, this reader could perhaps create a diagram or object that summarized the main point of the reading, to be shared during full-class conversations about that reading.

4. After readers determine their preference for oral or written directions, accommodate their cognitive processing strengths by ensuring that directions for each literacy task contain a visual description, an oral explanation, and one to three physical examples of writing.

5. Create one section of the classroom that has carpet or carpet squares, soft pillows, and an informal atmosphere for readers who are kinesthetic and enjoy reclining while reading/writing.

6. Offer options for students to work with a peer when reading/writing, as some readers with auditory preferences grow rapidly when they can discuss their literacy projects, plans, activities, and self-evaluations.

Readers/writers who are less accomplished need two things: educational experiences that mobilize their strengths to overcome obstacles, and a teacher who never gives up on them (Block, 2002a; Jensen, 2000). As Phinney (1988) reported:

> I worked with a brother and sister who read at least two grade levels below their peers until suddenly, in grade 5, they found themselves comparable with peers! It seems that their difficulty may have been caused by delayed specialization of the left hemisphere. When another brain growth spurt began, which typically occurs between ages of 10 and 12, the reading process came together for them.
>
> Such children begin early to think of themselves as failures. . . . Allowing [such readers/writers] to master the basic curriculum through alternative means would take pressure off both them and ourselves. (pp. 101–102)

Chapter Summary

There are several physical and cognitive variables that affect students' literacy development. Through careful diagnosis and adapted instruction, many neurological, visual, auditory, and cognitive difficulties can be overcome. Moreover, research has revealed that various dimensions of intelligence can be strengthened through effective instruction. This finding calls into question the practice of categorizing students based on traditional intelligence measures or standardized tests that assess only the visual–linguistic dimension of intelligence. By telling students how you puzzle over difficult materials or by performing think alouds, you can help students learn cognitive processes that you engage as a reader/writer. Such mentoring is valuable—as are serial books, predictable books, television series–based books, and big books. Because the relationships between cognitive processes and motivation, drive, and self-esteem are so intricate, Chapter 4 will describe how affective conditions can interact with cognitive differences to interfere with or to accelerate literacy learning.

Key Terminology

You may recall the meanings of some of the following terms after reading this chapter only once. If you do, place a check mark in the blank that precedes the term. If you are not certain of a meaning, turn to the page number that follows that term to review its meaning. If you learned 15 of these terms on your initial reading of the chapter, you have understood the intent of this chapter.

_____ congenital brain defect (page 56)
_____ attention deficit disorder (page 57)
_____ attention deficit disorder with hyperactivity (page 57)
_____ neuron (page 57)
_____ dendrites (page 57)
_____ axon (page 58)
_____ neurotransmitters (page 58)
_____ synapses (page 58)
_____ acuity (page 59)
_____ visual perception/discrimination (page 59)
_____ nearsightedness (page 60)
_____ farsightedness (page 60)
_____ astigmatism (page 60)
_____ strabismus (page 60)
_____ nystagmus (page 60)
_____ peripheral vision (page 64)
_____ minimal brain dysfunction (page 68)

_____ lateralization (page 70)
_____ schema (page 71)
_____ think alouds (page 72)
_____ verbal–linguistic intelligence (page 73)
_____ logical–mathematical intelligence (page 73)
_____ visual–spatial intelligence (page 73)
_____ musical–rhythmical intelligence (page 73)
_____ kinesthetic intelligence (page 73)
_____ interpersonal intelligence (page 74)
_____ intrapersonal intelligence (page 74)
_____ cognitive styles (page 75)
_____ field dependence (page 75)
_____ field independence (page 75)

 ## Case Study

Making Professional Decisions

Think alouds are important interventions for readers with cognitive differences. After reading the following think aloud by Evelyn Krieger, diagnose what type of physical or cognitive difficulty you think Sam may have had:

At home I had, as usual, eagerly begun reading the first chapter of the new Zindel book [that I wanted to read orally to my students]. [I was] highlighting vocabulary and writing notes in the margins, when suddenly it occurred to me that it might not be necessary to read the book beforehand. What would happen, I wondered, if I experienced this story for the first time with my students? What could I learn? What could my students learn? Perhaps my reading along with them in class would provide a model of what literature is all about: discovery and enjoyment.

I began my experiment by reading aloud a chapter each day while the students followed along. If a question came to me, I asked it. When I noticed an interesting description, I reread it. If I was confused by a passage, I let them know. If a scene reminded me of something, I shared my thoughts . . . [and] by thinking aloud, I was modeling the kinds of strategies a good reader naturally employs to construct meaning from a test: questioning, predicting, rereading, and reflecting.

My students also took turns reading [the book] orally. I encouraged them to ask any question that popped into their heads. When they stumbled on a difficult word, we discussed it on the spot, then added it to our vocabulary list on the chalk board. . . .

Then something wonderful happened. Sam, who always said he hated books, asked to take the book home. The next day, he announced to the class that he had read ahead a few chapters. "I just really got into it," he said bashfully. Soon he became the authority to whom the others went to check their predictions. I had a strong suspicion that Sam was reveling in the fact that he knew something his teacher didn't know. . . . In a sense I was saying to my students, "Look, I'm challenging myself. You can, too." I think they caught on and appreciated my experiment. They seemed more willing to extend themselves.

After you write your answer, you can check it by comparing it to the diagnosis given by Ms. Krieger in the Answer Key at the back of the book.

Thinking and Writing about What You Have Learned

Based on what you have learned in the first three chapters of this text, indicate which of the following activities would interfere with literacy growth for struggling readers/ writers. Then, for each activity you designate as ineffective, state why by citing something you learned from this chapter.

a. Whole-class spelling bees
b. Asking students to look up unknown words in a dictionary
c. Using textbook materials that are "inconsiderate" of readers because they assume knowledge the students don't have, are too dense, and do not provide connections between ideas
d. Activities that are simplistic—that do not involve real-world problems students face or do not challenge students' misconceptions about the world
e. Perfunctory tasks (such as visual–perceptual activities that ask students to draw lines connecting one picture to another) that have no proven impact on reading or on improving perception
f. Tasks presented with average increments of learning

For Further Reference

Standardized tests that can be used to detect auditory discrimination problems include the following:

Auditory Instruments, Auditory Instrument Division, Zenith Radio Corporation, 6501 W. Grand Ave., Chicago, IL 60635
Beltone Audiometers, published by Beltone Electronics Corporation, 4201 W. Victoria St., Chicago, IL 60646 (auditory acuity only)

Goldman-Fristoe-Woodcock Test of Auditory Discrimination, published by the Psychological Corporation, 555 Academic Court, San Antonio, TX 78204

Grason-Stadler Audiometers, published at 537 Great Rd., Box 5, Littleton, MA 01460

Kimmell-Wahl Screen Test of Auditory Perception, published by the Psychological Corporation, 555 Academic Court, San Antonio, TX 78204

Precision Acoustics, Precision Acoustics Corporation, 55 W. 42nd St., New York, NY 10036

Royal Industries Products, Royal Industries, Audiotone Division, P.O. Box 2905, Phoenix, AZ 85036

Wepman's Auditory Discrimination Test, published by the Psychological Corporation, 555 Academic Court, San Antonio, TX 78204

To detect students' difficulties in hearing variant pitches, audiometers have been made that calibrate frequencies at differing decibel levels. Such tests can be administered by school nurses. If a nurse administers one of the above tests and suspects a child of having a hearing loss, additional tests by a physician (or at a speech and hearing clinic, often housed on university campuses) can assist in furthering that child's literacy development.

 Onto the Information Superhighway

Teachers and reading specialists who work with students facing physical and cognitive challenges can often utilize resources; such as the following, which provide diagnostic and instructional assistance.

www.udel.edu/bkirby/asperger.html

www.autism.org

www.autism-society.org

www.autism-ppd.net

www.asperger.org

www.asw4autism.org/wiresorc.htm

www.canfoundation.org/newcansite/aboutcan/autism.html

www.ummed.edu/pub/o/ozbayrak/aspcrit.html

Lien and Diego are preparing a list of words they learned from a book they read together. They are going to use the book and this list to teach the names of animals to kindergarten children before they go on a field trip to the zoo.

Affective and Motivation Conditions That Create Differences in Literacy Achievement

A second grade teacher in Iowa described her "encouragement approach" to teaching. One boy's writing was totally
indecipherable. She said that in the past she would have be-
rated the boy for being lazy and incompetent. However,
since choosing a self-esteem approach, she now says,
"Johnny, this writing looks like it's getting a little better. I
bet in a week we'll be able to make out at least one letter."
A week later she was able to decipher several letters. She
said, "I bet in a few weeks we'll be able to make out a whole
word." Sure enough, it happened. The power of a positive
expectation was working miracles with the boy. The
teacher believed in him and he lived up to that expectation.

(Canfield & Wells, 1994, p. 12)

■ Chapter Overview: Key Points

The purpose of this chapter is to examine the affective aspects of students' literacy.
As Jean Piaget stated: "At no level, at no stage, even in the adult, can we find a behavior or
a state which is purely cognitive without affect nor a purely affective state without a cognitive element involved" (Piaget, 1967, p. 154). The domains of emotion and cognition
are especially entwined in the performances of less accomplished readers. Self-healing
seems to occur when these readers are supported by teachers who expand both the cognitive and affective dimensions of literacy simultaneously. Through effective diagnoses
and instruction, the commitment, interest, and confidence of struggling readers are for-
tified (Berliner, 1992; Block, 1992, 2002b; Wattenberg & Clifford, 1966).

In this chapter you will learn:

- How to build these readers' commitment to, interest in, and confidence for literacy
- How to diagnose true literacy difficulties as opposed to defense mechanisms and
  learned helplessness
- Instructional interventions that increase positive affect and motivation to read

Persistence will arise from increased (1) intrinsic motivation; (2) positive concept
of self as a reader; (3) positive attitudes; and (4) interest stimulation, and productive
emotions that deploy new cognitive commitment. By the end of the chapter, you will
have answers to the following questions:

1. What are the strategies that struggling readers/writers need to move from noncom-
   mitment, through marginal commitment, to total commitment to literacy?

2. How do choice and openness in the reading curriculum expand readers' interest in literacy?

3. How can confidence rise when students set their standards of success, overcome learned helplessness, and increase their confidence in themselves as readers?

4. How do the instructional guidance of discovery discussions, special attitude and interest assessments, and responsibility guides increase less accomplished readers' affect, achievement, and motivation?

How to Increase Struggling Readers' Commitment to Literacy

Motivation is the impulse to initiate and direct behavior with a drive toward competence that is sustained and augmented by deep feelings of self-efficacy (Bandura, 1994). **Self-efficacy** is the degree to which a person expects and values the successful completion of a task based on an assessment of past performances. It also involves the belief that success results more from ability and effort than from luck (Bandura, 1990). Motivation can be of two types, external and internal. Externally motivated readers are those who work for rewards they receive from others—such as praise from teachers, recognition from peers, or prizes from contests. Internally motivated readers are those who seek reading because of personal interest and desires to learn, relax, escape, or empathize.

Because most struggling readers have difficulty initiating, directing, and sustaining positive literacy experiences (regardless of the drive toward competence they exert), they quickly deplete their intrinsic motivation and positive views of themselves as readers (and about reading). In a study of 21,000 youths, one in five no longer had any significant level of intrinsic motivation to reading. Therefore, in addition to the reader in your class each year who has a physical difference and the student who has a cognitive difference (as described in Chapter 3), you will likely have at least five who will have such limited motivation that their literacy development is negatively affected (O'Neil, 1991). Fortunately, these affective factors are even more amenable to instruction than the cognitive/physical variables described in Chapter 3. With your guidance, students can reestablish a love for learning, develop resiliency, and begin to develop their own reasons for reading and writing. As one researcher noted: "Children of rich and poor alike are growing up amid daily breakdowns, divorce, and without a sense of direction. Physical poverty is killing our children's bodies, but spiritual poverty is squashing their souls" (Edelman, 1991, p. 32).

In Chapter 2 you read about practices that were followed historically when students became unmotivated to improve their literacy: They would be referred to special education, placed in a "low" group, given extra homework, and placed in programs that emphasized basic skills. Frymier (1992) found that many of today's teachers still use these instructional techniques and concluded that "the fact that general concern about the literacy problems of children at risk is so widespread in America suggests that such efforts are insufficient, ineffective, or both" (p. 259).

What, then, can we do to direct students to literacy as a tool for lifetime fulfillment? To start, we must be knowledgeable about the psychological attributes that move students from indifference to marginal commitment. We must be familiar with literacy self-esteem profiles so that students can move from marginal to total commitment. And we must determine the levels of emotional investment that are necessary for reluctant readers/writers to make a total commitment to literacy.

Psychological and Motivation Attributes

The self-concept of a student can be compared to a money sack filled with gold coins. All of a student's before-school experiences, physical and cognitive endowments, and socioeconomic variables have made either deposits or withdrawals from his or her "self-concept sack." Students with many deposits can afford to "spend" part of their self-concept in the risk-filled, unpredictable world of decoding, comprehending, and composing. These students could invest as much as 20 percent of themselves five times over before a negative level of self-confidence would emerge. The self-concepts of those with less enriched backgrounds, however, have often had more withdrawals than deposits. Thus, when these students are asked to read, they have no positive self-concept to spend.

Many students' first response to reading failure is either to decide never to invest any more self-concept coins in literacy or to get so mad that they pour all their coins on the table for a second try. If failure occurs in this all-or-nothing effort, students who are asked to engage in literacy for a third time often erect a self-defense of "This is stupid" (making no future commitment because it's too painful to make mistakes), "I don't want to" (taking no interest so as to not be found out that they really wish they could read but can't), or "It's sissy stuff" (acting-out or creating deflectors to distract from the negative self-concept that literacy arouses).

Psychologists have identified three levels of affect in readers/writers: indifference, marginal commitment, and total engagement.

INDIFFERENCE. Most readers and writers with low affect originally wanted to meet society's strict requirement and to be able to read and write by age 6. When they realize that they not be able to, so they project a demeanor of indifference (Maslow, 1956; Walz & Bleuer, 1992). They reason that if "I look like I don't care, people may assume my literacy failures are because I don't try instead of because I'm too dumb and stupid." Many struggling readers and writers believe they do not have the ability to do what others appear to do very easily.

Some teachers try to motivate indifferent students by tantalizing them with extrinsic rewards, or by trying to keep lessons from becoming boring by constantly changing the curriculum, bulletin boards, books, and daily routine. Too frequently, such changes are merely lateral (altering the content and lesson objectives) and the amount of coins a student must invest in the literacy tasks themselves still requires more self-concept than he or she has left to invest. As Brophy and Alleman (1991) explain: "Trying to make learning always fun is impossible and creates a counterproductive mindset in students. . . . Using extrinsic rewards conveys that learning is unpleasant and not to be pursued for its own sake" (p. 66).

Typically, unmotivated students do not respond to incentives or material rewards for reading or writing. While they may work to attain material rewards to avoid humiliation before peers, such enticements have not proven successful in moving them further along the literacy continuum (Guthrie, Schafer, Wang, & Afflerbach, 1995). More productive programs deemphasize extrinsic purposes such as grades, rewards, and competition (Deci & Ryan, 1987).

Another difficulty with extrinsic motivation is that some students may see reading only as a means to a more pleasurable end; that is, the reward becomes more important than reading (Grace & Buser, 1987). Some researchers believe that these students will turn into "reinforcement junkies" who must have extrinsic incentives to learn (Wlodkowski, 1986). There is also the concern that these reward systems establish false expectations of society, which does not always reward individuals in direct proportion to their ability or effort (Stipek, 1982).

MARGINAL COMMITMENT. What we must do, then, is to begin attracting indifferent students to a marginal commitment by scaffolding them to invest in just one particular literacy task. For instance, you might give a student a book that is easy to read and ask her to share it with the class; or you might allow a student to become the classroom librarian because he had mentioned that he would like to do that. Through the repetition of these individual connections to pleasure-filled reading and writing experiences, indifferent readers can learn to associate literacy (if only for a brief period) with positive emotions. When this occurs, indifferent readers can enter literacy by calling on different, richer resources than their depleted self-concepts. They can enter through the positive reservoirs of their care, pride, and ability to assume responsibility (McLaughlin & Aubrey, 1995).

Moreover, research has demonstrated that praise statements will be most effective for reluctant readers and writers if they specify the amount of effort that students put forth ("You have been working hard"), to the ability and strategies they exhibit ("You're good at decoding long words!"), or both ("You comprehend well when you consciously tie the meaning in one paragraph to the next") (Craven, Marsh, & Debus, 1991; Schunk & Cox, 1986). Unfortunately, without such feedback many young students view effort and ability as the same forces. As a result, many may elect not to apply effort to literacy tasks so as to avoid the implication that in the event of failure they really lacked the ability to succeed (McGinn, Winne, & Butler, 1993). Similarly, Krampen (1987) found that motivation increases for readers who receive self-referenced as opposed to norm-referenced feedback—that is, for students who are compared to themselves rather than to classmates ("You worked harder today than yesterday, and the result was that you enjoyed the book more today than yesterday"). In summation, the goal of your feedback is to build students' intrinsic motivation so that they advance from marginal commitment to total engagement.

Moving to Total Literacy Engagement

To move students from marginal to deeper commitments to literacy, you can demonstrate (through think alouds) the internal rewards literacy provides you—mental pictures, memories, vicarious experiences, feelings of empathy with literary "friends," and a growing awareness of oneself.

When you establish high expectations and suggest a realistic time frame for reading and writing growth, marginally committed readers can more easily engage momentary task-specific internal motivation to succeed. For example, Suzanne, a first grade indifferent writer, evidenced an internal motivation to write when she said, "I need to learn to spell my name." Upon hearing that goal, her teacher responded by stating a time frame and high expectation: "Do you know the first letter and can you write it?"

Suzanne said yes and wrote *S*.

The teacher asked again: "Do you know the second letter?"

"No," whispered Suzanne. The teacher wrote each of the remaining letters of Suzanne's name and then said with a big smile, "I'm not worried. I think you will know how to write your name by the end of next week."

Suzanne returned the smile and asserted, "I know I can, too! I can't wait. Next Friday, I'll show you I'm a writer!" She then busily engaged in repeatedly writing her name, as well as copying other words displayed in the room, for 2 weeks. Not only did her first written word appear at the next discovery discussion—but her first sentence was written as well.

BUILDING LITERACY SELF-ESTEEM. Ask students what they need to increase their literacy self-concept. Marginally committed readers know what they need in order to be better readers, so *we need to ask them*. Simply asking them, trusting their answer, and making changes based on it will move unmotivated readers to make a specific commitment to a task you or they design. The alternative of setting high expectations without student input can be devastating, as Jacob, a third grader, told me:

> My teacher kept giving me the same assignment night after night just hoping I would do it correctly. After a while I thought my teacher was goofy. I blamed not learning anything on that teacher because she gave me the same too-hard assignments over and over. This made me feel stupid and frustrated.

Sometimes these students cannot risk telling us directly what they need, but the comments they make provide clues. For example, when an indifferent student says, "I'm bored," you can rejoice! This really is a positive sign. This student has moved from indifference to a point where she feels safe enough to make a marginal commitment to reading. However, despite her commitment and positive self-concept, her interest level is still too low to sustain the risk of a reading failure. In such situations, avoid assigning "baby work." Instead, we can ask the student to read a high-interest, low-vocabulary book from Resource Card 5.

Similarly, when a student tells you that he is confused, you can inwardly rejoice. This response indicates that the student's self-concept and interest in literacy are strong; only his commitment is wavering. To increase his motivation, you can make your explanation as specific as possible, and tell him only what he needs to know at a specific point in the reading. These actions will reignite his perseverance.

In like manner, when a reader gets angry and abruptly closes a book, this student is demonstrating a commitment and interest in literacy, but the confidence in self is still low. Such readers may also have a high level of stress because they are afraid someone will make fun of them. As they grow older some avoid all literacy events that highlight their difficulties. They are more aware than anyone else of the reasons why they only get

RESOURCE CARD 5

**Top 25 Favorite High-Interest, Low-Vocabulary Books
Selected by Unmotivated Readers**

Blume, J. (1971). *Frecklejuice.* New York: Bantam.

Dalgliesh, A. (1954). *The courage of Sarah Noble.* New York: Scribner.

Estes, E. (1944). *The hundred dresses.* New York: Harcourt Brace.

Fleischman, S. (1986). *The whipping boy.* New York: Greenwillow.

Franklin Watts First Library. A series of science books on many topics. New York: Franklin Watts.

Keller, C. (1982). *Alexander the grape: Fruit and vegetable jokes.* Englewood Cliffs: Prentice Hall.

Lobel, A. (1970). *Frog and Toad are friends.* New York: HarperCollins.

MacLachlan, P. (1985). *Sarah, plain and tall.* New York: HarperCollins.

Monjo, F. F. (1968). *Indian summer.* New York: HarperCollins.

Naylor, P. (1991). *Shiloh.* New York: Simon & Schuster.

New True Books. A series of informational books on many science and social studies topics. San Francisco: Children's Press.

Parish, P. (1981). *Amelia Bedelia and the baby.* New York: Greenwillow.

Parsons, A. (1990). *Amazing cats— Eyewitness juniors.* New York: Knopf.

Peterson, J. (1967). *The Littles* (series). New York: Scholastic.

Schwartz, A. (1985). *All of our noses are here and other noodle tales.* New York: Harper & Row.

Schwartz, A. (1984). *In a dark, dark room and other scary stories.* New York: Harper & Row.

Sharmat, M. (1986). *Nate the Great stalks Stupidweed.* New York: Putnam.

Simon, S. (1979). *Animal fact/Animal fable.* New York: Crown.

Simon, S. (1980). *Einstein Anderson, science sleuth.* New York: Viking.

Sobol, D. (1977). *Encyclopedia Brown and the case of the midnight visitor.* New York: Dutton.

Take a trip to. A series of books on other countries. (1986). New York: Franklin Watts.

Thomas, J. R. (1981). *The comeback dog.* Boston: Houghton Mifflin.

Voigt, C. (1986). *Stories about Rosie.* New York: Atheneum.

Walsh, J. P. (1982). *The green book.* New York: Farrar, Straus, & Giroux.

Yolan, J. (1983). *Commander Toad and the big black hole.* New York: Putnam.

to read one paragraph of the textbook out loud while others read full pages to the class. By being as specific as possible and telling each student exactly what aspect of his or her literacy demonstration was meritorious, you may be the first ever to have celebrated the unmotivated student's present literacy strengths. Because you did, he or she will likely make a commitment to repeat that specific literacy process again—and probably at a more difficult level. Showing that you appreciate all the knowledge readers possess and all they have endured to arrive at any level of proficiency motivates them to reach higher and deeper.

A second benefit of sharing and celebrating with students whose self-concept is low is the *spillover effect*. When readers realize that you continuously point out "little great things" they do, they begin to read more, begin to agree that they are good, and begin to see their own evidences of growth. These newly enumerated strengths support a more positive self-image, which must be in place before students can move from specific to total commitment. Essentially your acknowledgments are depositing gold coins into their "self-concept sacks." Because of you, these students can have some positive self-images to invest in high-risk literacy challenges.

In summary, exposing oneself to possible failure *again* requires investments of positive self-concept and courage. When you acknowledge this courage, less accomplished readers/writers know you understand them, and most will work harder. Without your specific feedback concerning their strengths, however, these students will maintain low self-esteem and low literacy proficiency (Jongsma, 2000; Maynard, Tyler, & Arnold, 2000).

Levels of Emotional Investment

Before students can move from specific to total commitment, you must monitor their present level of positive emotional involvement and their level of frustration. Because students possess individual differences with respect to tolerance for challenge, their diagnoses can best occur in one-to-one conferences, or **discovery discussions** (to be discussed more fully later in this chapter). In these diagnoses, your goal is to ascertain how long a student can work on a task, and how difficult that task can become, before the student decreases his or her positive emotional investment, commitment, interest, self-concept, and intrinsic motivation.

Total literacy commitment comes from students who are willing to make high levels of positive emotional investment. To do so, they must construct meaning and sustain an interest in reading even when faced with decoding obstacles, increased readability levels, and decreased personal desire for success (Corno, 1993; Guthrie, Schafer, Wang, & Afflerbach, 1995; Turner, 1995). You can build students' volition by providing specific feedback, celebrating their effort and perseverance, and evaluating their performances by standards that you and they establish together (Block, 2001, 2002a; Zimmerman, 1994), as described in Box 4.1.

Before a total engagement in literacy evolves, students' affect must increase in four areas, as McGinn, Winne, and Butler (1993) report. Students' affect must expand relative to the following:

1. Task value and difficulty, as well as the extent to which products of the task are important for some goal outside the boundaries of the task per se (utility value)
2. The level of effort students are willing to exert to be successful, as well as how interesting or intrinsically valuable the task is judged to be (intrinsic or interest value)
3. The literacy strategies students feel that they command (literacy value)
4. Students' perceptions of the task's relevance to personal priorities (attainment value)

In summation, assisting students to improve the strength of their positive affect and level of positive emotional engagement is a multidimensional responsibility. Without

4.1 READING SPECIALISTS

Effective Feedback Strategies

To help students invest high levels of positive emotional energy, you can attribute their literacy successes to their effort and to the strategies they used rather than to luck (Michel, 1994; Worthy, 1996, 2000). In one-on-one intervention sessions, if you respond to a question by giving the correct answer quickly, struggling readers/writers assume that what is most important to you is to get their needs met as rapidly as possible so they can return to quiet seat work. Alternatively, if you respond by asking questions that suggest several options (such as, "What are all the different things you've tried?"), students assume that you want to help them think through literacy challenges themselves. It is also important to remember that your feedback must go beyond simple statements and check marks that say "Very Good." Your feedback will be most useful if it tells students which aspects of their reading or writing merit praise, which processes and strategies they used to reach a new level, and what they need to emphasize next to continue their progress (McCombs, 1995). With this feedback, students can raise their estimation of what they are capable of accomplishing.

Suppose a student approaches you during an independent work period or reading specialist Tier 3 or 4 support discovery discussion and says, "I'm having a lot of trouble. I don't know what to do. How do I do this?" As you read the following range of typical possible responses, select the one you would use to answer. Place a check mark before it. Pay particular attention to the implicit effect that each response could have on students' attitude toward literacy, based on the information in this chapter.

Response 1:

You say to yourself:	I'll just tell Joe the answer so he can get back to work.
Action you take:	[Tell answer, without explanation.]
Example:	"Just move the parentheses so that they come after the period."

Response 2:

You say to yourself:	I'll tell Elena and explain it one more time, in case she's not clear.
Action you take:	[Tell correct answer, with explanation.]
Example:	"To find the main idea, locate the sentence that summarizes all others or tells the most important point."

Response 3:

You say to yourself:	Perhaps if I give Bill several ideas or choices, it will help put him on the right track.
Action you take:	[Suggest several possibilities.]
Example:	"You can take a look at the workbook and review the different parts of speech, or you might look over the examples we did last Tuesday, or you might try writing each sentence on a separate piece of paper and looking at them one at a time, instead of while they are together in the paragraph."

4.1   READING SPECIALISTS

Effective Feedback Strategies *(continued)*

Response 4:

You say to yourself:	I'll get Carol to think on her own and realize exactly what she needs to do.
Action you take:	[Ask a yes/no or closed-ended question.]
Example:	"Did you try the two strategies we discussed yesterday?"

Response 5:

You say to yourself:	I'd like to help Ron try to think this through on his own, to see if he really can grasp it.
Action you take:	[Ask an open-ended question.]
Example:	"What are the different strategies you have tried so far to figure this out?" or "How do you think Magellan and the other great explorers might have thought to find this answer?"*

*Response 5 is the answer given by teachers whose students gained the most literacy strength in one year (Block, 2001).

your guidance, some may decide they would prefer not to know how to read or write rather than continuing to feel like a failure.

Increasing Interest in Literacy

When unmotivated readers and writers reach a level of total commitment, they often experience a simultaneous rise in **interest.** Interest has the power to (1) arouse and instigate behavior, (2) give direction or purpose to behavior, (3) continue to allow a behavior to persist, or (4) choose a particular, preferred behavior (Smey-Richman, 1988, p. 28).

Joseph Sottle (1987) asserted that "every child has a talent or interest that a thoughtful teacher can nurture" (p. 103). Trying to find out what interests students is an important dimension of promoting affective development; but "making things interesting" tends to "seduce them into remembering" only the less important details (Gardner, Alexander, Gillingham, Kulikowich, & Brown, 1991, p. 21).

One way to consistently build student interest in literacy is to use open tasks and student choice (Turner, 1995). **Open tasks** are those in which students decide which information they will use and/or what they want to read. Student choices occur when there are tasks with several available options. Such tasks can promote significantly greater engagement, reading strategy use, persistence, and volition by struggling readers/writers (Turner, 1995; Worthy 1996, 2000). The interest and motivational value of open tasks lie in students' ability to (1) seek challenges and self-improvement, (2) have autonomy over literacy, (3) pursue personal interests, (4) mold tasks to fit their interests, and (5) talk about what they read/wrote.

For example, in Turner's study, first graders could choose from several literacy activities during a weeklong celebration of *Clifford's Birthday Party* (Bridwell, 1988): They could write party invitations, describe the party they gave for Clifford, make a list of party supplies, draw and label Clifford's gifts, or read other Clifford books (Turner, 1995). Before outlining the choices, their teachers rehearsed the use of resources and how to plan; they also monitored the children's reading and evaluated their literacy growth on specific tasks. At the conclusion, teachers discussed successful and less successful choices and strategies students used and then asked children to suggest improved literacy tactics. These are the steps to become a "Sage at My Side," which is the effective teachers that struggling readers need. In contrast, when the same assignments are given to all students (closed tasks), there is little leeway (or need) for students to engage their own interest and affect.

Diagnosing True Literacy Difficulties as Opposed to Defense Mechanisms and Learned Helplessness

Most children enter school with self-integrated personalities and are eager to learn to read. For some of them, however, a progression of literacy failure and frustration culminates in a permanently negative emotional state. When success and approval are repeatedly denied, **learned helplessness** can result (students' belief that they cannot be successful no matter how much effort they exert) or **defense mechanisms** develop (negative behaviors or attitudes that divert students' own as well as others' attention away from their less-than-desired level of literacy achievement). Learned helplessness is demonstrated when students, in the face of uncontrollable and continual literacy failures, do not persevere, so as to appear as though they are making little effort to read or write (Kos, 1991; Weiner, 1986). Such defense mechanisms, which usually take the form of misbehavior, may be quite logical to students who have to make a choice between two evils. For these students, fear of reprisal from teachers or peers is less daunting than facing another unpleasant literacy experience (Kos, 1991; Winograd, 1994). A description of student traits that distinguish learned helplessness and defense mechanisms from true psychological or cognitive factors that limit literacy is shown in Box 4.2.

Learned helplessness and negative emotional responses also have biological consequences. They change adrenaline secretion, pulse rate, temperature level, and blood flow so that the body conditions a student into feelings that perpetuate "a habit of failing." When unmotivated readers completely disengage from reading and lose confidence in themselves, one effective strategy is to place them in a new environment that might generate different bodily responses to reading/writing (Bandura, 1994).

The early detection of defense mechanisms is also important. We can diagnose true literacy difficulties when less accomplished readers demonstrate more behaviors in the right column than in the left column of Box 4.2. First, try to identify what individual

4.2 DIAGNOSIS AND ASSESSMENT

Diagnosing Motivational Difficulties: A Learned Helplessness Checklist

Directions: For each item check the appropriate column. Count total check marks in each column. Diagnosis rests with the column that has the larger number of total check marks.

CHARACTERISTICS OF LEARNED HELPLESSNESS

____ Child asks for explanations regularly despite differences in subject matter.

____ Child asks for explanation of instructions regardless of style used, either auditory or visual.

____ Child's questions are not specific to material but appear to be mainly to gain adult attention.

____ Child is disorganized or slow in assignments but becomes much more efficient when a meaningful reward is presented as motivation.

____ Child works only when an adult is nearby at school and/or at home.

____ Individually administered measures of ability indicate that the child is capable of learning the material. Individual tests improve with tester encouragement and support. Group measures may not indicate good abilities or skills.

____ Child exhibits "poor me" body language (tears, helplessness, pouting, copying) regularly when new work is presented. Teacher or adult attention serves to ease the symptoms.

____ Parents report whining, complaining, attention getting, temper tantrums, and poor sportsmanship at home.

____ Child's "poor me" behavior appears only with one parent and not with the other; only with some teachers and not with others. With some teachers or with the other parent the child functions fairly well independently.

CHARACTERISTICS OF AFFECTIVE DIFFICULTIES THAT IMPACT LITERACY ACHIEVEMENT

____ Child asks for explanations in particular subjects that are difficult.

____ Child asks for explanations of instructions only when given in one instruction style, either auditory or visual, but not both.

____ Child's questions are specific to material, and once process is explained child works efficiently.

____ Child's disorganization or slow pace continues despite motivating rewards.

____ Child works independently once process is clearly explained.

____ Both individual and group measures indicate lack of specific abilities or skills. Tester encouragement has no significant effect on scores.

____ Child exhibits "poor me" body language only with instructions or assignments in specific disability areas and accepts challenges in areas of strength.

____ Although parents may find similar symptoms at home, they tend to be more sporadic than regular, particularly the whining and complaining.

___ Although the child's "poor me" behaviors may only appear with one parent or with solicitous teachers, performance is not adequate even when behavior is acceptable.

continued

4.2 DIAGNOSIS AND ASSESSMENT

Diagnosing Motivational Difficulties *(continued)*

_____ Child learns only when given one-to-one instruction and will not learn in groups even when instructional mode is varied.

_____ Although child may learn more quickly in a one-to-one setting, he or she will also learn efficiently in a group setting, provided the child's affective difficulty is taken into consideration when instructions are given.

_____ Total

_____ Total

It is crucial to realize that some children who truly have affective difficulties also acquire learned helplessness. The key to distinguishing between learned helplessness and affective challenges to literacy achievement is the child's response to adult support. If the child performs only with adult support when new material is presented, he or she is falling back on learned helplessness behaviors, whether or not there is also an affective challenge.

Source: Adapted from S. B. Rimm (1986), *Underachievement Syndrome: Causes and Cures,* p. 219. Watertown, WI: Apple Publishing. Permission to copy granted by Good Apple, 1204 Buchanan St., Carthage, IL 62321-0299. Materials copyright © by Good Apple. All rights reserved.

readers believe is the cause of their successes and failures (Weiner, 1980, 1983). Ask, "Why were you more successful today than yesterday?" The answers students give will usually attribute their success to one of four things:

1. Their own abilities, capabilities, or natural aptitude ("I know I read better today than yesterday because I am smart").
2. The amount of effort exerted ("I tried harder today").
3. The difficulty of the task ("The book wasn't as hard as the one I read yesterday").
4. Luck ("I don't know—just lucky I guess").

If a student attributes successes to ability and/or effort, you can support these positive responses, as explained earlier in the chapter, by providing feedback that states specific information about the parts of his effort and ability that most contributed to success (e.g., "Because you concentrated on gaining the full meaning of each sentence, your overall concentration improved, and you increased your ability to pause only at the end of sentences instead of after each word"). Because such students view success as internally controlled (have an *internal locus of control*), each literacy success generates self-confidence. However, when students view success as controllable through their abilities, each failure generates feelings of shame and hopelessness. No one else can be blamed. Whatever was lacking in their ability (and this "whatever" is usually unknown to students unless you describe it to them) will be lacking the next time they attempt a literacy task. Therefore, if students become failure-avoiding or develop learned helplessness, they either begin attributing failure to causes other than ability, to protect their self-esteem, or they stop trying.

If you continually ask them to "try harder," these students are forced to conclude that they are "just dumb" and regardless of how hard they try they will never be able to read. To avoid these deductions, match literacy tasks to students' ability, plus a small increment in either word density, paragraph length, or sentence complexity—but not all three simultaneously. For such students, the serial books described in Chapter 1, Box 1.3 are excellent choices. These books have the same main characters and same writing style, paragraph lengths, and sentence complexities. Only vocabulary alters.

If a student attributes her successes to the task's being easy or to luck, she views success as out of her control (she has an *external locus of control*). Success is perceived to be unstable, and students with this viewpoint experience each success with feelings of surprise or indifference. For such students, it is important not to suggest that a literacy task they are about to perform is easy.

Often, in an attempt to encourage students with a low self-concept, teachers emphasize the ease of literacy. Because task ease is an external factor, however, success at this task will not increase students' self-efficacy or internal control over literacy. Furthermore, if these students subsequently fail on what everyone knows is "so easy anyone should be able to do it," the failure is accompanied by feelings of shame and embarrassment. Some students then conclude that they lack even the bare minimum of ability in literacy. Similarly, wishing students "good luck" on a task generates ideas of an external and uncontrollable reason for success and will result in increased feelings of indifference and depressed self-esteem.

On the other hand, if we tell students that a task will be challenging (if indeed it will be for them) but that with reasonable effort they can be successful, increased internal locus of control, pride, and confidence can result. Students begin to value and believe in their own literacy abilities and the control that they can have over reading and writing.

Instructional Interventions

By reexamining their beliefs and restructuring tasks, as will be described in activities in this section, students with severe negative affective responses to literacy can change. The following interventions improve students' positive views of themselves as readers/writers.

Holding Discovery Discussions

Children who are close to, and trust, significant adults are heavily influenced by those mentors. These adults validate students for being who they are (Glenn & Nelson, 1994). In the past, when teachers met with students about literacy, these meetings were called *one-to-one conferences*. As explained in Chapter 1, I suggest that you label these times *discovery discussions* instead. This terminology does not have negative connotations. The word *conference* suggests that someone has come to another for help or advice. Readers at lower stages of literacy development have trouble accepting that their teachers would authentically come to them for advice. The term *discovery discussions,* on the other hand, communicates that teachers and students are partners in gaining new understandings.

One-to-one discovery discussions may be the only way unmotivated readers will express the depth of their literacy problems. Just as you may have experienced when faced with difficulty, when you need help you turn first to one person—not a group—to discuss that problem. Struggling readers are the same. They gain confidence in overcoming adversity in discussions that are one-on-one, as shown in this example:

> I think, for Eric, the reading process was still too invisible. Reading is often a solitary activity; it was hard for Eric actually to see how someone does it. Eric needed to sit side-by-side with a more accomplished reader, reading to discover information he truly needed. In short, he needed a reading apprenticeship. (Voss, 1993, p. 639)

Steps described below explain procedures for highly successful discovery discussions.

STEP 1: Establish a time during each day when impromptu discovery discussions, with you or with their peers, can be called by students. An optimal time is 10 minutes allocated during a 40-minute literacy period when students are engaged in self-selected reading/writing, working in centers, and/or preparing projects for presentations. At these times students will have signed up to engage in a discovery discussion with you or a peer. They ask questions and make requests to learn something about literacy.

STEP 2: Establish regularly scheduled times for student-to-teacher discovery discussions. Set aside part of one day each week for these meetings, and schedule them a month at a time. By doing so, you can be sure that at least once each month every student will have your undivided attention and expertise available to address their very specific literacy needs. Most students prepare for these scheduled discovery discussions for several days by deciding on a topic they wish to discuss—for example, asking for new reading strategies, sharing their reading successes, or asking for cues they can use to decode, comprehend, and compose.

Ms. Boyd, a second grade teacher, shared the following excerpt from a scheduled discovery discussion she held with Manuel. He wanted to read a book and share reading success in his discussion. Before this discovery discussion, he had difficulties reading three-letter consonant blends. Now, however, Manuel shared his success with Ms. Boyd:

> **Manuel:**   String. . . . String [as he turned to the next page and pointed to this word on two different pages].
>
> **Ms. Boyd:**   Very good. . . . Very good.
>
> **Manuel:**   I know how I done that.
>
> **Ms. Boyd:**   Tell me.
>
> **Manuel:**   I said "ring." Then I picked up "st" and said "string."

This discovery discussion unveiled Manuel's creativity. He demonstrated that he could develop his own strategy for decoding three-letter blends: Start with the last consonant in the blend and say the word that would result if only that consonant began it, then add the sounds of the two-letter blend in front of the word that was just pronounced. Had

Ms. Boyd not held a scheduled discovery discussion and allowed Manuel to set his own purpose for it, she might never have known Manuel's creative power and therefore would not have been able to develop it more fully as a decoding tool.

STEP 3: During each discovery discussion, allow for children to enjoy reading aloud to you. This is important because through this activity students can demonstrate ownership over books and reading. As a result, you are likely to frequently hear students exclaim, "I know this!" or "I can read this!" When you plan discovery discussions in this way, you avoid the temptation to approach each session with the intent of finding out what the child is doing wrong and what you can do to help (which is often the focus of traditional student conferences).

STEP 4: During a discovery discussion, if a student says they don't understand, respond by questioning, "Why do you think you don't understand?" This question is effective not just due to its content, but also because of its ability to communicate real interest in hearing *what the student has to say.* Try to detect patterns in the questions students ask, as well as in the answers they give. For example, a student might ask why her mind wanders when she is reading, and then she adds that this is why her comprehension is limited. You can reply by asking if she thinks her mind wanders because she is losing her place, or saying words to herself that do not sound right, or perhaps frequently skipping words she can't decode even if she wants to know the meaning and pronunciation. Through this continued-questioning method of pattern analysis, you can assist students to discover their own strengths and needs.

The following questions have been shown to be exceptionally valuable in assisting students to improve their writing abilities (Kucera, 1995). With limited modifications they can be used to improve readers' abilities as well.

1. What do you like best about your piece?
2. Why did you write it?
3. From where did you get your idea?
4. Who is your audience?
5. Did you have any particular problems with part or all of the piece? Are you stuck? Where?
6. Do you need help with grammar, spelling, capitalization, or punctuation?
7. What mood were you trying to establish?
8. One thing that I really liked about your piece was _____.
9. One thing I would like to know more about is _____.
10. I particularly appreciated the way you used the _____.
11. One question I have about your piece is _____.
12. I can see that you really _____. You must feel good about _____. All teachers would be glad [proud] to read this.

STEP 5: Allow for departures from a fixed agenda. Many struggling readers enter a discovery discussion bubbling over with something they want to share that is not directly related to reading. You may be amazed by the impact that your concern, the sharing of their ideas, and just having had an adult listen to them can have on students' reading ability. For example, one teacher wrote the following after holding several individual discovery discussions with Matt:

> We had a conversation first. Matt seemed to need to talk and have someone listen. He talked a lot about racing and race cars. He had never told me of this interest before.
>   He then read *All by Myself* to me. He had only one omission and one self-correction. The retelling was not much of a challenge. He remembered the story. I did have to ask a few questions (prompt him).
>   I enjoyed this session more than any before. I guess because he really wanted to just talk.

One week later this teacher sent me a copy of a note she had received from Matt's mother:

> I would like to thank you for working with my son. He had just about given up on school work. It is so nice to know someone really cares about his progress.
>
> Debbie

The sample discovery discussion record forms in Figure 4.1 demonstrate three ways to assess discovery discussions so that individual needs are addressed.

Analyzing Attitudes and Interests and Personalizing Instruction

A second instructional intervention for unmotivated readers is to administer attitude and interest assessments. To increase their effectiveness, follow the procedure explained here to ensure that your assessments increase students' commitment, interest, and confidence in self and literacy.

Gather as much information as possible about students' affective responses to literacy. To do this, you can first administer the attitude survey appropriate for their age level. Then prepare a note card for each student: As you read each survey, denote physical and cognitive limitations for each student on the left side of his or her card. For instance, one student may state "I do not like to read anything for too long because I get too tired"—so you would write "Refer for vision testing" on the left side of the card. On the right side of each card write the date and information about the student's level of commitment to literacy.

On a separate notepad, group students according to their interests, placing each student's name in as many different groups as his or her interests warrant. Subsequently, when you meet with each interest-based group separately, you can offer them a wide variety of books, at various readability levels, concerning their topics of interest. Use the work that readers complete in these first interest groups to assess their amount of self-initiated reading and their ability to set their own literacy goals. You can also use your assessments to determine what level of challenge aggravates their frustration.

Teaching Students to Set Their Own Standards

You can begin this instructional intervention by asking students to establish the standard of success they want to achieve in their next literacy experiences. This directive,

Form #1

STUDENT'S NAME: <u>David Carter</u>   WEEK OF: <u>2-23</u>

My goal for the week is: <u>to find a book I really like to read AND to learn why I do</u>

What I did: <u>I found Dear Mr. Henshaw. I really like it because it's so funny and I wish my</u>

<u>dad were at home too. It helped me.</u>

Teacher's comments: <u>I know another book you'll like. Mrs. B</u>

Form #2

| Student's Name: *David Carter* Conference Date: *Notes taken on Feb. 23*

What to check for next conference:
1. *increased comprehension*
2. *project with Susan and its progress*
3. *Read Dave's journal for progress on problem solving skills* | Issues Raised:
1. *Dave wanted me to read aloud to the class some poems from* <u>*Class Dismissed Two*</u>*; he really likes it.*

2. *Dave and Susan want to write an anthology of original poems together (see contract) based on* <u>*Class Dismissed Two.*</u>

3. *Dave had trouble resolving difference with Gary in discussion this week. He's not sure why.* | Action Taken/Goals Set:
1. *He's going to read some of his favorites to the class.*

2. *The project will be finished in two weeks (March 8); independent study, worth 10%.*

3. *Must monitor the next few discussions; talk to Gary; Dave will "track" the problem in his journal responses.* |

Form #3

OUTSTANDING READING FROM: <u>David Carter</u>

Deposit one outstanding example of my reading in action:

<u>*completed two self-selected readings in one week*</u>
                                          the reading
<u>*stated he enjoyed reading for very first time!*</u>
                                          action taken

Signature: <u>*Mrs. Bradford*</u>

Date: <u>*March 27*</u>

FIGURE 4.1 Teacher–Student Discovery Discussion Record Forms

MIDDLE SCHOOL and HIGH SCHOOL

Student Self-Responsibility Guides

Another effective intervention to increase students' affect toward literacy, developed by Elias and Tobias (1990), created self-responsibility charts to improve students' study skills and work habits. These charts have been selected by some secondary school struggling readers as their most helpful aids in increasing their self-confidence in literacy. Students complete the guides and bring them to a discovery discussion with you at the end of the grading period. These guides are used as outlines to follow as reading specialists analyze each individual's growth in self-selected literacy pursuits.

A sample guide appears here. It is helpful to remind students of the following facts before they write their guides:

1. Start simply to achieve initial success.
2. Old literacy habits take time to modify or to replace with effective strategies.
3. The "other" spaces can be used to write additional goals for this grading period.
4. Internalization and transfer of learning take considerable time; therefore, students should revisit their self-responsibility guides with you at least once each grading period.

Name: _____ Date: _____

Homeroom teacher: _____

Reading specialist: _____

Read the following list. Check the statements that apply to you:

_____ Not decoding well

_____ Forgetting what I read

_____ Coming late to school or class

_____ Reading too slow or too fast to comprehend

_____ Losing my books or forgetting to bring them

_____ Losing my place when I read

_____ Not writing complete sentences

_____ Not using vivid verbs and precise nouns

_____ Rambling when I write or speak

_____ Having limited interest in reading and writing

_____ Not reading or writing very often to solve problems in life or for personal pleasure

Other _____

Other _____

Books (or topics) I'd like to read _____

Activities I've enjoyed this week _____

coupled with your patience, cheers for progress, and strategies that support their positive self-esteem and established standards, can advance these readers' literacy, lower their anxiety, and eliminate their self-consciousness about potential mistakes.

Model how to set standards by writing on the board a few standards that students reached last week—such as increasing the amount of time spent reading silently by 10 percent, or writing one full paragraph with three details. The difference between setting goals and standards is that standards measure the next success in comparison to the most recent last attempt. Student responsibility guides are one means of doing so, especially for students who are in grades 5 through 12. An example used at Paladine Middle School in Paladine, Kentucky, appears in Box 4.3.

Chapter Summary

Most unmotivated readers need help from reading specialists and exemplary classroom teachers before they can understand and overcome their affective, attitudinal, emotional, and self-esteem obstacles. As Kathy Kirk, an outstanding reading specialist, stated: "I have to look inside myself, and use the activities in this chapter to help my students look inside themselves, to renew their desire to learn and to relate to literacy." This renewal comes through students' increased commitment, interest, and confidence in themselves and the pleasure and benefits that occur through pleasurable reading and writing experiences that were presented in this chapter.

Affective barriers are broken down when you guide students, through gradual commitment to you, in their selection of personally valued books and other literacy activities. You do this through (a) careful analysis and individual notes made about each student from attitude and interest assessments, (b) by holding unscheduled and scheduled discovery discussions, (c) by teaching students to set their own standards by asking effective questions, and (d) by monitoring students' self-expectations with self-responsibility guides. In the next chapter you will learn how to increase literacy abilities by encouraging every reader/writer to bring his or her cultural richness to comprehension and composing tasks.

Key Terminology

If you know the meaning of each term below, check it off. If you are not sure of the meaning, turn to the page indicated to review the term.

____ **motivation** (page 82)   ____ **open tasks** (page 89)
____ **self-efficacy** (page 82)   ____ **learned helplessness** (page 90)
____ **discovery discussions** (page 87)   ____ **defense mechanisms** (page 90)
____ **interest** (page 89)

Case Study

Making Professional Decisions

Brian, a middle school reader, provided an insightful summary of the effectiveness of the activities from this chapter that he had completed:

I *finally* see what literacy is all about. It's not so much learning to read and write or to become a good enough reader to have a career; it's more learning about myself. I'm teaching myself to become disciplined and curious at the same time. I'm focusing on my ambition to read better and in the process to become the best person I can.

What would you suspect Brian's major affective barrier was? What would be your next instructional support? Why? (If you would like to compare your professional judgment with that of Brian's teacher, turn to the Answer Key at the back of the book after writing your response.)

Thinking and Writing about What You Have Learned

1. Dr. Maxine Green, a renowned psychologist at Teachers College at Columbia University in New York, stated: "Self-evaluation is the most effective way to motivate a change in behavior because the evaluation comes from within the person, rather than external sources." Moreover, Dr. William Glaser, a famous physician at UCLA who specializes in learning differences, stated: "I have noticed that happy people are constantly evaluating themselves and unhappy people are constantly evaluating others." Relate both of these quotations to what you have learned in this chapter and describe how their messages apply.

2. Show how you can best integrate the information you have learned in the first four chapters of this textbook into your instructional program: Write a paragraph, draw a graph, or make a lesson plan for the first week of school to integrate what you've learned.

3. Based on what you have learned thus far in this book, explain what you would recommend to a colleague who came to you with this description of Dontay: "Dontay needs someone to believe in him; his confidence is boosted when others acknowledge his success. He rubs his eyes a lot, and his mind wanders at times."

4. Several diagnostic and assessment tools were presented in this chapter. How can you best schedule their use in your year's teaching plan?

5. Adapt and change the sample self-responsibility guide in Box 4.3 to meet your individual struggling readers' affective needs. Make them available to students throughout the year. Students can profit from storing the guides in their portfolios to document their progress throughout the year.

Onto the Information Superhighway

Many reluctant readers and writers overcome affective limitations when they complete Internet projects with the guidance of their classroom teachers and reading specialists working together. Such projects enable struggling readers to spend up to two periods in a typical day exploring topics of great personal interest. In so doing, they build vocabulary, comprehension, and in-depth breadth and depth of pleasure-filled, positive affective background experiences with literacy. These Internet projects can be developed from narrative and expository texts. They can also be created as collaborations by struggling readers in different countries. Three blueprints that can be followed by you and your reluctant readers appear in Figure 4.2.

Examples of Website-Related Projects

Flat Stanley

http://flatstanley.enoreo.on.ca

Read the book Flat Stanley *and then have your students send their own Flat Stanleys around the world to participating classrooms.*

Earth Day Groceries

www.earthdaybags.org

Students decorate grocery bags with environment-friendly messages and distribute these at local grocery stores just before Earth Day. A great social action project for a unit on ecology and the environment.

The Noonday Project: Measuring the Circumference of the Earth

http://k12science.stevens-tech.edu/noonday/noon.html

Students recreate the classic experiment Eratosthenes conducted more than 2,200 years ago. Collaborating with students from other schools throughout the world, they measure, gather and exchange data, and then estimate the circumference of the earth.

Journey North

www.learner.org/jnorth

Learn about the annual migration of many animals during seasonal changes.

Math Project Center

www.eduplace.com/projects/mathproj.html

A series of collaborative math projects with other classrooms.

Project Center

www.eduplace.com/projects

Links to many projects in reading, social studies, science, and math.

Spontaneous Projects

Spontaneous Internet projects are developed by individual teachers who then advertise for other classroom to join them. Spontaneous projects follow these steps: (1) Plan a collaborative project for an upcoming unit in your classroom and write a project description, (2) post the project description and timeline several months in advance at one or several locations, seeking collaborative classroom partners, (3) arrange collaboration details with teachers in other classrooms who agree to participate, and (4) complete the project in your own class while exchanging information with your collaborating classrooms. You can visit the following site to see how teachers develop, post, and join spontaneous projects around the world:

Global Schoolhouse Projects Registry

www.globalschoolhouse.org

Many popular projects are located at this site, including Newsday, Geogame, Letters to Santa, and Global Grocery List. (Note: *Your struggling readers may also enjoy following links to Lightspan's Collaborative Project site.*)

EXPLORING JAPAN

Internet Researcher: _____ Date: _____

News about Japan

Go to the bookmark I have set for *Kids' Web Japan* (http://www.jinjapan.org/kidsweb). Click on the button "Monthly News" (http://www.jinjapan.org/kidsweb/news.html) and read several recent news stories from Japan. Write notes about some of the news you discover, and be ready to share these with us during Internet Workshop.

_____

_____

_____

_____

Nature and Climate

Click on the button "Nature and Climate" and read a description of what it is like to live in Japan. Be certain to read answers to some of the questions at the bottom of this article. Write down notes about what you learn about the nature and climate of Japan. We will share these during Internet Workshop.

_____

_____

_____

_____

Your Choice

Let's discover what's cool among kids in Japan. Visit "What's Cool in Japan" (http://www.jinjapan.org/kidsweb/cool.html). Write down notes about what you discover is most popular among kids in Japan, and be ready to share this information during Internet Workshop.

_____

_____

_____

_____

Evaluation Rubric

I read and took notes for the first two items	2 points
I shared each item with my group	2 points
I did the "Your Choice" activity	1 point
TOTAL	5 points

FIGURE 4.2 An Example of an Internet Workshop Assessment

Source: Modified from "New Definitions of Comprehension Research and Practice," a handout distributed by Donald Lew, Preconventional Institute 15, International Reading Association's Annual Meeting, April 29, 2000, New Orleans, LA. Used by permission.

Information on this chalk-board is changed every week to expose all students to every language spoken by students in the classroom.

Embracing Readers' Social and Cultural Richness

Dear Dr. Block,

I just read that from the very first days of children's development, their language abilities build through students' self-created systems of uniting cultural and social behavior. Thus, literacy, as all language abilities, is "directed [by students] towards a definite purpose . . . refracted through the prism of children's environment. The path from object to child and from child to object passes through another person. This complex human structure is the product of a developmental process deeply rooted in the links between individual and social history" [Vygotsky, 1978, p. 30]. I must learn more about how culture influences all readers, especially those who are at Stages 2 and 3 in their development. This chapter taught me how to do it.

—Cathleen Cavanagh, teacher at
Starpoint School for Learning Disabilities

■ Chapter Overview: Key Points

The purpose of this chapter is to explore how reading specialists in clinical settings and classroom teachers in large/small group instruction can work together to build on the rich cultural and social knowledge of struggling readers to increase their literacy. As stated by one exemplary reading specialist, "Cultural appreciation is woven through everything that's done for my readers: room decor, available books, and interaction styles" (T. E. Napper, personal communication, July 19, 1995). Literacy is culturally framed and defined because different cultural groups differ in distinct ways in how they define literacy and what they perceive to be literate behavior. It is important, therefore, to understand how culture shapes the reading and writing behavior of struggling readers, and how it shapes the literacy events in their homes and communities. As educators, we can become more effective if we understand:

- The history of North America's growth in cultural influences on literacy achievement
- Present cultural and social influences on literacy achievement
- Interaction patterns influenced by cultural and social variables
- Ways to diagnose and instruct to capitalize on the cultural and social richness in struggling readers' lives

By the end of the chapter you will have answers to the following questions:

1. What cultural variables affect readers' development?
2. What social variables affect literacy success?
3. What instruction actions and diagnoses enhance students' literacy by building on individuals' cultural knowledge and social strengths?
4. What multicultural literature is preferred by less accomplished readers?

History of North America's Growth in Cultural Influences on Literacy Achievement

The first inhabitants of North America arrived 30,000 years ago. They were native Asians who crossed a land bridge that connected Siberia and Alaska. As they migrated across the vast fields of the Americas, the separation between tribes led to diverse cultures and languages. When the first Europeans arrived 29,500 years later, they viewed the multitude of cultures as one. Their mission was to conquer and convert the people—not just to Christianity but to the same values, including attitudes toward literacy, that they held. This belief led to the extinction of many literacy forms, especially the Native American use of storytelling, which did not spread into the European system of education.

In the next 300 years (1500–1800), the American population grew but remained relatively homogeneous. For example, the 1820 census revealed that four-fifths of the 9.6 million United States population was Protestant or Catholic and of northern or western European descent; one-fifth was African American.

By 1880 the total U.S. population had grown to more than 50 million. Then between 1880 and 1920, approximately 14.5 million immigrants entered the United States—fleeing poverty and religious or political persecution in Italy, Russia, Poland, and other southern and eastern European nations. Similar immigrations occurred in Canada. During those 40 years the U.S. population more than doubled, to over 106 million, and the immigrant population rose from 1.9 to 14.5 million people—an increase of approximately 315,000 a year, 26,250 a month, or 875 new immigrants each day from various cultural, national, and linguistic origins. Most immigrants lived in crowded, unheated city tenements and worked long hours at menial labor for low wages. They were labeled the "huddled masses" because they remained in city neighborhoods with people who came from their own country, held their own values, and spoke their native language.

Subsequent to this immigration, a law was passed (and remained in effect until 1965) that placed strict, narrow limits on the number of people who could come to the United States. During the years since 1965, North America has experienced another wave of immigration, one that has brought about very dramatic changes in our population composition. The majority of newer immigrants come from Third World (developing) countries. Many enter and remain in the United States and Canada as illegal aliens, which keeps them away from formal education and traditional literacy instructional experiences. If the current immigration trend continues, it is estimated that by the year 2050 the majority of U.S. citizens will have non-European cultural ancestry (Banks & Banks, 1995).

The first Asian immigrants to the United States were Chinese, coming during the gold rush of 1849. Immediately, they were prohibited from entering schools and were denied citizenship. The men usually could only get low-paying jobs as laborers, such as those who helped build the western portion of the transcontinental railroad. Less than 35 years after their arrival, the Chinese Exclusion Act of 1882 was passed, barring Chinese laborers from coming to the United States. This law was the first federal legislation to discriminate against a group of people based on cultural background. Only with the Immigration Act of 1965 would Chinese be allowed regular immigration procedures.

Until the end of World War II, most Asian groups settled on the West Coast. More recent groups of Asian Americans are war and political refugees from Korea, Vietnam, Cambodia, and Thailand; they have settled throughout the United States. This eastern Asian cultural group is the fastest-growing minority in the United States (U.S. Census Bureau, 2000).

Since September 11, 2001, North Americans have become more aware of the need to view the entire world as one body of humanity. And as reading specialists we have an even greater responsibility to build all students' abilities to read and write. Through our efforts, greater global understanding and sharing could occur in the future, resulting in fewer people turning to terrorist behaviors to deliver messages.

Present Cultural and Social Influences on Literacy Achievement

Today the United States is the most culturally diverse nation in the world. One of the most pressing challenges we face as educators is the need to increase the literacy of this changing population. We must assimilate various groups into the larger society without destroying individual students' identities and heritages. To illustrate the complexity of this task, in 2002 a randomly selected but typical large U.S. school district (60,000+ students) listed the cultural and social groups in its K–12 student population. The listing revealed 53 cultural heritages, and most classrooms contained 7 cultural heritages among 25 students. Unfortunately, although there has been increased attention to identifying the impact of culture on literacy, too many culturally diverse students are not performing at the reading or writing levels of their Anglo counterparts, and the gap is not closing (Garcia & Pearson, 1994; Jordan, Snow, & Porche, 2000).

Numerous studies have examined the relationship of various home and cultural factors on oral and written language development (Block & Pressley, 2002; Genishi, 1992; Heath, 1982, 1983; Morrow, 1993; Vygotsky, 1986). One study of children from three different communities and cultures within a 50-mile radius in one state revealed that different cultural groups have distinctly different home language routines and attitudes toward written language (Heath, 1983). For example, in a town called Gateway, children from African American and Caucasian families (the mainstream community) received early exposure to books, to written and oral narratives, to book reading behaviors, and to questioning routines. On the other hand, children from Roadville, a predominantly Caucasian mill community, were expected to learn to read by memorizing the alphabet letters and doing workbook-type activities. In that community, stories were viewed as representations of moral messages. As another contrast, Trackton children, who lived in a highly oral, predominantly African American mill community, were rewarded for storytelling that included embellishments, and they received more praise for verbal attention getting than for quiet, silent behaviors during reading. Few children in this Trackton cultural community were asked to write or read, nor were they praised for doing so.

Such differences in social and cultural orientations have many implications for diagnosing and instructing struggling readers (Cazden, 1993; Heath, 1983; Jordan, Snow, & Porche, 2000). How literacy is used in homes influences students' needs, motivation, and priorities for reading. Cultural and social factors also shape readers' assumptions about the reading process and their cognitive approach, social style, and attitudes while engaged in literacy activities (Field & Aebersold, 1990; Fillmore & Kay, 1981).

Culture can be defined as the "shared beliefs, values, and patterns of behavior that define a group, and that are required for group membership" (Peregory & Owen, 1993). **Socioeconomic backgrounds** are social backgrounds of students involved in the situations that arise as human beings live together as a group and deal with one another, such as social consciousness; and the history, development, organization, and problems of people living together as a social group, including the management of income, expenditures, production, distribution, and consumption of wealth and the satisfaction of material needs of a people.

At the community and family level, **sociocultural influences** on literacy include (1) spoken home language; (2) values, beliefs, and goals; (3) religion; (4) cultural traditions and experiences; (5) interpretations of transitions in students' life; (6) students' ways of responding to adults and displaying politeness; (7) use of literacy resources and time spent in literacy activities; (8) historical background; (9) children's perceptions of their teachers; (10) nature and importance of reading; (11) how a child should behave when an adult is speaking; (12) the desirability of answering when unsure; (13) the amount of competition or cooperation displayed to peers; and (14) the amount of control a child is to assert over his or her own destiny (Raphael et al., 2001; Reyhner & Garcia, 1989).

Cultural discontinuity describes the internal conflict a student can experience when a disparity occurs between the cultural and social values and activities taught at home and those promoted at school. In some cultural groups, parents and teachers expect a literal account of what students remember; other cultural groups expect students to explain reasons that underlie what occurred; and still others encourage a child to embellish the story by adding people and actions that were not a part of the story. If students' home cultural practices and values are incorporated into your classroom, some second-language parents will have stronger reasons to come to school and to support their children's academic pursuits, because they will no longer feel as if the environment is strange (Cazden, 1988, 1992; Heath, 1983; Reyhner & Garcia, 1989). When reading specialists and teachers value the richness of struggling readers' language, they assist them to reach higher levels of literacy success (Cazden, 1994; Heath, 1983; O'Neill, 1991).

Instructional Approaches to Cultural Diversity

There are four instructional approaches to culturally sensitive literacy instruction that can help eliminate cultural discontinuity for students from diverse backgrounds (Au, 1991; Banks, 1989; Rasinski & Padak, 1990). These approaches are as follows:

1. The *contributions approach* includes lessons and multicultural literature in which students are challenged to examine contributions others from their culture have made to society as well as the contributions they can make by using their own literacy abilities. Lessons move beyond learning about various holidays and leaders from different cultures to developing students' deeper understanding of their own and other cultural diversities.
2. In the *additive approach* lessons using multicultural literature are added to the existing curriculum (Rasinski & Padak, 1990); every unit of reading and writing instruction includes multicultural books. Often the teacher will choose to read these books aloud, especially if they are powerful and well written or if they accurately depict a cultural value shared by one or more of the students in the class.
3. In the *transformation approach* historical and contemporary issues are studied from the viewpoints of various cultures. Students may read and discuss books that describe an event in history from several points of view; for example, a class might read *Columbus* by Martin Labur (1994) or *Encounters* by Patricia Yolen (1994) with the objective of interpreting historic events from the perspectives of both Anglo American and Native American cultures.
4. In the *social action approach* students identify important social issues and use their literacy abilities and their diverse cultural perspectives to solve problems. For example, struggling readers might become concerned about the homeless and want to devote part of their literacy period to reading the want ads to and with these people. In the process of helping homeless people find jobs, students can observe the effects of illiteracy on people while they learn to mobilize their cultural values and perspectives to help others.

Multicultural influences on literacy also increase your responsibility to learn what your students believe and to be familiar with their literacy activities outside of school. To obtain this information, you can ask students at the beginning of the year to answer questions from attitude assessments such as those discussed in Chapter 4. Through initial discussion and sharing of their responses, students begin to see that they represent a wide variety of cultures and subcultures, and that no single label can describe all that they are as individuals.

There is little doubt that students who approach reading/writing from a cultural or social background different from that which is prominent in their school's climate, and from the materials they are expected to read/write, are at a disadvantage. To illustrate, answer the questions in Figure 5.1, which is a culturally biased test similar to those given in schools that are not sensitive to students' cultural heritages. When finished, count the number of your correct answers. Then pretend you are a reader who is not among the cultural groups for whom this test was designed. Imagine that based on the score you achieve on this first day of class, you will be placed in one of three groups for reading instruction: the Eagles, who soar; the Sparrows, who are ordinary; and the Vultures,

Assess your cultural awareness by answering the 10 true/false questions below. Although obviously limited in scope and number, these questions can provide you with a general sense of how culturally literate you are. (Answers to the questions appear at the bottom of the test.)

Answer true (T) or false (F) for each statement:

_____   1. The first clock in America was made by a black mathematician.
_____   2. Charles Drew was a black surgeon who performed the first successful heart operation.
_____   3. As a result of the Spanish-American War of 1898, the people of Puerto Rico and the Philippines finally rid themselves of Spanish colonial rule and willingly consented to having their countries become protectorates of the United States.
_____   4. The forced migration of the Sioux people from their homeland in Georgia to Oklahoma, during which one-fourth of them died of starvation, disease, and exposure, is known as the "Trail of Tears."
_____   5. During World War II the United States placed many innocent citizens in concentration camps and confiscated their property.
_____   6. There was no federal ruling protecting U.S. citizens' rights to marry a person of another race until 1970.
_____   7. There is some evidence that Africans may have established a colony in Mexico long before Columbus's voyage in 1492.
_____   8. The women's movement of the 1970s and 1980s was primarily a white middle-class movement.
_____   9. Mexican women have never been involved in political or labor struggles because their place has traditionally been in the home.
_____   10. During the fifteenth and sixteenth centuries, Timbuktu in the African kingdom of Songhay was one of the world's greatest cities, renowned as an intellectual and cultural center.

Answers: 1=T; 2=F; 3=F; 4=F; 5=T; 6=T; 7=T; 8=T; 9=F; 10=T

FIGURE 5.1 Test of Social and Cultural Background Knowledge

Source: Adapted from C. A. Grant & C. E. Sleeter (1989), *Turning on Learning: Five Approaches for Multicultural Teaching Plans for Race, Class, Gender and Disability* (p. 19). Columbus, OH: Merrill. Used with permission of B. H. Suzuki (author of the test).

whom no one likes. Which group are you in? If you got all 10 correct, you are an Eagle. If you got 7 to 9 correct, you are a Sparrow. If you got fewer than 7 correct, you are a Vulture. How do you feel?

Too often in the past, readers/writers have had their reading abilities assessed through tests that were culturally biased. From these test results alone they were labeled as being at lower stages of literacy development, merely because they were unfamiliar with the cultural and social background reflected in their reading material. To stop this cycle, you can implement the principles in this chapter. The interaction patterns described in the next section provide a basis for your increased understanding of how to use students' cultural strengths to expand their literacy.

Interaction Patterns Influenced by Cultural and Social Variables

Throughout the remainder of this chapter, you will read about instructional guidelines that build on individual students' literacy strengths that are culturally influenced. These guidelines are offered in full awareness that great diversity exists within all cultures. This information is not intended to categorize performances or people. As Lehr (1988) stated, "[Although] an awareness of the characteristics of groups of people is important, we must also realize that this knowledge helps us to understand groups, not individual learners" (p. 77).

The purpose of this chapter's recommendations is to help you understand individual readers' sociocultural richness and personalize instruction to capitalize on these students' strengths. However, keep in mind that just as none of us can be described merely by the social and cultural backgrounds we have experienced, neither do any of us possess all attributes of every other member of our social and cultural group. Thus, the information presented next is designed to increase your ability to individualize the diagnosis and instruction of literacy. As caring and effective educators, we have an obligation to be sensitive to cultural differences that affect how our students learn. The goal here is to suggest how cultural differences can be embraced as opportunities to build literacy rather than feared as obstacles to it. The larger issue is that school culture demands certain types of diagnostic and instructional interventions of students. This chapter was written to demonstrate how we can move away from some of the strict literacy performance demands and expectations in "school culture" and thus enable greater numbers of students to enjoy pleasure-filled reading experiences.

For some pupils, cultural differences may necessitate adapted instruction. Specific factors relate to learning preferences, such as sociocultural influences in students' attitudes toward confrontation, cooperation, competition, individual work, group work, turn taking, deadlines, and language use.

CONFRONTATION. Many students of European descent confront a problem directly, whereas in some Asian American cultures direct confrontation is avoided as much as possible. Students from other cultures may not express displeasure directly but may employ a go-between to speak for them. As a result, some may not feel comfortable expressing another point of view during literacy discussions. You can help students find culturally acceptable ways to express themselves using the activities described later in this chapter.

COOPERATION. Readers/writers are expected to be cooperative—but some cultural groups do not value cooperation on tasks that compromise their own principles, or on tasks at which they sense they should be working individually rather than cooperatively. By being sensitive to these feelings, you can offer such students a choice from a variety of tasks that involve more familiar solitary projects, then gradually move them into more challenging group-oriented literacy tasks.

COMPETITION. Competition is alien to many cultural groups, even though it is highly valued in the European American culture. For example, many Southeast Asians possess a strong sense of community that restrains them from winning at the expense of others. Similarly, many Hispanic Americans are group oriented and may not wish to be singled out; Native American children may value getting along in the literacy group more than gaining personal achievement. Many students from these cultures could have difficulty participating in literacy games and competitive activities and should be allowed to choose not to participate without negative consequences. Further, the Native American culture's concept of time and harmony with nature may lead to a pace of literacy performance that some could view as "reluctance" or "nonengagement." But if cultural lenses are used to interpret this behavior, you can understand that such readers/writers are not unmotivated (Gay, 1995). It might only be the time perimeters of the task that they are rejecting.

GROUP VERSUS INDIVIDUAL WORK. Not all cultures value working independently. Collaboration between students is often called cheating, but many groups encourage such strong group affiliations. If students with these cultural views are allowed to work in team activities, they can have a choice to collaborate and share. Another consideration is that readers from some home literacy cultures may have been taught only by rote memorization and therefore may have trouble adjusting to sharing information, developing independence, and communicating in a group situation. You can help by carefully explaining the roles of each member in a group, by making task directions explicit, and by giving every person a responsibility.

TURN TAKING. In a multicultural classroom there may be readers/writers who do not volunteer to participate, others who want to talk at the same time as the teacher, and some who want to answer every question. These students are influenced by their home literacy heritage and have very different ideas about turn taking. Try to provide opportunities for all turn-taking options. For instance, enable quieter students to be represented by more dominant students through pairings, whereby they can respond as a duo.

DEADLINES. Meeting deadlines is not a value commonly shared by all cultures. For example, some students from diverse cultures need your explicit instructions as to when work is due—and must know that this deadline is a specific time and not just an approximation or a suggestion.

QUESTIONS. European Americans are expected to ask questions to show that they are involved with learning. In other cultures (such as those of Southeast Asia), if students ask questions they are considered rude. In these cultures the teacher is to impart wisdom and students are to listen without voicing their ideas and opinions. You can assist reluctant readers/writers by checking their understanding, using discovery discussions, and employing paired learning. In this way, all students can be involved without being singled out.

Language Differences

An important aspect of divergence in a multicultural classroom is language, which has been called the "carrier of the culture" (Gay, 1995). By bringing other languages into the classroom, you acknowledge their importance and value.

There are many books in other languages that students of all language groups would enjoy. Such books have been described by Violet Harris (1993) as stories from the source—stories told from an ethnic perspective, placed within the context of ethnic life, and reflective of a particular group's language, culture, and beliefs. Harris beckons teachers to this wonderful early literacy resource with rich examples, such as Virginia Driving Hawk Sneve's portrayal of American Indian life as she has known it (e.g., *Dancing Teepees,* 1989) and Angela Johnson's depiction of African American children engaged in daily family activities (e.g., *The Leaving Morning,* 1992). She urges us to become familiar with multiethnic children's literature, to share it liberally with young children, and to develop long-range purchasing plans to ensure its presence in school libraries.

Students learning English as a second language need books with lots of repetition and patterns, as listed in Resource Cards throughout this book. They also enjoy teaching peers how to count and how to give greetings and write messages in their own native languages.

African American Culture

For some reluctant readers/writers from African American home literacy heritages, the self-initiated use of literacy for pleasure and growth may be strengthened by several instructional adaptations.

First, keep in mind that, *as a generalization,* many students in this culture tend to value approximations more than precision; spontaneity more than generating backup plans; completing a process more than creating a perfect end product; intuitive learning and nonverbal behavior more than analytical thinking and precise language; and exaggeration in stories they tell and read (Cazden, 1993; Heath, 1983; Hillard, 1989).

Further, some of these students may produce greater quantities of speech within teacher-absent peer groups than when their teachers are members of the group. As a result, the speech they use in conversations with you may be devoid of the rich nuances and connotations that are their language strengths (Cazden, 1995; Purcell-Gates, 1988). Knowing this increases the likelihood that your assessments will capture their African American students' true levels of responses to literacy.

Many African American readers/writers—and readers/writers from other cultural heritages as well—do not make continuous eye contact with teachers; they often look around the room as they talk, because they value others' appreciation for their vivid expressions and gestures or because they are embarrassed by their limited abilities to contribute to school culture's literacy standards (Banks & Banks, 1993; Block & Pressley, 2002). However, such cultural differences in speaking/listening style could lead to misunderstandings. For example, many struggling readers do not nod their heads or make responses such as "um-hmm" when listening to their teachers. As a result, their teachers may think that these readers are not concentrating or understanding, so they persist in explaining and reexplaining the same point. Some of these students then interpret the teacher's tendencies to dwell on the same point as "talking down" to them, and they become insulted (Hilliard, 1993; Ladson-Billings, 1995).

Another instructional adaptation you can make comes from awareness that some home cultures value body language and movement as an important communication medium. As a result, some students may excel in their ability to express feelings and interpretations of literary works through role plays, raps, and rhythmical chants that they create rather than in written responses (Cazden, 1994)—and you can capitalize on this cultural richness by regularly providing openings for these methods of expressing responses to print.

Be aware, too, that some readers (who wish to avoid ostracism from peers) develop elaborate coping mechanisms to draw attention away from their literacy improvements. For example, when praised before peers, many struggling readers may act like the "class clown," purposely do worse in the future, form alliances with other struggling readers/writers, share answers on tests, or stop doing the things that lead to literacy success. For these students, avoiding ostracism from peers is more important than improving their reading/writing abilities (Block & Pressley, 2002; Hilliard, 1992; Ladson-Billings, 1995). Also, in many African American communities children are not asked questions to which the parent or caretaker already knows the answer. Thus, children from Anglo households are used to questions like "Where is your nose?" or "Who did we read about today as well as last week?"—which are common question types in school—but African American students may not answer school questions like these because they could be ridiculed by peers.

Similarly, some reluctant readers/writers tend to learn *globally,* meaning they don't learn as well when information is presented in pieces. They profit from seeing the full picture first—flipping through and skimming a book before reading it, for example, or seeing samples of completed writing before they begin their own. They may also process information orally. For some students information isn't concrete until they have responded orally in some way; others enjoy repeating what the teachers say—and this can be disconcerting to teachers who like silence when they are talking.

Many students from orally rich home cultures value spontaneity and the worth of people as well as kinship. They have a strong sense of what is fair. Such students may also enjoy exaggeration in a story and appreciate more and more fanciful elaborated versions of stories above traditional versions (Block & Pressley, 2002; Heath, 1983).

You must ensure that these readers realize their best efforts will not go unrecognized or unrewarded. One effective program is called "Incentives for Improvement" (MacIver, 1992). It establishes individualized literacy goals for which students can aim, and it provides personalized, oral feedback. Too frequently in the past, many struggling readers/writers received feedback only as it related to their personality or to the neatness of their work, rather than to their work's academic quality (Jackson, 1993–94). Freppon and Dahl (1991), for example, teach vowel sounds by incorporating such values as the worth of people or the usefulness of body language. They suggest associating sounds with student names or physical movements—for instance, short *e* is taught by learning the word *Ethel* and short *i* by *itching.* In addition, an effective question to begin discussions of literature can be: "Who would like to be heard?" or "Pretend you are [author/main character] and you are eavesdropping on our class conversation about your book. What do you want to add?"

Another thing you can do is establish a "Culture Club" in which leaders from students' home communities come to your class to share books like those on Resource Card 6. You can also assign a project for reluctant readers/writers to locate literary resources in the

RESOURCE CARD 6

Books That Represent Orally Rich Home Cultures and/or African American Ethnic Background Experiences

Primary

Aagard, J. (1989). *The calypso alphabet.* New York: Holt.

Aardema, B. (1975). *Why mosquitos buzz in people's ears.* New York: Dial.

Adoff, A. (1973). *Black is brown is tan.* New York: Harper & Row.

Adoff, A. (1988). *Flamboyan.* San Diego, CA: Harcourt Brace Jovanovich.

Adoff, A. (1991). *In for winter, out for spring.* San Diego, CA: Harcourt Brace Jovanovich.

Aliki. (1965). *A weed is a flower: The life of George Washington Carver.* New York: Simon & Schuster.

Bang, M. (1983). *Ten, nine, eight.* New York: Greenwillow.

Bryan, A. (1986). *Beat the story drum, pum-pum.* New York: Atheneum.

Bryan, A. (1989). *Turtle knows your name.* New York: Atheneum.

Caines, J. (1982). *Just us women.* New York: Harper & Row.

Clifton, L. (1974). *Some of the days of Everett Anderson.* New York: Holt.

Clifton, L. (1983). *Everett Anderson's good-bye.* New York: Holt.

Daly, N. (1985). *Not so fast Songololo.* Middlesex, England: Puffin.

Feelings, M. (1981). *Mojo means one.* New York: Dial.

Flourney, V. (1985). *The patchwork quilt.* New York: Dial.

Greenfield, E. (1974). *She come bringing me that little baby girl.* New York: Lippincott.

Greenfield, E. (1974). *Sister.* New York: Crowell.

Greenfield, E. (1975). *Me and Neesie.* New York: Harper & Row.

Greenfield, E. (1978). *Honey, I love.* New York: Harper & Row.

Greenfield, E. (1988). *Grandpa's face.* New York: Philomel.

Grifalconi, A. (1986). *The village of round and square houses.* Boston: Little, Brown.

Grifalconi, A. (1989). *Osa's pride.* Boston: Little, Brown.

Hale, S. J. (1990). *Mary had a little lamb.* New York: Scholastic.

Haley, G. (1970). *A story, a story.* New York: Atheneum.

Havill, J. (1986). *Jamaica's find.* New York: Scholastic.

Howard, E. (1988). *The train to Lulu's.* New York: Bradbury.

Howard, E. (1991). *Aunt Flossie's hats (and crab cakes later).* New York: Clarion.

Hudson, C., and Ford, B. (1990). *Bright eyes, brown skin.* Orange, NJ: Just Us Books.

Johnson, A. (1989). *Tell me a story mama.* New York: Orchard.

Johnson, A. (1990). *Do like Kyla.* New York: Orchard.

Johnson, A. (1990). *When I am old with you.* New York: Orchard.

Jones, R. (1991). *Matthew and Tilly.* New York: Dutton.

Langstaff, J. (1987). *What a morning! The Christmas story in black spirituals.* New York: Macmillan.

Keats, E. J. (1964). *Whistle for Willie.* New York: Viking.

Keats, E. J. (1967). *Peter's chair.* New York: Harper.

Lewin, H. (1981). *Jafta.* Minneapolis, MN: Carolrhoda.

Mathis, S. (1971). *Sidewalk story.* New York: Puffin.

> ## RESOURCE CARD 6

Books That Represent Orally Rich Home Cultures and/or African American Ethnic Background Experiences *(continued)*

McKissack, P. (1986). *Flossie and the fox.* New York: Dial.

McKissack, P. (1988). *Mirandy and brother wind.* New York: Knopf.

McKissack, P. (1989). *Nettie Jo's friends.* New York: Knopf.

Mollel, T. (1991). *The orphan boy.* New York: Clarion.

Monjo, F. N. (1970). *The drinking gourd.* New York: Harper.

Ringgold, F. (1991). *Tar beach.* New York: Crown.

San Souci, R. (1989). *The talking eggs.* New York: Dial.

Schroeder, A. (1989). *Ragtime Tumpie.* Boston: Joy Street.

Shelby, A. (1990). *We keep a store.* New York: Orchard.

Steptoe, J. (1969). *Stevie.* New York: Harper.

Steptoe, J. (1980). *My daddy is a monster . . . sometimes.* New York: Lippincott.

Steptoe, J. (1987). *Mufaro's beautiful daughters.* New York: Lothrop, Lee & Shepard.

Steptoe, J. (1988). *Baby says.* New York: Lothrop, Lee & Shepard.

Wahl, J. (1991). *Tailypo!* New York: Holt.

Walters, M. P. (1986). *Justin and the best biscuits in the world.* New York: Lothrop, Lee & Shepard.

Yarbrough, C. (1979). *Cornrows.* New York: Coward-McCann.

Yarbrough, C. (1989). *Shimmershine queen.* New York: Putnam.

Intermediate

Adler, D. (1989). *Jackie Robinson.* New York: Holiday House.

Adoff, A. (1968). *I am the darker brother.* New York: Macmillan.

Adoff, A. (1970). *Malcolm X.* New York: Crowell.

Cameron, A. (1981). *The stories Julian tells.* New York: Pantheon.

Clifton, L. (1979). *The lucky stone.* New York: Dell.

Giovanni, N. (1985). *Spin a soft black song.* New York: Farrar, Straus & Giroux.

Greenfield, E. (1973). *Rosa Parks.* New York: Crowell.

Greenfield, E. (1977). *Mary McLeod Bethune.* New York: Crowell.

Greenfield, E. (1988). *Under the Sunday tree.* New York: Harper & Row.

Greenfield, E. (1989). *Nathaniel talking.* New York: Black Butterfly.

Guy, R. (1973). *The friends.* New York: Bantam.

Hamilton, V. (1967). *Zeely.* New York: Macmillan.

Hamilton, V. (1968). *The house of Dies Drear.* New York: Macmillan.

Hamilton, V. (1971). *The planet of Junior Brown.* New York: Macmillan.

Hamilton, V. (1974). *M. C. Higgins, the great.* New York: Macmillan.

Hamilton, V. (1983). *Willie Bea and the time the Martians landed.* New York: Greenwillow.

Hamilton, V. (1985). *The people could fly.* New York: Knopf.

Hamilton, V. (1988). *Anthony Burns: The defeat and triumph of a fugitive slave.* New York: Knopf.

Hamilton, V. (1988). *In the beginning: Creation stories from around the world.* San Diego, CA: Harcourt Brace Jovanovich.

Hamilton, V. (1990). *Cousins.* New York: Philomel.

community that reflect their culture and then share their findings with the class. They will likely appreciate being able to elect their own group spokesperson and plan their own oral or written presentations, which can then become events or happenings rather than being viewed by students as merely an assignment.

Hispanic Cultural Groups

According to data from the 2000 census, by the year 2030 cultural groups made up of people of Mexican, Cuban, Puerto Rican, or Central or South American descent will become the largest minority in the United States. In 1990, only 60 percent of students from these cultures graduated from high school; one in three were retained at least once in their school careers because of literacy difficulties; and 70 percent were placed in Tier 3 or 4 support classes with reading specialists, up from 56 percent in the 1950s (Garcia, 1991). As you read the information presented here, think about how you could create literacy instruction that builds on Hispanic cultural values.

Hispanic Americans comprise a wide variety of cultural groups with distinct national origins, socioeconomic statuses, and cultural backgrounds. Individual experiences vary greatly depending on the family's place of origin, occupation, and neighborhood. Hispanic Americans share an ethnolinguistic culture—they share ethnic similarities but do not necessarily speak the same language. Some people who identify with this culture do not speak Spanish. Similarly, people in cultural communities that date back to the settlement of California more than 200 years ago feel as if they have little in common with recent immigrants from Central or South America. As Tiedt and Tiedt (1995) state,

> It is not surprising, then, that there is much confusion over how to determine who is a member of this minority (Spanish-sounding last name, lack of knowledge of English, or birth in a Spanish-speaking country are some of the criteria that have been suggested) or what label to use to identify people (Latino, Hispanic, and Chicano have been some of the options). The Latino students [people speaking a variety of the Spanish language] that you have in the classroom may have lived in this country for a generation, immigrated from Mexico leaving most relatives there, or arrived as war refugees with no option but permanent settlement in this country. These origins affect the extent to which the students have already learned English and also the family's desire to maintain Spanish at home. (p. 177)

In Chapter 13 you will learn to build the literacy abilities of developing readers who speak Spanish as their dominant language. Meanwhile, the rest of this subsection will focus on strategies you can use with readers/writers from Hispanic cultures whose dominant language is English.

In an ethnographic study of a California high school located in an agricultural/suburban community, Matute-Bianchi (1986) found that approximately half of the students of Mexican descent rejected patterns of traditional literacy instruction such as participating in class discussions, carrying books from class to class, asking teachers for help in front of peers, and making it obvious that they were expending effort to do well in school. In these students' minds, to participate in both the dominant school culture and their own Chicano culture was not possible:

> To cross these cultural boundaries means denying one's identity as a Chicano and is viewed as incompatible with maintaining the integrity of a Chicano identity. Hence, school policies and practices are viewed as forces to be resisted, subverted, undermined, challenged, and opposed. Often the opposition takes the form of mental withdrawal, in which the students find themselves alienated from the academic content of the school curriculum and the effort required to master it. (p. 255)

In some Hispanic cultures, struggling writers/readers tend to sacrifice more to benefit classmates, judge others in terms of their personalities rather than their literacy accomplishments, and prefer teacher compliments about their personalities rather than their literacy products. Generally, the pace of work of these students is more relaxed and slower than that of some other students. Some are motivated by immediate feedback, pats on the back, and verbal praise, as opposed to written grades. Some Hispanic girls have difficulty demonstrating their knowledge before class or in a public forum or bidding for a turn to speak in group discussions. Some Hispanic students undervalue debating and analyzing the opinions of others when compared to students from the European American home literacy cultures (McConnell, 1989).

Most Hispanics place a high value on family unity and community bonding—which often creates conflicts for students who are asked to develop individual identities and self-awareness at school (Norton, 1993). A second conflict arises when these children give or receive sympathetic aid from a classmate, or repeatedly ask for guidance and direction from reading specialists and teachers. This cultural characteristic of cooperative achievement contrasts with individual critical and creative responses emphasized in the "school culture" of many literacy classrooms. These values can surface in subtle ways and may be misinterpreted. For instance, these children are taught to show respect for an adult who is correcting their behavior by looking down and not making eye contact.

One study identified common attributes of successful classrooms for readers/writers of Hispanic descent (Ruiz, 1993). In these classrooms, teachers emphasized functional oral and written communications as well as the development of strong oral and written vocabularies. Settings in small group projects and learning centers were informal and familylike; teachers rarely worked with groups larger than eight. Most of the time reading specialists and literacy teachers moved about assisting individuals, and full group instruction was confined only to start-up activities. Thematic units were selected by students in conjunction with their teacher. For instance, early in the year reading specialists and literacy teachers would ask, "What do you want to learn?" When readers agreed on a topic (such as "I want to learn about the chemicals my father has that are making my little brother sick—pesticides"), students would make a list of questions and specific learning goals. Over the next few weeks, struggling readers/writers would organize reading and writing assignments that addressed these learning goals in an integrated fashion, using books such as those listed on Resource Card 7.

Literacy abilities for some Hispanic readers will become more automatic if they are taught in conjunction with others, orally, and without a direct focus of attention on individual students as they work. For example, if students have difficulty comprehending

RESOURCE CARD 7

Compiled by Kathryn Meyer Reimer

Books That Represent Hispanic Cultures

Primary

Baylor, B. (1963). *Amigo*. New York: Macmillan.

Belpré, P. (1960). *Perez and Martina*. New York: Warne.

Belpré, P. (1965). *Dance of the animals*. New York: Warne.

Belpré, P. (1969). *Santiago*. New York: Warne.

Belpré, P. (1973). *Once in Puerto Rico*. New York: Warne.

Brown, T. (1986). *Hello amigos!* New York: Holt.

Delacre, L. (1989). *Arroz con leche*. New York: Scholastic.

Delacre, L. (1990). *Las Navidads*. New York: Scholastic.

dePaola, T. (1980). *The lady of Guadalupe*. New York: Holiday.

Dorros, A. (1991). *Tonight is carnaval*. New York: Dutton.

Martel, C. (1976). *Yagua days*. New York: Dial.

Rohmer, H. (1989). *Uncle Nacho's hat*. Emeryville, CA: Children's Book Press.

Intermediate

Cameron, A. (1988). *The most beautiful place in the world*. New York: Knopf.

Maestas, J. G., and Anaya, R. A. (1980). *Cuentos! Tales from the Hispanic Southwest*. New York: Knopf.

Meltzer, M. (1982). *Hispanic Americans*. New York: Crowell.

Mohr, N. (1977). *In Nueva York*. New York: Dell.

Mohr, N. (1979). *Felita*. New York: Dial.

Mohr, N. (1985). *Rituals of survival: A woman's portfolio*. Houston, TX: Arte Publico.

Mohr, N. (1986). *Going home*. New York: Dial.

Soto, G. (1990). *Baseball in April and other stories*. San Diego, CA: Harcourt Brace Jovanovich.

Soto, G. (1991). *Taking sides*. San Diego, CA: Harcourt Brace Jovanovich.

Thomas, P. (1978). *Stories from el barrio*. New York: Knopf.

---

longer sentences, and if you are aware that such a weakness is influenced by a lack of desire for using long sentences in their own oral expressions, you can increase students' comprehension abilities through oral modeling. For Hispanic students particularly, when they interact with you and classmates who model, the repetition will help them become familiar with the rhythm, pitch, volume, and tone of English. Repetitious reading will reinforce these rhythm and syntactical patterns. Moreover, because many idioms are not used in homes and communities where adults are Spanish monolingual or bilingual, it is helpful to preview material for Hispanic struggling readers so that you can explain the meanings of idioms, metaphors, or figurative language that they will read.

Hispanic performance on standardized tests of literacy can be adversely affected by several factors, including the content range of test topics, the use of paraphrased vocabulary in test questions and answer choices, and the number of culturally biased inferences required to determine answers. Also significant is the tendency of many Hispanic readers at lower stages on the literacy continuum to utilize a predominantly literal interpretation of the text to derive their answers. For all of these reasons, in some states nearly half of the students with limited English proficiency score below the 25th percentile on standardized tests (U.S. Department of Education, 2002).

Native Americans

The media have begun to portray Native Americans more accurately, helping to dispel negative stereotypical images of their culture. Difficulties in their educational level often remain, however. Many Native American groups experience the highest school dropout rates in the nation. Unfortunately, they also receive the least amount of adapted instruction that could utilize their cultural strengths (McCarty, 1993).

As a general rule, nature is held in high regard in Native American cultures; the concept of time carries only secondary importance to the activity in which they are engaged. As a result, some struggling readers/writers from this culture tend to conceive of time in large-scale blocks such as "morning," "afternoon," or "evening." Because of this, many do not realize the importance of completing assignments, for instance, within a 50-minute period. In addition, for many Navajo students, working in mixed-gender groups is against cultural values; same-sex groups are preferred.

For students whose primary language is the tribal speech, the bilingual approaches presented in Chapter 13 are proving successful. For Native Americans whose primary language is English, the following information may assist you to increase their literacy successes.

When instruction includes Native American literature such as that listed on Resource Card 8, you can expand all students' respect for the diversity among Native Americans. Enabling Native American students to use poetic expression in their writing and to experiment with multiple genres will capture their cultural value for intuitive knowledge. As an example, one student's summation of a thematic unit on Tomie de-Paola's *The Legend of the Indian Paintbrush* included the English and Navajo words for desert animals, plants, and environmental conditions.

Drama can be an effective strategy to increase comprehension and affective responses to literacy for many African American and Hispanic American readers/writers, although many Native Americans prefer to work behind the scenes or to write scripts individually rather than in groups (Block & Dellamura, 2001). Incorporating students' critiques as soon as possible after language is spoken or written will increase many Native American students' abilities to revise prior knowledge differences and also increase the sophistication of their literacy expressions. This process also expands Native American readers' knowledge of traditional English prose, plot structure, and methods of developing characterization better than direct instruction in story grammar.

Moreover, because in the English language authors portray story characters through subtle as well as explicit means, it is sometimes difficult for Native American readers to recognize how characterization evolves. By completing think alouds based on excerpts about characters from books, you can assist many students to see how descriptions, actions, conversations, and thoughts reveal character traits. Such think alouds are particularly valuable because they utilize oral language, which is the primary means by which ancient legends and traditions have been sustained in Native American culture.

A rewarding literacy activity that Native American struggling readers benefit from is transforming traditional folktales, legends, and fables into stories of contemporary

| RESOURCE CARD 8 | Prepared by Peggy K. Ford and Susan L. Ford Carr
Tarrant County Junior College |

Books Related to Native Americans' Home Literacy and Cultural Experiences

Aaseng, N. (1992). *Navajo code talkers.* New York: Walker. [Navajo]

Adler, D. A. (1993). *A picture book of Sitting Bull.* New York: Holiday. [Hunkpapa Sioux]

Ancona, G. (1993). *Powwow.* San Diego: Harcourt Brace. [Native American]

Ata, T. (1989). *Baby rattlesnake.* San Francisco: Children's Book Press. [Chickasaw]

Becker, J. (1994/1974). *Seven little rabbits.* New York: Walker. [Native American]

Begay, S. (1992). *Maii and Cousin Horned Toad.* New York: Scholastic. [Navajo]

Bierhorst, J. (1982). *The whistling skeleton; American Indian tales of the supernatural.* New York: Four Winds. [Pawnee, Blackfoot, and Cheyenne]

Blumberg, R. (1987). *The incredible journey of Lewis and Clark.* New York: Lothrop, Lee & Shepard. [Native American]

Bruchac, J. (1993). *Fox song.* New York: Philomel. [Abenaki]

Clark, A. N. (1991/1941). *In my mother's house.* New York: Viking. [Tesuque Pueblo]

Cohen, C. L. (1988). *The mud pony.* Illustrated by Shonto Begay. New York: Scholastic. [Skid/Pawnee]

Cohlene, T. (1990). *Quillworker: A Cheyenne legend.* New York: Watermill. [Cheyenne]

de Brebeuf, F. J. (1990). *The Huron carol.* Illustrated by Frances Tyrrell. New York: Dutton. [Huron]

DeFelice, C. (1990). *Weasel.* New York: Macmillan. [Shawnee]

dePaola, T. (1983). *The legend of the bluebonnet.* New York: Putnam. [Comanche]

dePaola, T. (1988). *The legend of the Indian paintbrush.* New York: Putnam. [Plains]

Dubois, M. L. (1994). *Abenaki captive.* Minneapolis, MN: Carolrhoda. [Abenaki]

Ekoomiak, N. (1990). *Arctic memories.* New York: Holt. [Inuit Eskimo]

Esbensen, B. J. (1989). *Ladder to the sky.* New York: Little, Brown. [Anishinabe/Ojibway]

Fradin, D. B. (1992). *Hiawatha: Messenger of peace.* Chicago: McElderry. [Iroquois]

Freedman, R. (1992). *An Indian winter.* New York: Holiday. [Mandans and Hidatsas]

Fritz, J. (1983). *The double life of Pocahontas.* New York: Putnam. [Powhatan]

George, J. C. (1987). *Water sky.* New York: Harper & Row. [Inupiat]

Goble, P. (1992). *Love flute.* New York: Bradbury. [Plains]

Hamilton, V. (1993). *In the beginning: Creation stories from around the world.* San Diego: Harcourt Brace. [Native American]

Hausman, G. (1994). *Turtle Island ABC.* New York: HarperCollins. [Native American]

Hill, K. (1990). *Toughboy and Sister.* Chicago: McElderry. [Athabascan/Alaskan Yukon]

Hinton, L. (1992). *Ishi's tale of lizard.* New York: Farrar, Straus & Giroux. [Yahi]

Hoyt-Goldsmith, D. (1993). *Cherokee summer.* New York: Holiday. [Cherokee]

Hurmence, B. (1994). *Dixie and the big pasture.* New York: Clarion. [Kiowas]

Jeffers, S. (1991). *Brother Eagle, Sister Sky.* New York: Dial. [Suquanish]

Jensen, R. E., Paul, R. E., & Carter, J. E. (1991). *Eyewitness at Wounded Knee.* Lincoln, NE: University of Nebraska Press. [Dakota/Sioux]

Joosse, B. M. (1991). *Mama, do you love me?* San Francisco: Chronicle. [Inuit Eskimo]

RESOURCE CARD 8

Books Related to Native Americans' Home Literacy and Cultural Experiences *(continued)*

Keegan, M. (1991). *Pueblo boy: Growing up in two worlds.* New York: Cobblehill. [Pueblo]

Keehn, S. M. (1991). *I am Regina.* New York: Philomel. [Nonschetto]

King, S. (1993). *Shannon: An Ojibway dancer.* Minneapolis, MN: Lerner. [Anishinabe/Ojibway]

Larry, C. (1993). *Peboan and Seegwun.* New York: Farrar, Straus & Giroux. [Anishinabe/Ojibway]

Lawlor, L. (1994). *Shadow catcher: The life and work of Edward S. Curtis.* New York: Walker. [Native American]

Liptak, K. (1990). *North American Indian survival skills.* New York: Franklin Watts. [Native American]

Littlechild, G. (1993). *This land is my land.* San Francisco: Children's Book Press. [Plains Cree]

Longfellow, H. W. (1986). *Hiawatha's childhood.* Illustrated by Errol LeCain. New York: Farrar, Straus & Giroux. [Iroquois]

Longfellow, H. W. (1983). *Hiawatha.* Illustrated by Susan Jeffers. New York: Dial. [Iroquois]

Lowry, L. (1993). *The giver.* Boston: Houghton Mifflin.

Lyon, G. E. (1993). *Dreamplace.* New York: Orchard. [Anasazi/Pueblo]

MacGill-Callahan, S. (1991). *And still the turtle watched.* New York: Dial. [Delaware]

Martin, B., Jr., & Archambault, J. (1987). *Knots on a counting rope.* New York: Holt. [Native American]

Martin, R. (1992). *The rough-face girl.* New York: Putnam. [Algonquin]

Mayo, G. W. (1987). *Star tales: North American Indian stories.* New York: Walker. [Native American]

McDermott, G. (1993). *Raven: A trickster tale from the Pacific Northwest.* New York: Harcourt Brace Jovanovich. [Pacific Coast Northwest]

Outhton, J. (1992). *How the stars fell into the sky.* Boston: Houghton. [Navajo]

Pitts, P. (1992). *The shadowman's way.* New York: Avon. [Navajo]

Roessel, M. (1993). *Kinaalda: A Navajo girl grows up.* Minneapolis, MN: Lerner. [Navajo]

Ross, G. (1994). *How Rabbit tricked Otter and other Cherokee trickster stories.* New York: HarperCollins. [Cherokee]

San Souci, D. D. (1994). *Sootface: An Ojibway Cinderella story.* New York: Delacorte. [Anishinabe/Ojibway]

Sewall, M. (1990). *People of the breaking day.* New York: Atheneum. [Wampanoag]

Seymour, T. (1994). *The gift of Changing Woman.* New York: Holt. [Apache]

Sloat, T. (1990). *The eye of the needle.* New York: Dutton. [Yupik Eskimo]

Sneve, V. D. H. (1993). *The Sioux: A first Americans book.* New York: Holiday. [Sioux]

Sneve, V. D. H. (1989). *Dancing teepees.* New York: Holiday. [Native American]

Stevens, J. (1993). *Coyote steals the blanket: A Ute tale.* New York: Holiday. [Ute]

Wood, T., & Afraid of Hawk, W. N. (1994). *A boy becomes a man at Wounded Knee.* New York: Walker. [Sioux]

Yolen, J. (1990). *Sky dogs.* San Diego, CA: Harcourt Brace Jovanovich. [Siksika/Blackfeet]

Young, E. (1993). *Moon Mother: A Native American creation tale.* New York: Perlman. [Native American]

American life (Collins, 1992c). Because these genres are prevalent in their culture, the students will enjoy altering the story's style, details, main events, setting, point of view, and characters' occupations to modernize the moral. Before the students begin, teachers can present several models by sharing some traditional stories and their modern transformations (e.g., *Cinderella/Princess Smartypants* or *The Three Little Pigs/The True Story of the Three Little Pigs*). Then reading specialists and classroom teachers work together and ask Native American struggling readers to draft their initial ideas; critique and synthesize them in group discussions; and script their concluding work as a dramatic enactment for the class. Upon completion, these writers ask their audience to identify the original folktale from which the transformation emerged.

Asian Americans

Like Hispanics and Native Americans, Asian Americans arrive at school from many separate, distinct home literacy cultures. As a group, Asian Americans value education for fostering self-improvement, developing self-esteem, and enhancing family honor. They also view learning and literacy as the strongest determiner in overcoming occupational discrimination, as demonstrated by the Asian proverb: "There is nothing without education. Education is more important than money."

In interviews, 100 percent of East Asian parents (as compared to 48 percent of Anglo parents) stated that a grade of C or a "Satisfactory" rating would be an unacceptable level of performance for their children (Fu, 1995; Yao, 1991). As a result, numerous studies report that East Asian academic performances, as measured on achievement tests and report cards, exceed those of all other cultural groups (Schneider & Yongsook, 1991). Furthermore, 10 times more Asian parents than Anglo parents said they strictly control their children's use of time outside of school and make sure the students study at home. Asian parents also support extracurricular activities that will enhance their children's social skills—including social service clubs, debate teams, and school newspaper staffs (Zane, Li-tze Hu, & Jung-Hye, 1991).

When you assist Asian American students, be aware that many of these children have been taught that responding with questions to a speaker shows lack of respect or implies that the speaker did not do a good job of explaining the topic. Some teachers wrongly assume that students do not understand or do not care if they do not ask questions (Fu, 1995). For immigrant students, however, language problems as well as lack of access to individualized teacher assistance can create tremendous strain. Chieu Huynh, a recently arrived Vietnamese student, described having to compete with classmates for scarce teacher and tutor time:

> Interviewer: Do you ask for help?
>
> Chieu: I ask her for help, but I still don't understand it. I try to see the teacher, but there are so many people. I can't ask him. Every problem is hard to understand, so I can't ask him every single problem. There's so many people in line. There's only one teacher. I don't get my turn, so I don't go in. So I get further and further behind. I can't catch up. (Phelan, Yu, & Davidson, 1994, p. 428)

Students from Urban Cultures

Distinct socially related attributes of urban city youth have been identified. Students raised in crowded inner cities, regardless of their cultural heritage, profit from instruction that emphasizes their sophisticated imaginations, performance-based activities, ability to work with others, oral skills, and gamelike structures. For example, a chance to serve as a group leader in charge of a Tier 1–4 literacy support activity will be esteemed by many urban struggling readers and will help build their reading motivation. Opportunities to tell about important events in their lives as well as the freedom to exercise their imaginations as they respond to reading/writing may also increase their literacy abilities.

For instance, Nicholasa Mohr, a Puerto Rican children's author who has lived in New York City's barrio (Spanish Harlem), in the Bronx, and in the Lower East Side, attributes her success with literacy to the nurturing power of her imagination. In an interview (Zarnowski, 1991), Mohr reminisced as follows:

> From the moment my mother handed me some scrap paper, a pencil, and a few crayons, I discovered that by making pictures and writing letters I could create my own world . . . like "magic." In the small crowded apartment I shared with my large family, making "magic" permitted me all the space, freedom, and adventure that my imagination could handle [and my crowded environment could not have given me without literacy]. (Zarnowski, 1991, p. 73)

In addition, when Mohr became aware of the economic problems within her home, she depended on her literacy abilities to make her life better:

> During those lean times, when the severe economic problems my family faced seemed too much of a burden on me, I turned to my creative ability. I used my imagination and was able to create something interesting and pleasing where previously there had been a sense of despair. After such a creation, life would seem a little better than before. (Nakamura, 1989, pp. 186–187)

Zarnowski (1991) recommends that you share the foregoing anecdotes with inner-city readers/writers and have them discuss the importance of literacy for people who have fewer material items in their lives than others. Although the cultural group depicted in Mohr's works is Hispanic, the inner-city experiences will be familiar to most urban children. Therefore, when they read books like those on Resource Card 7—in which Hispanic literary figures are central characters—students can discuss what part of their own experiences are universal, and which of those reported by Mohr are unique to urban life.

Haberman (1991), Brookhart and Rusnak (1993), and Block and Pressley (2002) have identified many lessons that correspond to what Haberman labeled the "seven make-or-break dimensions of teaching" literacy to struggling readers in urban settings:

1. Reading specialists and classroom teachers must persist longer in producing literacy gains; persistence must be consistent and stimulating. Curriculum must also include posing complex, meaningful problems; connecting with students' out-of-school experiences; modeling and scaffolding thinking strategies; encouraging students' multiple approaches to literacy; making dialogue the central medium for

teaching and learning; planning what students will be doing; applying ideals such as fairness, equity, and justice to the studies in the classroom; engaging activity rather than passivity; involving heterogeneous groups; questioning of assumptions; redoing, polishing, and perfecting work; and incorporating technology.

2. Literacy specialists must expect and receive students' respect for their authority.
3. Literacy specialists must have the teaching ability to move from theory to practice and back again within 15-minute minilessons (Block, 2002a).
4. Literacy specialists must have a resistance to burnout.
5. Literacy specialists must have effective strategies for each of the physical, cognitive, affective, cultural, and social variables discussed in Chapters 3 through 5.
6. Literacy specialists must have a professional persona.
7. Literacy specialists must be able to confront, admit in public, and ask students to help overcome fallibilities—their own as well as the students'.

As an example, one of the most effective urban teachers in Brookhart and Rusnak's (1993) study described the way she opens her literacy lessons for struggling readers:

> I give them a little scenario in the beginning saying when you criticize someone's poem you're not criticizing them. You're just looking at their work. Sometimes kids can get very unhappy, "He doesn't like my poem, he doesn't like me." We talk about that before I ever let them sit down in groups. . . . When I discipline them, I tell them that "I can't accept f—— you in this classroom. I can't accept that. I still like you. I want you to clean it up." . . . They know that if they write about an abortion, even though they are probably sure I'm anti-abortion, they know that I will still like them and try to help them through it. . . . I think they just want to tell somebody but they don't want that somebody to call Mommy. See, that's the key. You have to create an atmosphere where they trust you and they really want to learn, and that takes a long time. . . . There is a difference between saying, "Be quiet, please," and "Shut up." I don't use "shut ups"; they don't use "shut ups." (p. 24)

Results from other studies (Block & Graham, 1994) support the use of detailed planning and explicit instructions for inner-city students. Less accomplished readers/writers who live in urban settings appear to advance their literacy when their literacy teachers do not spontaneously alter a lesson during the duration of a Tier 1–4 support activity. These students do best with lessons that include clear objectives and procedures, and lessons that tie the activities to their lives through in-class discussions, modeling, and simulations.

Students from Rural Cultures

In 1986 the poverty rate in rural counties in the United States was 50 percent higher than in metropolitan counties. This rate remained higher, rose more rapidly, and fell more slowly than the metropolitan rate (De Young & Lawrence, 1995). Displaced rural workers were unemployed 50 percent longer than urban workers, and when they did return to work they were more likely than urban workers to take pay cuts and lose insurance benefits (Stern, 1994). Rural per capita income also declined substantially between the mid-1970s and the mid-1990s, with new jobs created in rural America typically paying little more than minimum wage (De Young & Lawrence, 1995). More than one-third of the rural Americans in poverty are children (Perkinson, 1991). The implications of these conditions are that many rural students come to school with economically impoverished homes in which parents cannot provide adequate health care. They are less likely to have received the educational background or print-rich home environments necessary to rapidly advance their literacy abilities.

Moreover, when rural children grow up in communities in which physical labor or government assistance is the predominant source of adult income, raising the aspirations of readers/writers to improve literacy is difficult. They often have fewer selections of quality literature from which to choose, fewer models of literacy's being used to improve lives, and less parental support to reach these highest levels of literacy than suburban peers. Frequently, only those rural students who want to leave their rural lifestyles are ready to accept literacy teachers' persistent claims that high levels of literacy and education are valuable, as reported by De Young and Lawrence (1995):

> In interviews that we have conducted in different parts of the country, we have found many parents who express mixed feelings about public schools that are dedicated to training their children for national purposes. Tom Goodwin, a fifth-generation Yankee from Tremont, Maine, voices such sentiments: "Our children are our greatest export. We feed them, we clothe them, we educate them, and [then] we send them away to find work. We pay three times in raising them: for their expenses, with taxes to educate them, and then in losing them." (p. 107)

For these reasons, some of the multicultural lessons later in this book are more difficult to implement in rural environments (such as reading folktales from many lands and going to ethnic grocery stores to experience the heritage of multicultural traditions).

However, at least two effective programs for rural readers were reported by Haas and Lambert (1995). One of these—PACERS (Program for Academic and Cultural Enhancement of Rural Schools, University of Alabama)—is being used in Alabama and from Appalachia to the Black Belt to the Wiregrass. In this program, readers/writers with limited literacy backgrounds and achievements study, research, and serve their own communities. They produce community surveys, newspaper stories, history projects, and photographic documentation for the community's newspaper, city government, and other agencies. They also use their literacy curriculum and reading class period to learn such things as how to build low-cost solar-heated homes, rehabilitate existing homes, operate greenhouses, conduct health screening, and test water. A third component enables these students to build parks, put on plays, and perform musical programs, thus adding to the beauty and entertainment opportunities for the community (Haas & Lambert, 1995).

The second program is REAL Enterprises (Rural Entrepreneurship through Action Learning). This project began and is used most widely in South Georgia, where predominantly African American pupils from low-income rural homes research, plan, set up, and operate businesses in their communities in cooperation with their high schools and community colleges. Businesses designed and operated by these students have included stores selling comic books, used books, and magazines; T-shirt printing operations; gift shops; and craft studios. The students are not the only beneficiaries, as community members have new goods and services that were not available before. Further, the program creates a closer bond between students, teachers, community, and school as more than 500 community leaders serve on a community support team for REAL and the schools (Haas & Lambert, 1995).

Embracing the Richness of Cultural Diversity

Struggling readers/writers from diverse backgrounds benefit from demonstrations that literacy instruction will not be separated from the home-based experiences, culture, and traditions that they value. In Tier 1–4 support settings, reading specialists and literacy teachers can assist such readers to view reading/writing as a valuable method of enriching present, documenting past, and projecting future cultural legacies. You can also help students see that literacy assists them to examine the full range of human experiences, and vicariously to discover diversities and joys beyond their immediate environments.

To do so, bear in mind two facets of diversity should be prized. First, because people should never completely be defined by their membership in a culture, each of your students' present cultural and social affiliations should become merely the starting points for your instruction. Through the literature and literacy experiences in your class, students can discover more of themselves, appreciate the links between themselves and others, and establish a quest for more information. Second, you can assist students who use social interaction patterns that are different from those you prefer in the classroom to adopt more acceptable forms. Explicitly teaching students school conventions and traditions of school life for which they will be held accountable is valuable to them.

You can also assist them by modifying those school conventions that are unnecessary and do not lead to higher literacy attainment. For example, literacy teachers in the past very often misinterpreted a lack of response from some students as evidence of deficiency, rather than as a culturally driven response to adult authority. Even though some students cannot verbalize that this is the reason they do not speak up or express their views fluently, you must be aware of this possibility and balance requests with respect.

Another adaptation you can make is to respect the fact that every child comes to you in the security of his culture, and that in his or her mind the world is a "very small place, complete in itself, and perfect in its completeness" (Taylor & Dorsey-Gaines, 1988). Children can best be led to literacy through their sense of wonder or through pleasurable, personal experiences with reading/writing, as will be demonstrated in the activities that end this chapter. Unpleasant literacy experiences either will be added to the trivia of commonalities that are irrelevant to the child's world, or will remain entirely outside the context of that child's view of the world.

These diversities bring important new obligations and opportunities to use the special talents each child has developed through his or her culture. An excellent example is found in one fourth grade class in which more than 80 percent of the students could not comprehend stories at a second grade readability level and were members of the African American cultural group. I had the privilege of watching these fourth graders mentor kindergarten children. Through gestures and dialect they accomplished more in one minute than I could have done in 9 months of instruction. Here is what happened:

Herbert, a struggling reader in our fourth grade class, won the leading role in *The Steadfast Tin Soldier,* a play the class wrote. He and 12 of the 24 class members completely rewrote the original plot of this story to match messages they wanted to convey about their culture to students younger than themselves. Using his unique abilities to improve and respond to present conditions more rapidly than students from other cultural heritages might, Herbert realized that at the climax of the play every child was completely engrossed, all eyes were on him, and every child awaited the main character's next words. At this moment, Herbert deviated from the script; jumped forward, as if to leave the stage and become himself rather than the steadfast tin soldier; and said, "I want you to know something really important before I tell you the end of this story. If I hadn't learned to read this year, I would not be able to be this actor and it really is fun to act today. You must learn to read this year, for me. Do you hear me! If you will do that for me, say 'Yes, Man' really loud!" All the kindergarten children responded loudly. Then, he quickly turned to me and asked, "Can I come back in 2 months and have everyone here read to me so I can be sure they know how?" I said yes; he jumped back in the cast, said the closing lines of the play, and came back in 2 months—and *every* child read a book he or she selected to share with Herbert.

Diagnosing and Instructing to Capitalize on the Cultural and Social Richness in Struggling Readers' Lives

This last section describes interventions that use students' cultural and social strengths to build their literacy abilities. First, it suggests titles you can order for your classroom library before school begins to ensure that students' cultural and social backgrounds are represented from the very first day of school. The section then presents lessons to use for opening the school year. These lessons will appeal to and capitalize on the strengths within the various cultural and social groups you will encounter in Tier 1–4 one-to-one and small group literacy sessions. The remainder of the chapter describes specific literacy activities to use as the year continues—activities that will help you personalize the literacy curriculum for individual students.

Before School Begins

To capitalize on cultural richness, prepare for the school year by selecting multicultural literature for your students, following the guidelines depicted in Figure 5.2. When you incorporate these principles, multicultural literature can become a powerful vehicle for maturing literacy abilities, increasing understanding across cultures, seeing the world in a new way, and "crawling inside the skins of persons [who are] very different from ourselves" (Huck, 1990, p. 3). Using these stories about vibrant people, you can root your instruction for struggling readers in a narrative set in the specific culture with which they are familiar—or you can introduce your students to lifestyles different from their own.

If you build a multicultural collection of children's literature you can also communicate to students that their cultures are not merely welcome but embraced in your room. Children's literature is one of the most powerful vehicles for transmitting your values to students, and such a library lets them know that you consider multicultural

- Cultural accuracy, both of detail and of larger issues
- Richness in cultural details
- Authentic dialogue and relationships
- In-depth treatment of cultural issues
- Inclusion of members of a "minority" group for a purpose that is central to the plot

FIGURE 5.2 Points to Consider When Selecting Multicultural Literature for Struggling Readers

approaches to literacy appropriate for receiving meaning and assessing who we are and what is important in our society. Moreover, students connect with books that represent their own experiences and culture.

Of the 2,000 new books published annually between 1979 and 1984, only 100 new titles (5 percent) concerned people of color or those of other ethnic origin. Today, although this number has doubled to 200, that figure still represents a small portion (only 6 percent) of the 3,400 annual publications of children's literature. Moreover, many of the 1979 publications were already out of print by 1984, and this trend continues. (Such books go out of print rapidly, because major bookstores generally do not operate in communities of color, rural areas, or inner cities.) Therefore, publishers are reluctant to add new titles to the 6,000 already marketed because sales bottom out, regardless of the number of titles offered, at 1.5 million a year (Harris, 1994).

To recommend specific titles for your collection, start by referring again to Resource Cards 6, 7, and 8. Each of the titles in these bibliographies has been recommended by librarians and educators and meets the criteria specified in Figure 5.2. Of all the people of color in the United States, African Americans have the most rapidly growing body of children's literature, many examples of which are on Resource Card 6. Native American literature demonstrates the appreciation, celebration, and protection of nature—central values in Native American cultures. Resource Card 8 has recommended titles.

Although the Mexican American and Asian populations in America are the fastest-growing populations, children's literature that depicts these cultures is the least represented. Resource Card 7 has a very limited number of books depicting Hispanic culture. Resource Card 9 provides at least one recommended title from each country in Asia. Also notice that Jewish American literature is included on Resource Card 10. The Jewish American community has produced numerous children's authors and illustrators. It also sponsors the National Jewish Book Awards, and the Association of Jewish Libraries Awards.

Opening School Activities

On the first day of school you can collect information about dates of students' birthdays, as well as special dates and celebrations that occur in their families. Record these dates on the calendar. (In the week preceding a student's birthday or a culturally based event the student observes, you can ask that student to write about it and read

RESOURCE CARD 9

Books That Represent Asian Cultures

Grades K–2

Boholm-Olson, E. (1988). *Tuan.* New York: Farrar, Straus & Giroux.

Friedman, I. R. (1984). *How my parents learned to eat.* Boston: Houghton Mifflin.

Hodges, M. (Reteller). (1964). *The Wave.* Boston: Houghton Mifflin.

Levinson, R. (1988). *Our home is the sea.* New York: Dutton.

Mosel, A. (1972). *The funny little woman.* New York: Dutton.

Sakade, F. (1958). *Japanese children's favorite stories.* New York: Tuttle.

Yashima, T. (1955). *Crow boy.* New York: Viking.

Grades 3–4

Bunting, E. (1982). *The happy funeral.* New York: Harper.

Chang, H. (1988). *Mary Lewis and the frogs.* New York: Crown.

Clark, A. N. (1979). *In the land of small dragon.* New York: Viking.

Coerr, E. (1977). *Sadako and the thousand paper cranes.* New York: Putnam.

Coutant, H. (1974). *First snow.* New York: Knopf.

Ishii, M. (1987). *The tongue-cut sparrow.* New York: Lodestar.

Louie, A.-L. (1982). *Yeh-Shen.* New York: Philomel.

Luenn, N. (1982). *The dragon kite.* San Diego, CA. Harcourt Brace Jovanovich.

Pratt, D., & Kuls, E. (1967). *Magic animals of Japan.* New York: Parnassus.

Vuong, L. D. (Reteller). (1982). *The brocaded slipper.* Palo Alto, CA: Addison-Wesley.

Yagawa, S. (1981). *The crane wife.* New York: Morrow.

Yolen, J. (1967). *The emperor and the kite.* New York: World.

Grades 5–6

Davis, D. S. (1982). *Behind barbed wire.* New York: Dutton.

Fritz, J. (1982). *Homesick.* New York: Putnam.

Garrigue, S. (1985). *The eternal spring of Mr. Ito.* New York: Bradbury.

Graham, G. B. (1970). *The beggar in the blanket & other Vietnamese tales.* New York: Dial.

Hodges, M. (Reteller). (1984). *St. George and the dragon.* New York: Little, Brown.

Huynh, Q. N. (1982). *The land I lost: Adventures of a boy in Vietnam.* New York: Harper.

Kogawa, J. (1986). *Naomi's road.* New York: Oxford.

Leaf, M. (1987). *Eyes of the dragon.* New York: Lothrop, Lee & Shepard.

Lord, B. B. (1984). *In the year of the boar and Jackie Robinson.* New York: Harper.

Maruki, T. (1982). *Hiroshima no pika.* New York: Lothrop, Lee & Shepard.

Nguyen, C. (1985). *Cooking the Vietnamese way.* New York: Lerner.

Tsuchiya, Y. (1988). *Faithful elephants: A true story of animals, people and war.* Boston: Houghton Mifflin.

Uchida, Y. (1985). *Journey to Topaz: A story of the Japanese-American evacuation.* New York: Creative Arts.

Yep, L. (1975). *Dragonwings.* New York: Harper & Row.

Yep, L. (1977). *Child of the owl.* New York: Harper & Row.

RESOURCE CARD 10

Books That Represent Jewish Culture

Bachrach, S. (1995). *Tell them we remember: The story of the Holocaust.* New York: Little, Brown.

Baylis-White, M. (1991). *Sheltering Rebecca.* New York: Lodestar.

Cohen, B. (1983). *Molly's pilgrim.* New York: Lothram.

Kimmel, E. (1989). *Hershel and the Hanukkah goblins.* New York: Holiday.

Lowry, L. (1989). *Number the stars.* New York: Harper & Row.

Oberman, S. (1995). *The always prayer.* New York: Harper.

Polacco, P. (1992). *Mrs. Katz and Tush.* New York: Bantam.

Rosenberg, M. B. (1995). *Hiding to survive: Stories of Jewish children rescued from the Holocaust.* New York: Clarion.

Schwartz, H., and Rush, B. (1991). *The diamond tree: Jewish tales from around the world.* New York: Harper.

Sherman, J. (1993). *Rachel the clever and other Jewish folktales.* New York: August House.

Singer, I. (1995). *Mazel and Shlimazel.* New York: Sunburst.

that information to peers.) Based on the information you receive from your students, you can place them in culturally homogeneous or culturally heterogeneous groups to discuss a topic of interest. On the second day of school, students can invite their parents or other adults in their neighborhoods to school, or can interview them about a specific culturally relevant topic their group selected. On the third day, students can write about these interviews and invite a few of the adults to come to school and describe their experiences to the class.

After students submit a list of their general interest areas, you can help them narrow down the list to a more specific topic. For example, if a group of students wants to learn about occupations and many of them come from Mexican American families whose members are involved in carpentry, roofing, masonry, house painting, architecture, or landscaping, you begin the next day's activities by meeting with this group and asking them questions about family members' jobs that they would like to explore. Then suggest that students with similar questions work and read together. Before you dismiss this group and convene the other interest groups, ask the students to describe how they would like to share their findings and to select a day on which this is to occur. The decisions they make will provide additional information on their self-efficacy, their learning style preferences, and the length of time they want to invest in learning new information.

Spend four or five additional days reading leveled books about three different areas of interest, and engage students in learning about people from their culture who were successful in these areas. Make booklets about outstanding people such as: Hank Aaron, Seiji Ozawa, Lee Trevino, Bill Cosby, Jesse Owens, Leonard Bernstein, Michael Jordan, Woody Allen, Whitney Houston, Jim Thorpe, Arna Bontemps, Marguerite de Angeli, Nicholasa Mohr, Mabel Leigh Hunt, John Tunis, Dorothy Sterling, Eloise Jarvis McGraw, Elise Greenfield, Laura Armer, Scott O'Dell, Ann Nolan Clark, Virginia Sorensen, Ellis Credle, and Jesse Stuart.

While students are working in interest groups for 3 to 8 days, you are collecting more information on an individual basis, using the observation guides discussed in Chapter 3, so that you can design personalized instruction for your students. In the process, ask students to share with you "tricks" they have invented that help them become better readers/writers. (Descriptions of these strategies will give you clues to students' learning strengths.) The class can share their strategies with one another throughout the year so that students have several methods of approaching specific literacy challenges.

Immediately following this unit, ask students to write or discuss any quotations or proverbs commonly heard in their family (e.g., "Two wrongs don't make a right" or "Early to bed and early to rise makes a man healthy, wealthy, and wise"). Depending on the literacy abilities of your students, they can copy their favorite from the board, discuss meanings behind their favorites, or create an original story that illustrates the single or combined message of one or more of their favorite proverbs.

"I" Books and Slit Books

Less accomplished readers/writers can make *"I" books* using the pattern provided in Box 5.1. In these little books, students describe themselves either by drawing a picture to complete each of the squares or by writing the words they want with assistance from you or a classmate. You can introduce this project by pointing out the values of learning literacy. Students can understand this concept more rapidly when they create their first book to express their own ideas or feelings.

Another easy activity is making *slit books,* as shown in Figure 5.3. This project permits students to produce booklets with more than four pages. Subject matter can be similar to that of the "I" books, or it can include a summary of what students read over a two-day period.

Students' work on these booklets can help you diagnose how home cultural influences interact with "school-based" literacy standards. Throughout the year, you can make similar diagnoses of new positive values and attitudes toward literacy that struggling readers are developing by means of culturally embracing assessments like that in Box 5.2.

Family Story Projects

Incorporating family story projects into the oral reading and sharing time of Tier 1 and 2 classroom sessions and of reading specialists' Tier 3 and 4 support interventions enables challenged readers to become stars. Family story projects are activities in which parents tell a story during the evening and the student writes that story in his or her journal. Alternatively, parents can write the story and ask the teacher to read it with their child. This story enables parents to share a personal interest and literacy experience with their child without having to leave their home or purchase a book. This activity has been demonstrated to significantly increase struggling students' literacy achievement (Jordan, Snow, & Porche, 2000). It enables you to root future instruction in the culture that the story illustrates, and it raises these readers' self-concept.

There are other benefits to writing family stories. In Navajo, Oglala, Sioux, and Yaquie cultures, competence must be developed to a high level before performances are allowed. For this reason, many children value observing and self-testing their literacy

5.1 DIAGNOSIS AND ASSESSMENT

Finding the Degree to Which Individual Struggling Readers' Home Literacy Culture Supports Literacy Achievement

Directions: The first week of school ask students to complete this assessment tool, which embraces their social and cultural richness. Count the number of times literacy is listed and record that number. Later in the year, ask students to write a second "I" Book. Compare the number of times literacy-related items are mentioned to the number from the first week of school.

"I" BOOK PATTERN

At home, I like	fold 2	In my room at home, I have
fold 1		fold 1
I can	fold 2	The books I read are about:

Use two sheets of 8½" × 11" paper.

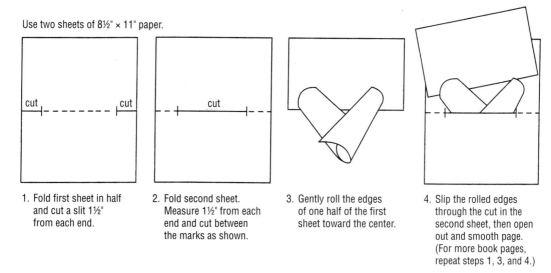

1. Fold first sheet in half and cut a slit 1½" from each end.

2. Fold second sheet. Measure 1½" from each end and cut between the marks as shown.

3. Gently roll the edges of one half of the first sheet toward the center.

4. Slip the rolled edges through the cut in the second sheet, then open out and smooth page. (For more book pages, repeat steps 1, 3, and 4.)

FIGURE 5.3 Easy Slit Book

Source: Modified from an original version in C. Block & JoAnn Zinke (1995), *Creating a Culturally Enriched Curriculum for Grades K–6,* (p. 220). Boston, MA: Allyn & Bacon.

abilities in private for an extensive period of time before they display them to you and others. Kwakuitl, Eskimo, Navajo, and Pueblo children may also have highly developed visual discrimination abilities, and the cooperative nature of Cherokee and Kwakuitl children may exceed other cultural groups (Lehr, 1988).

Hispanic students often prefer to work with others to achieve a common goal, and they are usually more sensitive to the feelings and opinions of others in group discussions than students from other cultural groups. This cooperative nature and sensitivity make family stories an excellent activity for these children.

Autobiographies and Biographies

Students reveal much to themselves by writing about their lives. Assign students to write their autobiographies, including the important parts of their lives and the aspects of their abilities that they value. Then pair each reader/writer with a partner and have the partners write each other's biographies. In these biographies the writers report the abilities and qualities of the other that they appreciate. When all have been finished, the partners read both of the autobiographies and biographies and discuss why differences existed and what they learned about themselves and their abilities through the process.

In conjunction with the biographies, ask parents about hobbies or books their children enjoy at home that they could bring to school to share with peers. Also, the public library has a list of children's authors and illustrators who live near your school. Your students can contact one of them by phone for an interview, or perhaps the author could come to class. Then, using notes collected during the phone interview or the

5.2 DIAGNOSIS AND ASSESSMENT

Identifying Struggling Readers' Use of Literacy Strategies When They Read Alone

Directions: Ask students to list the strategies and thinking processes that they used to comprehend a text as they read silently. Students then total the number employed to deduce meaning in all seven categories of semantic/syntactic/format clues. Repeat this diagnosis and assessment tool throughout the year. You should increase the number of strategies listed in each column as the year progresses.

Title of Book: _____

List and total the strategies you used as you read this book.

Rereading, Reflecting and Self-Correction	Author's Writing Organization and Style	Syntax and Mechanics of Sentences	Vocabulary	Illustrations	What Made It Easy to Read	What Made It Difficult to Read*	
1.	1.	1.	1.	1.	1.	1.	
2.	2.	2.	2.	2.	2.	2.	Grand
3.	3.	3.	3.	3.	3.	3.	Total of
4.	4.	4.	4.	4.	4.	4.	Literacy Strategies
5.	5.	5.	5.	5.	5.	5.	You Used
____ +	____ +	____ +	____ +	____ +	____ −	____ =	____

*Subtract total in this column.

classroom meeting, students can write a brief biography of that author. Box 5.3 has been used by many reading specialists in one-to-one intervention sessions to stimulate more home reading.

Student of the Week

According to the schedules presented in Chapter 8, Fridays should become special days for readers/writers in both Tier 1 and 2 classroom settings and reading specialists' one-to-one literacy support systems. In each Friday schedule you can set aside time to celebrate the successes and unique talents of each reader. One program to accomplish this goal is to announce one child each Friday as "Student of the Week" for the coming week. This student's parents are told ahead of time about the announcement so you can se-

5.3 READING SPECIALISTS

One-to-One Intervention Strategy to Build on Students' Home Literacy Richness

Name _____

	Book or Magazine and Author	Pages Read	Parent Signature	Parent or Student Comment
Monday				
Tuesday				
Wednesday				
Thursday				
Friday				
Saturday				
Sunday				

What did I do this week that good readers do? _____

_____

Parents' Comment: What my child did better as a reader or writer this week was _____

_____

cure items that will become that child's bulletin board (thus making a home-to-school connection).

The day of the announcement, all students in the class write a note to the parents of the "Student of the Week." Have them describe something they appreciate about the child, something the child does well, or something he or she did in class that was valuable to the class. You should proofread the notes and have students rewrite them in a "publishable," sharing form. Finally, these notes are sent home to the selected child's parents.

On the following Friday, just before the next "Student of the Week" is announced, the outgoing student tells about himself/herself—reading a portion of a favorite book to the class, telling important things he or she appreciated about the special recognition during the week, and discussing what he or she thinks is important about school and reading.

5.4 CLASSROOM TEACHERS

Resources for Materials in Tier 1 and 2 Settings That Embrace Students' Cultural and Social Richness

Directions: Ask reluctant readers and writers to correspond with one of the following agencies. By return mail, they will receive various pamphlets and books that they can read and share with peers.

The following references can increase your knowledge about specific cultures.

Southeast Asian Refugee Youth: An Annotated Bibliography. Southeast Asian Refugee Studies Project, Center for Urban and Regional Affairs, University of Minnesota, Minneapolis, MN 55401.

Los Angeles County Public Ethnic Resource Centers: The American Indian, Asian Pacific, African American, Chicano. Los Angeles County Public Library, ERIC ED 298 962.

Vietnamese Culture Kit. Iowa State University of Science and Technology, Research Institute for Studies in Education, Ames, IA, 50013, ERIC ED 149 602.

A Manual for Teachers of Indochinese Students. Intercultural Development Research Association, San Antonio, TX, 78284, ERIC ED 205 663.

Some Hints to Work With Vietnamese Students. Arizona State Department of Education, Phoenix, AZ, 85026, ERIC ED 133 383.

Teaching Multicultural Literature in Grades K–8. Edited by Violet J. Harris. Christopher Gordon Publishers, Norwood, MA, 02062.

Multicultural Review (a journal with reviews of multicultural children's literature, "dedicated to a better understanding of ethnic, racial, and religious diversity"). Greenwood Publishing Group, 88 Post Road West, P.O. Box 5007, Westport, CT 06881-5007.

Multicultural Publishers Exchange (publisher of books by and about people of color). Box 9869, Madison, WI 53715; 1-800-558-2110.

Hispanic Books Distributor. 1665 W. Grant Rd., Tucson, AZ 85745. (Selections are evaluated according to subject matter, literary quality, and format, with publications ranging from preschoolers to middle school readers, as well as resource books. Also has a *Hispanic Books Bulletin* to which you can subscribe.)

The Kiosk. 19223 DeHavilland Dr., Saratoga, CA 95070; 408-996-0667. (Publishes games, posters, diplomas, bookmarks, and stationery in several languages.)

Mariuccia Ioconi Book Imports. 1110 Mariposa, San Francisco, CA 94107; 415-285-7393. (Publishes Spanish-language records and books for children, including a "big book" series.)

Santillana Publishing Company. 901 W. Walnut St., Compton, CA 90220; 1-800-245-8584.

World Wide Games (exceptional handcrafted games from around the world). Colchester, CT 06415.

Third World Press. 7822 S. Dobson, Chicago, IL 60619.

Just Us Books. 356 Glenwood Ave., 3rd floor, E. Orange, NJ 07017.

Center for Applied Linguistics. Publication Program, 1611 N. Kent St. Arlington, VA 22209.

Center for Southeast Asia. 260 Stephens Hall, University of California, Berkeley, CA 94270.

Indochinese Materials Center. U.S. Department of Education, Region VII, 601 East 12th St., Kansas City, MO 64106.

JACP Inc. 414 East Third St., San Mateo, CA 94401.

Southeast Asian Learning Project. Long Beach Unified School District, 701 Locust Ave., Long Beach, CA 90813.

Teachers of English to Speakers of Other Languages. School of Languages and Linguistics, Georgetown University, Washington, DC 20009.

5.4 CLASSROOM TEACHERS

Resources for Materials in Tier 1 and 2 Settings That Embrace Students' Cultural and Social Richness *(continued)*

African Imprints Library Services. 410 West Falmouth Highway, Box 350, West Falmouth, MA 02574. (Provides recent children's books available from 20 African nations.)

Atheneum/Margaret K. McElderry Books. Macmillan Publishing Company, 1230 Ave. of the Americas, New York, NY 10020.

Farrar, Straus & Giroux. 19 Union Square West, New York, NY 10003. (Specializes in Swedish literature.)

Kane/Miller Book Publishers. P.O. Box 529, Brooklyn, NY 11231-0005. ("Cranky Nell" imprint.)

Lerner Publications Company/Carolrhoda Books. 241 First Avenue North, Minneapolis, MN 55401.

Tundra Books of Northern New York. Box 1030, Plattsburgh, NY 12901. (Specializes in Canadian, French/English bilingual books for children.)

Wellington Publishing Company. P.O. Box 14877, Chicago, IL 60614.

Chapter Summary

This chapter examined the home literacy cultural characteristics of readers from diverse backgrounds. Educators agree that many of these students process information differently—in ways that in many cases are in direct opposition to the "school cultures" in which they are learning. But rather than looking at these social and cultural patterns as obstacles to "school-dominant" literacy goals, we can embrace and build upon the richness that each child's life brings to the teaching of literacy.

As the information in this chapter demonstrated, evidence exists that students from different cultural and social groups value differ qualities about reading and writing experiences. Their literacy styles differ in cognition, values, and purposes. Without the knowledge gained in this chapter, you might have inadvertently caused students to respond negatively to reading/writing. This could have occurred because their cultural values and uses of literacy in their culture were incongruous or unrelated to the instruction you delivered. By using the knowledge in this chapter, however, you can provide more personally relevant and stimulating literacy experiences for your students.

To date, we have spent one-third of this text learning to diagnose the needs, behaviors, and literacy responses of less accomplished readers/writers. In Part 3, we will explore more specific instructional interventions that have proven to help students overcome obstacles and become highly successful literacy users.

Key Terminology

Now that you have completed this chapter, do you know the meanings of the following terms? If you do, place a check mark in the blank that precedes each term. If you are not certain, quickly turn to the page number that follows the term to review its meaning.

____ **culture** (page 107)   ____ **sociocultural influences** (page 107)

____ **socioeconomic backgrounds**   ____ **cultural discontinuity** (page 107)
(page 107)

Case Study

Making Professional Decisions

Reid was 9 years, 10 months old and in fourth grade when his mother brought him to the diagnostician on October 4.

During the initial interview Reid's parents reported that he had displayed difficulties in school since first grade. He was now receiving reading instruction in a second grade reader at his school, while most of his classmates were reading from a fourth grade book.

According to his parents, Reid was happy at home and there were few family conflicts. He had many friends, and got along well with his younger brother. Reid's father was his soccer coach and he enjoyed spending time in the outdoors with his two sons. Reid's mother reported that she spent hours reading to Reid and his brother. Reid seemed to find it difficult to pay attention and often could not remember the contents of the stories. When asked about behavior, neither parent could recall any specific behavioral problems. His parents said that Reid was slower in learning to talk than his brother.

During the interview, Reid's parents said that he had suffered three severe middle ear infections before age 3. His hearing was checked after the second and third infections by an audiologist and found to be within the normal range. His mother said that on two occasions Reid had not passed the school's annual hearing screening test. The school had referred him for further testing, but his parents had not had his hearing rechecked. Reid's only other health problem

was a recently discovered allergy to feathers, which caused a runny nose and clogged ears. His parents reported that he had always passed his vision screening tests at school.

The diagnostician reviewed his cumulative school records. The records showed that he had experienced problems in reading since he began school. The records also showed that he had excelled in math. The basal reader used in schools emphasized direct phonics instruction, especially in the primary grades. Reid's first grade teacher had noted that he had "trouble with sounds." He had seen a speech therapist for articulation difficulties with the sounds *s, sh,* and *f* and with the voiced and unvoiced *th* sounds.

The diagnostician interviewed his current fourth grade teacher. She reported that Reid was not verbally expressive and that his speaking abilities were generally below average. She also reported that he often did not pay attention and had difficulty following directions, which they attributed to his carelessness.

The diagnostician administered the following tests. Results were as follows:

INFORMAL READING INVENTORY
Word List

Independent level	Primer
Instructional level	Grade 1

Oral Reading Passages

Independent level	Preprimer
Instructional level	Primer

Silent Reading Passages

Independent level	Primer
Instructional level	Grade 1
Listening Level	Primer

During the testing, Reid was friendly and cooperative. However, the diagnostician noted that questions often has to be repeated.

Respond to the following questions, then check your responses against the Answer Key at the end of the book.

1. How severe is Reid's reading disability? Substantiate your answer.
2. Consider environmental, affective, cognitive, and physical variables. What evidence do you find that any of these may be associated with Reid's reading problems?
3. At what level would you begin instruction? Substantiate your answer.

Thinking and Writing about What You Have Learned

1. Chapters 1 through 5 have suggested several instructional activities. What plan can you develop to ensure that you use them systemically, whether in Tier 1 and 2 support settings or in Tier 3 and 4 special one-to-one interventions? Share your scheduling plan with peers in your class or school.

2. What will you do when an African American student's responses to a book tend to be more episodic than topic-centered during a literacy conversation about that book—or when the student talks about topics out of the sequence in which they were introduced? (Are you aware of the value of personally embellished statements? How would you respond to extraneous comments?) Write three actions you will take and present them to colleagues.

3. A teacher of a shy Asian reader said to the student: "Let yourself go more often, it becomes you." Was this a positive statement to make, in your opinion? Why or why not?

4. Throughout the first five chapters of this textbook, many benefits have been attributed to small group work for readers/writers from some backgrounds and capability levels. Identify which cultural group you think would benefit most from the group work strategy to enhance literacy described by this teacher:

   This is why I like for these students to do small group work without me being present in the group—to get them talking and interacting with one another. I think it also increases their depth of vocabulary and interest in the subject matter. It no longer becomes that they are doing this for me. They begin to see they have a role in what's going on in the classroom and with each other's learning. . . . I tell them that someone's ability to read and write is going to depend on the lessons they teach. I add that they really need to act as helpers to their friends; they need also to teach them why it is important to read and write. If you don't take part in this process, you're hurting the other person in some way. . . . [I try] to give them the sense that they could be teachers also, and that they do have something to say and some knowledge they can show. (P. A. Beardon, personal communication, October 3, 1995)

To find out what cultural group the teacher was discussing, turn to the Answer Key at the end of the book.

Onto the Information Superhighway

Multicultural Websites That Promote Literacy

African American Literature, Elementary School and Middle School

http://web.uflib.ufl.edu/cm/africana/children.htm

Latino Literature, Elementary School and Middle School

http://latino.sscnet.ucla.edu/Latino_Bibliography.html

The Pura Belpré Award List

http://ala.org

Descriptions of books by Latino/Latina writers whose work best portrays, affirms, and celebrates the Latino cultural experience.

Kay Vandergrift's Children's Literature Page

www.scils.rutgers.edu/special/kay/culture.html

Another strong resource on children's literature. Includes a section on gender and culture, with links to websites.

At Home with Multicultural Adolescent Literature

http://borg.lib.vt.edu/ejournals/ALAN/fall95/Ericson.html

Walk a Mile in My Shoes: Multicultural Curriculum Resources

www.wmht.org/trail/explor02.htm
www.weber.edu/mbe/htmls/mbe-books-pbyr-asian.html

Clearinghouse for Multicultural Bilingual Education. Picture books/young reader–Asian Pacific.

Oxfam America

www.oxfamamerica.org

Background and weekly updates on current crises.

Government of Guam Home Page

www.gov.gu

An excellent starting place to learn about Guam.

Federated States of Micronesia

www.visit-fsm.org

Official page of the Federated States of Micronesia, with links to Yap, Pohnpei, Kosrae, and Chuuk.

Bikini Atoll, Marshall Islands

www.bikiniatoll.com

A very interesting site about this island.

chapter

6

Readers and writers progress most quickly when explanations about ways to improve occur at the point of need.

Assessment to Inform Instruction

> Whaka Paohota oku painga, kia ngaro oku ngoikoretanga.
>
> [Highlight my strengths, and my weaknesses will disappear.]
>
> —Maori proverb
> from Hawaiian culture

■ Chapter Overview: Key Points

In Chapters 1 through 5 the historical, physical, cognitive, motivational, social, and cultural variables that influence the success of struggling readers/writers were described. The purpose of this chapter is to describe assessments that assist teachers in instructional decision making and in communicating with students, parents, and policy makers. The chapter contains a discussion of both informal and formal evaluations. They are presented as a single body of knowledge, because to separate them could communicate the misconception that these types of evaluations are more different than alike. Quite the opposite is true. Diagnoses of individual students' needs are best when drawn from the vast field of valid and reliable measures—both informal and formal.

Note that examples of assessment instruments have appeared in other chapters. These diagnostic and evaluative instruments were described at those points to demonstrate the continuous, inseparable relationship that should exist between assessment and instruction. Optimal appraisal occurs when students experience assessment as an integral, and often indiscernible, component in their ongoing instruction.

In this chapter you will learn:

- Principles of effective assessment and diagnosis
- Formal diagnosis, instruction, and assessment of students with special literacy needs
- Informal diagnosis, instruction, and assessment of students with special literacy needs

You will also learn why portfolios and performance instruments are particularly valuable for less accomplished literacy users; students can design demonstrations to showcase their literacy achievements. Last, you will examine grading and consider how to report achievement fairly when students have unequal abilities. By chapter's end, you will have answers to the following questions:

1. What are the most effective assessments for struggling readers/writers?
2. How can both standardized and informal tests provide direction to instructors, administrators, parents, students, and policy makers?

3. How can standardized tests, informal evaluations, and self-assessments reveal readers' and writers' new literacy growth?

Principles of Effective Assessment and Diagnosis

In the 1990s a call to restructure evaluation within U.S. schools powered one of the most extensive reforms of testing in history. Teachers have long suspected that standardized testing could have detrimental effects on students whose scores fall below the **national norm** (Smith, 1984)—the average score achieved by a group of same-age peers who take a test for the purpose of establishing performance standards. Research has documented the multiple negative effects of inappropriate uses of standardized achievement tests (Darling-Hammond & Wise, 1985; Haladyna, Nolen, & Hass, 1991; Shepard, 1991). The strongest criticisms of these standardized assessments are as follows:

1. They do not contain examples of the objectives that struggling readers are taught.
2. They evaluate these readers in timed settings with short passages, so the students cannot employ the special supports they use to demonstrate their best literacy.
3. They do not incorporate principles (described later in this chapter) that increase the authenticity, validity, and reliability of literacy assessment.

As educators grew more and more dissatisfied in the closing decades of the twentieth century, some sought to end the injustices by improving standardized tests; others developed new types of evaluative instruments. The goals of both efforts were basically the same:

1. To enable students to use their own knowledge and strengths in *authentic assessments* in which they are motivated to participate fully
2. To obtain more *valid* and *reliable* information about students' thinking processes
3. To evaluate students' problem-solving strategies about literacy

Authentic assessment is defined as a measure of competence in literacy obtained through activities, performances, processes, and situations that reflect reading/writing as it is used in students' lives outside school. **Validity** is the degree to which an activity reflects the domain of competencies in which it belongs. In other words, if an assessment is valid, professionals can clearly identify the purpose for which it was designed and agree that it represents the literacy domain from which it was selected. **Reliability** is the degree to which repeated administrations of a test will produce the same results.

By the early 1990s 40 states had begun legislation for statewide assessments designed to reach these goals (Pipho, 1992). Other nations developed new tests as well. This reform changed the focus of evaluation. Too often in the past, poor scores would create failure images and deflate the self-esteem of less accomplished readers/writers, but the new feeling was that standardized test scores should no longer be interpreted as failure to read, write, spell, or speak correctly. Instead scores should be interpreted as foreshadowing new learning possibilities. Each error should indicate that a student's zone of proximal development has enlarged so that he or she has noticed, although not yet mastered, a new concept (Vygotsky, 1978). Through instruction, this noticing can be transformed to understanding. Teachers should also ensure that every literacy assessment is a direct reflection of students' instructional program and informs the students of long-term goals—that it showcases their aptitudes and expertise.

The principles and assessment instruments presented here provide for such appropriate and effective assessments of less accomplished readers/writers.

New Principles for Assessment

Four actions relative to measurement can improve the power of diagnosis and assessment in advancing these readers' and writers' literacy.

1. *As you teach, gather as much diagnostic and evaluative information as possible from students while they work.* Such information blurs the lines between diagnosis, assessment, and attainment. When assessment occurs while students are actually engaged in reading, writing, and speaking purposefully, each incident of students' literacy can be used as an evidence of their growth. With this principle in mind, **diagnosis** can be defined as the process of collecting and reflecting on performance samples before there is any instruction targeted toward the objective being measured; on the other hand, **assessment** is the systematic process of gathering information about students' performances after instruction has occurred. Assessments indicate transfers of literacy strengths to novel tasks. Taken together, diagnosis and assessment enable you to form an appraisal of students' present literacy expertise.

To implement this principle, appraisal should be taken throughout an instructional program. For example, when students talk to one another you can diagnose the degree to which they transfer speaking abilities in school situations. When you document these comments in a systematic way they become anecdotal records—notes about literacy processes in action (to be discussed more fully later in this chapter) that provide specific incidents documenting a professional judgment you made at that time concerning an individual's literacy growth. When you believe that diagnosis, instruction, and assessment form parallel beams in the foundation by which everyone in your room will and can learn to read well, authentic performance assessment becomes easier. With this perspective, students can present their best to you through selecting, assembling, and exhibiting performances that reveal their highest level of capabilities.

2. *Do not interpret any single test score as a sole indicator of literacy.* It is becoming acceptable not to rely on standardized test scores as a dominant index of achievement for struggling readers/writers (Allington, 1995; Chall, 1993). A more valuable index is to report students' movement toward internally guided reading. For example, when students demonstrate their improved understanding of stories on the sports page of the daily newspaper through oral reading assessments and retellings throughout the year, it is a more informative appraisal of literacy growth than a standardized test score in reading comprehension that increases from 37 to 38. Moreover, such an authentic assessment reinforces students' affect; the praise students receive for growth is directly tied to daily reading activities in which adults engage. It is probable that students will view such reading/writing as an important, adultlike pursuit for their personal growth and pleasure.

3. *When you do not interpret errors as failures but as information about and opportunities for growth, less accomplished readers/writers tend to follow your lead.* Your assessment should include instruction in how students can use their strengths to overcome
weaknesses and to reach new goals they would like to attain. In the process, many students also begin to share ownership of their assessments; they become self-appraisers and
coappraisers. Such a position enables you to ask what they want to improve in a specific
diagnostic–instructional–evaluative activity, and why they would value this learning.
Through their answers you can gain important direction about future instruction and
students' present misconceptions. When something isn't working for a specific reader,
you have individual performance indicators that enable you to change it. These indicators also reduce unproductive thinking such as worrying about "what is wrong" with a
specific child, seeking to blame something else, or trying to bail out that child. Instead,
if verbal assessments and report cards document what struggling readers/writers know—
rather than what they don't know—their resistance to literacy decreases. Therefore,
encourage students' input about their abilities, and they will develop a desire to demonstrate their true literacy.

It is crucial that you do not overgeneralize a single literacy performance. Rather,
limit your statements to descriptions of literacy progress as evidenced by the contexts
in which the data were obtained. For example, in reporting results from the vocabulary
subtest from the Stanford Diagnostic Reading Test, instead of focusing on the overall
score, you could describe the types of words defined accurately and what these words
had in common. Then you could discuss with a student words that appeared on that
subtest that he or she would like to learn to define. By locating one or more such words,
the student will be indicating his or her zone of proximal development and new areas
of interest in word knowledge. If you carefully limit your comments to specific information, students will not overextend their aims or quickly find excuses for their errors.
Subsequent instruction in these areas will produce the most growth for less accomplished readers/writers (Goodman, 1989; Stanovich, 1993).

To determine how students have interpreted individual diagnostic–instructional–
evaluative activities, ask them to tell you what they could tell their parents that they have
learned. By partnering with parents you can capitalize on the observations and diagnoses
they make at home. Furthermore, when you interpret errors as information for growth and
not as failures, you assist parents to do the same.

4. *Diagnosis and assessment of struggling readers/writers should document the
processes of literacy in real-world contexts, using developmentally and culturally appropriate performance indicators and reports of individual students' growth along the literacy
continuum* (Harp, 1993). In the past, diagnosis for these readers typically occurred
through individualized standardized tests in Tier 3 support settings. Such settings are
more removed from the authentic situations in which these readers are expected to perform at school, as working adults, and in leisure pursuits.

Table 6.1 delineates the components of the foregoing principles. The next section
of this chapter will describe formal assessment instruments and literacy performance
indicators that adhere to these principles. The section after that discusses informal
assessment.

TABLE 6.1 Components of Effective Assessment

1. Continuous and ongoing assessments of literary processes are made while students are engaged in the processes of reading, writing, speaking, and listening.
2. Assessments are an integral part of instruction, so students have less stress due to test anxiety.
3. Assessments are authentic, reflecting real-life reading and writing that students will do as working adults and in leisure pursuits.
4. Assessments are interpreted with students and parents as indications of growth.
5. Assessments are developmentally and culturally appropriate.
6. Assessments identify students' strengths.

■ Formal Diagnosis, Instruction, and Assessment of Students with Special Literacy Needs

In the recent past, and in many schools today, group-administered, norm-referenced standardized tests are the most prevalent type of literacy assessment for struggling readers/writers. **Standardized tests** are administered in a controlled setting in which directions cannot be altered, and students respond to items they have not seen in instruction. These tests serve important functions, but if they are not properly used, misinterpretation of test scores can occur.

Moreover, because standardized tests are norm-referenced, an individual's score is compared to that of a large, representative sample of students. All students in this norming group take the test within the same 2-week period; their ethnic origins, genders, school settings, and socioeconomic backgrounds accurately reflect the percentages found in the United States or Canada.

Most standardized tests contain numerous subtests that cover separate skills related to the reading process. In recent decades these subtests have been criticized because they do not adequately measure students' processing and literacy performances; they contain only a few items, which cannot validly measure large domains of reading abilities. For example, in one standardized test a single question was used to measure students' ability to infer. The question was about a boy who was having a dialogue with a duck that followed him home. Here is the question:

> The boy told the duck what a good pet it would make, but pets were not allowed in the boy's rent-controlled housing project. He went on to explain that his family had had to wait two years to get into the project, and if he kept the duck, they would be kicked out and have no place to go. (N. Marshall, personal communication, 4/17/95)

Immediately after this passage, students were asked how the boy would solve his problem. Answer options included the following: (a) he would keep the duck; (b) he would give the duck to a friend; or (c) he would send the duck away. After reading the passage, what option would you pick to report the inference you made? Struggling readers in affluent areas tended to select the first option (keeping the duck), whereas those in urban areas selected the correct option (send the duck away). As one educator pointed out, "The readers in the affluent areas had no concept of rent-controlled housing projects, so they saw no reason for giving up the duck. After all, they tended to live in large, detached homes, and any moves made by their families tended to be to bigger, more expensive homes" (N. Marshall, personal communication, 4/17/95). Because these students were inferencing based on applications of the story to their own lives, they were penalized and scored as falling below the "norm" in inferencing abilities.

As a second example, complete the following items from a specific type of standardized test:

1. A hog is a hustler.   T   F
2. A chine is an automobile.   T   F

The first item is false and the second is true in inner-city dialect, according to *An Inner-City IQ Test* (1991) by Samuel D. Crawford and Robert H. Bentley. As these items demonstrate, answers students give on standardized tests are affected by the decontextualized situation in which testing occurs. Also, because the tests are designed to represent broad themes in the national curricula, their content does not provide a one-to-one match with the objectives in your program.

Similarly, in Michigan and Illinois only recently developed standardized tests for statewide assessment have methods of assessing prior knowledge, cultural background, ability to draw multiple interpretations, interests, creative thinking, and test-taking skills. These tests, and others, are finally beginning to "provide children with longer, noncontrived passages; assess their prior knowledge of the passage topics; ask questions based on a taxonomy of inferences; and evaluate children's awareness of reading strategies" (Armbruster, Anderson, & Meyer, 1991).

On the positive side, standardized tests do provide immediate general data for educational policy makers. They also serve as a reliable, uncomplicated, and efficient method for schools to gather information on large numbers of students. They enable administrators and legislators to have a single measure of achievement of various cohorts of students across their state, region, or nation. Also, as Chapter 14 will explain, standardized tests can provide information for instruction of individual readers/writers with literacy differences that require special instructional programs.

Should your less accomplished readers/writers have to take a standardized test, making them test-wise will assist their performance. Such instruction helps them recognize the complex wording of test directions, anticipate how test items will appear, and understand how the test is designed. This instruction will remove unfair obstacles to their performance.

The discussions of test categories that follow include information to help you interpret test scores that appear in these readers/writers' cumulative folders. If a parent mentions a test that has been given to a student in a Tier 4 support setting that does not match any of the descriptions here, approximately every 3 years the *Mental Measurement Yearbook* is updated with extensive information about standardized educational assessment instruments and can be referenced. The most recent edition, the *Thirteenth Mental Measurement Yearbook* (2002), is available in reference libraries. More information about various tests appears at the end of this chapter, so you can order those that are appropriate for individual students.

Category 1: Multiple-Subject Achievement Tests

Multiple-subject achievement tests are designed for grades K–12 and assess many subject areas (as shown at the end of this chapter). They contain several subtests that are often administered every day within a 1-week period. The reading content area is typically divided into phonic analysis, vocabulary, and comprehension.

Items are not designed to measure other strategies a reader could use to decode or comprehend. Therefore, when parents read the results of this assessment for individual readers/writers at early stages of development, caution them that many of the newer strategies their students are using (to be described in Chapter 9) are not measured by this test. Therefore, this test will likely not adequately measure the progress individual students are making toward independence in decoding, comprehension, and composing.

Category 2: Standardized Reading Survey Tests

Some standardized reading survey tests assess word recognition through the listing of nonsense words, reading passages, and supplementary word analysis and phonics tests. Although these tests can provide general measures of some components of reading ability, such as comprehension, word recognition, and reading speed, often they do little more than indicate the student's methods of decoding words in isolation, confirm or disconfirm the existence of a reading difficulty, and evaluate the student's sight word vocabulary. Specific items assess students' recognition of initial consonants, final consonants, consonant digraphs, consonant blends, initial consonant substitution, initial consonant sounds recognized auditorily, auditory discriminations, short and long vowel sounds, vowels with *r*, vowel diphthongs and digraphs, common syllables, phonograms, contractions, comprehension, blending, listening vocabulary, spelling, phonic spelling of words, visual memory of words, and other subtests. These tests may use words that a child has never read.

For example, in the Durrell Analysis of Reading Difficulty a tachistoscope (a machine that briefly flashes words on a screen that students are to read in isolation instantly) is used on the word recognition and word analysis subtests, and students' outcomes with words flashed this way do not provide information about strategies used. It is also important to explain to parents that in the past many people have turned to these tests to gain diagnostic information, and results should not be judged as achievement or lack of achievement.

Category 3: Specialized Standardized Tests

Most specialized standardized tests comprise lists of words and measure word pronunciation in isolation. They do not assess comprehension of oral reading; scores are only indications of word recognition ability. The **Formal Reading Inventory,** however, provides miscue analysis and data concerning silent reading comprehension.

An important caveat to give to parents when you, they, and their children interpret scores from these tests is that the terms *instructional* and *independent levels* are used differently from their customary use in informal reading inventories. Also, *potential level* (the level at which the student can listen and respond satisfactorily to questions) is also assessed differently. In these tests, *instructional* relates to concepts not yet mastered, *independent* connotes concepts mastered, and *potential* refers to the level of comprehension a student would have about the material in a passage if he or she did not have to read it but had it read to him or her.

How to Interpret Test Scores for Students and Parents

As parents read standardized test scores it is important that they understand several basic terms.

First, it is important to define *normed.* This means that the items were written with a difficulty level such that half of the children taking the test will get half or more of the items correct, and half of the students will get half (or more) of the items incorrect, as shown in Figure 6.1 and illustrated in Figure 6.2.

The number of items the child scores correctly on the test is called the **raw score.** If a child answered 8 out of 10 correctly, this raw score would seem to indicate that the student knew the material very well. However, the raw score does not indicate how well the student did in relation to peers. When the 8 correct answers are compared to the scores of all others taking the test who are the same age as that student, the comparison is called a **percentile ranking.** A percentile ranking can range from 1 to 99 and indicates the student's relationship to students in the norming group who were the same age. Therefore, in our example, a percentile ranking of 50 would indicate that answering 8 of 10 correctly places the student's performance as *better* than only 50 percent of all the other students who took the same test.

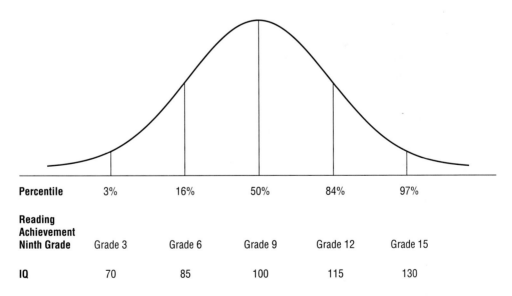

Percentile	3%	16%	50%	84%	97%
Reading Achievement Ninth Grade	Grade 3	Grade 6	Grade 9	Grade 12	Grade 15
IQ	70	85	100	115	130

There is a strong but far from perfect correlation between Reading Achievement scores and IQ. In other words, on average a ninth grader with an IQ of 85 tends to read about at the sixth grade level.

FIGURE 6.1 The Normal Distribution Curve

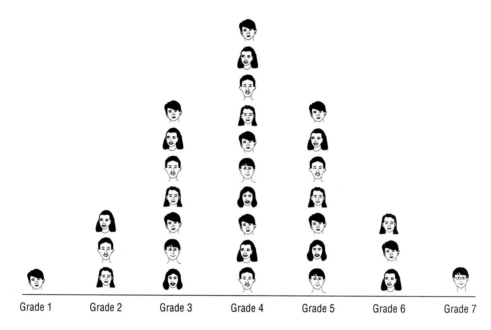

| Grade 1 | Grade 2 | Grade 3 | Grade 4 | Grade 5 | Grade 6 | Grade 7 |

FIGURE 6.2 Reading Abilities in a Typical Fourth Grade Class

It is also important for parents to consider the content in a specific subtest and the amount of exposure their child has had to that content compared to other students across the United States. For example, assume that a first grader speaks Spanish at home and has been in the United States just 2 months when a standardized English reading test is administered. Given that this student has been exposed to English for only 2 months, to score at the 50th percentile for all students in the United States of the same age should be interpreted as a momentous accomplishment!

Parents can also become confused by grade equivalent scores if they are not explained. A **grade equivalent score,** sometimes simply called a *grade score,* indicates achievement in school years and months. For example, the 50th percentile score for the first grader in our example would translate into a grade equivalent score of 1.2, indicating that this student has the average level of performance of first graders in the second month of school (when the test is administered). Problems of interpretation arise when a student's percentile score translates into a grade equivalent that is above or below the student's grade placement. To illustrate, suppose another first grader scores at the 80th percentile. That student's grade equivalent score translates to 3.1, which means this student performed on the test at the same average level of third grade students in their first month of school. When some parents hear this explanation, they misinterpret it to mean that their child should be working on material at a third grade level—but this is not a valid interpretation. Rather, the first grader's grade equivalent score of 3.1 indicates that he or she answered as many items correctly on this subtest as the average third grader. On some subtests, such as recognizing sight words, you would expect this to be the case, as there is a level of accuracy that first graders as well as third graders can attain equally well.

There are other terms that you should explain to parents. As mentioned earlier, *reliability* refers to consistency. To describe it to parents, explain that if their child took the same test (or a different form of the test) on a different day, the child should score approximately the same. Reliability is obtained by making the difficulty of items in all forms of the test the same. Test makers achieve this consistency by counterbalancing easy and difficult items so that equal numbers appear at the beginning, middle, and end of the test.

Also as mentioned earlier, *validity* means that a test measures what it is intended to measure. Test makers achieve validity by carefully selecting items so that the limited sample on the test adequately represents the subject area or literacy process being measured. *Face validity,* or criterion-related validity, means that the test looks like a test that should (and does) measure the process and product it attests to measure. Face validity is often achieved by comparisons to other tests reported to measure the same qualities. *Construct validity* refers to how well a test measures attributes that are not directly observable but can be inferred from the test. For example, a test will have construct validity in measuring comprehension if it samples from different genres. In doing so, it allows us to infer that students will comprehend as well on these types of materials when they are given longer to read them than the testing situation allows.

Distributions and indices of central tendency indicate how scores spread from highest to lowest, such as how norm-referenced tests report scores by spreading them out in a normal curve. Central tendency measures how many scores fall near the **mean,** or average score, and whether progressively fewer scores fall at the extreme high and extreme low ends of the continuum. The **median** score is the one exactly in the middle, with half of the test takers scoring below the median and half above it. **Mode** is the term to designate the most frequent score, the one received by the most students. The **range** of scores is the span from the highest to lowest, and the **standard deviation** is how far above or below the mean an individual's score fell, with increments from lowest to highest score being divided equally, as indicated by the vertical lines in Figure 6.1.

A standard deviation also indicates how many answers have to be missed before a student's results become significantly different from those of other students who took the test. For example, suppose the same first grade Spanish-speaking student discussed previously answered 7 of 10 correctly, which placed her at the 50th percentile, indicating that she correctly answered as many as the average student. To move one standard deviation below the average student, she would have had to answer 3 of 10 correctly, because almost everyone who took the test correctly answered at least 6 of the items (median was 4 and mean was 7). This indicates that on this subtest there was very little difference among all the students' performances.

When a child is several standard deviations above or below the mean, scores may need special interpretation for parents. Instead of indicating that the child is exceptionally bright or unintelligent, the score could have occurred because the content on that test had been either overrepresented in the child's curriculum and learned well or not included in the curriculum at all. Another equally valid interpretation for struggling readers/writers is that they differ significantly from the norming group as to the strengths they use to accomplish literacy tasks.

If parents exclaim that they don't understand how their child could do so poorly on a test, especially if the student answered most items correctly, you can explain by indicating that the score is a comparison only. Specifically, a score below the 50th percentile indicates that there were more of the child's peers across the country who had more correct answers than there were peers who had fewer correct answers than the student. Then suggest a conference with all of the student's teachers to identify strategies they can employ to increase the competencies measured on the test.

Always keep in mind that standardized tests are appropriate appraisal instruments when they are administered individually and are selected to assess distinct abilities for less accomplished readers/writers. If group-administered standardized tests are used, scores must be interpreted in light of both the restraints of the testing situation and the students' inability to use decoding and comprehension supports (described in Chapters 9 and 10) that would elevate them to maximum performance.

Informal Diagnosis, Instruction, and Assessment of Students with Special Literacy Needs

Informal diagnostic–instructional–evaluative instruments are assessments that do not have normative data. As described in the previous section, **normative data** are obtained when thousands of students, who represent the spectrum of possible test takers, take the same test during the same 2-week period. These test scores are used to derive standards by which all future test scores will be measured. In contrast, the informal assessments described in this section do not have a standard to which individual performances can be compared.

You will discover many informal assessment instruments in future chapters—and have already read about some in previous chapters. All of these instruments fall within nine categories:

1. Interest and attitude surveys (as described in Chapter 5)
2. Discovery discussions with anecdotal records and group assessments (as described in Chapters 4 and 13)
3. Teacher/student-made, curriculum-specific instruments (as illustrated in several chapters in this text)
4. Systematic observational record keeping
5. Informal reading inventories and informal writing inventories
6. Reading miscue inventories and running records
7. Retellings
8. Portfolios, performance assessments, and exhibits
9. Self-assessments

Collecting Observational Data

The first four categories overlap somewhat, and for discussion purposes these surveys and other observational tools are grouped together here. Observations are valued as an assessment tool both because they include the components of effective assessment listed in Table 6.1, and because they document the affective, cognitive, social, and cultural contexts in which the literacy event occurs. Policy makers can underuse such observations, however, if they are not recorded systematically (Klenk & Palinscar, 1994). Another limitation is that different teachers might study similar types of information but vary in their interpretations of what these records illustrate (Hiebert, Hutchison, & Raines, 1991). With these limitations in mind, observational records can validly demonstrate whether literacy objectives have been attained during a grading period, especially those that do not employ papers and pencils—such as increasing pleasure while reading, expanding reading/writing/listening interests, increasing reading rate, or eliminating a specific decoding weakness.

Anecdotal records, mentioned briefly earlier in this chapter, are systematically made observations; they are most instructive when new abilities unfold. These records differ from teacher-made instruments in that prior goals to assess may not have been set by you or students, so instead the anecdotal record (or observational note) is used to document spontaneous growths as they occur. Anecdotal records are also valuable diagnostic–instructional–evaluative tools because they are the easiest method to discover valid and authentic patterns in students' literacy behavior, attitudes, and abilities. Through anecdotal records, these readers/writers' achievements can be documented as they work naturally, exert only self-pressure, and develop their own independent control over problems within their self-initiated levels of confidence and tenacity. Many teachers report that they see individual students' reading progress more clearly and specifically when anecdotal records are used (Rhodes & Natenson-Mejia, 1990). These teachers report that they can make notations without stopping the student's literacy activity to ask questions.

Some teachers keep self-stick mailing labels in their pockets or carry a clipboard—then write individual student notes throughout the school day as literacy activity is observed. They attach these notes to students' anecdotal record folders at the end of each school day.

The most valuable anecdotal records comprise a statement such as "When [student's name] was engaged in [activity description] at [specific time and date] with [description of material and group size], I noticed that _____." The record also notes the number of times this incident has occurred previously, how frequently, or how the intensity of this behavior distinguishes itself from previous incidents.

To illustrate, ask yourself what could have been included in the following anecdotal record to increase its effectiveness as an assessment of Juanita:

> I saw Juanita close her book just as she finished reading it. She clung to it and pulled it to her chest. She bowed her head down as if to block out all distractions as she relished the memories she had just read.

You likely wanted to know the context in which that reading occurred—what the book was about, how long the book was, what made the book so enjoyable, and so forth.

Let's try a second example. Consider what you would document about the following observation:

> I overheard Josie whisper to Monica, "You'll really like *The Cat in the Hat*. It's just like *Green Eggs and Ham!*"

Here is what Josie's teacher, Mrs. Rogers, actually wrote:

> On September 3, 2002, Josie recommended Dr. Seuss's *The Cat in the Hat* to Monica. This was the first time she connected two books to the same author and saw the similarities between two books. I asked why she recommended that book to Monica and she said it was because this was the first time she and a friend had to talk about a book they'd read. I asked if she'd like to read a book with Monica every Thursday and talk about it with her, then they could tell me what they learned on Friday. She said "Yes, that would be wonderful!" and smiled beamingly as she and Monica skipped outside hand in hand.

Many teachers also develop touchstone words to use in anecdotal records so that patterns between entries can be discerned (e.g., "No attempts were made today to _____" or "Sincere attempts were made today to _____ and were somewhat sustained" or "Attempts were successful today because _____ and engagement in _____ continued for _____ minutes").

Another way to increase the effectiveness of anecdotal records is to find convenient times in your instructional program and in your daily schedule to record your observations. For example, you could divide the number of students for whom you will make anecdotal records by the number of days in each week in which you direct the students. Then note in your lesson plan book to observe Michael and Joshua on Monday of the first week but on Tuesday, Wednesday, Thursday, and Friday of subsequent weeks so that you can detect performance levels on different days. Ideally, by varying the days on which you make anecdotal records, your assessments could assist students and their parents to discover patterns of performance at different times of the week.

For readers/writers at lower stages of development, you may find it helpful to begin with a checklist (see the sample in Table 6.2). As growths are noticed, extended comments about individual students can be made in the right column and then placed in a file box, notebook, or folder. Many teachers find it helpful to start slow, requiring themselves to notice only one student a day. It is also wise to establish a definite time and place for filing records, such as checking to be sure all students' records have been placed in their folders just before you turn out the light to go home every day.

Another type of anecdotal record is a group anecdotal record, such as that shown in Figure 6.3. Group anecdotal records document cooperative work and social development during literacy activities, two accomplishments that many struggling readers/writers seek.

Another record-keeping form is "kid watching," popularized by Yetta Goodman (1989). "Kid watching" is valuable because you do not establish in advance that you will observe a specific child on a certain day. Instead, you mingle and record literacy progress for several students. A variation is to give Figure 6.4 (p. 157) to an observer who is not normally involved in daily classroom activities—such as a parent, colleague, principal, or curriculum director. This person writes about accomplishments of individual students while they interact on self-initiated literacy activities, providing a fresh perspective for you and your students.

A final type of observational record that is particularly valuable for struggling readers/writers is obtained when you establish a weekly exchange between yourself and other literacy mentors of individual students (e.g., parents, older classmates, or resource teachers). Give these mentors checklists on which you have recorded specific goals. Then each student's instruction and assessments throughout the week (in Tier 3 and 4

TABLE 6.2 Assessing Levels of Emergent Reading		

Name _____

	Date Observed	Teaching Strategy

Recurring Principle
   Does the child use the same stroke creating
     "recurring" text in scribbles?
Directional and Flexibility Principles
   Does the child move his hand or head from left
     to right when viewing text and write/scribble
     from left to right?
   Does the child point to the left side as he or she
     attempts to read?
   Has vertical writing ceased?
   Does child recognize "I" and "T"?
Contrastive Principle
   Does the child write lowercase letters and capital
     letters correctly?
   Does the child say different sounds for different
     printed letters?
Abbreviation Principle
   Does the child draw a picture or lines that
     represent an idea?
   Does the child leave spaces between words?
Sign Principle
   Do written attempts resemble familiar signs
     (i.e., billboards, advertisements) available to
     the child?
   Does the child label objects in his/her picture?
   Does the child recognize labels in the room?		

support settings and at home) can be coordinated to these objectives. See Table 6.3 (p. 158) for an example of such a checklist, which Mr. Flores used to assess reading strategies for a group of his students. For some, however, the more open-ended format of Figure 6.4 is preferred, as it has the advantage of unrestricted, unprompted recall on the part of each mentor and allows more serendipitous accomplishments to be noted.

Informal Reading and Writing Inventories

Informal reading and writing inventories are among the most widely used forms of informal reading/writing diagnosis for struggling readers/writers. Many readers require this one-to-one diagnosis to reveal the depth of their strengths, potential, and personal

Were the team members' remarks relevant? Explain.

Yes, they were. They all expressed relevant ideas that were contributions to the group. Surprisingly, there was very little straying.

What was each student's level of participation?

There was pretty level participation from all the students. They all wanted to say their piece about the topic.

Explain your observations of the use of eye contact in speakers and listeners in your group.

There wasn't very much eye contact. Most of their eye contact was in passing. They pretty much kept their eyes on the books and worksheets they were working on.

Describe your observations of the students' participation in active listening.

The children made eye contact with the person speaking. They were absorbed by the person's words and came up with ideas that sprouted from the listening and raised questions.

Describe an incident that illustrates the sharing of ideas.

The children were learning how to use the Spanish articles Lo, Los, and Las. They talked and sounded out the articles' positions together. They put their ideas together to find an answer they found suitable.

Were the students able to accept diversity? Example.

Not applicable

Did the students "take turns" during the discussion? Explain.

The students did take turns on the discussion. They all had information they wanted to contribute and did so in an orderly fashion.

When did you observe an exchange of ideas? Example.

The children exchanged ideas throughout the entire lesson. They all gave something to the lesson to help them finish the project.

Give an example of a student's use of synthesis in rephrasing an idea(s) as presented.

At one point, one of the students was trying to explain an idea that two other students didn't understand. He restated the idea and used an example in a right and wrong way.

Comment on other aspects of your experience as a group observer.

All students worked surprisingly well together and finished the project very well!

FIGURE 6.3 Anecdotal Record Form for Group Interactions

Source: Adapted from B. C. Hill & C. A. Ruptic (1994), *Practical Aspects of Authentic Assessment,* p. 102. Norwood, MA: Christopher-Gordon. Copyright © 1994 by Christopher-Gordon Publishers, Inc. Used with permission.

1. BRYAN "My name's Bryan"	2. ROBERT "I wanna be a fish"	3. PRISCILLA "I like 'My Favorite House'"	4. DAN "I like to play with my dog"	5. STEPHEN "My favorite sport is basketball"	6. LADRAEYLN "Football & baseball"
7. LATICIA "Like to watch 'The Power Rangers'"	8. KRISTA "Color inside books" (Barney)	9. ADRIANNA "I like to spend time w/ Mom"	10. ANH THU "Like to play"	11.	12.
13.	14.	15.	16.	17.	18.
19.	20.	21.	22.	23.	24.

FIGURE 6.4 Kid-Watching Record Sheet

On the first day of school, to discern first grade students' level of literacy, Mrs. Ward asked students: "What do you like to do when you read and write?" or "What is it that makes you special?"

literacy barriers. **Informal reading and writing inventories** are commercially prepared or teacher/student-made tests in which students read orally and retell and/or answer comprehension questions over a passage. The purpose of the assessment is to identify the student's decoding and comprehension strengths and weaknesses, to ascertain the level at which the student functions independently and instructionally, and to observe how the student copes with frustration.

Informal reading inventories (IRIS) have been used widely since the mid-1940's. Typically, the commercially prepared IRIs differ from teacher/student-made versions in that they contain graded word lists and at least two passages that correspond to grade-leveled readability from preprimer through grade 6, 8, 9, 12, or adult levels.

Commercially prepared IRIs include the following and can be purchased from the publishers:

Analytical Reading Inventory (Merrill Publishing Company)
Bader Reading and Language Inventory (Macmillan Publishers)
Basic Reading Inventory (Kendall-Hunt Publishers)
Classroom Reading Inventory (William C. Brown Publishers)
Flynt-Cooter Reading Inventory (Gorwisch Publishers)
Ekwall Reading Inventory (Houghton Mifflin)

TABLE 6.3 Reading Strategies Checklist

Name _____

E = uses strategy in a consistently *E*ffective way

S = strategy is *S*ometimes used effectively and sometimes ineffectively

I = uses strategy in consistently *I*neffective way

N = *N*ot observed to use strategy

	Text & Date *Christina*	Text & Date *Connie*	Text & Date *Cristobal*	Text & Date *Peter*	Text & Date *Reyna*	Text & Date *Larry*
Looks back	S	S	S	S	E	S
Rereads	S	S	S	S	E	S
Skips	N	N	N	S	N	S
Substitutes word	N	S	N	S	N	S
Asks for help	N	E	N	S	S	N
Uses graphophonic cues	S	E	S	N	N	N
Uses pictures/visual cues	S	E	S	S	N	N
Uses context	N	S	S	N	N	N
Uses background information	S	S	S	N	E	N
Self-corrects miscues	E	S	S	S	S	S
Recognizes miscues	S	S	S	S	S	S

Recommendations

These children are good at looking back and rereading. They don't use graphophonic cues or context or background information very well. Perhaps it is because of the transitionary period that they are in. They recognized miscues and self-corrected them well. All of them were eager to read, which pleased me.

Informal Reading-Thinking Inventory (Harcourt Brace College Publishers)

Qualitative Reading Inventory (Scott Foresman)

Traditionally, the procedure for administrating an IRI goes something like this:

1. The student silently reads a grade-leveled passage from a commercial IRI or a 200-word passage that you have duplicated from a book you determine to be at or a little below the student's instructional reading level.

2. The student rereads the same passage orally, as you mark oral reading errors on your own copy of the passage.
3. The student answers 5 to 10 comprehension questions over the 200-word passage and/or retells the story.
4. Based on your observations, you determine readability levels for the student: *instructional* (just right), *independent* (easy), or *frustration* (too hard).
5. You then identify instructional objectives that use the student's demonstrated strengths to eliminate literacy barriers in decoding, comprehension, and affect.

In addition to knowing the foregoing steps, you will also need to develop a consistent system for noting observations when you administer an informal reading inventory. (Administering informal writing inventories will be covered in Chapter 11.) Symbols such as those that follow are helpful for marking miscalled words and make recording and analyzing results easier and more accurate.

USING SYMBOLS TO INDICATE DECODING ERRORS. The basic symbols presented here indicate specific types of reading errors. Refer to Figure 6.5 to see how they would be used to mark an IRI story. After reading the example in Figure 6.5, see Figure 6.6 for an analysis of the student's strengths and weakness. Then, as you read about the following symbols, try to detect the thinking done by Mr. Flores, the fifth grade teacher who completed the IRI in Figure 6.7 (p. 163).

○   *Circle any words the student does not read orally.* As the student reads the IRI story aloud, draw a circle around omitted words. (For instance, in Figure 6.7 the child omitted the word *the* and Mr. Flores circled it.)

Students can omit words for many reasons, and it is important that you correctly identify the reasons when you administer an IRI to a struggling reader. One question you can ask yourself for each omitted word is "Does the omission interfere with meaning?" If it does, the omission can be interpreted as evidence that this student is allocating too much attention to decoding, or perhaps that a previous decoding error resulted in loss of meaning. If omitting the word does not interfere with meaning, the student is likely concentrating so much on the meaning of the story that less important words are not spoken or are overlooked. This is not as serious an error as the former, but be aware that such errors could indicate the student is overrelying on past experiences with this subject matter to bolster his or her comprehension. Such errors could also mean that the child is reading too narrow a range of topics; if so, broadening his or her reading interests could be an advantageous goal.

∧   *Use a caret (the proofreading mark for insertions) to insert any words the student adds.* As the student reads the story, make a note of words he or she says that do not appear in the text. (For example, in Figure 6.7, Mr. Flores inserted the word *too* in the fifth line of the story when the student said it.)

To analyze insertion errors, again pay attention to meaning-related issues. In addition, if the inserted word adds to the meaning (by placing emphasis in a specific direction), this could indicate that the student is discerning the authors' unstated intentions and thus is understanding implied meanings. Insertion errors can also indicate that the student is very involved in the story, which is a good, not negative, quality. Unfortunately,

Air Pollution

refined
In the 16th century, Queen Elizabeth often ~~refused~~ to visit the city of London. She said that
A *dirty*   *A* *dirt*   *fowls*
the air was too ~~polluted~~. The ~~pollution~~ came from smoke from burning coal fires. When ~~fuels~~ are

A   *poison*
burned, they emit smoke that has ~~poisonous~~ gases. Most pollution today is caused by the same

thing.

pollution
About 85 percent of the air ~~pollutants~~ in the United States are found in smoke. The main
products   *and*
~~producers~~ of dangerous gases are cars, factories, and power plants. ⟨The⟩ burning of trash and

in
garbage also adds pollutants ~~to~~ the air.

blow   *R*
Some air pollutants ⟨are⟩ ~~blown~~ away by the wind. When the wind is not blowing, the smoke
Smōg   *Smōg*
does not go away. ~~Smog~~ results from a mix of fog and smoke. ~~Smog~~ usually happens in very large

cities. It looks like a dirt⟨y⟩ cloud.

sc
smōg   *harming*
The pollutants in smoke and ~~smog~~ ⟨can⟩ cause disease. Air pollution is ~~harmful~~ to the nose,
sc
throut   *treat*
~~throat~~, and lungs. It is a ~~threat~~ to our health.

146 words

Substitutions	10	Repetitions	1
Additions	1	Reversals	0
Omissions	4	Self-corrections	2
Words aided	3		

FIGURE 6.5 Informal Reading Inventory Story

insertions most often indicate that the student has lost his or her place in the text or is "buying time" while trying to decode an upcoming word that would fit the context. This student may be overrelying on context clues to the exclusion of other decoding strategies.

    //   *Use double slashes to indicate inappropriate pausing that interrupts the flow of sentences.* If the student pauses long enough when reading aloud to disrupt meaning, indicate the spot with two slash marks. (In Figure 6.7, for example, note the double slashes in the third and fourth lines of the story.)

Student *Mary*   Date of testing *8/16/93*

Passage grade level *5*

Text Word	Student's Response	Semantic Appropriateness	Syntactic Appropriateness	Graphic Similarity	Comments
refused	*refined*	*no*	✓	✓	*missed medial sound*
fuels	*fowls*	*no*	✓	✓	*missed medial sound*
poisonous	*poison*	✓	*no*	✓	*missed ending*
pollutants	*pollution*	✓	✓	✓	*ending*
producers	*products*	✓	✓	✓	*ending*
blown	*blow*	✓	*no*	✓	*ending*
smog	*smōg*	*?*	*?*	✓	*medial sound*
dirty	*dirt*	✓	*no*	✓	*ending*
threat	*treat*	*no*	✓	✓	*"thr"*

(continue on back if needed)   Reading Level: _____ Ind. _____ Inst. __✓__ Frus.

Word accuracy rate (number words correct/total words in passage) = *130/146 = 89%*

Self-correction (SC) rate (number self-corrections/total errors) = *2/19 = 10%*

Words aided or prompted (words given by examiner): *polluted   pollution   emit*

Comprehension accuracy rate (number correct/total questions) = *50%*

Solving strategies used (see questions to determine solving strategies):

  attends to graphic, particularly the initial sounds

  uses meaning clues

(continued)

FIGURE 6.6 Oral Reading Behavior Analysis Form

— 1. What causes air pollution? (burning gases; poisonous gases)
   smog

— 2. What is smog? (a mixture of smoke and fog)
   when the wind doesn't blow

— 3. Why does smog occur? (The pollutants are not blown away by the wind and they mix with the fog.)
   don't know

+ 4. Why does smog usually happen in large cities? (There's a lot of smoke from the factories and more cars in bigger cities.)
   They have lots of cars.

+ 5. Why is air pollution harmful to our health? (We breathe poisonous air and it can harm our lungs, etc.)
   It's bad for your health, your lungs and stuff.

— 6. What does *emit* mean? (give out; send out)
   have

+ 7. How is pollution today the same as pollution in the 16th century? (They burned coal which gave off pollution and we burn coal, oil, gasoline, and other gases.)
   because we burn things

+ 8. What is the main idea of this passage? (Air pollution is caused by the burning of fuels.)
   Air pollution is bad for us.

Oral Reading Summary Sheet

Student __Mary__	Grade __4__	Sex __F__
Birthdate __2/18/92__	Chronological Age __10__	
School __Fairfield Elem__	Teacher __Flores__	
Test Administered by __Gonzalez__	Date of Testing __8/16/02__	
Independent reading level __3.4__	Instructional reading level __4__	
Frustration reading level __5__	Listening level __N.A.__	

Reading Strengths

   - uses meaning cues, visual cues (graphic)
   - attends to initial phonic cues, comprehension skills

Reading Needs

   - some medial sounds may need review
   - few self-corrections (Is she monitoring as she reads?)

Instructional Recommendations

   Review medial sounds, perhaps review analogy method, work with metacognitive strategies. Increase silent reading opportunities and give a structured vocabulary program.

FIGURE 6.6 *(continued)*

MOTIVATIONAL STATEMENT: When this story begins, a man has just brought a dog to Jack and Ned. Read to find out more about them.

Jack looked at (the) little dog.

"We take care of all pets."

$$\overset{P}{}$$
All day Ned and Jack//took dogs.
$$\overset{SC}{}\ \overset{P}{}$$
They//took big dogs.
$$\overset{SC}{}\ \overset{SC}{}\ \overset{too}{}$$
And they took many,little dogs.

Ned looked at the dogs.

(Then) he looked at Jack.

"We have many dogs," said Ned.
$$\overset{P}{}$$
"How many do we have?"

"One, two, (three) . . .

"One, two, (three) . . .

Oh, Ned. I don't know.

Let's say we have fifteen dogs."

$$\overset{SC}{}$$
"Look, Jack," said Ned.

"Here is a man with a big cat.
$$\overset{R}{}$$
We don't want to (take) care of a cat, do we?"

"Oh yes," said Jack.
$$\overset{took}{}$$
"We take care of all pets."

Source: From R. H. Ross & M. LaPray (1978), "Pet-sitters Take Care of All Pets," in *Magic Rings and Funny Things,* pp. 16–19. Chicago: Rand McNally.

COMPREHENSION QUESTIONS

_____ main idea   1. What were Jack and Ned doing all day? (They were taking care of big and little dogs.)

_____ detail   2. What type dogs did Jack and Ned take? (big and little dogs—all kinds)

_____ detail   3. How many times did Jack try to count the dogs? (twice)

_____ detail   4. How many dogs did they think they had? (fifteen)

_____ detail   5. Did the boys know exactly how many dogs they had? (no) Why did you say that? (They gave up counting and Jack said he didn't know.)

__X__ sequence   6. What was the last pet that was brought to Jack and Ned? (a big cat)

_____ detail   7. How did Jack answer the question "We don't want to take care of a cat, do we?" (Yes. We take care of all pets.)

__X__ inference   8. Why might Ned not want to take care of a cat? (Dogs don't like cats and they had many dogs; Ned thinks they have enough pets to care for.)

Note: Do not count as miscues mispronunciation of the names *Jack* and *Ned.* You may pronounce these words for the student if needed.

FIGURE 6.7 Sample of Informal Reading Inventory

Pauses that are appropriately placed (so as to not interrupt meaning) but are inappropriate in length usually indicate that the student lacks confidence in his or her reading ability. On the other hand, excessive and inappropriate pausing can indicate that the student has lost the meaning of the passage, has become confused, or cannot decode the next word and is buying time in hopes you will pronounce it.

R   *Use an R to indicate repeated words.* When the student repeats a word that he or she just read, write an *R* above that word. (For example, when the student repeated the word *to* near the end of the story in Figure 6.7, Mr. Flores wrote an *R* above it to note the error.)

When the repeated word does not disrupt meaning—such as "oh, oh, my" instead of "oh, my"—it could simply be that the student is reading according to his or her own dialect or oral language pattern; such errors are not serious. Most often, however, repetition indicates that the reader cannot decode the next word without hesitating, and so uses the repetition to buy time. This student may have somewhat more confidence than peers who pause inappropriately, but basically most repetitions indicate limited decoding abilities or a loss of place through mind wandering, confusion, or lack of comprehension. By noticing the types of words or beginning consonant/vowel patterns that characterize the words after pauses and repetitions, you can obtain data on which to base the student's future decoding instruction.

took   *Write the word the student says when it is not the word in the passage.* When the student says the wrong word, write that word above the correct word. (In our example in Figure 6.7, Mr. Flores wrote "took" above the word *take* when the student misread it.)

A student's saying words incorrectly is a very valuable clue to that student's decoding and comprehension processes. If the substitution extends the meaning by providing a richer word, this suggests that the printed word may be known but just overlooked in lieu of a word that more accurately describes the vivid image the reader has in mind. For example, if a reader enjoys books about horses and substitutes "stable" for the word *barn* in "Jim took the horse to the barn," the substitution provides only limited evidence of a specific problem in decoding or comprehension. On the other hand, if the word does not maintain meaning, you have an indication that instruction to strengthen use of context clues would be valuable.

SC   *Use SC to indicate words the student self-corrects.* When the student miscalls a word the first time but self-corrects before reading the next word, write *SC* above it. (In our example in Figure 6.7, the student made self-corrections in the fourth and fifth lines of the story.)

Self-corrections are not counted as errors by some reading experts. You may wish to note them to help you determine if attention and comprehension are sustained to the end of each sentence. If so, the student's self-corrections will be evenly spaced among the sentences read. On the other hand, if self-corrections occur only in short sentences, you have evidence that understanding complex sentences may be difficult. Other patterns can be discerned from self-corrections as well. For instance, try to determine whether self-corrections are made only on sight words, or only with words you know have appeared in books the student has previously read, or only with phonetically regular words.

P   Use a P *to indicate words you pronounce for the student.* When you have waited for 5 seconds (and counted that time by lowering your five fingers, slowly, out of sight of the student's eyes), pronounce the word for the student and write *P* above it. (In Figure 6.7, you can see that Mr. Flores had to pronounce the word *took* for his student.)

When you have to pronounce a word for a student, you have good evidence that the word is unknown to this reader. By analyzing why this word may have been at the student's frustration level, you can determine which activities from Chapter 9 should be included in future instruction.

DISCUSSING THE STORY WITH THE STUDENT. After the student has finished reading the IRI story aloud, you should ask comprehension questions and/or ask for a retelling of the story, as specified in the five steps in administering an IRI that were presented earlier. Record the student's answers and statements.

Then show the student the symbols you marked and explain them. Perform think alouds as to the types of thoughts the student could have been having at the time each oral and comprehension error was made, then ask the student if your think alouds are correct. Suggest what the student could think about when similar words and concepts occur in future reading. You can also ask the student to reread the passage and explain his or her thinking as he or she corrects (or remakes) each error. As the student reads, take notes as to points of improvement in decoding, reading speed, and strategy use that you want to discuss. As soon as this second oral reading is complete, ask the comprehension questions again and write any comments, beyond the answers given on the first reading, that the student makes. Then discuss your observations with the student and point out the improvements made.

You can also show the student how you determined whether this story should be read by him without anyone's assistance (independent level), with assistance (instructional level), or not until later in the year (frustration level). (You will learn to make these calculations in the discussion that follows.) Ask if the student notices a pattern in the errors made. Discuss the pattern you think exists. Establish an instructional goal for the week based on the IRI's data. Complete the summary sheet in Figure 6.6 and file it in the student's folder. Also, if you are able to use a separate tape for each child during the entire school year, place the tape in that student's folder as well.

DETERMINING READING LEVELS FROM AN IRI. The most popular formula for computing reading levels appears in Table 6.4. In recent decades some have questioned the number of errors used as criteria for determining a student's independent, instructional, and frustrational reading levels. Reviews of research by Powell and Dunkeld (1971) and McKenna (1983) conclude, however, that reading levels established half a century ago are still valid, if not rigidly adhered to, and that Powell's (1968) criteria can be used to account for student differences in sociocultural backgrounds. Specifically, if a student repeatedly omits the same word a total of 11 times but makes no other errors, the passage could still be considered at the child's independent level if the error did not disrupt meaning. Using the criteria in Table 6.4, you can determine each child's

TABLE 6.4 Betts's and Powell's Criteria for Reading Levels

The Betts Criteria

Reading Level	Word Recognition (percent correct)	Comprehension (percent correct)
Independent	99% and above	90% and above
Instructional	95–98%	75–89%
Frustration	90% and below	50% and below

To use the Betts criteria, the teacher compares the percentage of correct scores to those in the chart. For example, Brian, a third grader, scored 100 percent on word recognition and comprehension on the third grade passage. Then on the fourth grade passage, which had 215 total words and 8 comprehension questions, he had 12 word recognition errors and 6 comprehension errors. According to the formulas, Brian had 94 percent correct in word recognition and 25 percent correct in comprehension:

$$\frac{215 - 12}{215} = 94\% \qquad \frac{8 - 6}{8} = 25\%$$

When Brian's performance is compared to the chart, he is close to the instructional reading level in word recognition on the fourth grade passage but definitely at a frustration level in comprehension. Based on these results, Brian should be placed in a high third grade reader.

The Powell Criteria

To use the Powell criteria (Powell, 1968), the teacher applies the same formulas for word recognition and comprehension percentages as when using the Betts criteria. Powell, however, established differentiated criteria according to the level of the passage as shown in the table below. The teacher locates in the left column the grade level of the passage administered to the child. Next, the teacher compares the student's word recognition and comprehension scores with those to the right of the passage level. This comparison determines the child's reading level.

Passage Grade Level	Word Recognition (percent correct)	Comprehension (percent correct)	Reading Level
2nd and below	94% and above	81% and above	Independent
	87–93%	55–80%	Instructional
	below 87%	below 55%	Frustration
3rd to 5th	96% or greater	85% and above	Independent
	92–95%	60–85%	Instructional
	Below 92%	below 60%	Frustration
6th and above	97% or greater	91% and above	Independent
	94–96%	65–90%	Instructional
	below 94%	below 65%	Frustration

Source: Adapted from L. Bader (1994), *Bader Reading and Language Inventory,* p. 10. Columbus, OH: Macmillan. Used with permission.

performance on individual IRIs. The reason Powell's levels are more lenient is that they take into account the increased familiarity older students bring to reading because of their more extensive exposures to different content, genre, and print structures than younger students.

To illustrate and practice determining the levels of readability, start with word recognition. Take the total number of words in the passage read, subtract the number of errors made, and divide by the number of words in the passage. Then assess comprehension by taking the total number of comprehension questions asked, subtracting the number missed, and dividing by the total number asked. Multiply these answers by 100 to determine percentage. For simplicity's sake, use Figure 6.7 as an example; it was a 100-word passage with 8 comprehension questions. The student made 15 errors in decoding and 2 in comprehension, so the formulas to determine word recognition and comprehension would look like the following:

$$\frac{100 - 15 \times 100}{100} = 85\% \qquad \frac{8 - 2 \times 100}{8} = 75\%$$

Therefore, because this child is a first grade student, this passage and similar books would fall within the student's instructional level of readability.

When readability levels have been computed, remember that it is important to interpret this information for the student. You can do so by explaining that the student can read independent reading level materials by himself or herself with fluency and good comprehension. With such books this student will likely experience the pleasure of problem-free reading. Also point out that if a book is slightly more difficult, the student may need to ask for assistance with word meanings from a peer or you. At this point, you may want to teach the "five-finger method" of judging book difficulty. Explain that when the reader selects a book, that reader should hold up five fingers and turn one in towards the palm each time he or she comes to an unfamiliar word. If all five fingers are turned in before he or she has read a full page, that book is likely at the student's frustration level: Literacy limitations may make the reading less pleasurable than with another book on the same topic. You can close this discovery discussion by defining **frustration level** as the point at which a book has so many difficult words and concepts that even with several supports in place the main ideas may not be understood.

SETTING NEW INSTRUCTIONAL OBJECTIVES. The procedure for administering an IRI ends with your analysis of the student's decoding and comprehension errors to determine instructional objectives. Work out a program that utilizes the student's demonstrated strengths to eliminate the student's literacy weaknesses. There are several ways you can use the IRI data to accomplish this.

To start, point out at least three strengths you noticed in your student's reading. For example, in Figure 6.7 notice that the student comprehended all major details, identified the author's main idea, and had the confidence to self-correct four times (or at least once every 25 words). You could share this information and your praise to open a discovery discussion with this reader. Ask if he or she agrees that these are newly developing literacy strengths. Ask the student how these strengths developed, why they are valuable, and how he or she can use them to continue to improve.

Another way to use the IRI data to set instructional objectives is to look at the type of error made most frequently and ask the student if he or she is aware of using this strategy when difficulties occur in reading. If so, ask why it is used and what the student would like to learn to avoid having to rely on it. For example, in Figure 6.7, the most frequent error this student made was to omit words. You would ask the student why he or she did not read these words orally.

You should analyze words on which the student made errors to see if there is a common characteristic. For example, in Figure 6.7 this student made errors when a word began with the letters *t, th,* or *thr.* By asking if the characteristic you identify is causing difficulties, you can move closer to an instructional directive that will increase this student's reading power.

Compare misread words that were self-corrected to those that were not. If no pauses or other miscues preceded or followed the self-correction, you can assume that the student is using phonic clues. If the student paused before the self-correction, phonic analysis is inaccurate or ineffective for the student's processing of this particular passage. Similarly, if the student substituted words that are semantically and grammatically unacceptable, contextual clues are not operating effectively for this reader.

If you determine that oral reading interferes with the student's comprehension or is word-by-word, then reading fluency instruction will assist the student with both decoding and comprehension accuracy. To discern if lack of fluency is a result of decoding weaknesses, ask the student to read a text that is very easy for that student to read. If fluency problems continue, you have eliminated the possibility that decoding weakness is the cause.

As you analyze the IRI data, ask yourself if any errors were dialect-related or a result of the reader's second-language clues. If the miscue simply reflects a different sound system in the reader's dialect, additional instruction relative to that word and its word family members may not be warranted. Alternatively, if the dialectical error reflects imperfect knowledge of English grammar, additional instruction can eliminate future difficulties. For example, some of the most common dialectical and second language errors that you may want to instruct include the following:

- Use of an incorrect verb ending (e.g., "he wanted to goed")
- Omission of individual letter sounds in words (e.g., "picher" for *pitcher* or *picture*)
- Improper verb agreements (e.g., "she are going")

If previous instructional strategies included changes in the student's reading time, now is a good time to discuss these changes with the reader. Ask whether the increase or decrease in reading time seems to be an improvement and why. Also ask what new strategies the student has learned in this session that should be included in weekly goals. Consider all the IRI data you obtained, and ask the student to write a summary report with you to go in his or her conference folder as well as to parents and other adults he or she identifies.

Reading Miscue Inventories and Running Records

After IRIs, the next most widely used informal tests are miscue inventories and running records. **Reading miscue inventories** (RMIs) were first published in 1973 but revised by

Goodman, Watson, and Burke in 1987. While the RMI is very similar in its procedures to the IRI, the RMI coding system is more extensive. Also, RMIs focus more on analyzing the types of miscues individual students make than on obtaining a measure of reading ability. Comprehension is measured through student retellings and probing questions, with the analysis of miscues suggesting strategies a student uses to comprehend (Goodman, 1989).

A weakness of RMIs is that the *RMI Manual* (1983) and *RMI Alternatives* (1973) by Kenneth Goodman provide few instructional guidelines, and many of the grammatical and semantic forms of miscues are too complex to explain to students. Although some teachers find that RMIs extend their understanding of individual students' strengths and weaknesses over time, others consider IRI data to be sufficient. Because the data that RMIs, running records, and IRIs provide are similar to each other, you may prefer to develop expertise in conducting only RMIs, running records, or IRIs first. Then, if you desire additional information concerning the specific types of miscues individual students are making, and/or the reasons why comprehension may not be developing adequately, you can read an RMI manual or ask that other types of individualized oral reading and comprehension measures be administered by a reading specialist in your district. Some districts prefer that all students receive IRIs, RMIs, and running records from a reading specialist.

Running records were developed by Marie Clay and are described in depth in *The Early Detection of Reading Difficulties* (1985) and *Reading Recovery: A Guidebook for Teachers in Training* (1993b). They are similar to miscue inventories in that they enable you to analyze every word a student reads, whether each word was read properly or improperly, and how each word supported or interrupted comprehension. Running records provide information about vowel errors, consonant errors, insertions of extra sounds in a word (e.g., "black" is said for *back* or "flat" for *fat*), omissions of sounds in a word (e.g., *brought* is pronounced "bought"), and strategies students depend on when their decoding and comprehension are impaired. Clay noted in 1985 that running records are "more adapted to the teacher's needs in day to day activities of the classroom, particularly for those who teach young children" (1985, p. 17). Since that time, however, many upper-grade teachers have also found running records equally effective for older readers.

RUNNING RECORD PROCEDURES. After reading through Figure 6.8, make two photocopies of a 100- to 200-word passage and ask a student to read the passage aloud from the original book as you tape-record the reading and mark the errors (described in the next paragraph). Although running records were originally designed to use a blank sheet of paper to mark these errors, many teachers prefer to make a copy of the passage and to mark errors above each word, as shown in Figure 6.8.

To take a running record, make a check above the text (or on the blank sheet of paper) for each word that the student reads correctly. For each word read incorrectly, you can use the same symbols used in IRIs. Here are the steps to follow:

1. Write every word miscalled, and place a check above every word read accurately.
2. Write *A* if the child appeals for your help, and *T* if you told the word.
3. If the child finger-points, place a dot over the word.

Name of child: _David L_____   Name of teacher: _____

Date of observation: ___6 Nov 2002___

No. of words: ___172___   Words per minute: ___190 seconds; 53.4 wpm___

Story title: ___Seeing the School Doctor___

✓   everybody ✓ ✓ ✓
1. Yesterday everyone in our grade

went (SC) ✓ ✓ ✓   ✓
had to see the school doctor.

✓ nu —(SC) ✓ ✓ ✓ ✓✓
         noise
2. The nurse took six children at a   Looked at
                                             pictures
✓ ✓ ✓ ____ ✓   to decode
time to the spare room.   nurse.

✓ thr (T) ✓ ✓ ✓ ✓ ✓
      though
3. We thought we were going to have   Studied
                                       picture of
   (T)   int—sons   syringe.
injections. inc—   in—ter—s
             in—ter—s

R ✓ ✓ ✓ (arksed) ✓ ✓ ✓ ✓ the
4. First the nurse asked us to look at (a)
                                        Picture below
chain (SC) (TTA)   text. Turned
chart.   page without
                                        reading text.
                                        Returned to
                                        missed page.

✓ ✓ ✓ ✓ ✓
5. She was testing our eyes.

✓ ✓ checkerd ✓ ✓ R✓ hear (SC) ✓
      check-er
6. Then she checked our ears to see if

✓ ✓ see (SC) ✓ (SC) from end of
we could hear properly.   sentence

Maria (T) ✓ (T) ✓ ✓ ✓
7. Mario and Toula did not understand

✓ ✓ ✓ ✓ ✓ didn't
what she was saying. They don't

✓ ✓
speak English.

✓ ✓ ✓ ✓ ✓ ✓✓ ✓ ✓
8. Next she looked at our hair to see if

✓ ✓ ✓
it was clean.

✓ ✓ ✓ ✓ ✓✓ ✓
9. She undid my pony tail so she

                              Pot
✓ ✓ ✓ ✓ ✓ po— (T)   Looked all
could look at my hair properly. over page
                                 for clues.

✓ ✓ ✓✓ ✓ ✓ were (SC)
10. Then, one at a time, we went

R ✓ ✓ ✓ ✓ ✓
behind the screen to the doctor.

✓ ✓ saw (SC) ✓ ✓ ✓ ✓✓ ✓
11. The doctor was a big man in a white

✓
coat.

Ax (T) ✓ ✓ ✓ ✓ ✓✓ ✓
12. Alex cried. He would not take off his

✓   Giggles
clothes.

✓ ✓ ✓ ✓ ✓ •
13. The nurse had to undress him.   Laughing

✓ ✓ ✓ ✓ ✓ • ✓
14. When it was my turn I undressed

✓ • ___ ✓ under✓ ✓ ✓ ✓• started
myself right down to my T-shirt and finger-
                                     pointing
✓ •
pants.

R ✓ • ✓ • (TTA) ✓ ✓ ✓ ✓
15. The doctor listened to my heart.
                                   Looked at
✓ ✓ ✓ at ✓ ✓ ✓ in ✓ pictures
Then he looked in my mouth and my for
                                   listened
• ✓   and then
ears.   heart.

✓ ✓ ✓✓ ✓ ___ ✓
16. He told me I was very healthy.

FIGURE 6.8 Sample Running Record

Source: Adapted from L. Wilson (1991), "Seeing the School Doctor," in *City Kids.* New York: Scholastic.

4. Compute the error-to-accuracy rate using the same formulas as for IRIs. An accuracy rate of less than 90 percent indicates that this text was too difficult for the student to understand fully.

5. Compute the oral reading fluency rate, self-correction rate, and teacher intervention or dependence rate. You figure these rates by counting the number of words read and dividing that number by the number of minutes it took to read those words (200 words in 10 minutes is an oral fluency rate of 20 words per minute); counting the self-corrections made in a sample of 100 words and dividing the number of self-corrections by 100 (7 self-corrections in 100 words is a self-correction rate of .07, or 7 percent); and counting the number of teacher interventions in a sample of 100 words and dividing that number by 100 (10 teacher interventions in 100 words is a dependence rate of .10, or 10 percent).

6. After a period of instruction with the student using other reading material, return to the second photocopy you made of the original story and complete a second running record. Compare results.

When self-correction rates increase, you know the student is seeing errors that he or she may not have considered previously. If insertions and omissions make a difference to meaning, you can assume that the student is not using prediction skills well. Alternatively, if meanings are not altered and mainly redundant words are omitted, you have an indication that the student's reading power is increasing; the child's expectations and predictions about the text are becoming stronger and more accurate because he or she is not relying on every word in the text. Similarly, the nature of substitutions is critical; if nouns are substituted for nouns and verbs for verbs, for instance, then the child is aware that syntactic patterns need to be preserved; if these substitutions are close in meaning, then you know that the student is also using semantic clues. See Box 6.1 for instructions on how to administer and use running records to inform instruction.

DeFord (1993) cautions that interpretations made from running records are highly subjective. You will construct reasons for students' errors based on your philosophy of what good reading is. You make decisions through inferences about readers' behaviors—for example, explaining errors as not looking for all the visual clues, not monitoring comprehension, not self-correcting, or not searching for alternative meanings. To illustrate, in DeFord's research six teachers cited six different explanations as to why a reader called "like" for the word *all*.

Retellings

While running records provide in-depth information about readers who are weak decoders, you can use retellings to evaluate readers with weak comprehension abilities. **Retellings** are informal assessments in which you ask students to tell in their own words, what they just read in a passage. Some teachers tape-record students' retellings for extended analysis.

If you want to assess students' abilities to summarize, retention, and other metacognitive processes, listen to their retellings of longer passages. If you want to assess students' inferencing abilities and vocabulary knowledge, listen to their retellings of shorter passages. Irwin and Mitchell (1983) recommend that you assign levels to

6.1 DIAGNOSIS AND ASSESSMENT

Analysis of Running Records for Instructional Intervention

Record everything a student says while reading aloud.

Accurate reading	✓ ✓ ✓ The cat is . . .	Mark every correct word with a check.
Substitution	was were	The word attempted is written over the word in the text.
Omission	— oven	Record an omission with a dash above the word in the text.
Insertion	a —	The word inserted is placed above the line and a dash is placed below.
Self-correction	ran ∣ sc running ∣	Write the word said, then "sc" for self-correction. No error is counted.
Repetition	ro rock ∣ R2 ro rock ∣	A repetition is not an error and often results in self-correction.
Told	— ∣ fled ∣ T	If the student makes no attempt, tell him or her to try it. If the student is still stuck, tell him or her the word and write "T."
Appeal and told	— ∣ A ∣ rabbit ∣ ∣ T	If the student appeals for help, tell him or her to try it. If the student cannot continue, tell him or her the word.

When you look at each miscues and self-correction tally the number of times that struggling readers used the following strategies:

	M	S	V

- **M** for meaning—does this make sense? (semantics)
- **S** for structure—does this sound right? (syntax)
- **V** for visual information—does this look right? (graphophonics)

The category with the highest total indicates the student's first strength in decoding; the lowest total is his or her weakest strategy and may indicate an area for instructional intervention.

evaluate the "richness of retellings" (p. 394), as shown by the categories in Table 6.5. In this way students are given credit for the summarization, elaboration, and inference processes they demonstrate. Students can also use these criteria to establish new goals for higher levels of comprehension.

TABLE 6.5 Judging Richness of Retellings

The matrix below evaluates retellings in a holistic fashion on the basis of criteria similar to a procedure used to grade written compositions. This technique is an alternative to questioning for assessment of student comprehension of both narrative and expository text.

	5	4	3	2	1
Generalizes beyond text	X				
Thesis (summarizing) statement	X	X			
Major points	X	X	X	?	?
Supporting details	X	X	X	X	?
Supplementations	Relevant	Relevant	Relevant	Irrelevant	Irrelevant
Coherence	High	Good	Adequate	Some	Poor
Completeness	High	Good	Adequate	Some	Poor
Comprehensibility	High	Good	Adequate	Some	Poor

Source: P. A. Irwin & J. N. Mitchell (1983), "A Procedure for Assessing the Richness of Retellings," *Journal of Reading, 26,* p. 395. Reprinted by permission of the authors and the International Reading Association.

As you interpret each retelling, ask yourself the following questions:

1. *Is this student merely telling me what he or she thinks I want to hear?* If you believe so, when the student finishes, add one additional prompt and say: "That is good. If I were not here and you were talking to the author of the book, what would you want the author to know?"

2. *Is the student reporting only facts because he or she may think that is the appropriate behavior in "testing situations"?* If you think so, when the student is finished, ask: "What was the most important message the author gave, in your opinion?"

3. *Does the student seem uncomfortable using this form of oral assessment?* If so, ask the student to write what he or she remembers from the story. If the student is still uncomfortable, ask three students to work together to write a group retelling. You can use this group retelling to tell you the depth and breadth of their comprehension. On the next day, ask for individual retellings.

4. *Have I considered this student's individual needs and personality in my interpretation?* Try to give prompts that will elicit the student's full understanding.

One of the most important values of retellings is that they capture dimensions of comprehension ability that are not always obvious when students are required to answer specific questions about a reading that was not important to them. Moreover, if you rely too heavily on written responses to assess interpretations—especially with second-language readers—the invalidity is increased (Garcia & Pearson, 1993).

❖ Ideas for the Collection Portfolio ❖

- Writing samples
  - *A writing process "package" showing an assignment taken from rough draft through the editing and revision process to the final polished draft*
  - *Writing samples showing different parts of the process*
  - *Writing prompts and rubrics associated with samples*
  - *Writing done for content areas such as social studies or science*
  - *Writing inventory or checklist*
  - *Research reports*
  - *Interview notes*
  - *Writing samples reflecting different genres*
  - *Journal or learning log entries (photocopies)*
- Reading inventories or checklists
- Responses to reading
  - *Book reports/reviews*
  - *Open-ended questions with scoring rubrics*
- Tape recordings of oral reading
- Photographs of projects and activities
- Videotapes of skits, activities, etc.
- Mathematics checklist and mathematics problem-solving samples
- Introductory note to potential audience
  - *Parents*
  - *Interested educators*
  - *Guests*
  - *Explanations of criteria for selection*

❖ Ideas for the Showcase Portfolio ❖

- A selection of items from the Collection Portfolio
  - *Best work*
  - *Growth over time*
- Student's reflections on selections or general progress
- The self-esteem folder
  - *Memorabilia*
  - *Newspaper clippings and photos*
  - *Team photos*
  - *Awards*
  - *Snapshots*
  - *Playbills from productions they wrote*

❖ Ideas for the Teacher–Student Assessment Portfolio ❖

- Photocopies of material from the Showcase Portfolio
- Anecdotal records
- Conference records
- Interest inventories
- Teacher-made tests
  - *Unit tests*
  - *Open-ended tests*
  - *District test scores*
  - *Standardized test scores*
- Student evaluations of teacher and self

❖ Ideas for the Teacher Resource Portfolio ❖

- Reference to passages in books
- Student evaluations of teacher
- Notes from peer coaching
- Articles from education magazines and journals
- Notes from education classes and in-services
- Copies of administrative evaluations

FIGURE 6.9 What to Put in Portfolios

Source: Adapted from B. C. Hill & C. A. Ruptic (1994), *Practical Aspects of Authentic Assessment,* p. 15. Norwood, MA: Christopher-Gordon. Used with permission.

Portfolios

Student portfolios and performance assessments are particularly valuable to struggling readers/writers. They focus on each student's achievements over time instead of comparing individual performances to those of other students. Portfolios include anecdotal records, notes from teacher observation and teacher–student conferencing, book logs, and student samples. They may include logs of students' voluntary reading, journals, videotapings of book dramatizations, student writings, research projects, laboratory reports, science learning logs, and oral histories, as shown in Figure 6.9. In Figure 6.10 you see how to use portfolios to document each student's literacy growth and communicate this information to the student, parents, and colleagues. To illustrate the variety of items possible, even at the first grade level, one teacher during the first recording period placed the following items in a struggling reader's portfolio: student drawings of themselves as readers, results of oral interviews about their understanding of literary concepts, a parent questionnaire, standardized test results, first writing sample of the year, and a reading record form.

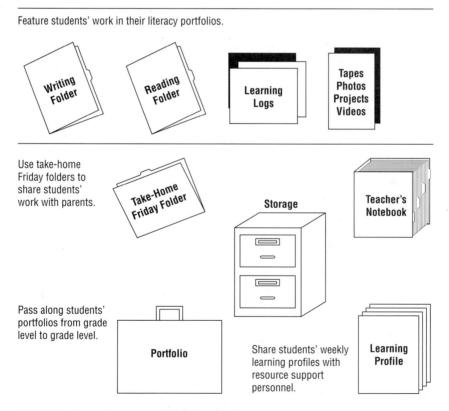

FIGURE 6.10 How to Utilize Portfolios

Source: Adapted from B. C. Hill & C. A. Ruptic (1994), *Practical Aspects of Authentic Assessment,* p. 27. Norwood, MA: Christopher-Gordon. Used with permission.

Portfolios provide multiple lenses so that you (and your students) can see a broader spectrum of the achievements each reader makes to visualize a wider potential. They demonstrate three types of progress. First, students can select and highlight their best work in the showcase portfolio (Valencia, 1990). Second, evidence of student progress over the entire grading period or year can become a documentation portfolio. Third, a process portfolio can be made so students can store and explain sections of an ongoing project or process goal that they are working to achieve. In addition, some teachers have a section in the portfolios of less accomplished students for documenting transfer of literacy to other content areas and out-of-school contexts.

Valencia (1990) explains another value of portfolios for struggling readers/writers:

Developing artists rely on portfolios to demonstrate their skills and achievements. Within the portfolio, the students include samples of their work that exemplify the depth and breadth of their expertise. They may include many different indicators: work in a variety of media to demonstrate their versatility, several works on one particular subject to demonstrate their refined skill and sophistication, and work collected over time to exemplify their growth as [literacy] artists. Within such rich sources of information, it is easier for the critics and the teachers, and most importantly, the artists themselves, to understand the development of expertise and to plan the experiences that will encourage additional progress and showcase achievements. A portfolio approach to the assessment of reading assumes the position that [struggling readers/writers] deserve no less. (p. 338)

Evidence suggests that portfolios enable readers/writers to explain and appreciate their ongoing development, understand the complexity of literacy products they have mastered, and reflect collaboratively with teachers and parents about what they want to learn (Au, 1994; Paris et al., 1992; Valencia, Hiebert, & Afflerbach, 1994). Portfolios providing information about the following:

- The number and diversity of genres students are exploring in their reading

- The length of the books students read in a given week, grading period, or year

- Less successful students' feelings about reading/writing as it relates to individual works they select

- Ways that next year's teacher can begin to tie instruction more closely to struggling readers/writers' zones of proximal development in writing and reading competencies

- How the steps and stages in reading/writing development are unfolding for each student, and what holes exist in the reading program

- What students have learned and retained from individual lessons, as evidence of the effectiveness of specific teaching methods for individual students

- The strength of students' decision-making abilities as they compare and contrast entries in portfolios

- Students' perceptions of themselves as readers and the degree to which they feel they control their abilities to understand what they read and to express their ideas/feelings/positions in writing (Valencia, Hiebert, & Afflerbach, 1994)

Because they can include items of virtually limitless variety, portfolios are the type of informal assessment that captures the scattered pattern and breadth of individual students' literacy profiles. For instance, California English and language arts teachers reported that portfolios enabled them to individualize writing instruction, have documents available for parent conferences, give importance to daily writings, reduce the grading of paperwork, coordinate schoolwide projects such as writings for the community, and make the zone of proximal development for individual readers visible (*Portfolio News,* 1990). In classrooms that do not keep portfolios, 63 percent of teachers attributed the successes of struggling readers/writers to medication or Tier 3 or 4 pull-out programs. With portfolios, 82 percent credit these readers' successes to the quality and quantity of objectives that they and the student accomplished together. Moreover, when less accomplished readers were not assessed at least in part by portfolios, they and many of their teachers could not cite specific growths and goals for the upcoming week (Place, 1993). Alternatively, those who had portfolios reflected on specific ways they still wanted to improve, and many realized the importance of practicing their reading. They also began to assume greater responsibility for their own learning (Dewitz & Palm, 1993).

IMPLEMENTING PORTFOLIO ASSESSMENT. Perhaps the most difficult aspect of portfolio assessment is to ensure that portfolios do not merely become extremely large folders. Students must learn to select and explain entries for portfolios so that others understand the significance of each piece. Through the implementation presented here, portfolios will accomplish this function and teach less accomplished students how to take responsibility for their own literacy learning.

To begin, you can hold at least one full-class conversation about portfolios every grading period. Describe the following three areas of development that should be in their portfolios:

1. Showcasing the best work
2. Demonstrating progress over time
3. Documenting ongoing, individual literacy processes and product goals

At these assessment conversations, demonstrate how students can select and compare items within their portfolios to address these three areas (Henning-Stout, 1994).

You should also instruct students to date pieces as they are entered, then to select samples that demonstrate specific reading/writing abilities. For example: "Please select one piece in the next few weeks that shows me how good a writer you are. Be sure to include the date you wrote this sample. Staple a cover paragraph to it that explains what growth this writing demonstrates." Or: "Select one section of all your tape-recorded readings that illustrates the power of your reading ability. Wind your tape to the beginning of that segment and put it in an envelope on which you have written the date it was recorded and what you particularly want me to notice about your reading."

Teach students how to give reasons for their selections. Model this lesson by giving several different types of rationale statements for each of the three sections of their portfolios. Swain (1994) reported that with modeling, struggling readers double the number of their reflections per piece and shift the content of their reflections from surface level, mechanical issues (i.e., spelling, punctuation) to writing style issues (i.e., use of genre-specific elements, writing process features, quality of revisions, depth of personal insight, and growth in literary style). When these guidelines are followed, a large proportion of readers, even below age 10, can describe and assess their own strengths and future goals in reading/writing (Dewitz & Palm, 1993). The following explanations, written by struggling readers/writers, can be used as samples for your students when you model for them:

> I like and dislike this poem. I like it because it has a lot of feeling and I think other kids that have to stay home by themselves at night could relate to it. I dislike this poem because I don't like to be reminded of staying home alone and it makes me mad. But for now, I will keep it in my portfolio because it's about an important idea. I don't want to put it into final draft yet. If ever.
>
> This piece is important to me because it is the first time I ever had characters talk to each other. You know with quotation marks. I even went over their conversations in my sleep! The other extremely important thing about this paper is that I actually wanted to do a revision. Two revisions. And I liked the final copy. I've never done a revision on purpose before. I usually have just thought about it, and said I'll do better next time, but this time I wanted to fix it right away. I just didn't get tired of this piece like I have with other pieces. I also really liked the characters, Sam and Nicky, and wanted them to get to do something exciting. I didn't want them to have to be in a boring story. Sometimes I still think of other things Sam could do and how Nicky would save the situation. Maybe a sequel? (Hill & Ruptic, 1994, p. 45)

End the portfolio assessment conversation and each one-to-one discovery discussion by establishing new goals for the next recording period. List at least three alternative methods students suggest to reach goals.

As often as possible, send portfolios home and ask parents to write their reflections about the progress they see in their child's literacy development. Parents who are asked to comment on their child's portfolio tend to be stronger in their beliefs that the child has improved in literacy, with improvements also being evidenced in students' motivation, self-confidence, and more positive attitude toward literacy (Dewitz & Palm, 1993). Parents who participate in portfolio assessment also usually feel that they have a clearer understanding of their child as a reader. Parents also report that they appreciate checklists and book logs, because they give them more information about more global aspects of their children's reading and writing progress.

One teacher sends "Friday folders" home to parents every 2 weeks (Hill & Ruptic, 1994). Students (and this teacher) select pieces from their portfolios and place them in a file folder; students explain why their pieces were chosen. Accompanying each student's selections is a comment sheet on which parent comments will be written. On open house visiting days, three students and their parents can sit together at a table and share their portfolios. In this way, parents learn about other students in the room while they are encouraging their less accomplished readers/writers to press toward higher goals (Graves, 1994).

The first week that Friday folders are sent home, the teacher includes an explanatory letter similar to this one:

Instructions about Friday Folders
Dear Parents,

This is your child's Friday Folder. The Friday Folder contains your child's schoolwork and will come home every 2 weeks for your viewing pleasure. This folder also contains a letter to you from your child describing recent learnings and activities.

The Friday Folder needs to be returned to school on Monday with work intact. The reasons for work coming back are threefold. First, some of the work is still in process. Second, your child will be taking time to reflect on his/her work and to set future learning goals. Finally, your child will also be selecting several pieces from the Friday Folder to keep in his/her classroom portfolio.

The classroom portfolio is an organizational tool that will help me, you, and your child to view growth in all areas throughout the entire year. The portfolio will contain pieces that are significant to your child, either because the pieces showed improvement or because your child feels they are among his/her "best." Each piece in the portfolio will be described and be accompanied by a self-reflection. Your child may take his/her portfolio home at the end of the year.

On the back of this letter is a place for you to comment every 2 weeks as you review the work with your child. Your observations and insights are important to me and your child.

Patricia Kamber

EVALUATING PORTFOLIOS. It is important that your struggling readers and writers know the special values portfolios hold for them. Most believe grading is mysterious and something "done to them" because they have difficulty viewing their reading/writing objectively and metacognitively without your help.

A first step to build self-assessment abilities is to use small Post-it notes on which students note one of three things:

1. Why they like the piece
2. A self-reflection about the growth evidenced at this point in the book log
3. A new goal this specific portfolio selection helped them establish

Because these first assessments are only one sentence in length, metacognitive thinking becomes less threatening.

Once readers have completed several of these brief assessments, they will be ready for a discovery discussion in which they justify the grade they would award themselves on the full portfolio or on an individual selection. Also, ask them what they think they could do to raise that grade before the next grading period. Stress that they know themselves, their level of effort, and the amount of growth they achieved as well as, if not better than, other people. In this way, portfolio assessment builds students' reliance on their own effort for future success—which is very important for less accomplished readers, as described in Chapter 4. Conclude this discovery discussion by asking what types of

Student name __Juanita Morez__ Course name __Reading__ Grading period __4__

Birthdate _____11-1-93_____ Current grade placement __Fourth Grade__

Below is a written record of student reactions to their work and student–teacher assessment conferences.

A. **Reading Response Journal**
   1. What do you feel is important about your RRJ's?   _Telling me deep thinking_
   2. Do you write in your RRJ at each opportunity?   _Most times_
   3. Do you include a summary about what you read?   _yes_
   4. Do you write your opinions or feelings about what you read or about why you didn't read?   _yes_
   Teacher comments: _accurate record_

   Reading Response Journal Grade ___B___

B. **Writing Workshop**
   1. Put a star on the writing that represents your most important writing and describe why you believe this.
   2. Show me evidence of prewriting activities (concept map or brainstorming).   _I did_
   3a. Show me an example.
   3b. How do they help you write drafts?   _Make me think deeper_
   Teacher comments:

   Writing Workshop Grade ___A___

C. **Class and Group Activities**
   1. Group projects and whole class activities   _Generative Curriculum on Peace in the USA_
      a. Describe the activity you liked best and tell why.   _Visiting homeless people because they appreciate what we taught them._
      Teacher comments:
      Grade ___A___   _Juanita was a leader and grew tremendously._

   2. Participation and ability to use K-W-L and other comprehension strategies independently
      a. Which strategy helped you the most and why?   _KWL_
      b. Show me the notes from the K-W-L's or other comprehension activities in which you have participated.   _Included_
      Teacher comments: _used only KWL_

   Combined Class and Group Activities Grade ___C___

D. **Sustained Silent Reading**
   1. What kind of material did you like to read most and why?   _Horse Book_
   2. Why do you think we read every day?   _To improve our comprehension_
   3. Do you read the entire SSR period? Why or why not?   _yes_
   Teacher comments: _Improving in her reading abilities_

   Sustained Silent Reading Grade ___A___

E. **Goal for Next Grading Period**
   1. What do you want to accomplish this next six weeks?   _To comprehend more strategies_
   2. How do you plan to do this?   _Discovery Discussions and expert group meetings_
   Teacher comments: _These will be scheduled on Friday of each week_

Teacher Signature __Ms. McDonald__ Date _1-7-96_

Student Signature __Juanita Morez__ Date _1-5-96_

FIGURE 6.11 Reading Portfolio Record

Source: Adapted from S. Mathews, J. P. Young, & N. D. Giles (1989), *Student Literature Recorders: Providing Tools for Brighter Futures*, p. 109. Kansas City, MO: Kansas City Public Schools.

activities and support you can provide that would assist them to attain the goal they desire in the next recording period.

If readers answer the following questions before the discovery discussion, the quality of the portfolio assessment process will improve:

1. Why do you think I asked you to engage in sustained silent reading every Friday, and what goals did you accomplish through this activity? (Alternatively, you could ask some other question relative to the content you assigned during this grading period.)
2. Explain specific reasons why a particular method of reading/writing instruction was so valuable to you.
3. Pick a book or story that was difficult for you and place a Post-it note at the point where you could not understand what the writer was saying. Explain the reasons why you think this reading was difficult for you.
4. Select an unfinished writing and describe the problem that stopped you. What would you like to learn so you will not face that problem again?
5. Select your best work and describe what was different about the process you used to complete it, which increased its quality. If you could continue to work on this, what would you do next? Why?
6. When you look over your portfolio or reading/writing selection, what do you feel about yourself as a reader/writer and why?
7. What makes you unique as a reader? As a writer?

Then, just before you begin the discovery discussion, ask students to end their reflections by asking you a question about their reading and writing. Record all these responses on one of the report forms shown in Figures 6.11 and 6.12.

Self-Assessments

The way you know that you know something is to go someplace deep inside your body to find that feeling—the one that tells you that you know. That's what learning is.
        From a discovery discussion between two 7-year-old girls (Henning-Stout, 1994)

Students need to learn how to evaluate themselves and to evaluate themselves better. As adults, most of the assessment they experience will be either self-assigned or self-evaluations. Another benefit of self-assessments is that struggling readers/writers learn they can accurately diagnose problems and articulate whether corrections are effective (Kos, 1991). In addition, self-assessment releases students from being dependent on others to evaluate how they are doing. For example, suppose you overhear a less accomplished reader say, "That was a hard one. I liked getting it done!" You can see that self-assessment enabled this student to demonstrate the degree to which he is purposefully thinking, reading, writing, and comprehending knowledge, as well as what his purposes were.

Self-appraisal and self-regulation also improve confidence. This confidence evolves because it enables students to reflect on and evaluate the reasons for their beliefs. Through such reflection, students come to develop their own standards of quality, which Berliner (1994) has identified to be one of the most powerful motivational forces students can have to expand their literacy. He states: "I have always believed that the ability

Name _____ Date _____

I. **Process evaluation** (20 points). Rate each area.   **Points**
   A. Sharing artifacts and reflections with peers. (5 or 10 points)   _____
   B. Submitting portfolio for two interim reviews. (5 or 10 points)   _____

                                                                  Total _____

II. **Product evaluation** (30 points).
   A. Aspects of the portfolio (8 points). Rate each area for 1 or 0 points.
      1. Literacy autobiography (1 point)   _____
      2. Reading for different purposes (1 point)   _____
      3. Writing for different purposes (1 point)   _____
      4. All stages of writing process (1 point)   _____
      5. Use of word processing system (1 point)   _____
      6. Oral interpretation of children's literature (1 point)   _____
      7. Significance of role models (1 point)   _____
      8. Talking and listening for different purposes (1 point)   _____

                                                                  Total _____

   B. Reflections on artifacts (12 points). Choose one.
      ➤ All reflections are substantive and well composed. (12 points)
      ➤ Most reflections are substantive and well composed. (9 points)
      ➤ Some reflections are substantive and well composed. (6 points)
      ➤ Few reflections are substantive and well composed. (3 points)

                                                                  Total _____

   C. Summative reflective piece (10 points). Choose one to represent your evaluation of
      (a) what you learned about your own literacy, (b) how your literacy experiences
      might affect your teaching of literacy, and (c) personal literacy goals and plan of
      action.
      ➤ Each of the three areas is adequately elaborated, and the
        writing is carefully composed. (10 points)
      ➤ Each area is addressed in carefully composed writing. Two
        areas are adequately elaborated; one area needs further
        development. (8 points)
      ➤ Each area is addressed. The writing style is adequate. Two areas
        need further elaboration. (6 points)
      ➤ Each area is addressed. The writing style is adequate, but all
        three areas need further elaboration. (4 points)
      ➤ One or more areas are not addressed. Writing style is not
        satisfactory. (2 points)

                                                                  Total _____
                                                            Grand Total _____

Points possible = 50

FIGURE 6.12 Criteria for Evaluating a Literacy Portfolio

Source: Adapted from B. J. Wagner (1994), *Drama as a Learning Medium,* p. 373. Washington, DC:
National Education Association. Used with permission.

to be partially free of external evaluation—the praise and criticism of friends, family, teachers and others with whom we interact—is the ultimate in personal agency" (p. 323). When readers come to know this sense of personal agency in their reading/writing, literacy becomes intrinsically valuable, and they establish higher goals for themselves than we could for them. As Berliner points out, "Powerful thinking is more likely to occur among people that have learned they can judge things for themselves and that others do not always set the standards for their behavior" (1994, p. 372).

PROCEDURES FOR SELF-ASSESSMENT. Not withstanding these positive benefits from self-assessments, there are limitations of time that must be overcome. It can take several days to complete an accurate self-assessment, as Margarita, a first grade reader, observed—especially if self-assessment is set for only one period during what may not be your best day:

> I didn't get a good grade today. I want to be better and sometimes I feel strong inside. When I'm strong I go with my feelings and I sound out every word. I'm not feeling strong now. I have days when the words just come to me and I don't even think I'm reading. I never want that feeling to end. That didn't happen today. I don't know why. I didn't get a star today.

A key in self-assessment procedure is that students must choose what they want to evaluate. The more options students can choose from, the more useful information they will provide about their reading and writing processes (Johnston, 1992).

When puzzled looks cross readers' faces, you can provide information about what the student is doing well. For example, you can ask struggling readers/writers to tell what is difficult for them and what is easy. Ask them if there are any common elements. For instance, perhaps it is always hard or always easy to do one of the following:

_____ Read little words like *to, the* and *that*

_____ Read short sentences

_____ Read faster

_____ Write more information

_____ Put meanings of words together in a sentence

_____ Put feelings into words better

_____ Feel less self-conscious when reading orally

_____ Find good books to read

_____ Have better beginning sentences

_____ Select what should go in the portfolio

_____ Not get mad at yourself when you can't read something

Last, you can demonstrate how to use the self-assessments in Tables 6.6 and 6.7. Then allow students to use the form they prefer. Choosing the form they like best enables students to present themselves in their most positive light because the form matches their personality and evaluation style.

TABLE 6.6 Self-Assessments: After Reading or Writing

After Reading

Date _____ Name _____

I _____ in reading today.

Things that went well were _____

_____

_____

Difficulties I had were _____

_____

_____

Tomorrow I plan to _____

_____

After Writing

Date _____ Name _____

I _____ in writing today.

Things that went well were _____

_____

_____

Difficulties I had were _____

_____

_____

Tomorrow I plan to _____

_____

Source: Modified from forms in B. C. Hill & C. A. Ruptic (1994), *Practical Aspects of Authentic Assessment,* p. 105. Norwood, MA: Christopher-Gordon. Used with permission.

◼ Grading Readers/Writers with Literacy Challenges

Ella, an eleventh grade struggling reader at Schenley High School in Pittsburgh, described how grading assisted her development:

> In the beginning I [wrote], but basically it was for a grade because at the time I couldn't find my own style. . . . As time went on I began to do the work for myself, not for the grade, but to see how well I could become an artist. (Gardner, 1993, p. 1)

TABLE 6.7 Skills I Use

Skills	Dates	With guidance ≪——≫ Independently
I label my pictures with words.		
I write phrases and sentences.		
I use my sounds to write.		
I use spaces between words.		
I use titles to tell my main idea.		
My writing has a clear beginning, middle, and end.		
I use a variety of forms: journals		
lists		
observations		
stories		
poems		
letters		
reports		
directions		
I share my written work with others.		
I use spaces to show individual words.		
I write neatly.		
I use capital letters: to begin sentences		
for proper names		
I use punctuation: periods		
question marks		
exclamation points		
quotation marks		
I use the sounds of letters to help me spell.		
What I want to learn next:		Next step:

Source: Adapted from B. C. Hill & C. A. Ruptic (1994), *Practical Aspects of Authentic Assessment*, p. 81. Norwood, MA: Christopher-Gordon. Used with permission.

For many less accomplished readers/writers, if individual grades on literacy products are made public, the grades communicate that some students are "smarter" than others. Grades also pressure some to push themselves into new zones of proximal development before they are ready because they are striving for an A. Unfortunately, many also misinterpret grades as rewards or punishments for their literacy performances. According to one study, "the pursuit of the rewards and the avoidance of the punishments overwhelm the search for understanding" (Bratcher, 1994, p. 56). The purpose of this last section is to describe how you can make the pursuit of rewards in reading and writing intrinsically motivating and avoid these negative consequences.

Struggling readers/writers can be graded more appropriately by analysis of parts of their literacy processes and products or by holistic analyses. *Holistic grading* measures the quality of a reading, writing, speaking, or listening performance by the success with which that specific literacy activity achieved its objective and/or surpassed its goal. Such holistic measures can be of three types (Bratcher, 1994).

The first is called **analytical grading.** In the example appearing in Figure 6.13, one of three symbols is recorded for each process within the reading continuum, indicating that the process is fully developed (FD), in beginning stages of development (BD), or not present (NP). When this grading system accompanies readers and writers from grade to grade, specific zones of proximal development for each student can be identified, and personalized instruction in those areas can begin more rapidly.

The second type of holistic grading is called **anchor grading.** You help students recognize quality in a literacy performance (e.g., what a good attempt would resemble or what would demonstrate specific growths). A *narrative report card* is one type of anchor grading. Literacy categories are listed at the top of a narrative report card, and the teacher checks off categories as appropriate to indicate achievement. The bottom half of the card contains the teacher's description of the student's achievements within that grading period. For example, Mr. Morris, a fourth grade teacher, wrote the following about Peter, a hardworking but struggling reader and writer:

NARRATIVE REPORT CARD: PETER S.
Peter is a quiet sensitive child who is developing in positive ways. His attitudes towards language, learning, and other children are commendable and are responsible for his development academically.

Peter has shown that he can work independently. He is resourceful when organizing time and resources in contract work, makes appropriate use of reference material within the room, borrows regularly from the school library, and is very considerate of the needs of his fellow students.

Peter likes to read fiction books and writes mainly in this genre. He has however produced a nonfictional descriptive piece, a spillover reaction to nonfictional retellings done in Term 1.

Peter's great strengths lie in discussion/sharing time where he loves to explain his opinions and interpretation—everything he says is considered and justified, backed up with evidence.

Peter is coming to grips with simple punctuation and uses speech marks almost automatically. He does not have strong control of basic spelling forms, although at the same time he is becoming more adventurous in his vocabulary. (Daly, 1989)

Student's name: _____ Date administered: _____

Preconventional   **Comments**

Dates grades were given

			Holds book; correctly turns pages
			Chooses books and has favorites
			Shows start/end of book
			Listens and responds to literature
			Knows some letter names
			Interested in environmental print

Beginning

Dates grades were given

			Reads early-reader books
			Relies on print more than illustrations
			Uses sentence structure clues
			Uses meaning clues
			Uses phonetic clues
			Retells beginning, middle, and end
			Recognizes names/words by sight
			Begins to read silently
			Understands basic punctuation

Emergent

Dates grades were given

			Pretends to read
			Uses illustrations to tell story
			Participates in reading of familiar books
			Knows some letter sounds
			Recognizes names/words in context
			Memorizes pattern books and familiar books
			Rhymes and plays with words

(continued)

FIGURE 6.13 Reading Continuum Checklist

Developing

Dates grades were given

			Sees self as reader
			Reads books with word patterns
			Knows most letter sounds
			Retells main idea of text
			Recognizes simple words
			Relies on print and illustrations

Proficient

Dates grades were given

			Reads complex young adult literature
			Moves between many genres with ease
			Integrates nonfiction information to develop a deeper understanding
			Interprets sophisticated meaning in young adult literature with guidance
			Participates in complex literary discussions

Independent

Dates grades were given

			Voluntarily reads and understands a wide variety of complex and sophisticated materials with ease
			Evaluates, interprets, and analyzes literary elements critically

Fluent

Dates grades were given

			Reads most young adult literature
			Selects, reads, and finishes a wide variety of materials
			Uses reference materials independently
			Understands literary elements and genres
			Begins to interpret deeper meaning in young adult literature with frequent guidance
			Participates in guided literary discussions

FIGURE 6.13 *(continued)*

Expanding

Dates grades were given

				Comments
			Reads beginning chapter books	
			Reads and finishes a variety of materials with frequent guidance	
			Uses reading strategies appropriately	
			Retells plot, characters, and events	
			Recognizes different types of books	
			Makes connections between reading, writing, and experiences	
			Silent reading for short periods	

Bridging

Dates grades were given

			Reads medium level chapter books
			Reads and finishes a variety of materials with guidance
			Reads and understands most new words
			Uses reference materials to locate information with guidance
			Increases knowledge of literary elements and genres
			Silent reading for extended periods

Grading Symbols
FD = Fully developed
BD = Beginning to develop
NP = Not present

FIGURE 6.13 *(continued)*

Source: Adapted from B. C. Hill & C. A. Ruptic (1994), *Practical Aspects of Authentic Assessment,* pp. 69–72. Norwood, MA: Christopher-Gordon. Used with permission.

The third type of holistic grading is **cluster grading,** in which the teacher collects samples that demonstrate a student's achievement and determines grades by comparing one demonstration to another. Portfolios, retellings, and other types of informal assessments described in this chapter can be cluster graded.

All of these three grading systems share a common trait: They do not require struggling readers/writers to reach arbitrary literacy standards that might be outside their zones of proximal development, and they do not require these students to demonstrate success by competing against more internally guided users of literacy. Any time these students must compete for grades against internally guided peers, grading becomes more appropriate if you give two grades for each literacy performance—one based on the arbitrary grading standards used for all students and one to indicate this student's own individual improvement.

For example, consider a reading specialist's group of third grade students who established the goal of increasing their amount of self-selected reading. These students came largely from households at lower socioeconomic levels; they had few books at home and no public library in their rural area. They fell in love with William Armstrong's book *Sounder,* from which the class read orally each day. Mr. Armstrong was making a public appearance in a nearby city, so the specialist challenged each member of her group to read 1,000 pages of self-selected reading material in the 6 weeks prior to Mr. Armstrong's visit. Those who did could go to meet him and would receive the grade they had contracted for during the discovery discussion that began this grading period. To make this competitive grade more appropriate for these readers/writers, this reading specialist brought 60 Caldecott books from a library in the nearby city for the students to read. They were allowed to stay after school to read, or they could come at lunchtime for assisted reading with her and a group of sixth graders who volunteered to help for 15 minutes during the lunch period. On the day before the 6-week deadline, all but one student, Charles, had reached their literacy goal. On this day, Charles and his teacher stayed at school until 5:30 p.m. reading his last 150 pages together. Charles and all the other readers in the group attained success in this competitive environment and were graded on the same scale of improvement as their peers—movement from point a to point b on their individual literacy continuum, regardless of where points a and b were located at the beginning of this grading period.

Using the grading systems presented here rewards struggling readers/writers for their hard work and progress. Grades should become more than arbitrary measures of achievement; they should provide feedback as to the student's strengths and needs. Whenever possible, these readers should also be allowed to choose what they want to have assessed. When choice is provided, grading becomes less threatening.

Chapter Summary

Recent reforms in assessment have led to the creation of new methods of analyzing literacy for readers/writers, including IRIs, RMIs, running records, retellings, and portfolios. Standardized tests have been redesigned to measure the process of literacy as well as to be more sensitive to cultural and socioeconomic background variables that affect individual student performances. Educators and legislators have come to agree that present and future assessments must serve two functions: (1) to determine whether individual students are achieving or growing toward desired standards of performance, and (2) to provide relative measurements for groups of students at the school, district, state, regional, national, and international levels. When inappropriate uses of norm-referenced achievement tests occur for struggling readers/writers, you can assist students and parents to interpret the validity, reliability, and relevance of individual student scores.

In addition, carefully administered performance assessments—such as portfolios, anecdotal records, narrative report cards, anchored grading, self-assessments, and holistic grading—can provide information during instruction that is not available through other assessment avenues.

In the final analysis, the goal of assessment is to identify all readers' strengths, potentials, literacy barriers, and self-assessment abilities. The assessment tools presented in this chapter will assist you to achieve this goal and to make highly effective decisions about future instruction for every reader.

Key Terminology

Now that you have completed this chapter, see if you know the meanings of the terms listed below. If you do, place a checkmark in the blank that precedes the term. If you are not certain, turn to the page number that follows the term to review its meaning. If you have learned 20 of these on your initial reading of the chapter, you have understood the chapter's content.

_____ national norm (page 143)
_____ authentic assessment (page 143)
_____ validity (page 143)
_____ reliability (page 143)
_____ diagnosis (page 144)
_____ assessment (page 144)
_____ standardized tests (page 146)
_____ Formal Reading Inventory (page 148)
_____ raw score (page 149)
_____ percentile ranking (page 149)
_____ grade equivalent score (page 150)
_____ distributions (page 151)
_____ mean (page 151)
_____ median (page 151)

_____ mode (page 151)
_____ range (page 151)
_____ standard deviation (page 151)
_____ normative data (page 152)
_____ anecdotal records (page 153)
_____ informal reading and writing inventories (page 157)
_____ frustration level (page 167)
_____ reading miscue inventories (page 168)
_____ running records (page 169)
_____ retellings (page 171)
_____ analytical grading (page 186)
_____ anchor grading (page 186)
_____ cluster grading (page 189)

 ## Case Study

Making Professional Decisions

Meisong was 9 years old and beginning the third grade when her mother brought her to the diagnostician. She had repeated first grade. Although Meisong had received extra Tier 3 instruction in a small group after school for the past two years, she had made little progress. Her most recent assessment indicated that she was reading at a primer level. Most of her classmates were reading at or above grade level.

An interview was conducted with Meisong's mother. The mother reported that her pregnancy with Meisong was difficult and that she had taken med-ication to prevent a miscarriage. She described the birth as "long and complicated" and suspected that she might have had inadequate oxygen during the birth process. Meisong walked and talked somewhat later than most children, and her mother described her as awkward and uncoordinated. Despite these problems, Meisong was well adjusted and said she had a happy family life.

Meisong said that she liked to read, even though reading was hard for her. She said she was eager to learn to read better and she hoped this teacher could help her so she wouldn't "be dumb any more."

The results of the tests administered are presented below:

INFORMAL READING INVENTORY

On the preprimer level of the Word Recognition List, Meisong recognized only 5 of 20 words correctly on the timed presentation. When words were presented without time constraints, she made no attempt to correct her responses. Errors had little resemblance to the target words, with only initial consonant sounds employed as a strategy for identifying unknown words. Even this strategy was inconsistent. In passage reading, Meisong became frustrated at the preprimer level. When she encountered an unfamiliar word, she made no attempt to figure it out and just waited for teacher help. In the Listening Comprehension test, Meisong understood passages read to her at the first grade level.

EMERGENT LITERACY ASSESSMENT

Because of Meisong's poor performance on the informal reading inventory, portions of the Emergent Literacy Assessment were administered. First, Meisong was presented with a random set of upper- and lowercase letters. She could identify all the letters of the alphabet, but she reversed lowercase letters *b* and *d*, *p* and *q*, and *s* and *z*. When asked to write the letters, she had difficulty with *S*, *Z*, and *J* in both upper and lower cases.

On the Book Reading task, Meisong was asked to read a short book with predictable patterns by rereading each sentence after the teacher read them, and she was asked to point to the words as she read. She was able to repeat what the teacher said, but she could not point to the words successfully as she read them. She frequently lost her place while reading. When asked to identify specific words after reading, Meisong was successful in only 2 of 10 attempts.

Next, Meisong was asked to identify beginning letters and their corresponding sounds. She was presented with a list of 10 words and was successful in providing both the beginning letters and sounds for all 10.

Meisong was then asked to identify ending sounds in a list of 10 words. When she could not do so for the first 4 items presented, the test was stopped. When she was asked to identify the individual sounds in single-syllable words, she was unable to segment the sounds. In addition, when presented with individual sounds, such as /b/-/a/-/t/, she could not blend these sounds into the word *bat*.

Throughout the diagnosis, Meisong appeared to be easily distracted. She stood up to see over the partitions whenever she heard the slightest noise and she constantly looked out the door to see what was happening.

Respond to the following questions, then check your responses against the Answer Key at the end of the book.

1. What does Meisong's performance on the Informal Reading Inventory indicate about her reading level? What strategies would you recommend to improve Meisong's sight word recognition?
2. Should phonics be taught?
3. What instructional interventions do you recommend?

Thinking and Writing about What You Have Learned

1. Which of the assessment instruments in this chapter do you want to use and why?

2. Which grading system do you judge to best complement your teaching style and why?

3. What is the difference between the mean score on a standardized test and that test's standard deviation?

4. What is the difference between analytical, anchored, and cluster grading?

5. Do you agree with each of the categories shown in Figure 6.13, the Reading Continuum Checklist? If so, you may want to incorporate these into your grading program for readers. If not, you may want to develop your own.

6. Including students in the design of their own portfolio assessment system increases the value of portfolios for less accomplished readers/writers. How would you go about including these readers/writers in the design and assessment of their portfolios?

For Further Reference

The following list of tests and assessment instruments should be useful to teachers, reading specialists, and other educators. It was compiled by Gloria B. Smith of Rider College. It lists formal tests first, then informal tests. They are arranged by category and alphabetically by title within each category.

FORMAL TESTS

Intelligence Tests

California Test of Mental Maturity (CTB/McGraw-Hill, 1997). Provides separate IQs for reading and nonreading tasks. Grades K–16, six levels. Group intelligence test.

Kaufman Assessment Battery for Children, by Alan S. Kaufman and Nadeen L. Kaufman (American Guidance Services, 1996). Five global areas of functioning: sequential processing, simultaneous processing, mental processing, composite (sequential plus simultaneous) achievement, and nonverbal. Individual administration.

Raven Progressive Matrices, by J. C. Raven (Psychological Corporation, 2000). Nonverbal intelligence test to measure intellectual capacity to form comparisons and reason by analogy. Three forms, available for ages 5–adult. Group or individual administration.

Slosson Intelligence Test, by Richard L. Slosson (Slosson Educational Publications, 1981). Provides IQ, mental age, and an analysis of items for information, arithmetic, similarities and differences, vocabulary, digit span, comprehension. All ages—infant to adult. Individual administration.

Stanford-Binet Intelligence Scale, by Robert L. Thorndike, Elizabeth P. Hagen, and Jerome A. Sattler (Riverside Publishing, 1999). Provides measurement of cognitive abilities and single IQ score for very young child to adult. Individual administration.

Test of Nonverbal Intelligence (Language Free), by Linda Brown, Rita J. Sherbenou, Susan K. Johnson (Pro-Ed, 2000). Problem solving by identifying relationships among abstract figures. Individual administration.

Wechsler Intelligence Scale for Children (WISC-R), by David Wechsler (Psychological Corporation, 2000). Intelligence test for children; gives verbal score which includes information, comprehension, arithmetic, and similarities.

Reading Tests: Comprehension

California Achievement Test (Reading) (CTB/McGraw-Hill, 2000). Subtests: vocabulary, comprehension, English usage and mechanics, spelling, and mathematics. K–12. Group administration.

Comprehensive Tests of Basic Skills, Spanish edition, developed by Norwalk-LaMirada Unified School District in Southern California (CTB/McGraw-Hill, 2000). A series of achievement tests to estimate basic skills of Spanish-language students.

Durrell Analysis of Reading Difficulties Test, 3rd ed., by Donald D. Durrell and Jane Catterson (Psychological Corporation, 1980). Provides intensive analysis of reading difficulties: silent reading, oral reading, and listening comprehension. Individual administration.

Gates-MacGinitie Reading Tests, 2nd ed., Forms 1, 2, and 3, by Walter H. MacGinitie (Riverside Publishing, 2000). Provides measures of silent reading comprehension and total reading scores for grades 1–12. Group and individual administration.

Iowa Test of Basic Skills, (Houghton Mifflin Company, 2000). Achievement battery includes vocabulary, comprehension, work–study skills. Grades 3–9.

Metropolitan Achievement Test (Reading), by Irving Balow, Roger Farr, Thomas Hogan, and George Prescott (Psychological Corporation, 2000). Eight levels—vocabulary, word analysis, comprehension, spelling; also mathematics, social studies, and science in upper-grade levels. K–12. Group administration.

Nelson-Denny Test, by James I. Brown, J. Michael Bennett, and Gerald S. Hanna (Riverside Publishing, 2000). Silent reading tests for high school students. Self-administered, individual or group.

Stanford (Diagnostic Reading Test), by B. Karlsen, R. Madden, and E. F. Gardner (Harcourt Brace Jovanovich, 2001). Two forms and four levels, for ages 7–9. Complete battery for diagnosis of decoding skills, vocabulary levels, and comprehension. Individual and group administration.

Reading Tests: Word Analysis and Decoding/Word Recognition

Peabody Individual Achievement Tests (Subtest: Word Recognition), by Lloyd M. Dunn and Frederick C. Markwardt, Jr. (American Guidance Service, 1999). Word lists. Individual administration.

Roswell-Chall Diagnostic Reading Test of Word Analysis Skills, by Florence Roswell and Jeanne S. Chall (Essay Press, 1978). Measures decoding and word recognition skills: grades 1–4. Individual administration.

Slosson Oral Reading Test, by Richard L. Slosson, revised ed. (Slosson Educational Publications, 1999). Oral reading of word list. Individual administration.

Woodcock Reading Mastery Tests—Revised (subtests: Word Identification, Letter Identification, Word Attack Skills), by Richard W. Woodcock (American Guidance Service, 1999). Individual administration.

Reading Tests: Vocabulary–Semantic

Gates-MacGinitie Reading Tests, 2nd ed., Forms 1, 2, and 3, by Walter H. MacGinitie (Riverside Publishing, 1999). Timed vocabulary tests for grades 1–12. Individual or group administration.

Peabody Picture Vocabulary Test, revised ed., Forms L and M, by Lloyd M. and Leota M. Dunn (American Guidance Service, 1999). Measures vocabulary and verbal ability. Individual administration.

Spelling Tests

Diagnostic Spelling Potential Test, by John Arena (Slosson Educational Publications, 1999). Four subtests: spelling, word recognition, visual recognition, and auditory–visual recognition. Individual administration.

Test of Written Spelling, by Stephen Larsen and Donald Hammill (Slosson Educational Publications, 1999). Subtests for spelling of predictable words, unpredictable words, and combined sets of words. Individual or group administration.

Writing Tests

The Picture Story Language Test (PSLT), by Helmer Myklebust (Grune & Stratton, 1980). Measures language disorders—using picture-card stimulus—as well as productivity, syntax, and abstract–concrete language. Individual or group administration.

The Test of Written Language, by Donald D. Hamill and Stephen C. Larsen (American Guidance Service, 2000). Six subtests: thematic maturity, spelling, vocabulary, word usage, style and handwriting, and total writing quotient.

Auditory Tests

Audiometer, by Maico Hearing Instruments (Maico, NA). Individually administered screening for preschool through adult. Using audiometer, can provide information about auditory acuity. Screening only: Evidence of hearing loss should be confirmed by hearing specialists.

Auditory Discrimination Test, by Joseph M. Wepman (Language Research Associates, 1999). Measures child's ability to discriminate between sounds. Individual administration.

Goldman-Fristoe-Woodcock Auditory Skills Test Battery, by Ronald Goldman, Macalyne Fristoe, and Richard W. Woodcock (American Guidance Service, 1993). Five subtests: Auditory Selective Attention Test; Diagnostic Auditory Discrimination Test, Parts 1, 2, and 3; and Auditory Memory Test. Individual administration.

Test of Auditory-Perceptual Skills, by Morrison F. Gardner (Children's Hospital of San Francisco, 1985). Test of auditory number, sentence, and word memory; also auditory word discrimination, processing, and interpretation of directions. Also includes a hyperactivity scale.

Visual Tests

Bender-Gestalt Test for Young Children, by Elizabeth Koppitz (Grune & Stratton, 1997). Used to assess visual–perceptual skills and perceptual–motor integration. Individual administration.

Keystone Visual Screening Tests, by Keystone View (Keystone View, Division of Mast Development Company, 1989). Visual screening test for preschool through adult levels. Uses a Keystone Telebinocular machine and provides screening tests for far-point and near-point vision and fusion. Individual administration.

Test of Visual-Perceptual Skills, by Morrison F. Gardner (Special Child Publications, 1998). Measures visual discrimination, visual memory, visual–spatial relationships, visual form constancy, visual sequential memory, visual figure–ground perception, and visual closure. Individual administration.

Motor Skills Test

Bruininks-Oseretsky Test of Motor Proficiency, by Robert H. Bruininks (American Guidance Service, 1999). For ages 4–15. Assesses motor performance and fine and gross motor skills. Individual administration.

Tests for Infants and Preschool Children

Bayley Scales of Infant Development, by Nancy Bayley (Psychological Corporation, 2000). Provides mental scale, motor scale, and infant behavior record. Individual administration.

Gesell Developmental Schedules, by Arnold Gesell and recently revised by Knobloch, Stevens, and Malone (Gesell Institute, 2000). Measures infant responses for motor, language, adaptive, and personal–social behavior. New version distinguishes fine-motor from gross-motor behavior. Used in medical settings. Individual administration.

McCarthy Scales of Children's Abilities, by Dorothea McCarthy (Psychological Corporation, 1999). Used for preschool children. Measures cognitive abilities, including verbal, perceptual/performance and quantitative, memory index, and motor index. Individual administration.

Learning Disabilities Tests

Slingerland Screening Tests for Identifying Children with Specific Language Disability, by Beth H. Slingerland (Western Psychological Services, 2000). Four forms (A–D) for grades 1–6. Provides information on student's ability to copy from near and far point; tests visual–perception–memory linkage, auditory–perception–memory linkage, and auditory–visual linkage. Group or individual administration.

Oral Language Tests

Assessment of Children's Language Comprehension, by Rochana Foster, Jane Giddan, and Joel Stark (Consulting Psychologists Press, 1972). Assesses receptive language disorders in young children. Individual administration.

Language Assessment Battery, Spanish-Language Tests, by Staff of the New York City Board of Education (Riverside Publishing, 1999). Provides measure of communication skills for Spanish-speaking students. Individual administration.

Peabody Picture Vocabulary Test, revised ed., by Lloyd M. and Leota M. Dunn (American Guidance Service, 1999). (Listed also under Reading Tests: Vocabulary–Semantic.) Individual administration.

Stanford-Binet Intelligence Scale, by Robert L. Thorndike, Elizabeth P. Hagen, and Jerome Satter (Riverside Publishing Co., 1999). (Listed also under Intelligence Tests.)

Test for Auditory Comprehension of Language, by Elizabeth Carrow-Woolfolk (Teaching Resources, 2000). Assesses auditory comprehension of language—both English and Spanish tests available. Individual administration.

INFORMAL TESTS

Self-Concept Scales

Coopersmith Self-Esteem Inventories, by Stanley Coopersmith (Consulting Psychologists Press, 1990). For ages 8–15. Shows relationship of academic achievement and personal satisfaction in school. (There is an adult form of this inventory, but there are no normative data for it.) Self-administered; group or individual administration.

Piers-Harris Children's Self-Concept Scale, revised ed., by Ellen V. Piers and Dale Harris (Western Psychological Services, 1999). Children report on conscious self-perceptions. Six subscales: Behavior, Intellectual and School Status, Physical Appearance and Attributes, Anxiety, Popularity, and Happiness and Satisfaction. Individual or group administration.

Reading Miscue Inventory: Alternative Procedures, by Yetta M. Goodman. Dorothy J. Watson, and Caroline L. Burke (Richard C. Owen Publishers, 1987). Oral reading miscue analysis, individual administration. Apple computer system disk available.

Oral Language

Oral Language Evaluation, 2nd ed., by Nicholas Silvaroli, Jann Skinner, and J. O. "Rocky" Maynes, Jr. (EMC, 1985). Establishes a beginning oral language level in English or Spanish. Assesses beginning oral language, diagnoses language needs, and prescribes instructional activities.

Spelling

Spellmaster, by Claire Cohen and Rhoda Abrams (CTB/McGraw-Hill, 2000). Tests three categories of words: regularly spelled words, irregularly spelled words, and homonyms.

The Beginnings of Writing, by C. A. Temple, R. G. Nathan, and N. A. Burris (Allyn & Bacon, 1999). Informal measures for prephonemic spelling, early phonemic spelling, letter name spelling, and correct spelling.

Writing

Stanford Writing Assessment Program Guide, by Eric Garder, Robert Callis, Jack Merwin, and Herbert Rudman (Psychological Corporation, 2000). Assesses students' writing, grade 4 through high school. Four types of informative writing are assessed—describing, narrating, explaining, and reasoning. Six dimensions of writing are assessed—general merit, quantity and quality of ideas, organization, wording, syntax, and mechanics. Scoring must be by at least two rating teachers.

Test of Written English, by Velma Andersen and Sheryl Thompson (Slosson Educational Publications, 2000). An informal test for assessing capitalization, punctuation, written expression, and paragraph writing.

Attitudinal Inventory

Dulin-Chester Reading Attitude Scale, Form 3, by K. L. Dulin and R. D. Chester (International Reading Association, 2000). Test of middle and secondary school pupils' attitudes toward reading. Group administration.

Visual–Perceptual and Visual–Motor Materials

Fitzhugh Plus (Allied Educational Press). Programmed workbooks in matching, completing, analyzing shapes.

Frostig Program for the Development of Visual Perception (Modern Curriculum Press). Written activities develop visual and auditory perception.

Pictures and Patterns (Modern Curriculum Press). Exercises for body awareness, visual–motor coordination, figure–ground discrimination, etc.

Auditory–Perceptual Materials

Auditory Discrimination in Depth (DLM). Multisensory program by Lindamood and Lindamood develops auditory skills including phonological awareness. Filmstrips and cassettes included.

Auditory Perception Training (DLM). Two graded sets teach memory, motor skills, imagery, etc.

High Hat Early Reading Program (American Guidance Service). Originally *Goldman-Lynch Sounds and Symbols Development Kit.* Teaches sounds to symbols and symbols to letters associations. Puppets, cassettes, etc.

Semel Auditory Processing Program (Modern Curriculum Press). Assesses and remediates basic language disorders.

Sound-Order-Sense (Modern Curriculum Press). Develops auditory perception for disabled older students.

Special Remedial Approaches

The Basic Reading Series (Science Research Associates). Workbook and six books of basal series uses phonics approach in structured format. Uses stories, poems, plays.

Breaking the Code (Open Court). Uses synthetic, highly structured phonics approach. Alphabet cards teach letter sounds rather than names.

Corrective Reading. Decoding ABC (Science Research Associates). Thirty-five to 45 daily lessons with teacher scripts. Three graded levels move from word attack basics (A), to decoding (B), to skill applications (C).

chapter 7

Creating Optimal
Learning Environments

Only three of these four children are reading. In this chapter, you will learn activities to ensure that on subsequent days all students will be engaged in reading.

Dear Dr. Block,

I feel rather helpless after this week. I wish I had more time to spend with Steven. It is amazing how a little bit of one-on-one helped him as well as me. It is unbelievable how much insight I gain through discovery discussions as to exactly what he needs next.

—Paula Maury,
seventh grade teacher

Chapter Overview: Key Points

The purpose of this chapter is to show how classroom organization can remove limits on readers' capabilities. In previous chapters you obtained information about differences between struggling readers/writers and higher-performing peers. This chapter will explain the following:

- Principles to follow in organizing time and routines so students can overcome literacy barriers
- Qualities of effective instructional groups
- Ways to solve classroom and one-on-one learning difficulties

By chapter's end you will have answers to the following questions:

1. How do you find time to engage frequently in discovery discussions with struggling readers/writers?
2. What characterizes effective learning environments for students who read at lower stages on the literacy continuum?
3. What lesson plans, classroom schedules, and time management strategies enable students to overcome physical, cognitive, affective, cultural, and social challenges to literacy?
4. How can you alter the learning community so *everyone* will self-initiate reading and writing purposefully and pleasurably?

Principles of Organization, Time, and Routines

In the past, alternative instructional strategies were delayed until an extensive testing program for readers was complete and an appropriate label was assigned to each child. Today, we know that the longer effective instruction for these readers/writers is delayed, the greater the differences become between the achievement levels of these students and those of their peers (Madden, Slavin, Karweit, Livermon, & Dolan, 1989; Pinnell, Lyons, DeFord, Bryk, & Seltzer, 1994; Walmsley & Walp, 1990).

From the following four options, if you could use only one variable to increase your students' literacy abilities, which would it be?

- Studying the results of a performance measure of students' abilities
- Having a standardized assessment profile that describes students' decoding and comprehension grade-level equivalency
- Implementing a new program such as Reading Recovery, Success for All, Writing Workshop, or Workshop Way
- Allowing students to spend 90 minutes a day engaged in reading, writing, and literacy activities at their instructional level

If you chose the last option, your understanding of these readers/writers is consistent with findings from recent research. In fact, three instructional actions have been shown to enhance less accomplished readers' success and will now be described.

ORGANIZATIONAL ACTION 1. Provide 90 minutes a day for reading and writing. The most effective action you can take to advance struggling students is to increase the time they spend in quality-driven literacy instruction (Guthrie, Martuza, & Seifert, 1979; Leinhardt & Bickel, 1989; Zieme, 2000). Researchers report that even a moderate increase in silent reading time of 5 minutes per day results in achievement gains that average a month's growth in literacy power by the end of the year (Pinnell, Lyons, DeFord, Bryk, & Seltzer, 1994).

Research also indicates that the more academic *engaged time* less accomplished readers/writers have, the greater their literacy gains will be (Rosenshine & Stevens, 1984). **Engaged time** or **engagement** is time spent in intense, purposeful concentration and comprehension. Effective teachers use discovery discussions to identify the most appropriate reading materials for each student and then maximize engaged time by scheduling more silent reading of self-selected books. Unfortunately, time allocated to effective reading activities for readers at all levels is limited. For example, silent reading time accounts for only 6 to 15 percent of total school time (Blanton & Moorman, 1990; Goodlad, 1984). Even more critical is that during this limited silent reading time, many struggling readers/writers spend most of their time either looking at the teacher, waiting for the teacher to "come and answer" their raised hands, or reading not books but single xeroxed pages (Fitzgerald, 1995; Ruddell & Ruddell, 1995).

In addition, many other special instructional actions described in this chapter are not used in most of today's classrooms (Baker & Zigmond, 1990; Durkin, 1978–79; Mason,

1984). Instead, directed learning often occurs in full-class groups with **round-robin reading** (children take turns reading consecutive paragraphs orally). Another widespread instructional activity is to assign the same reading to all readers and then ask a series of questions prepared by textbook authors or teachers, telling answers to these questions if students do not know them, and usually sending five or six readers to pull-out programs outside the classroom to complete their worksheets. When interruptions and travel time are factored out in these programs, special instruction for struggling readers/writers typically lasts only 15 to 30 minutes a day (Lehr & Harris, 1988). Thus, planning to increase the amount of time these readers actually *read*, including sufficient class time for them to talk and write about what they read, should be among your first instructional priorities.

ORGANIZATIONAL ACTION 2. Give these readers extra time to complete literacy assignments without allowing their slower pace to be perceived as a deficiency by you or by their peers. Tell them literacy growth can occur rapidly and through persistence. Teach them how to manage their learning time (Coleman, 1992). One way to do so is to schedule "dress rehearsal" checks a few minutes (or a few days for longer assignments) before projects, readings, and writings are due. These checks enable you to monitor, scaffold, and improve students' time management, reading, and writing. Similarly, by scheduling small group meetings once or twice a week, you can give less accomplished readers/writers opportunities to report their progress and to ask for new literacy and task management strategies before projects and reports are due.

Because struggling readers' growth is usually not incremental, your support is important when their goals are not achieved while those around them are succeeding. Such support keeps students' commitments, interests, and self-concepts high. If these readers are taught that there is no universal "right time" for certain literacy abilities to evolve, comparisons to peers will be less likely, and students will be less likely to reduce their self-initiated literacy time and positive values for reading and writing.

ORGANIZATIONAL ACTION 3. Become a better time manager. The better a classroom manager you are, the more time less accomplished readers/writers have to develop their reading/writing abilities. Research has shown that such readers make more progress when their teachers provide structure, clarity, redundancy, appropriate pace, and maximal student engagement (Scruggs & Mastropieri, 1994).

You can improve time management by taking a few simple, commonsense steps. One is to schedule self-selected silent reading times immediately after a recess or lunch period. Instruct students to place materials for their sustained silent readings on their desks before recess so they can begin reading as soon as they enter the room. Another time-management strategy is to assign one student per table to distribute papers and supplies—rather than one or two students for the entire class—so that less successful students can begin reading instructions for the lesson immediately. Utilize time normally spent waiting and create authentic reading experiences for these readers. For instance, instead of standing in bus lines for 20 minutes after school, allow students to read a favorite book to a group of younger schoolmates in the cafeteria until their bus number is called. Time management can further work for the benefit of these readers if you allow them to study new material the day before it is introduced to the full class.

Box 7.1 lists specific actions that reading specialists and classroom teachers have taken to increase classroom management so struggling readers/writers can have the

Assessing Your Ability to Create Optimal Learning Conditions for Struggling Readers/Writers

Place a number in the appropriate column to show how many days per week you currently use each procedure. Each day equals one "point."

	Frequently (4 to 5 days/ week)	Sometimes (2 to 3 days/ week)	Rarely (0 to 1 day/ week)
COMMUNICATING			
■ I clearly define activities for students.	_____	_____	_____
■ I post assignments where students can see them, and they know where to turn in work.	_____	_____	_____
■ Standards for form and neatness are understood.	_____	_____	_____
■ I have a system for absent students to make up assignments.	_____	_____	_____
■ Consequences for incomplete or late work are defined, and students know what they are.	_____	_____	_____
■ I make decisions without hesitation and delegate responsibility where appropriate.	_____	_____	_____
■ I clearly display students' work.	_____	_____	_____
■ I provide various forms of feedback to students.	_____	_____	_____
MONITORING			
■ Each day, I list and prioritize tasks to be done the next day.	_____	_____	_____
■ I rank daily tasks and complete the most important tasks first.	_____	_____	_____
■ I have a procedure to monitor students' work in progress.	_____	_____	_____
■ I know when students have completed assignments.	_____	_____	_____
■ Students keep individual records of their work.	_____	_____	_____
■ I use the grading policies and procedures defined by my school.	_____	_____	_____
■ I set time aside for myself every day.	_____	_____	_____
■ I have a procedure for sending students' work home to parents.	_____	_____	_____
MANAGING MATERIALS			
■ My desk and teaching area are neat and organized.	_____	_____	_____
■ I put materials back where they belong after I use them.	_____	_____	_____
■ Students know where to get pencils when theirs break.	_____	_____	_____

Total Points _____ + _____ + _____ = _____%
of time you are optimizing learning for struggling readers

necessary uninterrupted blocks of time to refine their reading strategies. Use Box 7.1 to assess how efficiently you are managing your classroom. Place a check mark in the appropriate column for each of the actions or policies currently used in your classroom. Were there any you did not check?

Your students' learning environment will improve if you develop a procedure to incorporate into your classroom the strategies you have not yet adopted. Such procedures give you more time to spend with less accomplished readers/writers. For example, after Kelly Austin, a dynamic second grade teacher, completed Box 7.1, she developed the following strategy to make more efficient use of the first several minutes of the school day, when students are arriving and getting settled:

> I implemented the buddy-reading grouping system to increase reading time in my class. Now, from the moment students arrive, they know to select a partner and read together. The first child to arrive each day works with me. The remaining pairs are chosen only by the order in which students enter the room—that is, the first two that enter are paired, and then the next two, and so on. If there is an odd number, the third student reads with me and my partner until another student arrives. This paired reading continues until 5 minutes after the official school day begins and increases daily silent reading time all readers by 5 to 15 minutes.

Once you have established an optimal learning environment for readers, the next consideration is how to plan lessons that can improve less accomplished readers' literacy capabilities.

Designing a Quality Curriculum

A quality literacy curriculum for struggling readers consists of six steps, as detailed below. Before lessons begin, remember that less advanced readers' growth usually occurs through self-initiated actions and requests for special instruction. This is true because large gains in reading ability result from split-second insights that correct these students' misconceptions about reading and writing. Before many of these insights are possible, the students must experience some degree of modeling by you or their peers. In classrooms that follow the six steps on the lesson plan, such modeling is almost continuous, because students set goals, monitor their own progress, and usually ask for help whenever they experience blocks to their literacy progress.

As you make lesson plans, you might also ask yourself questions such as these:

- What will I do in this lesson to help students establish their voice and maintain attention to print?
- What will I do to keep the classroom or clinical setting comfortable and orderly as struggling readers/writers explore their literacy goals?
- What can I do in this lesson—such as bringing in more concrete experiences—to help students value this particular literacy experience more?

You are now ready to implement the six steps to design quality-driven lessons for struggling readers/writers.

Step 1: Attract Less Advanced Students through Choices and Open Tasks

Students form strong conceptions about literacy and the material they read early in life. These beliefs and theories are difficult to dislodge (Shaughnessey, 1994). Thus, to attract less advanced students to literacy, you must help them move from stereotypical and misconceived conceptualizations toward deeper comprehension. Help your readers/writers in Tier 1 and 2 support settings to choose topics with great care, and spend sufficient time with literacy tasks so that misconceptions can be disproved through exposure to a volume of facts. You should teach them to approach topics in numerous ways and provide varied opportunities for them to display their understanding. Activating and organizing students' background knowledge before they read will also assist comprehension.

To appreciate the importance of choice in lessons, compare your affective response to a meal you select from a menu to a meal that someone else chooses for you. Choice is even more crucial for less accomplished readers/writers, because materials of high personal interest are easier for them to comprehend. Moreover, through topic selection readers come to understand that reading is for a specific use *right now* (Turner & Paris, 1995). Also, when students read within the contexts they choose, they will internalize new reading strategies faster (Block, 1994; Marzano, 1992). One method of including choice in lessons is to involve students in topic and material selections. You can also ask them to describe what they want to learn about reading and writing, you can give them options about what they want to reemphasize in their free and content area readings, or you can coordinate their choices with Tier 3 support teacher.

Instead of singlehandedly trying to adapt instructions for 24 individuals, let students assist you by making adaptations they value. Making selections also allows students to see that they can indeed make good choices concerning their reading materials, reading abilities, and reading purposes. In such classrooms, students are more likely to judge reading and writing to be fun. Further, these students report that they learn new stories and word meanings because they get help from their friends (Morrow, 1993).

To illustrate, second grade readers in Tier 3 and 4 support settings in Pittsburgh were given a choice about their learning goals, including the chance to decide which tasks they would work on at any given moment. As a result, these students completed more learning tasks in less time than a comparison group (Maynard, Tyler, & Arnold, 2000). In like manner, when inner-city students were taught to self-assess their reading, they missed less school and scored better on a national test of basic reading skills than those in conventional classrooms (Block, 2001; Corno, 1994). Similarly, readers who participated in decisions about schoolwork scored higher on standardized tests than peers who did not (Boggiano, 1992). They were more likely to continue working even when tasks were not self-selected (Bandura, 1994).

Step 2: Help Struggling Readers Set Goals and Standards

Have students state what they want to accomplish, the method they will use to accomplish it, and how they will judge that they have been successful. In this way, less accomplished readers can articulate what and how they want to learn and can integrate self-assessment into their ongoing learning processes.

The most difficult aspect of guiding students in goal selection is that they tend to create goals that are too vague or general (Block, 2001). To address this tendency, direct readers/writers to state their goals as follows: "I want to understand or appreciate _____ by _____. I will know I have reached my goal when I can _____." Sample goals set by struggling readers from grades K–8, which your students can use as models, are shown in Table 7.1.

It is also helpful if all students know what they should do if they achieve their individual goals before the class is ready to move to the next activity. For example, students in the lower grades can be taught that early finishers are to go to the "special box" that contains constantly changing puppets, props, costumes, and flannel board figures; or that they should go to the drama center and prepare a one-minute presentation for Sharing Time. Older students can be taught to grab a buddy and a book and move to a quiet corner and read orally or silently together.

Step 3: Plan a Special Support

The most readily available types of special supports are (1) students in the class, (2) adult volunteers, (3) older schoolmates who spend 15 to 30 minutes as teaching assistants for small groups, (4) reading materials that cover a wide range of readability levels, and (5) technology. In planning special supports for lessons, it is helpful to ask yourself questions such as these:

> Does this support provide opportunities for struggling readers and writers to reach their own goals?
>
> Do the texts I've selected challenge, inspire, and empower students to take risks?
>
> Does the support enable me to ask more from them than they would ask from themselves?
>
> Does the support sustain engagement for at least 30 minutes longer than would be possible without it?
>
> Does the quality of the literature, in and of itself, lead students into other topics, stories, or lives?
>
> Do I compare other books to pieces I've selected and find them lacking?
>
> Do I keep thinking about the content in this lesson myself?

Step 4: Provide Time to Read

Give students time to read alone, with you, or with peers before full-class conversations; doing so strengthens the voices of these readers/writers. Before students begin this reading time, you can ask them what they want to discuss when the reading session ends, or perhaps you can tell them an idea you want to discuss with them. In this way, these readers will have established a purpose for reading. With repeated practice of Step 4, most students will begin to establish their own purposes for reading.

TABLE 7.1 Sample Goals Formulated by Struggling Readers/Writers

Goals of Students in Grades K–2

Learn to write my name
Hold book and turn pages alone
Keep my eyes on my book
Pick a book I can read
Skip unknown words
Read favorite books again
Figure out words by sounding out, asking someone, skipping and coming back, using letters
  for clues, using the pictures, covering half the word, looking at the shape of the word
Read more by myself
Try not to make silly mistakes
Make my writing more legible so I can read it
Tell the story out loud to someone
Read new kinds of books
Read longer books
Read chapter books
Publish a book that looks almost as good as an actually published book
Try not to write myself into a corner (plan ahead)

Goals of Students in Grades 3–6

Get help sounding out words
Read at home every night
Stick with a book
Choose more "just right" books
Skip unknown word and come back to it
Substitute a word
Skim or skip uninteresting parts
Read more books by _____
Read with expectation
Recommend books to other kids
Ask myself, "Does this make sense?"

Goals of Students in Grades 7–9

Read regularly for enjoyment
Read at least one novel or nonfiction book of my own choice
Identify the main ideas in printed text
Understand the ideas of character and plot in literature
Learn to use a wide range of words about people
Understand and use imaginative language
Extend vocabulary with new words found in print
Collect information about people from the newspaper
Locate and use relevant information from a variety of texts
Give honest, thoughtful views about my reading

Step 5: Assess Activities

When you have completed the literacy activity, assess the results. Struggling readers/writers appreciate literacy assessments that include self-evaluations. For example, in one survey, more than 2,000 4- and 5-year-olds were asked whether, if they could evaluate their reading achievements, they would be able to and would want to. They were also asked if they thought their evaluations would be accurate. The results were overwhelmingly positive. Even young readers say they want their teachers to let them decide more. They want more time to read, and they want to evaluate what they achieve. They also want teachers to trust their evaluations (Daly, 1989). Moreover, Strommen (1994) discovered that when children worked at hands-on activities, presented examples of the literacy behaviors and goals they had learned, and assessed their purposes, they made more reasonable speculations as to their next developmental goals. (Examples of types of assessment from which readers/writers can select were presented in Chapter 6.)

Step 6: Ask Questions about What Worked Best

Have students explain orally or in writing what activities and experiences worked best for them in this lesson and why. Their feedback will assist you to incorporate their preferred learning modalities into the next lessons.

In addition to following this basic lesson plan, you can also use other strategies to accelerate literacy development. The next section will present five grouping systems that create optimal learning environments for these students.

▤ Qualities of Effective Instructional Groups

Through carefully considered grouping practices, struggling readers and writers can develop trust in their own abilities to solve literacy problems, take more literacy risks, learn "how to learn," adapt to changes, communicate about material they read, and ask questions (Allington, 1995; Block, 2001). Unfortunately, in some classrooms the same readers are placed together in the same small group every day. This grouping system is called **homogeneous** because theoretically all students in each group have the same level of reading ability. Research indicates, however, that no two students have the same literacy abilities, so that truly homogeneous grouping can never really occur (Allington, 1995; Chall, 1993).

Moreover, a growing body of research suggests that such ability grouping does not increase students' achievement—and in fact is likely to have detrimental effects on the self-concept and achievement of some readers (Berghoff & Egawa, 1991; Clay, 1993b; Olson, 1994). One reason is that whereas less accomplished students need to learn new ways to organize information, make valuable contributions to conversations, and write and read more challenging words, expert peer modelers are absent in most homogeneous groups. These deficits of homogeneous grouping were articulated well by two struggling readers:

Sometimes you get stuck with the leftover people when other people don't want us in their better reading groups. It's just sort of depressing. And then you sort of start not wanting to work at all. (West & Oldfeather, 1993, p. 54)

I am in the slow readers' group
My brother is in the football team
My sister is a waitress at The Blue Dragon Diner
I am in the slow group in reading.
That is all I am in and
I hate it!

—*Allan Ahlberg,* second grader (Booth, 1989, p. 3)

Homogeneous instructional grouping should be replaced with more flexible arrangements and supplementary assistance such as parental aides or Chapter 1/Title 1 teachers. You can also maximize the individual help readers receive through one-to-one discovery discussions and tutor–tutee pairs. When you use effective grouping practices, struggling readers/writers receive the following benefits:

- Students have more role models from which to learn.
- You will spend less time managing behavioral problems stemming from the lowered self-esteem that homogeneous grouping creates.
- Students will not impose lower expectations on some members of the class.
- Students will have more opportunities to see examples before they attempt strategies independently (Texas Education Agency, 1994).

Each of the following grouping systems provides additional individual benefits for these readers/writers. Keep in mind, however, that none of these grouping systems is a panacea and therefore none should be used exclusively. To help you decide how to use the grouping plans most effectively, a listing of the benefits and pitfalls of each plan follows the descriptions.

Reading Response Groups

Reading response groups, or **literature response groups,** are heterogeneous small groups of five to seven students who meet to discuss books they elect to read. These groups are also called *literature circles, conversation circles, book clubs,* and *reading workshops.* In these groups members read the same selection of children's literature. Usually, 4 days are set aside for students to read the book (independently or in pairs) with a peer group leader; students set daily obtainable goals for how many pages to complete. Then the group meets to discuss their interpretations of the book. Through these reading workshops children learn the following literacy skills:

- To enjoy discussing books read in common
- To respond orally and in writing to quality children's literature
- To analyze the structure of stories, poetry, or nonfiction
- To recognize the theme or main ideas in stories, poems, or nonfiction

- To describe how they came to understand the book
- To write their own fiction, nonfiction, and poetry inspired by what they have read

Furthermore, this grouping system can be modified to discuss students' writing as well. Writers' workshops are best when they take place among a small circle of friends with differing levels of ability. No more than three students should be in the group, as in-depth critiques and suggestions are more likely then. To begin, reluctant writers read their work or ask peers to read it. The other group members describe what they liked best, what confused them, and what advice they have for improvements. Then the other students share their work, and the cycle repeats. It's important that reluctant writers in each group go first so that they do not lose their confidence to share.

The reading response group format can be "free recall" discussion (Raphael, Florio-Ruane, Kehus, George, Hasty, & Highfield, 2001), in which students express personal responses without a focus question from you to open the discussion. In some instances a more effective format may be student-led "conversation circles" or "literature conversations" in which student- or teacher-generated questions open the meeting—questions such as these:

What does the author do to make you feel like you're right there in the book?

What is the most captivating aspect of the book's plot?

What do you think is the theme of the book?

How does the author reveal changes in character?

How did this reading experience improve your reading ability?

There are several adaptations you can make to expand the benefits of reading response groups for less accomplished readers. For instance, it will be beneficial if you allow these students to read parts of the book with you or an adult aide, so they will not fall behind more able decoders/comprehenders and thus limit their participation in group discussions—and will not have to *pretend* they have read their assigned chapters just to save face. After the response group concludes its discussion, these readers could reread the material—and they could then open the next group meeting with a synopsis of what was discussed. Another adaptation is to plan for some meetings to discuss several books on the same topic, at various readability levels; this way, less successful readers can select a book on their individual reading level and present unique facts from that book during the discussion. When less advanced readers have a chance to choose from several selections concerning the same topic, or from several works by the same author, these readers can profit from the increased schema provided from multiple exposures to the same content or writing style.

Regardless of the type of reading response group you use, to be most effective you should monitor how much struggling readers read each day. You can do this unobtrusively by walking around the room at the end of the silent reading period and noting the page number each student is on. Also remember that it is usually not wise to continue discussion of any one reading for more than 3 days, as personal responses to the chapter or other selection are usually exhausted in 3 days or less.

Reading response groups can provide benefits for less accomplished readers, as listed below. The limitations to be overcome are also described.

Benefits for Struggling Readers/Writers

1. Because these readers' responses are valued by peers, social status in class often improves.

2. Students take ownership of their reading/writing and make many self-efficacy choices concerning literacy each day.

3. Students learn varied interpretations, make multiple applications to real-world situations, and share personal experiences—but do not have to defend their claims or make connections as often as in other grouping systems.

4. These students may read an entire book for the first time in their lives and develop personal values for literacy that they carry with them throughout their lives.

Potential Pitfalls to Address

1. Recognizing and recording individual literacy strengths and weaknesses is difficult.

2. Scheduling is difficult—such as what to do when one group finishes reading its book before others.

3. There is little or no individual instruction to overcome individual literacy problems in decoding and comprehension strategies.

4. Reading high-level books may be too frustrating, unless you make modifications during silent reading time. (Because of this, struggling readers may fake having read their books.)

Box 7.2 includes guidelines for diagnosing and assessing benefits received by a reluctant reader from a specific reading response group discussion.

Cooperative Groups

Cooperative groups differ from reading response groups in that every student in the group is accountable for a portion of the learning responsibilities and every student's effort is necessary for the highest achievement and grade. A group's grade is based on a group presentation, product, or project. Since the mid-1980s, cooperative learning has received considerable attention as a grouping system to provide academic and social benefits for less accomplished readers/writers (Johnson & Johnson, 1995).

Unfortunately, some students tend to be nonparticipatory (Matthews, 1992; Stevens & Slavin, 1995). One effective strategy to get around this problem is to assign a number to each member of the cooperative group and a different number to designate each group. Then pose a question. All cooperative group team members are to put their heads together, examine the possibilities, and construct an answer. You then pick numbers by drawing cards from a stack. The first number drawn designates the person from each group who will give the group's answer; the second number specifies which group will respond first (Garmston & Wellman, 1994).

7.2 DIAGNOSIS AND ASSESSMENT

Assessing a Reluctant Reader's Participation in Reading Response Group Discussions

Student's name: _____ Date: _____

Rater (self, teacher, or peer): _____ Total score: _____

ACTIONS TAKEN TO INCREASE THE QUALITY OF THE CONVERSATION	SCORE (1 point for presence of action; 2 points for quality use; 3 points for internally guided mastery)
1. Identified associations between characters, themes, and his/her life	_____
2. Responded to classmates' contributions and used strategies to respond positively to others' seemingly "incorrect" comments	_____
3. Shared his/her own literary voice and/or life story	_____
4. Constructed chains of reasoning between classmates' comments	_____
5. Expressed empathy for a classmate or literary character	_____
6. Asked a question or expounded/justified a personal position	_____
7. Was an equal partner in the conversation, not dominant or withdrawn	_____
8. Made comments that were not straight recalls or retellings of text	_____
9. Used complex language/expression	_____
10. Gave bases for statements, predictions, and hypotheses	_____
	TOTAL: _____ of 30 possible

Interpretation: Instructional intervention should occur for any item on which a struggling reader does not score 3.

Suggested responsibilities for struggling students that will maximize their participation include the following:

- *Initiator:* Reexplains assignments and manages turn taking in the group
- *Researcher:* Obtains examples and facts the group does not know collectively

- *Procedure developer and resource engineer:* Handles all materials and routine tasks for the group, arranges seating, and manages props for group presentations
- *Creative design artist:* Is responsible for illustrations and any art, graphics, banners, charts, or examples needed by the group
- *Recorder:* Keeps notes on group discussion; prepares first drafts for all group presentations
- *Overseer and assistant:* Assists any of the above members who request help, and assumes responsibility for any of the above jobs when a student is absent.

Before the first cooperative group occurs, teach strategies for how to construct good questions, learn vocabulary, and identify literary elements. It is helpful to establish a time limit in which products and processes are to be completed and to not waver from it (e.g., cooperative groups must complete oral discussions in 10 minutes and written first drafts in 15). The group should meet every day. It is best if less successful readers remain in the same cooperative group for only one week each month, as they need supports from varied grouping systems to grow most effectively. By assigning specific tasks so every student has a responsibility, rotating members so that everyone eventually performs each duty, and requiring a concrete product at the end of each cooperative group meeting, you can reduce the potential inefficiencies in this grouping system.

Another strategy for establishing cooperative groups that build readers' commitment to learning is to use **sociograms**—methods of identifying which students are closest friends in a learning community. To employ this method, provide multiple topics and ask students to select three that interest them. Second, have students write names of three people with whom they want to work. When you arrange groups based on your students' choice of the person or topic to work with, you ensure that students will get at least one topic of choice or be able to work with at least one person they choose.

Two variations of cooperative groups in reading specialists' settings and self-contained classrooms that are exceptionally effective for struggling readers are *base groups* and *buddy systems.* **Base groups** are cooperative groups that stay together at least a half year. Students work together several times a week in every subject area, but not every day because of the need to incorporate the benefits of other types of grouping systems. Individual student talents develop through the bonding that occurs, as well as through group goal setting and the social skill sessions that are integral to base groups. Students also learn how to expand on discussion topics, accept varied points of view, draw each other out, and effectively acknowledge individual comments. Often base groups begin the year by designing their group ad, song, motto, goals, name, and awards (Bellanca & Fogarty, 1990).

Buddy systems are cooperative, heterogeneous groups in which all people are responsible for everyone else's learning, even to the extent that they consult one another before asking the teacher, edit one another's work, and read one another's assignments before they are turned in (Fader, Duggins, Finn, & McNeil, 1976). Both buddy systems and base groups can be used spontaneously throughout the day in all subject areas (e.g., "Move to your base groups and prepare a summary of key points learned today for your daily grade in our Science Lab"). The benefits and limitations of cooperative groups for reluctant readers and writers follow.

Benefits for Struggling Readers/Writers	Potential Pitfalls to Address
1. Students exhibit increased self-esteem, tolerance for others' opinions, and appreciation for varied literary responses.	1. Less accomplished readers may come to rely on more able peers for answers.
2. Students learn how to work well in groups, and this instruction transfers to real-world situations.	2. Monitoring of individual student and group growth is difficult if not planned carefully in advance.
3. More able students become actively involved with less accomplished readers by modeling, encouraging, and assisting them in literacy development.	3. It is difficult to develop group goals that challenge all students continuously.
4. Students show significant gains in reading comprehension and composition (Johnson & Johnson, 1982; Slavin, 1990).	4. End products must be broad-based in their objectives but must also include more complex and sophisticated coverage so that students at all levels of the literacy continuum are challenged.
5. Students experience decreased alienation from school and peers (Putnam & Markovchick, 1989).	5. Because individual member responsibilities are beyond some readers' zone of proximal development, these students may become embarrassed before peers.

Expert Groups

When you form **expert groups,** struggling readers/writers become authorities on a topic and are acknowledged by peers for this expertise. To begin, the class first decides on a general topic for study. Then you assign students to heterogeneous groups of four, with each group studying a different aspect of the topic. Within groups, the subtopics are further broken down and each member is assigned a specific content area to read about and share with others in the group. In other words, each group member becomes an expert on one specific aspect of the general topic under study. The expert grouping system is beneficial for reluctant readers/writers because they can receive shorter but interesting books that they read either silently or orally with another person.

When students complete their reading, they teach their content to others in their group. All gain from the increased background knowledge provided by others. The group ends with a group-constructed synopsis of all the information they gathered on their aspect of the group's subtopic. After these summaries are made, each member of the expert group becomes a member of a new group, and members again teach their area of expertise to classmates, as depicted in Figure 7.1.

Two special types of expert grouping systems are *research groups* and *group communal writings.* **Research groups** are special in that group size depends on the number

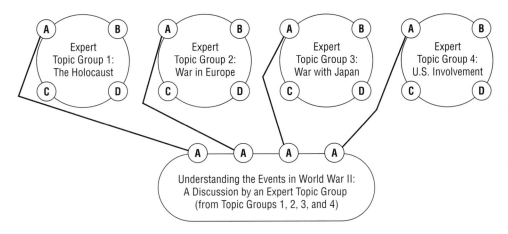

FIGURE 7.1 How Expert Groups Work

of students who select a specific topic to explore; large groups and two-member research groups can be engaged simultaneously. In research groups, however, every student answers a unique question that he or she generates—not one selected from a list of topics in a curriculum guide. Similarly, **group communal writings** can consist of a varied number of students. In these groups students contribute their particular strengths to one written product. For example, one student who enjoys outlining and organizing thoughts before writing listens as each group member describes what he or she wants to say, and this student creates a basic outline to guide each writing; another who enjoys and is proficient in language mechanics edits all group members' work. As one student reported:

> I loved holding the sessions because I was helping someone and I felt good about myself because I had read. I usually don't read that often, but I felt like I would be letting my group members down. They depended on me, and I depended on them. I hope we do this more often. We put our heads together and it is more exciting because three heads are better than one. (Hicks, 1991, p. 148)

Another excellent variation of expert grouping puts students together on the basis of a reading ability they want to learn. These readers' ability groups can be called *Word Wanters, Meaning Makers, Breadth Builders, Speed Mavericks, Memory Menders, Critical Analyzers,* and so forth—depending on the group's objective. One day a week one of the above objectives is listed on the board, and less accomplished readers who want to increase their abilities in that area can elect to join heterogeneously grouped peers with the same objective. The group meets with you for as long as it chooses to explore strategies students can use to improve that reading or writing ability. In these groups all members model what they do and then ask you and other group members questions to gain even more expertise in that area. These objective-based groups can be coordinated with Tier 3 support work so that individual readers can discuss the same area of need on the same day. Such groups maintain their memberships until reteaching has been successful, students have developed strengths in their selected area, and students can perform the literacy competency independently.

The benefits and limitations of expert grouping systems for less advanced readers follow.

Benefits for Struggling Readers/Writers	Potential Pitfalls to Address
1. Readers develop high affect for reading because of the instant benefits—such as overcoming a weakness instantly because someone edited their writing perfectly, or learning information to share that is important to others.	1. Readers often do not read all the material independently, so future readings in that subject may be hampered.
2. Reading and writing integrate with self-esteem because struggling readers may be seen as experts for the first time; they will be asked questions that no one else in the group can answer. Further, becoming an expert at school often supplants students' needs to join destructive community gangs.	2. Students must be guided in literary selections, as many books at different levels of difficulty are available.
3. Students learn to synthesize data.	3. It is difficult to recognize and record individual students' growth in reading comprehension abilities, because much is learned through oral presentations.

Desktop Learning Centers

Desktop learning centers are created by one or more readers/writers who explore a single concept with displays placed on a desk located at the side or back of the room (like a museum exhibit). This grouping system is particularly valuable for readers with physical and cognitive differences, as discussed in Chapter 3, because when students share their work they become stars of the class. It is also valuable in that concentrated reading in a single area increases these students' decoding ability, vocabulary, background knowledge, imagery, and comprehension.

Desktop learning centers begin when a student asks you about something he or she wants to learn. You then ask this student to study that topic, either independently or with a partner or partners, and to prepare a desktop learning center for classmates. Then these students spend two 90-minute periods reading and writing about that topic. On the third and fourth 90-minute periods, students collect, make, and label as many objects as possible to display at their desktop learning center. On the fifth day, the class hears the students' presentation, studies the display, and asks questions of the "experts" who prepared it. Examples of the types of centers created by Block (1993a, 2001) and Vukelich (1993) for younger students appear in Box 7.3.

CLASSROOM TEACHERS

Teachers' Instructional Interventions: Desktop Learning Centers

Instructions: Set a desk to the front and left of the classroom. Allow one or two struggling readers to read and write books about one of the topics below. The students do not share their books with peers until a week's study is completed.

RESTAURANT
Reservation book
Telephone book
Menus
Play money
Pens, pencils, markers
Order pads
Telephone message pads
Calendar
Paper of various sizes
Books about food

SHOE STORE
Foot-measuring device
Checkbooks
Receipt pads
Play money
Pricing tags
Credit cards
Paper of various sizes
Shoe posters
Repair forms
Claim checks
Shoe labels
Books about clothing

CAMPGROUND
Name tags
Fishing license application forms
Fishing licenses
Calendar
Entrance passes
Diaries
Paper of various sizes
Books, pamphlets, magazines
Maps
Postcards

Stationery
Observation log
Books about nature

LIBRARY/ BOOKSTORE
Sign for book fines
Children's books, magazines (with card pockets and date due slips)
Date stamp and stamp pad
Book return box
Cash register
Play money
Library cards
Books about individual student hobbies or cultural interests

BANK
Teller window (use puppet stage)
Passbooks
Checks
Play money
Roll papers for coins
Deposit slips
Money bags
Books about math

OFFICE
Typewriter, calculator
Business checkbook
Clipboards, open/closed signs, calendars
File cabinets for alphabetical ordering
Index cards, business cards
Post-its
Address labels
Paper, paper clips
Books about careers

Source: Adapted from C. Block (1993), *Teaching the Language Arts,* pp. 432–435. Boston: Allyn & Bacon.

The benefits and limitations of desktop learning centers for struggling readers and writers follow.

Benefits for Struggling Readers/Writers

1. Students are not limited by their literacy weaknesses in the contributions they can make to the class. Also, hobbies can come to school to enhance literary appreciation.

2. Less accomplished readers can develop intense and sustained friendships with more advanced readers, who can also teach vocabulary that these students could not read without aid.

3. New genres are discovered and appreciated, and instruction is authentic.

Potential Pitfalls to Address

1. It is not always easy to find time to hold meetings so that intense bonding, learning, and sharing occurs.

2. Learning centers must become more than glorified show-and-tell days. Reading must occur, and in many different genres, so that students can add new knowledge to their interest areas.

3. Some schools have set a time each week for same-age meetings. To be most effective, time should also be made for struggling readers to teach younger peers.

Paired Groupings

There are many types of paired groupings, including pairs, dyads, study buddies (Block & Dellamura, 2000/2001; Jensen, 1992), and think–pair–share groupings (Lyman, 1990). In these groupings readers are assigned or select a partner with whom they complete a certain literacy project.

If they work as a **pair,** two different grades can be given and students can read materials at different levels of difficulty. If they work as a **dyad,** students receive the same grade and usually read the same reading selection. Two effective activities for pairs and dyads are assisted reading and repeated readings. **Assisted reading** occurs when one student reads one page orally and his or her partner reads the next page. In **repeated reading** one student reads a page and then the second rereads the same page (see also Chapter 10).

Study buddies meet at school to begin homework assignments and also exchange phone numbers so they can consult each other at home. Each is responsible for being sure the study buddy receives and completes all the work for days he or she is absent. In schools that do not assign homework, struggling readers/writers benefit from study buddies by being allowed to pair with a person who has the same hobby or reading interests. They can meet to share work on their hobbies at home. They can also keep each other informed of upcoming television and community events relative to the hobby area.

Think–pair–share groupings (Box 7.4) include four steps. First, students are paired and listen while you pose a question. Second, each person has a set time to think of a response. Third, pairs discuss both of their responses. Last, they share their responses with the entire class. In this paired grouping system, these readers learn how to rehearse responses mentally before sharing—unlike traditional question-and-answer periods, in which reluctant readers have limited time to think through their own answers to a question before other answers are given and the discussion moves

7.4

MIDDLE SCHOOL and HIGH SCHOOL

Using the Pair Share Strategy to Optimize Learning for Reluctant Readers and Writers

- After students have engaged in a reading or writing activity, they can pair with partners to share ideas, opinions, or questions they may have.
- Then the partners can come back to the group and report the information they shared to the whole class.

- The teachers can write the pairs' concerns or ideas on poster paper or in the format of a semantic web.

Step 1:

Share in pairs

Step 2:

Share with a group

Step 3:

Share with the class

on. This system also gives these students opportunities to share many of their own ideas with others. This grouping system also makes participation in conversations less threatening.

Tutorials pair readers so as to let them meet their literacy needs in ways that go beyond small groups. Tutorials enable these students to continuously make connections, supplant ineffective strategies, ask questions, and reconsider (Getsie, Langer, & Glass, 1985). As you might expect, to be most effective, tutor–tutee pairs should be taught how to engage in interactive, explanatory discussions and how to provide feedback and think alouds. When this occurs, less accomplished readers will ask up to 240 times as many questions about their own reading as they will in any other grouping system (Graesser & Pearson, 1994).

Tutorials for these readers are different, however, from those for higher-achieving peers in two significant ways. First, as mentioned, these readers serve as both tutor and tutee. When they serve both roles, their self-concept is enhanced instead of reduced, which often occurs when they are only the tutee. Second, students are taught to *listen* and not talk when they are tutors. Instead of teaching, tutors ask tutees to tell what the most difficult part was for them and what they want to learn. Thus, instead of teaching/telling/talking about areas of need, tutors listen as tutees explain strategies they attempted and reasons why they think these strategies were not successful. Struggling readers benefit from listening to others' explanations of strategies as well as from having to explain their own.

Tutorial pairs can be formed in several ways. First, you can pair students in cross-age groupings. In these tutorials struggling readers transfer what they have learned to younger schoolmates. In another tutorial format students can become "secret mentors." In this system each student in the class selects the name of a classmate from a jar. On each slip of paper, below their names, individual students have described a particular difficulty they are having with literacy. You meet one-on-one with each secret mentor to develop ways to overcome the tutee's problem and develop a lesson plan. For a full week, for 10 minutes a day while students are writing freely, secret mentors can elect to write about strengths they value in their secret tutee. At the end of the week, the secret mentors are revealed; they spend the class period that day assisting tutees with their difficulty—with students alternating between being the mentor and the tutee so that each student is both.

In a variation of the tutorial format, reluctant readers can become tutors to their full class or a small group. Each student chooses something to read and learn about that would benefit the class in some way. For example, one student read the directions and learned how to make individual blackboards (using blackboard paint and 11×14 heavy cardboard squares)—and then led the class in making their own blackboards. This reader used literacy in a way that he valued and also for the benefit of others. Now all students in the class have personal blackboards on which to write answers and take notes during full-class conversations, so all can share their thoughts.

Through tutorial plans struggling readers increase their self-esteem; add verification that reading is a valuable, enjoyable pursuit; and significantly increase their decoding and comprehension competencies (Labbo & Teale, 1990). At the end of each session, tutors and tutees can answer the following questions:

- What did you like least about this tutoring session?
- What did you appreciate/learn the most?
- How will you improve the session next time and why?

Tutors and tutees can also write more extensive assessments periodically to gain more diagnostic information (see Chapter 6).

The benefits and limitations of tutorial settings for less accomplished readers/writers follow.

Benefits for Struggling Readers/Writers

1. Students receive direct instruction in the specific areas where their needs occur.

2. Students need not participate in several one-to-one discovery discussions concerning the same topic; you economize instructional time.

3. Close, caring friendships often develop—which support other literacy growths.

Potential Pitfalls to Overcome

1. Keeping readers in homogeneous groups for too long could reduce self-concept and affect for literacy.

2. Instruction must provide multiple ways to apply concept because these readers' more able peers may not be present during instruction.

3. Off-task behavior can occur.

Each of these grouping systems can enhance literacy for struggling readers/writers. Each creates large blocks of time for students to engage in literacy at their own pace and appropriate developmental level along the literacy continuum. Within any group, however, problems can arise. A description of solutions to address them follows in the next section.

Solving Classroom and One-on-One Learning Difficulties

There are five general problems that often occur in large or small group settings:

1. No one wants to share.
2. Too many students share simultaneously.
3. Comments are not understood by others.
4. A few dominate the conversation.
5. Students may give predictable answers.

There is a subtle but effective way to solve the problem of students' not sharing. When your students draw a blank and duck their heads during a discussion, ask them to turn to a partner and share the first (even if nebulous) thought they have relative to the topic. This less threatening scenario will break the ice. Then pairs can share, or you can continue the discussion by asking students to pull four pairs together. These groups identify similarities among their thoughts on the board. After all groups have written their thoughts, the entire class discusses these ideas and/or the students turn to their original partners and together write a summary of what they have learned. Reluctant

7.5   READING SPECIALISTS

Responding Appropriately and Effectively to Students' Incorrect Answers

1. **"Think Again."** When students have sufficient background to answer a question, respond to their first "less than correct" attempts by asking them to "think again." This response reassures students that they can produce an effective response, if only allowed a little more time and thought. Use this strategy to respond to a student's insufficient answer when you are 99 percent certain that the student can respond more effectively with a second try.

2. **Give a relevant prompt.** If students give a partial answer, provide a relevant fact about the topic and then reask the question. For example: "Why do you think Cinderella didn't run away from her wicked stepmother and stepsisters?" Students do not answer. You prompt by saying, "Placing yourself in Cinderella's shoes will help you understand what she could have thought."

3. **Reword the question.** When you ask a question and a student's answer suggests that your wording was vague, acknowledge this student's attempt and say, "Good try. Let me clarify my question. I think it confused you."

4. **"Could you expand your answer for us? Why do you think so?"** When students' answers appear to be off the point, ask them to explain their thinking. In many cases the answer is relevant when the thoughts that support it are explicated.

5. **"Remember that. I'm going to return and ask for this information again."** When the several answers students give demonstrate that they misunderstand major concepts in a discussion, provide more information. Once you provide this added material, tell students to remember it because you will call on them to state thoughts about it be-fore the class is over. Then as the class ends, you again ask for their thoughts about that information and the original concepts.

6. **"That would have been correct if. . . ."** If you recognize the reasoning behind a student's answers, follow the insufficient answer with "That would have been correct if I had asked . . . but I am asking . . ." (restating your original question). For example, if you ask, "What do you do to organize paragraphs when you write?" and a student answers, "Combine sentences to make them less redundant," you respond by saying, "That is an effective sentence-revising strategy, but what I was asking for was a strategy you use at the paragraph level."

7. **Give examples and nonexamples of possible solutions.** This discussion strategy can be used to close a lesson or as a review of previous information. It is based on a multiple-choice testing format in that you supply several answers to a question you ask, and students select one of the choices or generate a better solution. To illustrate: You are reviewing a student's language arts portfolio at the end of a grading period. You suggest three future goals and ask the student to decide which he or she most values.

   Nonexamples are used to stimulate students' thinking by stating what a discussion is *not* designed to cover. For example, you begin a class dialogue by stating, "Yesterday we covered some of the ways you can decode words. Today we want to extend our discussion. I *do not want you to tell us the names of the decoding strategies on your thinking guide.* Instead, I want you to tell us a specific word for which you used one of the decoding strategies."

readers/writers benefit by contributing continuously throughout the class period and by receiving peer support for their literacy abilities.

When too many students want to share simultaneously, stop conversations and ask everyone in the class to number off from 1 to 5. Then select one student to begin. After that student expresses his or her opinion, he or she will randomly call out a number from 1 to 5. All students with that number in the count-off express their opinion in response to that student's comment. The last student in that round calls out another number, and those with that number have the opportunity to express their opinion. The class can continue this procedure until everyone has had the opportunity to speak and the discussion is completed. During this process all students have the right to pass.

Whenever individuals make comments that are not understood by others or when a few dominate the conversation, try to discern the reason why this is happening. When reading specialists diagnose why some comments are distracting others, they help struggling readers/writers to correct their misconceptions by employing the feedback statements in Box 7.5.

Some reluctant readers/writers with lower self-esteem tend to respond with predictable answers, or they may quickly judge their comments to be wrong when in actuality they were not. To overcome these limitations, ask these students to explain the connection their comment had to prior comments, or ask open-ended questions that have more than one correct answer. This decreases the likelihood that such students will be completely wrong when answering and will thus encourage them to participate more freely.

An important instructional intervention by reading specialists and literacy teachers is to teach struggling readers to voice associations they identify between characters, themes, and their own lives; to be responsive to classmates' contributions; to share their own literary voices and life-stories; to construct chains of reasoning between classmates' comments; to express empathy for classmates or literary characters; to ask questions; to justify or expound on personal positions; and to give the bases for their statements, predictions, and hypotheses. Box 7.6 is a diagnostic and instructional tool that has been used effectively in secondary school Tier 1–4 special supports for less accomplished readers.

Chapter Summary

Optimal learning environments in one-to-one and small group instructional settings for struggling readers/writers can extend engagement in profitable and enjoyable literacy instruction for at least one to two times longer than without them. Many students need you to increase their self-direction and time-management skills, and all depend on the effective grouping systems described in this chapter. An optimal learning environment also allows students to choose their own reading materials, goals, and standards for success—with time being scheduled in creative ways so they can thoroughly read materials before participating in full-class discussions of them.

These readers' lessons contain special features. They are designed to repeatedly build students' commitment, interest, and confidence in themselves as readers/writers.

7.6

MIDDLE SCHOOL and HIGH SCHOOL

Individual Interventions for Struggling Writers

Use this self-assessment form when you finish teaching a new literacy strategy. Students can also complete the self-assessment at the end of a full week's work, and it can be used to plan next week's instruction.

Student name: _____   **Date:** _____

Describe your specific goal for today/this week/this project. _____

_____

What would you like me to teach you? _____

_____

What do you want to do after you finish reading as a postreading activity? _____

_____

COMPLETE THE FOLLOWING SELF-ASSESSMENT:

I met or did not meet my goal because _____

_____

From this experience, I learned _____

_____

My level of satisfaction with what I accomplished today is _____

_____

The strategy that worked best for me when I read or wrote today was _____

_____ because _____

_____

What I want to learn next is _____

_____

They enable students to establish their own goals, to overcome literacy barriers that are important to them, and to select relevant materials. At the end, students also assess their literacy, engage in postreading activities, discuss how they can improve their reading/ writing in the next lesson, and report what worked well for them that day.

Although there is no single grouping system that is best for all struggling readers/ writers, several small group arrangements, as described in this chapter, have proved to support these readers' literacy growth. Among the most important are tutorials, special types of small groups, expert groups, and base groups.

The goal of this chapter was to describe instructional actions, a lesson plan, and grouping systems that advance less successful readers' literacy. This instruction ensures specific individual needs can be identified.

Key Terminology

Now that you have completed this chapter, see if you know the meanings of the terms listed here. If you do, place a check mark in the blank that precedes each term. If you are not certain, turn to the page number that follows the term to review its meaning. If you have learned 15 of these on your initial reading of the chapter, you have understood the chapter's content.

_____ **engaged time** or **engagement**
(page 201)
_____ **round-robin reading** (page 202)
_____ **homogeneous** (page 208)
_____ **reading response groups**
(page 209)
_____ **literature response groups**
(page 209)
_____ **cooperative groups** (page 211)
_____ **sociograms** (page 213)
_____ **base groups** (page 213)
_____ **buddy systems** (page 213)
_____ **expert groups** (page 214)

_____ **research groups** (page 214)
_____ **group communal writings**
(page 214)
_____ **desktop learning centers**
(page 216)
_____ **pair** (page 218)
_____ **dyad** (page 218)
_____ **assisted reading** (page 218)
_____ **repeated reading** (page 218)
_____ **study buddies** (page 218)
_____ **think–pair–share groupings**
(page 218)
_____ **tutorials** (page 220)

 ## Case Study

Making Professional Decisions

David had just turned 10 years old and completed the fourth grade. During their interview his parents reported that David's reading problems had persisted through his school history. They said his physical development was normal except for an operation he had when he was an infant to correct a "cross-eyed" condition.

David's parents reported that he was a very happy, likable boy. Before starting school David had been enthusiastic about reading, but he had developed an aversion to it as he experienced failure. Now he avoided reading. When he was required to read a book, he selected easy ones with large print.

David's mother reported that David had always passed the hearing screening test that was administered at his school. However, he had been referred to an ophthalmologist after his last vision screening test. The ophthalmologist told David's parents that his near point vision, far point vision, and color perception were all in the normal range, but that he had problems with depth perception and binocular vision at both the far point and near point ranges.

When David's cumulative school records were examined, they confirmed that he had experienced continuing problems in reading. However, he was more successful in other academic areas. In an interview his fourth grade teacher described him as having a bad attitude toward reading. She also said that at the end of the year, David was reading with the lowest group in the last half of a second grade reader, while the remainder of the class was on grade level. She said David had particular problems with oral reading and frequently lost his place in the text.

David said he did not want to meet with the diagnostician. He said he read outside of school, and that he only read things when they were assigned. He was quite reluctant to participate in the diagnosis, particularly when asked to read longer text and in reading orally; a great deal of time was spent convincing him to cooperate and to read the passages presented.

Tests administered and their results are presented below:

INFORMAL READING INVENTORY

Word Recognition List

| Independent Level | Primer |
| Instructional Level | Grade I |

Oral Passage Reading

| Independent Level | Primer |
| Instructional Level | Grade 1 |

Silent Passage Reading

| Independent Level | Grade 1 |
| Instructional Level | Grade 2 |

| Listening Level | Grade 5 |

David's word recognition broke down at the third grade level. Consequently, he was unable to comprehend at that level. An analysis of his miscues at all levels of the IRI showed that he rarely tried to sound unknown words. However, he supplied words in the text that made sense contextually.

Respond to the following questions, then check your responses against the Answer Key at the end of the book.

1. Considering both environmental and individual factors, what factors might be related to David's reading problem? Substantiate your answer by citing evidence.
2. Is David a struggling reader? Substantiate your answer.
3. What seems to be David's major area of reading difficulty? Substantiate your answer.
4. At what instructional level would you begin in Tier 1 and 2 support settings? Why?

Thinking and Writing about What You Have Learned

1. Reflecting on what you have read, what do you consider to be the most important action you can take to assist students who have not yet learned to read at the level needed to comprehend books at their grade placements?

2. What principles will you follow to organize classroom time so that students are more effectively engaged in their own self-directed literacy development?

3. What types of record-keeping systems and evaluation methods (Chapter 6) will you choose to overcome the pitfalls described in the grouping systems of this chapter? (After you've made your list, review Chapter 6 to check your response.)

4. What teaching methods and scheduling strategies can meet the needs of children at divergent literacy levels in a self-contained classroom?

5. What could you do to provide an outline of the lesson plan steps for less accomplished readers/writers so they can use it to guide their self-directed learning?

6. Design a daily schedule and grouping system. After you've selected the classroom schedule you prefer, insert the type of small groups you want to use first. Then insert the times at which you will conduct full-class conversations, tutorials, and discovery discussions with struggling readers/writers.

7. Loretta is 12 years, 4 months old. She is in the fifth grade because her second grade teacher retained her. After repeating second grade, she withdrew from peers and reading. Her best friend, Suzette, is in the sixth grade and lives in the apartment across the hall from Loretta, Loretta's mother, and Loretta's two younger brothers. Loretta and Suzette baby-sit her brothers until 7:00 p.m. each night and on Saturdays. Loretta has considerable difficulty understanding her social studies, science, math, and health textbooks. She pretends to read some selections of children's literature. You have learned all this because you made a home visit, read her cumulative record folder, and mailed Loretta two interest inventories that she returned to you during the summer.

   What type of differences, as described in Chapters 3 and 4, would you want to analyze because they may be affecting Loretta's literacy? And what type of grouping system would be most valuable for her? After you have answered these questions, compare your answers to those Loretta's teacher, Mr. Nicholas, actually prepared for her. This answer appears on the Answer Key in the back of the book.

chapter 8

Enhancing Emergent Literacy

Senior citizen after-school programs have proved profitable for many struggling readers at the emerging reading level, including students like Malcolm, above, who is older but still reading at the beginning levels of proficiency.

Dear Dr. Block,

My time with Darlene, a first grade student in my class, has been an invaluable experience. As I look back, I realize I should've put more planning into my work before we met in our discovery discussions each Thursday. I wish I had done more creative games and activities with her—yet Darlene always just seemed so happy to be alone with me. At first, she always wanted me to read (through assisted readings) all the books I brought. By the end of 10 sessions, she had completed a desktop learning center, set and met 10 goals, and grabbed the books from my arms to *read to me!*

—Ann Brewer,
first grade teacher

■ Chapter Overview: Key Points

In this chapter you will learn about the beginning stages of literacy development—the concepts that must be understood before students can move on to full literacy success—and how you can assist students at all ages to master the stage labeled *emergent literacy.* Most textbooks speak about emergent reading and writing as concepts developed and taught prior to and during preschool through first grade years. However, many older students (and even adults) enter schools unable to break the code of printed English. Moreover, many students do not learn these concepts during the first year of schooling. For these reasons the basis of emergent literacy has been defined as the fundamental concepts taught to students of any age who have not yet learned to read the simplest words. As Juel (1988) found, if a child is still in the nonreading or emergent reader category at the end of first grade, the probability is 8 in 10 that he or she will remain among the lowest 10 percent of readers, even until fourth grade. This low level of performance persists even if a child is placed in different supplemental reading programs. The reason Juel cited is that "children who did not develop good word recognition skills in first grade began to dislike reading and read considerably less than good readers both in and out of school" (p. 49).

In this chapter you will learn strategies and intervention programs that increase emergent reading abilities. These strategies and programs are more intensive than developmental literacy instruction and should be implemented as soon as you detect that a child is unable to read any words. With such early intervention, further literacy problems may be prevented.

This chapter describes:

- Emergent literacy concepts
- Literacy interventions for less accomplished emergent readers and writers
- Tier 1–4 supports for less accomplished students who are reading at the emergent literacy stage
- Diagnosing emergent readers' needs

By chapter's end, you will have answers to the following questions:

1. What instruction is needed for less accomplished emergent readers?
2. What bridges can be built so struggling readers use their newly evolving literacy at home to obtain extra practice as well as support for and enjoyment of reading and writing?
3. What are the most effective Tier 1–4 activities and programs for nonreading students and those who have not learned to decode?

Emergent Literacy Concepts

Emergent literacy is a continuum of understandings that lead to a student's ability to associate letter sounds and meanings to printed words and to read and write successfully (Block, 2001; Morrow, 1987; Teale & Sulzby, 1986). The reason the term *emergent literacy* replaced *reading readiness* as a description of preliterate behaviors is that we now know that literacy is a continuous process—one that begins during the first months of life and continues through kindergarten and first grade (Adams, 1993) and beyond. Chapter 3 indicated the depth of research presently under way on the oral language acquisition processes a student must master. There are a comparable number of studies concerning emergent literacy and how young children come to understand written language. A review of this research follows.

Research now indicates that children begin to learn to read and write as early as 2 years of age; writing abilities often develop before reading; many students spell before they read; and reading and writing can be learned in conjunction with speaking. Most children enter preschools and kindergartens already recognizing 14 of the 26 letters of the alphabet. Moreover, kindergarten children's literacy develops rapidly. For example, when a one-word label can no longer bear the weight of students' accumulated word knowledge, they begin to use complete sentences and paragraphs. Similarly, most students, by age 5½, have established a desire to write (Barillas, 2000; Hilliker, 1986). By age 5, most print in uppercase letters, and a few use both hands interchangeably for handwriting. Your responsibility as a kindergarten teacher is to help children develop hand dominance and fine motor skills, using the letters and words students write. If a kindergartner has not established hand dominance, consult with school specialists and parents to ensure that this slower evolving ability is not misinterpreted as a type of learning disability. Young children can easily become frustrated because their motor skills cannot keep up with the thoughts and ideas they want to write. In such cases, you can invite older students into the room to scribe for them.

Reading Readiness versus Emergent Literacy

From the 1930s through the 1970s, educators believed that there was a "best time" to initiate reading and writing (and to some degree, speaking and listening) instruction. Educators believed that students had to reach a level of "readiness" before literacy concepts would "imprint" (Morphett & Washburne, 1931). This philosophical position, known as the theory of *reading readiness* or *language readiness,* was based on the premise that children had to acquire a basic set of mental skills before instruction in reading and writing could begin. These competencies were believed not to be in place until students reached a mental age of 6½ years for reading and 9 years for writing instruction. During the early 1980s, however, new research documented that students do not need a benchmark of accumulated life experiences before literacy instruction can begin. Rather, as explained earlier, acquiring literacy is a continuous process that gradually emerges over time (Reese, Garnier, Gallimore, & Goldenberg, 2000; Texas Education Agency, 2000).

The first 6 years of a child's life are extremely important, because that is when most language is acquired. Linguists and psychologists have also found that emergent literacy follows a similar path regardless of the language a child is learning. Also, early literacy experiences support subsequent achievement regardless of whether the time spent on literacy activities was at school or home (Reese et al., 2000). Signs of word recognition appear at about 26 to 28 months of age. At approximately the same time, children create their first scribbled words. Many children join words together by 4 years of age. Approximately 2 years later, students master language to such an extent that they can speak and "write" sentences they never used before (Travers, 1982). What is even more amazing is that although children may have difficulties with other tasks during this 6-year period, mastery of the language comes easily and naturally.

Because 4- and 5-year-olds talk to integrate subject matter, substantive conversations assist students to transform their declarative into applied knowledge (Newmann, 1991). Research has demonstrated that children who are advanced in oral language tend to achieve better in literacy than those who have not used literary concepts prior to first grade. Studies also indicate that some children enter school having spent only 2 to 3 hours interacting with print and text, while others have as many as 2,000 to 3,000 hours of such exposures (Teale, 1986). Research further suggests that students in this first group rarely recover from the disadvantage they carry into kindergarten (Adams, 1990; Block, 2001).

Emergent reading competencies are summarized in Figures 8.1 and 8.2. Using these instructional guides, you can build a personalized curriculum for every emergent reader. Each time a student demonstrates one of the concepts listed in Figures 8.1 and 8.2, enter the date it occurred and a brief comment as to the quality of that demonstration in the appropriate column. In this way, you will have a guide for instruction that scaffolds each student into discovering new facts about print and lays a solid foundation for future pleasure and success in reading.

NAME	PRECONVENTIONAL • Book awareness • Letter names • Responds to stories • Chooses favorites • Interest in environmental print	EMERGENT • Pretends to read • Some letter sounds • Plays w/words/rhymes • Memorizes books • Pictures = story	DEVELOPING • Reads predictable books • Sees self as a reader • Concept of words • Recognizes simple words • Print + pictures = story • Retells main idea	BEGINNING • Reads early reader books • Expands word recognition • Develops sense of story • Begins to read silently • Uses phonics and some other strategies	EXPANDING • Easy chapter books • Uses varied strategies • Reads silently • Increased fluency and expression • Retells story
1					
2					
3					
4					
5					
6					
7					
8					
9					
10					
11					
12					
13					
14					
15					
16					
17					
18					
19					
20					
21					
22					
23					
24					
25					

FIGURE 8.1 Emergent Reading Development

Source: Adapted from B. C. Hill & C. A. Ruptic (1994), *Practical Aspects of Authentic Assessment*, p. 63. Norwood, MA: Christopher-Gordon. Copyright © 1994 by Christopher-Gordon Publishers, Inc. Used with permission.

NAME	PRECONVENTIONAL
	• Scribbling
	• Pictures = meaning
	• Pictures w/"words"
	• Random letters
	• Tells about writing
	    or
	BMTYZ = WORD
		EMERGENT
		• Copies names/words
		• Pictures + print
		• Mainly uppercase
		• Beginning/ending
		  consonants
		• Pretend-reads writing
		WD or YD = WORD
			DEVELOPING
			• Directional conventions
			• Upper- and lowercase
			• Uses some spacing
			• Some letters based on
			  sounds
			• Reads own writing
			WRD = WORD
				BEGINNING
				• Others can read
				• Complete thoughts
				• Punctuation experiments
				• Inventive spelling
				• Some words spelled
				  correctly
				WERD = WORD
					EXPANDING
					• Awareness of spelling
					  patterns/rules
					• Capitals/periods
					• Beginning/middle/end
					• Add-on revision
					• Begins to write fluently
					WORD = WORD

1					
2					
3					
4					
5					
6					
7					
8					
9					
10					
11					
12					
13					
14					
15					
16					
17					
18					
19					
20					
21					
22					
23					
24					
25					

FIGURE 8.2 Emergent Writing Development

Source: Adapted from B. C. Hill & C. A. Ruptic (1994), *Practical Aspects of Authentic Assessment,* p. 65. Norwood, MA: Christopher-Gordon. Copyright © 1994 by Christopher-Gordon Publishers, Inc. Used with permission.

Emergent Writing

Most students demonstrate many literary understandings in the preschool and kinder-garten years. They evidence their awareness that writing has meaning when they use the same marks repeatedly or when they realize that "real writing" is made up not of only one mark, but of various marks that face different directions.

As students become more aware of print, they also realize that "adult writing" is ordered—and so they place their letters horizontally in an attempt to reproduce what they have seen. At this point, however, they may not be clear about the left-to right prin-ciple of English. Therefore, although young children know their writing is to be written horizontally, they aren't sure where to begin. You will notice that some students write backwards, beginning on the right and moving across the page to the left; or they do the "wraparound" trick, writing to the margin of a page and then putting letters vertically; or they write from left to right, then from right to left below the line just completed.

Once students become aware of ordering principles, they turn their attention to in-dividual letters. Marie Clay (1975) reported that it takes students considerable time to understand fully how to make each letter and which features distinguish one letter from another. When they first begin to write, for example, children do not realize that *I* and *T* are different. When students begin to realize that there are contrasts between letters, they tend to make comments such as "An *a* and an *o* are a lot alike."

The last developmental phase in emerging writing is the stage when students intend their works to be read by others. They discover that others should be able to read back what they wrote, and that writings are like signatures of thoughts.

Discovering That Print Has Meaning

Most children begin school with an intense desire to learn to read. NFL quarterback Bernie Kosar once recalled, "The third day of first grade, I came home, threw my lunch box down in the kitchen, and declared: I'm *not* ever going back to school." "Why?" asked his father. Kosar's response: "Because they didn't teach me how to read" (*Dallas Morn-ing News, 1993*).

Students who are functioning at the emerging reading level differ from readers at higher stages of the continuum in three basic ways: (1) They cannot decode indepen-dently; (2) they have a sight vocabulary of fewer than 50 words; and (3) they cannot dis-tinguish individual letters and sounds. Many emergent readers need the activities in this chapter before they can progress toward reading fluency and effective writing. Before students can move beyond the emergent reading level, they must master the following concepts:

1. **Recurring principle:** Nonreaders must understand that writing involves not only making but also repeating more than one type of mark—that letters consistently contain downstrokes, curves, slants, and vertical as well as horizontal lines. When stu-dents write different types of marks on their papers, you have one indication that they know the recurring principle. They have discovered that print contains many different marks that rotate directions and combine to convey meaning. Often when students be-gin to write with differing lines, shapes, and letters, they also experience their first sat-isfactory encounter with literacy. Because they can now decipher and manipulate print,

they want to know how to consistently replicate this new pleasurable image-making ability, so they seek to learn more about letters.

2. Directional and flexibility principles: Students must learn that words are read from left to right, that text begins at the left side of the page, and that meaning begins again to the left when the right margin is reached. Until they develop this understanding students may write in any direction. And when they play "reading," they may start at the middle or end of a book and turn pages from back to front. One of the first indications that a student has discovered that print flows in a definite direction occurs when you are reading a book to him or her: If the student points to the next word that you are about to read before you say it and asks you to say it, the student knows the direction of print.

About the time students recognize that print is read horizontally, they begin to take inventory of their own writing. One sign that directionality is developing is seen when students write the same letter (or series of letters) over and over again to create a long line of text. Some students make long lists of all the letters they know. They also write and say all the combinations of letters and words they have memorized. You will also notice that all of their scribbles are horizontal and move from left to right.

The flexibility principle is in place when students realize that individual letters and their features represent meaning—for example, when they recognize that *I* and *T* are different because *T* does not have the horizontal line at its base. Students who have these two concepts in place will demonstrate them unaided. In contrast, readers who are not yet aware that print features can be rotated and attached to each other may very easily and proficiently copy letters but cannot produce them through their own initiation. To help students develop this concept, show them why letters such as *I* and *T* are not the same, and explain why letters like the one-letter words *I* and *a* have different meanings.

3. Contrastive principle: Students who know the contrastive principle will make the appropriate letter-to-sound matches in their pretend readings and writings. For example, as they read they will say different sounds when they see the words *a* and *oh*. The sound may not be the correct pronunciation for these words, but the students will not say the same sound for different printed letters. Similarly, in their writing, nonreaders who know the contrastive principle will use a capital letter to begin the word and not place any more capitals at the center or end of words.

4. Abbreviation principle: When students leave spaces between the lines, letters, and words that they write, this is an indication that they have learned the abbreviation principle—that sets of marks are grouped to represent different ideas. They have learned that space between words is necessary.

5. Sign principle: When this concept is in place, your students will cross a major threshold in reading. They will write with the intention of having it read by others. In addition, their writing will become very personal and they will be come upset if others misread their scribblings. Another characteristic of this stage is that students begin to write words below their pictures, labeling the main concept their picture represents. A student's work illustrating the sign principle appears in Figure 8.3.

Once these five principles are in place, students develop other literacy concepts (i.e., word, sentence, story) and can recognize that words can be broken into sounds.

FIGURE 8.3 Example of the Sign Principle

Source: Cathy Collins Block, *Teaching the Language Arts.* Copyright © 1993 by Allyn and Bacon. Reprinted by permission.

THE CONCEPT OF WORDS. Research has demonstrated that students who recognize the spaces between words as boundaries signaling the ending of one meaning and the beginning of another will learn some words just by seeing them in print (Ehri & Sweet, 1991; Morris, 1981; Reutzel, Oda, & Moore, 1989). Other students can learn words if items around the room are labeled. You could, for instance, put name tags on lockers and ask students to find the names that are most like theirs; or you could have students give names to parts of the room that are used for special purposes, then put up signs with these names in the appropriate spots. Such labels reflect the environmental print that students have read prior to beginning school. **Environmental print** comprises the words in your students' home and community settings that they see each day, such as *McDonald's, Stop,* or *Cheerios.* Emergent readers learn these words through the many clues for meaning in which they appear. Similarly, when their classrooms are rich in print that labels objects, students can use the strategies they have already mastered to attach meaning to new words such as *door, listening center, desk, table,* or *author's chair.* (See Barr, Kamil, Mosenthal, & Pearson, 1991, for a review of research concerning environmental print and its value in developing emergent literacy concepts.)

Research demonstrates that students who are developing the concept of words will also attend to pictures, rhythm of language, and songs to predict meaning (Morrow, 1993; Osborn & Chard, 2001; Teale & Sulzby, 1986). These language forms develop students' schemas, and when their schemas are enriched, students can move from relying on pictures to using their memory of words as their predominant decoding strategy (Elster, 1994; Sulzby, Branz, & Buhle, 1993). Thus, emergent readers who have not yet developed a sight vocabulary of 100 words will grow toward this ability most rapidly when predictable picture books are used for instruction. As Elster (1994) discovered, emergent readers can develop the concept of words through predictable books because they deploy moment-to-moment shifts of attention from pictures to past experiences to memorizing word images that predict what word should be printed at that spot on the page. It is just as important to note, however, that such books are not as effective for emergent readers who are above age 8 (Fielding & Roller, 1992). The humiliation of reading such a book before peers is too great, and the content in many predictable books is not age appropriate. For these reasons, desktop learning centers (discussed in Chapter 7) and the activities in this chapter specified for older students are more effective. Resource Card 11 lists predictable books and picture books; Resource Card 12 contains wordless books with complex pictures that have been shown to significantly increase less accomplished readers' sight word knowledge.

THE CONCEPT OF SENTENCES. Emergent readers learn the concept of sentences when they watch their teachers read to them from big books and charts. Through the pauses teachers place at the end of sentences and the rhythm of language that they hear, struggling emergent readers discover that grammatical rules impose restrictions on the permissible sequences of words in sentences. They also realize that capital letters, punctuation, and paragraph indentions clue that new thoughts are about to begin. Some emergent readers will not develop such awarenesses unless they are taught these concepts directly. Otherwise, many of these students assume that every word is entirely unique and must be decoded without any syntactical and semantic aids. Therefore, they view each new text as mountains of single new words to be learned. For these readers, hopelessness rapidly mounts as each consecutive word in a sentence is encountered.

Alternatively, when students are taught that English follows basic sentence rules, these students gain confidence that they really will learn to read soon. To impart this knowledge, you can explain basic syntactic information as you read with them. For instance, explain that when "Wh" sentences (those beginning with *When, Where, Why, What,* or *Who*) end with a question mark, we know a detail is being asked for. Or when reading a book aloud, teach them that "Oh!" or "Wow!" or similar expressions are actually one-word sentences. Explain how the subject of a sentence is a noun and usually comes first, and that the word *the* often precedes nouns—then they can use this fact to decode the word, because when they see *the* they'll know the next word is probably a noun.

THE CONCEPT OF PHONEMES AND GRAPHEMES. Emergent readers also learn that sounds, **phonemes,** are represented by letters, **graphemes.** At the most basic level of phonemic awareness, students recognize that an individual letter represents a distinct sound. You can help emerging readers develop phonemic awareness when you ask them to repeat printed rhymes. You can point to individual letters at the beginnings and ends of words from books read chorally, such as those on Resource Card 13, which contain the most frequently occurring vowel and ending patterns in our language.

The second level of phonemic awareness includes blending sounds. You can help students practice blending different beginning consonant sounds with the same ending pattern by making oral games. For example, ask them to read from a word card with

RESOURCE CARD 11

**Picture Books and Predictable Books for
Less Accomplished Emergent Readers**

Alexander, M. (1968). *Out! Out! Out!* New
York: Dial.

Aliki. (1983). *Use your head, dear.* New York:
Greenwillow.

Aliki. (1984). *Feelings.* New York:
Greenwillow.

Allen, P. (1983). Who *sank the boat?* New
York: Coward-McCann.

Ardizzone, E. (1970). *The wrong side of the
bed.* New York: Doubleday.

Asch, F. (1988). *Mooncake.* New York: Aladdin.

Borden, L. (1989). *Caps, hats, socks, and mit-
tens: A book about the four seasons.* New
York: Scholastic.

Borden, L. (1991). The *watching game.* New
York: Scholastic.

Bottner, B. (1987). Zoo *song.* New York:
Scholastic.

Brown, D. (1993). *Ruth Low thrills a nation.*
New York: Ticknor & Fields.

Bunting, E. (1990). *The wall.* New York:
Clarion.

Burningham, J. (1985). *Slam bang, skip trip,
sniff shout, wobble pop.* New York: Viking.

Carlson, B. (1982). *Let's find the big idea.*
New York: Abingdon Press.

Charlip, R., & Joyner, J. (1994). *Thirteen.*
New York: Aladdin.

Cooper, S. (1983). *The silver cow: A Welsh
tale.* New York: McElderry Books.

Delacre, L. (1991). *Nathan's balloon adventure.* New York: Scholastic.

Demarest, C. (1991). *No peas for Nellie.* New
York: Aladdin.

DeSantis, K. (1985). *A doctor's tools.* New
York: Dodd.

Dodd, A. (1994). *Footprints and shadows.*
New York: Aladdin.

Faulkner, M. (1991). *The moon clock.* New
York: Scholastic.

Gibbons, G. (1983). *The boat book.* New
York: Holiday House.

Ginsbury, M. (1983). *The magic stove.* New
York: Coward-McCann.

Greenfield, E. (1981). *Daydreamers.* New
York: Dial.

Guarino, D. (1989). *Is your mama a llama?*
New York: Scholastic.

Guy, R. (1981). *Mother crocodile: An Uncle
Amadou tale from Senegal.* New York:
Delacorte.

Gwynne, F. (1990). *A little pigeon toad.* New
York: Aladdin.

Hoban, T. (1975). *Dig, drill, dump.* New
York: Greenwillow.

Hoban, T. (1984). *I walk and read.* New
York: Greenwillow.

Hoban, T. (1989). *More than one.* New York:
Greenwillow.

Hopking, L. (1984). *Surprises.* New York:
Harper & Row.

Hurwitz, J. (1990). *Busybody Nora.* New
York: Morrow.

Hutchins, P. (1972). *Rosie's walk.* New York:
Weston Woods.

Kingman, L. (1953). *Peter's long walk.* New
York: Doubleday.

Kraus, R. (1974). *Owliver.* New York:
Windmill.

Louie, A. (1982). *Yeh-Shen: A Cinderella
story from China.* New York: Philomel.

Maestro, B., & Maestro, G. (1978). *Busy day:
A book of action words.* New York:
Crown.

Redmond, I. (1993). *Elephant.* New York:
Knopf.

Rockwell, H. (1975). *My dentist.* New York:
Greenwillow.

Sendak, M. (1963). *Where the wild things
are.* New York: Harper & Row.

RESOURCE CARD 11

**Picture Books and Predictable Books for
Less Accomplished Emergent Readers (continued)**

Shannon, M. (1993). *Elvira*. New York: Ticknor & Fields.

Sharmat, M. (1975). *I'm not Oscar's friend anymore*. New York: Dutton.

Sobel, H. L. (1975). *Jeffs hospital book*. New York: Holt.

Spier, P. (1982). *Peter Spier's rain*. New York: Doubleday.

Stevenson, J. (1981). *The wish card ran out!* New York: Greenwillow.

Tapio, P. D. (1975). *The lady who saw the good side of everything*. New York: Seabury.

Watanabe, S. (1981). *What a good lunch!* New York: Philomel.

Wild, M. (1993). *The slumber party*. New York: Ticknor & Fields.

Wild, M. (1994). *Our granny*. New York: Ticknor & Fields.

Zolotow, C. (1981). *One step, two. . . .* New York: Lothrop, Lee & Shepherd.

several beginning consonant flip cards over it—such as *[c]ar, [st]ar, [b]ar,* and so on. Then you and they can make up a story using several words from the same word pattern—such as "Old MacDonald had a *rake,* which he used at the *lake* to *make* a *snake* go away. His wife asked him to *bake* a *cake* to *take* to the *lake.* They ate the *cake* and lived happily ever after." As emergent readers say this story with you, have word cards with the pattern *-ake* and the letters *r, l, m, sn, b, c,* and *t* ready to hold up rapidly at appropriate times. On the second reading, do not say the word but allow students to blend the sounds for each word unaided.

Research indicates that students who can write letters learn phonemic concepts faster than those who don't scribe (Clark, 1988; Griffith & Olson, 1992; Walsh, 1988). Furthermore, teaching the names of the letters of the alphabet is an important tool. Readers who are developing phonemic awareness need to ask how to write certain letters, how to reproduce the sound of a letter called by a specific name, and how to ask for a new letter they want to write. Without these names, students' zone of proximal development in phonetic knowledge will be restricted (Peterson & Hanes, 1992). Students also develop phonemic awareness through the practice of invented spelling and through playing orally with sounds of letters (Ehri & Wilce, 1987; McGee & Reiglls, 1990).

Music, environmental print, and rebus stories teach phonemic–graphemic awareness rapidly (Block, 2001). Cognitive scientists attribute the value of music and rebus stories for struggling emergent readers to the fact that they make the rhythm of English explicit for use in decoding; the helpfulness of environmental print stems in part from the power of logos to enhance memory (Bransford & Stein, 1993). **Rebus stories,** for instance, use pictures of nouns in sentences instead of the printed word (see Figure 8.4 on p. 242). Music builds phonemic awareness through repetition; students at the emergent reading level enjoy singing the same songs repeatedly. Similarly, music, environmental print, and rebus stories increase readers' phonemic–graphemic awareness by tying written language to students' normal speaking vocabulary and life outside of school.

RESOURCE CARD 12

Wordless Books That Struggling Emergent Readers Enjoy

Anno, M. (1983). *Anno's U.S.A.* New York: Philomel.

Aruego, J. (1971). *Look what I can do.* New York: Scribners.

Ayers, P. (1987). *Guess what?* New York: Knopf.

Briggs, R. (1978). *The snowman.* New York: Random House.

Brown, C. (1989). *The patchwork farmer.* New York: Greenwillow.

Brown, R. (1982). *If at first you do not see.* New York: Holt.

Butterworth, N. (1991). *Amanda's butterfly.* New York: Delacorte.

Day, A. (1985). *Good dog, Carl.* La Jolla, CA: Green Tiger Press.

Day, A. (1989). *Carl goes shopping.* New York: Farrar, Straus & Giroux.

dePaola, T. (1981). *The hunter and the animals.* New York: Holiday.

Florian, D. (1984). *Airplane ride.* New York: Crowell.

Geisert, A. (1991). *Oink.* Boston: Houghton Mifflin.

Graham, A. (1991). *Full moon soup, or, The fall of the Hotel Splendide.* New York: Dial.

Heller, R. (1989). *How to hide a butterfly and other insects* (series). Mexico: Grijalbo.

Hoban, T. (1971). *Look again.* New York: Macmillan.

Hoban, T. (1990). *Shadows and reflections.* New York: Greenwillow.

Hoban, T. (1992). *Look up, look down.* New York: Greenwillow.

Hutchins, P. (1991). *Changes, changes.* New York: Macmillan.

Keats, E. (1985). *Kitten for a day.* New York: Four Winds Press.

Koren, E. (1972). *Behind the wheel.* New York: Holt.

Krahn, F. (1981). *Here comes Alex Pumpernickel.* Boston: Little, Brown.

Mari, I., & Mari, E. (1990). *The apple and the moth.* New York: Pantheon.

Mayer, M. (1974). *Frog goes to dinner.* New York: Dial.

Morris, T. (1980). *Lucky puppy, lucky boy.* New York: Knopf.

Oakley, G. (1980). *Graham Oakley's magical changes.* New York: Atheneum.

Ormerod, J. (1981). *Sunshine.* New York: Lothrop, Lee & Shepard.

Pragoff, F. (1989). *Odd one out.* New York: Doubleday.

Raskin, E. (1966). *Nothing ever happens on my block.* New York: Atheneum.

Ruben, P. (1978). *What is new? What is missing? What is different?* Philadelphia: Lippincott.

Sara, S. (1991). *Across town.* New York: Orchard.

Sis, P. (1992). *The ocean world.* New York: Greenwillow.

Spier, P. (1986). *Dreams.* Garden City, NY: Doubleday.

Turkle, B. (1976). *Deep in the forest.* New York: Dutton.

Young, E. (1983). *Up a tree.* New York: Harper & Row.

Because speaking is the communication system emergent readers rely on to express information at home, you should create classroom activities that make the relationship between reading, speaking, and everyday experience more vivid. For example, younger emergent readers enjoy bringing environmental print to class and pasting advertising

RESOURCE CARD 13

**Favorite Books to Introduce Less Accomplished
Emergent Readers to New Concepts**

Ahlberg, A. (1990). *The black cat.* New York: Greenwillow.

Ahlberg, A. (1990). *The pet shop.* New York: Greenwillow.

Ahlberg, A. (1991). *Dinosaur dreams.* New York: Greenwillow.

Ahlberg, A. (1991). *Mystery tour.* New York: Greenwillow.

Anholt, L. (1990). *Good days, bad days.* New York: Putnam.

Barton, B. (1990). *Bones, bones, dinosaur bones.* New York: Cromwell.

Carle, E. (1987). *The tiny seed.* Natick, MA: Alphabet Press.

Florian, D. (1992). *At the zoo.* New York: Greenwillow.

Ginsberg, M. (1992). *Asleep, asleep.* New York: Greenwillow.

Guy, G. (1991). *Black crow, black crow.* New York: Greenwillow.

Hoban, J. (1990). *Buzby.* New York: Harper & Row.

King, B. (1991). *Sitting on the farm.* New York: Orchard.

LeTord, B. (1989). *A brown cow.* Boston: Little, Brown.

Lewis, T. P. (1988). *Frida's office day.* New York: Harper & Row.

Marshall, J. (1991). *Rats on the roof, and other stories.* New York: Dial.

Marshall, J. (1992). *Fox outfoxed.* New York: Dial.

Oxenbury, H. (1989). *Pippo gets lost.* New York: Macmillan.

Oxenbury, H. (1989). *Tom and Pippo and the dog.* New York: Macmillan.

Oxenbury, H. (1989). *Tom and Pippo in the snow.* New York: Aladdin.

Oxenbury, H. (1989). *Tom and Pippo make a friend.* New York: Macmillan.

Paterson, K. (1991). *The smallest cow in the world.* New York: HarperCollins.

Rose, A. (1992). *Hide and seek in the yellow house.* New York: Viking.

Stadler, J. (1991). *Cat is back at bat.* New York: Dutton.

Van Leeuwen, J. (1990). *Oliver Pig at school.* New York: Dial.

Weiss, N. (1989). *Dog, boy, cap, skate, sun, sand, sea, sail.* New York: Greenwillow.

Wiseman, B. M. (1988). *Morris and Boris at the circus.* New York: Harper & Row.

Ziefert, H. (1990). *Who can boo the loudest.* New York: Harper & Row.

logos in blank books. Use this cut-and-paste activity to make rebus stories—and as they work, ask students to tell you what the images convey. For instance, you would read, "We buy our clothes at _____," and if the Wal-Mart logo was used in this rebus the children would say "Wal-Mart" when you pointed to it. Then you would write the words readers say in letters the same size as the letters in individual logos, so that the words you write are as similar as possible to those in each logo. After students read all the rebus stories, ask them to tell you something important that they would like to share with someone outside the classroom, such as the principal, a relative, or a friend. Write this sentence on the last page—so that students can read aloud several pages of sentences with environmental print plus the last page, which is an important message (using print

FIGURE 8.4 A Rebus

alone) that they want to give to someone else. Discuss why their printed message will communicate their idea to that person better than an oral message would (e.g., because the person can keep the book forever), and then talk about other ways they could use reading and writing in their lives.

Because rebus stories have long been used as an activity for young children (see magazines such as *Humpty Dumpty, Weekly Reader,* and *Highlights*), they are often viewed as "baby work" by older students. However, you can modify and upgrade this instructional technique so that older emergent readers can learn the phonemic–graphemic concept more speedily. One adaptation might be to use pictures in recipes to represent the ingredients, utensils, or steps (see Figure 8.5). Thus, when students read the words on the recipe card and see the pictures of a bowl, knife, spoon, bunch of grapes, and so forth, they can associate the rebus images with the semantic clues supplied through simple sentences. After students have read and made their first recipe, they can modify it to construct a new recipe for another group in their class. After their creations are prepared and eaten, they can read their recipes to other class members who copy them. If the food and recipes are taken home to share with their families, students have an instant application of the value of print in their lives.

Another way to create an authentic reading experience for older emergent readers is to take a highlighter and mark content-specific sight words in one of three sports stories or one of three lifestyle stories from the newspaper. These content-specific words should be common to all three stories (e.g., *opponent, victory, winning, defeated,* and *goalpost;* or *family, friends,* and *neighborhood*). Using the highlighted story, help students learn these words through context and graphemic similarities to other words (e.g., *goal post* is two words just as the goal post itself has two legs; or *winners* has the base word *win*). Once students recognize the highlighted words in the first story, hand them the second story and ask them to read it to you, a peer, or adult volunteer. Have them notice how many new words they decode instantly. Then, ask them to read the third story and explain how knowing content area words by sight, knowing the similar phonemes and graphemes in some words, and knowing that some words frequently reappear in

Fruit Salad

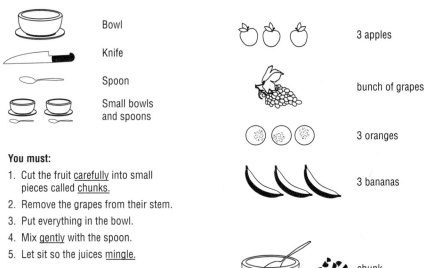

You need:

Bowl

Knife

Spoon

Small bowls
and spoons

3 apples

bunch of grapes

3 oranges

3 bananas

chunk

grape

You must:

1. Cut the fruit <u>carefully</u> into small
   pieces called <u>chunks.</u>
2. Remove the grapes from their stem.
3. Put everything in the bowl.
4. Mix <u>gently</u> with the spoon.
5. Let sit so the juices <u>mingle.</u>

Then you can:

1. Put the fruit salad in small bowls.
2. Eat and enjoy.

FIGURE 8.5 Using a Modified Version of Rebus Stories to Teach
Content-Specific Sight Words to Emergent Readers

Source: Adapted from T. Salinger (1992), "Critical Thinking and Young Literacy Learners." In
C. Collins & J. Mangieri (Eds.), *Teaching Thinking: An Agenda for the Twenty-First Century*,
p. 321. Hillsdale, NJ: Lawrence Erlbaum Associates, Publishers, Inc. Used with permission.

specific subject areas can rapidly increase their decoding abilities and use of
phoneme–grapheme matches.

A modification of this technique is to have older readers make graphics that depict
meanings of words for younger classmates or use them in a series of directions for a project. By creating such text on computers or in manuscript, older emergent readers learn
basic sight words and phoneme–grapheme matches and then reinforce this knowledge
through the experience of teaching the words to younger students.

THE CONCEPT OF STORY. The concept of story encompasses the knowledge that print
records important events and that narrative stories have an opening, setting, character
descriptions, body of events, climax, conclusion, and purpose. When emergent readers
begin to orchestrate their own knowledge of phoneme–graphemes, print, and story,
many also start to view reading not so much as a chore but as an adventure. If this
adventure—like most other new adventures in life—is presented as requiring assistance

from others to be accomplished most successfully, less accomplished emergent readers will be less hesitant to ask for help with literacy.

To develop the concept of story most rapidly, emergent readers profit from having others read aloud to them and with them. If one of your emergent readers has few available adults with whom to read, you can meet his or her literacy needs by setting aside 5 minutes each recess period for a private discovery discussion during which you (or an older schoolmate) and the student can read. (This brief period has proved to be the only instructional supplement many readers need to move up on the literacy continuum.) During these one-to-one readings, allow students to reread the same books as often as they desire.

Notice that at this point in students' literacy development they do not word-call (decode words but not know their meaning) because they do not feel a need to limit their attention merely to phonics. They are reading to tell a story. When a student begins to merely call words and not search for or retain the meaning, he or she is demonstrating a need for instruction in comprehension.

Literacy Interventions for Emergent Readers/Writers at Home and School

The number of children coming from diverse backgrounds and from homes functioning at the poverty level increased dramatically between 1980 and 2000. Also, fewer children today have access in their homes to print and literacy experiences mediated by an adult (Gay, 1995). These conditions necessitate multiple instructional approaches designed to help children develop emergent literacy abilities. Also needed are strong parent partnerships; working with parents helps literacy specialists understand each child's unique home literacy profile. Through close communication with teachers, parents can provide Tier 4 supports and opportunities for extended periods with print. This is necessary for students who are progressing at a different pace from their peers along the literacy continuum.

For more accomplished emergent readers, it may be enough that parents are kept abreast of their children's literacy progress. With less successful emergent readers, however, it is important to bring home environments and parents to school—figuratively and, if possible, literally—for several reasons. First, many parents of students with emergent literacy abilities may not understand or be able to reinforce the instructional strategies used at school, because they were not exposed to the same kinds of curriculum when they were in school. Second, parents or other adults can provide knowledge about students' progress to guide your instruction. Without this close communication, there might be misunderstandings among you, parents, and students that could impede students' progress. Moreover, because students' language foundation is acquired at home, not at school, the more home-to-school bridges you can construct with parents, the fewer bridges emergent readers will have to build by themselves. Equally important, without a strong home-to-school literacy connection, many struggling emergent literacy users could find themselves in two different language worlds. Misunderstandings occur when a teacher's best intentions of introducing new language patterns and words are interpreted by the student or parent as an effort to change the culture or dialect of the home. Thus, by understanding students' language foundation, you can more effectively use concepts that are important at home to teach new words and literacy processes at school. As a teacher, you are in the best position to erect bridges to the child's home and community. Many parents will not reach out to you—not because they don't care, but because they don't know how or cannot find time to initiate the contacts.

In addition, when you reinforce the home language foundation you enhance the literacy foundation for students who do not have adult literacy models. For example, Todd, a ninth grade student with emergent literacy abilities, needed such a teacher. When he returned to school following a jail sentence for a gang-related assault, a reading specialist worked with him daily to teach the concepts presented in this chapter and Chapters 9 and 10. Through this teacher's personal kindness, consistent work, and high expectations, Todd became a contributing member of his classroom and community— in fact, he received an award for his work repainting and repairing the homes of retired older adults in his neighborhood. Todd credited his teacher, who enabled him to use his newly developed emergent reading/writing skills to assist others; thanks to this teacher, Todd no longer found it necessary to seek security in violent street gangs (Burke, 1991). As you endeavor to assist emergent readers/writers, there are many ways you can build school, parent, and community partnerships.

Taking Literacy Home

It is important to help parents use the limited time they have at home to support emergent literacy abilities. This help begins by ensuring that parents understand what they can do at home to reinforce concepts learned at school—and how important it is that they do so. You can promote understanding occurs by making home visits, sending newsletters written by you and students, and providing resources.

HOME VISITS. Home visits take the most time but provide distinct and valuable information. By visiting a student's home you can learn about his or her domestic responsibilities, the types of literacy items in use, family stories that you can use as examples to introduce new concepts throughout the year, and literacy resources near the home. These visits may also help you raise your expectations for readers/writers who come from lower-income homes, as you experience the rich culture and unique resources— such as strong family values and highly developed common sense—found in the home environment. In addition, you can learn about the unique ways a child learns at home and come to understand other factors, such as why a student has frequent absences, as related in the following report:

> The drama teacher said that Leticia was irresponsible. She signed up to be in the Drama Club after school and has only been to two meetings. After my visit to Leticia's home, I told her drama teacher Leticia's younger brother was hospitalized for a series of operations. When the mother had to leave, she left Leticia in charge of caring for her two younger siblings. In fact, her missing after-school rehearsals was an act of responsibility, obedience and loyalty to her family [and not at all a sign of irresponsibility]. (Gonzales et al., 1993, p. 15)

Home visits enable you to learn about students' interests, talents, hobbies, pets, and home activities. These subjects can then be used to reduce emergent literacy users' reticence to contribute to class discussions and to ensure that their background vocabulary is present in books you read aloud or that they choose to read.

Some teachers visit the homes of future students during the summer preceding the school year. They follow these visits with letters to the future students telling them how much they look forward to having them in their class. For some emergent literacy users this letter will be the first they have ever received. In and of itself, this letter makes literacy a part of that student's home experiences.

NEWSLETTERS AND LETTERS HOME. As frequently as possible, it is valuable for students with emerging reading and writing abilities to add their own messages to the bottom of letters you send home. If their writing skills are developed enough, you can also tell them the message you want their parents to have and let them write it in their own words, proofreading it before it goes home. These efforts build students' appreciation of reading and writing as purposeful activities. Similarly, newsletters that you write to describe the most important things students learn at school, as shown in Figure 8.6, build partnerships with parents. Such newsletters also serve the practical purpose of enabling emergent literacy users to deliver important messages about school events to their parents.

Other types of written notices include assessments that parents make about their child; an example is shown in Figures 8.7. In addition, students enjoy summer calendars in which they write something they want to do at home each day to improve their literacy, as shown in Figure 8.8 (p. 249).

PROVIDING RESOURCES. Another way you can take literacy to students' homes is by providing resources to parents. The primary resource is *information* about emergent literacy that assists parents to support their child's literacy abilities at home. A practical way to present this information is to make an audiotape, so busy parents can listen to it as they drive or ride to work, fold the laundry, or engage in other daily activities. Whatever format you use, however, there are several useful suggestions you should include.

First, to share books most effectively with emergent readers, parents need instruction (Block & Dellamura, 2000/2001; Neuman & Gallagher, 1994). This instruction can be an audiotape or videotape of their child reading with you at school; after the demonstration, you could end the tape by describing important actions you took (and they can take at home) that made the experience beneficial to their child's literacy development. Alternatively, parents could come to school and watch as you read with their child. Or you could mail a list of instructions. Be sure to include the following recommendations for parents:

1. Center any discussion of the book around ideas the child initiates and that are personally relevant to that child (Neuman & Roskos, 1993). As you read, the child may point to a word and interrupt your reading to ask what it is or may look intensely at a single word. Allow this study and continue reading only when you have taught the meaning and pronunciation of the word and your child's interest is satisfied. Sometimes it helps to move your finger below the words as you read so the child can look at each word as you read it.

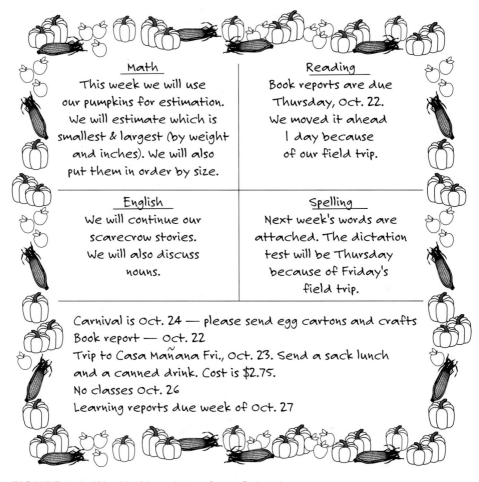

Math

This week we will use our pumpkins for estimation. We will estimate which is smallest & largest (by weight and inches). We will also put them in order by size.

Reading

Book reports are due Thursday, Oct. 22. We moved it ahead 1 day because of our field trip.

English

We will continue our scarecrow stories. We will also discuss nouns.

Spelling

Next week's words are attached. The dictation test will be Thursday because of Friday's field trip.

Carnival is Oct. 24 — please send egg cartons and crafts
Book report — Oct. 22
Trip to Casa Mañana Fri., Oct. 23. Send a sack lunch and a canned drink. Cost is $2.75.
No classes Oct. 26
Learning reports due week of Oct. 27

FIGURE 8.6 Weekly Newsletter from School

2. Tell your child stories, particularly stories about ways you solved literacy problems when you were a child (or as an adult). Add details about what you thought and did to overcome reading and writing obstacles (Neuman & Roskos, 1993). Also, if you use literacy in any way to solve problems or to add pleasure to your life, include these details in your stories.

3. When you read with your child, remember that your praise is more important than your instruction. You need not teach the part of the word your child said wrong or the details from a story your child omitted. Notice improvements, and describe the improvement you see in notes sent to school for the teacher's information. Emergent literacy users are often unable to recognize their growth unaided, so praise from you becomes their major clue that they are learning (Roskos, 1992).

Name: _____   Date: _____

Teacher: _____   Grade: _____

My Child as a Reader

With a vertical slash on the line, indicate where you see your child's interest and participation in the reading process. Make comments or give examples of behaviors observed.

Never	Seldom	Sometimes	Often
(shows little interest)		(shows enthusiasm and attention)	

1. My child likes me to read to him or her (e.g., brings books from school library to share; likes regular bedtime stories).

2. My child reads stories to me (e.g., shares stories he or she has read at school; reads or attempts to read his or her own books and library books).

3. My child attempts to read in everyday situations (e.g., street signs, store signs, cereal boxes, etc.).

4. My child can retell a story so that I can understand it (e.g., retells a story heard at school; retells a story to a brother, sister, or friend).

5. My child figures out new words he or she sees (e.g., uses letter sounds and meaning clues to read a store or street sign; perseveres in figuring out unknown words in a story).

6. When my child reads, he or she "guesses" at words, but they usually make sense in the story (e.g., the story might say "John was racing home" but child reads, "John was running home").

Comments:

_____

_____

_____

_____

FIGURE 8.7 Parent Assessment Form: Observational Guide

Source: Adapted from L. K. Rhodes & N. L. Shanklin (1994), *Windows into Literacy: Assessing Learners K–8,* p. 27. Portsmouth, NH: Heinemann Publishers. Copyright © 1994 by Heinemann Publishers, Inc.

SUMMER READING

June

Sunday	Monday	Tuesday	Wednesday	Thursday	Friday	Saturday
1	2	3	4	5	6	7
				Read the TV Guide. Choose a program to watch.	Read something that comes in the mail.	Read a magazine.
8	9	10	11	12	13	14
Read the names of appliances you find around the house. 15	Read through this calendar. 16	Read quietly for 15 minutes. 17	Read cartoons from the newspaper. 18	Rest for 30 minutes. Read as you rest. 19	Read a recipe to mom. Help her make it. 20	Read a funny book. 21
Read an ad from the Sunday newspaper. 22	Make a bookmark. 23	Read 20 minutes outside. 24	Read road signs next time you take a walk or a ride. 25	Spend some time reading at the public library. 26	Read a note. Have dad write one to you. 27	Read to someone for 20 minutes. 28
Write and read a letter to a pet. 29	Read all sides of a cereal box. 30					

FIGURE 8.8 Summer Literacy Calendar

Adapted from calendar created by June Cash. Used with permission.

4. The more directive you are and the more instructions you give, the less your child will interact with you and the printed material (McCarthey, 1992). Therefore, it is more effective to have pleasurable discussions about a book than to teach many new words from the book (Neilsen, 1993; Teale & Sulzby, 1987; Yaden, Smolkin, & Conlon, 1989).

5. One night a week, have the entire family discuss literature. You can begin by reading aloud from a book, magazine, or newspaper article; then pass the text around so everyone can see it. The next week another family member would lead the discussion, perhaps talking about his or her favorite book. When it is your child's turn, he or she can create a story from a picture book (such as those on Resource Card 12) and share it with the family.

6. Vary the way you read books with your child. One week you **echo read**—that is, you read aloud one line at a time and your child reads the same line aloud immediately after you. The next week use the same book and **choral read**—that is, your child reads aloud along with you. The third week, read a predictable book (see Resource Card 11) that your child brings home. About halfway through the book, when you come to the phrase that is frequently repeated, stop and ask your child to read that phrase. The fourth week, read a book to your child and then ask him or her to retell the story using the illustrations as prompts. Then, the next month you can repeat the cycle or allow your child to choose the type of reading he or she wants to do each time.

Another way to support parents is to assist them in selecting good literature for their children. The first method of doing so is to mail book lists periodically and suggest that parents take these lists to the library to use as guides for locating high-quality books their children will like. You can also send home copies of books that you are reading with their children at school. In this way emergent readers have twice the amount of exposure to each book, because they can read it again at home.

Another resource for parents is the traveling story box. You or your students place a book, an item relative to the book (such as a stuffed animal), and a blank journal in a box or large envelope. Students are allowed to check out one of these traveling boxes and read the book at home with a parent. The parent and child write their reactions to the book and a question to you, if you and they desire, in the journal.

Another good resource that reading specialists distribute to parents is a list of ideas for providing a literate environment at home, as illustrated in Figure 8.9.

Chapter 13 will offer additional suggestions for building bridges between school and home—bridges for students and parents whose first language is not English, for parents who cannot read English, and for those who resist coming to school because they didn't have good experiences as students.

Bringing Home to School

Fully as important as reinforcing literacy at home is bringing family members and home experiences to the classroom. Among the most effective means to accomplish this are conferences, parent visits to school, and telephone calls.

CONFERENCES. Traditionally, *parent–teacher conferences* have been the main means by which home cultures have come to school. These conferences will be most helpful to emergent readers if they achieve three goals:

1. Exchanging knowledge about emergent readers' strengths
2. Providing support and enrichment opportunities so emergent readers can have successful literacy experiences at home and school
3. Developing joint goals and plans of action

1. Comment on reading to stimulate interest.

2. Play reading games in the car.

4. Let you children see you writing for real-life experiences.

3. Read at bedtime.

6. Create a special reading and writing place.

5. Always be an adoring audience.

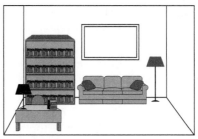

7. Hold daily, meaningful conversations.

FIGURE 8.9 Parents' Suggestion List Distributed by Reading Specialists

Building parent–teacher support through conferences can increase student achievement. Following such meetings, emergent readers tend to read more at home and thus increase their reading proficiency (Anderson, Wilson, & Fielding, 1988).

To accommodate parents' working hours, it is helpful to provide both day and evening conference times. Doing so at least twice a year demonstrates your sensitivity to parents' busy schedules. Moreover, if you give them the assessment form provided in Figures 8.7 a few days before the conference, parents can become equal partners in planning the content of the meeting. Without such joint planning, parents tend to believe that communication is only one-way—or, as one Spanish-speaking parent put it:

> *Yo sigo lo que la escuela me manda, lo que la escuela me pide que haga. Es como si yo fuera una alumna también en la escuela.* [I follow what the school tells me to do, what the school asks of me. It's as if I were also a student in the school.] (Rueda & Garcia, 1992, p. 90)

You can open parent conferences with the following request: "Tell me about your child" (or "Tell me about your child since we last met"). Parents respond well to this opening because it communicates that you see their child as a vibrant human being whose actions and thoughts at home are important to the work they do at school. Moreover, if a child has suddenly begun to have a literacy difficulty, the parent can discuss possible causes, such as a traumatic incident or a new medication. In this way you do not have to ask the difficult question: "Has anything happened at home that might affect your child's schoolwork?" After you have discussed strengths, shared information, and established mutual goals, end the conference by asking the parent: "Is the child I described the same as the child you see at home?" The answer to this question can illuminate any unintentional biases you may hold about an emergent reader.

PARENT VISITS TO SCHOOL. It can be rewarding for parents to visit your classroom during the school day. Parents appreciate and profit from watching your instruction. If possible, describe your objectives for the lesson to them before it begins.

Many parents appreciate being asked to write comments comparing the literacy their child demonstrates at school to what the child employs at home. You can also show parents some activities relative to the lesson that they can do with their child at home to accelerate their child's literacy. While they are at the school, parents can practice performing one or more of these activities with their child, and you can provide feedback as to their effectiveness. This will help the at-home experiences of emergent readers/writers become even more productive.

TELEPHONE CALLS. Many teachers have established the practice of calling parents to report good news about their children. This practice is particularly valuable for emergent readers/writers because of their limited ability to discern their own progress. You can involve the parents in your classroom routine by telling them about new letters decoded, concepts mastered, or other skills their children are developing.

If you phone in the evening hours, it is valuable also to speak to your students. In this way you can explain how proud you are of them and that you are calling to tell their parents about a specific growth made recently. Doing so provides concrete evidence to the children that their parents are closely involved with and informed about the work they do at school.

Tier 1–4 Supports for Emergent Readers/Writers

Many effective activities and programs can be used in Tier 1, 2, 3, and 4 settings to advance the literacy abilities of struggling emergent readers/writers.

Reading Classmates' Names

Although the amount of print in books and charts can be overwhelming for students at the emerging level, you can help them learn the concepts described in this chapter more rapidly if you include classmate names on charts and other materials. Use sign-in sheets for daily attendance, check-in sheets for participation in activity centers, check-out lists for the classroom library, names on desks, names beneath personal identity shields that students create and display on their classroom lockers, and names in large letters to identify works posted on the bulletin board. The reason learning to read classmates' names is such a valuable activity is that these words are abstract nouns; learning to read them requires processes and concepts similar to those students will use to read nonpictorial nouns.

To encourage students to read classmates' names, ask them to assist you. For example, when you are returning papers, handing out refreshments, and so forth, ask students to distribute the items to their classmates as you read each name. As these students become more literate, they often ask to do these tasks alone, as in this instance:

> While Jevon continued to sit at the back of the circle in the Story Corner, and apparently found little meaning in storytime, he was becoming "name literate" in our classroom. . . . When I scanned the list [of classroom names] I was preparing, I puzzled out loud what name I'd left out, Jevon suggested randomly it might be Coby's. I gave him the [list] . . . and he looked the list over, saying confidently: "Nope, there it is!" Sure enough, beneath his finger was Coby's name. . . . When it was his turn to be leader and fill in the chart, he would rally his friends to help him; when one of his friends was the leader, he was there ready to offer his help in turn. He found his name and all of his classmates' names on the message board and the sign-up sheets. Reading the center selections that his friends had made for art, writing, or math center time gave him information he wanted to consider before making a choice himself. (White, 1990, p. 18)

Another power of name literacy for struggling emergent readers is that these words can be used to help others. By reading the names, these students can show classmates where things belong and to whom they belong.

If some students are unable to write their own names, make it a point to be beside their desks each time you collect work from the class. While the rest of the class finishes their work, you can write the student's name (or guide the student's hand to write it) in the upper left-hand corner of the paper—so the student will develop the habit of looking to that part of all printed materials first.

As students learn to read names and become more literate, move beyond merely labeling objects in the room to writing phrases. For example, if two guinea pigs are brought to school as pets, instead of writing simply GUINEA PIGS on tagboard beneath their cage, write JENNY—FEED GUINEA PIGS AT 2:00 (with Jenny being the name of the student who is responsible for pet care that week).

Alphabet Strips and Word Strips

An important point in emergent readers' development is the stage when they begin to recognize individual letters in their own and their classmates' names. Many do so more rapidly if the alphabet is printed on a sentence strip on their desks. In this way peers can also easily point to individual letters when struggling emergent readers work together or with others. Similarly, to assess a student's level of reading development, listen to the type of questions he or she asks about letters (e.g., "Is that the second letter in my name?"). In response, refer to letters as being either present or absent from his or her name.

Then, to help students move from name and letter literacy to word literacy, use word strips. Create phrases for objects in the room, name them, and label these objects with tagboard. For example, when it is time to feed the guinea pigs, if you notice that students are having trouble opening the cage with their hands, call an emergent literacy user to your side and suggest that the children find a special pencil to use as a tool—the "guinea pig cage opener." When the child finds the pencil that works best, write GUINEA PIG CAGE OPENER on an index card (or allow the student to write it if desired), and help the student attach it to the pencil with yarn. This student then announces to the class what the new object is and where it will be stored and places it there for classmates' future use.

You can also use tagboard strips on the first day of school. Distribute them to students, and then pass each desk individually and ask what word or phrase each student wants to learn to read. Write it on the strip. Students at the emergent stage can then leave school on the first day with a word or phrase to take home to read—and avoid the disillusionment voiced by Bernie Kosar earlier in this chapter. Before they take their word strips home, ask students to read them to you as they leave. Instruct them to read their words to their parents to show how well they can read.

▪ Diagnosing Emergent Readers' Needs

Asking questions about the print that an emergent reader has expressed interest in is among the most sensitive and effective diagnostic and instructional tools. Students' responses to questions such as "How did you know that?" or "What do you think will come next in the story?" or "Why was that important to the story?" reveal the concepts that these emergent readers have mastered. Other assessment instruments are checklists like the form shown in Box 8.1, in which reading specialists record individual accomplishments of students. Such checklists convey progress without negative and often invalid connotations about the speed with which a child learns (such as that a student's progress is advancing at an "inappropriate" rate). This form can be used in many ways and can help you regroup students according to need.

A second diagnostic tool is in Box 8.2. It also provides instructional guidelines to increase students' literacy development. Notice that the checklist in the right-hand column includes skills and concepts the student has mastered; those in the left-hand column are things the student wants to work on. Each week emergent readers should take stock of their competencies and check off the appropriate entries in the right-hand column. As students need these literacy skills, they will be taught them.

Intergenerational Programs

An article in the magazine *Children Today* (November/December 1988) described model programs that utilize intergenerational friendships to provide instruction for emergent readers. In the Massachusetts cities of Agawam and Springfield, and in White

8.1 DIAGNOSIS AND ASSESSMENT

Diagnosing Struggling Emergent Readers

Name _____

Teaching Strategy _____ Date Demonstrated _____

1. *Recurring Principle*
   Does the child use the same stroke, creating recurring text
       in scribbles?

2. *Directional/Flexibility Principles*
   Does the child move his or her hand or head from left to right
       when listening to text and write/scribble from left to right?
   Does the child point to the left side as he or she attempts to read?
   Has vertical writing ceased?
   Does the child recognize *I* and *T*?

3. *Contrastive Principle*
   Does the child write lowercase letters and capital letters correctly?
   Does the child say different sounds for different printed letters?

4. *Abbreviation Principle*
   Does the child draw a picture or lines that represent an idea?
   Does the child leave spaces between words?

5. *Sign Principle*
   Do written attempts resemble familiar signs (e.g., billboards,
       advertisements) available to the child?
   Does the child label objects in his or her picture?
   Does the child recognize labels in the room?

Settlement, Texas, these programs serve students from low-income single-parent families. The students go to a retirement facility for after-school care until their parents pick them up. During this time, retired citizens read to students and assist them with writing. These adults are taught the strategies presented in this chapter, so that they can reinforce the program used at school. The results are positive for both the students and adults. As one senior citizen states:

> The children have become part of our lives! There was a void here before. They literally light up our lives and we kind of give them security. We bridge the gap. It's being with someone, being loved by someone. They bring love and laughter into all our lives. (p. 201)

8.2 DIAGNOSIS AND ASSESSMENT

Diagnosing the Needs of Struggling Emergent Readers

Name: _____

Next Time Needs Specific Help with . . .

1. _____ Short vowels
2. _____ Long words
3. _____ Meanings of words
4. _____ Remembering what I read
5. _____ Remembering what I read yesterday
6. _____ Writing longer sentences
7. _____ Reading faster
8. _____ Other: _____
   _____
   _____
   _____
   _____
   _____
   _____

Describe what you want to learn next week:

No Longer Needs Help With . . .

A. _____ The letters of the alphabet
B. _____ Sounds of consonants
C. _____ "I," "A," "The"
D. _____ Blending sounds of letters together
E. _____ Reading "ch," "sh" and "th"
F. _____ Meanings of lots of words
G. _____ Understanding what I read
H. _____ Reading a full book alone
I. _____ Spelling
J. _____ Handwriting
K. _____ How to study
L. _____ Concept of words
M. _____ Concept of sentences
N. _____ Concept of story
O. _____ Writing a sentence
P. _____ Reading silently for 5 minutes
Q. _____ Reading orally for 1 page without missing a word.
R. _____ _____
S. _____ _____
T. _____ _____
U. _____ _____
V. _____ _____
W. _____ _____
X. _____ _____
Y. _____ _____
Z. _____ _____

In this kind of intergenerational program, each student is paired with a senior citizen who enjoys a similar hobby or interest. Every afternoon the children and retired persons enjoy snacks together and tell about their day. Then they read at least one book together about their mutual hobby or interest, engage in an activity related to that hobby, and write a sentence about what they did. Later, the children do their "homework" with their special person (whom they affectionately call "Aunt," "Uncle," "Grandpa," or "Grandma"). This homework includes special notes the teachers write to the older adult concerning the next day's schoolwork. The senior citizens work with the

children, and thus students can be prepared for the next school day's ever
ple of such homework appears in Figure 8.10.

One principal stated that he can definitely tell a difference in his students as a result of this program. He says their attitudes and reading abilities have improved. (For
specific information about initiating this program, contact the American Association of
Retired Persons, 601 E Street N.W., Washington, DC 20049.)

Transitional Programs

Transitional and developmental classes are programs that have significantly increased
the reading achievement of students at the emergent reading stage (Barillas, 2000; Clay,
1991; DeFord, Lyons, & Pinnell, 1991; Lee & Neal, 1993). Many schools have created a
developmental class that provides an additional transitional year of instruction between
kindergarten and first grade (without the need for children to repeat or "fail" kindergarten) for students who have not yet broken the code to read and write English. Transitional and developmental classes reduce the negative implication that some students
are "behind" in life (as early as age 5!).

The concepts presented in this chapter cannot be timed, and individual students'
abilities to develop these concepts relate less to their intellectual capacities than to factors described in Chapters 1 through 7. Nonetheless, if a student exhibits the following
behaviors after a full year of instruction, a transitional class may be the correct instructional plan:

- Dawdles while at school
- Cries or has difficulty separating from people and objects
- Tires easily or is easily provoked into cranky behavior
- Is tense much of the time when engaged in literacy activities
- Has developed mastery of only one or two of the concepts described in this chap-
  ter (see Boxes 8.1 and 8.2)
- Expresses a dislike for school
- Compensates for lack of literacy by becoming a loner or class clown (Allington,
  1995; Ruddell & Ruddell, 1995)

A transitional program is valuable for such students because they can continue to
explore literacy at the emergent level without being forced to decode words before they
are ready (Au, 1991; Cazden, 1994; Texas Education Agency, 2000). It can also forestall
the need for costly remediation in later years, and it averts the decrease in self-esteem
that is associated with grade retention. Teachers can also be more sensitive to the unique
learning styles and learning rates of individual students in these classes, because transition classes contain fewer students than regular first grade classes. As already noted in
this chapter, however, communication between school and parents must be effective
and should precede any decision for transitional class placement. Also, such classes
should not exceed 15 to 17 students so that each child can receive individual literacy
supports.

Chase 10-8-02

1. big

2. pig

* 3. fit fit fit fit

4. did

5. swim

6. six

7. dig

8. win

* 9. sit

10. hit

* 11. been been been

* 12. October

Please work with Chase on the words that have a "*" beside them. I worked with Chase today during school. He is doing an excellent job in spelling!!!

Keri Mcjennis

FIGURE 8.10 Sample Homework Communication between Teachers and Members of the Senior Citizen Program

Chapter Summary

This chapter described emergent literacy as well as the diagnosis and instruction of students who struggle at this level. Reading specialists and literacy teachers assist struggling emergent readers to recognize that letters are made from more than one type of mark, are written horizontally, have blank spaces between them, and can result in words that label ideas. Emergent readers also learn that they can obtain meaning from words, that words are arranged into sentences, that certain letters and sounds correspond, and that all these concepts combine to result in stories that make sense. These concepts evolve more rapidly when parents become partners with the school through home visits by the teacher, student-composed letters to parents, newsletters, parent assessments of their child's development, literacy calendars, school visits, parent–teacher conferences, and telephone calls.

Through Tier 1 and 2 supports in literacy classrooms, struggling emergent readers can be more successful in learning to read classmates' names, as well as in learning to read and write other words they want to know. Transitional and intergenerational programs can also assist emergent readers to develop decoding and comprehension abilities more rapidly.

Chapter 9 will describe special adaptations for decoding.

Key Terminology

Now that you have completed this chapter, see if you know the meanings of the terms listed below. If you do, place a check mark in the blank that precedes the term. If you are not certain, review the term's meaning by turning to the page number shown. If you have learned at least eight of these on your initial reading of the chapter, you have understood the chapter's content.

____ **emergent literacy** (page 230)
____ **recurring principle** (page 234)
____ **directional and flexibility principles** (page 235)
____ **contrastive principle** (page 235)
____ **abbreviation principle** (page 235)
____ **sign principle** (page 235)

____ **environmental print** (page 236)
____ **phonemes** (page 237)
____ **graphemes** (page 237)
____ **rebus stories** (page 239)
____ **echo read** (page 250)
____ **choral read** (page 250)

 ## Case Study

Making Professional Decisions

Ramón was a 15-year-old high school student who was beginning his sophomore year when he was re-ferred to the high school diagnostician by his homeroom teacher. According to the teacher Ramón seemed to be trying hard, but his teacher felt he would need more individual help to pass the school's competency test in order to graduate.

The diagnostician interviewed Ramón's parents with the help of a Spanish interpreter. The family had immigrated to the United States when he was 10 years old. Both parents were employed. Although they had received little formal education themselves, they wanted Ramón to finish high school and college.

In the interview the parents said that Ramón had had only 2 years of schooling in his native country before their emigration. When Ramón enrolled in his American school, he was placed in fourth grade. He learned English on his own after he came to the United States. He had never been retained.

The parents could not recall anything unusual about Ramón's physical and family history. He was a popular boy and had many friends. The parents said he used English only at school and spoke Spanish at home. They described Ramón as a "good son" who frequently helped his father at work. There were no reported signs of behavior problems or adolescent rebellion.

In their initial interview his parents indicated that Ramón had passed both the vision and hearing screening tests at his school.

An examination of Ramón's cumulative records revealed that his elementary level teachers thought he was a serious and industrious student who experienced difficulties in keeping up with his peers in science, social studies, and math word problems. They noted that he was an accurate and fluent oral reader, although comprehension seemed to be an area of difficulty. His current high school teachers acknowledged that although Ramón worked hard, he was not succeeding in his courses. They described him as polite but shy, especially with teachers.

Ramón described himself as "dumb" and probably the "worst reader in the school." He said he was embarrassed by his poor reading. The specialist administered the IRI provided in Chapter 6 of this text. The results of the test are presented below:

INFORMAL READING INVENTORY

Word Recognition List

Independent level	Grade 6
Instructional level	Grade 6

Oral Reading Passages

Independent level	Grade 5
Instructional level	Grade 7

Silent Reading Passages

Independent level	Grade 5
Instructional level	Grade 6

Ramón's word recognition scores were consistently higher than his comprehension scores. Ramón's overall instructional level as measured by the IRI was sixth grade for silent reading and seventh grade for oral reading.

In addition to the informal reading inventory, Ramón was administered the *Gates-MacGinitie Reading Test,* a formal measure of comprehension and vocabulary. The results of this test are presented below:

GATES-MACGINITIE READING TEST, LEVEL 10–12, FORM K

Vocabulary	7.2 grade equivalent
Comprehension	6.6 grade equivalent
Total score	6.8 grade equivalent

The results of this standardized test indicated that Ramón was reading at the sixth grade level.

The high school diagnostician asked Ramón to bring a textbook from his classes to their next meeting. He brought a social studies text. The specialist asked him to read a social studies selection of about 300 words and then to retell what he had read. His retelling was extremely sparse and nonsequential. The specialist then asked Ramón several questions about the selection. He was able to answer very few without looking back in the text. When allowed to look back, Ramón was able to find answers that he had not known or to correct erroneous ones.

The diagnostician then modeled the think-aloud process for Ramón. She chose another selection and read it orally while Ramón followed along. She stopped after each paragraph and said what she had thought about as she read the text. She modeled several different types of think-aloud comments. She paraphrased or summarized the paragraph and connected the topic to her prior knowledge. She made inferences and noted parts that she found difficult. She asked questions and indicated when she found the answers in further reading. The specialist asked Ramón to join her in thinking-aloud. Ramón seemed to find the entire process enjoyable, although he generally restated the examiner's comments in his own words or said, "I thought that too." After several pages of thinking aloud together, the specialist asked Ramón to do this on his own. He found it extremely difficult.

1. Considering all social, motivational, cultural and physical/cognitive variables, which appear to be associated with Ramón's reading problems? Why?

2. What are Ramón's most pressing literacy needs? Substantiate your response.

3. Do you recommend group or individual instruction? Why?

4. At what level would you begin instruction? Substantiate your response.

5. What strategies would you use to instruct Ramón?

Thinking and Writing about What You Have Learned

1. What will you use to build partnerships with your students' parents, and why are these activities compatible with your teaching style (and your present students' needs, if you are teaching)?

2. What are three classroom activities you can use for emergent readers, and why did you choose these?

3. Which materials and work samples from activities in this chapter would you include in a struggling emergent students' literacy assessment and/or portfolios, and why are these important to you?

4. To assess your ability to diagnose emergent readers, study the writing samples in Figures 8.11, 8.12, and 8.13. Write the first concept in the sequence of literacy knowledge you would teach to each child and the activity from this chapter you would use to instruct it. Once you've completed your diagnosis and instructional plan, turn to the Answer Key at the end of the book to learn the concept taught and instructional activity that was actually used to move this student to the next level of literacy understanding.

FIGURE 8.11 Student Writing Sample 1

Translation: The ichthyosaurus always has to be doing stuff.

FIGURE 8.13 Student Writing Sample 3

Translation: She has a tennis racket.

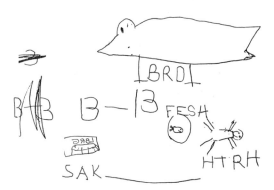

FIGURE 8.12 Student Writing Sample 2

Translation: Larva, bird, fish [in egg], hatched, and signature.

Enhancing Decoding Abilities

When you post and explain semantically rich, complex words around the room, students can use the contexts in which these words appear to learn the words (just as they use the contexts of sentences in books to obtain clues to meaning).

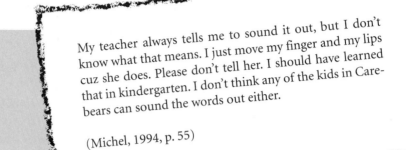

My teacher always tells me to sound it out, but I don't know what that means. I just move my finger and my lips cuz she does. Please don't tell her. I should have learned that in kindergarten. I don't think any of the kids in Carebears can sound the words out either.

(Michel, 1994, p. 55)

■ Chapter Overview: Key Points

Before students can become avid readers, they must self-initiate decoding strategies. Strategies in this chapter are particularly effective in helping dependent readers become internally guided because they are more intense and targeted than those designed for students who already decode independently. This chapter presents:

- Explanation of why some readers need special decoding strategies, and an introduction to the six specific strategies to be described
- Special Tier 1–4 diagnostic and instructional approaches to teach sight word strategies
- Special Tier 1–4 diagnostic and instructional approaches to teach semantic and syntactic context strategies
- Special Tier 1–4 diagnostic and instructional approaches to teach structural analysis strategies
- Special Tier 1–4 diagnostic and instructional approaches to teach phonics strategies
- Special Tier 1–4 diagnostic and instructional approaches to teach students how to use dictionaries and thesauruses
- Special Tier 1–4 diagnostic and instructional approaches to help struggling readers put all decoding skills to use in concert

Decoding does not mean merely that students use phonics, sight words, structural analysis, and/or context clues. To decode most effectively, students must use certain strategies with certain words and continuously check their decodings against understandings about life, about story structures, and about what would make sense with other words in the story. Decoders must also apply the four rule systems that govern the English language: the phonological (sounds in words), syntactical (position a word holds in a sentence), semantic (the specific meaning of a word in a particular context), and pragmatic (the practical and most common uses of words and most frequent word choices by an author) systems.

In this chapter you will learn how to build students' understandings about decoding. The special Tier 1, 2, 3, and 4 support strategies presented will guide students to realize that reading is not just saying words or using a few ideas to make a best guess at a word. Rather, when they read they create meaning from the words; they may have to change their ideas when the word they think the author has used does not make sense. By the end of the chapter, you will have answers to the following questions:

1. Which diagnostic strategies and instructional methods increase struggling readers' use of content-specific, basic, and signal sight words?

2. How can Post-it notes, clozes, and other tools strengthen struggling readers' context clue knowledge?

3. How can students use compound words, affixes, and structural analysis more effectively in decoding?

4. What portion of students' decoding strategies should be based on phonics?

5. How can you increase struggling readers' use of the dictionary and thesaurus when they read and write?

6. How can less accomplished readers learn to use decoding strategies synergistically and automatically?

▩ Why Some Readers Need Special Decoding Strategies

Let's analyze the limitations of past instructional programs for struggling readers to see how these approaches often added to students' difficulties rather than alleviated them. An actual one-on-one discovery discussion with one of these readers will start the analysis. As you read the dialogue that follows, put yourself in the place of Suzanne, the student receiving this instruction. What are you learning about the reading process, and how do you feel?

The teacher began by stating that the objective of this session was to identify the ending sound of printed words. Notice, however, that throughout the session no printed words were read. The entire instructional session was oral, and proceeded as follows:

Teacher: Suzanne, if I say the word *book*, what do you hear at the end of the word?

Suzanne: L.

Teacher: No . . . b-o-o-kkkkkk.

Suzanne: T? I?

Teacher: No, try again: b-o-o-kkkkkkk.

Suzanne: K.

Teacher: Now, I want you to go back and do the skill cards at your seat. First, look at the picture. Say what the picture is. Then listen for the ending sound of the picture. Write the letter of the sound you hear at the end. . . . What do you do when you get back to your seat?

Suzanne: I write the letter of the picture.

Teacher: No, you say the word of the picture. First you look at the picture. Then, say what the picture is. Then, listen for the ending sound of the picture word. Then, write the letter of the sound you hear at the end. Now, what do you do?

Suzanne: Say the letter at the end.

Teacher: No, you listen for the letter at the end, then write it in the space. . . . What do you do when you go back to your seat?

Suzanne: Say the picture and write the letter you hear.

Teacher: Write the letter you hear where?

Suzanne: At the end.

Aside from the incorrect concepts about decoding that were communicated by the teacher (such as saying sounds in isolation), if you had been this reader, how would you have felt after giving five incorrect answers and receiving four negative feedbacks, and having only two correct answers (following three prompts) in this 80-second instructional session? What would you have learned about reading and decoding? Would your positive attitude toward reading increase? Would you now understand how reading gives people lifelong joy and information? In similar research, during a typical 20-minute lesson, struggling readers were told 57 of the 461 words they were to read. In addition, 69.9 percent of this typical lesson was allocated to giving instruction about tasks unrelated to reading, such as where to sharpen the pencil, where to write the heading, and what to do when finished (DeFord, Lyons, & Pinnell, 1994; Hennings, 2000).

When readers who are only beginning to become independent are taught to decode in such environments, reading becomes an endless combination of isolated and meaningless letters and sounds, lacking the synergism and spontaneity that come when students integrate multiple language clues. Moreover, these readers tend to use a single decoding strategy—context, phonics, or picture clues—regardless of the power of that strategy. Whenever it is impossible to use it, these readers usually fall back on their own personal experiences and guess at words (Adams, 1993; Allington, 1980; Goodman, 1989; Lindsey, 1999). When no experience-to-word match exists, struggling readers have to abandon all risk taking to avoid negative feedback from others who might discover that they really don't understand what they are reading. They begin to distrust the few reading strategies they know how to use.

To reduce these negative effects, it is important that in the material you use for decoding instruction, only 1 in every 10 to 20 words is outside the student's reading vocabulary. This is necessary because the typical reading experience for less internally guided readers is overly challenging. By ensuring that these students can read with no more than one error in every 15 words—that is, that approximately 93 percent of the words are familiar—you can enable most struggling readers to risk making meaning and engaging several decoding processes simultaneously.

This chapter will present special Tier 1–4 diagnostic and instructional decoding strategies that can assist less accomplished readers. It is important that your students internalize the rationales for these decoding processes and the ways these processes can work interactively. Later in the chapter you will find special lessons designed to encourage students to practice using their favorite strategies in concert.

Key Strategies for Decoding Success

Decoding success is a prelude to positive attitudes toward literacy. Without decoding accuracy, students lose interest in reading (Adams, 1993; Anderson, Hiebert, Scott, & Wilkerson, 1985; Lesgold & Resnick, 1982; Lundberg, 1987). As readers gain more confidence in their decoding abilities, however, they not only sustain positive attitudes but also persist in predicting difficult words from context by using letters as clues. They will also be able to explain what they have learned about reading and how they know they are good readers.

Research shows that speed of word recognition is related to high levels of comprehension for students as early as first grade (Bosch, Bon, & Schreider, 1995; Lesgold & Resnick, 1982), but most struggling readers need your support before they can become fully independent decoders (Biemiller, 1970; Chall, 1989; Juel, Griffith, & Gough, 1986; Stanovich, 1985). Through your decoding program, students will learn that our language is rich with information and provides many clues that assist in decoding. The following decoding clues can unlock the meaning of most words in our language:

1. Basic sight words (comprising the 400 most frequently occurring words in our language)
2. Content-specific sight words (building strong mental images when new material is read)
3. Signal sight words (acting as verbal "highways" to carry meanings)
4. Syntactic and semantic context clues (telling students what is possible to appear in certain spots in a sentence)
5. Structural analyses (adding meaning to base words with prefixes and suffixes)
6. Phonics and letter-to-sound correspondences

In addition, two other effective decoding strategies to be discussed in this chapter are dictionary/ thesaurus usage and decoding methods.

Sight Word Strategies

There are three types of sight words: content-specific, basic sight, and signal sight words. These sight vocabularies are essential for less accomplished readers, for without them they are forced to stop frequently while reading. These stops lock students' short-term memory into processing single words—and thus limit their ability to gain meanings from sentences or to make sense from the rhythm of printed words' match to spoken language.

Teaching Content-Specific Sight Words

The sight words taught least often are content-specific sight words. **Content-specific sight words** appear only when particular subjects are read—so you can teach struggling readers that when they are reading and come to a rather long word they have never seen before, they should first try to determine if it is a content-specific sight word. The subject of the reading material can be a decoding tool because often these words are names of objects associated with that subject, descriptive words that give details about the subject, or events that occur relative to the subject. With this instruction, students can learn the meaning of content-specific words independently. Box 9.1 describes how reading specialists and classroom teachers can diagnose decoding problems and provide Tier 3 and 4 one-to-one instructional interventions.

Another approach for Tier 1–4 support is to teach content-specific sight words through word imagery. As shown in Figure 9.1, content-specific sight words are more easily remembered when their meaning is portrayed in drawings attached to the words. After showing the meaning-associated image, ask students to discuss how the image relates to the word's meaning. If a reader has difficulty remembering a word, you can ask him or her to draw a picture that comes to mind depicting the word's meaning.

9.1 READING SPECIALISTS

Diagnosis and Instructional Interventions to Build Sight Word Knowledge

Diagnosis: Ask students to read the words listed in Table 9.1. Students should be able to read 100 words by the end of kindergarten, 200 by the end of first grade, and 300 by the end of second grade. If a student is less accomplished than desired, the following Tier 3 and 4 instructional interventions can be initiated.

1. For younger struggling readers, create activities. Provide an experience for a student, talk about the experience, have the student dictate a story about the experience, and read the story.

2. Use Visual, Auditory, Kinesthetic, and Tactile Experiences.

- Print unknown words on index cards.
- Tell students to look carefully at each word as you hold it up and pronounce it.
- Then ask them to close their eyes and picture the word.
- Have students try to write the word from memory.
- Last, show each index card to the students again for comparison with the original word.

3. Label objects. Label objects around your classroom and have students attach the printed word to the object. Have students create picture dictionaries or folders: They can cut pictures from magazines and newspapers; paste them into a book or inside a folder using a separate page for each letter, then label the pictures.

4. Create word banks. Word banks are student-selected collections of words they want to learn to recognize at sight. When a student recognizes a word, the teacher writes it on an index card. This index card is placed on a ring or in a box as the student's own personal collection.

5. Have students make their own fishing pole game. All the students need is a string and piece of Velcro (or a magnet) tied to the string for the pole. They can make word cards shaped like fish, with Velcro (or paper clips) fastened to the head area of the fish. Using the fishing pole, the student catches a fish and reads the word printed on it.

6. Have students locate words in newspapers. Ask students to locate words in newspapers and create stories from words found in articles, headings, or ads.

FIGURE 9.1 Using Images to Teach Content-Specific Sight Words

Teaching Basic Sight Words

Recognizing a word by sight means that the reader has identified the word instantly by the unique configuration of its shape (e.g., elephant) or by the unique combination of its letters together with their location in sentences (e.g., "Once upon a time . . ."). Unfortunately, many basic sight words (e.g., *the, to, that*) do not contain a picturable meaning. Therefore, readers must memorize their images and learn to decode these words automatically.

If you follow the criteria mentioned earlier—that materials used for decoding instruction should contain 93 percent familiar words—then when less internally guided readers know the 5,000 most frequently occurring English words by sight, virtually all reading material they select will have 93 percent recognizable words. For this reason alone, the time your readers spend learning the basic sight words will be very profitable. For a complete list of the most frequently occurring English words see *3,000 Instant Words*, by Elizabeth Sakiey and Edward Fry (1984).

Basic sight word instruction is most effective, however, when you teach the most frequently appearing words first. These words have been identified by Fry, Fountoukidis, and Polk (1985) and appear in Table 9.1. You can reassure struggling readers by telling them that when they can read the first 25 of these words by sight, they will be able to read rapidly about one-third of all the words they will ever encounter in printed materials. Then share with them that when they can read the first 100 words, they will know about half of all the words they will ever read.

The following Tier 1, 2, 3, and 4 support strategies are those that have proved most effective and valuable in diagnosing struggling readers and helping them learn basic sight words.

TABLE 9.1 The Instant Words: Most Frequently Used Basic Sight Words

These are the most common words in English, ranked in frequency order. The first 25 make up about a third of all printed material. The first 100 make up about half of all written material. Is it any wonder that all students must learn to recognize these words instantly and to spell them correctly also?

First Hundred

Words 1–25		Words 26–50		Words 51–75		Words 76–100	
the	on	or	can	will	make	number	now
of	are	one	said	up	like	no	find
and	as	had	there	other	him	way	long
a	with	by	use	about	into	could	down
to	his	word	an	out	time	people	day
in	they	but	each	many	has	my	did
is	I	not	which	then	look	than	get
you	at	what	she	them	two	first	come
that	be	all	do	these	more	water	made
it	this	were	how	so	write	been	may
he	have	we	their	some	go	call	part
was	from	when	if	her	see	who	over
for		your		would		oil	

Common suffixes: *-s, -ing, -ed*

Second Hundred

Words 101–125		Words 126–150		Words 151–175		Words 176–200	
new	most	great	tell	put	why	kind	page
sound	very	where	boy	end	ask	hand	letter
take	after	help	follow	does	went	picture	mother
only	thing	through	came	another	men	again	answer
little	our	much	want	well	read	change	found
work	just	before	show	large	need	off	study
know	name	line	also	must	land	play	still
place	good	right	around	big	different	spell	learn
year	sentence	too	form	even	home	air	should
live	man	mean	three	such	us	away	America
me	think	old	small	because	move	animal	world
back	say	any	set	turn	try	house	high
give		same		here		point	

Common suffixes: *-s, -ing, -ed, -er, -ly, -est*

TABLE 9.1 *(continued)*

Third Hundred

Words 201–225		Words 226–250		Words 251–275		Words 276–300	
every	tree	left	begin	until	river	idea	mountain
near	never	don't	life	children	four	enough	cut
add	start	few	always	side	carry	eat	young
food	city	while	those	feet	state	face	talk
between	earth	along	both	car	once	watch	soon
own	eye	might	paper	mile	book	far	list
below	light	close	together	night	hear	Indian	song
country	thought	something	got	walk	stop	real	leave
plant	head	seem	group	white	without	almost	family
last	under	next	often	sea	second	let	body
school	story	hard	run	began	late	above	music
father	saw	open	important	grow	miss	girl	color
keep		example		took		sometimes	

Common suffixes: *-s, -ing, -ed, -er, -ly, -est*

Source: Adapted from E. Fry, D. Fountoukidis, & J. Polk (1985), *The NEW Reading Teacher's Book of Lists,* pp. 147–149. Englewood Cliffs, NJ: Prentice-Hall. Copyright © 1985 by Prentice-Hall, Inc. Used with permission.

These instructional experiences also enabled these students to focus on learning basic sight words through instant recognition without use of additional decoding strategies.

LESSON 1: STUDENT-CREATED GAMES. To build sight word vocabulary, struggling readers often enjoy and profit from reading and rereading familiar stories. The first reading enables teachers and/or peers to diagnose difficulties and list unknown words, which can then be taught in this and subsequent lessons. Because most sight words do not change meanings when placed in contextual situations, gamelike activities reinforce rapid recognition of each word's unique visual image and increase basic sight word knowledge. In Figures 9.2 and 9.3 you will find games that fourth grade readers created to teach to younger schoolmates. These games were selected as among the "top five favorite activities" by students in grades 1 through 5 (Block, 2001).

LESSON 2: CONFIGURATION. In addition to allowing students to use games, sight words can also be learned through configuration. **Configuration** is defined as the visual shape formed by the letters in a word—for example, the configuration of the word *the* is the and the configuration of *that* is that. To turn configuration into an instructional tool, you and readers can select words from Table 9.1 or words that are phonetically irregular and unknown by the students, such as a, that, one, it, and therefore. Then, you can ask students to draw their personalized, unique configuration around

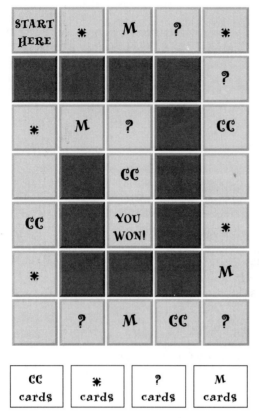

Needed:

1–4 players, game pieces, dice, cards, enlarged game board.

How to Play:

Roll the dice to decide who should go first. Player 1 rolls dice, moves a game piece the designated number of spaces, then does what the space he or she lands on says. On a space with a ?, ✳, M, or CC, the player is to select that card. For example, on a ✳ (decoding) square, the player picks a ✳ card. The player then reads the card to decode the sentence or the word. ("M" or meaning cards ask the player to define the meaning of the word. "CC" or context clue cards give a sentence with a word in it, and the student is required to define the word. "?" or question cards can be a decoding, "CC," or "M" card.) If Player 1 gets the right answer, he or she moves ahead the number of spaces on the card. Then it is the next player's turn. The first player to the center wins.

FIGURE 9.2 Candyland Word Game

each one that will assist them to remember that word's meaning and sounds. For instance, because the word *a* means "only one," Andy, a first grade reader, drew the following configuration to learn the word *a:*

Students write each of these words with its unique configurations on one side of an index card. Immediately after each configuration is drawn, have the student turn the card over and just print the word without its configuration. When all words have been completed, ask the students to study their configured words by looking at each word and saying it orally or silently until they feel they can recognize it instantly. Then you can have students read each word from the side of the card that does not contain the configuration to a partner. If they cannot read a word, ask them to look again at the side with the configuration. After they feel they know all the words, have them read a page from a selected work of children's literature orally to their partners. For any word that is missed, partners are to show the reader the configured version without giving any

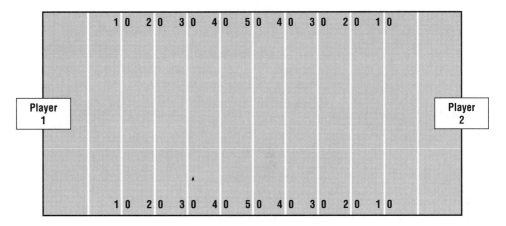

Needed:

1–5 players, paper footballs (one for each player), book or magazine.

How to Play:

If playing alone, the student should begin reading the book. Once a word is learned or a paragraph is comprehended, the student moves the football ahead 10 yards from the goal line. For every missed word or paragraph misunderstood, there is a regression of 10 yards. The student is finished once a touchdown is scored. For two players, flip a coin to decide who will go first. Whoever wins the coin toss is Player 1. Then have student place their paper footballs on opposite goal lines. Player 2 gives an example (an unfamiliar word or a paragraph to express meaning) from a book or magazine to Player 1. If Player 1 demonstrates he/she knows the word or understands the paragraph and can explain the meaning, he/she move ahead 10 yards. The first player to score two touchdowns wins. If more than two people play, two teams are created and each player on the team writes the meaning. The teacher is the referee. The teacher reads all answers and moves the team ball ahead 10 yard for every correct answer given. Students can add to this game by creating their own rules for penalties, field goals, and extra points.

FIGURE 9.3 Football Word Game

other prompt. If the configuration does not lead to an immediate recall, partners are to describe the position the word holds in the sentence. If neither of these prompts is effective, you can ask readers to explain what they were thinking when they drew the configuration and work with them to make the configuration more distinctive.

LESSON 3: THE OMNIBUS STRATEGY. The Omnibus strategy (Manzo & Manzo, 1993) is described in Table 9.2. This strategy is called Omnibus because it uses every learning modality to build sight word recognition ability. The only addition to this strategy that proves valuable for struggling readers is to end the session by asking students to explain the meaning that the word holds for them. When asked to give their own meanings for even the most indescribable words, such as *of* or *that,* readers remember them better. For

TABLE 9.2 The Omnibus Strategy to Sight Word Automaticity

This sight word activity can be done with one or more students. The teacher holds up a flash card or writes a word on the chalkboard:

Teacher:	See this word? The word is *and.* Everyone look at this word, and say it together.
Students:	*And.*
T:	That's correct. Now say it five times while looking at it.
S's:	*And, and, and, and, and.*
T:	Good. Now say it louder.
S's:	*And!*
T:	Come on, you can say it louder than that!
S's:	*AND!*
T:	OK, I have three other cards here [again, answer, arrange]. When I show a card that is not *and,* say "No!" in a loud voice. But when you see *and,* say the word *and* in a whisper.
S's:	No!
S's:	No!
S's:	[whisper] *And.*
T:	Great. Look at it carefully, and when I remove it, close your eyes and try to picture the word under your eyelids. Do you see it? Good. Now say it in a whisper again.
S's:	*And.*
T:	Good. Now spell it.
S's:	A . . . N . . . D.
T:	Now pretend to write it in the air in front of you with your finger while saying each letter.
S's:	A . . . N . . . D.
T:	Good. Now describe the word. The way you would describe a new kid to a friend who hasn't seen him yet.
S1:	It's small.
S2:	It has a witch's hat in the beginning.
S3:	It has a belly at the end.
T:	What's its name again?
S's:	*AND!*
T:	Let's search for *and*'s throughout the day and even after you go home tonight. We'll ask you later if you found any in school and again tomorrow morning if you found any at home.

Source: Adapted from A. V. Manzo & C. Manzo (1990), *Content Area Reading*, p. 323. Boston, MA: Prentice Hall.

example, Clarion, one very articulate reader, stated: "*That* is a word that tells me something is about to be said about the words that came before it. *Of* usually means only a little bit, such as only one detail will be told to me and I know I won't have to concentrate so long when I see *of*! I like *of*'s best!"

Teaching Signal Sight Words

The third type of sight words are those that clue, or send a signal, that (1) cause–effect relationships are being described; (2) a specific ordering of ideas is important; (3) a summation, more of the same, or something different is coming; or (4) changes in thoughts or new thoughts are about to occur. Table 9.3 displays signal sight words that readers profit from learning.

You can diagnose how many of these words students know by creating sentences in which signal words are used to indicate order or sequence. If students do not know the meaning and function of signal sight words, you can use the following Tier 1–4 support lesson to teach the words' meanings, and purposes.

TABLE 9.3 Signal Sight Words

Comparison	Contrast		Simple Listing
as	but	notwithstanding	and
similarly	on the other hand	though	too
at the same time	in spite of	yet	I, II, III . . .
like	conversely	regardless	finally
as well as	despite	whereas	furthermore
likewise	however	although	first, second . . .
both	nonetheless	in contrast	1, 2, 3 . . .
all	on the contrary	unlike	
by the same token	instead	for all that	
furthermore	rather	even though	

Cause–Effect	Conclusions		Time Order
because	in brief	before	immediately
accordingly	in the end	after	formerly
since	in summary	now	later
thus	to reiterate	previously	subsequently
for this reason	in conclusion	last	meanwhile
consequently	to sum up	next	presently
hence	finally	then	initially
resulting	therefore	when	ultimately
therefore	thus		
as a result	as already stated		
so			
then			

1. Make an overhead of a page from a selection of children's literature that you just read or will read to the class.
2. Highlight a few words that appear in the different categories in Table 9.3, color coding them. For instance, you could highlight a "comparison" word with a yellow highlighter and a "time order" sight word with a pink highlighter.
3. Ask students to explain the difference between these words and what these words signal about the upcoming words in text.
4. Ask what students will think, in the future, when these words appear. The goal is to enable students to decode these words independently to make sense.
5. Ask students to read silently. When they come to a word in this lesson, have them raise their hand and tell you what it means and what they are thinking.

Semantic and Syntactic Context Clues

The next decoding strategy employs context clues. You will probably find that most struggling readers have difficulty verbalizing what they think when they use context clues. Some may say that they "read to the end of the sentence," but in reality they may simply be moving their eyes without using the semantical and syntactical clues that sentences lend. When you teach these readers to use context clues, merely introducing them often enables many students, for the first time, to independently combine word meanings. For example, Mario, a less accomplished first grade reader, completed the sight word lessons presented earlier and was beginning to independently decode words in predictable books from Resource Card 14. However, he set the goal of learning to "work out all the hard words" in other books he wanted to read. After completing the instructional sessions in context clue usage, Mario enthusiastically exclaimed: "Guess what! Guess what just happened! I was reading along looking at each word like I already do. Then, my brain began knowing the words even before I did! My brain knows what the word means before I even see all of it! That's powerful context clues!!"

Teaching Semantic Context Clues

The instructional lessons that follow are quite effective in diagnosis and instruction of struggling readers (Block, 2001; Hennings, 2000; Lindsey, 1999). It is important to teach these students, however, that although semantic context clues are valuable decoding tools, when used as the sole decoding tool they can predict only about one-fourth of content-specific words (Gough, Alford, & Holly-Wilcox, 1981).

LESSON 1: BIG BOOKS. To assist readers to tie the meanings of several words together through semantic context clues, you can use a **big book** (Holdaway, 1979). A big book is about 18 by 24 inches—big enough so that all students can see the words. To begin this lesson you cover certain words in the big book with Post-it notes. (You cover all but the first letter in semantically rich words.) For first grade readers, you can cover five such words in five distantly spaced sentences, so the chance that students can guess each word from the preceding semantic clues is high. For second graders, you can cover six words;

RESOURCE CARD 14

Books That Build Readers' Abilities to Use Semantic and Syntactic Context Clues

Adams, A. (1971). *A woggle of witches* (139).* New York: Scribner.

Barrett, J. (1970). *Animals should definitely not wear clothing* (65). New York: Atheneum.

Brown, M. (1995). *Arthur's Christmas cookies* (150). Boston: Little, Brown.

Carle, E. (1995). *The fireflies* (107). New York: Harcourt.

DeRegniers, B. S. (1964). *May I bring a friend?* (151). New York: Atheneum.

Emberley, B. A. (1995). *Drummer Hoff* (30). New York: Simon & Schuster.

Hogrogian, N. (1971). *One fine day* (150). New York: Macmillan.

———. (1995). *Good-night, Owl* (51). New York: Simon & Schuster.

Keats, E. (1962). *The snowy day* (157). New York: Viking.

———. (1967). *Peter's chair* (153). New York: Harper & Row.

———. (1969). *Goggles* (149). New York: Macmillan.

Kellogg, S. (1973). *Leo, the late bloomer* (78). New York: Dutton.

———. (1974). *The mystery of the missing red mitten* (128). New York: Dial.

Lobel, A. (1968). *The comic adventures of Old Mother Hubbard and her dog* (91). New York: Bradbury.

McPhail, D. (1972). *The bear's toothache* (111). Boston: Little, Brown.

Sendak, M. (1963). *Where the wild things are* (139). New York: Harper & Row.

———. (1973). *Noisy Nora* (103). New York: Dial.

*The numbers in parentheses following each title indicate how many words are contained in the story.

---

for third graders, seven words; fourth graders, eight words; and for fifth grade and above, you can cover nine words in separate and distantly spaced sentences. Then you can model how, when students come to a word covered by the Post-it note, they should say the sound of the first letter, pause, and then keep on reading—with the intent of using the first letter's sound and the meanings of other words in the sentence to decode the unknown word.

An example of such a modeling session is illustrated in the following scenario. The teacher holds up the big book and proceeds:

I have covered some words on this first page to illustrate what you will say to yourself and think when you come to words you don't know. You can put together the meaning of all the other words in the sentence to figure these words out—which is called using context clues. I'll show you how to do it. [Teacher has covered all letters in the word *queen* except for the *q*. Teacher points to the word.] If I didn't know this word I'd read to myself: "Once upon a time, a handsome king and beautiful /q/ [pause] lived in a large castle on the top of the highest hill in all the land." By reading to the end of the sentence, using what I know from previous stories, and the sound of the first letter of my unknown word, I know that the word has to be *queen*. When we come to the next covered word, use context clues with me to decode the word—and explain to me what you thought as you read.

LESSON 2: DOES THIS MAKE SENSE? Another way to teach context clues is to have struggling readers ask themselves, "Does this make sense?" as they read. To build readers' use of semantic context clues in this way, follow your oral reading of a book with a discovery discussion with one or more readers. You begin by asking these students to retell what you just read; you write their sentences on a chart. Then have them read their retellings. Before this reading occurs, model how you used semantic context clues to decode the most semantically rich word in the first sentence on the chart. Then instruct the pupils to do the same as they read the remaining sentences orally. Last, hand them a page from the book and remind them that many of the words they just read to you will be on this page as well. As they read independently, work with each student as they perform think alouds and ask themselves, "Does this make sense?" as they read.

This activity is a modified version of the *language experience activity* (LEA). In **LEA**, readers tell a story that you write for them. Immediately after the dictation, the students read their stories. Most will be able to do so without difficulty, because the words are a part of their own speaking and listening vocabularies. LEAs provide the most enriched contextual clues for reading.

LESSON 3: CLOZE AND MAZE PASSAGES. A somewhat more time-consuming instructional activity involves *cloze and maze passages,* which are similar to the big book activity using Post-it notes. With **cloze passages** you type up sentences of text, but instead of covering some of the words you systematically insert *blanks*—perhaps for every 5th or 10th word, or for words that serve a specific semantic context function. When students come to a blank they must integrate all the decoding tools available—especially author's writing style, the purpose of the text, and context clues—to deduce a word that would make sense. A sample cloze sentence is "The dog chased a _____ up the tree as the _____ meowed." **Maze passages** are similar, except that below each blank are several words from which students can choose.

When cloze passages are constructed to target only one type of semantic or syntactic context clue, or only one type of *content* word (such as only nouns), they encourage students to think strategically about this category of words in the future. For example, Fayetta, a second grade reader, exclaimed at her lesson's end: "Now I know how to get all the hard words by myself! I just read around and around them until I see what they are supposed to add up to and what this author is trying to tell me!" Similarly, if you delete only *function* words (such as only conjunctions, only pronouns, only noun determiners, only prepositions, or only auxiliary verbs), you will encourage students to use syntactic clues, inflectional endings, and grammar changes to deduce meaning. When you create function word clozes, ask: "What if you come across a word at this point [the blank] in sentences in the future—what would you expect to see at this point in the sentence and why? How does knowing this about our language help you decode words like this better?"

You can also use clozes to teach phonics and graphophonic cues in concert with semantic and syntactic context clues. To teach phonics, cover only the first letter of words that all have the same first letter, or cover only the endings of those words with the same ending. In this way students use common English spelling patterns to deduce meaning. You can also use clozes as a decoding assessment. Have students write or tell you what they thought as they identified each word for every blank (use about 10 blanks in a 200-

word passage). You can increase the difficulty of any cloze passage by making the deleted words call for a progressively more integrated use of language cues to build more of a student's independent learning strengths.

Readers who enjoy kinesthetic learning experiences may profit from removing the Post-it notes themselves. For example, one first grade teacher reports as follows:

> I think today was one of our most successful discovery sessions. When working with Darius, I used the Post-it notes to teach semantic clues. To my surprise, Darius instantly experienced tremendous success using this strategy. I was surprised and proud because for the lesson he selected a book that was way above his independent reading level. It was the predictable book *Boss for a Week* by Lindy Handy, and by learning to use semantic clues so rapidly he read every word correctly! Darius predicted the covered words in the text rapidly, partly because he was anxious to pull off those Post-it notes to see if he had guessed the "right" word. I now know his lessons need to include kinesthetic learning aids.

Maze passages can become an important instructional tool for readers who rely too heavily on their own background experiences to decode. Because maze passages require students to choose from among words they would not normally say themselves, the lesson teaches them to make meaning through reflection rather than just quickly inserting words that are common in their oral vocabulary. Many such readers also increase their reading vocabulary when they eliminate words that would not make sense in a specific context. To understand the mental processes involved in maze and cloze reading, complete the following maze activity yourself, noticing the reflection and selection strategies you use to make sense. (The example is taken from the *Hunter/Grundin Literacy Profiles: Reading for Meaning: Level Three* [Literacy Assessment Corporation, 1992], which contains many maze sentences.) You can teach these strategies to your students through your think alouds before you give readers their first maze.

He cleaned the windows _____ a week and dusted _____ every evening.

very	furniture
twice	potatoes
then	towels
while	robots

You can also increase the instructional value of maze passages by modifying incorrect answer choices. For example, if a specific reader overly relies on initial consonants to decode words, make all the options in a maze passage begin with the same initial consonant so that graphemic clues are neutralized, forcing this student to develop other methods of decoding words. Similarly, if a student has trouble using syntactical clues, ensure that one incorrect answer choice comes from the same grammatical class as the correct answer, and one incorrect choice comes from a different syntactical category. Then, you can praise the student on correct discrimination based on selection of the correct grammatical class, so he or she knows what strategy was used. This feedback increases the student's independent application of syntactical context clues in future independent silent readings.

9.2 READING SPECIALISTS

Diagnosis and Instructional Interventions to Build Semantic and Syntactic Context Clue Use

Diagnosis: **Selecting pictures** Orally present 10 sentences to students, leaving out a word in each. Students must select a picture that correctly completes the sentence. Discuss why the specific picture was selected. If a student misses 3 or more, offer the instructional interventions listed below. For example:

>   Pictures: a cat, a dog, a car

>   We drove to the store in a _____.

Diagnosis: **Selecting words to complete a series of sentences** (grades 2–12). Write 3 sentences, each with a word missing, and show the students 3 different words or phrases to be used in completing the sentences. Be certain all 3 terms begin with the same letter. Read the sentences to the students, then have them select the word that properly completes each sentence. Example:

>   Words: fruit, forty-yard dash, football

> 1. We played _____ at the park.

> 2. We ate _____ for dessert.

> 3. We ran the _____ for the track team.

If students do not get all 3 correct, offer the following instructional interventions.

1. Supply missing words in sentences. Have the students read sentences with a word missing. They should then enter words into the blank spaces and tell how they knew the correct choice in each case. Example:

>   Our car is _____.
>   red
>   blown
>   crying

2. Supplying missing words that contain the same initial consonant. Give students a sentence with a word missing, but supply an initial consonant for the missing word. Students must supply an appropriate word that begins with that initial consonant. Then ask them to write a second sentence that could follow the first one, also using the word in the blank. Then ask the students to tell you how they knew that sentence would make sense.

>   The dog b_____ at the gray cat.

3. Homograph sentences. Write pairs of sentences that contain homographs (words that are spelled the same but pronounced differently). Then encourage students to use context as they read the pairs of sentences while pronouncing the homographs correctly.

4. Silent reading time. Provide silent reading time so that students can practice reading words in context. Students may want to engage in buddy reading or read with their reading specialists beside them during this time. Instruct the readers to stop and discuss each time they decode an unknown word using semantic and syntactical context clues. The readers' partners (or the specialists) are to write down the words decoded correctly by semantic and syntactical clues.

LESSON 4: SYNTACTIC AND SEMANTIC CONTEXT CLUES. Most struggling readers profit from learning to use semantic and syntactic context clues. Using **semantic clues** means using the meanings of other words in a sentence or paragraph to deduce the meaning of unknown words. **Syntactic clues** involve the positions and grammatical roles that words hold in a sentence, which can help readers deduce their meanings.

Box 9.2 describes how to diagnose and instruct students who lack the ability to utilize these clues. When those methods are not successful, the following Tier 4 activity often helps less accomplished students in grades 1–9. First, teach them where **naming words** (nouns and noun phrases) can be found in sentences. You can do so by highlighting these words in yellow on a few photocopied pages from selections of children's literature. Next, teach them where **painting words** (adjectives and adverbs) are located in sentences by highlighting these words in blue. Last, teach them where **doing words** (verbs) are located by highlighting these words in pink. Ask students to read all the highlighted pages aloud with you and to state discoveries about what all words of the same color have in common. Then have them write their own rule for syntactic context clues, based on the pattern these words revealed. Finally, in a discovery discussion, have students read a page without highlighting and ask them to do think alouds each time they stop to decode a word. Continue these think alouds until the students regularly include references to the rule they created for using syntactic context clues.

In this lesson you can also help struggling readers combine syntactical and semantic clue use with sight word knowledge. You can make charts similar to the one in Figure 9.4, underlining or highlighting all sight words, to help readers use the syntactical information interactively with basic sight words to decode unknown words.

LESSON 5: TRANSFORMING SENTENCES. Transformation is borrowed from the Reading Recovery program. To begin this activity, ask students to select the most difficult sentences from a book just read. Then write these sentences on sentence strips and have students point to the section that was most difficult for them. Instruct about the syntactical features of that phrase placement, then cut that sentence into parts and ask students to put it together so it will make sense. As they put the sentence together using different phrase placements (see Figure 9.5), readers learn about permissible English phrase patterns.

Our Class Today		
is	–	Michael <u>is</u> happy.
the	–	<u>The</u> big pillow is on <u>the</u> chair.
said	–	Meisong <u>said</u>, "I read to the class today."
in	–	The puppet is <u>in</u> the box.
was	–	The sun <u>was</u> shining yesterday.

FIGURE 9.4 Using Syntactic and Semantic Context Clues with Sight Words

Phase 1
Recording of sentence.

Discussion of theme. Teacher helps in recording of sentence. Sentence written on sentence strip.

Phase 2

| it was raining when we went to the football game and I got soaked |

Phase 3
Rehearsal.

Reading of sentence practiced if necessary. Phrases indentified and cut out.

Phase 4

| it was raining⟩when we went⟩to the football game⟩and I got soaked |

Phase 5

Nouns, pronouns, verbs, & their markers identified and cut out.

| it/was raining⟩when we went⟩to/the football game⟩and I/got soaked |

Phase 6

Individual words identified and cut out.

| it/was/raining⟩when/we/went⟩to/the/football game⟩and/I/got/soaked |

Phase 7

Picking up named words

| it was | | when we went to the | | and I got | |

Phase 8
Rearrange.

Jumbled words to be put into original order

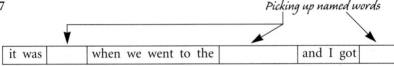

Phases 9 and 10

Re-order into

| when⟩we⟩went⟩to the⟩football game⟩it⟩was⟩raining⟩and⟩I⟩got⟩soaked |

new sentences

| we⟩went⟩to the⟩football game⟩when⟩it⟩was⟩raining⟩and⟩I⟩got⟩soaked |

FIGURE 9.5 Summary of Procedures in Transformations

Source: Adapted from M. M. Clay (1993), *Reading Recovery: A Guidebook for Teachers in Training,* pp. 68–69. Portsmouth, NH: Heinemann.

Structural Analysis

Structural analysis uses the meaning contained in prefixes, suffixes, base words, and compounds to determine the meaning of the words in which they appear. Structural analysis also employs the meaningful units in unknown words as a tool to decode them. Less accomplished readers profit from being taught that whenever a word is long, structural analysis is often the most effective means of identifying that word's meaning. Structural analysis instruction is important for these students because longer words evince more fears of decoding failure than do shorter words. Moreover, these readers are more likely to use context clues to guess at shorter words, but without the following lessons in structural analysis they tend to skip longer words, thus limiting their comprehension. Box 9.3 describes how to diagnose difficulties with longer words and offers activities to teach structural analysis. The following lessons are to be used in conjunction with the activities in Box 9.3 so that students receive two different experiences a day to build their abilities.

LESSON 1: TEACHING COMPOUND WORDS. To introduce structural analysis, coach students to look within words for prefixes, suffixes, base words, and compound words that

9.3 DIAGNOSIS AND ASSESSMENT

Diagnosis and Instructional Intervention to Build Structural Analysis Skills

Diagnosis: Ask students to read and tell the meaning of 20 words from Tables 9.4 and 9.5. If they miss more than 15 words, teach the following activities.

1. **Sentence changing.** The teacher reads a sentence using two individual words instead of contractions. Students change the sentences by inserting the contraction in place of the individual words.

   She <u>did not</u> have a cat.
   She <u>didn't</u> have a cat.

   Perform the same activity by writing two sentences in which one sentence contains a word without an affix and the second sentence contains the word with an affix from Table 9.5. Have the student describe why the meaning changed.

2. **Contraction scavenger hunt.** Have students search newspapers and magazines for word combinations that can be changed into contractions or contractions that can be changed into two separate words. Students can highlight or underline these words.

3. **Collages, sentences, paragraphs.** Students might create a collage, sentences, or paragraphs using words containing prefixes and suffixes taken from Table 9.5 and share their results with you or a peer.

clue the meaning of a word. Among the most effective and enjoyable small group lessons is to demonstrate how meanings in picturable compound words can be decoded when the meanings of the two words within a compound word are combined. Students enjoy the challenge of being the first in the group to recognize a compound word's meaning.

To implement this activity, display the words in Table 9.4 on the overhead. Explain that as soon as anyone looks within a word and puts two meanings together, he or she

---

TABLE 9.4 Compound Words

snowshoe	battlefield	drugstore	counterclockwise
snowman	firearms	paperback	baseball
snowflake	fireside	horseback	basketball
snowfight	sailboat	bareback	football
snowstorm	lifeboat	nowhere	neighborhood
snowplow	mailman	cupcake	handwriting
doghouse	fireman	shortbread	supermarket
greenhouse	spaceman	gingerbread	handbag
playhouse	sandman	grandfather	filmstrip
courthouse	bellhop	grandmother	cowboy
birdhouse	motorboat	sidewalk	cowgirl
farmhouse	policeman	inside	pigsty
lighthouse	footman	outside	sandbox
henhouse	watchman	beside	hatbox
schoolhouse	fisherman	mountainside	playmate
schoolyard	milkman	cornfield	teammate
playground	doorman	armchair	classmate
playpen	typewriter	fireplace	classroom
today	whichever	blacksmith	cannot
tonight	whenever	broomstick	tiptoe
into	notebook	rainstorm	lunchroom
something	schoolbook	nightmare	bedroom
sometimes	pocketbook	fishhook	bathroom
somewhere	workbook	seashore	stoplight
somehow	cookbook	seaport	meanwhile
someone	textbook	seashell	barnyard
anybody	bookmark	seaplane	proofread
anything	bookworm	oceanfront	firewood
anyway	bookcase	bedtime	silkworm
anyhow	bookkeeper	nighttime	championship
anyplace	bookstore	daytime	worldwide
anywhere	storybook	anytime	bathtub
bedside	everything	rainbow	skycap
butterfly	everyone	clockwise	

may write that word in a sentence to challenge other group members to read. Each sentence is written on a separate sheet of paper or sentence strip and held up for peers to read silently and to raise their hands when they can deduce the word's meaning. Once students learn the picturable compound words in Table 9.4, you can also teach the nonpictorial compound words in the table.

LESSON 2: TEACHING AFFIXES. In another structural analysis lesson, struggling readers can skim a book of their choice to locate as many long words that contain recognizable affixes as they can. **Affixes** are morphemes (the smallest units of meaning in our language) that can be added to either the beginning of a word (prefix) or to the end of a word (suffix) to alter the meaning of the root word (base word). With each word, you can ask readers to describe what they were thinking as they decoded the words in a passage that you read together. This section of the activity is to build students' confidence that they can decode long words and to reinforce the value of using structural analysis as an aid in doing so.

You should teach your struggling readers the meanings of prefixes and suffixes. Interestingly, while the English language has many inconsistencies, when a word contains a prefix, 60 percent of the time that prefix will have the meaning of *not (un-, im-, in-, ir-, il-), again (re-),* or *opposite of (dis-)* (White, 1989). Because prefixes are spelled consistently and occur at the beginning of words, they are relatively easy for readers to learn. As a result, most struggling readers' confidence increases when you teach them how dependable and consistent the meanings of prefixes are. The affixes that these readers need to know appear in Table 9.5. They are the most frequently used in our language and will be contained in 90 percent of all the affixed words students will ever read.

LESSON 3: CHALLENGING MORE ACCOMPLISHED READERS. Older struggling readers also enjoy challenging more accomplished students to decode long words that appear on television, in grocery stores, or in print around their home—words such as *antiperspirant, superstar, forehead, automobile,* and so forth. On a specified day of the week, you can ask these readers to bring one or more such words and present each one, written on a card in a sentence that re-creates the context in which they learned it, for classmates to decode. Then they can write their words under the appropriate heading on the blackboard: "Prefix Gave Me a Clue," "Compound Word Gave Me a Clue," or "Suffix Gave Me a Clue." This activity is valuable for these readers because it allows them to challenge more able readers and to lead the class successfully in literacy.

Similarly, when struggling readers/writers need more practice using structural analysis, they can highlight long words in a newspaper or magazine story. When the article is completed, these students share with a tutor their explanation of the decoding strategies they used to discern the meanings of the highlighted words. When students incorrectly assign meaning to a word, the tutor can ask questions to help these students discover how they overapplied or underapplied the meanings of prefixes, suffixes, base words, or compound words in that instance.

LESSON 4: WORD ARCHITECTURE. Another valuable activity that older readers value and that leads to automatic use of structural analysis and is called **word architecture** (Block, 1996). In it, students combine prefixes, root words, and suffix meanings into

TABLE 9.5 Order for Teaching Suffixes and Prefixes

Grade 1	Grade 2	Grade 3
Final consonant doubled (run/running)	Final *Y* changed to *I* (family/families)	*Suffixes* *-able:* able, capable of (lovable)
Suffixes	*Suffixes*	*-er:* noun forming; person or thing that is or does (teacher)
-s: plural form of nouns (dogs)	*-en:* verb forming; cause a specified condition (ripen)	*-ful:* filled with (colorful)
-es: plural form of nouns (witches)	*-en:* adjective forming; made up of, having (earthen)	*-less:* lacking, free from, without (hopeless)
-ed: past tense of verbs (walked)	*-er:* comparative form of adverbs and adjectives (taller)	*-ment:* act, action, or state (retirement)
-ing: forms present participle of verbs (talking)	*-est:* superlative degree of most adjectives and adverbs (sweetest)	*-ness:* state, quality, or condition of being (kindness)
-ing: noun forming; the act or an instance of (camping)	*-ful:* filled with, able (colorful)	*-ous:* having, full of (grievous)
	-ly: adjective forming; resembling, characteristic of (daily)	*Prefixes*
	-ly: adverb forming; in a specified way or time (annually)	*dis-:* opposite to (disorderly)
		im-, in-, il-, ir-: lacking (illiterate, inbreed)
	Prefixes	*in-, on-:* toward (inland, onboard)
	re-: back, again (return)	*mid-:* in or at the middle (midair)
	un-: not (unusual)	*mis-:* wrong, bad (mistake)
		over-: too much or above (overhead)
		pre-: before in time (preheat)
		under-: beneath, below (underachiever)

Grade 4	Grade 5	Grades 6/7
Suffixes	*Suffixes*	*Suffixes*
-ic: of, like, pertaining to (historic)	*-al:* like, pertaining to (comical)	*-ary:* related to, connected with (missionary)
-ish: of or belonging to; like (childish)	*-ance:* the act, quality, or condition of (inheritance)	*-ist:* a person who does, makes, works with (manicurist)
-tion: the act, process, state (digestion)	*-ent:* adjective and noun forming; same as (consistent)	*-ize:* make or change into; make similar to (alphabetize)
	-sion: the act, process, or result of (division)	

TABLE 9.5 *(continued)*

Grade 4	Grade 5	Grades 6/7
Prefixes	*Prefixes*	*Prefixes*
de-: away from; the reverse (decompose)	*for-:* preceding in time, place, or order (forerunner)	*anti-:* against (antibody)
en-, em-: put into or on; be within (encase, empower)	*inter-:* together, mutual(ly) (interact)	*centi-:* hundred or hundredth (centipede)
im-, in-: in, into (inbreed)	*semi-:* half (semicircle)	*com-:* with (companion)
non-: not (nonsense)	*sub-:* under, below, beneath (submarine)	*en-:* put into or on; cover with (endanger)
out-: beyond (outstanding)	*tele-:* from or across a distance (telephone)	*equi-:* equal (equilateral)
super-: above, over; better or more than usual (supernatural)	*trans-:* across, over; above and beyond (transport)	*ex-:* out of; not (exhale)
		geo-: of the earth (geology)
		mal-: bad, badly (malfunction)
		micro-: extremely small (microfilm)

words that are common in our language. As shown in Table 9.6, each prefix, root, and suffix is numbered; students refer to these numbers and combine them into words. For example, *tele-* is #14 of the word architecture components and is a prefix of Greek origin meaning "far." *Gramma* is #24 of word architecture and is the Greek root word meaning "letter" or "writing." Thus, to build the first item in the word architecture activity, combine #14 and #24 into the word *telegram* (see the Table 9.6 answer key), which is a letter or writing that is sent far away.

TABLE 9.6 Word Architecture

Use the architectural components to build words, as follows:

1. 14 + 24	14. 31 + 38	27. 10 + 33	40. 15 + 48
2. 3 + 18 + 44	15. 13 + 18 + 46	28. 18 + 40	41. 12 + 22
3. 11 + 23 + 49	16. 10 + 27 + 45	29. 8 + 34 + 43	42. 6 + 29 + 46
4. 10 + 30	17. 4 + 26 + 39	30. 13 + 18	43. 14 + 33
5. 9 + 34	18. 14 + 32	31. 5 + 21	44. 18 + 29 + 50
6. 12 + 19 + 46	19. 15 + 47 + 41	32. 16 + 28 + 40	45. 23 + 43
7. 5 + 24	20. 6 + 32 + 50	33. 32 + 40	46. 11 + 29
8. 31 + 42	21. 26 + 30	34. 4 + 23 + 39	47. 7 + 35
9. 17 + 29 + 50	22. 20 + 28 + 50	35. 8 + 22	48. 5 + 29
10. 31 + 48	23. 27 + 24	36. 20 + 28 + 40	49. 3 + 24
11. 12 + 23 + 39	24. 19 + 37	37. 4 + 34 + 43	50. 36 + 25 + 50
12. 8 + 19	25. 16 + 17 + 25 + 50	38. 11 + 22	
13. 32 + 25	26. 7 + 21 + 40	39. 13 + 35	

continued

TABLE 9.6 *(continued)*

Prefixes	Roots	Suffixes
1. *a-, ab-* (L. not, without; away from)	15. *alere* (L. nourish)	37. *-ant* (used to form noun, adj.; one who performs; condition of)
2. *bi-* (L. two, twice)	16. *autos* (Gk. self)	
3. *ana-* (Gk. on; up; backward)	17. *bios* (Gk. life)	38. *-arch* (ruler)
4. *de-* (L. away from, remove, reduce)	18. *chronos* (Gk. time)	39. *-ate* (used to form adj., noun, verb; characterized by having)
5. *epi-* (Gk. upon, over, after)	19. *cognoscere, cognitus* (L. know, knowing)	
6. *eu-* (Gk. well, good)	20. *demos* (Gk. people)	40. *-ic* (of the nature of)
7. *hypo-* (Gk. under, beneath)	21. *dermos* (Gk. skin)	41. *-ary* (pertaining to)
8. *in-* (L. not; into, in)	22. *fundere, fuses* (L. melt together, pour)	42. *-ician* (specialist)
9. *ob-* (L. against)	23. *genere, gignere* (L. be born, beget)	43. *-ion* (act of, state of)
10. *peri-* (Gk. around)	24. *gramma* (Gk. letters, writing)	44. *-ism* (doctrine; characteristic of)
11. *pro-* (L. before, in front of, forward)	25. *graphein* (Gk. write)	45. *-ium* (scientific unit)
12. *re-* (L. back, again)	26. *hydro* (Gk. water)	46. *-ize* (subject to; become like)
13. *syn-* (Gk. with, together)	27. *kardia* (Gk. heart)	47. *-ment* (state, quality, condition)
14. *tele-* (Gk. far)	28. *kratos* (Gk. power)	48. *-mony* (resulting thing; abstract condition)
	29. *logos* (Gk. word)	49. *-or* (state or quality of, one who)
	30. *meter* (Gk. measure)	
	31. *pater* (L. father)	50. *-y* (used to form adj., noun; inclined to; instance of)
	32. *phone* (Gk. sound)	
	33. *skopein* (Gk. look at, see)	51. *-able* (that can be, tending to)
	34. *struere* (L. pile up, build)	
	35. *thesis* (Gk. laying out; a proposition)	52. *-al* (used to form adj., noun; relating to; process of)
	36. *tomos* (Gk. cutting; section)	

Answer Key

1. telegram	14. patriarch	27. periscope	40. alimony
2. anachronism	15. synchronize	28. chronic	41. refund
3. progenitor	16. pericardium	29. instruction	42. eulogize
4. perimeter	17. dehydrate	30. synchronic	43. telescope
5. obstruct	18. telephone	31. epidermis	44. chronology
6. recognize	19. alimentary	32. autocratic	45. generation
7. epigram	20. euphony	33. phonic	46. prologue
8. patrician	21. hydrometer	34. degenerate	47. hypothesis
9. biology	22. democracy	35. infuse	48. epilogue
10. patrimony	23. cardiogram	36. democratic	49. anagram
11. regenerate	24. cognizant	37. destruction	50. tomography
12. incognito	25. autobiography	38. profuse	
13. phonograph	26. hypodermic	39. synthesis	

▇ Phonics

Up to this point in decoding instruction, you have focused on whole words or word parts as clues to meaning, because efficient readers decode words as wholes. Because English is an alphabetic language, however, matching sounds to letters, or **phonics,** is a necessary decoding strategy.

The need for phonetic decoding abilities is not disputed; there is disagreement, however, as to which types of phonetic instruction are best and how much of total instructional time should be devoted to phonetic analysis. As reported in *Becoming a Nation of Readers* (Anderson, Hiebert, Scott, & Wilkerson, 1985) and *Beginning to Read* (Adams, 1993), it is not important that children be able to cite the phonetic rules that govern our language, but they do need to be able to use them.

Equally important, some struggling readers rely too heavily on phonic analysis; they attempt *all* decodings by sounding individual letters. When the curriculum overemphasizes phonics, many students infer that "sounding it out" should be the first and only strategy used to derive pronunciation and meaning. Even more damaging is thinking that if only they were good enough readers, "sounding it out" would be all they should have to use. The reality is that at best, only approximate pronunciations of most English words are possible through sole reliance on phonetic analysis. As with all decoding strategies, only when it is used in concert with other approaches can phonics strengthen the word recognition abilities of less accomplished readers. Therefore, although it is important to teach phonetic analysis, you should teach only phonic generalizations that are more than 50 percent consistent in English. Those generalizations appear in Table 9.7 and should be taught in the context of reading materials that students select.

TABLE 9.7 Phonic Generalizations

Phonic Generalizations	Utility Percentages*
1. When *c* and *h* are next to each other, they make one combined sound: *charge, mechanic*	100%
2. When *c* is followed by *o* or *a,* the sound of *k* is likely to be heard: *canal.*	100
3. When *ght* is seen in a word, *gh* is silent: *tight.*	100
4. When a word begins with *kn,* the *k* is silent: *knife.*	100
5. When a word begins with *wr,* the *w* is silent: *wrap.*	100
6. When a word ends in *ck,* the *ck* has the same sound as *k: lock, neck.*	100
7. When *ture* is the final syllable in a word, it is unaccented: *future.*	100
8. When *tion* is the final syllable in a word, it is unaccented: *notion.*	100
9. When the first vowel element in a word is followed by *th, ch,* or *sh,* these syllables are not broken when the word is divided into syllables and may go with either the first or the second syllable: *fashion.*	100
10. In most two-syllable words that end in a consonant followed by *y,* the first syllable is accented and the last is unaccented: *paltry.*	98

continued

TABLE 9.7 *(continued)*

Phonic Generalizations	Utility Percentages*
11. When two of the same consonants are side by side, only one is heard: *dollar.*	97
12. If the last syllable of a word ends in *le*, the consonant preceding the *le* usually begins the last syllable: *gable.*	96
13. Words having double *e* usually have the long *e* sound: *meet.*	95
14. When *a* is followed by *r* and final *e*, we expect to hear the sound *are*, as in *bare.*	95
15. When *c* is followed by *e* or *i*, the sound of *s* is likely to be heard: *glance.*	93
16. When *y* is the final letter in a word, it usually has a vowel sound: *lady.*	90
17. When the last syllable is the sound *r*, it is unaccented: *ever.*	90
18. In *ay*, the *y* is silent and gives *a* its long sound: *spray.*	89
19. If *a, in, re, ex, de,* or *be* is the first syllable in a word, it is usually unaccented: *reply.*	85
20. When there is one *e* in a word that ends in a consonant, the *e* usually has a short sound: *held.*	84
21. *Ch* is usually pronounced as it is in *kitchen, catch,* and *chair*, not like *ck: pitch.*	83
22. The *r* gives the preceding vowel a sound that is neither long nor short: *part.*	82
23. When the letter *i* is followed by the letters *gh*, the *i* usually stands for its long sound and *gh* is silent: *light.*	81
24. In most two-syllable words, the first syllable is accented: *bottom.*	80
25. If the first vowel sound in a word is followed by two consonants, the first syllable usually ends with the first of the two consonants: *dinner.*	77
26. The letter *g* is often sounded as the *j* in *jump* when it precedes the letters or *e: gem.*	74
27. When a vowel is in the middle of a one-syllable word, the vowel is short: *bed.*	69
28. When a word has only one vowel letter, the vowel sound is likely to be short: *crib.*	65
29. One vowel letter in an accented syllable has its short sound: *banish.*	63
30. The first vowel is usually long and the second silent in the digraphs *ai, ea, oa,* and *ui: claim, beat, roam, suit.*	62
31. When there are two vowels, one of which is a final *e*, the first vowel is long and the *e* is silent: *cradle.*	61
32. If the only vowel letter is at the end of a word, the letter usually stands for a long sound: *go.*	61
33. The two letters *ow* often make the long *o* sound: *row.*	55
34. When a word ends with silent *e*, the preceding vowel is long: *amaze.*	52

*Utility percentages are the averages of the percentage calculations done by the three researchers cited in the table source note.

Source: Data from M. H. Bailey (1967), "The Utility of Phonic Generalizations in Grades One through Six," *The Reading Teacher, 20*, pp. 413–418; T. Clymer (1963), "The Utility of Phonic Generalizations in the Primary Grades," *The Reading Teacher, 16*, pp. 252–255; and R. Emans (1967), "The Usefulness of Phonic Generalizations above the Primary Grades," *The Reading Teacher, 20*, pp. 419–425.

An important guideline for phonics instruction is not to ask students to memorize the phonic generalizations, but rather to help them understand, use, and rely on the information these rules provide about our language. Research concerning less accomplished readers documents that they do in fact use syllable units and individual letter-to-sound correspondences simultaneously to decode phonetically regular words (Adams, 1993; Ehri, 1993; Pearson, Barr, Kamil, & Mosenthal, 1994; Stahl, 1994). It appears, however, that the speed of their decoding increases when they also learn to instantly combine letter combinations at the beginning of words—called **onsets** (such as *ch* or *fa*)—and vowel patterns at the end of words—called **rhymes** (such as *-am* or *-in*)—selectively with sight words, contextual clues, and structural analysis to discern meaning (Ehri, 1980, 1993).

Moreover, because consonants are more salient clues to instant recognition of phonetically regular words than are vowels, only when a word is still unknown after consonants are recognized should an analysis of vowels come into play. Typically, readers use their prior knowledge of letters and letter patterns to trigger a complete visual image from the partial single-letter data that their eyes supply (Biemiller, 1993; Stanovich, 1991). For example, you can show your less successful readers how much decoding information they can get from consonants by sharing the following illustration: Th__ b__g bl__ck d__g r__n aft__r th__ c__t.

Let's look more closely at how reading specialists and classroom teachers can work together to diagnose and build students' phonics skills.

Instructional Principles for Teaching Phonics

Good instructional activities lead readers to appreciate and automatically employ phonic generalizations. As you will notice, the lessons that follow assist phonetically weak readers to decode words by simultaneously combining the information available to them in print with phonic generalizations. The applications of phonics that you teach will generally include the use of orthography (spelling patterns, as shown in Table 9.8),

TABLE 9.8 Vowel Sound Spellings at the Initial and Medial Positions

Long Vowel Sounds in the Initial Position

ā	ē	ī	ō	ū
āble	ēvil	īce	ōcean	ūniverse
āche	ēven	īvy	ōkay	ūnicorn
āce	ēvening	īvory	Ōklahoma	ūnite
ācorn	ēqual	ītem	ōver	ūse
ācre	ēquation	īcing	ōbey	ūseless
āge	Ēgypt	īdentify	ōh	ūsual
āpe	ēcology	īdea	ōld	ūkelele
Āpril	ēgo	ī	ōpen	Ūtah
Āsia	ēve	īrish	ōval	ūniform
āte	Ēdith	īodine	ōboe	ūnicycle

continued

TABLE 9.8 *(continued)*

Long Vowel Sounds in the Medial Position

ā	ē	ī	ō	ū
cāke	Pēte	līke	cōne	cūbe
rāce	Stēve	nīne	stōve	mūle
gāme	bēēt	whīte	nōte	cūte
plāce	trēē	rīde	hōme	fūme
cāge	fēēt	bīke	nōse	mūte
gāte	sēēd	kīte	smōke	fūse
fāce	mēēt	mīle	hōpe	flūte
sāve	swēēt	wīpe	stōne	dūke
snāke	grēēn	līne	vōte	tūne
lāke	whēēl			

Short Vowel Sounds in the Initial Position

ă	ĕ	ĭ	ŏ	ŭ
ăpple	ĕlephant	ĭgloo	ŏctopus	ŭmbrella
ăs	Ĕskimo	ĭt	ŏx	ŭncle
ăstronaut	ĕnter	ĭs	ŏn	ŭs
ăfter	ĕxit	ĭf	ŏstrich	ŭnder
ănt	ĕdge	ĭnvade	ŏlive	ŭmpire
ălligator	ĕggs	ĭll	Ŏctober	ŭgly
ăctor	ĕnemy	ĭtch	ŏbject	ŭp
ăm	ĕngine	ĭmprove	ŏdd	ŭnlucky
ăfternoon	ĕscape	ĭgnore	ŏtter	ŭntil
ănniversary	ĕnergy	ĭnsect	ŏpera	ŭsher

Short Vowel Sounds in the Medial Position

ă	ĕ	ĭ	ŏ	ŭ
băd	pĕt	bĭg	pŏt	bŭs
băt	tĕn	shĭp	fŏx	tŭb
blăck	tĕll	tĭn	blŏck	pŭppy
căp	bĕd	hĭll	bŏx	jŭmp
căt	hĕlp	sĭt	tŏp	mŭch
căn	stĕp	stĭck	dŏll	sŭm
clăp	rĕd	pĭg	sŏck	cŭp
dăd	slĕd	kĭt	mŏp	dŭck
făn	spĕll	wĭn	hŏt	cŭt
măp	yĕs	pĭn	shŏp	rŭg
răg	wĕst	dĭg	rŏck	drŭm
tăn	tĕnt	hĭd	lŏck	clŭb
săd	hĕn	bĭt	drŏp	fŭn
măn	wĕll	wĭll	spŏt	bŭt

phonological principles (the most prevalent sounds of individual letters in the alphabet, as depicted in Table 9.9), sight words, and semantic and syntactic information. What distinguishes struggling readers is that they have not learned how to use this information effectively to meet the decoding demands in each reading experience.

To ensure that students realize that phonetic generalizations are not to be used in isolation, the instructional activities in this section demonstrate how each type of printed language information facilitates the use of others. For example, using what has been comprehended in previous paragraphs assists the interpretation of letter-to-sound knowledge in upcoming difficult words. Similarly, recognizing the specific meaning of a word the author chooses to communicate his or her idea enhances the use of context clues to interpret future words and implied meanings.

 # 9.4 CLASSROOM TEACHERS

Teaching Specific Phonic Generalizations or Phonetic Elements

- Select the phonic element you with to teach.
- Tell your students the name of the phonic element you will be teaching them, and write the letters that stand for it on the board.

Th   th

- Write a list of words containing the element. Pronounce the words for students. Then have the students pronounce the words along with you while they listen to the sound being taught.

their   think
thump   Thanksgiving

- Ask students to contribute additional words that contain the same sound.
- Finally, have students listen as you say words. Some of the words should contain the sound; some should not. Have students identify those words containing the sound.
- Next, you can play WORD-VOWEL BINGO. To do so, make bingo cards that contain words with blank spaces where the vowels belong. Instead of using blank chips for markers, students use markers with vowels and vowel combinations printed on

them. As a word is read, students spell the word on their card, using the appropriate vowel or vowel-combination marker.

b__d	b__t	e		a	oa		ea
h__te		m__t					

- Then you can play VOWEL CHECKERS. Place words containing the vowel sounds on which you are working on the spaces where students move the checkers. If a student hops over or lands on a space, he or she must think of another word that contains the same vowel sound.
- Or you can play BINGO. Give students bingo cards with different consonants on them. As you read a word, the student covers the appropriate consonant heard at the beginning of the word. (This activity can be expanded to include consonants at the end or middle of words.)
- You can also play RIDDLES. For example, following a review of the hard and soft sounds of c and g, you might say, "I am thinking of something that begins with the sound of a hard g. It has four legs. It has horns, and it can be found on a farm. It likes to eat just about anything. What is it?" (Answer: goat)

TABLE 9.9 More Advanced Consonant and Vowel Sound Spellings

Consonants	Variant Consonants *c, g, s*	Digraphs with *h*	Digraphs with First Letter Silent	Blends—Initial	Blends—Final	Special Combination of Consonant and Vowel
b bat		*ch* chair	*ck* deck	*r* break	*ld* sold	*ci* special
d dent	*c* cat	scheme	*gn* gnome	*l* clean	*lk* walk	*si* mansion
f fall	city	chandelier	*kn* knife	*s* skate	*nd* send	*ti* station
h hit	got	*gh* ghost	*wr* write	scrape	*nk* thank	
j jam	*g* giant	*ph* pharmacy		*tw* twirl	*nt* meant	
k kite	*s* us	*sh* ship	**Digraph Cluster Following a Short Vowel**			
l land	his	*th* thick	*dge* bridge			
m mat	sugar	these	*tch* stitch			
n name		*wh* what				
p pan		who	**Additional Digraph**			
qu quite			*ng*			
r road						
t top						
v vane						
w well						
x box						
z zebra						

Vowels	Single—Short	Schwa ə in Unaccented Syllables	Digraphs/Diphthongs with a	Digraphs with e	Cluster with i	Digraphs and Diphthongs with o	Diphthongs That Encode /ōō/
a	ă act	a əbout	ai a/ā/ maid	ēe as/ē/ sleep	igh as/ī/ sight	oa as/ō/ coat	ui fruit
e	ĕ end	e ticket	ay as/a/ stay	ea as/ē/ leaf		oi as/oy/ oil	ue blue
i	ĭ it	i pencəl	au as/aw/ vault	/ĕ/ head		oy as/oy/ boy	ew stew
o	ŏ olive	o aprən	aw as/aw/ draw	/ā/ great		oo as/ōō/ moon	
u	ŭ upon			ie as/ē/ relief		/ŏŏ/ look	
ə				/ī/ lie		ou as/ow/ around	
	Single—Long			ei as/ē/ (after c) receive		/ŭ/ young	
	ā able			/ā/ vein		/ō/ soul	
	ē even			ey as/ē/ donkey		/ōō/ group	
	ī icy			/ā/ prey		ow as/ow/ cow	
	ō omen					/ō/ low	
	ū and ōō unit						
	rude						
	Single—3rd Sound						
	a ä always						
	o ōō do						
	u ŏŏ push						

y as a Consonant, Vowel, Digraph, Diphthong	r-Controlled with Single Vowels	r-Controlled with a	r-Controlled with o	r-Controlled with Digraph ea	r-Controlled with Digraphs
Consonant at the beginning: yellow	her fir purse worse	fär câre	stôre doctər	hear learn bear	ai or ee
Vowel: mystery, apply, carry	/er/ /er/ /er/ /er/	/fär/ /âr/		/ē-r/ /er/ /âr/	hair peer
Digraph: play, obey					/âr/ /ē-r/
Diphthong: employ					

Source: Adapted from M. Miller (1993), unpublished manuscript, p. 20. Des Moines: University of Iowa. Reprinted by permission of Marcia Miller.

The largest limitation of phonetic analysis shows up when less able readers apply the proper generalizations but are up against a word that is not within their listening vocabulary. At these times, unless such readers have learned to automatically apply context, comprehension, sight word, syntax, and other decoding strategies, frustration rises quickly and they often resort to guessing. Therefore, to begin instruction on spelling of consonant and vowel sounds, you can be most successful by demonstrating how each sound appears in the initial position (refer again to Table 9.8). Because struggling readers already tend to isolate the first sound in a word, using a strategy they already rely on will make learning individual letter-to-sound correspondences easier.

In addition, because making letter-to-sound associations is difficult for some children, highlighting with pictures that represent consonant and vowel sounds in initial positions assists these students. These pictures can be used with a selection of children's literature to introduce each letter. High quality children's literatue that repeats specific vowel spelling patterns can be used to reinforce students' learning. Students can select books in which they will have repeated opportunities to read words that feature the letter-to-sound correspondence taught that week. Similarly, if you post these picture associations on a chart, students can reference it when they write. For example, if students do not know the sound represented by *b* and want to read or write a word that contains a *b*, they can reference the letter printed on the chart with the picture of a bird. The picture clues the sound represented by *b*.

The first consonant sound spellings you should teach are the **continuants**— consonants that produce sound by the constant release of air (i.e., the letters *b, d, f, h, l, m, n, s,* and *v*, depicted in Chapter 14). Then teach the letters that are **stop consonants**— those that stop the flow of air, producing sounds that are less easily glided and blended into words than continuants. Stop consonants are *p* and *t*. The third instruction segment covers *blends* and *digraphs*. Research indicates that these are the most difficult consonants to learn because they require very fine sound differentiations (Ehri, 1993; Treiman, 1988). Students should be able to recognize a few words with beginning blends or digraphs by sight before direct instruction is provided; the easiest for students to learn are *dr, tr,* and other blends that do not begin with *s;* digraphs such as *ch, sh,* and *th;* and *s* blends such as *sl* and *sc* (Cunningham, 1995).

It is also better to introduce short vowels before long vowels in medial position. The reason short vowels are best taught first is because they are the most frequently occurring and are governed by only one phonetic generalization—namely, a vowel will sound short if it appears between two consonants or before a single consonant.

Another thing to remember is that many phonetically weak readers will have trouble differentiating letters that resemble each other, and that therefore it is not a good idea to introduce similar letters one after the other. For instance, when you introduce the letter-to-sound correspondence of /b/, students may confuse it with other letters that have a similar visual feature, such as /d/, /p/, or /q/. Similarly, when you introduce /t/, wait a few weeks before teaching /f/. When students begin to confuse two letters that have common features, you can create a mnemonic to reinforce the correct letter-to-sound correspondence. For example, if students confuse the letters *b* and *d*, write "bed" and then demonstrate that the "headboard" is the straight line in the letter *b* and the "footpost" is the straight line in the letter *d*.

The following lessons provide specific activities to develop phonetic awareness.

LESSON 1: WRITING FOR PHONICS. Allow students to apply phonetic generalizations in their own written compositions as soon as possible after each rule has been introduced. Because some readers are more interested in writing than in overcoming reading difficulties, writing activities that foster phonic awareness increase reading abilities (Adams, 1993; Anderson et al., 1985; Durkin, 1987; Goodman, 1986).

Synthetic phonics approaches as described earlier are not effective for all phonetically weak readers. Some have difficulty isolating and blending individual sounds. For these students, the following analytical approach will be more successful, especially because it incorporates writing. In this approach, students learn words' pronunciations and meanings by combining larger sound units in words. For example, instead of learning the word *catch* by sounding the individual letters, analytically based readers would either say "cat-" and add the "-ch" sound, or say "c-," "-at-," and "-ch."

To begin this lesson in analytical phonics, select a book in which a single letter is repeated many times. As you read the book to the class, each time you come to the repeated letter write it on the board and have students write it on their papers. Then, combine it with other letters. If it is a consonant, for example, write that letter with each vowel (e.g., ma____, me____, mi____, mo____, mu____). These will become categories in which students will recall, say, and write words from the book you just read. As each word is said, students take turns coming to the board to write the word in its proper category. Others write each word on their paper as it is written on the board. Next, describe meanings and encourage students to draw stick-figure illustrations beside picturable words to assist in their recall of the word and its meaning; older students can generate a sentence for each word. When most words containing that letter sound are listed, ask students to write their own sequel to the book, containing the words on the board. Younger students can pair to create their writings.

A related writing activity that is valued by some struggling readers places phonics in the context of reading. To begin, write a sentence on the board from a book the students have just read or had read to them. The sentence should have words representing at least four phonetic generalizations (e.g., "The cat went into the yard."). Students say and/or write that sentence. Then ask them to substitute other words that adhere to the underlined phonetic generalizations that would also make sense in the sentence. For instance, a reader could suggest "The cat went into the barn" because it demonstrates the use of the *r*-controlled vowel principle. Another student could say "The men went into the yard" because it demonstrates the use of the cvc principle. Students write each new word under the principle it demonstrates as they repeat the entire new sentence orally. Some readers enjoy pairing with a partner and/or competing with others to generate as many applications of the phonetic principles as they can.

LESSON 2: COMPARING AND CONTRASTING VOWEL PATTERNS. When many readers come to an unfamiliar word, they do a fast mental search through their schema to locate words with similar letters. If a student does not know the word *beak,* for instance, but recognizes that it looks like *peak* (which she does know), she says "beak."

In a recent study, some readers were taught spelling patterns through rhyming words, as follows:

mane   = crane = plane = cane
bright = night = light = fight
sing   = king   = thing = ring

Other readers were asked to read words that begin with the same consonant and vowel combinations, such as *bat, back, bam*. Others were taught to rely on vowel generalizations to recognize words that all begin with the same consonant, such as *fat, far, farm, fake, fit, foam, fare, fair* (Bruen & Treiman, 1992).

Children in the last group performed best; the first group showed the poorest performance. The researchers concluded that because the rhyme recognition method was easiest, readers in that group were less mindful of their processing of the words, leading to overall weak growths in word recognition. The superiority of the third group was explained by evidence that phonetically weak readers in this group used links between graphemes and phonemes as clues to decoding rather than relying on the sound-to-letter combinations of larger graphemic units (Bruen & Treiman, 1992). Thus, the group taught to attend to vowel differences abstracted more information about grapheme and phoneme connections than other groups.

Because vowel graphemes and vowel phonemes are the most difficult to learn, the readers in the study profited more from this small-unit segmentation strategy than from a larger-unit spelling strategy. Moreover, it appears that these students also learned more patterns in words and learned not to treat these patterns the same as words, but rather to use them as a decoding tool. When these readers can see that one pattern is not identical to another, they have a broader range of possible pattern-recognition skills and responses available, and they bring better and more flexible problem-solving tools to each unknown word. They also become better at envisioning possibilities and predicting consequences.

The following analogy to an expert applies here. As we are aware, professional bird watchers, chess players, and proficient readers can recognize patterns even with only rapid exposure to partial bits of information, because they know where and when to look for particular patterns and pieces of information. Just as chess players do not spend time thinking how to knock out the king on their first move (because he is so well guarded), bird watchers do not waste time trying to find eagles in flat, treeless terrains. Through learning the sounds of common spelling patterns, readers will no longer need to see every single letter in a word to decode it. Thus, rhyme patterns are not the best means of learning common spelling patterns, because readers focus too much on pronouncing the word they already know, rather than on recognizing common spelling patterns in unknown words. However, as Bruen and Treiman (1992) concluded, "rhyme-based analogies do have some role to play in teaching children to pronounce words [as] teaching methods based on rhymes can help to show beginners that one can sometimes pronounce unknown words based on known words" (p. 179).

Remember, when readers fall into the habit of just pronouncing the first consonant and then guessing at the remainder of the word, they will profit from your instruction to combine the sounds of the first two or three letters by thinking of other words that begin with those letters. For example, when a phonetically weak reader comes to the word *band* and cannot pronounce it, instruct him to say other words that begin with /ba/ such as *barn, bat,* or *banner.* Recalling the /ba/ sound will be a more powerful decoding tool than thinking of words that could rhyme with *band.*

LESSON 3: MAKING PHONICS TACTILE AND KINESTHETIC. By using the pictures in Figure 9.6, (posted on a class chart), you can reintroduce letter-to-sound correspondences for readers who need more intensive instruction in phonetic generalizations. You

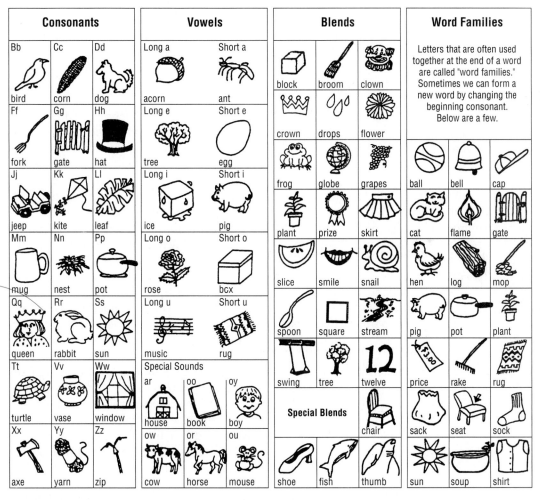

FIGURE 9.6 Using Picture Association to Teach Letter Sounds

Source: From "Class Acts," *Fort Worth Star Telegram,* p. 17E, September 8, 1993, Fort Worth, TX. Reprinted by permission of the Fort Worth Star Telegram.

will know which students need this instruction because they will be the ones who incorrectly apply letter-to-sound correspondences repeatedly to the same word, assigning random letter sounds for the consonants and calling, for instance, "bat;" "tab," "cat," "bot," or "dab" on different occasions.

To begin this lesson bring the real object depicted in Figure 9.6 for each letter sound to class—for example, a stuffed bird for /b/ and a leaf for /l/. Next, ask students who require this intensity to hold each object, using Figure 9.6 for reference if necessary, as they write the beginning letter and first vowel of this word on an index card. Then ask them to lay their cards near the objects. Check each student's work when finished. For every object labeled incorrectly, bring in other objects the child can see, hear, smell, or use that contain that opening letter sound. If the child misses the /gr/ blend in *grapes,* bring in green grapes that the student eats, sees, and smells. Write the words and say the words. Then ask the student to grate a carrot. When all objects are labeled correctly, ask students to say the beginning consonant and vowel sounds on all cards. When all sounds are pronounced correctly, take away the physical objects and ask students to use only the pictures on Figure 9.6 as aids for saying the letter sounds. Last, ask students to say the cv patterns on all the cards without object or pictorial prompts.

LESSON 4: BLENDING MADE EASY. As mentioned previously, blending is difficult for many readers. Gliding sounds together is an abstract concept that can be hard for a student to learn just by watching the movement of someone else's mouth or by seeing the steady movement of a hand beneath a word as it motions the blending of its parts.

Past instructional approaches have not been as effective as desired. Because these approaches asked students to say every sound of every letter separately, students' blendings often did not result in recognizable words. For example, say each of the following sounds separately: /p/, /e/, /a/, and /t/. Now say the sounds rapidly together. Did you say "peeaht" instead of "peat"? Another difficulty in blending lessons is that whenever students were asked to separate a stop consonant phoneme (i.e., /p/ or /t/) from other letters they had to say the /uh/ sound before they could blend it back to the next letter in the word. For example, say these letter sounds slowly and separately: /t/, /e/, /a/, /r/. Now say the sounds separately again but a little bit faster. Did you say "tuheear"? Therefore, regardless of how hard teachers pushed readers to say separate sounds faster and faster, correct blending did not result; many words never approximated the spoken word they represented.

However, Rosenshine and Stevens (1984) and the Commission on Reading (Anderson et al., 1985) found that time spent in blending activities (for students functioning at a first and second grade reading level) results in higher achievement test scores. And Miller (1993) developed a more effective method of teaching blending. In it, you can ask readers to say the correct medial vowel sound first, based on their knowledge of phonic generalizations of the cvc, cvcc, and cve patterns. Then have them attach the beginning consonant sound to that vowel sound and blend these two phonemes together. Thus, with the word *dad,* the student would first say the sound /a/, and then say /da/ as a single, blended sound. Last, the student would be asked to add the last sound: /dad/. Miller suggests extending this activity by showing how changing one phoneme changes the word—for example, *dad* can become *had.*

Another activity for strengthening readers' blending abilities is to have students change words that begin with a single consonant to words that begin with consonant blends or digraphs. For example, on a sheet of paper you would write words that could be contained in other common words that begin with consonant blends. Then you ask students to say the first word, then blend the consonant to get the longer word:

> top   ___top   (stop)
> eat   ___eat   (treat)

Moreover, you can teach phonetically weak readers that only 120 major word patterns and 3,000 basic sight words account for the majority of words that they will ever read. To illustrate this reality, you can readminister the foregoing activity a week later and have students determine how much their blending abilities have improved by comparing the total number of words read and meanings given correctly on both occurrences.

To diagnose phonic skill, administer pretests and posttests to see visible results of how much pupils know. An informal test is the Name Test (Cunningham, 1990), which is presented in Box 9.5. The assessment evaluates phonic analysis abilities in a nonthreatening format. When students need additional assessment and instruction, a special Tier 4 program shown in Box 9.6 can be used.

Using Dictionaries and Thesauruses

Research documents that direct instruction in efficient dictionary use builds the decoding and composing abilities of less accomplished readers/writers, as well as their oral and writing vocabularies (Anderson & Pearson, 1984; Beck & Dole, 1992). Prior to becoming your students, however, many may have been dissuaded from seeking dictionaries and thesauruses as reading and writing tools for a variety of reasons. They may have developed negative associations with the dictionary because other teachers required them to look up words they didn't want to look up ("Look up and write the definition of every word in your spelling list this week"—and the next week, and the next week, etc.). Some may have been handed a dictionary or thesaurus as soon as they were asked to revise their writing and may have misinterpreted this to mean that their teachers did not think they could write well enough without it—especially if they have been told to use a dictionary more than classmates. Others may not feel comfortable using the dictionary because they never had proper instruction as to how to find meanings and understand the diacritical pronunciation markings. Still others may associate the dictionary with punishment ("Copy two pages from the dictionary instead of going to recess today").

Through the instructional activities that follow, however, less accomplished readers can come to enjoy and value the dictionary and thesaurus. This instruction requires approximately 2 weeks. During this time you can teach dictionary and thesaurus skills as separate lessons and enable these readers to practice alone or in pairs so each skill can become automatic as soon after its introduction as possible.

Diagnosis of Phonic Decoding Abilities: The Name Test

In an article in *The Reading Teacher,* Patricia Cunningham proposed a new, brief, informal decoding assessment device. This device assesses a student's ability to decode names. The use of names may have some advantages over conventional word lists and nonsense words (pseudowords). In some instances, names may encourage a student to put forth a better effort while decoding than do nonsense words. Although there are no specific norms for this test at this time, the Name Test has been found to be very reliable (.98 reliability coefficient).

CONSTRUCTING THE NAME TEST

1. Type or print 25 names on a piece of paper or posterboard. Make sure that the print size is appropriate for the age or grade level of the student being tested.
2. If you think it would be helpful, type or print each of the names on an index card so that it can be read individually.
3. Prepare a scoring sheet. Type the list of names in a column and, following each name, draw a blank line on which you can record the student's responses.

ADMINISTERING THE NAME TEST

1. Administer the Name Test on an individual basis. Choose a quiet, distraction-free environment.
2. Explain to the student that he or she is to pretend to be a teacher who must read a list of the names of the members of his or her class. Have the student read the names as if he or she were taking attendance.
3. Have the student read the entire list. Tell him or her that you will not be able to help with difficult names, but to make a guess at each name if possible.
4. Place a check on the answer sheet for each name the student reads correctly. Write phonetic spellings for each name that is not pronounced correctly.

SCORING AND EVALUATING THE NAME TEST

1. Count a name as correct if all of the syllables are pronounced correctly regardless of where the child placed the accent. As an example, the name *Westmoreland* is correct whether it is pronounced "WEST-more-land," "west-MORE-land," or "west-more-LAND."
2. For words in which the vowel pronunciation depends on which syllable the consonant is placed with, count the response as correct for either pronunciation. For example, either "Ho/mer" or "Hom/er" is counted as correct.
3. Count the number of names read correctly, and analyze those mispronounced, looking for patterns indicative of decoding strengths and weaknesses.

SAMPLE NAME TEST

Jay Conway _____	Wendy Swain _____	Fred Sherwood _____
Glen Spencer _____	Chuck Hoke _____	Kimberly Blake _____
Yolanda Clark _____	Flo Thornton _____	Grace Brewster _____
Dee Skidmore _____	Roberta Slade _____	Gus Quincy _____
Homer Preston _____	Ned Westmoreland _____	Troy Whitlock _____
Ron Smitherman _____	Cindy Sampson _____	Ginger Yale _____
Chester Wright _____	Vance Middleton _____	Bernard Pendergraph _____
Zane Anderson _____	Patrick Tweed _____	
Stanley Shaw _____	Tim Cornell _____	

Source: Adapted from Patricia Cunningham (1990, October), "The Name Test: A Quick Assessment of Decoding Ability," *The Reading Teacher, 44* (2), pp. 124–130. Copyright by the International Reading Association.

Tier 4 Phonic Programs: Teaching Students with Extreme Reading Difficulties

The following methods and approaches are effective structured, multisensory, and alphabetic Tier 3 and 4 supports.

ALPHABETIC PHONICS-BASED METHODS

Academic Language Therapy Association, 4020 McEwen, Suite 105, Dallas, TX 75244 Telephone: 972-907-3924

ALPHABETIC PHONETIC STRUCTURAL LINGUISTIC APPROACH TO LITERACY (APSLA-L)–DERIVED PROGRAMS

Mr. Tony Kemper, The dePaul School, 1925 Duker Avenue, Louisville, KY 40205 Telephone: 502-459-6131

Mrs. Joy Martello, Shelton School, 5002 West Lovers Lane, Dallas, TX 75209 Telephone: 214-352-1772

Patricia Hardman, Ph.D., Hardman & Associates, Inc./Dyslexia Research Institute, 4745 Centerville Road, Tallahassee, FL 32308 Telephone: 850-893-2216 Fax: 850-893-2440

Brighton Academy, 9150 Bereford Drive, Baton Rouge, LA 70809 Telephone: 504-923-2208

THE ASSOCIATION METHOD

Maureen K. Martin, Ph.D., Director, DuBard School for Language Disorders, The University of Southern Mississippi, Box 10035, Hattiesburg, MS 39406-0035 Telephone: 601-266-5223 Fax: 601-266-5224 E-mail: dubard@usm.edu

THE HERMAN METHOD

Renee Herman, Director, Herman Method Institute, 4700 Tyrone Avenue, Sherman Oaks, CA 91423 Telephone: 818-784-9566

LINDAMOOD-BELL LEARNING PROCESS

Paul Worthington, 416 Higuera Street, San Luis Obispo, CA 93410 Telephone: 805-541-3836 or 800-233-1819 Fax: 805-541-8756

ORTON-GILLINGHAM APPROACH

Diana Hanbury King, Executive Director, Academy of Orton-Gillingham Practitioners and Educators, P.O. Box 234, East Main Street, Amenia, NY 12501 Telephone: 914-373-8919 Fax: 914-373-8925

PROJECT READ/LANGUAGE CIRCLE

Liz Sund, P.O. Box 20631, Bloomington, MN 55420 Telephone: 612-884-4880 or 800-450-0343

THE SLINGERLAND APPROACH

Clara McCulloch, executive Dean, The Slingerland Institute, Security Pacific Plaza, 411 108th Avenue, N.E., Bellevue, WA 98004 Telephone: 425-453-1190

THE SPALDING METHOD

Mary North, Ph.D., Research and Curriculum Director, Spalding Education Foundation, 2814 W. Bell Road, Suite 1405, Phoenix, AZ 85023 Telephone: 602-866-7801 Fax: 602-866-7488

STARTING OVER

Joan Knight, Director, 317 West 89th Street, #9E, New York, NY 10024 Telephone: 212-769-2760 Fax: 212-877-5030

WILSON READING LANGUAGE SYSTEM

Barbara Wilson, Director, 175 West Main Street, Millbury, MA 01527-1943 Telephone: 508-865-5699 or 800-899-8454

LESSON 1: TEACHING DICTIONARY USAGE. The specific objectives in dictionary instruction, as well as suggestions for teaching them, are as follows:

- Teach how the definitions of each word are ordered. For example, some dictionaries arrange definitions from the most general to the most specialized. You can ask students to bring a word to school that they heard on TV, on radio, or from an adult. Then use these words to demonstrate how the definitions of a word are arranged.

- Teach various ways to identify which definition an author had in mind. For instance, you can tell students to consider how subtle the author's writing style is and thus how likely it is that the author would choose less commonly used meanings of words.

- Teach how to use a word's first letter to know where to open the dictionary at the most efficient place. One method for doing this is the game Dictionary Sword Drills, to be described shortly.

- Teach/review alphabetical order, including how the first, second, and third letters in a word, and so on, determine where the word appears in the dictionary. You can select several words that have the same first three letters and model how you would look to the fourth letters in these words to locate their entries in the dictionary.

- Teach about guide words and their function. Explain how the left guide word is the first on the page and the right is the last.

- Teach the diacritical markings and primary/secondary/tertiary accents. A pronunciation guide is in Table 9.10.

- Teach how to find the parts of speech that a word can take. Look up a familiar word and show where parts of speech are listed in the entry.

- Teach how to use the information contained in the preface and appendixes of the dictionary.

- Teach how to find a word's synonyms and antonyms at the end of each definition.

In addition, throughout the year, it is valuable for students to watch how, and for what reasons, you turn to the dictionary. Research also suggests that struggling readers/writers understand words better when dictionary definitions are translated into the language that students normally use (McKeown, 1993). For example *Webster's New World Dictionary of the American Language* defines *animosity* as "spirited, strong hatred, ill will, open or active hostility *syn.* see ENMITY" (2001, p. 63). These readers would learn this word more rapidly if this definition were translated into simpler language.

When you have instructed your students as described above, bring in as many dictionaries as possible for your readers to use. If possible, also keep a variety of types and sizes of dictionaries in your classroom, which you can rotate by checking them out from public and school libraries. Allow students to choose and "adopt" a specific dictionary for their own use, as some readers enjoy softcover versus hardback versions, thick versus thin, smaller versus larger sizes, and so forth. A list to begin your collection appears at the end of the chapter.

Struggling readers enjoy learning how to use dictionaries through a game called Dictionary Sword Drills. In this game you ask students to apply a specific dictionary-use

TABLE 9.10 Diacritical Marking System and Pronunciation Guide

Short Vowels and Regular Consonants (no marks)					
A applé	G gírl	M midnight	S sâw	Y bäby	
B Bill	H hat	N nest	T täblé	Z zēbrá	
C coơkiès	I Indian	O ox	U umbrellá		
D Daddy	J jar	P penny	V valèntiné		
E egg	K kittén	Q quēen (qu)	W windōw		
F fish	L Lindá	R Rickéy	X box (ks)		

Long Vowels (bar over)
Ā ápron   Ē ēar   Ī īce cream   Ō Ōceán   Ū Ūnited States

SCHWA (comma over)
À ȧgo   =   È ėnőughh   =   'O òthėr   Can also be used when any vowel, not a *u*, makes a short *u* sound. Examples: sòme frònt

Letter *Y*
y in yes (consonant)   ȳ in mȳ (long vowel)   funny (note y = E not marked)

Diphthongs (underline both)
OI = OY   OU = OW
boil   boy   out   owl

Broad *O/A* (circumflex)
Â
âll âwful âuto   =   Ô
lông   ôr

Long and Short *OO* (one and two dots)
One-Dot U or Short OO   U̇ = Ȯ
pùt   goơd

Two-Dot U or Long OO   Ü = Ö = Ë
Jünė   roơm   nëw

R-Controlled Vowels (*r* acts as vowel)
AR AR IR ER UR
far vāry fĭr hėr fŭr

Digraphs (underline)
SH shŏé   CH chāir   WH which   TH that (voiced)
TH thing (unvoiced)   NG sing   PH = f phōné

Second Sounds of Consonants (underline)
C (c = s) cent
S (c = z) is
G (g = j) gem

Silent (slash)
còmé right hėr

Exceptions (+ over)
wòmèn actiòn ŏne stopped ŏf

Source: Adapted from E. Fry, D. Fountoukidis, & J. Polk (1985), *The New Reading Teacher's Book of Lists*, p. 403. Englewood Cliffs, NJ: Prentice-Hall. Used with permission.

strategy they just learned to a specific word that you say. Then the first person/pair to find the word wins one round in Dictionary Sword Drills. For example, assume your students have just learned to use the first letter of a word as a clue to the best place to open the dictionary: A–G words open near the beginning, H–R words open near the middle, and S–Z words open near the end. You say "zebra" and the first student/pair to find that word and read its definition wins that round.

If you schedule lessons on using dictionaries during November or sooner, your students will receive an added benefit. At the end of the lessons you can ask readers to write the title, author, publisher, place of publication, and publication date of their favorite dictionary on a piece of paper. Unbeknownst to students, you can then mail this information to their parents, along with a letter explaining that this is the dictionary their child prefers and suggesting they consider purchasing it as a Christmas, Hanukkah, or Kwanzaa gift. In this way students could have their favorite dictionary available for home use.

Last, you may not want to require readers to refer to a dictionary when they write unless they choose to do so or unless you are able to assist them in locating the word they want to spell. The frustration of trying to find words they cannot spell can lower students' positive attitudes toward literacy. On the other hand, most less accomplished readers/writers come to discover and internalize the importance of using dictionaries when they self-initiate looking up words to express their thoughts more exactly. By leaving dictionaries at writing centers, in the library corner of your classroom, and on your desk, you will help students come see dictionaries as permanent partners in decoding and writing. When readers self-initiate this partnership through their desire to understand the precise meanings of words, they also come to appreciate the hard work their favorite authors put into selecting "just the right" word—and how this makes their writings so good!

LESSON 2: TEACHING THESAURUS USAGE. By third grade, reluctant readers should also be introduced to the thesaurus. **Thesauruses** are books that contain synonyms and antonyms. When students learn to make use of these books, their vocabulary increases, as does their specificity in word choice when writing.

Struggling readers/writers can best learn to use a thesaurus in conjunction with a writing project. When they identify a word that expresses an idea they want to communicate, you and this student can look up the word in a thesaurus and read its synonyms. The student sees that there are more than just one or two words to express an idea and can then select some of these new words to incorporate into his or her vocabulary. When students compose on a computer, the use of dictionaries and thesauruses in word processing programs can also be taught.

Pulling It All Together

The purpose of teaching each decoding skills separately is to ensure that struggling readers understand each of the available decoding approaches. The activities in this section are equally important because through them you can assist these readers to select and use the most effective set of strategies for decoding individual words. These lessons also help students apply their decoding strategies interactively. Although some students may need only one of these lessons before all decoding strategies are at their command instantly and interactively, others may require repeated practice with all of them before they develop decoding automaticity. The activities have been shown to be most effective when conducted in Tier 2 needs-based groups or discovery discussions.

LESSON 1: WHEN I DON'T KNOW A WORD. Distribute copies of Figure 9.7 to students who have learned the strategies it lists. Encourage students to refer to a class chart that you have posted (made by enlarging this figure). Explain that the strategies can be used

FIGURE 9.7 When I Don't Know a Word

together to unlock the pronunciation and meaning of words. Ask struggling readers to read the strategies with you, and ask for students' questions about this information and the figure. Then share the following five points with your students:

1. As a general rule, basic sight words must be memorized. Therefore, when students see words that appear often, they should ask themselves: "What clues about that word can help me memorize its pronunciation and meaning?" You can help readers understand that trying instantly to recognize sight words will be among their most effective decoding strategies. Thus, whenever they see small words that occur regularly, they should ask you or a classmate for a clue as to how to recognize and remember that word.

2. As a general rule, students should analyze words with familiar spelling patterns phonetically by comparing and contrasting the word parts that follow regular English patterns. Therefore, when struggling readers see words that have vowel and consonant patterns similar to those of other printed words, they should ask themselves: "What other word that I know how to pronounce has letters like this word? What generalization have I learned that could apply to this word, and what would make sense using context clues?"

3. As a general rule, students should decode long words through structural analysis. Therefore, when less accomplished readers see long words, they should ask themselves: "Is there any section of this word that I recognize—such as a prefix, base word, suffix, or part of a compound word?" By recognizing and/or pronouncing a part of the word, readers can use that part's meaning to key the full word's meaning with the help of other context clues.

4. As a general rule, struggling readers should look at the other words in a sentence and the role the unknown word serves in the sentence as clues to meaning. Therefore, as readers try to apply sight word vocabulary, phonic generalizations, and/or structural analysis they should reread the sentence in its entirety. When they come to an unknown word, they can say the sound of the first letter, pause, and then read on until they gain enough context clues to discern the meaning of the unknown word. Often, reading to the end of the paragraph will be helpful.

5. As a general rule, if the preceding strategies are unsuccessful, struggling readers should ask a friend, ask you, or look in the dictionary. If the meaning is still vague when these resources are used, readers should reread the entire sentence to try to understand the word's meaning in the context that it appears.

Next in this lesson, you can instruct readers to ask themselves the following questions when they come to a word they do not know:

"What type of word is this?" (e.g., It is a long word).

"Which strategy should I use first to decode this word, while I also think of all the clues I have thus far?" (e.g., If it's a long word, I know I should first apply structural analysis).

"Using what I know about the author's writing style, what word makes sense and begins with the first letters in this word?"

Once students understand how decoding strategies interact, how to ask themselves the questions above, and how to review the class chart (or their copy of Figure 9.7) whenever they have trouble decoding, they can practice using these strategies interactively with a partner. Specifically, you can have pairs select a book to read; one student reads orally as the second follows along silently. When students come to a word neither one of them knows, they should ask the three questions listed above, and together they can follow Figure 9.7 to decode the unknown word. As students read, move from pair to pair to assess their decoding abilities and to answer queries. After 10 minutes of reading, ask partners to switch roles and continue the activity. To close the lesson, you can ask volunteers to meet with a small group of younger schoolmates to teach them what they have learned about how to select appropriate decoding strategies. While the volunteers are in this other classroom, you can meet with the remaining struggling readers to discuss what they have learned and how confident they are in their independent decoding abilities. You can also ask them to identify strategies at which they would like to become more proficient, and schedule additional activities to model these strategies.

LESSON 2: READER-SELECTED MISCUES. This lesson is a literacy event that asks students to identify words and sentences they do not understand (Rhodes & Shanklin, 1994). After students have been introduced to the strategies in this chapter, you can ask readers to select a book they want to read, at a readability level that is not too easy or too difficult for them. Then distribute to each reader five acetates and an acetate pencil or felt-tip marker. Demonstrate how students should lay an acetate over the first page they read from the book, and how they should underline difficult words or sentences as they read. When they have read and marked five pages, instruct them to bring their books to you, with the acetates in place on the appropriate pages. When they do so, you quickly identify and categorize the common difficulties individual students mark. Discuss the results of your analysis with them and assist each student to decode and understand each of the difficult sections in his or her reading by sharing a decoding tool that may work well for this reader.

In addition, as you and the student sit side by side and share a book together, the student will associate greater warmth and security with books and feel freer to ask questions. An example from one of my students illustrates:

> Tommy was in the sixth grade and a nonreader. As his teacher, I tried everything. Every Thursday from September to March we worked on specific decoding goals Tommy set. We met in small groups, with others who wanted to learn the same comprehension strategies as Tommy. In April, Tommy came to me with his gym shoes tied across his right shoulder, for he was captain of our sixth grade football team and on his way to recess. He stopped because he wanted to learn how to read "Humpty Dumpty." I wrote the nursery rhyme on the board and underlined all the words that had the same ending sound. His face lit up, and without my prompting a single word Tommy read the entire nursery rhyme without an error.
>
> "I got it! I got it! I didn't know that letters at the end of the word needed to be read and that I could use what I read in the first line to understand the rest! All I've been doin'

is saying the first letter to myself and guessin' what the word might be. You can read all the letters and then you know the word." My heart jumped with joy and I asked why he never read to the end of words. He said he didn't think he was supposed to!

I later learned that when Tommy was in first grade he developed pneumonia and was out of school from November to February. During the first 3 months of school he had learned all the sounds of beginning letters. In his absence, his school's reading program introduced ending sounds and blending. By February, students were reading full words by sight. Thus, Tommy felt he was dumb because he couldn't do as well as classmates.

From that day in April to the end of the year Tommy increased his comprehension abilities until he could read everything he wanted to read—and he read avidly.

LESSON 3: EXPLAINING FAVORITE DECODING TOOLS. There is a difference between simply knowing the name and definitions of the decoding clues and being able to explain how they are used. Through the process of explaining, less accomplished readers come to understand *how* and *why* they read as they do. If a student has difficulty explaining how he decodes, focus on a specific word in a book you read together.

For example, in one session after David correctly read the word *lioness,* I asked him to explain how he decoded that word. He said he knew the word *lion* was in the word and that the word meant more than a lion. He also knew (from the context) that the word referred to a mother—and then he thought how *prince* means "royal" and *princess* means "woman," so *lioness* meant "lady lion."

After these discovery discussions, students can also share their self-created decoding clues with peers, as doing so often increases confidence in their own decoding abilities. For example, less accomplished fourth grade readers cited these strategies:

- Look for small words that you know in the word and add on the rest of the letter sounds with your own best guess.
- Think about where you could have seen this word before.
- Think about a good word you already know that is very similar in its letters.
- Read what you can of the word and use the rest of the sentence to figure it out.
- Quickly skim ahead to get an idea of where the author is going. If he uses the word again on the page you'll have two contexts to use for figuring it out.

LESSON 4: WHAT'S IN MY HEAD? Marjorie Downing, an elementary teacher at Benchmark School in Media, Pennsylvania, and Pat Cunningham, reading professor at Wake Forest University, created this activity for struggling readers. Its purpose is to assist these students to integrate decoding strategies through mental word imaging. These readers enjoy the challenge it poses and the gamelike format.

To begin this activity, select 25 words. These words can be ones your students want to learn, ones that will appear in a selection they will read, or words that provide background for a new subject unit. Introduce these 25 words to your class in groups of 5 over a 5-day period. Teach their meaning and pronunciation. Make a large chart for each group of five words, showing them underlined in a sentence to reinforce their meanings; mount the charts on the wall.

On the fifth day, explain to students that they can recognize unknown words by thinking about all the decoding strategies they have learned and imagining the word in their minds. Then ask students to number to five on their papers and tell them you will give five clues for each of the five words you want them to write—one word from each of the five charts on the wall. Begin with the most general clue and progress in specificity until the last clue, which—when combined with the previous four—will eliminate all but one word.

The types of clues you give first might be telling students how many syllables the word has, whether it contains a prefix or suffix, or another structural analysis decoding skill. The second clue you give should be designed to integrate students' knowledge of phonetic generalizations—such as stating that a word begins with the same sound as another word you say, ends with the same sound, rhymes with another word, and so on. The third clue integrates students' knowledge of syntactical clues and endings of words in that you tell students the grammatical function the word serves in the sentence on the wall or perhaps the vowel spelling pattern it contains. The fourth clue identifies some aspect of the semantic function the word serves—but the semantic information you supply should relate to at least two words on the wall. For example, you could say that the word names one of the birds the class read about this week. The fifth clue will give the definition of the word, so that no other word on the wall matches that definition.

To illustrate, see Figure 9.8, in which five clue cards for five different words appear along with the master list of words.

Word Lists

		eyes
		world
List 1:	bed	walls
	room	
	day	
	teeth	*List 4:* stop
	yellow	supper
		good
		sent
List 2:	king	start
	forest	
	kind	
	boat	*List 5:* mother
	thing	max
		most
List 3:	claws	made
	wild	magic

(continued)

FIGURE 9.8 What's in My Head? Sample Words and Clues

Clue Cards

List 1: Clue #1 – It is a short word.
Clue #2 – Begins with the same sound as "bike."
Clue #3 – Rhymes with the word "head."
Clue #4 – It can be found in a house.
Clue #5 – It is something you usually sleep on.

List 2: Clue #1 – It is a short word.
Clue #2 – Begins with the "K" sound.
Clue #3 – Rhymes with the word "ring."
Clue #4 – It has four letters.
Clue #5 – It usually goes along with a queen and it wears a crown.

List 3: Clue #1 – It is a plural word.
Clue #2 – It begins with the same sound as "club."
Clue #3 – Rhymes with the word "jaws."
Clue #4 – It is part of an animal, like a tiger.
Clue #5 – An animal can scratch with these.

List 4: Clue #1 – It is a one-syllable word.
Clue #2 – Begins with an "S" sound.
Clue #3 – Rhymes with the word "pop."
Clue #4 – You do this at a traffic light in a car.
Clue #5 – The traffic light is red when you do this.

List 5: Clue #1 – It is a two-syllable word (long).
Clue #2 – Begins with an "M" sound.
Clue #3 – Rhymes with the word "another."
Clue #4 – It is the name of someone.
Clue #5 – It is sometimes called "mom," "mama," or "mommy."

FIGURE 9.8 *Continued*

Chapter Summary

Readers profit from instruction that provides explicit explanation and practice of decoding strategies that unlock word meanings and pronunciations. This chapter described six types of decoding strategies, as well as providing lessons that increase students' abilities to decode. Three of these decoding strategies involve sight words. The first focuses on content-specific sight words, which can be taught through word imagery and by associating unknown words to the central topic. The second strategy emphasizes the 3,000 most frequently used words in our language, which can become part of struggling readers' sight vocabulary through memorization facilitated by student-created games, student-constructed configurations, and the Omnibus strategy. The third sight word strategy stresses signal words, which give the reader information as to the direction the reading material will take. An effective method of teaching signal sight words is by placing words in categories.

The fourth type of decoding strategy uses the information conveyed by semantic and syntactic context clues. Semantic context clues can be taught through several types of activities, including the cloze technique and the maze technique. Syntactic context clues can be taught by identifying words as either naming, painting, or doing words and by using sentence transformations. The fifth decoding strategy is structural analysis, in which students learn the meanings of most common compound words, as well as English prefixes and suffixes. Other structural analysis activities are the Word Architecture game and challenging classmates to identify meanings of affixed words. The sixth strategy is phonics, and the chapter included a table of the most reliable phonic generalizations in our language. Also discussed were four activities that increase less accomplished readers' abilities to analyze words phonetically: writing for phonics, comparing and contrasting vowel patterns, making phonics tactile and kinesthetic, and blending made easy.

After exploring these six strategies approaches, the chapter turned to another useful decoding tool: proficiency in self-initiated use of dictionaries and thesauruses. The use of these important references can be taught in a 2-week unit that includes modeling, explicit instruction, sword drills, school-to-home reinforcements, and word processors.

The chapter ended with a discussion of one more decoding approach: integrating all the other approaches to decode words independently. The final section described four activities that increase readers' abilities to use all of the methods interactively as they read.

Key Terminology

Do you know the meanings of the following terms from this chapter? If you know a word's definition, place a check mark in the blank that precedes it. If you do not know its definition, take a few moments now to review it on the page number provided. This immediate rereading will increase your retention.

_____ **content-specific sight words** (page 267)
_____ **configuration** (page 271)
_____ **big book** (page 276)
_____ **LEA** (page 278)
_____ **cloze passages** (page 278)
_____ **maze passages** (page 278)
_____ **semantic clues** (page 281)
_____ **syntactic clues** (page 281)
_____ **naming words** (page 281)
_____ **painting words** (page 281)

_____ **doing words** (page 281)
_____ **structural analysis** (page 283)
_____ **affixes** (page 285)
_____ **word architecture** (page 285)
_____ **phonics** (page 289)
_____ **onsets** (page 291)
_____ **rhymes** (page 291)
_____ **continuants** (page 296)
_____ **stop consonants** (page 296)
_____ **thesauruses** (page 306)

Case Study

Making Professional Decisions

Mary was 9 years old and in the fourth grade when she was referred to the school reading teacher by her classroom teacher. She had fallen seriously behind her classmates. Her teacher stated that Mary occasionally reversed letters such as *b* and *d* while reading. School records indicated that Mary had experienced reading problems throughout her school years.

When Mary's mother was interviewed, she stated that several family members had experienced reading problems in school. Mary's health and emotional history appeared normal in general, and her environment seemed to be supportive of literacy activities. Mary's mother reported that Mary had always passed the vision and hearing screening tests at school.

An interview with Mary showed her to be bright and friendly but frustrated by her reading problems. She said the source of the difficulty was that she could not "sound out words."

The results of tests administered are presented below:

INFORMAL READING INVENTORY

Word Recognition List

Independent Level	Grade 1
Instructional Level	Grade 2

Oral Reading Passages

Independent Level	Grade 1
Instructional Level	Grade 2

Silent Reading Passages

Independent Level	Grade 2
Instructional Level	Grade 3
Listening Level	Grade 4

Mary had trouble pronouncing many of the words on the second grade oral reading passage. She frequently hesitated and stopped to "sound out" unfamiliar words with extreme difficulty. She was extremely frustrated by the words in the third grade passage. She vocalized words during the third grade silent reading passage. Excellent comprehension was maintained throughout the second grade passage. However, it appeared that the many words she missed on the third grade passage affected her comprehension at that level.

An analysis of miscues made on the Word Recognition List showed Mary had difficulty with multisyllabic words and word endings. An analysis of the miscues made during her oral reading also showed that Mary had some difficulty with words of more than one syllable. She seldom used context to try to identify words. She often ignored endings, such as *-est, -ly,* and *-ment,* and she reversed the letters *b* and *d* once.

Spelling Test   Grade 1

On the spelling test Mary performed well on Level 1, but she became frustrated on Level 2. She had problems with *r*-controlled vowels and with less frequent vowel patterns, such as *ow, aw,* and *all.* She also had problems with multisyllabic words and word endings.

Respond to the following questions, then check your responses against the Answer Key at the end of the book.

1. What areas of word recognition seem to be most in need of help? Support your conclusion with evidence.
2. Outline a plan to instruct Mary in one of the areas indicating instructional need.
3. Do you think that Mary needs to be taught not to vocalize? Why or why not?
4. Do you think that instruction should emphasize eliminating letter reversals? Why or why not?

Thinking and Writing about What You Have Learned

1. Can you list on a chart the strategies that can increase decoding abilities? In the middle column of your chart, can you list instructional activities that strengthen readers' use of each clue? If so, when finished, make copies of this form to use as an assessment record of individual students' progress. You can write the date that each instructional activity was taught and the effects.

2. After having read the information in this chapter, pretend that you are at a party and a man asks you how students learn to decode words. The man has just heard a TV news story that phonics instruction is on the rise again.

3. Read the following research finding and decide which decoding clues this boy was using to teach himself to read:

   > Experts have begun to examine in detail what happens when children learn to read on their own, and why they can be successful without a teacher. One of the best documented cases concerns a boy from a poor home in a southern state of the USA who became an expert reader by learning the words of the TV advertising slogans by heart and reciting them as they appeared on the screen. (Meek, 1982, p. 31)

   Assuming this reader was enrolled in your second grade class, which activities in the chapter would you teach him, and why? (See the Answer Key at the back of the book to check your answers.)

4. It would be helpful to team up with other teachers and make clue cards for the "What's in My Head?" activity. By working together and making multiple copies, you all could use one another's clues. In this way it wouldn't take long to accumulate the resources needed to teach the 240 major and minor phonograms in our language.

5. You may want to duplicate the student-created games in this chapter to stimulate your students' thinking as to decoding games they could make and enjoy with peers. Why do you think student-created games were not suggested as an activity to teach phonic generalizations? Which products from activities in the chapter would be most appropriate to include in readers' portfolios as assessment documents, and why?

For Further Reference

The following lists of dictionaries and thesauruses that students recommend to their peers can help you select appropriate reference books for your own classroom.

PICTURE DICTIONARIES

My First Dictionary (contains approximately 600 words), published by Grosset & Dunlap

Picturebook Dictionary (contains approximately 1,000 words), published by Rand McNally

BEGINNING DICTIONARIES

(Note: This group contains most words that students will read through third grade readability levels.)

The Ginn Beginning Dictionary, published by Silver Burdett Ginn
My First Dictionary, published by Houghton Mifflin
Beginning Dictionary, published by Houghton Mifflin
Scott Foresman Beginning Dictionary, published by Scott Foresman
Webster's New World Children's Dictionary, published by Prentice-Hall

INTERMEDIATE DICTIONARIES

Scott Foresman Intermediate Dictionary, published by Scott Foresman
Webster's Intermediate Dictionary, published by Merriam-Webster
The American Heritage School Dictionary, published by Houghton Mifflin

ADVANCED DICTIONARIES

Webster's Third New International Dictionary, published by Merriam-Webster
Merriam-Webster's Collegiate Dictionary (Tenth Edition), published by Merriam-Webster
The American Heritage Dictionary of the English Language, published by Houghton Mifflin

THESAURUSES

In Other Words: A Beginning Thesaurus (third grade reading level), published by Scott Foresman

In Other Words: A Junior Thesaurus (fourth grade reading level), published by Scott Foresman

My First Thesaurus (third grade reading level), published by McDougal, Little
Young Writer's Thesaurus (fourth grade reading level), published by McDougal, Little
Roget's International Thesaurus (sixth grade reading level), published by Thomas Y. Crowell

Onto the Information Superhighway

Websites to Increase Reading Specialists' and Classroom Teachers' Abilities to Teach Phonics

www.learningpyramid.com/factfile.html

www.touchphonics.com/mag.html

www.phonicsworld.com/index.html

www.papajan.com/Reading-Phonics/resources.html

www.intensive-phonics.com/index.html

Some comprehension abilities struggling readers need can be learned informally when students talk about books, as they read them, with their friends.

Enhancing Comprehension

One day in May, Darren picked up Thomas Locker's *The Boy Who Held Back the Sea.* When I stopped at his desk during reading workshop, he read the page perfectly. "What's happening in this story?" I asked. The old patterns of confusion appeared on Darren's face. "I don't know." Then, he pointed to an illustration and said, "a boy who lived in the town, he acted like that boy."

"Tell me more about the boy," I said. Darren shook his head as though trying to clear his thinking. "My head doesn't work sometimes," he said. . . . "It gets all mixed up for me."

(Avery, 1993, p. 355)

Chapter Overview: Key Points

The purpose of this chapter is to "unmix" literacy messages for Darren—and for other readers who do not comprehend as well as they desire. *Comprehension* can be defined as readers' ability to understand what they read and to connect this understanding with their lives and with previous information they have learned. *Comprehension processes* are the thinking processes readers/writers use to sequence, prioritize, summarize, organize, and retain the information presented as well as to make meaning for themselves and others. Research demonstrates that such meaning-making can be interrupted for several reasons. These disruptions occur when readers do not or cannot (1) decode accurately; (2) activate past experiences to build stronger personal connections to the text, both mentally (efferent responses) and emotionally (aesthetic responses); (3) recognize and integrate the text's structural and vocabulary clues to guide meaning-making; or (4) self-initiate cognitive and metacognitive strategies to overcome confusion (Allington, 1993; Beach & Hynds, 1991; Block, 2001; Gambrell & Bales, 1986).

In this chapter you will learn diagnosis and intervention methods that assist readers to overcome these barriers, understand what they read, and value their own reading responses. This chapter will present strategies to help students move from reticent to reflective readers/writers. Key areas covered are:

- Overcoming comprehension barriers
- Tilling the text
- Expanding content vocabulary

- Reflecting before, during, and after reading; developing metacognition
- Using comprehension strategies interactively
- Diagnosing and assessing comprehension

By the end of the chapter you will have answers to the following questions:

1. What instructional activities help readers "till their texts" and use the format of the printed page to improve comprehension?
2. How can struggling readers activate prior knowledge effectively so that differences between their backgrounds and those of literary characters do not interfere with comprehension?
3. How can struggling readers/writers increase their vocabularies prior to, during, and after reading and writing?
4. How can these readers/writers use story maps, story frames, and paragraph functions to improve their comprehension?
5. What cognitive and metacognitive strategies improve comprehension and composing abilities for these readers/writers (e.g., asking oneself questions, summarizing, inferring, predicting, interpreting, imaging, and using "fix-up" strategies)?

Overcoming Comprehension Barriers

As described in Chapter 2, until the 1980s most comprehension instruction consisted of drilling readers on isolated skills to improve their meaning-making. In recent decades, however, educators have come to understand that comprehension is a constructive process, in which readers create interpretations by relating the words they read to their own past experiences. Educators also know that the meanings readers bring to the text, the meanings they want to receive from it, and the meanings they establish beyond it are important factors in readers' comprehension abilities.

For this reason, recent work in assisting struggling readers to become more internally guided has focused on developing strategies students can use to bring more to the text (1) before they read ("tilling the text" by nurturing prereading ideas such as establishing one's own purpose, analyzing printed format, and identifying vocabulary and conceptual loads), (2) while they read, and (3) as they reflect on what they learned after they have read.

Before the pleasure of full comprehension occurs for less accomplished readers, many will need the supports and strategies in this chapter. The stages of comprehension ability closely parallel the levels of literacy ability and are as follows (Block, 2001; Block & Pressley, 2002):

Stage 1: Meaning-making is frequently disrupted by decoding difficulties, absence of enough external comprehension supports, interrupted concentration, unfamiliarity with the purpose of textual features, and/or lack of personal goals and pleasures from reading.

Stage 2: Literal comprehension occurs, but it may not be retained or may be incomplete because only a mental (efferent) connection has been made to the information in a selection.

Stage 3: Inferential comprehension occurs when students can "read between the lines" to make accurate predictions and interpretations.

Stage 4: Applied meaning-making occurs when students make an emotional (aesthetic) connection and response to reading, and when they reflect on new ways to use the knowledge gained.

Stage 5: Self-initiated, value-filled meaning-making results when emotional (aesthetic) and mental (efferent) connections and responses to a selection occur before, during, and after reading—with cognitive and metacognitive strategies being self-initiated the moment comprehension is interrupted for any reason.

To move into increasingly higher levels of understanding, readers must move beyond the first two stages of comprehension, with most benefits of internally guided reading being received at Stages 4 and 5. Students at lower stages can reach these highest stages by "tilling the text" before they read (or write), by making meaning while they read (or write), and by reflecting after they read (or write).

Tilling the Text

The preparation known as **tilling the text** helps enable students to fully comprehend each selection they read (and to fully compose each thought they want to write). To reach Stage 5 in comprehension, readers must till the text—just as soil is tilled and nourished before planting so nutritious fruits (meanings) can be produced. To help prepare students for higher levels of comprehension, model (through think alouds) the following thought processes they should engage in before reading:

- What motivates me to want to read? Or, how do I establish a personal purpose for an assigned reading?
- How do I activate prior knowledge before, during, and after reading?
- How will I build my text-specific knowledge and vocabulary?
- How do I intend to focus (and refocus) my mind on meaning-making?

In essence, readers' comprehension will advance when they learn how to till the text to do the following:

1. Attend to the author's writing style as they read
2. Establish a purpose for reading material

3. Overcome word-calling
4. Be aware of ways in which their own background knowledge can interfere with or expand meaning-making
5. Expand their content-specific vocabulary knowledge

The need for each of these abilities, as well as methods to increase their use by readers, will be described next.

Attending to Authors' Writing Styles

Among the first steps in tilling a text is to look at subheadings and print features (such as the length of paragraphs and amount of white space) to determine the conceptual density of a reading. This enables readers to understand how an author divides the topic into subtopics. To perform this analysis, many readers must also learn that dense concepts and writing styles will require more intense comprehension and metacognitive processes, and that each writing was built by an author who had a specific message.

BECOMING LESS REALITY-BOUND.   Attending to an author's writing style includes appreciating how the author depicts literary characters. It is often more difficult for struggling readers to like and understand literary characters because these students are more reality-bound than internally guided readers (Block & Pressley, 2002; Culp, 1985; Hunt & Vipond, 1985)—in other words, they find it difficult to become personally involved in the story.

This inability to identify with characters is compounded by struggling readers' tendency *not* to select texts that have characters they admire—partly because they have not been taught to till their text, and thus they spend less time selecting books. Also, these students often fail to understand characters' motives because most authors leave these to inference—and these readers are not yet comprehending at Stage 3. Another barrier is that these students rarely stick with a book long enough to truly get to know the characters. Finally, these readers are less likely to vary their reading rates in order to "savor" certain passages and hence do not give themselves the opportunity to become captivated while reading (Nell, 1988).

Establishing a Purpose

Another step in tilling the text is to identify the purpose for reading it. One of the most important actions you can take is *not* to tell less accomplished students the purpose for reading a piece of material. When you establish these readers' purposes too often, they may not learn to do so themselves—as it often takes repeated trials before they trust themselves enough to decide on their own what is important to comprehend. To help them assume such ownership before they read, remind them of the thought processes (listed earlier) that you modeled and instruct them to scan the text to discern which parts capture their mind and attention. In the process, you can also remind them to be alert to which sections are likely to require more intense concentration for them.

TRUSTING THEIR OWN TILLINGS. We can better understand why self-trust is so difficult for such readers when we consider how their attention to print differs from that of readers who are more internally guided. First, struggling readers often allocate less attention to the general meaning of sentences because they must allocate more concentrated effort to decoding the meaning of individual words. As a result, they cannot extend their attention to the full number of textual clues that are available, and thus they less frequently think about the relationships between larger units of meaning in phrases, sentences, and paragraphs than do internally guided readers. Moreover, whenever confusion begins, many readers tend to focus even more intently on individual words and letters. Unfortunately, such overconcentrated attention to decoding has repeatedly let them down in the past—and so they don't really trust it to help this time either. Often, when these readers become confused and must stop reading to "sound out" a word and can't, they will lift their eyes from the page or may just pretend to be reading. The best indicator that such readers are overdependent on decoding as their primary comprehension tool occurs when they lift their eyes from the page during a silent reading period; when you ask them why, they respond: "I don't know this word."

At this point, you know that these students will profit from learning to till the text. Such instruction will make the content and context of larger meaning-making units more salient. In the process, students come to believe that they *are* capable of internally guiding themselves away from confusion during meaning-making. When this assurance arises, students can experience major breakthroughs in comprehension. It seems that once these readers put all the pieces of knowledge and strategies about comprehension together for the first time, they switch from mainly decoding to comprehending. In addition, their affect surges to complement this cognitive growth. With this surge, readers at Stage 1 move to Stage 5 of comprehending almost immediately—and often become avid readers thereafter.

Overcoming Word-Calling

Word-calling is defined as reading every word accurately but not comprehending the words' collective meaning. In most cases word-calling problems emerge at some point after second grade, and often in students who have not been taught tilling-the-text strategies. Specifically, by third grade struggling readers move into material that contains words and topics for which they cannot merely guess at meanings by using their common sense and past personal experiences (Chall, 1983). Also, because they have not been taught the textual differences between expository and narrative text, many content-area reading materials become too conceptually dense for them to comprehend.

Because these readers tend to read infrequently, they need the strategies in this chapter to supplement their more limited conceptual knowledge base. Further, unless these readers learn metacognitive strategies (presented later in this chapter), most will not stop when they come to something they don't understand (Allington, 1993; Baker & Brown, 1983). Similarly, many word-callers become so obsessed with reading for accuracy that they literally *forget* to comprehend (Dymock, 1993; Goodman, 1973;

Rosenbaum, 2001). As Adams (1995) and Graves, Cooke, and Laberge (1983) have demonstrated, students who preview their text make better inferences about the material read, and this strategy assists these readers to relate new vocabulary to over-arching concepts.

Mere exposure to predictable or below-grade-level narrative books, however, will not eliminate word-calling. These books tend to reinforce readers' ideas that reading should always be predictable from personal experiences and that all words are to be memorized. Therefore, although such books have a place in the decoding portion of in-struction, they should not be relied on to build comprehension abilities. As a matter of fact, for some readers above the second grade, predictable pattern books reduce com-prehension (Roller, 1994).

Using Prior Knowledge to Expand Meaning-Making

As presented in Chapter 4, there are many methods of increasing less accomplished readers' abilities to apply prior knowledge to literacy, and it is important to teach these methods. Because Stage 5 comprehension requires an interaction of readers' tilling of the text, prior experiences, and printed material (visual information), the more auto-matically prior knowledge can be elicited while reading, the more comprehension in-creases. However, many readers are unable to continuously integrate these tools because (1) their culturally driven out-of-school experiences are too disparate from school texts; (2) text is not clearly written so as to move distinctly from point to point; (3) vocabu-lary introduced before a reading session does not relate to the central idea of the book (e.g., teachers may try to introduce *all* the words that might cause trouble); or (4) metacognition is not engaged so that word recognition errors are left uncorrected (Palinscar & Brown, 1984; Zieme, 2000).

Equally important, such readers may need to be taught how to recognize when their prior knowledge contains naive or incorrect information. In the process they must learn how to reconcile and conflicting information successfully new. Without this instruction some students will ignore new vocabulary because they believe they already have the needed information; or, when a conflict in information occurs, they will stop thinking about what they are reading. To help students discern naive background knowledge you can do any of the following:

1. Demonstrate how students can probe their beliefs before reading
2. Model how you know when your background experiences are inadequate to help you "read between the lines" in a book
3. Encourage students to place themselves in the story
4. Identify the questions students want to ask while they read

Another method of building background knowledge is to assist students to activate their schemas and to ask what they are thinking as they read. For example, if students can identify what background knowledge they are applying at a particular moment in a text, they can better understand whether that knowledge is adequate for reflecting about the material and remembering more of what they read. Similarly, once they learn to make predictions as they read, they can analyze whether their initial predictions were accurate. If they were, they know their background knowledge is interacting effectively with the author's.

When students activate their schemas, they can also use more of their background knowledge to decode new words and expand their vocabulary. Strategies and special supports that you can teach them for this purpose are described next.

Expanding Content Vocabulary

Dear Mrs. J.,

I think my vocabulary is growing. I read much faster now. I feel my eyes move across each line. I'm not afraid of trying any book in the library. Also, sometimes when I talk, I hear myself use words I've never used before. Even my parents noticed [that] I speak differently.

Love,
Marie

(Stiles, 1991, p. 31)

Appropriate vocabulary instruction increases students' comprehension abilities (Nagy & Herman, 1987). The following instructional lesson enables readers who are just beginning to develop independent comprehension ability to integrate decoding, prior knowledge, and tilling of the text to increase comprehension. These students learn more new words through such teaching than when left to learn new terms through independent reading (Carver, 1994, 1995; Nagy & Herman, 1987). Specifically, without your instruction it would take these readers about *12 years* of daily reading—learning the meanings of at least seven new vocabulary words each day of every year—to reach the level of reading vocabulary that Stage 5 readers possess by fourth grade. Thus, without the activities in this chapter, struggling readers may never develop the vocabulary they need to fully appreciate and enjoy reading materials beyond fifth grade readability (Nagy & Herman, 1987; Raetkin, Simpson, Alvermann, & Dishner, 1985; Raphael & McKinney, 1983).

Optimal vocabulary instruction uses the lessons presented here to teach only those words central to the theme and purpose of specific reading selections (Beck & McKeown, 1991a). Such instruction should also occur in the contexts of sentences that have vivid, memorable meanings that are relevant both to the text and to students' lives (Nagy & Herman, 1987). Moreover, when words are taught thoroughly so that these readers see relationships between new terms, students can more frequently verbalize and supply their own meanings for words, without merely memorizing the definitions told them. Instruction should also include postreading activities in which less accomplished readers can return to new terms they read to add connotations they have created. Each lesson can be taught before, during, or even after reading, depending on the interest level of students and density of the text (Beck, McKeown, McCaslin, & Burkes, 1979). These lessons should identify words that these readers want to learn and think are important and should enable students to predict the meanings of words from possible dictionary definitions by using the context in a reading (Adams, 1995).

Another guiding principle of effective vocabulary development is that meanings should be conveyed in multiple contexts—"knowing a word is mastering its use in a multitude of contexts: word mastery is a matter of degree" (Dymock, 1993, p. 93). Instruction that calls for deeper, more meaningful uses of words as they are introduced is the most durable, creates the most affinity for reading (Mezynski, 1983; Stahl & Fairbanks, 1986), and increases the beauty and enjoyment of writing (Duin & Graves, 1987; Stevenson Learning Skills, 2000).

The following vocabulary lessons assist readers at Stages 1 and 2 to reach higher levels of comprehension. You can develop new strategies based on adaptations of these methods. Once readers cultivate a method of vocabulary development that they prefer and can guide internally, direct instructional time prior to and after reading can be shortened. Until readers employ one or more of the following methods without your prompting, however, the goal of your curriculum should be to reintroduce at least one of them once a month until familiarity increases students' self-initiated use. Also, monitor readers' use of their preferred method when they read silently from assigned and self-selected materials.

LESSON 1: IT'S KIND OF LIKE _____. In this method you teach students to ask themselves the following questions to learn new words:

What is it kind of like?

When would I use it in my life?

What is it a part of?

What function does it normally perform? (Is it a naming, painting, or doing word?)

When you say "It's kind of like _____" to introduce new words before reading, you can allow students to volunteer answers to each of these questions, in a group session, to develop their automatic reference to context clues when they read silently. Through this sharing, students gain ideas from peers as to ways that words can apply to their lives as they read.

LESSON 2: SEMANTIC MAPS. The goal of vocabulary instruction is to connect words in relational patterns to improve readers' comprehension and to help readers relate these mental patterns to experiences in life. Asking students to use their senses to form mental images as they learn a word increases such transferability. It is from experiences that concepts are attached to labels, and making semantic maps enables the vicarious experiences in reading to originate new concepts labeled by words.

Semantic maps, also known as *concept maps* or *webbing,* are diagrams in which a main idea is surrounded by supporting concepts in categorical patterns (see Figure 10.1). This map may be completed before, during, or after reading. Students can also relate words in their personal life to the 5 or 10 words chosen to be mapped from the reading material. Alternatively, students can receive an incomplete map they can use to

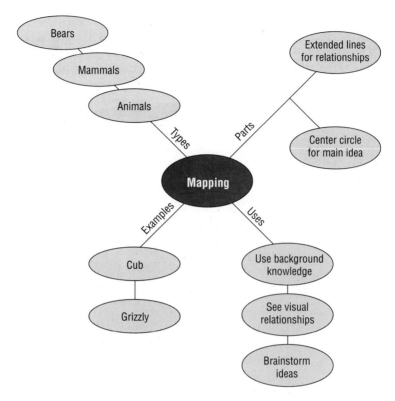

FIGURE 10.1 Semantic Mapping Format

deduce the meaning of new words from an upcoming reading, as each new word is placed in a semantic relationship with the other words that appear on the map. Thus, the purpose of a semantic map (Raphael, 1984) is to help students use context clues, examples, and their own backgrounds to increase their vocabulary.

LESSON 3: GRAPHIC ORGANIZERS. Once readers are comfortable with mapping, they can expand their vocabularies by using **graphic organizers.** Graphic organizers are outlines or semantic maps. You can make a graphic organizer of key words and subtopics from a passage, then introduce the hierarchical relationships among these words and topics by explaining that the lines between words and topics represent classifications and examples of meaning. Then, after readers have read the passage, you can also ask them to suggest other words the reading called to mind that can enhance the relationships among the words on the original graphic organizer.

Box 10.1 describes further vocabulary-building activities reading specialists and classroom teachers can introduce to diagnose and teach middle and high school students.

MIDDLE SCHOOL and HIGH SCHOOL

Instructional Strategies That Increase Vocabulary Knowledge

10.1

1. Create a Word Market. Each week, the children must "purchase" five new words. They must learn to spell the words and learn their definitions. They will record their words in their own personal dictionaries. They may trade in old words that they have learned for new words.

2. Use the students' own writing samples. Circle five words out of their writing each week that they must replace with a new word. Provide them with dictionaries and thesauruses as references.

3. Make a bookmark. When the children read, have them write down the words that they do not know and would like to learn. They can record their words on a bookmark that they have made, and can use it to keep their place while they read.

4. See special vocabulary programs such as *Word Search and Worldly Wise* (Grades 1–12); see also Rosenbaum's (2001) word map approach.

Source: Created by Malitha DeSilva, an early childhood education major at Texas Christian University, Fort Worth, TX.

Making Meaning While Reading

When you assist readers with weaker comprehension skills to understand connections between the events in a story and the writing structures the author uses, you can increase these readers' abilities to predict while reading. They begin to think ahead more frequently and gain a greater sense of control over reading (Loxterman, Beck, & McKeown, 1994). To build this understanding you teach story grammar, authorial patterns, paragraph functions, and directed readings.

Story Grammar in Narrative Texts

Story grammar is the underlying structure and connection between events in a writing through which the author moves meanings from one idea to the next until the concluding episode is reached. Just as English grammar describes how sentences can be constructed, story grammar delineates acceptable story orderings—such as flashbacks; narratives; sequential, spatial, and cause–effect relationships; historical fiction; and so on. Because the mind will automatically store images in patterns and in order, when weak comprehenders learn to recognize an author's intended ordering, their confusions and misunderstandings during reading are reduced.

Moreover, researchers have demonstrated that Stage 4 and 5 comprehenders can decipher typical story grammars without instruction because of their repeated exposures to specific genres (Block, 1996; Block & Pressley, 2002). Proficient readers come to expect that the next story they read will conform to the traditional framework they have experienced in past readings. On the other hand, less accomplished readers will not internalize these structures without direct instruction (Baumann & Bergeron, 1993; Mandler, 1978).

The **story frame** or **story map** displays features of expository as well as narrative texts in separate boxes (see Table 10.1). It is particularly valuable for less accomplished

---

TABLE 10.1 Story Frame Example

This story frame was filled out by a group of fourth grade struggling readers.

> Setting: (When and where does the story take place?) The story takes place during the war with the Nazis in France.

I know this because the author uses these words: "Choisi-le Roi, just outside of Paris."

> Main Characters: (Who are the important people in the story?) Monique, Sevrine, Marcel (Monique's mother).

continued

TABLE 10.1 *Continued*

I know they are important because: The whole story is about them.

> The Problem starts when: Monsieur Lendormy sees Monique and Sevrine in Monique's bedroom window.

or

> The Main Character's goal is: Monique is trying to be a friend to Sevrine and keep her safe from the Nazis.

The Plot: (What happened?)

> Event 1:   Monique and Sevrine let a butterfly go out the window and Monsieur Lendormy saw them.

After that . . .

> Event 2:   Sevrine and her mother and daddy had to leave Monique's house where they were hiding.

Next . . .

> Event 3:   Sevrine's mother and Daddy went with Pere Voulliard. Sevrine left with Monique and her Mother.

Then . . .

> Event 4:   Sevrine, Monique, and Monique's mother walked a long distance until a car came to help Sevrine.

Turning Point: (How I know the plot is reaching a solution?)

> The Resolution: (How did it end?)   Monique and her mother finally made it to the train station and returned home safely.

I know this because the author uses these words: finally

> Author's Moral or Purpose (or, Purpose for Me):   It is important to help other people.

I think this is the moral because: The story was about how Monique and her mother helped keep Sevrine and her parents safe from the Nazis. Sevrine and her parents were Jews.

readers because after they label episodes from the story in the appropriate boxes, these students can write beneath each box the clues from the story that helped them identify that aspect of the story's grammar. After using story frames as few as three times, many readers can identify central narrative elements in children's literature without prompting (Baumann & Bergeron, 1993). The story frame also increases readers' abilities to write narratives (Graves, 1995). You can re-create or adapt Table 10.1 and let your students practice using story frames to increase their comprehension.

A related activity that weaker comprehenders enjoy uses story cue cards on which elements of story grammar appear (see Figure 10.2). Note that each element appears on a separate card. The value of entering each element separately is that readers can experience success each time they complete a card instead of feeling only one sense of accomplishment for completing a full story frame after a full day's reading.

In Figure 10.2, notice how few words Arcus used when he completed his story cue cards for the book *Go Away, Dog*. Such limited writing will be typical of your less

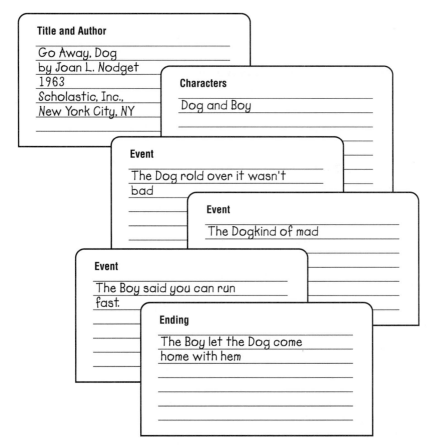

FIGURE 10.2 Story Cue Cards

Each card has an example given by Arcus, a fifth grade developing reader.

accomplished readers. From this activity they learn to use story grammar to connect ideas—a skill they can transfer to other stories. In addition, story cards can become valuable supports when students give retellings and when they write. If a reader has particular difficulty recognizing one aspect of story grammar, you can provide a copy of Resource Card 15, which lists books that demonstrate individual aspects of story grammar. These books present story elements so distinctly that after students read just a few of these titles, their abilities to recognize separate parts of story grammar increase rapidly (Block, 1993a, 1993b). For example, students who have difficulty recognizing settings can read *Bringing the Rain to Kapiti Plain* by Verna Aardema; in this book the author

RESOURCE CARD 15

Books That Demonstrate Individual Aspects of Story Grammar for Students with Comprehension Difficulties

Settings

Aardema, V. (1981). *Bringing the rain to Kapiti Plain.* New York: Dial.

Anderson, H. (1986). *The ugly duckling.* New York: Random House.

Babbit, N. (1975). *Tuck everlasting.* New York: Farrar, Straus & Giroux.

Eifert, H. (1995). *The teeny-tiny woman.* New York: Viking.

George, J. (1972). *Julie of the wolves.* New York: Harper & Row.

L'Engle, M. (1962). *A wrinkle in time.* New York: Farrar, Straus & Giroux.

Paterson, K. (1977). *Bridge to Terabithia.* New York: Crowell.

Themes and Plots

Chaucer, G. (1991). *Chanticleer and the fox.* New York: Disney.

Hutchinson, V. (1976). *Henny Penny.* Boston: Little, Brown.

Lawson, R. (1972). *Rabbit hill.* New York: Viking.

Lewis, C. (1950). *The lion, the witch, and the wardrobe.* New York: Macmillan.

White, E. B. (1952). *Charlotte's web.* New York: Harper & Row.

Good Beginnings, Middles, and Endings

Cane, M., Ed. (1964). *The Call of the Wild and other selected stories.* New York: Harcourt Brace & World.

Gag, W. (1977). *Millions of cats.* New York: Coward, McCann & Geoghegan.

Galdone, P. (1974). *Little Red Riding Hood.* New York: McGraw-Hill.

Potter, B. (1963). *The tale of Peter Rabbit.* New York: Golden.

Sendak, M. (1963). *Where the wild things are.* New York: Harper & Row.

Gallo, Donald R. (1984). *Sixteen short stories.* New York: Delcorte.

Sequential Patterns

Baskin, L. (1972). *Hosie's alphabet.* New York: Viking.

Carle, E. (1979). *The very hungry caterpillar.* New York: Philomel.

Domanska, J. (1985). *Busy Monday morning.* New York: Greenwillow.

Galdone, P. (1986). *Over in the meadow.* Englewood Cliffs, NJ: Prentice-Hall.

develops a setting that is so vivid readers can locate and imagine it easily. Students enjoy having their own copy of this Resource Card to refer to when they select books from the library.

Authorial Patterns in Expository Texts

Once readers feel comfortable with narrative story grammars, you can introduce other types of authorial patterns that are used in expository texts: descriptive, cause–effect, compare–contrast, definition–example, problem–solution, problem–solution–result, and time-order. When these patterns are presented, the major differences between expositions and narrations should be emphasized. For example, narrations have clearly defined conclusions, whereas expositions comprise a repetition of similar ideas using paragraphs that adhere to different patterns (story grammars) in the ordering of ideas and events.

Struggling readers learn the expository patterns faster when they are presented separately. Once all expository grammars have been introduced, you can also do think alouds with readers before they read a selection so that they learn how you identify which pattern is being used and how knowing this ordering in advance will increase their comprehension. You can demonstrate using the first page of the material to be read, as most weak comprehenders can duplicate this modeling after having seen your examples only a few times. To check that your readers are in fact using knowledge of the authorial pattern to aid comprehension, you can ask each student to do a think aloud (in a discovery discussion or tutorial support setting) about what that student is thinking as he or she reads.

Paragraph Functions

In like fashion, students find it easier to make meaning when they recognize the functions of single paragraphs. If students consciously identify these functions when reading, their abilities to inference and apply what they read increase (Block, 2001). When you provide the information presented here, it will often be the first time some students understand that sentences are put together in a predictable manner. In turn, for some, reading comes to be viewed as possessing the valuable quality of predictability.

The most frequently occurring types of English paragraphs are the following:

- *Introductory:* Provides an overview for the entire text and tells readers the purposes of paragraphs that follow.
- *Explanatory:* Gives reasons for an event, an outcome, a position, or an author's ideas. (Keywords in this paragraph are *for example, specifically, for this reason.*)
- *Descriptive:* Delineates features and individual points after a main purpose or idea has been stated in a previous paragraph.
- *Cause and effect:* Presents the results of one or more causative agents or features that lead to a specific event. (Keywords are *because, since, so that, so,* if, *as, for.*)
- *Conditional:* Specifies what would happen if something else occurred or states the limits to the ideas presented in a previous paragraph. (Keywords are *if . . . then, unless, although, only if.*)

- *Time or spatial sequential:* Relates the time order in which particular events or ideas occur or the order in which objects exist in a given space. (Keywords are *first, second, third, then, finally, next, before, after, during, another, also, in addition, when, until, meanwhile, always, following, finally, initially.*)

- *Question and answer:* Begins with a question; answers the question in subsequent sentences.

- *Summarizing or concluding:* Reports the most important points from previous paragraphs. (Keywords are *hence, therefore, as a result, thus, in summary, in conclusion, accordingly, consequently, finally, to sum up.*)

As you read a story orally to the class (and display the text with an overhead transparency), you can pause to model how you identified the paragraph you just read. Then you can make the identification of subsequent paragraphs into a game, asking weaker comprehenders to read along with you and identify upcoming paragraphs. You can conclude by asking students how knowing the purposes of paragraphs will assist them as they read silently.

Directed Reading Thinking Activity (DRTA)

The *directed reading thinking activity* is a lesson that teaches less accomplished readers to use the details to predict what will happen next (Stauffer, 1969). To begin this lesson, ask these readers to till the text and set a purpose for reading. Then have students read a section of a story or content area material. Ask them to stop at a point where you feel they should have enough information to make an accurate prediction about the next section to be read. At this point, encourage students to share their predictions and justify them. Next, they can discuss why they did or did not read previous points in the message accurately, what distracted them, and which strategy they will use in the next segment to strengthen their comprehension.

For example, a second grade teacher met with readers who were not predicting while they read. He performed the directed reading activity with *The True Story of the Three Little Pigs.* He combined the DRTA strategy with story frames and tilling the text. While reading the first page aloud, he modeled how he discerned the author's organization. He also made three columns titled "First Pig's Actions," "Second Pig's Actions," and "Third Pig's Actions," where he would record details so as to make more accurate predictions as he read. Then he asked his students to use all these strategies together as they read to page 17, then to close their books and write their predicted ending.

Reflecting before, during, and after Reading: Developing Metacognition

Weaker comprehenders are no longer taught separate skills as in the past—such as circling the main idea sentence on a worksheet, underlining a topic word, or locating "who did what, to whom, when, and where." Instead, they are taught *strategies*—organized, purposeful sets of actions readers perform to make meaning. Strategies (1) are intentional and deliberate, (2) are flexible and adaptable, (3) employ reasoning, and (4) involve metacognition (Dole, Buffy, Roehler, & Pearson, 1991). Metacognition during reading (to be discussed at length later in this section) refers to two specific types of reader thought processes: (1) being aware of what they are thinking and why they are thinking about it as they read; and (2) controlling their reading so that disruptions in comprehension are overcome through internally guided, self-initiated cognitive strategies (Baker & Brown, 1984; Jacobs & Paris, 1987).

Several studies have shown that struggling readers have less knowledge than more able readers about how to consciously organize such cognitive strategies and metacognitions while reading, and that they do not know how to think to eliminate interruptions in meaning-making (Block, 1994; Johnston, 1985; Palinscar & Brown, 1989). Thus, whereas expert readers use the following strategies without being instructed to do so, the strategies remain secrets to readers in Stages 1 and 2 of comprehension ability (Collins, 1991a; Johnston & Winograd, 1985). Unless you teach strategies to less accomplished readers, they often infer that simply putting the meanings of individual words together is the ultimate outcome of reading. Moreover, many will have great difficulty integrating efferent and aesthetical thoughts with literal comprehension, so Stage 5 comprehension will remain beyond their reach (Block, 1993; Borkowski, Carr, & Pressley, 1987; Carr & Ogle, 1987; Scardamalia & Bereiter, 1984; Wittrock & Alesandrini, 1990; Wong, 1987).

Students will learn these strategies faster if the teacher or reading specialist presents them through direct instruction, using graphic and descriptive illustrations (thinking guides), explaining why a strategy is useful, and describing the types of reading situations in which each approach will be most effective (Block & Mangieri, 1995; Schunk & Rice, 1991).

STRATEGY 1: EXPLAINING. When readers are asked to explain their thinking, comprehension is enhanced (Block, 2001; Block & Mangieri, 1995; King, 1994; Pressley, Johnson, Symons, McGoldrick, & Brown, 1989). In the process students discern important details. You can also assist students' detail recognition by telling them that the purpose of details is to identify who, what, where, when, how, and why, as they relate to the reasons that actions and ideas occur in a story. You should not, however, ask students to locate specific details because this is not an authentic task. Instead, ask readers to point out details they found important, interesting, effective, suspenseful, creative, or humorous. Then if they desire, they can analyze differences between detail types as a group and discuss what characterizes the most effective way to use details for explanations.

Students can then practice giving effective explanations that incorporate the following principles:

- Explanations don't just tell what something is or describe it—they tell the *how* and *why* about it.

- Explanations should be in our own words—not just repeating something we have heard and memorized.

- When we explain something, it is often helpful to use information we already have to make what we are explaining clearer—comparing the new information to something we already know

STRATEGY 2: SUMMARIZING. When readers learn to make mental and written summaries of their readings, retention increases by 16 percent, on the average. These summaries also become a record keeper of thoughts, which enhances the application of readings to life (Block & Mangieri, 1995; Stein & Kirby, 1992).

An effective activity to establish the summarization strategy is to use the K-W-L (Know–Want–Learn) Strategy Sheet shown in Table 10.2. In the two left columns of the K-W-L Strategy Sheet (Ogle, 1986), students list what they know prior to reading and

---

TABLE 10.2 K-W-L Strategy Sheet

This K-W-L sheet was completed by a group of fourth grade struggling readers before and after reading P. Lauber's *Volcano: The Eruption and Healing of Mount St. Helens.*

What We Know	What We Want to Find Out	What We Learned or Still Need to Learn
1. Volcanos erupt. 2. Lava comes out. 3. Mount St. Helens is in Washington State. 4. Lava is molten rock.	1. Why did it erupt? 2. Will it erupt again? 3. Was anyone killed? 4. What do animals do when a volcano erupts?	1. Differences between igneous, metamorphic, and sedimentary rocks and soil. 2. Shifting in continental plates cause eruptions. 3. It has erupted only once in 150 years (about). 4. 57 people died. 5. Animals fled or were killed by lava, heat, or "stone winds." 6. It took a long time for animals and plants to grow back but some like insects, moss, fungi, and woodpeckers came back soon.

Categories of Information We Expect to Use in Our Report and Future Reading:

A. Description of how volcanoes erupt
B. How people and animals die
C. How terrains change after a volcano
D. Types of animals that came back first
E. Plants that came back first
F. How we can avoid losses of lives of people, plants, and animals in the future
G. How long it will take before Mount St. Helens is back to top form

Summary of What We Learned:

Volcano taught us why Mount St. Helens erupted, what happened when it did, and how it is healing itself with the help of nature, man, animals, and plants.

Source: Adapted from D. Ogle (1986, February), "K-W-L: A Teaching Model That Develops Active Reading of Expository Text," *The Reading Teacher,* pp. 564–567. Reprinted with permission of Donna Ogle and the International Reading Association.

what they want to find out. In the third column they put what they learned or still want to learn after they've read. You can also teach weaker comprehenders to write summaries about their reading using the format shown in Figure 10.3. They can do so in conjunction with 2-minute and 10-minute writes (to be described later in this chapter). For

1. DELETE DUPLICATION.
   Example: There was a rabbit and in the beginning he was really splendid. He was fat and bunchy as a rabbit should be.

   Summary: The splendid rabbit was fat and bunchy.

2. COMBINE IDEAS WITH THE SAME SUBJECT.
   Example: He had a brown coat with white spots. He had thread whiskers and his ears were lined with pink satin. His spots made him stand out among the plain red stockings.

   Summary: His brown coat, white spots, and pink-lined ears made him stand out among the plain red stockings.

3. RESTATE IN FEWER WORDS.
   Example: There were other things in the stocking, nuts and oranges, and a toy engine, and chocolate almonds, a mouse and candy canes, but the rabit was the best of all.

   Summary: The stocking was filled with Christmas treats, but the rabbit was the best gift.

4. USE SUMMARY WORDS.
   Example: Summary words include: *almost all, in conclusion, in brief, the main point, on the whole, ultimately, to sum up.*

5. REMOVE DETAILS THAT ARE NOT ABOUT THE MAIN SUBJECT.
   Example: On Christmas morning when he sat wedged in the top of the boy's stocking with a sprig of holly between his paws, the Velveteen Rabbit looked charming.

   Summary: The Velveteen Rabbit looked charming.

   A great summary sentence could be:

   _____

   _____

   _____

FIGURE 10.3 Summarizing

Source: From C. C. Block & J. N. Mangieri (1996), *Reason to Read: Thinking Strategies for Life Through Literature, Volume 2,* p. 138. Palo Alto, CA: Addison-Wesley. Used with permission.

example, in Table 10.2 (which a group of fourth grade weaker comprehenders completed before and after reading the Newbery Honor book *Volcano: The Eruption and Healing of Mount St. Helens* by Patricia Lauber), this strategy increased students' comprehension and vocabulary significantly, as demonstrated by the depth of vocabulary and specificity in the right-hand column and in the summary at the bottom of the table.

The reason this form of the K-W-L strategy (which includes summative thinking) is so valuable for these readers is that in writing their summaries they are reviewing the material read and learning to shift main ideas to the forefront—two skills these readers need to improve.

STRATEGY 3: INFERRING, PREDICTING, AND INTERPRETING. *Inferring* is the process of judging, concluding, or reasoning from given information and is the first step in constructing meaning that is not literally stated. *Predicting* is a special type of inference in which the next event, action, or idea is deduced. *Interpreting* is another type of inference in which literal information is connected to background knowledge and opinions are used to make a reasoned judgment about the literal information. Weaver and Kintsch (1991) analyzed text and found that as many as 12 to 15 inferences can be contained in every expressly mentioned statement in a passage. Therefore, it is important that the inferring strategy become a cornerstone in readers' strategic thinking before higher levels of comprehension are possible. The K-W-L Strategy Sheet in Table 10.2 visually displays inference processes and can be shared with students as you model inference, interpretation, and prediction strategies and processes for them.

You can also teach young readers to infer by showing them how they already make inferences in their own lives. For example, you might say something like this:

> If your mother, father, grandmother, or grandfather told you to take your umbrella to school, your brain would automatically think of rain, although no one said that word. This is an *inference*—a secret thinking process and strategy you use to make meaning, called *inferring,* and you can do this when you read and listen. To infer, you take what the author says plus what you know and end up with what was meant. For example, listen to this sentence: "Nibbsie came running, with the stick in his mouth." You hear what I say and your mind adds a few things—based on what you know. You come up with an entirely new thought. I did not tell you that Nibbsie is a dog; you know this because there were clues that he was a dog. As you read and listen in the future, look for clues and use more than one clue as you think. When you do so you are inferring.

Another method is to give students a first-person story in which the narrator is only identified as "I" and students must infer to uncover who "I" is. You can divide the story into paragraphs and have readers use the first paragraph as their first infer ring clue; then discuss their ideas and how they silently thought as they read to come up with these ideas. Continue to discuss subsequent inferences in this manner, one paragraph at a time, until the correct narrator is identified and the inferences that lead to this identity are explained by individual readers.

In a similar exercise, you can lay separate paragraphs (each with clues as to the narrator's identity) on a table and ask struggling readers to come get them, one at a time—reading each one, working at their own pace, and thinking about the information they read until they are sure they have inferred the correct first-person narrator. When they are ready to predict the identity of the narrator, you can ask them to come whisper it in your ear. Then you can record the amount of time it took each student to make that inference. Allow them to change their minds if they wish and to choose whether to read on or reread previous paragraphs after their first inference. When all students have inferred at least once, ask the first few who accurately identified the narrator to explain the inference processes and strategies they used. After students have practiced their inferring skills for a week as they silently read other texts, you can reinitiate this activity. Present a second set of cut-up paragraphs on the table for students to read again in the same manner. When they have identified the correct narrator, record their times again and encourage them to describe their improvements in inferring. Table 10.3 contains a story that can be used in this activity. The correct answer appears in the Answer Key at the back of the book.

Readers should also explain the reasons behind their inferences and predictions, as such vocalizations transfer to faster mastery of this metacognitive strategy (Block &

TABLE 10.3 First-Person Narrative

Clue #1
Lunch made me sleepy, so I curled up to take a nap. With sleep came a wonderful dream. I was stretched out on a lovely green lawn with the sun warming my body. Birds were singing gaily overhead, and little yellow daffodils peeked out through the grass. I reached out to touch one—and suddenly there was no sun.

A heavy shadow had shut out the light. Something grabbed me and I cried out, fighting to get free. It was no use; I was traveling through space. This was no dream. It was real. I had been captured, and there was nothing I could do about it.

Clue #2
Soon I felt something solid at my feet. I could move, but it was hard to stand. My legs felt limber. Where was I?

Cautiously, I stepped forward. OUCH! I bumped into a wall and went in the other direction, but every time there was a wall. Four walls and no door. I'm in a cell!

All of a sudden there was a blast of cold air from above. I looked up but could see nothing. Where was the air coming from? Suddenly I knew: there was no roof on my cell! I had discovered a way out.

continued

TABLE 10.3 *Continued*

Clue #3

Stepping carefully toward a wall, I attempted to reach the opening. I wasn't tall enough, so I sat down again to think. The cell was still rocking. Maybe I could throw myself against one of the walls and tip the cell over. Again and again I rushed at the wall, but I finally gave up, defeated.

Sitting down, I tried to gather the energy for one more try. If that didn't work—Wait, the movement stopped!

A minute later I heard an earthshaking bang as I felt a different motion. My cell was moving up and down, not back and forth. I couldn't keep my balance. I said to myself I'd conquer whatever it was. I'd be ready. In an instant there was a horrible crunch, and the wall nearest me was ripped away. Beyond the opening I could see a dazzling light.

Clue #4

"Now's your chance," I told myself, cautiously crawling to the opening. At first, I saw nothing but a shiny wood floor. Then I saw *them!*

Feet! Giant feet! They seemed about to surround me, so I quickly retreated. I could be ground to smithereens out there! Of course, that's what they were planning—that's why they made it easy for me to escape! Well, I'd fool them; I wouldn't move.

Clue #5

No, I couldn't stay. I had to try to get out.

Once again I crept to the opening, but the feet were still there. Then I noticed something else. Near two of the feet, four round posts rose from the floor. The posts were topped by a thick, low roof. I could easily squeeze under it, but those giant feet couldn't.

I took a deep breath and moved quickly. Racing out of my cell, I skidded under the thick roof. I made it! My legs felt like rubber again, but I was safe for the moment.

Clue #6

What would happen next? I wondered. I didn't have long to wait, however, for I heard voices high above the roof.

"Oh, Donald, she's afraid of us!"

"Well, naturally," came the reply. "That must have been a very frightening trip for such a little _____."

Pressley, 2002). An example of one reader's explanation of predictions is shown in Figure 10.4. It can serve as a model for your students. Figure 10.5 outlines the inferring process.

Older students can be taught to make inferences by reflecting on how they inferred specific traits of literary characters and friends. Describe how authors want readers to

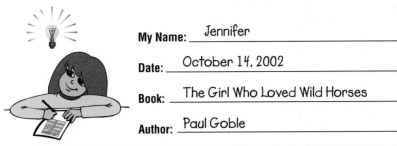

My Prediction	Why Did I Make That Prediction?
I think the book is about a girl who loves horses.	Because pictures of horses look dreamlike.
I predict she gets a horse.	Because on the picture on back of the book she is on a horse.
I predict she's really a princess.	There is a "Princess" word in here.
I think I am going to like it.	The sentences are like music playing.

FIGURE 10.4 Sample of a Reader's Explanation of Her Predictions

infer characters' traits through the relationships they form with other characters. Books that students enjoy reading to practice inferring include the following:

The Great Gilly Hopkins

Sarah, Plain and Tall

The Eighteenth Emerging

Goodbye

Chicken Little

Julie of the Wolves

One-Eyed Cat

Sea Glass

The Summer of the Swans

Each of these contains many inferences students can discuss in small groups.

In addition, you can ask readers to make inferences from pictures that are age appropriate. Readers who are weak comprehenders have demonstrated that they can make

FIGURE 10.5
Thinking Guide:
Drawing Inferences

Thinking Guide

Drawing Inferences

Name: _____   Date: _____

Look for clues when you read!

Use more than one clue.

Put the clues together with what you already know to draw an inference.

inferences from pictures just as well as internally guided readers do (Beal, 1990; Holmes, 1987). Another instructional activity is to remove the dialogue from the last two sections of a cartoon, ask readers to write their inferences on them, share their completed cartoons with each other, and explain their inferring processes and strategies.

STRATEGY 4: IMAGING. *Imaging* is making mental pictures of information in a text. Images make text realistic and more retrievable in memory. Imaging helps students integrate information (Pressley, 1977), detect inconsistencies (Gambrell & Bales, 1986), enhance comprehension (Gambrell & Jawitz, 1993), and increase retention (Sadoski, Goetz, Olivarez, Lee, & Roberts, 1990). Moreover, when instructions to image are given before students read, literal comprehension increases significantly, with males benefiting more than females (Gambrell & Koskinen, 1982). These increased abilities resulted from the experimental subjects' expanded abilities to detect inconsistencies in text through imagery. Imaging also enabled these students to focus their attention on important information in texts and to reorganize the information into useful mental models (Gambrell & Jawitz, 1993). Teaching imaging involves assisting readers (through your modeling) to place themselves in the scenes of their reading by using all their senses and prior knowledge to create vivid representations of prose.

Images of feeling are the most powerful connectors between the cognitive and emotional aspects of life and learning (Broudy, 1987). The reason imaging instruction is so important to struggling readers and writers is that it induces them to think actively while reading. For some, this instructional event will be the first time they have done so. It also integrates emotional experiences with attitudinal and logical experiences in readers' lives. Images enable readers to become immersed in the experience evoked by the language process, rather than in the language process itself (Fleckenstein, 1991). Moreover, because imaging evokes emotions it is the best strategy to increase readers' positive, aesthetic response to reading, as reflected in this excerpt:

> As I wrote, the scenery came back as it was all set to be, and the emotions started pouring in. When I got to the part about turning around, I lost the fact that I was writing and started reliving the whole thing on paper. . . . Right when I mentioned my mom I could picture her. A feeling of warmth came over me. (Fleckenstein, 1991, p. 214)

One method to increase imaging is to tell readers that they will learn how to paint pictures in their minds *as they read* to better remember what they read, and that these pictures are called images. Then you can ask students to read picturable nouns and describe the images these words evoke (McNeil, 1986). After students have described to a partner images that these words produced, have them read an entire paragraph and describe how their images changed as they read each successive sentence. When they feel comfortable and competent in image making, you can silently read a book along with each student. Instruct the student to stop your reading whenever he or she has a vivid mental image to share. After the student's explanation, share and contrast yours. Diagnose whether the student's image contains enough of his or her sensual information and prior experiences to ensure that an emotional connection to the text has been made. If these are not present, conduct a minilesson about imaging and engage in two or more periods of silent reading and descriptions of mental images so this student can practice improving his or her imagery with your support.

Another instructional method is to have students write similes to describe main ideas they read. For example, Natalie, a first grade student, wanted to describe how she had arranged all the snowballs she wrote about in her story. She wanted to communicate the splendor of this final product, which had taken her an hour to create. She wrote: "I formed 25 snowballs. I put them side by side in a perfect half-circle. It glistened in the sun. It was beautiful." But Natalie was not satisfied with this description. She said: "I wanted people to really see it, so I added 'It looked like a huge diamond necklace for a giant princess.' " By using the word *like* and knowing how to use similes to create effective mental images, Natalie completed her writing experience with strong feelings of accomplishment and pride.

A third way to develop imaging is to ask readers to tell you about an event they are going to write about. The process of describing the unfolding action often creates an image in their minds. For instance, Cedric, a fifth grader, described the following image when this method was implemented in a Tier 3 setting: "The second time Michael Jordon shot from the foul line he missed it. Patrick Ewing jumped up and wrestled it away from everyone else!" Following his oral description, Cedric wrote about this scene, including more details from his vision.

Bellanca and Fogarty (1990) use guided imaging in a gamelike activity in which students assign human traits to an animal or inanimate object. This adaptation increases the speed and vividness with which students imagine new information while reading. For example, the first student might say: "An elephant is riding a bike." Then a second student explains why the image is beneficial ("That's a good idea because the elephant can get around faster.") and then gives another trait the elephant possesses: "He can also talk and says 'What's for lunch?' " Then a third student explains why the last trait was a good idea ("That's a good idea because the elephant can communicate with people and other elephants as he rides past.") and gives another trait to add to the visualization: "He flies kites as he rides his bike." As the ideas are expressed, one student writes them on a chart. After all students in this Tier 2 small group lesson have contributed, they orally read the chart and compare the images that this reading created in their minds.

Increasing Metacognition

Metacognition is the awareness and deliberate, conscious control of one's thinking and cognitive strategies while reading, thinking, and learning (Flavell, 1976). Brown (1980) delineates specific metacognitive thoughts related to the act of reading, as follows:

1. Clarifying the purposes for which one is reading
2. Understanding and monitoring the demands of decoding and comprehending
3. Consciously searching for, and focusing attention on, the most important information
4. Monitoring ongoing information to determine whether meaning and purposes for reading are being achieved
5. Engaging in planning, review, and self-interrogation, and taking corrective action when confusion and unknown meanings of words occur
6. Recovering from interruptions and disruptions in meaning
7. Pausing to reflect, respond, and apply what you read to your life

Most struggling readers lack metacognitive self-direction and strategies. This situation is especially alarming when related to the findings that (1) metacognition is crucial to the development of Stage 5 comprehension; (2) learning how to learn, a highly advanced metacognitive ability, has the most enduring effect on student achievement; and (3) the development of metacognition enhances readers' motivation as well as their positive attitudes toward reading (Chipman & Segal, 1985; Cullinan, 1992; Presseisen, 1987; Smey-Richman, 1988). Because so many benefits result from increased metacognition, four lessons to increase struggling readers' metacognitive abilities follow.

LESSON 1: INTRODUCING METACOGNITION. To introduce metacognitive reading strategies, ask what students already know about thinking while they read. Follow their descriptions with feedback: Explain that they are already thinking about their own thinking as it relates to reading, and that such thinking is important and is called metacognition. End the discussion by asking them what types of metacognition they would like for you to model. For instance, if you were modeling what to think when students come to a word they don't know, you would say something like this:

> I think to myself about what I should do, which is metacognition. I first look at the length of the word and its letter pattern to determine if I should use phonic generalizations, sight word memories, or structural analysis to pronounce the word. While I'm making this decision I move my eyes back to the first of the sentence and reread the other words so I can put their meanings with sound of the first letter in the unknown word. If I still do not know the word, I read to the end of the paragraph and by that time I have made the decision whether I know the word or am going to ask someone for the meaning, look it up in a dictionary, or read on to gain more context clues.
>
> Now, tell me what you would think to figure out this word [pointing to a word in a book a student has selected to read].

Helping less accomplished readers talk about their metacognitions often requires repeated prompts, but eliciting such explanations helps them learn to do so on their own, as illustrated in this exchange:

Teacher: Jimmy, can you tell us one of the things we talked about that can help us figure out a new word?

Jimmy: First letter.

Teacher: I'm not sure I understand what you mean. Could you give me some more words that will help us understand how the first letter can help figure out a new word in reading?

Jimmy: Look at the first letter.

Teacher: How would looking at the first letter help us figure out a new word in reading?

Jimmy: Look at the first letter and think about what sound it makes. Then try to think of a word that starts with that letter and makes sense in the sentence.

Teacher: Good Jimmy! Now you've given enough words for us to understand how the first letter helps us figure out a new word. (Feitler & Hellekson, 1993, p. 7)

LESSON 2: RECIPROCAL TEACHING. **Reciprocal teaching** is a procedure that assists readers to integrate the strategies of asking questions, summarizing, clarifying, and predicting (Palinscar & Brown, 1989). In this activity, students become the teachers and report their metacognitive thinking to peers. As each student completes a turn at teaching, he or she selects the next teacher by asking, "Who will be the next teacher?" Through this control, readers' self-esteem is built as they choose to help others and share when they are ready.

The reciprocal teaching activity begins when you (and subsequently each student who becomes the teacher) initiate a discussion about the next section of a text to be read and ask questions about its content. Then the group discusses the questions, raises additional ones, and resolves disagreements and misunderstandings by reading the text. Next, the discussion leader summarizes to identify the gist of what was read, clarifies words and ideas that others misunderstood, and predicts upcoming content. After others also make and share their predictions, the leader asks for a new leader to volunteer for the next section of text, as illustrated in this scenario:

Mrs. Mackey: (reading the following text) "The pipefish changes its color and movements to blend with its surroundings. For example, a pipefish that lives among green plants changes its color to a shade of green to match the plants."

Clare: (the "student teacher" who is leading the discussion) "One question that I had about this paragraph is: What is special about the way that the pipefish looks?"

Keith: (clarifying) "Do you mean the way that it is green?"

Andy: (elaborating) "It's not just that it's green; it's that it's the same color as the plants around it, all around it."

Clare: (resuming) "Yes. That's it. My summary is that this part tells how the pipefish looks and that it looks like what is around it. My prediction is that the next part will be about its enemies and how it protects itself and who these enemies are."

Monty: (adding to Clare's summary) "They also talked about how the pipefish moves . . ."

Keith: (rejoining) "It sways back and forth."

Andy: (adding) "Along with the other plants . . ."

Mrs. Mackey: "OK! Let's see if Clare's predictions come true. Who will be the teacher?" (Hiebert, 1991, p. 125)

Reciprocal teaching models competent use of comprehension and metacognition. It also supports students' efforts to explain text and their thinking; pushes for deeper understanding, reflection, and metacognition; continuously and consciously releases more control of comprehension to students; and increases students' abilities to lead group discussions.

LESSON 3: "YOU BE THE COUNSELOR." This lesson builds metacognition because it enables readers to walk in another person's shoes and to think as that person likely thought. The purpose of "You Be the Counselor" is to assist readers to understand the reasons behind literary characters' actions; to separate facts from opinions, assumptions, and beliefs; and to question these facts, assumptions, and beliefs as they read.

In this activity you ask students to assume that a main character in a fictional book came to them for advice, or that they were called to analyze the causes behind an event in a nonfiction reading. "You Be the Counselor" assists students in connecting their thoughts to the story in several ways. First, students must place themselves in the story and identify with the main character's emotions, motives, and actions. Second, students must discern how their opinions, emotions, and responses to the events in the story will likely differ from the character's. Last, most will imagine a future event upon which their advice and projections rest. The more frequently students practice these metacognitions through repeated participation in this activity, the more rapidly these strategies became a part of their automatic comprehension processes.

LESSON 4: SELF-MONITORING AND EXPLAINING METACOGNITIONS. This activity begins by introducing the following symbols:

✓ = I know that I understand this paragraph

? = I know that I don't understand this paragraph

As students read, have them write the appropriate symbol beside each paragraph in the margin of pages xeroxed from a book (or on an acetate that covers a page in a book) to indicate how well they comprehend it. After students mark about 10 paragraphs, ask them to meet with you for a discovery discussion to analyze what the paragraphs they misunderstood had in common. If students have difficulty describing their reasoning, you can also ask the following questions to increase their metacognitive awareness:

- Are any sentences in this paragraph more important than others?
- What could you do to better comprehend this paragraph?
- Can you tell what the author thought was important in this paragraph by tilling the text of the paragraph that comes before it and the one that follows it?

As you interact with readers on a one-to-one basis (during this and subsequent activities and as they read silently and orally), the following responses can assist them to initiate metacognitive thinking:

- "Describe an example so I can understand what you are thinking."
- "Yesterday you had a lot of difficulty understanding _____ as you read. Today you seem to have had far less difficulty. What did you think as you read today that helped you?"
- "I noticed that you skipped the word _____ and kept right on reading. Remember when you used to just come to a word and stop reading until I told you that word? What does that tell you about your reading ability now? What are you thinking when you keep on reading?"
- "Why do you think that I gave you the prompt that I did just now? What prompt can you give yourself in similar situations when you're reading and I'm not here with you?"
- "Did you ask yourself why you are reading this book before you began reading? Why did you [or did you not] ask yourself that question?"

- "What were you thinking while you read and before you began to read this book that helped you understand it so well?"
- "While you read, what did you do if you didn't understand a paragraph?"
- "What were you thinking when you came to this word you didn't know?"
- "After you read, what did you do to help you remember what you read?"

The cognitive and metacognitive strategies presented in this chapter can move students to Stages 4 and 5 of comprehension ability. For the students to become internally guided readers, however, they must till the text before they read, make meaning while they read, and reflect after they read. They must also employ these strategies interactively, and the next section of this chapter describes how you can assist them to do so.

Using Comprehension Strategies Interactively

Internally guided comprehenders are more flexible in their strategy use than less accomplished readers and are more likely to activate a variety of strategies when texts become difficult (Kletzien, 1991). The following activities have been proved to increase these readers' abilities to use comprehension strategies interactively. These students also prosper by repeating these activities frequently.

LESSON 1: REVERSE THINK ALOUDS. Throughout this book think alouds have been proposed frequently as valuable teaching tools. In this activity think alouds are reversed: Instead of your *telling* what you are thinking, students *ask* you what you are thinking at a particular time while you and they read. To begin this lesson, you can sit beside a struggling reader and explain that the student is to read along silently while you read orally. The student is to stop you during the reading to ask questions about how you decoded a particular word or to ask what you are thinking to comprehend, clarify an author's point, or summarize. Such questions will illuminate strategy use at the exact point that the individual reader needs to know which strategy to use and will enable you to diagnose what strategies are important to this reader.

If some readers have not asked you a question by the end of the first page, stop reading and rephrase the instructions, emphasizing that at any word or point in the reading, if they do not understand something, they can ask you what you are thinking (e.g., which strategy or type of metacognitive thinking is assisting you and how you knew to use it). Then begin to read again and have them stop you.

LESSON 2: TWO-MINUTE OR TEN-MINUTE WRITES. Ms. Marjorie Downing, a primary teacher at Benchmark School in Media, Pennsylvania, created this integrative lesson. It starts by asking students to write for 2 or 10 minutes after hearing a story read aloud by you or a peer. You will also write—and everyone explains what was most important about the book, the most important thoughts gained from it, or what the concluding episode is likely to be and which strategies were used to make this prediction.

When writings are complete, you ask students to read their work to others. You can read your writing about halfway through the sharing experience. When all who wish to read their writings have shared, discuss differences between the thoughts, comprehensions, and metacognitions used by the group.

If students do not see the differences between two or more interpretations, you can identify a couple of salient differences and demonstrate how a detail in the reading possibly held more meaning for one person than another, which could have led to different personal responses. Similarly, if readers do not write their most important thoughts or prediction, ask if they would like to hear a think aloud about how you make decisions about what is most important to you as you read.

Books that have proven highly successful for 10-minute writes include *Frederick* by Leo Lionni; *Leo the Late Bloomer* by Leo Lionni; *Alexander and the Terrible, Horrible, No Good, Very Bad Day* by Judith Viorst; *The Lazy Bear* by Brian Wildsmith; *Sylvester and the Magic Pebble* by William Steig; and *The Giving Tree* by Shel Silverstein.

Figure 10.6 is an adaptation of the 10-minute write lesson. Ms. Carey, a fourth grade teacher, and Ashlee, a fourth grade reader, read the book *The Lazy Bear* together and did the first 10-minute write to report how they predicted the story would end. After sharing their writings and then reading the author's ending, Ms. Carey and Ashlee also wrote what they learned from performing the activity. As you will notice in the second writing, Ashlee was unable to express what she learned. This is an indication that she needs additional instruction to improve her metacognition.

LESSON 3: TAPE-RECORDING IMPROVEMENTS. This activity can be used as assessment before and after the activities in this chapter have been taught. It consists of asking students to select books they would like to read and tape-recording their readings for one minute. At the end of this time, students can tell what they thought about their reading and the content of the book. Tape-record these answers immediately following the reading so that levels of each student's comprehension, understanding, and strategic reading are documented. Next, you can ask each student to return to his or her seat and count the total number of words he or she read as well as the average number of words per page in the book that the student selected. Then students write this information (along with the counter numbers on the tape in which their reading can be found) in their portfolio or on a record form to be kept until the end of the year. Last, before calling the next student to perform the tape-recorded reading, fast-forward the tape recorder for three times the number of counter spaces each students' reading and answers used. In this way, you have blank spaces between each student's reading so that posttest readings can be recorded on the tape immediately following the student's first reading.

After you have taught all the lessons in this chapter, you can reimplement this lesson, allowing students to choose any book they would like to read. Ask them to describe what they were thinking as they read and what they think about the content of the book, just as before. When each student has finished, ask him or her to again count total number of words read as well as the average number of words per page of the book selected. Then, you and the student assess growths in readability of books chosen, in oral readings, and in answers given. If the student desires, he or she can hear

In the first 10-minute write, Ms. Carey, a fourth grade teacher, and Ashlee predicted how the story would end. In the second part of the lesson, they wrote what they learned from the activity.

1st Ten-Minute Write

I think that the bear is going to jump in the pile of leaves. He will probably go home with some leaves on his body and his mom will find out. He might get in trouble, but I don't know. I know this because the author choose to use the words "paused to think about the fun that he could have in the leaves."

2nd 10-min Write

Everybody can interpret the story differently. A story can have many different meanings. This is important to me because it makes me feel like I can comprehend and think about the exact points that I think are most important. The ending to this story surprised me, and I would have never guessed what the author said. This may mean that I may have missed some subtle meanings or inferences the author wanted me to understand.

Ashlee

He is going to have something in his hand's. His mom will say that is neet. Were did you get that it will be a cup. The will be rich to. The will tall everybody. The will say neat. Someone wills till it.

2nd 10-min Write

What we remibed and we read good We read good to it was long and we read it.

FIGURE 10.6 Two-Part 10-Minute Write Lesson

both the pretest and posttest recordings. Some readers will prefer to listen only to the posttest.

When these oral readings have been reviewed, you and students can use the following assessment tools as additional evaluations of their comprehension achievement.

Diagnosing and Assessing Comprehension

The assessments in Tables 10.4, 10.5, 10.6, and 10.7 engage struggling readers in their own evaluation of their comprehension strengths and weaknesses. They also enable these students to judge how well they are using cognitive and metacognitive strategies interactively.

TABLE 10.4 Assessing Cognitive and Metacognitive Strategies during Reading

Student _____ Grade _____

Examiner _____

Directions: Observe students' oral reading four times a year. Ask the student to perform a think aloud about how he/she prepares to read to assess 1 and 2 below. Stop the oral reading and ask for a prediction to assess 3. Ask for a sequence of details and a main idea from the text to assess 4 and 5. Stop the reading at the next to the last page of a chapter's or book's end, and ask the student to describe what they are picturing mentally. At the end of the reading, ask students to summarize what was read to assess 7.

	Obs. I Date ____	Obs. II Date ____	Obs. III Date ____	Obs. IV Date ____
DA = Developing Adequately NI = Needs Improvement				
1. Links prior knowledge before reading	_____	_____	_____	_____
2. Develops purpose for reading	_____	_____	_____	_____
3. Uses titles and/or illustrations to predict content/events	_____	_____	_____	_____
4. Sequences	_____	_____	_____	_____
5. Locates main ideas	_____	_____	_____	_____
6. Creates visual images	_____	_____	_____	_____
7. Summarizes	_____	_____	_____	_____

Summary _____

_____

_____

_____

_____

Recommendations _____

_____

_____

_____

_____

TABLE 10.5 Metacognitive Rating Sheet

Directions: Explain each item to students. Give an example with think alouds from a text before students are to complete *The Metacognitive Rating Sheet* alone.

Reading Strategies

Name: Sasana   Date: 10-19-2002

Reading selection: *The Cat's Purr*

Before Reading

I used pictures, titles, and headings to help me think about what
I'm going to read. Specifically, I _____.

I think about what I already know about this content.
I thought about _____.

I set my own purpose, and it is _____.

During Reading

I thought about what might come next, and _____.

I revised my predictions and/or make new
ones, such as when _____.

I imaged pictures of what I'm reading, such as when _____.

I looked for author clues to what will happen/be
coming. For example, _____.

I picked out important ideas by _____.

I skipped hard words/parts _____ times.

I noticed when something doesn't make sense,
such as when _____.

I went back and reread on pages _____.

I asked myself questions on pages _____.

After Reading

I asked myself what I understood, and the
theme was _____.

I compared what I read with what I predicted,
and I discovered that _____.

I discussed with others or wrote about what I most
valued in this text. What I valued was _____.

TABLE 10.6 Metacomprehension Strategy Index

Directions: When presenting this self-assessment to a student, introduce it as follows: "Think about what kinds of things you can do to help you understand a story better before you read it. Read each of the lists of four statements and decide which one of them would help *you* the most. *There are no wrong answers.* It is just what *you* think would help the most. Circle the letter of the statement you choose."

In each set of four, choose the one statement that tells a good thing to do to help you understand a story better.

1. Before I begin reading, it's a good idea to:
   A. See how many pages are in the story.
   B. Look up all of the big words in the dictionary.
   C. Make some guesses about what I think will happen in the story.
   D. Think about what has happened so far in the story.
2. Before I begin reading, it's a good idea to:
   A. Look at the pictures to see what the story is about.
   B. Decide how long it will take me to read the story.
   C. Sound the words I don't know.
   D. Check to see if the story is making sense.
3. Before I begin reading, it's a good idea to:
   A. Ask someone to read the story to me.
   B. Read the title to see what the story is about.
   C. Check to see if most of the words have long or short vowels in them.
   D. Check to see if the pictures are in order and make sense.
4. Before I begin reading, it's a good idea to:
   A. Check to see that no pages are missing.
   B. Make a list of the words I'm not sure about.
   C. Use the title and pictures to help me make guesses about what will happen in the story.
   D. Read the last sentence so I will know how the story ends.
5. Before I begin reading, it's a good idea to:
   A. Retell all of the main points that happened so far.

   B. Ask myself questions that I would like to have answered in the story.
   C. Think about the meaning of the words that have more than one meaning.
   D. Look through the story to find all of the words with three or more syllables.
6. While I read, it's a good idea to:
   A. Decide on why I am going to read the story.
   B. Use the difficult words to help me make guesses about what will happen in the story.
   C. Reread some parts to see if I can figure out what is happening if things aren't making sense.
   D. Ask for help with the difficult words.
7. While I read, it's a good idea to:
   A. Check to see if I have read this story before.
   B. Use my questions and predictions as a reason for reading the story.
   C. Make sure I can pronounce all of the words before I start.
   D. Think of a better title for the story.
8. While I read, it's a good idea to:
   A. Think of what I already know about the things I see in the pictures.
   B. See how many pages are in the story.
   C. Choose the best part of the story to read again.
   D. Read the story aloud to someone.
9. After I read, it's a good idea to:
   A. Practice reading the story aloud.
   B. Retell all of the main points to make sure I can remember the story.
   C. Reread the names of the people in the story.
   D. Decide if I have enough time to read the story.

Note: Answers that demonstrate the most advanced and effective metacomprehension strategy use are (in order) c, a, b, c, b, c, b, a, and b.

Source: Adapted from C. Temple & J. Gillett (1996), "Metacomprehension Strategy Index Appendix A" in *Language and Literacy: A Lively Approach,* pp. 415–419. New York: HarperCollins. Copyright © 1996 by HarperCollins College Publishers. Reprinted by permission of Addison-Wesley Educational Publishers Inc.

TABLE 10.7 Comprehension Strategies Assessment Forms

These are two types of self-assessment forms that can be adapted in many ways by changing the strategies evaluated. They are to be used separately on different days to provide opportunities for students to express their abilities in their own words.

Name _____ Date _____

Book title _____

Comprehension Strategies

1. Underline all the strategies you used today to help yourself understand the book you are reading. Circle the strategy you used the most.
   - I thought about what I already knew.
   - I made predictions and read to find out if they came true.
   - I reread what I didn't understand.
   - I made pictures in my head.
   - I asked someone to explain what I didn't understand.

2. Give an example of how you used one of the strategies you underlined or circled.

   _____

   _____

   _____

- -

Name _____ Date _____

Book title _____

Comprehension Strategies

1. What strategies did you use today to help yourself understand the book you are reading?

   _____

   _____

2. Explain how one of the strategies you listed helped you understand something in the book.

   _____

   _____

   _____

Source: Adapted from L. Rhodes (1994), *Windows into Literacy: Assessing Learners K–8*, p. 102. Portsmouth, NH: Heinemann.

Chapter Summary

This chapter described five stages of comprehension ability and presented ways to assist weak comprehenders to overcome comprehension barriers. These methods include tilling the text before reading, making meaning during reading, and reflecting after reading—students should use these strategies interactively and with their own initiative.

Tilling the text prepares readers to comprehend fully the selection they are about to read. It involves attending to authors' writing styles, establishing a personal purpose for reading, overcoming word-calling, applying prior knowledge, and expanding content vocabulary. When readers engage in meaning-making while they read, they pay attention to story grammar, authorial patterns, and functions of various paragraph styles. They also apply comprehension strategies such as DRTA. Reflecting after reading encourages struggling readers to explain, summarize, infer, predict, interpret, and utilize imaging. Increasing metacognitive abilities is also a goal.

In the next chapter you will learn how to assist reluctant readers/writers to improve their writing abilities.

Key Terminology

The following vocabulary terms were introduced in this chapter. If you know a word's definition, place a check mark in the blank that precedes it. If you do not know its definition, take a few moments now to review it on the page number provided. This immediate rereading will increase your retention. If you learned six of these terms on a first reading, you have comprehended well. Congratulations.

_____ **tilling the text** (page 321)
_____ **word-calling** (page 323)
_____ **semantic maps** (page 326)
_____ **graphic organizers** (page 327)
_____ **story grammar** (page 329)

_____ **story frame** (page 329)
_____ **story map** (page 329)
_____ **metacognition** (page 344)
_____ **reciprocal teaching** (page 345)

Case Study

Making Professional Decisions

Marcus, age 8, was in the second grade when he was referred to the school reading specialist.

When the reading specialist interviewed Marcus's mother, his mother reported that his physical and developmental histories were normal. When Marcus was in preschool, both parents had spent much time with him and encouraged him to read. However, changes in the family situation in the past 2 years had limited the amount of time the parents

could devote to Marcus. His mother had gone to work, and his father had accepted a job in a different city and was able to get home only occasionally.

Marcus's teacher reported that he was popular in school but that he seemed to lack motivation for schoolwork. Because he rarely completed his assignments, he was having difficulty.

In the interview, Marcus said he disliked reading and thought it was too hard. He never read for pleasure and could not imagine why anyone would do so. His only area of interest was baseball. He said he was a good shortstop and said he followed professional baseball closely. He had memorized many facts and records and seemed to have a keen interest in the strategy behind the game.

The results of tests administered are presented below:

INFORMAL READING INVENTORY

Word Recognition List

Independent Level	Grade Primer
Instructional Level	Grade 1

Oral Reading Passages

Independent Level	Grade Primer
Instructional Level	Grade 1

Silent Reading Passages

Independent Level	Grade Primer
Instructional Level	Grade 1
Listening Level	Grade 3

His word recognition was perfect at primer level, but he exhibited severe problems with comprehension.

Marcus was asked to bring in his social studies textbook and show how he studied it. He began with the first page of the chapter and continued to laboriously read the rest of the chapter by making up stories abour the pictures. When questioned on the chapter, he remembered little of it and was unable to distinguish between important and unimportant information. When asked to reread a paragraph, he could not identify the main idea. He seemed to have little grasp of the concepts presented in the chapter.

Although Marcus cooperated with the reading specialist, he was unenthusiastic about the diagnosis.

Respond to the following questions, then check your responses against the Answer Key at the end of the book.

1. With which aspects of comprehension does Marcus need help?
2. What strategies would you use to help Marcus with his comprehension abilities? Would these focus on narrative or expository text?
3. How would you plan to help Marcus with his social studies course? Give suggestions for both the reading specialist and the content area teacher.
4. What strategies would you use to help Marcus with his comprehension of narrative text?

Thinking and Writing about What You Have Learned

1. Why is it important to teach readers to "till their texts," apply their prior knowledge, and use story structures to increase their comprehension?

2. Can you recall the cognitive and metacognitive strategies that advance readers' comprehension?

3. What types of instruction assist readers to use comprehension strategies interactively?

4. When your students are ready to experience harder books, what have you learned in this chapter that will enable them to do so with less difficulty?

5. Which of the assessments in this chapter do you want to include in your teaching repertoire, and why?

6. This chapter suggested activities that could also be used as pre and post assessments and could be used as evaluative work samples in students' portfolios. Which lessons

and assessments (in this chapter) do you want your students to include in their portfolios, and why?

7. Read the following assessment of Loretta's progress. Loretta was taught some of the activities in this chapter. What would be the next actions you would take if you were Loretta's teacher?

> Dear Dr. Block,
>
> Even though Loretta did not perform very well on our last day together, I did feel like I witnessed some improvement in her reading.
>
> Honestly, she was very sporadic and inconsistent, but I think she came away from our discovery discussion with a new awareness about print.
>
> Even though she may not do it all the time, Loretta knows it is important to be able to identify the who, what, why, when, where, and how of a story. She knows there is something wrong if she gets to a point in her reading and she's lost track of what's going on. She does not always know how to solve her problem, but she does know she needs to back up, reread, and slow down.
>
> I see this as a definite improvement because Loretta used to speed through her reading no matter what. She was just trying to tackle the words, not the meaning.
>
> At least now she knows there is more to reading than letter sounds. She knows her job is to make meaning out of each sentence. I am not saying she is capable of this, but at least the awareness is there.
>
> —Ms. Guitterez

When you have written your answer, check the Answer Key in the back of the book to compare it to the actions Ms. Guitterez took immediately after making this assessment.

c h a p t e r 11

Jin is working diligently to overcome his writing barriers. His teacher used the activities in this chapter to assist him.

Assisting Reluctant Writers

> "Tell me why writing is too hard," I persisted.
> "You have to think too much to write," [the third grade boy] responded. "You have to find all the words yourself. When you read—somebody's already done that for you so you don't have to think when you read."
>
> (Bean & Hamilton, 1992, p. 203)

■ Chapter Overview: Key Points

Writing is one of the most difficult academic subjects (Bereiter & Scardamalia, 1987; Harris & Graham, 1992). This is especially true for students who have difficulty in simultaneously negotiating the rules of English, generating ideas, organizing sentences, establishing purposes, and presenting a perspective that they value for which they intend a response (Applebee, Jenkins, & Mullis, 1990; Scardamalia & Bereiter, 1986; Scheid, 1991).

This chapter will present:

- Special Tier 1–4 supports for reluctant writers
- Special supports during prewriting and first-draft writing
- Special supports during the revising process
- Encouraging creativity in reluctant writers
- Diagnosing and assessing reluctant writers' needs

By the end of the chapter, you will have answers to the following questions:

1. What classroom supports increase the composition abilities of students who are struggling with writing?
2. What special supports are needed in first-draft writing to help students overcome writer's block?
3. What questions can reluctant writers ask themselves to help make their revising process more effective?
4. How can students' confidence be increased so that they can write significant ideas to real people for important purposes?
5. What types of feedback are most valuable to reluctant writers?
6. How can these writers' creativity be increased and measured?

Special Tier 1–4 Supports for Reluctant Writers

Instruction for reluctant writers must move beyond basic implementation of pre-scribed stages of prewriting, producing a first draft in 20 minutes, revising it with a peer, editing, and "publishing." Each student needs you to tailor your teaching to his or her individual needs by finding exactly what works and does not work for that individual. In this way you can avoid teaching "*the*" writing process, which is likely to have become as much of a standardized, senseless routine as diagramming sentences was for struggling writers before the 1970s. You will have succeeded when your students share many valuable ideas confidently and proficiently as writers.

Researchers have studied reluctant writers by comparing their compositions to those of normally developing writers. These studies demonstrate that struggling writers' products are as creative as those of their more accomplished peers—but are less polished, expansive, and coherent (Block, 2001; Harris & Graham, 1992; Kobrin et al., 1993). Studies also suggest that these writers do not know how to narrow their topics and that they tend to spend less time and do shallower thinking during the prewriting stage than better writers (Fitzgerald & Markham, 1987; Morocco & Neuman, 1986; Stotsky, 1989). Reluctant writers also have a tendency to "tell" knowledge that they hear or read rather than to express their own ideas (Englert & Raphael, 1988). Equally important, they need help with learning to do the following:

- Select more vivid, expressive verbs
- Remove redundancies
- Overcome spelling difficulties
- Translate the rhythm of spoken language to standard written English
- Reduce the tendency to be satisfied with first drafts (Block, 2000; Graves, 1995)
- Think of revision as more than just throwing a writing away
- Not give up when burdened by the mechanics of grammar, penmanship, story grammar, or spelling (Walvoord & Singor, 1984)

On a positive note, reluctant writers have shown that they can develop these competencies and can realize significant growth in written expression when special supports are present in their instructional program. These supports enable them to trust their own ideas, their classmates, and their teachers (Calkins, 1991). This trust will also increase their desire to reflect before, during, and after writing. If such trust isn't present, however, these writers tend to say, "What am I supposed to write?" instead of "Listen to what I think." Therefore, instruction to improve the expressive abilities of less accomplished writers begins with and depends on making it clear that they can describe what they know and feel and what they want to express to their audiences.

Providing this support means praising individual word choices and remembering that for struggling writers merely beginning a composition takes more structure and encouragement than for proficient writers, because less accomplished writers have difficulty committing to a topic. They also tend to make selections based on what they think you will view as important (Downing, 1995). The more you compliment their best words and sentences, the more they will dare to expose a part of themselves and risk evaluation. This confidence will come most rapidly when they write for at least 35 minutes 4 days a week (Graves, 1991).

The following subsections describe additional Tier 1–4 instructional actions that create a supportive classroom atmosphere.

Developing Their Voice

Most reluctant writers need continuous support to discover their own voices (Barger, 1991). A successful **writing voice** involves the ability to write with the quality, clarity of focus, originality, and articulation necessary to say what you want to communicate. This voice emerges as writers learn to communicate their exact message by integrating thoughts and emotions. Students will have established their voice when repetitions and stereotypical writing features—such as beginning each sentence with the word *I*—disappear (Graves, 1995; Quintero & Rummel, 1993).

The reason reluctant writers need your support to discover their voice is because without it most such writers will not freely experiment, think, feel, and play with language; nor will they use writing as a tool to establish order in their lives (Fine, 1995; Rief, 1994). Once confident that they have your positive response to their deeply felt ideas, most of these writers reduce their sense of inadequacy and vulnerability; they begin to share and not to demand attention; and they want to learn how to revise their ideas. No amount of money or materials can remove these writers' tendency to hide who they are—only you can do that. You do so by listening to their stories before they write them and by giving their literary characters voices when you read orally. In the process, you should not reward students for suspending their social and emotional selves or mistake a student's broken and self-protective spirit as one that is merely shy and cooperative.

You may notice that your struggling writers' first step in self-expression is to report mundane (safe) events in their lives. In one research study, however, after only 40 class periods of keeping daily journals, reluctant writers abandoned imitation and began to write what they truly thought and believed. When this shift in content occurs, writings may become shorter and more stilted. Knowing that this retrenchment actually represents a growth in writing ability enables you to provide positive feedback to writers at this stage in their development. This feedback, in turn, often enables them to share more in-depth thinking that is important to them (Peregory & Owen, 1993).

You can also support these writers by creating shared life experiences in class (e.g., by talking about significant problems in class discussions or reading books that elicit empathy and catharsis) so that these discussions can become memorable episodes students can report in their writings.

ALLOWING MORE TIME. As you help your students develop their writing voice, remember to be patient. Most less accomplished writers need more time than proficient writers to believe they can learn new writing strategies and to develop their compositions. Most also need extra time before they begin to think of themselves as writers; they need to establish a new self-image before they can value their ideas enough to communicate them. This is true because before they reach you they may have experienced many writing activities in which they failed. They may have learned that they should not expect too much of themselves as writers and probably felt that others did not either.

Through your continuous support, however, and with extended periods of time to write each day, a moment usually arises when negative responses to writing are broken, as illustrated by this example:

> Marcy cried silently every time the class [wrote]. She whispered "I can't" when asked what was wrong. . . . I stooped in front of her desk and . . . said:
>
> "Do you live alone?" I asked in a no-nonsense voice.
>
> "No."
>
> "Who lives with you?"
>
> "My mom."
>
> "Write it down." I said. Marcy wrote "Mom."
>
> "Anyone else?"
>
> "My cat." Marcy wrote "cat" without my direction.
>
> Then, she looked up and said, "I used to have a dad, but he died when I was a baby."
>
> "Oh, yeah?" I replied. Barely audibly, Marcy started telling the stories of her dad, stories she had been told over and over again about the father she didn't remember. I listened. A few moments later, she wrote about her dad and at the end of the workshop shared her story with the class. The tears stopped that day. Marcy confidently participated in *all* the class activities, especially writing [from that moment forward]. (Avery, 1993, p. 113)

Struggling writers need such responses to their writings, responses that are not sentimental or instructional, but sensitive and sincere.

Identifying Unique Communication Strengths

Reluctant writers need your help in identifying their unique communication strengths. For example, Karen, a seventh grade reluctant writer, organized her ideas well orally but not in written compositions. She also made good inferences. When her teacher pointed out these strengths, Karen began dictating her writing to a peer so she could use her oral organizational skills to prompt her insights and rehearse her ideas before she wrote.

Similarly, most writers need your assistance to learn what their strengths are and how they can devise new methods of using them to improve their writing.

Accepting Different Viewpoints

This support may be more difficult than it seems. When we invite students to write with passion about things they really understand and to which they have an emotional connection, we may read things we don't want to see.

It's important that you examine your beliefs and attitudes before the year begins. By communicating what you will accept in your classroom before students write their first thoughts, you will eliminate problems that may arise if a student submits a piece whose content you cannot tolerate. On the other hand, you should be tolerant of students' ideas even when they differ from yours. Mutual respect and acceptance will reduce feelings of rejection and will enhance writers' self-esteem.

Also, you communicate acceptance if you refrain from walking around, peeking over writers' shoulders as they work. Doing so only decreases their risk taking.

Providing Explanations

Your own explanations are an excellent classroom support. By modeling, demonstrating and explaining special strategies, you can expand these writers' abilities to do the following:

- To overcome writer's block
- To question themselves when revising
- To improve the quality of their first drafts
- To write significant ideas for important purposes
- To create more interesting openings and powerful sentences
- To improve their spelling abilities
- To employ correct grammar

The checklist in Table 11.1 provides a good reference for you to verify how well you are using the supports presented thus far in the chapter. Once these basic classroom supports are in operation, it is time to turn your attention to assisting struggling students to develop prewriting strategies.

TABLE 11.1 Checklist to Develop a Classroom Atmosphere That Supports Reluctant Writers

1. Do you have areas or centers for reluctant writers that promote literacy and are quiet?

   Do students begin to trust themselves?
   Do students trust classmates to respond?
   Do you respond favorably to what they write?
   Do students trust you to give them time?
   Have you taught new writing strategies?

2. Does your classroom promote a writing attitude in which individual literary voices can emerge?

   Do you accept students' ideas?
   Do students see you write?
   Do students know they are partners in learning?
   Do you help students identify authentic reasons for writing?
   Do you notice and praise their writing?

3. Do you read aloud from a wide variety of genre that serve as writing models?

4. Are reluctant writers increasing confidence and positive self-images as writers?

   Is there less stereotypical writing?
   Are there fewer comments like "I can't" or "I don't know how"?

continued

TABLE 11.1 *Continued*

5. Have you identified each writer's unique strengths?

6. Are you prepared to accept what students write when their viewpoints differ from yours?

7. Do you provide uninterrupted writing time:

   Daily? _____

   If not, how often? _____

   35–40 minutes? _____

   If not, how long? _____

Areas where I need to improve:

_____

_____

_____

_____

Special Supports during the Prewriting Stage

Reluctant writers experience writer's block more often than their more proficient peers. The most frequent causes of their difficulty are beginning a writing task before their ideas are organized and attempting to write about topics that they do not know well. Organization evolves more easily when students base their writing on personal experiences, or when they read a book (such as an *All About* book) on the topic they have chosen and then use that author's organizational method as a guide. Facts and ideas become more specific (Block, 2001; Linden & Whimbey, 1990).

In addition, some students profit from using a word processor or tape recorder (Meltzer & Solomon, 1988). As a matter of fact, in a survey completed by IBM, 82 percent of teachers reported that word processors improved motivation, creative thinking, and self-confidence in reluctant writers. Bilingual students also benefited because they could compose their thoughts in their native language and then could type the English translation more rapidly than if using penmanship. Moreover, some such writers prefer drawing a picture to using word processing as a means of rehearsing and organizing their ideas before they write (Gaskins, Gaskins, & Gaskins, 1991).

Other special strategies that assist these writers to spend more time planning what they will write and to overcome writer's block follow. Many teachers list these strategies on a chart in the classroom so they can be consulted whenever a student experiences writer's block.

1. *Make a list.* Designate the front pages of students' journals as topic pages. Whenever an original idea comes to mind or if students encounter something they feel deeply about, they can jot this topic on the front page of their journal. Then, when they wish to write or are asked to write but cannot think of a topic, they can refer to this list.

2. *Create a semantic map.* Whenever struggling writers experience writer's block they can create a semantic map to depict the depth of their feelings and ideas about a topic. Because the map connects their ideas subordinately, categorically, and/or graphically, it organizes their thoughts so they can begin an organized composition.

3. *Revise previous writings.* By rereading a prior work, writers see how their style and the depth of their ideas have developed, as well as how they have improved their ability to refine works for a specific audience. If reluctant writers know they can revise former works on days when they have less creativity and interest in composing a new message, their writing improves more rapidly.

4. *Do an unfocused or focused freewrite.* **Unfocused freewriting** occurs when students write, rambling from topic to topic for 5 to 10 minutes, until they find an intriguing idea. Similarly, **focused freewriting** develops and expands a single idea by writing in a stream of consciousness about that idea.

5. *Read what you have so far to a peer.* When struggling writers pause to read aloud to a classmate, their ideas appear to emerge more rapidly.

6. *Create and revisit a chart of starter sentences.* Early in the year, ask students to create a chart of self-generated starter sentences that can be used over and over again to **jump-start** their thinking. Whenever they face writer's block, they are to write one of these sentences on their paper—and by finishing it, they will have begun to write, which can lead them to an original idea. Post this chart in a prominent place for students to consult as they write. Starter sentences (and some starter activities) that other writers have made into charts for their classmates include these:

"I really don't know what I want to write next because . . ."

"I remember a time in my life when . . ."

"I know a person who acted like this, and if [my main character] were just like him/her, he/she would . . ."

Draw until you think of something to write.

Talk with a friend for no more than 5 minutes to discuss your idea for writing.

7. *Jot down the event that first triggered your thinking.* Teach these writers to begin descriptive writings by jotting down the scene, incident, or detail that first triggered their thinking. Explain to students that this initial thinking will likely be very vivid and thus may open the way to deeper meanings for their entire composition. Also, this description can be later moved to a specific section in the writing. As Calkins (1991) explains, the reason to put the most specific detailed experience first is that "by lingering long enough [with it] to capture the vivid, sensory particulars of a scene or an experience . . . [struggling writers] begin to know the fullness of the experience for [themselves] and make [their] own new meaning from it" (p. 279).

8. *Have a special section of the writing notebook in which students record sentences from children's literature that made them laugh, moved them to think, or convinced them.* These sentences help less accomplished writers identify specifics about style, tone, and clarity of writing. Ask students to identify why they like certain sentences. How did the author create this suspense? How did he make them laugh? Then ask them to write what they can do to include that element in their own writing. For example, one writer, Joseph, read the following excerpt from Beverly Cleary's *Dear Mr. Henshaw* and broke into laughter:

> Mrs. Badger said, "Why don't we all go help ourselves to lunch at the salad bar?"
> What a mess! Some people didn't understand about salad bars, but Mrs. Badger led the way and we helped ourselves to lettuce and bean salad and potato salad and all the usual stuff they lay out on salad bars. A few of the younger kids were too short to reach anything but the bowls on the first row. . . . When we carried our plates back to our table, people at other tables ducked and dodged as if they expected us to dump our lunches on their heads. All one boy had on his plate was a piece of lettuce and a slice of tomato because he thought he was going to get to go back for roast beef and fried chicken. We had to straighten him out and explain that all we got was salad. (Cleary, 1983, pp. 116–117)

When Joseph and his teacher talked about what Beverly Cleary had done to make this paragraph so funny, Joseph discovered that by picturing a funny event in his mind and writing details vividly, he too could create humorous works.

9. *Have special places in the room for writing.* Students and you should designate several areas in your classroom where they can go (if they wish) when they want to write. Through this choice, these writers feel more in charge, have a greater sense of solitude, and can move more rapidly into the still and concentrated state of reflection that is necessary to begin their writing (Calkins, 1991).

Always bear in mind that reluctant writers have significantly greater difficulty beginning to write than do proficient writers and need special strategies during the prewriting stage. You do not provide the support these writers need simply by introducing writing periods with statements such as "Take five minutes to jot down your ideas for someone else in our class to read" or "Spelling won't count" or "Just put down anything and no one will read it if you don't want." Nor does it help if you are always trying to motivate them with pep talks while they write, walking around the room reading over their shoulders, interrupting them, or commenting on sections that aren't complete. During this time you should be working on writing too—so you can model for students how you work (and sometimes struggle) and demonstrate that you value writing, too. In doing so, you allow these writers time to discover something thrilling that they want to write about with the help of the nine strategies enumerated above. With these supports in place, most struggling writers will begin to reach for an exact word and will feel pleasantly surprised by what emerges on their pages as they relate new ideas to others.

Special Supports during First-Draft Writing

This section of the chapter will describe seven strategies that provide support for reluctant writers during the first-draft stage of the writing process. Unfortunately, in most of today's pull-out programs, these strategies are not used, and students receive only limited time to read literature and to write and refine their compositions (Allington, 1994; Applebee, 1993). To combat this trend, you can ask struggling writers to carry their first drafts to in-class small group meetings with you or to resource teachers. There students can receive instruction in the seven strategies, which can significantly improve the power of their writing: (1) dictating their ideas; (2) writing their own "Choose Your Own Adventure" book; (3) using dialogue journals; (4) storytelling; (5) creating personalized bookmarks to cue their thinking; (6) writing for authentic reasons; and (7) practicing tricks of the trade.

Dictating

Kindergarten teachers have long known the power of allowing young children to dictate their thoughts. This practice instills a joy for reading and writing. And research has demonstrated that older writers, too, can profit from dictating their stories. When a student is stumped at a point during the writing of a first draft, you can assist by asking the student to tell you what he or she wants to say and then writing that section for the student. In this activity you and the student become partners. You write the words, examples, and goals; the student provides ideas, insights, and the passion from which the power of the writing springs (Cooper, 1993).

Each dictation should take from 3 to 12 minutes, so these writers' thinking about their work moves forward rapidly. After this period, ask students to either continue writing or reread and revise the ideas you wrote. You can also set aside 12 minutes three times a week, on a regularly scheduled basis, to do subsequent dictations until individual students feel comfortable that they can write their own thoughts independently.

If you have performed dictations for two students on the same day, they can read their dictations to each other on the next day and revise their pieces together. Through this sharing, struggling writers quickly expand their repertoires by borrowing writing conventions from each other.

Writing a "Choose Your Own Adventure" Book

Reluctant writers can learn how to develop fuller plots by writing their own "Choose Your Own Adventure" story, alone or with others. As an example, show students the flowchart in Figure 11.1. To introduce this chart, ask students to generate and list qualities common to the "Choose Your Own Adventure" books that they have read. Explain the flowchart by saying that each box represents one page and one episode in their "Choose Your Own Adventure" story. During the next few days, have students pair to each page and assemble them into a book. Remind them to end each page (except for the endings) by offering readers two directions in which the story may proceed. Then writers should tell readers which page to turn to for the option they select.

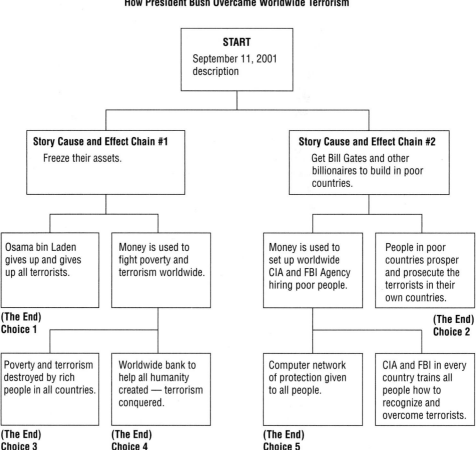

Title:
How President Bush Overcame Worldwide Terrorism

FIGURE 11.1 Flowchart for a "Choose Your Own Adventure" Book

To teach students to recognize multiple causes and effects, have them write a series of episodes with alternative outcomes as in the "Choose Your Own Adventure" books. A flowchart can serve as an outline, as shown in this example created by fifth graders Chad and Taylor.

Source: Designed by Rachel Escamilla, administrative assistant at Texas Christian University, Fort Worth, TX.

Gradually introduce other genre writing in this same manner, beginning with fairy tales ("Once upon a time" stories), autobiographies, biographies, informational report writing, fiction, and then poetry.

Using Dialogue Journals or Scribble/Doodle Boards

Another way to improve students' first-draft writing is to use dialogue journals. A **dialogue journal** is a journal in which a writer expresses an idea to you or a peer; then the next entry in that student's journal is your (or the peer's) response to that idea. The third entry will be the writer's new idea, and the cycle continues. Such journals make a bridge from oral speech to written communication, because journaling does not depend on complex story structures to produce successful written communications (Staton, 1982). Dialogue journals also enable students to build a more empowered conception of themselves as writers because they are communicating and being understood by others regularly. Box 11.1 describes scribble boards, which assist in the same manner.

However, such growth will not naturally unfold for some until you provide external prompts (Anderson, 1992/1993). You can stimulate the thinking process by writing three stimuli (such as those that follow) on the board each day (Ardizzone, 1992). On each subsequent day you can eliminate one and add another so that students have the opportunity to respond to each stimulus for 3 successive days. Some example stimuli are these:

Make an entry that describes or depicts pictorially a possession you own or a value you treasure.

Recall an event so important to you that it helped to shape who you are today.

Record information you learned recently that is important to you.

Write a letter to a specific person and give the letter to that person sometime today.

Pretend you are someone else and tell what you would do if you were that person and why.

Share a personal thought or feeling you had recently.

Mimic a section of a book or poem you read recently that you particularly enjoyed.

Retell a story from your family's life, from your experiences, or from a reading about which you want someone else's opinion.

Share an experience you had that was very similar to something you read recently that describes a quality of human behavior.

Play with language to create a funny rhyme, riddle, or phrase that you've never heard before, and ask someone else to add another line to it.

Complete the sentence, "I wonder . . ."

Complete the sentence, "What puzzles me is . . ."

Answer the question, "What would happen if . . ."

Reread and analyze your writings to date: Describe how you write and why you write as you do.

Record information about your emotions—such as what types of events make you cry (e.g., when someone works hard and wins, when you see someone being kind, when you see something beautiful).

11.1   READING SPECIALISTS

Instructional Intervention for Reluctant Writers

SCRIBBLE/DOODLE BOARD ACTIVITY

This activity helps students learn to prewrite and fosters the creation of richer first drafts.

- Place a sheet of large poster paper in front of each group of students.
- As a story is being read to them, have the students draw or write anything that they feel or think. This will allow struggling writers to express their opinions about the story without being embarrassed or feeling that their ideas are incorrect or stupid.
- Express to the students that there is no right or wrong to this activity.
- The scribble/doodle board gives reluctant writers the chance to express their ideas in drawings or scribbled notes rather than in formal prose.
- Have students share what they drew and why with their group.
- Then have each group share with the whole class.
- Hang the paper up in the class so students can add to it when they feel the need to.

Step 1:

Step 2:

As a class, share the ideas.

Step 3:

Hang the poster paper scribble boards on the walls.

The students can add to them when they think of new ideas.

Source: Adapted from activity created by Summer Sides, reading specialist, Fort Worth, TX. Used by permission.

Storytelling

The fourth support strategy for the first-draft stage is to allow reluctant writers to tell their stories orally before they begin to write. The interest displayed by their audience increases students' confidence that they can also write significant ideas for important purposes.

This activity is important to such writers because they have many feelings and insights that they may not have had the opportunity to examine. Through telling their thoughts they come to appreciate their own value in helping others, and they establish more reasons to write. For example, if a situation arises in class or school to which a struggling writer responds with uncommon wisdom and insight, ask the student to write down what he or she said.

Creating Personalized Bookmarks

Often, reluctant writers feel very deeply about issues but have difficulty expressing how they feel. You can assist by asking them to make the bookmark in Figure 11.2. This bookmark can be personalized in many ways, with individual words or phrases that the writer wants to use to express ideas and feelings. Each consecutive use of this strategy can challenge students to add new ideas to each box.

Writing for Authentic Reasons

Optimally, you can nurture struggling writers through several revisions until they judge a work to be polished enough to submit for publication. Often city newspapers have student writing sections or may publish student works in the Letters to the Editor section. Also, you can suggest that students write letters to the publication sources listed at the

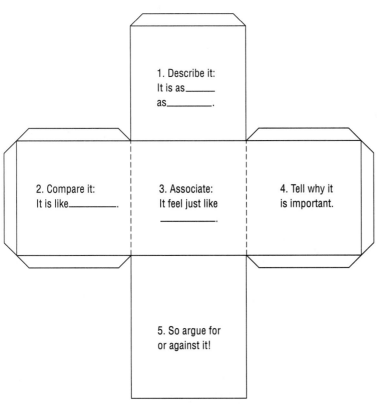

FIGURE 11.2
Bookmark That Helps Writers Express Their Ideas More Specifically

A few sample strategies are shown here; new strategies from this chapter can be added or substituted after they are taught.

1. Describe it:
It is as_____
as_____.

2. Compare it:
It is like_____.

3. Associate:
It feel just like
_____.

4. Tell why it is important.

5. So argue for or against it!

Fold toward center at broken lines.

end of the chapter, which also publish students' work. In addition, you can ask them to write letters to community agencies (selected from published compilations of sources of free and inexpensive material books that you bring to class) to obtain resources for topics under study.

Your reluctant writers can become scribes for full-class communications. For example, whenever you would normally write a letter on behalf of the class, ask a less accomplished writer to write it, and then you cosign. To illustrate, your reluctant writers could write to the Reading Is Fundamental (RIF) program, which can provide children's literature for them and their classmates to read at home. Instead of writing the letter yourself, ask a pair of students to write to this address:

Reading Is Fundamental
2500 L'Enfant Plaza
Smithsonian Institute
Washington, DC 20560

Similarly, list the names of all class members on a sheet of paper. Then ask struggling writers to become record keepers and assume the responsibility of noting what each student is to do the next day during writers' workshop (e.g., Donna will be in the revising center, Michael will complete his pictures, etc.). This record will be used daily, and the students can see that their writing is valuable each day.

A principle you may wish to adopt is that during each grading period you will ensure that struggling writers have had at least one writing experience in which they express their ideas to people outside of the classroom. These writers also profit by bringing their outside writing experiences into the classroom. For example, middle school students asked me if they could learn to complete job applications. They wanted to have summer jobs when they turned 16. They collected real job applications and asked me to demonstrate how to write in limited spaces so as to make their writing clear and convincing. Box 11.2 illustrates how reading specialists can create short paragraph exercises in an authentic way: Reluctant writers can write one-sheet newspapers as shown in the example.

Practicing Tricks of the Trade

The last special support for first-draft writing involves helping reluctant writers to overcome individual weaknesses by demonstrating tools that professional writers use. One of the most distinguishing differences between reluctant and proficient writers is that the former will not ask for help even when they do not understand something (Block, 2001). Also, because they often write more slowly than peers and it takes them so long to express themselves, they complain about writing in the hope that they will have to do only the minimum. Such complaints should become a first indicator that a student has the desire to write but needs special tools before he or she can become proficient.

Depending on the needs of individual writers, you can teach these tricks of the writing trade through direct or indirect means. Indirect instruction involves working through discovery discussions, asking: "What do you want me to teach you so you can write what is important to you?" You can also pair a writer with a more accomplished peer. When students work together on authentic writing projects (as opposed to tasks

Strategy to Assist Reluctant Writers

UNUSUAL UNBELIEVABLE UNREAL

April 1998	Literature at its best	Free

Tailor Kills Seven at a Blow
The Brave Little Tailor

Readers can meet new friends both real and imaginary within the section **Unbelievable Characters**. Titles include: Lou Gehrig: The Luckiest Man, The Most Beautiful Roof in the World: Exploring the Rainforest Canopy, Willy's Silly Grandma, The Ghost on Saturday Night, Dancing With Great Aunt Cornelia, The On-Line Spaceman and Other Cases, The Brave Little Tailor, and Happily Ever After.

Girl Makes Flying School Bus
Junk Pile

Characters found in the section **Coping With Adversity** struggle with adverse situations requiring unusual talents or unbelievable experiences. Titles include: Junk Pile, Breath of the Dragon, Travels with Rainie Marie, Moving Mama to Town, Spaceman, and The Heart is Big Enough.

Horse Helps Man Become Tsar of Russia
The Little Humpbacked Horse

The fantasy of fairy tales and traditional folklore is appealing for its invitation for readers to transcend reality and experience **Unreal Tales From Real Places**. Titles include: The King of Ireland's Son, The Cricket's Cage, The Gold at the End of the Rainbow, Little Folk: Stories From Around the World, and The Little Humpbacked Horse.

Fish & Frogs Fall from Sky
Strange Mysteries From Around the World

What may seem unreal to many might actually be a mysterious natural phenomenon. Titles in the **Unreal Phenomena** section include: Strange Mysteries From Around the World, The Moon Book, Batwings and the Curtain of Night, A Drop of Water, Eye of the Storm: Chasing Storms With Warren Faidley, Flood, and Disappearing Lake: Nature's Magic in Denali National Park.

INSIDE
Unbelievable Characters
Coping With Adversity
Incredible Accomplishments
Unreal Tales From Real Places
Unusual Plants and Animals
Unreal Phenonmena
Transformations
Too Good to Miss

Healthy Looking Girl Can't Get Out of Bed
Westminster West

The **Transformation** section has a trio of fascinating times and places where mysterious changes occurred. Titles include: Westminster West, The Orphan of Ellis Island, and Blue Lightning.

Desert Trees From Sprouting Twig
The Never-Ending Greenness

Incredible Accomplishments of characters real and fictitious, contemporary and historical are highlighted in this section's books. Titles include: If Sarah Will Take Me, The Neptune Fountain: The Apprenticeship of a Renaissance Sculptor, The Never-Ending Greenness, A Distant Enemy, Hell Fighters: African American Soldiers in World War I, You Must Remember This, Spike Lee: By Any Means Necessary, Danger Along the Ohio, Mississippi Mud: Three Prairie Journals, and Journey to Nowhere.

Toothless Whale
Big Blue Whale

Books in this section are sources of information about **Unusual Plants and Animals**. Titles include: Katya's Book of Mushrooms, Chameleons on Location, Komodo Dragon on Location, Animals You Never Even Heard Of, Big Blue Whale, and An Extraordinary Life: The Story of a Monarch Butterfly.

Mysterious Footprints Found on Shore After Fatal Shipwreck
Ghost Canoe

Some books are just **Too Good to Miss**. Such is the case for the last section. Titles in this section include: Seedfolks and Ghost Canoe.

Special thanks to W. Quinn White, Franklin Elementary School, Van Wert, Ohio, USA, for creating this graphic.

A one-page newspaper gives reluctant writers an authentic purpose for composing brief snippets and single-paragraph items.

Source: From E. B. Freeman, B. A. Lehman, & P. L. Scharer (1998, April), "Children's Books: Unusual! Unbelievable! Unreal!," *The Reading Teacher,* 51(7), pp. 588–597. Used by permission.

without real-world applications), reluctant writers tend to ask their partner many questions about writing (such as "How can I write _____?" or "How could we say _____?"). Alternatively, if others prefer to work alone, you can allow them to come back from lunch early to finish their compositions.

In a similar vein, when you notice that struggling writers are embarrassed because their writing is more simplistic than peers', you can ask them to select one word a day from anything they have read that they want to use in their own compositions. Next, have them write that word at the top of their journal entry that day along with its synonym, antonym, and definition, and have them use it in a sentence in a writing. For older writers, you can distribute a copy of Table 11.2 and ask them to select an item and practice using it to improve their writing. In addition, you can teach the following tricks of the trade.

TRICK OF THE TRADE 1: WRITING EFFECTIVE OPENINGS. Just getting started is a major hurdle for reluctant writers. To assist these students to create good openings, you can ask them to bring their favorite books to a small group meeting. As they read the openings (or paragraphs) that they most enjoyed, ask why they enjoyed these so much. Then allow students to incorporate these styles into their writings. With older students you can share the strategies in the first part of Table 11.2, which authors use to strengthen their openings.

A strong image makes a good opening. Similarly, when writers have difficulty making a strong ending, teach them to capture a specific image that ties the piece together (Wilde, 1993).

TRICK OF THE TRADE 2: CREATING MEMORABLE CHARACTERS. When writers create one-dimensional characters, you should encourage them to provide depth to their characters and plots. Ask them to describe the character's personality at the outset, an event that altered the character's personality, and how that alteration changed the character. Students also benefit from learning about the characters that their favorite authors and peers describe. To teach them, use a small group of students who need to expand their characterizations. Discuss how most authors develop characters.

It is also important to know that many student writers typically use characters who are not identified or are their friends. Second graders and sixth graders tend to write most extensively about themselves. By fourth grade many of these writers begin to create dialogues as well as names for fictional characters, and they continue to do so in later grades. In like manner, fifth grade writers typically begin to use internal character reflections to develop their characters.

A similar small group meeting can assist writers who have difficulty creating conflict in their plots. In a small needs-based group with peers, writers learn that conflict can be created in three ways: by making a character's desires (1) restrained by nature, (2) resisted by other characters, or (3) resisted by conditions in his or her life. Following a discussion of these plot variations and examples from their favorite books, movies, and television shows that illustrate each, struggling writers can write about a character they create who battles and then resolves an issue. Last, you can have them write about how this conflict reveals a trait their character possesses.

TABLE 11.2 Tools Professional Writers Use

I. For a good opening sentence I can:

   a. Describe a person or scene.

   b. Write a dialogue.

   c. Describe an action.

   d. Dispel a misconception: "You may believe the moon causes waves but it doesn't."

   e. Use a short sentence or single word: "It was glorious!" or "Whew!"

   f. State my position boldly: "The most important point I'll make is this: _____."

   g. Explain the purpose of the piece and then add a smile or surprise for the reader: "The list of things about which I am ignorant is much much longer—but I don't want to boast."

   h. Issue a challenge: "By any reasonable standard, no one would want to read 20 pages about how to make a cake."

   i. Add an odd fact I was able to unearth.

   j. Give precise details and unexpected imagery.

   k. State an opposite: "I've often wondered what it takes to have a successful reading program. Now that I know, I wish that I didn't."

   l. Paraphrase or give an exact quote from a book.

   m. Ask a question.

   n. Give a personal anecdote.

   o. Say something unpredictable.

   p. Use humor.

   q. Share a novel idea.

II. Other tools professional writers use are:

   a. Use specific, concrete language. Instead of *supermarket,* use *Tom Thumb.* Instead of *cereal,* use *Cheerios.* This way readers can see images and vicariously experience an event with you.

   b. Place important words or ideas at the beginning or the end of a sentence or paragraph to highlight them.

   c. Cut the clutter.

   d. Use the most vivid verbs and most specific nouns possible.

   e. Remember that three is the magic number for a list, and use only three adjectives or less before a noun.

   f. Be a detector, so every word you write is exactly what you mean.

   g. Vary sentence lengths. Do not write sentences longer than 19 words. Use some very short ones as well.

TRICK OF THE TRADE 3: WRITING RICHER SENTENCES. Effective writers know how to use rich, vivid words to communicate subtle meanings. They also know how to put words together to get their ideas across clearly and concisely. Reluctant writers can learn these skills when you teach the following strategies:

1. Be specific and use exact words to paint pictures.

    Original: I ate lunch.

    Revised: I took tiny bits off my cheeseburger because I wanted it to last a long time. It was the only time this week we would have my favorite lunch served at school.

2. Use painting, doing, and naming words, or specific nouns and vivid verbs.

    Original: I saw a bird.

    Revised: I watched a baby sparrow spread its wings and soar on its very first flight.

3. Use no more than three ideas in a single sentence.

    Original: My mother told me to clean my room and before I could do anything else she also told me that I had to help her take out the trash and set the table for supper and feed the dog and wash my hands.

    Revised: My mother told me to clean my room, take out the trash, and set the table for supper. Before I could begin, she also asked me to feed the dog and wash my hands.

4. Put two short sentences with the same subject together.

    Original: I woke up. I ate breakfast.

    Revised: I woke up and ate breakfast.

5. Use transitional phrases like these to move the action along:

    Meanwhile . . .

    As a result, . . .

    Whenever . . .

    Because . . .

    Although . . .

    Before . . .

    During . . .

    In addition, . . .

One way to teach the foregoing strategies is to give your writers a writing assignment and, after the compositions are complete, demonstrate how the five methods above could have benefited their work. Next, provide time for students to skim their compositions, revising one or more of their sentences using each strategy. When the revisions are complete, ask for volunteers to read "before" and "after" sentences from their writing. Make a large chart titled "Making Writing SHOW Instead of TELL." List the five strategies on the chart, and post some of your students' sentences as examples of effective writing.

The second part of Table 11.2 includes other ideas for better writing.

Special Supports during the Revising Process

If reluctant writers are not taught effective strategies for revising their ideas, daily writing can actually *decrease* their expressive power. Specifically, without strategies for creating more effective openings, transitions, and endings, repeated writing experiences reduce these writers' sentence variety, idea complexity, and use of correct spelling (Block, 1996; Kucera, 1995). Their expectations decrease as well—until they eventually create works that cannot be easily understood by anyone but themselves. This in turn reinforces their negative self-image as a writer.

To break this cycle, you can teach them that their first goal in writing is to get their ideas down as soon as possible; it is not to solve all mechanical and organizational problems. Then you can teach the developmental stages of revision, how to benefit from self-questioning, and how to make connections and transitions. Finally, always provide positive feedback while they work on their revisions. With this series of instructional actions, struggling writers will likely begin to value the revising process.

Stages in the Revising Process

Through observing and documenting reluctant writers' normal development, researchers have identified four revising abilities that evolve over time (Block, 1996; Downing, 1995; Graves, 1995). These researchers also report that direct instruction in small group minilessons (or discovery discussions) enables less accomplished writers to develop these revising strategies more rapidly. For this reason, you can greatly enhance these writers' revising skills by indicating to them what stage they are presently demonstrating and explaining how they can develop more advanced revising strategies.

REVISING STAGE 1: ADDING TO THE END. Ask students to look at their first draft to find where they wrote any new ideas that were added after the first day. If they find that all afterthoughts were written at the end of their composition, compliment these writers that they are at the first stage of revising ability. Then teach them how to revise by inserting new thoughts into their texts in the natural sequence in which they would normally occur and would add most value.

REVISING STAGE 2: MAKING INSERTIONS. Ask students to reread a sentence that they added to their ending and to point to the place in the text where that sentence could be moved to add more impact or to make the meaning clearer. When their fingers mark that spot, teach the caret editing symbol that adults use to insert sentences when revising. After students have marked their insertion location with a caret, demonstrate how their pencil can circle the sentence to be moved, as if their pencils were ropes used to lasso the sentence. Then draw a line connecting it to the caret.

REVISING STAGE 3: HIGHLIGHTING THE MAIN IDEAS. Explain that besides adding new ideas and inserting these ideas at appropriate spots in the text, another part of revising is to help their readers find the most important points in the text. For instance, writers can highlight their main idea by moving it to the first or last sentence of the piece. Demonstrate how you rearrange sentences so that the most important points either open or close individual paragraphs (or the entire composition).

Also, relate a trick they can use to identify their main idea: They can ask themselves, "What do I *really* want people to know?" The answer to this question will usually become their main idea sentence or will enable them to write one.

REVISING STAGE 4: DELETING AND REWRITING. Sometimes the revision process calls for more than merely inserting additional ideas or rearranging sentences. Deleting and/or rewriting larger portions of text may be necessary. For instance, a composition may be repetitive, may lose its focus, or simply may not communicate what the writer intended.

Reluctant writers tend to begin most of their sentences with the same word. Because of this, their writing reads like a panoramic camera surveying a scene: "I ate Froot Loops. I ate Pop Tarts. I drank milk. I ate a lot. I ate fast. I ate the most." Your instruction should assist students to focus on their main idea. To this end, you can have them write their main point either at the beginning or at the end of the paragraph or selection. To make their writing more captivating and powerful, they should always require themselves to delete or rewrite at least two subsequent sentences so as to pull the reader toward their most important ideas and increase the focus and power of their writing.

You could use the breakfast foods example for a demonstration. In this instance, you could state that the main idea of this writing was to tell the reader that breakfast is your favorite meal. Thus, revision begins with putting the main idea first and rewriting at least two sentences. The final draft would read: "Breakfast is the meal I like best. I eat a lot, too. Today I ate Froot Loops, Pop Tarts, and milk!" Students will realize that the meaning of the revised version was clearer.

Self-Questioning

An effective revising strategy is for students to ask themselves questions that can help organize their ideas and improve the writing. Before they pick up their pencils to revise, reluctant writers should ask themselves the following questions:

Can I make my words more specific and vivid so my ideas become crystal clear?

Does each paragraph contain vibrant details and a main idea?

Can I shorten any sentence to make it more direct and easier for my readers to understand?

Can I make connections between ideas, phrases, sentences, and paragraphs so my reader does not have to infer the connections I intended?

Can I use an example to make it easier for readers to understand?

Which section contains my most important idea—the ending, the middle, the third sentence?

What is it that I want my readers to experience from this writing?

If I read my title as if I am a reader, and then ask myself what I expect from this title, has my writing delivered this?

When I find something that is awkward and doesn't say what I want precisely, do I rewrite or eliminate it?

Which word, phrase, or sentence matters the most to me? Which one do I think communicates best? What did I do to create it, and how can I apply this strategy to other sections of this writing?

Make a chart of these questions and post it in the room, or give copies to writers to place in their writing notebooks and on their desks for reference as they revise.

Making Connections and Transitions

Another good revising strategy is to help struggling writers make connections between their ideas. To do so, you can explain and demonstrate the following steps:

1. Identify and clearly describe the conflict.
2. Reread the writing to see if it can be more informative, entertaining, or persuasive.
3. Reread the revision while thinking about a specific person in the audience to whom you want to communicate; then picture that person reading the work.
4. Write the solution to the conflict as if personally involved, including references to your own experience, if applicable.
5. Reread the revision with an eye to injecting more passion and imagination into the piece.
6. Reread while thinking about what you want readers to learn from the piece and how the writing will answer a tough question or explain a complication in the world.

In addition, when reluctant writers have difficulty composing complete paragraphs, you can ask them to select a chart in the classroom that they value and to copy that chart and write it in paragraph form. After students repeat this lesson a few times, they can begin to write longer connected paragraphs without outside prompts. For example, Joyellen, a second grade struggling writer, enjoyed the Friday afternoon recipes our class made. I asked if she would like to copy her favorite recipe and read it to her grandfather when she got home. Her eyes lit up and she copied the steps meticulously in paragraph form. She drew a picture to accompany it and wrote why she liked this snack the most. Then I asked her to ask her grandfather to write to me about what he liked best about her note to him and the recipe. The next day, when I read the grandfather's note to the class, Joyellen's face beamed and four other writers asked if they could copy this week's recipe to read at their homes. From that day forward, whenever Joyellen did not know what to write, she wrote recipes. Eventually these culminated in a booklet of recipes and poems she created and gave to the class, titled "We Have the Triple-Decker, Super-Duperest Class of All."

Giving Feedback

Your feedback should be plentiful, positive, and specific. As Diederich (1991) stated: "I believe very strongly that noticing and praising whatever a [struggling writer] does well improves writing more than any kind or amount of correction of what he does badly because they need all the encouragement they can get" (p. 24). Moreover, Johnston (1992, p. 23) suggests that this feedback should explain any confusion about a section of writing. For example, "The part in the middle about the horse made me feel very sad, but I feel a bit confused about the part where you were going home." This statement will be more helpful than asking, "Why did you write the part about going home in that way?"

Encouraging Creativity in Reluctant Writers

The need for sensory, creative learning at all grade levels is becoming increasingly well understood (Adams, 1993; Collins, 1991a, 1991b, 1992c; Gardner, 1993). *Creativity* is the wellspring that generates original ideas and products. It can arise from a variety of sources, including these:

- A seemingly simple and surprising event
- An ability to generate and recognize undervalued ideas
- A desire to avoid joining the crowd
- Redefining problems
- Insights
- Beliefs
- Ambiguity
- A willingness to excel and grow (Sternberg & Lubert, 1991)

While creativity has long been a topic of interest to educational and psychological researchers, there has been a phenomenal growth in knowledge about this subject in the last 40 years. For example, as of 1980 about 250 studies were completed each year (*Annual Review of Psychology,* 1981). During 1965 and 1966 the total number of studies on creativity equaled all that had been attempted during the 10 years prior to that time (1955–1965), which in turn equaled all that had been completed over the preceding 100 years! Fortunately, you can use our new understandings to elevate the abilities of reluctant writers to contribute innovatively to our world.

Research indicates that creative people maintain high standards, accept confusing uncertainty, and view the higher risks of failure as part of the process of accomplishment. Highly creative individuals also approach what they perceive to be important aspects of their work with considerable intensity and engagement. They exhibit an internalized license to challenge the conventional and to express their own insights, which they undertake with real creative engagement. This attitude induces *constructive discontent,* a condition needed for creativity (Adams, 1993).

Albert Einstein reported that fantasy was more important in his work than genius. Similarly, Nikola Tesla, inventor of the AC induction motor and the Tesla coil, reported that he used creative language constantly, to "project before my eyes a picture complete in every detail of a new machine I want to create." Tesla tested devices mentally—by having them "run" for weeks, after which time he would examine them thoroughly for signs of wear—"before he began to create his invention through work and words" (Adams, 1993, p. 36).

One limit to struggling writers' creativity in spoken and written language is that they cannot determine probable consequences of their creative acts. Thus, many tend to talk and think just like peers. Others squelch creative ideas before they are expressed. Moveover, because creative ideas or acts are often imperfect, many of these writers do not yet have the confidence to project themselves creatively. This fear of making a mistake has kept many, even into their adult years, from fashioning solutions and advancing new ideas in their writing and speaking.

Fortunately, several components of creative thinking are amenable to instruction.

1. Creative and innovative thinking tools
   a. Substituting (putting ideas together or in place of one another)
   b. Adapting to make a slight variation
   c. Modifying or magnifying
   d. Rearranging
   e. Estimating, anticipating, forecasting, predicting
   f. Taking a calculated risk
   g. Brainstorming and synthesizing
2. Generative processes
   a. Generating hypotheses
   b. Planning
      • Selecting strategies to fulfill a specific goal, product, or process by organizing time, materials, and effort
   c. Composing or building
      • Developing a composition
      • Recasting new information and ideas that come into play
      • Recognizing what the objectives are
3. Innovative thinking
   a. Exploring a subject
   b. Mulling over a subject
   c. Making discoveries about form, rules, restrictions, values, and ideas

The **Carlson Analytical Originality Scale,** described in Box 11.3, can be used to assess creativity.

Diagnosing and Assessing Reluctant Writers' Needs

What criteria should struggling writers have in mind when they define their goals and the quality of their writing? What standards do these writers use to judge whether they are effective or not? Unfortunately, without instruction in self-assessment, the evaluations

11.3   DIAGNOSIS AND ASSESSMENT

Diagnosing Writing Abilities:
The Carlson Analytical Originality Scale

You can use the **Carlson Analytical Originality Scale** (Carlson, 1993) to isolate the aspects of students' writing that demonstrate the most creativity. The Carlson Analytical Originality Scale ranks many components of creativity and has five divisions: Story Structure, Novelty, Emotion, Individuality, and Style of Stories.

Under *Story Structure,* five items are included: unusual title, unusual beginning, unusual dialogue, unusual ending, and unusual plot.

The *Novelty* portion of the originality scale includes 16 items: novelty of names, novelty of locale, innovative punctuation and expressional devices, new words, novelty of ideas, novel devices, novel theme, quantitative thinking, new objects created, ingenuity in solving situations, recombination of ideas in unusual relationships, picturesque speech, humor, novelty of form, inclusion of readers, and unusual related thinking. A few illustrations (including point values for various degrees of creativity) follow:

- Ingenuity in solving situation or predicament.

  0 – No imagination used.

  1 – Situation solved in usual pattern:

  Then she woke up—it was a dream.

  Then the knight killed the dragon.

  3 – Unusual ideas used to solve situations:

  Natives of the Jingle-Jangle tribe dug a pit, put meat on a pole, and captured the lion.

  5 – Ideas used involving ingenuity:

  Grandma made a Gooba to capture the wolf, as wolves are afraid of Goobas.

- Recombination of ideas or things in unusual relationships.

  0 – No odd combination or ideas organized into new relationships.

  1 – Odd ideas combined but in a rather usual relationship:

  The bunny put on her apron.

  3 – Unusual combination of ideas or objects:

  Father made alphabet soup so the boys could learn the alphabet. The bunny wore a mauve hat.

  5 – Combinations of ideas or things into relationships that are unusual:

  Billy had a circle of pure, solid gold spinning around his head. Was he an angel? He couldn't be, for in his left hand he had a slingshot, and in his right hand was a rock.

Emotion on the originality scale consists of four items: unusual ability to express emotional depth, unusual sincerity in expressing personal problems, unusual ability to identify with problems or feelings of others, unusual horror theme.

The *Individuality* section includes four items: unusual perceptive sensitivity, unique philosophical thinking, facility in beautiful writing, and unusual personal experience.

The final division, *Style of Stories,* includes seven items: exaggerated tall tale; fairy tale; fantasy turnabout of characters; highly fantastic central idea or theme; fantastic creatures, objects, or persons; personal experience; and individual story style.

of most reluctant writers are not specific enough to assist them to grow as writers. For example, Helgers (1984) and Brown and Cambourne (1989) found that these writers' most frequent measures of writing "goodness" were the following:

- Self-satisfaction with their writing ("I like the first page")—22 percent of all students surveyed
- Surface features ("It has all the periods"; "It's a bit longer")—19 percent
- Story grammar or book structure ("I have chapters")—14 percent
- Content ("It's exciting")—11 percent
- Value they assign to the global piece ("It's my best"; "It's kind of weird")—8 percent
- Having had fun writing it—5 percent

As the year moves on and activities in this chapter are implemented, writers can be taught how to assess the content and clarity of their ideas more specifically. To assist in this process, in one assessment you can ask each student to evaluate an anonymous peer's work and use the comments the student makes as evidence of his or her knowledge of writing conventions and quality of ideas. For example, Daly (1989) suggests that you say something like this:

> This is writing done by a child of your age who has [revised and] edited it as well as [he/she] can. If you were the only person who could help [him/her] improve the writing, what advice would you give? (p. 93)

Similarly, you can create another assessment based on curricula students have just completed in which they must write their culminating thoughts for a real audience. For instance:

> Pretend you are a member of the Save the Environment Club at your school. The club has been reading and discussing how important the rain forests are to our environment. The principal has asked you to present a talk at the next parents' meeting informing the parents about why everyone should be concerned with what is happening to the rain forests. So that you will remember to include important details, your principal has asked you to write out your talk first. Use information from your reading to help prepare the talk. (Valencia, Hiebert, & Afflerbach, 1994, pp. 265–266)

For a third assessment you might hold a discovery discussion. During that discussion you would ask as many of the following questions as you wished in order to elicit struggling writers' depth of abilities:

- What other things did you like about your writing this grading period?
- What things did you wrestle with? (Shannon, 1991)
- How do you want to end your pieces?
- What kind of examples are your best and why?
- Could you explain what you wanted to do in this piece and how you feel others could evaluate your success in reaching that goal?

Fourth, assist students to assess peers' writings during sharing time. To do so, student evaluators should time the length of the reading, note the depth of discussion the piece generated, and judge the quality of a writer's answers to the following questions:

- What do you want from us as an audience to improve your writing ability?
- What did you attempt for the first time or refine in your writing style with this piece?
- What part of the paper did you like best and why?
- What part of the paper gave you the most difficulty and why?
- What are some ways that you can improve on any weakness you see in this paper?
- Would you like us to tell you what you did to make your meaning so clear to us?

To diagnose individual students' needs, you can follow these sharings by making assessment cards such as the examples in Box 11.4, in which students evaluate one aspect of their writing for a week. You can also ask them to make a list in their journals of "Things I Do Well in Writing" and "Things I Am Working On."

Fifth, some reluctant writers prefer to respond to tape-recorded questions and comments from you, and to have you respond to their answers and follow-up questions on the tape as well. The advantage is that these writers receive a more complete explanation of the revision tips you suggest than would be possible if you tried to write all your ideas on their papers. Another advantage is that taped comments do not take as much time as other types of assessment. Unfortunately, tape-recorded assessments do not allow dialogue between you and the student concerning suggestions you both offer (Bratcher, 1994). The forms in Figure 11.3 and Table 11.3 (p. 387) enable students to respond to teachers' criteria. Although you could vary the criteria, the weight allowed each aspect of writing on Table 11.3 is an effective ranking for writers.

Chapter Summary

As an educator, you now have the ability and opportunity to assist students for whom writing is a difficult and ineffective method of communication. Some students already enjoy oral storytelling and judge themselves to be capable, persuasive orators—yet they need your help in overcoming writer's block, so their desire to communicate doesn't evaporate. With your help, such writers can move through the prewriting stage by learning to do the following: (1) make a list; (2) create a semantic map; (3) reread previous writings; (4) do an unfocused or focused freewrite; (5) read what they have written so far to a peer; (6) consult the chart of starter sentences; (7) jot down an event that triggers thinking; (8) designate a section of their writing notebook to record examples of techniques they like; and (9) select places in the classroom where they want to write.

Most reluctant writers must also learn to trust their own writing abilities, their classmates, and their teachers. They also need assistance to discover their own voice—

11.4 DIAGNOSIS AND ASSESSMENT

Identifying Reluctant Writers' Needs through Self-Assessment Cards

Directions: These self-assessment cards can be used each time students compose for longer than 15 minutes. Students are to complete one of the two cards at the end of a writing experience. The first card is a wholistic assessment; the second is an anchor assessment. The second card can be written to assess other composition abilities, such as "writing stronger sentences" or "making more vivid descriptions for the setting and within the plot."

Name _____ Monica _____ Date 2-3-02

Title of your piece _____ Ramona Rides Again _____

In our discovery discussion today, you gave several suggestions about things that might make your piece better.

In the space below, write down one suggestion that you plan to use in revising your piece. Tell why.

All my sentences were the same—all boring!! I want
to write better grammar so they'll begin differently and
some will be short and some will be long.

Name _____ Monica _____ Date 2-4-02

Title of your piece _____

STRONG VERBS

1. For the last week you have been working on using strong verbs in your writing. How did you do with that while you were writing today?

   Instead of writing said I wrote gasped.

2. Give an example of a sentence from your writing in which you used a strong verb. Copy the sentence in the space below and underline the strong verb.

   Ramona pondered and pondered.

Source: Modified from L. K. Rhodes & L. Shanklin (1993), *Windows into Literacy,* p. 95. Portsmouth, NH: Heinemann. Copyright © 1993 by Heinemann. Used with permission.

Name _____ Costobal Costillo _____ Date 8-8-02 ____

I've checked the items that I think have improved since my last writing.

_____ My writing describes my thoughts clearly to an objective audience.

_____ I have included a main thought in each paragraph and have provided ample details to support that thought.

_____ If someone else read my writing, they could clearly understand these points: _____, _____, and _____.

_____ I have not reused vocabulary repeatedly.

_____ My ideas used descriptive, imaginative vocabulary.

__✓__ I have checked and rechecked my writing to be sure I used complete sentences.

__✓__ I have included a title that depicts and represents what my writing is about.

__✓__ I am proud of my writing.

My goal for my next paper is
to write a famis story _____

_____

_____

_____

_____

FIGURE 11.3 Questions to Assess My Own Writing

Source: Adapted from form developed by Cathleen M. Cavanagh, graduate student at Texas Christian University, Fort Worth, TX. Reprinted by permission of Cathleen M. Cavanagh.

with sufficient time and specific feedback directed to this end. Because they have not yet appreciated and cultivated their own voice, they need longer periods within the school day to write. This extended time can be provided through discovery discussions and small, needs-based groups. Similarly, writers become more proficient when they are taught how to overcome writer's block, to improve their first drafts, to make effective revisions and edits, and to self-assess. Students realize they can write significant ideas for important purposes and that they can use writing to resolve personal and professional issues throughout their lives.

Support strategies to assist first-draft writing include (1) dictating; (2) writing "Choose Your Own Adventure" books; (3) using dialogue journals; (4) storytelling; (5) creating personalized bookmarks; (6) writing for authentic purposes; and (7) practicing tricks of the trade. As their writing power increases, students also need your

TABLE 11.3 Writing Rubric for Teacher Evaluation and Student Self-Assessment

Focus

(1)	2	3
No! This piece goes all over, or it is too big.	Focus is pretty clear. Only a few things don't fit.	Very clear focus. It stays on track and isn't too big.

Details

1	2	(3)
Very few details (1 to 3).	Some good details (4 to 6).	Lots of great details (7 plus)!

Lead

(1)	2	3
Needs work!	Just okay. Good try.	Great! It catches readers' attention and gives a clue.

Ending

1	(2)	3
No end in sight. It just stops.	Pretty good. I can tell it is finished without "The End."	Awesome! The end is tied to the beginning and pulls the whole piece together.

Spelling

1	2	(3)
Tons of mistakes.	A few mistakes.	Very few mistakes.

Punctuation and Capitalization

1	2	(3)
Lots of missing periods, capitals, commas.	Only a few missing periods, capitals, commas.	Almost no errors on periods, capitals, commas.

Additional Comments: From this assessment I see I need to work on writing better first paragraphs!

Source: Adapted from S. Downing (1995), "Teaching Writing for Today's Demands," *Language Arts, 72,* pp. 200–207.

guidance in revising their ideas. You can provide this support by helping them increase the number of questions they ask themselves as they compose and teaching them to make connections and transitions between the ideas they write about. Encouraging creativity is also an important strategy you can teach.

Key Terminology

Now that you have completed this chapter, do you know the meanings of the following terms? If you do, place a check mark in the blank that precedes each term. If you are not certain of any term's meaning, you would benefit by quickly reviewing it on the page indicated. If you have learned four of these on your initial reading of this chapter, you have understood the chapter's intent.

_____ **writing voice** (page 361)
_____ **unfocused freewriting** (page 365)
_____ **focused freewriting** (page 365)
_____ **jump-start** (page 365)

_____ **dialogue journal** (page 369)
_____ **Carlson Analytical Originality Scale** (page 382)

 ## Case Study

Making Professional Decisions

What strategies from this chapter would you select to assist Juan, a fourth grade reluctant writer? Juan began the fourth grade rejecting writing, but through one of the activities you've read thus far in this chapter, by the second month of school he was using the writing pattern of his Mighty Mouse cartoon book to write journal entries such as the following:

To day it was ranning. why? The only men who can tell us is faster dan a speeding bullet. More bigger dan a penut smaller dan my hand. It middy mouse. Yes hes baaack beeter dan ever. Faster dan ever.

He' parner jast like! But! more dumer dan middy mouse. Its supper Juan. Yes he's back more dumer dan ever. Middy mouse can't belive I he's parnter.

[*Translation:* Today it was raining. Why? The only man who can tell us is faster than a speeding bullet. More bigger than a peanut; smaller than my hand. It is Mighty Mouse. Yes, he's back, better than ever. Faster than ever.

His partner is just like him! But! more dumber than Mighty Mouse. It's Super Juan. Yes, he's back, more dumber than ever. Mighty Mouse can't believe I am his partner.]

Now, as you read Juan's second writing, think of the type of feedback you would provide and identify the clues in this writing that indicate he is developing his voice:

To day I got up. I whast to, I took a shower. I help my brother get dress, and I got dresset too. My mom left me some money. It was five dollars in cash. I went to the story to buy my brother a pice of candey. We got on the bus we came to school and played. Her I am writing this for you.
P.S. See you later!!!

[*Translation:* Today I got up. I washed, too; I took a shower. I helped my brother get dressed, and I got dressed, too. My mom left me some money. It was five dollars in cash. I went to the store to buy my brother a piece of candy. We got on the bus. We came to school and played. Here, I am writing this for you.

P.S. See you later!!!] (Peregory & Owen, 1993, pp. 102–103)

What feedback would you provide? What evidence exists that Juan's voice is developing? What strategies would you use? Check your responses against the Answer Key at the end of the book.

Thinking and Writing about What You Have Learned

1. Recall and list as many strategies as possible that assist reluctant writers to (a) overcome writers' block, (b) improve their first drafts, and (c) revise their compositions. For those that did not come instantly to mind, review their discussion in this chapter. If you recall 10 strategies, you have comprehended the information in this chapter well. If you recall more than 10, you are well on the way to developing a teaching repertoire that will address many needs of your struggling writers. Congratulations. To check yourself, compare your list to the following summary, adapted from a list created by Tricia Nail, a second grade teacher.

    Supports for Reluctant Writers
    > Helping them learn to trust their ideas
    > Helping them discover their own voices
    > Allowing them time to learn writing strategies
    > Helping them identify their writing strengths
    > Accepting other viewpoints
    > Modeling and explaining special writing strategies

    Strategies to Overcome Writer's Block
    > Make a list on paper or tape
    > Create a semantic map
    > Reread previous writings
    > Do an unfocused or focused freewrite
    > Read to a peer what you have so far
    > Consult the chart of starter sentences
    > Jot down the event that triggered your thinking
    > Keep a section of a writing notebook for examples of powerful writing
    > Select the place where you want to write

    Activities during First-Draft Writing
    > Dictating
    > Writing a "Choose Your Own Adventure" book
    > Dialogue journaling
    > Storytelling
    > Personalizing bookmarks
    > Composing letters of request
    > Practicing tricks of the trade

Supports during Revising
Teaching the developmental stages in revising
Encouraging self-questioning
Helping students make connections and transitions between topics
Teaching students how to write effective leads and endings

2. The National Writing Project (a federally funded program to develop teachers' abilities to instruct the writing process) has regional offices throughout the United States. These offices disseminate innovations in classroom practices for struggling writers. They also maintain addresses and publications from exemplary schools in their areas. These schools welcome visitors and provide ideas that enhance instruction for others with similar student populations. If you write to the director in your region, he or she could become a continuous resource for your professional development. The names and addresses of the National Writing Project's regional directors are:

Northeast Region *(Connecticut, Maine, Massachusetts, New York, Rhode Island, Vermont)*

Joseph Check
Institute of Learning and Teaching
University of Massachusetts, Harbor Campus
Dorchester, MA 02125

Mid-Atlantic Region *(Delaware, District of Columbia, Maryland, New Jersey, Pennsylvania, Virginia, West Virginia)*

Robert Weiss
West Chester University
West Chester, PA 19383

Southeast Region *(Alabama, Florida, Georgia, Mississippi, North Carolina, South Carolina)*

Samuel Watson
Department of English
University of North Carolina
Charlotte, NC 28223

Mideast Region *(Illinois, Indiana, Kentucky, Michigan, Ohio, Wisconsin)*

B. J. Wagner
English Department
National College of Education
Evanston, IL 60201

North Central Region *(Iowa, Minnesota, North Dakota, South Dakota, Manitoba [Canada])*

Keith Tandy
English Department
Moorhead State University
Moorhead, MN 56560

Mid-Central Region *(Colorado, Kansas, Missouri, Nebraska)*

Michael Vivion
English Department
University of Missouri
Kansas City, MO 64110

South Central Region *(Arkansas, Louisiana, New Mexico, Oklahoma, Texas)*

David A. England
223 Peabody Hall
Louisiana State University
Baton Rouge, LA 70803

Pacific Region *(Arizona, California, Hawaii, Nevada)*

Sheridan Blau
Graduate School of Education
University of California
Santa Barbara, CA 93106

Northwest Region *(Alaska, Idaho, Montana, Oregon, Utah, Washington, Wyoming)*

William Strong
Secondary Education
Utah State University
Logan, UT 84322

3. Encourage your students to keep a writing portfolio in which they collect both drafts and final compositions. At the middle and end of the year, assist them to identify ways in which their writing has improved by listing special strategies they are using.

4. After reading the poem that follows—written by Robert, a fifth grade reluctant writer—assess its creativity and decide which strategy from this chapter you would teach to Robert. After you have written your answer you can compare it to the strategies used by Robert's teacher; see the Answer Key at the end of the book.

> There is a woman sitting in a chair.
> She had yellow hair.
> The chair was really red.
> She looked like she was dead.
> Maybe she had a scare.

For Further Reference

These companies publish student writings:

Merlin's Pen, 98 Main St. East, Greenwich, RI 02818
Scholastic Inc., 730 Broadway, New York, NY 10003-9538

Writer's Voices, Literacy Volunteers of New York City Inc., Attn: Publishing Department, 121 Avenue of the Americas, New York, NY 10013

Young Publish-A-Book Contest, Raintree Publishers, P.O. Box 1367, Milwaukee, WI 53201-1367

Onto the Information Superhighway

In the time it takes you to read this sentence, type in www.funbrain.com. You will be amazed at what new and exciting images await you. In seconds you will be introduced to Spellaroo, The Plural Girls, The Translator Alligator, and other games and lessons to enhance your curriculum.

Literacy Games and Animal Connections

www.funbrain.com

Funbrain is an interactive cross-curriculum website that will support your classroom literacy plan. Activities include Grammar Gorillas, Con-nect the Dots, Word Confusion, Spellaroo, What's The Word?, 2 Bee or Not to Be, Sign the Alphabet, Wacky Tales, The Translator Alligator, Paint By Idioms, The Plural Girls, Captain Fredo, and Writer's Block. To add to the fun and appeal of this site, have a box with website information inside of the box. Have the border of the box be dancing animals and books to catch the attention of reluctant writers.

Source: Adapted from information compiled by Nicole Devlin, early childhood education major at Texas Christian University, Fort Worth, TX.

Spelling difficulties can be overcome when teachers highlight and explain the spelling patterns and irregularities in words.

Assisting Students Who Face Spelling, Grammar, and Handwriting Challenges

A reluctant writer said: "Teachers often complain that struggling writers work inconsistently. Teachers say that one day we can do everything while the next we cannot spell or read the same material that we did the day before. This can happen because often we do not have the energy or concentration to function at one hundred percent. While other students can work consistently with eighty percent effort, we must be functioning at full capacity to be effective spellers and writers. I wish teachers would understand this fact rather than exasperate the problem by saying: 'You knew how to do this yesterday! What's wrong?'"

(Adapted from Lee & Jackson, 1992, p. 106; co-author Lee is a reluctant writer)

■ Chapter Overview: Key Points

In Chapter 11 you learned how to support the writing development of students who are struggling with writing. In this chapter you will learn how to improve these students' spelling, grammar, and handwriting. You will also learn about the resources and methods available to support students' efforts with spelling, use of conventions, and letter formation.

Key concepts addressed in this chapter are:

- Spelling development
- Tier 1–4 supports for spelling development
- Diagnoses and instruction of grammatical principles
- Improving handwriting

By the end of the chapter you will have answers to the following questions:

1. What activities increase struggling writers' spelling abilities?
2. What methods improve these writers' grammar usage?
3. What methods improve these writers' penmanship?

Spelling Development

Research has demonstrated that improved handwriting and spelling ability, or **orthography,** not only assists students' knowledge about word structures but expands their efficiency and speed of writing and reading. This, in turn, enhances the growth of their self-concepts (Gentry, 2000; Henderson, 1990; Uhry & Sheperd, 1993). Spelling instruction can also expand their speaking, listening, reading, and writing vocabularies (Templeton, 1992).

As shown in Figure 12.1, students progress through parallel stages in writing and spelling development. In the **scribble stage** of writing, when children are scribbling in an attempt to communicate, they are simultaneously in the **precommunicative stage** of spelling, beginning to learn that lines and scribbles are different from numbers and words. When they are in the **isolated-letter stage** of writing and are beginning to write letters (usually linked to drawings), they are also becoming aware of the **directional principle**—that letters move left to right to form words—and are said to be in the **semiphonetic stage** of spelling. Likewise, when letters, numbers, and unique symbols are interspersed in otherwise recognizable sentences, children have entered the **transitional stage** of writing; this occurs roughly at the same time that they enter the **phonetic stage** of spelling, when they begin to use basic phonograms and learn that every word has spaces before and after it (even if they spell a word with only a single letter). In the **stylized sentence stage,** which immediately precedes writing proficiency, traditional sentence structures are used; at the same time, students are in the **transitional stage** of spelling, in which most words are spelled correctly (although some spellings are only approximations). If the correct spelling pattern is not selected, an acceptable English representation will appear (e.g., "bote" for *boat*). Finally students reach writing and spelling proficiency in the fifth and final stages. Until a student's developmental stage is diagnosed, instruction is less effective in assisting that child's writing and spelling to advance rapidly (Graves, 1994; Henderson, 1990).

A difference between spelling/grammar/handwriting and the other language arts is that the former skills require strong visual memories. Specifically, if a student is to acquire full spelling ability from reading books, the student needs both a strong visual memory and an immediate recall of sound-to-letter correspondences. Most reluctant readers/writers do not have these natural strengths. Also, to study a word and to learn its spelling, it is necessary for students to be able to read that word. Furthermore, unlike the pattern with reading, students grow as spellers by learning one principle and then another. You best reveal these principles by teaching some words directly as **exemplars,** representative examples of the spelling generalizations. Some students with weaker visual memories will require five or more exposures to these exemplars before they can understand the difference between their invented spelling and the correct form of a word.

Poor spelling affects students' grades throughout school as well as people's assessment of their capabilities outside of the classroom. Therefore, when a spelling problem is diagnosed and instruction is targeted to correct it, more than students' writing abilities can improve. This instruction is best when (1) delivered in the meaning-centered context of students' own writings, (2) conducted in relatively short periods of time, and (3) accompanied with specific feedback about students' improvements.

WRITING	SPELLING	SAMPLE
1. *Scribble stage* • Unrecognizable letters • Writing is represented as lines, scribbles, and scrawls • Writer can decipher scribbles, but meaning does not hold over time	**1.** *Precommunicative stage* • Realization that letters spell, not lines or numbers • Little or no knowledge of sound-to-symbol relationships • One or more letters are written to represent a word • L/R directional principle may or may not be understood • Repetitive use of known letters, usually uppercase letters	Sample of Stage 1 (Translation: Child could not remember the meaning of what she wrote.)
2. *Isolated-letter stage* • Letters appear, usually linked to symbols or numbers • Purpose of writing is understood • Drawing becomes prevalent in writing • Illustrations assist writer to hold meaning over time	**2.** *Semiphonetic stage* • L/R directional principle is understood • Sound-to-symbol relationships appear and are known • Words, sounds, and syllables are represented by single letters (e.g., *b* = bee, *c* = sea)	Sample of Stage 2 (Translation: Katrice's birthday story: I will go to Red Lobster and I will eat some ice cream and my friend will come too with me and my cousin will come to Red Lobster.)
3. *Transitional stage* • Stage is easily overlooked • Common words are spelled correctly at the beginning of the writing • Isolated letters, numbers, and symbols continue to exist • Drawings always hold meaning to writer	**3.** *Phonetic stage* • Basic phonograms are used (e.g., /an/, /in/, /on/) • A letter or word is visible for each thought • Word spacing is consistent • Letters are assigned as they are heard (e.g., brd = bird)	(Translation: Dear Rabbit, I waited 5 years for a three wheeler. I want one. Please Rabbit. Brian Breton) Sample of Stage 3

FIGURE 12.1 Developmental Stages in Writing and Spelling

WRITING	SPELLING	SAMPLE

4. *Stylized sentence stage*
- Sentences begin to form around familiar words, repetitive phrases, and sentence beginnings
- Writer can read message over time

4. *Transitional stage*
- Transition occurs from reliance on sound to visual patterns
- Correct letters are used but may be reversed
- Vowels are inserted in every syllable
- Rules for capitalization and punctuation appear
- Learned words are spelled frequently
- Approximations indicate reliance on visual memory (e.g., paly = play)

my mom is realea helips us bekus sheiis a nurse, well She yustoo be but now She isa nursing assistant teacher. I Love her. She reeds to me She tux me in at nite. She is rile bise. She is a verel good cook. She pras with me She givs me mune if I do my work. She bis me toys and School ekwimint. And plas gams with me

(Translation: My mom is really helps us because she is a nurse. Well, she used to be but now she is a nursing assistant teacher. She reads to me. She tucks me in at night. She is real busy. She is a very good cook. She prays with me. She gives me money if I do my work. She buys me toys and school equipment. And plays games with me.)

Sample of Stage 4

5. *Writer stage*
- Writing is creative
- Writing becomes an independent activity
- Approximated and conventional spelling is used
- Writer's voice is evident through an interest in expressing own ideas

5. *Correct stage*
- Self-initiated proofreading thinking about spelling while writing occurs
- Knowledge of prefixes, suffixes, silent consonants, contractions, irregular spelling, compound words, and complex sentences is utilized
- Wide variety of words spelled correctly

(Translation: Nike© vs. Reebok© Reebok makes a long lasting shoe but if you take a shoe like the punks it is not worth it to spend that kind of money. Nike makes a sport shoe. It is a better company than Reebok and it is worth every penny you spend on Nike. And if you take the air compartment you will find Nike makes a good shoe. Ever since Nike Air and the Air Pack came out Nike has a better chance of getting to the top.)

Sample of Stage 5

FIGURE 12.1 *(continued)*

Sources: S. Bratcher (1994), *Evaluating Children's Writing,* p. 71. New York: St. Martin's Press. Copyright © 1994 by St. Martin's Press. Used with permission. K. Rockos & B. J. Walker (1994), *Handbook for Understanding Reading,* pp. 10, 103. Englewood Cliffs, NJ: Merrill. Copyright © 1994 by Merrill. Used with permission.

Types of Spelling Difficulties

Many writers experience one of the following five difficulties that impair their spelling ability. Specific instructional supports, discussed a little later in this chapter, can be used to overcome these difficulties.

AUDITORY INATTENTION. Some writers cannot transpose individual sounds to letters. Their minds seem not to understand or attend to subtle differences between sounds. If auditory confusion is the cause of spelling difficulties, most letters in the words the student writes will follow correct English spelling patterns, but the word itself cannot be pronounced (e.g., *should* is written as "shuoed").

VISUAL INATTENTION. Students who have visual inattention hear sounds distinctly but cannot remember how these sounds are written in words. The words they write can be sounded accurately, but do not contain correct English spelling patterns (e.g., *should* is written as "sshhoooodt").

SPELLING RULE INATTENTION. Some students spell incorrectly because they **overextrapolate;** that is, they extend the rules of English spelling patterns into situations for which they are not valid. For example, such a student would overextrapolate the ending sound in *should* as the past tense ending morpheme "-ed" and would spell *should* as "shouled."

USE OF HOMOPHONES. Some writers substitute a homophone for the word they intended to write. Students who, for example, substitute "bear" for *bare* may be writing so rapidly that they are unaware of their error; or they may not be using meaning as a clue in spelling.

NO PATTERN TO ERRORS. Some students have such poor handwriting that letters cannot be distinguished. Because of this problem, no error pattern can be discerned. You should assist writers in this category to recognize and reproduce the specific letter formations that are common to most of the words they spell incorrectly.

Instructional Supports for Specific Spelling Problems

As noted previously, students in different stages of writing and spelling development think differently about language. To advance their understanding, the instructional supports will vary.

Transitional spellers in second grade or above can profit from taking the spelling dictation test in Box 12.1. After you analyze the cause of errors and the readability level at which most errors occur, encourage these students to read books at this level. For example, if a writer who is a transitional speller in the fifth grade scores at the second grade level on the spelling grade placement test in Box 12.1, that student can be helped to advance in spelling ability by reading books at the second grade level at least once a week. After reading a book the student can challenge himself or herself to spell from memory 10 words read or to write as many words as he or she can remember and then check the spellings by rereading the words in the book.

When a student's level of spelling development and cause of spelling errors have been diagnosed, instruction can be targeted. Strategies to employ include mnemonic devices, word sorts, multisensory instruction, and pictorial aids. Writers who use these strategies significantly increase their spelling abilities (Cunningham, 1995; Gentry, 2000; Henderson, 1990).

Spelling Dictation Test for Grade Placement

PURPOSE: To determine the grade level at which the student spells when writing dictated sentences

ACCURACY: No more than one spelling error in one sentence

TIME: Your discretion

DIRECTIONS:

1. Give the student paper and pencil and say: *I'm going to dictate some sentences and I want you to write them. Do the best you can to spell each word correctly.*
2. Then dictate the sentences listed below, one at a time, pausing and repeating as many times as you think would be helpful for the student.
3. Stop the test when the student misspells more than one word in one sentence. Do not penalize for omitting capitalization or punctuation, as the objective of this test is to measure only spelling dictation proficiency.

SENTENCES FOR DICTATING:

1. *Look at the big nut.*
2. *We found a blue coat and red dress.*
3. *The clown could not catch the horse.*
4. *The smaller truck was waiting, as it had come early.*
5. *The purpose of this visit was to compare the two offices.*
6. *They prepared a very interesting program for the balance of the day.*
7. *It was impossible for her to keep the schedule, so she asked that they consider getting a substitute.*
8. *He received a certificate of appreciation at their graduation for the fine work he had done.*

GRADE PLACEMENT: The highest-numbered sentence in which there is no more than one misspelled word corresponds to the student's spelling dictation grade level. If that is sentence 8, then the student is at grade level 8; if it is sentence 7, then the student is at grade level 7; and so on.

NOTES: *Individual administration.* You can save time by anticipating the highest grade level at which the student will be able to spell 100 percent of the words correctly and then beginning the test at that level. If your original estimate proves to be too difficult, drop down one level at a time until a "basal" (100 percent success) level is established. Then continue testing at higher levels until the student makes more than one error in a sentence.

   Group administration. When you give this test to a group of students, it is best to begin at the first level and dictate all sentences.

Source: Adapted from E. Fry (1994), *The Spelling Dictation Test.* Laguna Beach, CA: Laguna Beach Educational Books. Used with permission.

FOR WRITERS WHO SPELL PREPHONEMICALLY. Most writers who are in second grade and above should demonstrate only an occasional prephonemic spelling error. If they are making this kind of error often, your first instructional goal is to assess whether the student's spelling is **dysgraphic** (neurological in origin) and needs more intensive instructional intervention than the school can provide. In general, prephonemic spellers in preschool through second grade need to learn that books and print carry meaning. Such students profit from selecting books they would like to have read to them—and having you, an older schoolmate serving as a tutor, a senior citizen "adopted grandparent," or a classmate read these books to them for 30 minutes daily. After 25 minutes of reading in which the reader moves his finger beneath each word as it is read, ask the prephonemic speller to write from memory the words that were learned through this reading. Most will begin by writing only single words, but usually will write full sentences within 4 weeks of this daily intervention.

When possible, immediately following these oral reading experiences, ask prephonemic spellers to complete a dictation, as described in Chapter 11, and to draw a picture to illustrate the words they dictated. After their pictures are complete, allow them to write a caption for the picture. In this caption they will likely produce correct spellings.

FOR WRITERS WHO SPELL PHONEMICALLY. Students who spell phonemically know that print represents sounds, but problems arise either when they cannot match individual phonemes to letters or when they can write only about half of the alphabet, so even if they know a letter-to-sound correspondence they may not have the ability to present it in writing. The first instructional objective for these writers is to ask them to read a line of print and then write their favorite word from that sentence. Then ask them to write other words, leaving a blank for parts they can't write or don't know how to spell (e.g., for *dog* they might write "d-g"). By congratulating them for every correct letter ("You spelled all the sounds you heard! I am proud of how many letters you wrote correctly!"), you can assist these spellers. This encouragement tends to increase future requests they make of classmates to help them spell all the sounds in words correctly.

FOR WRITERS WHO SPELL BY LETTER NAMES. Once reluctant writers reach the letter name stage, most write enthusiastically. Their words tend to be creative and often lack spaces between them, because at this stage most beginning spellers do not attend to word features. It is important to help move these writers into the next stage of their development by challenging them with a variety of writing formats, because they will need to attend to correct spelling. The best formats are letters to go home, notes in the suggestion box for you to read, journal entries, recipes, science experiments, self-evaluations, and so forth.

FOR WRITERS WHO INSERT IMPROPER VOWELS. Some struggling writers may begin to insert incorrect vowels in their words. To address this difficulty, help these writers learn to read and spell basic sight words and survival words through the "What's in My Head?" activity (see Chapter 9) to increase mental imagery.

FOR WRITERS WHO DO NOT ATTEND TO VISUAL FEATURES. "Decorating" difficult words to associate visual images with their meanings is particularly valuable for struggling writers whose errors occur from visual inattention. These writers can decorate words that are difficult for them to spell in several ways, as shown in Figure 12.2: They can (1) choose to draw pictures of whole words' meanings, (2) make images over difficult letters within a word, or (3) use different fonts to depict a word's meaning. As soon as visual inattenders misspell a word several times or come to a word they want to learn, model this method by drawing a graphic in one of these ways. Then challenge students to do the same. Writers who are visual inattenders benefit from creating these images directly on their compositions during the editing stage (and before they write their final drafts).

FOR WRITERS WHO DO NOT ATTEND TO AUDITORY CLUES. When you diagnose a specific spelling pattern that consistently poses a problem for a struggling writer, it may result from auditory inattention. Ask the student to picture a word that comes to mind when he or she hears the sound that the spelling pattern represents (e.g., a thumb for /th/, a church for /ch/, or a shoe for /sh/, as shown in example 4 of Figure 12.2). Then have this student write several other words with this same spelling pattern beneath that image on a sheet of paper. Once the writer has discussed these words and can write them, you can create a challenge of six new words that contain the same letter pattern. Last, the student can draw these pictures and spelling patterns in the top margin of his or her journal to remind the student of their spellings in subsequent writings. This method is particularly valuable for auditory inattenders because it associates a picture to the part of a word that is difficult for them to spell. Because visual images are their strength, auditory inattenders can use these pictures as they spell.

FOR WRITERS WHO VIOLATE SPELLING RULES AND WRITERS WHOSE ERRORS HAVE NO PATTERN. Word sorts are very helpful for writers who violate spelling rules and for writers whose errors show no pattern. One word sort activity involves word cards that students can take home or take to tutorial sessions for added instructional support. To begin this activity, place a set of blank index cards in the writing center or table at the back of the room. Any time writers want to learn the spelling of a word, they write their name on one of the cards and write the spelling for that word, which a peer or you dictate to them. After the student has used the card to write this word in a composition, the card is placed in a box next to the blank cards. After approximately 20 cards have been made by classmates, ask a reluctant writer in the transitional stage to sort the index cards according to the spelling patterns that gave classmates difficulty. Words with the same pattern are then put together on a slotted word chart or poster board (e.g., *may, day, say,* and *pay* are put together). Then the appointed reluctant writer presents his or her hypothesis about why each set of words was difficult. The student can also suggest a graphic or picture clue (see Figure 12.2 again) to help classmates remember words within this family.

In another word sort activity, less accomplished students write the correct spelling of every word they have misspelled on their last three compositions on the left-hand side of a sheet of notebook paper, trying to list words with similar spelling patterns

1. One way for struggling writers to learn difficult words is to draw pictures that capture whole words' meanings.

2. Silent or confusing letters are highlighted by pictures that aid visual recall, which is particularly valuable for visual inattenders.

famïly
It is hard to hear the *i* sound when *family* is pronounced. The *i* becomes a person in the family, and it is easier to remember.

Wørld
World is difficult to spell because the *er* sound is spelled *or*. The *o* becomes a globe of the world as a visual clue.

¢ent
Cent and *sent*—which word refers to money? That's easy to remember when the *c* becomes a ¢ sign.

3. Some visual inattenders also enjoy varying their writing script to convey the meanings of words they want to learn. For example, they would write *holler* and *whisper* as follows:

HOLLER   *whisper*

4. Decorating can also be used to help students master letter patterns.

th   sh   ch   challenge
wh	th		w	sh		wh	ch		in	ch
t ee	th		c a	sh		m a	ch		ba	th
p a	th		f o	sh		s a	ch		ru	sh
			fr e	sh				fla	sh
								di	sh

FIGURE 12.2 Decorating Difficult Words

Source: Example 2 modified from C. E. Quinn (1988), "Sight Word Spelling Tricks," *Academic Therapy, 23* (3), p. 288. Copyright 1988 by PRO-ED, Inc. Reprinted by permission.

together. Next, students get another sheet of paper and slit it vertically into three equal sections, then staple or tape it on top of their list. Under the left-hand flap will be the student's word list; blank space will be under the other two flaps. The flaps are labeled, from left to right: "Look and See in Your Mind," "Write and Draw," and "Write Word and Check." Then students lift the left-hand flap ("Look and See in Your Mind") just enough to see the last word on their list. They view this word, close their eyes, then spell the word in a mental image. Next, they lift the middle flap ("Write and Draw") and write the word, along with a graphic or pictorial image that will help them remember the spelling. Finally they lift the third flap ("Write Word and Check") and write the word; they also write another word that is spelled similarly next to that word (e.g., if *say* is the word, the student writes "say" and "day"). Students continue in this manner, working their way up until the entire sheet is complete. If students write their name on their flap sheet, you can detach it after the activity, to be stored with you until next time.

■ Tier 1–4 Supports for Spelling Difficulties

Whereas the foregoing supports were designed to address specific causes of spelling difficulties, others are more general in their application. The next three have proved successful with many different types of spelling problems and can be used with many struggling writers.

MULTISENSORY EXPERIENCES. Although writing in the air does not increase spelling abilities, feeling letters through different textures does. Specifically, many writers profit from making words with letters cut from sandpaper, molding letters from clay, or writing letters on paper plates with pudding or whipped cream. As they write in these media, you can also ask these students to say the word and its meaning, say each letter as they write or mold it, close their eyes and visualize their finished product (each word), and then repeat these steps with no more than five words at a time. After five words have been constructed, you can have students write these words from memory on index cards. For any word a student writes incorrectly or cannot remember, have a partner show the word again so the student can write it again in a chosen medium (e.g., pudding). Then the index card is attempted again. The last step is to study only the words on the cards. When these writers are confident they can spell a word, they turn the card over and write that word in a sentence. Any word missed at this point is added to the student's word list, to be used the next time you implement the "flap sheet" word sort activity described earlier.

MNEMONIC RULE TRICKS. To teach spelling rules most effectively, you should introduce only one rule a day. Instruction is further enhanced when you give a struggling writer the responsibility of planning the instruction for peers with you. You and this student meet to select a strategy and to create a mnemonic device to remember the spelling generalization. By having this student subsequently teach the rule and the trick to classmates, you will help him or her learn it faster.

Two examples of mnemonic rule tricks you can suggest to get students started creating their own are the following:

1. *Rule:* When a one-syllable word ends in a consonant, or when a word with more than one syllable ends in a consonant and is accented at the end, double the consonant before adding a suffix (e.g., sit + er = sitter; refer + ing = referring). When a one-syllable word ends in a vowel other than *e,* or when a word with more than one syllable ends in a consonant but is not accented on the last syllable, do not double the last letter (e.g., do + ing = doing; travel + er = traveler).

Mnemonic trick: Tiny words ending in a consonant want to have a twin letter to make them stronger. As for longer words that sound loudest at the end, they want to be seen, just like loud people at a party. On the other hand, a word that has two syllables and speaks softly at the end does not want to draw added attention to itself, so it does not double its last letter to make itself longer before the suffix is added.

2. *Rule:* When a word ends in a consonant and *y,* change the *y* to *i* before adding a suffix, unless the suffix begins with *i* (e.g., dry + er = drier; fry + ing = frying).

Mnemonic trick: If you cannot pronounce a word after adding the suffix, the word is misspelled (e.g., *trying* is okay, but not *triing*).

Teaching Grammar

Grammar is the description of the structure of our language—including word choice, word order, usage, sentence structure, sentence type, dialect, paragraph form, and paragraph function. To increase writers' use of more effective grammatical structures, they should be taught about the power of the following three broad aspects of grammar:

1. Choosing vivid words (*traditional* grammatical principles)
2. Using multiword phrases for subjects or predicates (*structural* grammatical principles)
3. Considering how the sentence's meaning is altered slightly by choosing from several possible words, then using the one that conveys exactly what you mean (*transformational* grammatical principles)

The purpose of this section is to demonstrate how struggling writers can improve these grammatical components of their writing.

When these students recognize that their sentences are less gracefully styled than those in the books they read, many credit the differences to their own stupidity rather than to an inadequate use of grammatical principles. To eliminate these negative self-perceptions, it is important to create a comfortable, risk-supportive setting for these writers. Then you can open a full-class conversation concerning what students do know about proper grammatical usage. Begin by complimenting students on what they are already doing well in their use of conventions. From this point your lesson can diverge in one of two directions. If your students are already motivated to add more power to their writing, you can model how to use phrase placements; or perhaps you could discuss colons, semicolons, capitalization, or another convention. You can display a page from a book you are reading to the class and ask the students to describe the impact a specific convention made on the meaning of that page.

Alternatively, if students need to discover for themselves a reason to use more powerful conventions and grammatical principles, you can display a piece of writing with a particular convention removed (e.g., with all commas or all periods whited out), then ask for students' comments about that writing and what they would add.

If students want to learn to use more vivid phrases, refer to the parts of speech listed in Table 12.1. Also, teach students to notice the various sentence structures and

---

TABLE 12.1 Parts of Speech

Understanding the functions of the parts of speech helps students gain precision in word choice.

Nouns

Traditionally, a noun is defined as the name of a person, place, or thing.

I. *Derivational Affixes*

-age	coverage, village
-ance	clearance, importance
-ee	trustee, employee
-er	employer, dancer
-ment	pavement, government
-ce	independence, insolence
-cy	*democracy, lunacy*
-ity	*vanity, scarcity*
-ness	stillness, silliness
(also	-ster, -ism, -ist, -ship)

II. *Inflectional Affixes*

To make plurals:

-s	coats, pigs
-es	dishes, ditches

But note the irregular plural forms:
children, women, oxen, men, deer, geese, feet, mice

Also, *mass nouns* are not commonly pluralized: communism, milk

III. *Sentence Test Frames*

The _____ couldn't hide its _____.

One _____ had many _____.

Sharon was in _____.

Verbs

Traditionally, verbs are defined as words that name actions or states of being.

I. *Derivational Affixes*

-ize	socialize, criticize
-ify	*classify, mystify*
-en	darken, lighten
-ate	hesitate, navigate
en-	enlist, enlarge
be-	belittle, bedazzle

II. *Inflectional Affixes*

-s	*runs, moves*
-ed	flagged, started
-ing	flagging, starting
to ____	to run, to fall

III. *Auxiliary Verbs*

be/is/am/are/was/were	is going, was talking
have/has/had	have taken, has talked

might/may	might run, may rain
shall/should	shall fight, should speak
will/would	will run, would stall
can/could	can find, could lose
must	must begin

IV. *Sentence Test Frame*

$$(\text{The}) \text{ noun} \begin{Bmatrix} \text{may} \\ \text{will} \\ \text{must} \\ \text{can} \end{Bmatrix} \text{\_\_\_\_ (the) (noun)}.$$

Note that parentheses ( ) mean "may choose this element." Braces { } mean "must choose one of these elements."

Examples:

The aardvark *whistled* the tune.

Rain must *fall*.

continued

TABLE 12.1 Parts of Speech *(continued)*

Adjectives

Traditionally, adjectives are defined as words that modify nouns.

I. *Derivational Affixes*

-y	funny, crazy
-ive	active, passive
-able	comfortable, agreeable
-ful	bashful, cheerful
-less	helpless, thoughtless
-ar	regular, circular
-ary	ordinary, legendary
-ic	civic, terrific
-ish	childish, fiendish
-ous	fabulous, hideous
-en*	wooden, woolen
-ed*	beloved, aged
-ing*	*charming, interesting*

II. *Inflectional Affixes*

-er	fuller, smaller
-est	biggest, tallest

III. *Sentence Test Frame*

A _____ noun seems very _____.

Examples:
    A *stingy* person seems very *stingy*.
    (But not: A *telephone* man seems very *telephone*.)

*Not to be confused with verb inflectional affixes.

Adverbs

Traditionally, adverbs are defined as words that modify verbs, adjectives, or other adverbs.

I. *Derivational Affixes*

a-	ahead, away
-ly	slowly, happily
-ward	backward, skyward
-where	somewhere, nowhere
-wise	clockwise, likewise

II. *Sentence Test Frame*

_____ the noun _____ verbs the noun _____.

Examples:
    Sometimes the clock disturbs the baby.
    The clock *greatly* disturbs the baby.
    The clock disturbs the baby *now*.

Prepositions

Traditionally, prepositions are defined as words that show a relationship between a noun or pronoun and some other word in the sentence.

Sentence Test Frames

The first frame identifies all but 9 of the 42 prepositions.

1. The ant crawled _____ the door.

    Prepositions that will fit this slot are:

about	behind	from	round
above	below	in	through
across	beneath	like	to
after	beside	near	toward
against	beyond	off	under
along	by	on	underneath
around	down	opposite	up
at	for	over	with
before			

Prepositions that will not fit the slot are these:

among	of
but (meaning *except*)	regarding
concerning	since
during	until or till
except	

Some of the second group will fit the slot in this test frame:

2. The old man was silent _____ the war.

The others—*among, but, except,* and *of*—will fit the slot in this one:

3. No one was talking _____ the girls.

Source: Adapted from C. Block (1993), *Teaching the Language Arts,* p. 254. Boston: Allyn & Bacon.

TABLE 12.2 Sample of Structural and Transformational Grammatical Rules

Rule	Example
Noun–verb (subject–predicate)	Dogs eat.
Noun–verb–adjective (subject–linking verb–noun modifier)	Flowers are fragrant.
Noun–verb–adverb (subject–predicate)	John walks slowly.
Noun–verb–noun (subject–predicate)	I eat hamburgers.
Noun–verb–noun–prepositional phrase (subject–predicate)	Daddy threw the ball to Susie.
Noun–linking verb–noun	Martha is a policewoman.
Noun–linking verb–adjective	The mountains are awesome.

connections between words, as depicted in Table 12.2. To introduce this table and to help students understand the differences between the types of sentences they can write, ask them to picture a white furry rabbit in their minds. Then ask them to come to the board and write a sentence that describes what they pictured. When each student has written on the board, discuss how the placement of subjects and predicates change the emphasis of each student's message. Students' sentences will likely resemble the following:

The rabbit is furry and white.

The furry rabbit is white.

The white rabbit is furry.

The rabbit I see is furry and white.

When I saw a rabbit, it was furry and white.

My rabbit is white and furry.

Then explain how transformations enable writers to stress the exact part of a meaning that they want to emphasize to their readers by placing the most important part of an idea at the beginning or the end of a sentence. Teach transformational grammar through demonstration of how phrase placements create subtle changes in meaning. Discuss the examples in Table 12.3, and then have students locate similar sentences in their favorite books and their own writings.

Once these introductory grammar lessons have been completed, you may want to share a passage from your own writing and demonstrate how you used grammar to convey your meaning.

TABLE 12.3 Transformation of Sentences

Transformation	Description	Sample Sentence
Simple Transformations		
Negative	*Not* or *-n't* and auxiliary verb inserted	Lions roar. Lions don't roar.
Yes–no question	Subject and auxiliary verb switched	The lion stalked the jungle. Did the lion stalk the jungle?
Wh- question	*Wh-* word (*who, what, which, when, where, why*) or *how* and auxiliary verb inserted	Lions roar. Why do lions roar?
Imperative	Unsaid *you* becomes the subject	Lions give cubs meat. Give cubs meat.
There is...	*There* and auxiliary verb inserted	Lions are cautious. There are cautious lions.
Passive	Subject and direct object switched and the main verb changed to past participle form	Lions make cubs hunters. Cubs are made hunters by lions.
Complex Transformations		
Joining	Two sentences joined using conjunctions such as *and, but, or*	Lions roar. Tigers roar. Lions *and* tigers roar.
Embedding	Two (or more) sentences combined by embedding one into the other	Lions are animals. Lions are cautious. Lions are cautious animals.

Diagnosis and Instruction of Grammatical Principles

If students are experiencing difficulties with grammar, you can provide classroom supports as well as one-to-one activities to improve their proficiency. Following are two supports that have proved to be effective; you may also want to refer your students to the books listed in Resource Card 16.

SHOW ME WHAT YOU ALREADY KNOW ABOUT GRAMMAR. This "show me what you already know" support has been shown to produce significant growths in grammatical awareness (Block & Mangieri, 1995). This activity begins with one-to-one discovery discussions in which you ask students to describe the rules about word placement, punc-

RESOURCE CARD 16

Books for Students with Different Dialects or Who Have Difficulty with English Speaking Patterns

Armstrong, W. (1987). *Sounder.* Santa Barbara, CA: ABC-Clio.

Barrett, J. (1980). *Animals should definitely not act like people.* New York: Atheneum.

Bernstein, J. (1992). *Dmitry: A young Soviet immigrant.* Philadelphia: Lippincott.

Bouchard, T. (1989). *The boy who wouldn't talk.* New York: Viking.

Childress, A. (1973). *A hero ain't nothin' but a sandwich.* New York: Coward, McCann & Geoghegan.

Clifton, L. (1975). *My brother fine with me.* New York: Holt, Rinehart & Winston.

Clifton, L. (1977). *Amifika.* New York: Dutton.

Fredericksen, H. (1970). *He-who-runs-far.* New York: Young Scott.

Galbraith, C. K. (1971). *Victor.* Boston: Little, Brown.

Gammell, S. (1983). *Git along, Old Scudder.* New York: Lothrop, Lee & Shepard.

Grahame, K. (1989). *The wind in the willows.* New York: Aladdin.

Greenfield, E. (1988). *Nathaniel talking.* New York: Black Butterfly Children's Books.

Guy, R. (1973). *The friends.* New York: Holt, Rinehart & Winston.

Gwynne, F. (1970). *The king who rained.* New York: Windmill.

Hamilton, V. (1983). *The magical adventures of Pretty Pearl.* New York: Harper & Row.

Heide, F. (1978). *Secret dreamer, secret dreams.* Philadelphia: Lippincott.

Herman, C. (1994). *What happened to Heather Hopkowitz?* Philadelphia: Jewish Publication Society.

Horwitz, E. L. (1987). *When the sky is like lace.* Philadelphia: Lippincott.

Jacobs, H. (1994). *Cajun night before Christmas.* Boston: Houghton Mifflin.

Johnson, C. (1955). *Harold and the purple crayon.* New York: Harper & Row.

Jordan, J. (1971). *His own where.* New York: Crowell.

Juster, N. (1961). *The phantom tollbooth.* New York: Random House.

Lasky, K. (1981). *The night journey.* New York: F. Warne.

Lattimore, E. F. (1960). *The Chinese daughter.* New York: Morrow.

Levine, E. (1992). *I hate English!* New York: Scholastic.

Miles, M. (1971). *Annie and the old one.* Boston: Little, Brown.

Parish, P. (1963). *Amelia Bedelia* (series). New York: Harper & Row.

Simon, N. (1967). *What do I say?* Chicago: Whitman.

Steig, W. (1971). *Amos and Boris.* New York: Puffin.

Steptoe, J. (1974). *My special best words.* New York: Viking.

Thomas, J. (1973). *Lordy, Aunt Hattie.* New York: Harper & Row.

Wiseman, B. (1970). *Morris goes to school.* New York: Harper & Row.

---

tuation, and capitalization that they used in their favorite composition and why they used each one. As they describe their thinking you can also challenge them to explain how they knew to use those particular principles at those points in their writings (e.g., "I noticed that in the closing paragraph, you said, 'When all is said and done, I'm glad

I did that.' Why did you put your phrase at the beginning of the sentence?"). Research has also demonstrated that struggling writers are challenged to continue to grow when you end these discovery discussions by asking this question: "What do you want to learn next to become a better writer?" (Graves, 1994). If students do not have an answer, you can demonstrate a new type of transformation they may want to consider from Table 12.3 or one of the tricks of the trade from Chapter 11.

IMPROVING CORRECT USE OF CAPITALIZATION. Reluctant writers enjoy discovering capitalization rules on their own by reading examples of capitalizations and writing rules to describe the examples. Once these rules have been created, most of these writers enjoy making "Capitalization Sheets" to use when editing their own and peers' writing. In this way, they think more frequently about capitalization in the context of composing their own thoughts.

Improving Handwriting

Illegible handwriting usually results from improper posture, pencil grip, or paper placement.

Proper posture includes a straight and tall seating position. For comfort, the student's back should be against the back of the chair; to reduce fatigue, shoulders should not lean forward. Desk height should enable the arm to lie flat and not to be lifted at a strange angle to reach the desktop. Similarly, if the desk is too low students' postures will slouch.

Proper pencil grip must occur as well. This includes both the angle and pressure with which the pencil is held. When the pencil is positioned at a 45-degree angle (not perpendicular) to the paper, students' downward thrust is reduced and fewer pencil leads break. You can diagnose whether students are holding their pencils with improper pressure by watching their hands as they write. If they are gripping the writing utensil too tightly, their handwriting will be too dark, and/or their writing will be slow. Conversely, if these writers are gripping their utensils with proper tension, you should be able to take them from their hands without having to pull hard.

As shown in Box 12.2, right-handed students need to place their paper slightly to the right of the midline of their body, turned to the left at a 25-degree angle. This positioning ensures that only the small muscles of their hands (and not the large) are used in penmanship. Also, before handwriting can improve significantly, these writers must develop the habit of resting both the wrist and forearm on their papers so as to free small muscle movement.

Without your special assistance, left-handed students may write by placing their hand below the writing line or hooking their hand over it. You must teach left-handed writers to place their paper properly, grip their pencil, and slant correctly. You can place masking tape (see Box 12.2) on left-handed students' desks to mark the position where the upper left-hand corner of the paper should be each time they begin to write. (You can also use masking tape to help right-handed students who don't position their paper properly.) The upper right-hand corner of the paper should be in line with the cen-

12.2   CLASSROOM TEACHERS

Guide to Paper Placement for Improved Penmanship

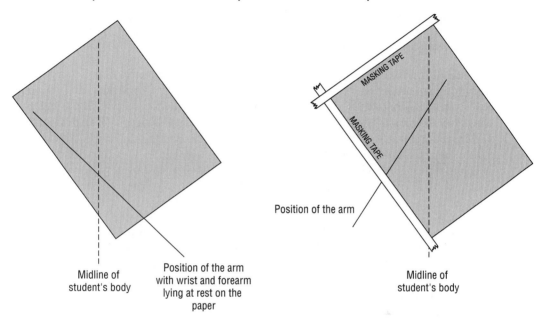

Midline of student's body

Position of the arm with wrist and forearm lying at rest on the paper

MASKING TAPE

MASKING TAPE

Position of the arm

Midline of student's body

Source: Adapted from D. Graves (1994), *Fresh Look at Writing*, p. 301. Portsmouth, NH: Heinemann.

ter of the student's body. Once the student has used the paper in this position for a few times, remove the tape and have students determine their own paper position, as each will prefer a slightly different placement from this mean positioning. Once a correct, personalized position is established, replace tape to mark both edges of the upper left-hand corner for at least the next grading period.

It is a good idea to group left-handed students together for handwriting instruction so you can observe them and so they can help each other during instruction. The following strategies are designed to address the special problems of left-handed writers:

1. Left-handed students' elbows should be kept close to the body as they write. The blunt end of the pencil or pen should be directed back over the shoulder. The desk should be high enough for the child to see the pencil or pen as it touches the paper.
2. In manuscript writing (printing), "circle strokes" should be made from the left to right clockwise instead of counterclockwise as right-handed writers do.

3. Ask left-handed writers to write four sentences. They are to make a tiny vertical line at the point where they place their pencil to begin each letter. Study these markings to analyze if letter strokes are beginning at the proper position for left-handed writers.

4. Demonstrate to students that their upward strokes will be pushing strokes rather than pulling strokes, as is the case for right-handed writers.

5. It is becoming increasingly acceptable for left-handed students to use manuscript writing indefinitely when they find it easier than cursive.

6. Ask students to compare their writing samples to a handwriting model and to identify one letter they wish to improve.

To improve both right-handed and left-handed students' individual letter formation, you can also provide an oral stimulus by modeling how to make each letter in a word as the children see the visual features of each letter you are creating. These students can say the letter strokes as they subsequently write the word you modeled. Instruction will be more effective if students view and then replicate a model, as described here, rather than tracing difficult letters. However, merely viewing and trying to copy a letter will not significantly change penmanship. Students need to be shown how to make each feature of their troublesome letters, such as how to make the downstrokes, circles, and stems that each contains (Peck, Askov, & Fairchild, 1980).

Finally, erasers can be a problem for teachers and students. When struggling writers get in the habit of erasing, their writing speed is slowed and holes in their papers destroy meaning. You should demonstrate the process of crossing out errors to eliminate this problem.

Manuscript Writing

Although several important readiness aspects of handwriting instruction occur in early childhood education programs, manuscript instruction traditionally begins in first grade. One reason manuscript writing, or printing, is usually taught before cursive is that young students' small muscles are less well developed than older students'. Therefore, many primary students have trouble guiding their writing utensils to make all the angles required for cursive writing. Another reason is that printed letters look more like the typeset letters students have read in books (Askov & Peck, 1982; Duvall, 1986).

Researchers have found that giving beginners "giant" pencils will not improve their penmanship, as most poor handwriters prefer small, adultlike writing utensils. In fact, first and second grade students tend to write longer stories if they use ballpoint or felt-tip pens as opposed to pencils (Askov & Peck, 1982).

The first manuscript letters to be introduced should be uppercase letters because large muscles are involved in their formation more than in their lowercase counterparts. Capitals should be taught and practiced one at a time as students learn to write their own and classmates' names. The easiest letters for first grade students to write (and the suggested order in which to introduce them) are *l, o, h, d, i, v,* and *x*. The most difficult letters for young students to write—and therefore those that should be introduced last—are: *q, g, p, y, j, m, r, k, b, u,* and *a*. Even as late as 9 years of age, many children continue to have difficulty in forming *r, u, b,* and *t*. Some struggling writers may require that you guide their hand as they learn to write these letters.

Cursive Handwriting

Instruction in cursive handwriting usually begins in late second or early third grade but can begin earlier. Cursive words are written laterally, formed at a 60-degree angle. The strokes of looping, retracing, rounding, and closing letters are taught separately, following the same basic methods used to teach manuscript writing. The most frequent errors in cursive writing are faulty endings, incorrect undercurves, mixed slants, failure to produce letters in the center of a word, incorrect formation of initial strokes, poorly formed capital letters, and failure to use appropriate downstrokes.

Students can learn cursive writing more easily when they practice less complicated letters first. For example, you can begin by asking them to write several short words that contain the same letters, such as these:

add, all, at, call, cup, dad, did, do, got, go, had, hall, hid, hunt, it, lad, late, little, oat, old, pad, pat, pig, pill, tall, to, tooth, and *up*

Once you complete this lesson, you can also teach struggling writers that most legibility errors occur through five types of misstrokes (Hillerich, 1985). Students can identify whether they have a problem with any of these five strokes through the following activity:

1. Ask students to write the words *darling, good, guide,* and *adding.* Ask them to look at their words and determine if their letters are closed at the top. If they are not, these students need to practice circle strokes.
2. Next, have them write *nothing, nautical, many,* and *number.* Then ask them to look at the letters *m* and *n.* What happens if their tops are not rounded? If writers do not like how these words appear, they can practice rounded strokes.
3. Now ask the students to write the words *item, triangle,* and *time.* Have them study the letters *t* and *i* and determine if these two letters are the same size. If they are, writers need to practice proper line height.
4. Have them write the words *ladder, letter,* and *left.* Students should analyze the loops on the letters *l* and *e* to see if they are open. If they are not, these students need to practice backstrokes.
5. Pupils write the words *umbrella, underwater,* and *runner.* Then they study each of the letters that they made. They are to describe what could happen if the tops of the *u* are not pointed. If they are not pointed, writers can improve their handwriting by practicing upstrokes and subsequent retracings.

Chapter Summary

This chapter described important aspects of instruction that have proved to increase the spelling and grammar proficiency of struggling writers. The chapter discussed developmental writing stages and contained several strategies for diagnosing types of spelling difficulties. Several special supports to build spelling power were also described, including imagery, mnemonic aids, and word sorts. Grammar and handwriting difficulties were explained, as well as special classroom and one-to-one supports that can improve writers' grammatical proficiency and penmanship.

Key Terminology

Now that you have completed this chapter, do you know the meanings of the following terms? If you do, place a check mark in the blank that precedes the word. If you are not certain of a term, review its meaning by turning to the page number that follows it. If you have learned at least 10 of these on your initial reading of the chapter, you understood the chapter's intent.

____ **orthography** (page 395)
____ **scribble stage** (page 395)
____ **precommunicative stage** (page 395)
____ **isolated-letter stage** (page 395)
____ **directional principle** (page 395)
____ **semiphonetic stage** (page 395)
____ **transitional stage** (in writing) (page 395)

____ **phonetic stage** (page 395)
____ **stylized sentence stage** (page 395)
____ **transitional stage** (in spelling) (page 395)
____ **exemplars** (page 395)
____ **overextrapolate** (page 398)
____ **dysgraphic** (page 400)
____ **grammar** (page 404)

Case Study

Making Professional Decisions

Please refer to the writing sample from Jennifer, a second grade reluctant writer in Figure 12.3. [Translation: Dear Lacy, I miss you very much. I want you to go to my house. Love, Jennifer.] What stages in writing and spelling does this writing sample indicate? What do you think is the cause of Jennifer's spelling problems, and what activities would you use to improve her spelling? Explain your answers.

When finished, answer the same questions for the other struggling writers whose work is shown in Figure 12.3: Matthew, a fifth grader, and Freddie, a fourth grader.

Thinking and Writing about What You Have Learned

1. What are the five types of spelling difficulties, and what special strategies assist struggling writers to overcome these difficulties?

2. What are the three broad aspects of grammar that, once understood, can improve the compositions of beginning writers?

3. When you hold parent–teacher conferences, showing the chart of writing and spelling stages in this chapter can assist parents to understand their child's present level of ability.

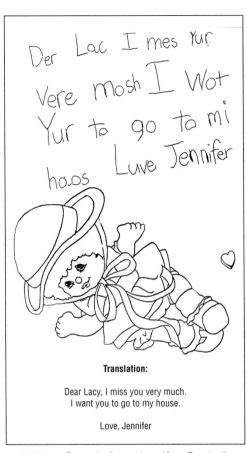

Der Lac I mes Yur
Vere mosh I Wot
Yur to go to mi
haos   Luve Jennifer

Translation:

Dear Lacy, I miss you very much.
I want you to go to my house.

Love, Jennifer

Writing Sample from Jennifer, Grade 2

If i have a problem i triy to solve
it by, doing a vendiagram,
weighted-characteristics test, or
talke it over with someone. Like
this weekend i was at my dads
and my 2 little brothers wanted
lunch and i said mcdonals Anthony
said taco bell Michal said taco bell
sow my dad said figur it out sow i
listed all the pluses for mcdonals,
and taco bell. i said to my self
they do got the best tacos and
buritous and finely i decided that
we should get taco bell for lunch.

Writing Sample from Matthew, Grade 5

11-16-02
Freddie
witing

I would become a great rider if
I could spell beder and I lison beder
some times.

I won't to learn how to
spell beder So I can be
a beder rider.

Translation: I would
become a great writer
if I could spell better
and I listen better
sometimes. I want to
learn how to spell
better so I can become
a better writer.

Writing Sample from Freddie, Grade 4

FIGURE 12.3 Writing Samples from Reluctant Writers

Nisha is leading her group orally for the first time all year. Her teacher has implemented the activities in this chapter to assist her in overcoming her oral language challenges.

Assisting Students Who Face Oral Language Challenges

When I was a young teenager, I had a terrible stutter. I used to avoid answering questions in class. It was too embarrassing. I was written off by an awful lot of people as somebody who was not going to succeed. . . . There were a couple of teachers, one in particular, who just decided they were not going to give up on me. They spent long hours with me after class. They helped me gain self-confidence by showing me in every way that I could be just as important and have as much self-esteem as anyone else. These teachers were as responsible as my parents or anybody else for anything I have been able to do since. . . . If we can mentor students with adults who show them that they care about them as human beings, then we will have done an awful lot to solve a number of special literacy difficulties.

Thomas H. Kean,
Governor of New Jersey
Paraphrase from Crossroads Conference, 1992

Chapter Overview: Key Points

When students improve their reading and writing abilities, they seek to share the discoveries they make with others—and these sharing experiences most often occur through oral presentations and conversations. For this reason, it is important to build students' oral communication and listening abilities. Chapter 13 is designed to explain the pathologically related difficulties, developmental delays, dialectical differences, and second language interferences that can hamper students' oral communication. The chapter also describes instructional processes that enable them to overcome each of these difficulties.

One in five struggling readers/writers also has speaking difficulties (Pierce & Gibbs, 1992). Their underdeveloped abilities to communicate orally inhibit these students' literacy development in several ways. Basically, well-developed oral language abilities enable readers to sort ideas, emotions, experiences, and written words for easier storage. Talk ignites the processes of comprehension. It has been shown, in fact, that many readers/writers who would normally be considered "at risk" can significantly increase their literacy when they are taught to use conversation effectively in reading group activities (Heath, 1988). For example, when they engage in meaningful conversation, less accomplished literacy users will have high-level thinking discourses in which they contemplate, "What would happen if . . . ?" and explore multiple causes—which are the most rapid means of building experiential background. Moreover, such talks enable students to show people who they really are, make sense out of their lives, and present their insights.

While you should not make literacy users overly conscious of their differences in speaking, you can help them to become clearer and more effective speakers of Standard English (Peterson, 1992, p. 52). By doing so you can reduce the risk that students' way of speaking will be rejected or become a source of humiliation. You can also use the activities in this chapter to assist these students to shape their ideas for various audiences. Such activities begin with your offering support and insisting that students speak their own meanings and share their literary voices.

Key concepts addressed in this chapter are:

- Problems in attaining oral proficiency
- Developmentally related speaking difficulties
- Pathologically related speaking difficulties
- Second-language speaking difficulties
- Dialectically different language learners
- Increasing oral reading fluency

Thus, the purpose of this chapter is to increase your ability to help students speak more effectively. By the chapter's end you will have answers to the following questions:

1. What are the most pervasive problems struggling readers/writers have in achieving speaking proficiency?
2. What classroom experiences enable these literacy users to sustain stimulating conversations and eliminate stage fright?
3. What actions can you take to assist students who have dialectical or second-language speaking difficulties?
4. Why is drama important for less accomplished literacy users?
5. How can you assess students' oral language growth?

Problems in Attaining Oral Proficiency: An Introduction

Oral language problems in less accomplished literacy users are of four types:

1. Developmentally related speaking difficulties
2. Pathologically related speaking difficulties
3. Second-language speaking difficulties
4. Dialectical differences

Developmentally related difficulties limit students' abilities to understand more sophisticated linguistic and literary structures; they usually are due to environmental differences in a student's previous language use or a lack of opportunity for self expression in school in previous years. Pathologically related difficulties, in contrast, require special language instruction; they often involve listening difficulties as well as physical deficits that inhibit speech. Other categories of difficulty are encountered in students whose first language or dialect varies from that of the majority of oral speakers in their class. In this chapter you will learn methods of meeting the special needs of students within each of these groups.

Developmentally Related Speaking Difficulties

Christopher Lee, a 22-year-old who was having difficulties with oral expression, wrote: "I wish someone would have worked with me to find my language strengths rather than trying to change my [expressive] system to theirs" (Lee & Jackson, 1992, p. 84). Halliday (1973) has identified seven basic language functions, as follows:

1. *Instrumental*—to control others ("Give me")
2. *Regulatory*—to control situations ("I'll be your friend if you give me your toy")
3. *Interactional*—to define social interactions ("Do it with me")
4. *Personal*—to talk about oneself ("I like books")
5. *Imaginative*—to pretend ("Today I am a princess")
6. *Heuristic*—to find out about things ("What is it?" "Why?")
7. *Informative*—to tell something learned ("Lemons are sour!")

Developmentally related speaking difficulties—limitations in communicating for any of these purposes—can occur when appropriate, effective methods of communicating have not been modeled or taught.

By the time students are in the second grade, typically they should use oral language for all seven functions with ease. If students don't use their oral language effectively, you can ask them to do one of several things:

- Share ideas, as when they volunteer to share their responses to a reading
- Clarify their points of view and use their speech to clarify points of confusion with others
- Discuss main themes of stories, writings, and events in class
- Relate their ideas to others and to printed sources
- Critique ideas and authors
- Identify purpose in conversations and print media
- Relate others' ideas to personal experiences and feelings
- Connect new knowledge to prior knowledge (Raphael et al., 1992)

Many literacy users who are developmentally delayed also develop some degree of shyness or stage fright that interferes with their speaking effectiveness. The following teacher actions have assisted students to overcome shyness and stage fright—which is a first step toward stronger oral communications:

1. Allow less accomplished speakers to rehearse with you or a peer before they have to speak before the class.
2. Allow these students to work in small groups, instead of alone, so that they have the support of the group during oral presentations.
3. Ask for volunteers to go first.
4. Give less advanced literacy users something to say that the class has never heard or read.
5. If silence occurs, give an individual student a choice in which there is no wrong answer, such as, "Based on what you've told us about Templeton, do you think he would be happiest on sunny days or rainy days?"
6. Allow them to videotape their speaking first and review it with you so they can overcome apprehension.
7. Provide a structured dialogue, except for a section in which they can choose to add one creative, surprise part for the class.
8. If you feel that a group activity is going to be loud, take the students outside. Being outdoors allows them to be freer to throw themselves into the activity, even to be silly, and may loosen inhibitions. By taking them outside, you can let students experience the fun of acting and the novelty of being outside the classroom. This setting also places speaking in a more authentic, free-flowing context.
9. Within reason, allow students to rehearse oral presentations as long as they need. When granted this freedom, most struggling literacy users will tell you when they are pleased enough with their work to present it.
10. Share the following books with students. They all feature main characters who use creative strategies to overcome their stage fright:
    a. *Stage Fright* by Ann Martin (Holiday House, 1984) tells how fourth grader Sara learns that her shyness and fear of the stage is a common, healthy thing and that she can overcome it.
    b. *What Do You Do When Your Mouth Won't Open?* by Susan Pfeffer (Avon, 1981) is a humorous treatment of dealing with the fear of speaking before a group.
    c. *You Mean I Have to Stand Up and Say Something?* by Joan Detz (Atheneum, 1992) is a humorous treatment of the fear of speaking before a large group.
11. Ask less accomplished students to write a creative piece using a new format (such as a television advertisement), which they can read orally before the class. Because these students will be the first to read these types of writings in class, the novelty usually sparks classmates' immediate attention and positive comments.

Communication Apprehension

A more serious phase of shyness is called **communication apprehension (CA)**, or *stage fright*. You can diagnose this difficulty by administering the Communication Apprehension Test (Box 13.1), which can help students understand and overcome their fears of communicating orally. This instrument consists of 23 statements that describe feelings about communicating. As you read each one, ask students to indicate how much each statement applies to them by marking 1 through 5—where 1 is *Strongly agree,* 2 is

13.1 DIAGNOSIS AND ASSESSMENT

Diagnosing Speaking Difficulties: The Communication Apprehension Test

1. I dislike participating in group discussions.
2. Generally, I am not comfortable while participating in group discussions.
3. I am tense and nervous while participating in group discussions.
4. I do not like to get involved in group discussions.
5. Engaging in a group discussion with new people makes me tense and nervous.
6. I am not calm or relaxed when I am called on to express an opinion at a meeting.
7. Generally, I am nervous when I have to participate in a meeting.
8. Usually, I am not calm or relaxed when I am called on to express an opinion at a meeting.
9. I am afraid to express myself at meetings.
10. Communicating at meetings usually makes me uncomfortable.
11. I am not relaxed when answering questions at a meeting.
12. While participating in a conversation with a new acquaintance, I feel very nervous.
13. I have a fear of speaking up in conversations.
14. Ordinarily, I am very tense and nervous in conversations.
15. Ordinarily, I am very calm and relaxed in conversations.
16. While conversing with a new acquaintance, I do not feel very relaxed.
17. I'm afraid to speak in conversations.
18. I have no fear of giving a speech.
19. Certain parts of my body feel tense and rigid while giving a speech.
20. I do not feel relaxed while giving a speech.
21. My thoughts become confused and jumbled when I am giving a speech.
22. I face the prospect of giving a speech with little confidence.
23. While giving a speech, I get so nervous I forget facts I really know.

Agree, 3 is *Undecided,* 4 is *Disagree,* and 5 is *Strongly disagree.* Encourage students to respond quickly with their first impressions; there are no right or wrong answers.

When you have read all 23 items, have students add up their points. Any total score above 65 indicates that the student is generally more apprehensive about communication than the average person. Scores above 80 indicate a very high level of communication apprehension; scores in this range may suggest that students will have some difficulty implementing some of the activities in this chapter. Special paired settings and one-to-one meetings can provide the extra support these students may need to overcome their anxiety. Extreme scores (below 50 or above 80) are abnormal. This means that the degree of apprehension may not be a realistic response to the situation. For example, people with very low scores may not experience apprehension in situations in which perhaps they should, and people with very high scores may experience apprehension when there is no rational reason for the anxiety. About 20 percent of the population falls in each extreme category.

Once they are diagnosed, you can assist students with CA by presenting sentence completions related to books they have read. Through this instruction, these students will eventually generate such oral sentences without your aid. For example, following the silent reading of a book, you could ask students with CA to complete the following sentences, which are listed from least to most difficult:

I wonder why [story character] did _____.

I wish I had known _____ about _____.

I wish I knew why [story character] did _____.

I wish I knew why [story character] did _____ because I _____.

The story took place at _____, which is like _____ that I know.

The most important part for me was _____.

I thought about _____, which wasn't in the book.

Another action you can take is to appoint a student with CA to be the person who will show a new student around the school. Being responsible for someone else makes it important for the anxious speaker to talk.

Using Drama to Increase Speaking Abilities

Once shy or developmentally delayed students are engaged in creating a dramatization of a book they read or a story they wrote, other educational objectives become more important. Specifically, through the excitement of the drama, the discipline it requires, and the rewards from the successful performance, previously uninspired students often become motivated to reach higher academic achievements. For example, after St. Augustine School in South Bronx (the poorest congressional district in the nation) introduced arts education, 98 percent of its students met New York State grade-level academic standards. During the same year, in another elementary school only a few blocks away, fewer than half of the students from the same neighborhood were reading at their grade level. Similar results have occurred through the Arts Connection for inner-city youth in New York City, the Artists-in-Residence Program of the Music Center of Los Angeles, and in the Sampson County Schools of North Carolina (Hanna, 1992; Surace, 1992).

These results occur because through drama, less accomplished literacy users feel "a sense of specialness, capability, achievement, and empowerment to make changes in their lives; they acquire self-discipline and new learning strategies; their attendance improves; they exhibit more mature behavior, including caring about others, a sense of responsibility, and an acceptance of delayed gratification; they are willing to 'work hard' and complete tasks; and their academic achievement, as measured by standardized reading tests, is equal to or exceeds that of their peers" (Hanna, 1992, p. 603).

Drama also enables students to actively construct meaning while emotionally engaged with literacy (Beyersdorfer & Shauer, 1993). It provides oral experiences that build from prior knowledge about concepts and the reading/writing behaviors (Glazer,

1989). Drama assists struggling literacy users to understand plot structures, inner feelings of literary characters, story themes, and how to use oral language to express important ideas and emotions. It also enhances their recall of oral and written words. Such literacy users also report that they enjoy the sociability of working with friends who "helped them get the hard words." Revising their scripts increased their writing abilities (Browning & McClintic, 1995; Shands, Deines, & Zuckerman, 1994).

Moreover, for the few minutes it takes these students to enact their drama, they exercise some control over their lives. Their use of literacy also commands the attention and applause of peers. In addition, when they invite others to participate in a play they author and direct, they can have final say over a literacy event. Equally important, drama enables students to move one of their private experiences into a public forum in which issues are discussed and new oral language forms mastered.

Dramatic activities should begin with few print prompts, and you should add props only as play practices enfold. Students can use the story frame presented in Table 10.1 (in Chapter 10) to outline their play. They can also choose a book on Resource Card 17, as these are books that struggling literacy users in grades K–8 selected as their favorites for adapting to drama.

For students with communication apprehension and second language difficulties, confidence increases more rapidly when puppets and masks are added to the production. Simple masks and puppet stages can be developed in only a few minutes, as illustrated in Figure 13.1. The grading system for dramatic productions shown in Table 13.1 can be used to enhance students' assessment and self-assessment.

Readers' Theater is a type of drama in which students read parts from a play or book. Everyone is on stage at the same time, but all except the person speaking have their backs to the audience. The books on Resource Card 17 can also be adapted as scripts for Readers' Theater for less accomplished literacy users.

RESOURCE CARD 17

Favorite Books for Adapting to Drama

Babbitt, N. (1975). *Tuck everlasting.* New York: Farrar, Straus & Giroux.

Blume, J. (1972). *Tales of a fourth grade nothing.* New York: Dutton.

Brittain, B. (1983). *The wish giver.* New York: Harper & Row.

Coerr, E. (1977). *Sadako and the thousand paper cranes.* New York: Putnam.

Fleischman, S. (1986). *The whipping boy.* New York: Greenwillow.

Gilson, J. (1983). *Thirteen ways to sink a sub.* New York: Lothrop, Lee & Shepard.

Marshall, P. (1983). *Reena and other stories.* Old Westbury, CT: Feminist Press.

Morrison, T. (1974). *Song of Solomon.* New York: Knopf.

Naylor, G. (1988). *Mama day.* New York: Ticknor & Fields.

FIGURE 13.1 Puppet Stages and Masks Students Can Make

Source: Simple masks taken from P. J. Finn (1993), *Helping Children Learn Language Arts,* p. 129. New York: Longman. Copyright © 1993 by Longman Publishing Group. Reprinted by permission of Addison Wesley Educational Publishers Inc.

TABLE 13.1 Grading System to Assess Students' Oral Language Development through Puppetry, Plays, Readers' Theater, and Other Productions

	Performance		
	Poor	*Average*	*Excellent*
Script well written (accurate, creative)			
Puppets or play well constructed and executed			
Works well in group			
Adequate preparation for performance			
Smooth presentation during show			
Stays within time boundaries			
Proper introduction and closing used			
Adequate sound projection			
Participation in practices			
Correct grammar usage			

Grading: Poor = 3, Average = 4, Excellent = 5, Not demonstrated = 0; total possible points = 50.

Source: Adapted from grid created by Dr. Lucinda H. Rose, College of Education, Mississippi State University, 1992.

Pathologically Related Speaking Difficulties

Students who have physically related articulation problems (e.g., cleft palate, lisp) should be referred to a language specialist to ensure that basic language skills are not impaired. Moreover, students who frequently stop and start over when telling stories may have a language difficulty beyond mere shyness or communication apprehension. Such symptoms should not be ignored. Similarly, although some students have difficulty attending to oral directions, others may be tuning out because they have quit trying to engage their listening abilities. To understand the words others say seems impossible. Only speech therapists and neurologists can identify the causes of pathologically related problems. You can employ the following instructional supports, however, while students receive special support outside of the classroom.

SUPPORT 1: MODIFIED SHARED READINGS. While pathologically related problems are being diagnosed, you can have less accomplished literacy users participate as often as possible in **shared readings** with you and groups of no more than four students. You can begin by reading the first few pages and asking for students' predictions. Whenever possible you can phrase questions so that students with pathologically related problems can answer with one word (e.g., "Suzanna, is the prediction you are making in your mind more like Jason's or Joanna's?").

Then, by the middle section of the book, you can emphasize the pronunciation of new vocabulary words, which are repeated orally by all members of the group in unison. Then, on the last pages, you can ask students to come to you, one-on-one, with a pointer and book, and have them read their favorite section of the book aloud. If possible, they can tell why it was their favorite. Soon many developing speakers will gain confidence to read this book or another before the class. (You will have suggested that they practice doing so at home with their families first.)

SUPPORT 2: SHARINGS. To initiate sharings, meet daily with speakers who have pathologically related difficulties developmentally delays to read a book that they selected (preferably one without chapters). Introduce this book by deciding which of the seven oral language functions (see page 419) it can help this student to develop. Then read a few pages with the student. Say that you are going to write a note to his or her parents about what you would like them to do tonight with the book. In the note, describe a type of conversation the family could have about this book, in which one of the seven functions of oral language could be practiced. Last, ask the parents and student to write you in return about their conversation about this book. Place your note and the book in a manila envelope.

As a result of this activity, many students for the first time have something so important to report about this at-home activity that they want to and do share in front of the class. When you follow this lesson with the following Tier 1 full-class support, these students continue to grow.

SUPPORT 3: ONCE-A-WEEK BOOK/EVENT/MOVIE/TV CONVERSATIONS. During weekly full-class conversational times, students have the opportunity to share something exciting, funny, emotional, or thought-provoking that they experienced through talking with another person. To begin this activity, ask students to share conversation about a book, event, movie, or TV show in pairs, then in groups of four, instead of following the traditional method in which one child speaks and the whole class listens. In this activity everyone talks and the most speakers have to address is four people. By midyear most less accomplished students are able to share their thoughts in groups of eight. Also at this time, you can introduce how to be an effective group leader and how to include many speakers in a conversation.

Second-Language Speaking Difficulties

In 1974, Public Law 93-380, the Bilingual Education Act, made provisions to enable students with limited English proficiency (LEP)—otherwise known as students acquiring English (SAE)—to have their learning needs met in the least restrictive possible environment. This law specified that oral language needs must also be met in such a way as to account for the different cultural factors that influence students' purposes for speaking, as described in Table 13.2.

TABLE 13.2 Program Models for Second-Language Speakers

Program Model	Student Population	Type of Instruction	Instructional Setting	Teacher
Bilingual education	LEP or SAE	Dual language instruction	Primary language is the medium of instruction only until the student masters English. This transitional model is the most common in the United States.	Bilingual
Maintenance bilingual program	LEP or SAE	Dual language instruction	Learning in both languages is supported and encouraged. Bilingualism, including biliteracy, is the goal.	Bilingual
Immersion strategy	LEP or SAE	All instruction in target language	Language is taught through the content lesson. Use of the native language is limited to case-by-case needs. Mainstreaming occurs after the first or second year.	Has specialized training in ESL and receptive skills in the students' primary languages
Bilingual Immersion Program (BIP)	LEP or SAE	Elementary programs of dual language instruction	Learning is based on the student's natural language, culture, background, and interests. This model consists of three major components: native language cognitive development, English language arts, and sheltered content area instruction in English.	Bilingual
English as a Second Language (ESL)	LEP or SAE	All instruction in target language	ESL programs are not bilingual programs, because instruction is not provided in two languages. ESL programs are English language development programs. The goal is to accelerate the acquisition of conversational language and equip students with the necessary skills to succeed in the regular all-English curriculum.	ESL-trained bilingual or English-speaking
Sheltered English	LEP	Modified form of English to ensure that language is comprehensible	This approach is often used in districts where LEP students speak many different languages.	ESL-trained bilingual or English-speaking

Source: Adapted from J. L. Smith & H. Johnson (1994), "Models for Implementing Literature in Content Studies," *The Reading Teacher (48)*3, pp. 198–209.

Language acquisition has been described as a subconscious process, learned informally in the context of its functional uses (Chomsky, 1975; Halliday, 1975). It also appears that students develop oral competence by focusing on the meaning of the message, not on its form or grammar. Thus, one theory of second-language acquisition holds that students acquire language by understanding messages or by receiving "comprehensible input" (Krashen, 1985). Stimulated by the sheer exposure to print in and out of school, many students acquire language and literacy incidentally, without formal instruction, connecting their first language to what they perceive in their environment (Krashen, 1989). For less accomplished literacy users, however, the amount of input they receive is partially a function of the linguistic competence they bring to their second language. For example, Cummins (1979) argues that if a child's first language vocabulary and concept knowledge is limited, he or she may have difficulty assimilating decontextualized or metaphorical language and also may not have insight into the English written language, which has different rules from English speech. Thus, many of these children may be "confronted by nonsense" (Smith, 1977) in the task of speaking and reading English. There is no way for them to relate the printed symbols to a known spoken phenomenon.

In addition, children for whom English is a second language need motivation to learn and to identify with members of their second-language group (Cummins, 1986; Trueba, 1987, 1989). Fearing failure, some children may construct an "affective filter" or defense system that prevents them from utilizing the input they receive for language acquisition (Krashen, 1985). In order to lower the filter, Krashen suggests that oral language programs become highly motivating and nonevaluative, and that they involve children in ways that help them temporarily "forget" they are hearing or reading another language—such as when they are engaged in drama, conversations, and small group rehearsals outdoors. Similarly, higher levels of English proficiency are associated with greater vocabulary gains. Data suggest that for students who are not increasing their competence in English, word knowledge through incidental learning tends to follow the "rich get richer" pattern (Shefelbine, 1990; Stanovich, 1986; Walberg & Tsai, 1983).

Although Spanish is the predominant second language represented in schools, more than 20 other home languages may be present in your classroom ("Numbers and Needs," 1991). The gap between second-language users and their English-speaking peers widens increasingly throughout the school years (Boldenberg & Gallimore, 1991). To help narrow this gap, many reading specialists teach second-language users phrases in oral and written English with the help of books such as those listed in Box 13.2.

Diagnosing Second-Language Learners' Speaking Needs

To assess the level at which second-language speakers can read English when they enter your room, ask them to write a list of 10 English words. Analyze their vowel/consonant writing to detect overgeneralizations. Also, ascertain which vowel sounds in each student's native language do not exist in English—and vice versa. This will help you coach second-language learners in the vowel sounds they need.

Not only students' home language but also their home culture and values may differ significantly from your language goals at school and may interfere with Standard English principles. Students will have serious difficulties if you ask them to abandon

13.2 READING SPECIALISTS

Instructional Interventions for Bilingual Students

The books listed here help teach English idioms and phrases to second-language learners.

CONVERSATIONAL POEMS FOR CHORAL READING

Fleischman, Paul. *I Am Phoenix*. Illus. by Ken Nutt. Harper, 1985.

———. *Joyful Noise*. Illus. by Eric Beddows. Harper, 1988.

Hoberman, Mary Ann. "An Only Child" in *Fathers, Mothers, Sisters, Brothers*. Illus. by Marylin Hafner. Little, Brown, 1991.

Hopkins, Lee Bennett. *Side by Side: Poems to Read Together*. Illus. by Hilary Knight. Simon & Schuster, 1988.

Joseph, Lynn. "Pulling Seine" in *Coconut Kind of Day*. Illus. by Sandra Speidel. Lothrop, Lee & Shepard, 1990.

Merriam, Eve. *You Be Good and I'll Be Night*. Illus. by Karen L. Schmidt. Morrow, 1988.

———. "Windshield Wiper" in Kennedy, X. J., *Knock at a Star*. Little, Brown, 1982.

"O Won't You Sit Down," African American spiritual, in Bryan, Ashley, *All Night, All Day*. Atheneum, 1991.

There's a Hole in the Bucket. Illus. by Nadine Bernard Westcott. Harper, 1990.

Weil, Zaro. *Mud, Moon, and Me*. Illus. by Jo Burroughs. Houghton Mifflin, 1992.

Wolman, Bernice, Ed. *Taking Turns: Poetry to Share*. Illus. by Catherine Stock. Atheneum, 1992.

IDIOMS

Ciardi, John. "This Man Talked about You" in *I Met a Man*. Illus. by Robert Osborn. Houghton Mifflin, 1973.

Kennedy, X. J. "Telephone Talk" in *The Kite That Braved Old Orchard Beach*. Illus. by Marion Young. M. K. McElderry/Macmillan, 1991.

Lee, Dennis. "The Secret Place" and "Secrets" in *The Ice Cream Store*. Illus. by David McPhail. Scholastic, 1991.

Livingston, Myra Cohn. "I Never Told" in *I Never Told and Other Poems*. M. K. McElderry/Macmillan, 1992.

———. "Secret Passageway" in *Worlds I Know and Other Poems*. Illus. by Tim Arnold. M. K. McElderry/Macmillan, 1985.

McCord, David. "Secret" in *All Small*. Illus. by Madelaine Gill Linden. Little, Brown, 1986.

Prelutsky, Jack. "I Had a Little Secret" in *Beneath a Blue Umbrella*. Illus. by Garth Williams. Greenwillow, 1990.

Seabrooke, Brenda. "Clues" and "Secrets" in *Judy Scuppernong*. Illus. by Ted Lewin. Cobblehill/Dutton, 1990.

Viorst, Judith. "Secrets" in *If I Were in Charge of the World and Other Worries*. Illus. by Lynn Cherry. Atheneum/Macmillan, 1981.

their language, culture, and values at school, however; and having to make such a choice will be counterproductive to their learning and self-esteem. You must, therefore, make modifications in your instruction to adapt to special needs of students with limited English proficiency.

Addressing Second-Language Learners' Speaking Needs

In the 1990s educators moved to Banks's Integration of Ethnic Content program, in which students not only learn the heroes, holidays, and discrete cultural elements within many groups, but also view concepts, issues, and events from many cultural perspectives before they make classroom and personal decisions on important social issues. (See Banks, 1991, and the discussion in Chapter 5 of this textbook for more information about this multicultural education perspective.)

Students with limited English proficiency can be served by the following programs:

1. *English as a Second Language (ESL):* In these homogeneously grouped classes, instruction emphasizes learning of English exclusively. Second-language users are exposed to learner-centered activities stressing everyday communication of meaning in English.
2. *Bilingual Education:* In these classes both English and the native language are used, and instruction is given in both languages. Some of these classes include students who are not limited in their English proficiency so that they can learn two languages (Reyes, Laliberty, & Orbanosky, 1993).
3. *Education of the Bilingual Program (EBP):* In these classes instruction occurs only in English but takes into account the linguistic and cultural features of the native language. The differences in speaking patterns between languages are taught within the content of holidays, heroes, and values of the native language, along with topics discussed at home relative to the first language. Some of these programs follow a "guarded English" model in which English is taught in a simplified version. Some follow a "structured integrative approach" in which English content area words are taught with connecting words in the first language of the child. Some are taught through "immersion"—in which, from the moment students enter the room, only English can be used by everyone in the room.

Other specific instructional supports and activities are also effective in addressing the needs of students with second-language speaking difficulties, including the following.

USING BOOKS IN SPANISH AND ENGLISH. Using books in Spanish and English is a Tier 2 support method utilizing peer tutors. To start, students should select a book from Resource Card 18, which contains books in Spanish and English that second-language readers and their tutors have recommended as their favorites.

Before the first tutoring session, teach students how to read together by distributing copies of Figure 13.2 and demonstrating how they are to begin a page by reading one line in Spanish and then the corresponding line in English. Then they are to stop and ask what the line means. Students proceed in this manner to the end of the page. Then tutors read the complete page in English alone, allowing tutees to refer silently to the Spanish if they desire. Second-language learners describe what they comprehended. After all separate pages have been read in English once, tutors and tutees read the full book together in English and discuss the meaning of the book as a whole. You can close this introduction by modeling as a tutor while all pairs watch you and a second-language learner engage in the full process.

Evaluating pairs at the end of every 3-week period is valuable. In doing so you can record the number of books read, the number of new English words learned, increased

RESOURCE CARD 18

Favorite Books in Spanish and English

Blanco, A. (1992). *The desert mermaid.* San Francisco: Children's Book Press.

Cruz, A. (1991). *The woman who outshone the sun.* San Francisco: Children's Book Press.

Dana, D. (1974). *The elephant and his secret.* New York: Atheneum.

de Brunhoff, L. (1965). *Babar's Spanish lessons.* New York: Random House.

Dorros, A. (1991). *Abuela.* New York: Dutton Children's Books.

Du Bois, W. P., & Po, L. (1972). *The hare and the tortoise and the tortoise and the hare.* New York: Doubleday.

Eastman, P. D. (1982). *Big dog . . . little dog.* New York: Random House.

Frasconi, A. (1955). *See and say: A picture book in four languages.* New York: Harcourt Brace.

Hofer, G. B., & Day, R. P. (1992). *Listen children, a unique collection of Mother Goose rhymes, poems, songs, jingles, and riddles.* Austin, TX: Eakin.

Joslin, S. (1966). *There is a bull on my balcony.* New York: Harcourt Brace.

Mistral, G. (1972). *Crickets and frogs.* New York: Atheneum.

Nardelli, R. R. (1966). *The cat in the hat beginner book dictionary in Spanish.* New York: Beginner Books.

Prieto, M. (1975). *The fleas of the panther.* Englewood Cliffs, NJ: Prentice Hall.

Rohmer, H. (1982). *The legend of Food Mountain.* San Francisco: Children's Book Press.

Sheheen, D. (1984). *A child's picture dictionary.* New York: Adama Books.

Williams, L. (1984). *The little red hen.* New York: Aladdin.

Tortillitas para Mama and other nursery rhymes. (1981). New York: Holt, Rinehart & Winston.

comprehension evidenced, increased joy in literacy witnessed, and the degree to which pleasant interpersonal exchanges are occurring between pairs. Alter partnerships if any of the above are not occurring.

Other activities that tutors and tutees can complete together include (1) talking in both their first language and English while writing and creating drama; (2) writing to pen pals in both their first language and English; (3) listening to English audiotapes of books as they read along in a book that is printed in either their first language or English; (4) labeling objects in the room with English and first-language phrases; and (5) assuming leadership positions as a class officer or introducer of adult guest speakers.

USING CAPTIONED TELEVISION. If possible, you may wish to incorporate captioned television broadcasts into your program. Information about obtaining decoders can be obtained from the source provided at the end of the chapter.

Research indicates that closed captions significantly increase reading comprehension for second-language students who are reading at or above third grade level (Jensema, 1983; National Captioning Institute, 1990). There are additional benefits:

Brilla, Brilla, Estrellita

Brilla, brilla, estrellita,
Un milagro, tan bonita.
Tan lejana, ay te cante,
En el cielo, un diamante.
Brilla, brilla, estrellita,
Un milagro, tan bonita.

Twinkle, Twinkle, Little Star

Twinkle, twinkle, little star,
How I wonder what you are.
Up above the world so high,
Like a diamond in the sky.
Twinkle, twinkle, little star,
How I wonder what you are.

FIGURE 13.2 Reading Spanish–English Texts in Pairs: An Example

Captioned television also increases listening comprehension and speaking fluency, as reported by Neuman (1990). For example:

> Mary had little confidence in her reading ability. . . . After having watched captioned television three different times, Mary was observed to be absorbed in reading the captioning and read aloud. It seemed that her confidence was increasing to the point where she was proud of her fluency and wanted others to know about her success. She even wanted to read a book to me. (p. 51)

These viewing sessions can be used in a variety of ways to develop reading, writing, and speaking. To begin, you can review the "thinking aloud" activities recommended by the National Captioning Institute, which are presented in Table 13.3.

Struggling second-language literacy users can choose whether they want to learn 10 spoken words or 10 written words as they watch each captioned TV segment. Regardless of their selection, during the viewing you request that each student write on a sheet of paper 10 words they want to learn as well as clues to each word's meaning or pronunciation. Immediately after the viewing ends, ask students and their partners to read and discuss each other's lists. Then those who wish to increase their oral language can prepare an oral presentation for their partner in which they use their words to describe an event that could occur or has occurred in their life. Those who wish to increase their written language can use their words to write a story in which they are the main characters. Table 13.3 can be also used without captioned television to develop reading, speaking, and writing abilities for second-language users and dialectically different students.

TABLE 13.3 Thinking Aloud

The focus of this activity for second-language learners is to build both comprehension and oral expression. These students need to develop the kinds of strategies that good readers use to make meaning from material. By "thinking aloud" the teacher can model productive strategies and thus can encourage students to develop self-monitoring strategies in comprehension.

1. To begin this classroom activity, watch a captioned program with a highly predictable plot. Periodically stop the video, using the pause button after a particular scene. "Think aloud" about the meaning of the program to students. There are many possible strategies that might be helpful, including the following:

   ■ Demonstrate how to use prior knowledge.

     For example, "Now I know the robber will get caught because it's a mystery, and that always seems to happen at the end."

   ■ Show how to monitor comprehension strategies.

     For example, "I'm not sure I really understood the part about carbohydrates and energy. Maybe I should wait to form an opinion about it, until I get more information."

   ■ Describe how to use context clues to guess at unfamiliar vocabulary.

     For example, "I really don't know what 'fatigued' means, but from the way it's used in the program, I would guess it means 'tired.'"

   ■ Demonstrate that it is appropriate to predict and guess what may happen next, even if it turns out not to be correct.
     For example, "From what I've seen so far, I think the man in the blue shirt is going to win the prize. There were several clues that make me think so. . . ."

     You might wish to use this modeling technique on a regular basis, modeling one or two reading strategies per lesson.

2. Following this demonstration, encourage students to try to monitor their comprehension. Using a different highly predictable program (they'll have more success with this type of show, especially in the beginning), stop the tape after several brief episodes. Ask students general questions, such as:

   ■ What do you think will happen next?
   ■ Why do you think so? What is your proof?
   ■ Do you have any questions?

   Students will enjoy predicting future events in a free-flowing way. Tell them that they are using very complex comprehension skills and succeeding in monitoring these processes as they watch.

Source: Adapted from National Captioning Institute (1990), "Thinking Aloud" from *The New English Teacher: A Guide to Using Captioned Television with Language Minority Students*, p. 6. Vienna, VA: The Institute. Reprinted by permission of National Captioning Institute.

Dialectically Different Language Learners

Dialectically different literacy users have qualities in their spoken versions of English that interfere with others' understanding their message. Students for whom there may be special dialectical instructional needs are rural, African American, Appalachian, migrant, Native American, Inuit, emigrant, or Cajun. Oral language differences can also interfere with these students' reading comprehension, speaking effectiveness, and writing power.

Talking, reading, and writing serve specific political, personal, social, and cultural purposes. Language is formed by many contexts, such as societal norms, communities, and individuals' social and personal identities (Luke, 1995). An individual student's language culture consists of learned systems of meaning, communicated by means of cultural, language, and other symbol systems that have "representational, directive, and affective functions and are capable of creating cultural entities and particular senses of reality" (D'Andrade, 1984, p. 116). Students use these personal language resources to index the beliefs, lifestyles, patterns, and values of their particular groups; these resources are also employed as students form an identity and assert their difference. Most important, if a student reads or hears something that someone else communicates and does not understand it, or if a student's own language is misunderstood or ridiculed, or if communication is prohibited, teachers have a responsibility to remove any obstacles without devaluing the breadth and diversity of that student's language use. For example, occasionally students attempt to interject statements of their backgrounds and histories into the books they read at school. When this occurs teachers must recognize that these expressions are statements of their backgrounds and histories. These students had the courage to display their identity in the "public domain of school" (Luke, 1995, p. 38). When these expressions are interpreted by educators as individual differences and personal voices, students can use their language to read, interpret, and make sense of themselves and their surroundings.

When dialectically different students enter school, they are confronted with a language that replaces the familiar with something they experience as artificial. Some researchers suggest that the result is a cultural collision by which some students come to associate literacy with a rigid and distant set of standards, expectations, and purposes; they do not grasp that reading and writing are tools for self-realization (Tonnessen, 1995).

Moreover, the influence of cultural, social, and dialectical background knowledge on reading comprehension is particularly problematic for students whose home language or language variety differs markedly from the mainstream standard language that is taught in most schools and that is reflected in the literary texts taught in these schools (Applebee, 1988). Research has demonstrated that students' participation in instructional discourse is severely impeded when teachers did not take into account the language variation of their students (Cazden, 1986). Also, if the school language interferes with comprehension, students will use more elaborate language when they are with their peers without a teacher being present.

The term *discourse* implies a "dialect of both linguistic form and social communicative practices . . . that are constructed in moment-to-moment interactions" (Hicks,

1995, p. 51). Many scholars of language and linguistics acknowledge that words have semantic content, which we refer to as their dictionary meanings. However, when a word, phrase, or sentence is uttered or written, it assumes meaning that is inherently social in nature. Words will make sense for students only as they acquire their meanings through social usage (Bakhtin, 1986; Hicks, 1995).

As an example, Black English has five major social devices that contribute to its artistic qualities and reflect an attitude toward verbal behavior that speakers of this language commonly possess (Paznik, 1976):

1. The manipulation of language to engage the sympathies of another
2. The indirectional figure, such as use of double entendre and irony
3. The orational figure, such as extensive use of exaggerated language and heightened deliveries
4. The use of rhythm, meter, and repetition to achieve aesthetic effect
5. The imagistic figure, or figurative language used to create word pictures (Lee, 1995)

Black English also demonstrates a unique richness; it values the playful possibilities of language, manipulation of language for its own artistic merit rather than simply as a tool of literal communication, manipulation of the symbolic functions of language, and use of densely imagistic and figurative language to express complex ideas in a few words (Lee, 1995). Proverbs and figurative language are also used routinely in this social cultural discourse and as socializing tools in family life (Smitherman, 1977; Smitherman-Donaldson, Daniel, & Jeremiah, 1987). For example, many mothers quote proverbs to their children and use them as child-rearing devices to teach rapidly and in no uncertain terms about life and giving (e.g., "A hard head makes a soft behind," "If you make your bed hard, you goin' have to lie in it," "Still waters run deep," and "God don't like ugly"). Use of proverbs can be traced to West African roots; they are densely metaphoric and aphoristic and clearly involve plays on language, and they "drive home the points with short, succinct statements which have the sound of wisdom and power" (Smitherman, 1977, p. 95).

The first instructional adaptation for assisting dialectically different learners is for teachers to empower students who may be academically at risk (in part because of cultural and language differences) by making their expectations explicit. Another way to empower is to encourage students to support their responses to the complex problems of interacting with texts and to draw on their knowledge of the social world of the texts so that all meanings are valued. As one researcher put it: "Insisting that students consistently articulate how they knew something was true imposed a kind of conscious regulation of their language and strategy use as an ongoing monitoring of their level of understanding" (Lee, 1995).

When mismatches occur between the child's life-based experiences and those presented in books, the problem is that to accept what they read, some students must contradict a part of who they are. Even more difficult to resolve is the situation that results if dialectically distinct readers try to read with a preoccupied mind or have different conceptions about a reading topic. Conceptual change must take place if meaning is to occur, and such readers must have the freedom to voice their personal understandings as near the point of initial reading contact as possible (Bransford & Stein, 1993). Many may not be aware that they hold different conceptions unless these concepts are explicitly contrasted with the author's meaning in the text (Beck & Dole, 1992). You can help make these conceptual gaps explicit by asking questions like these:

- What did you notice in the story that was important, interesting, surprising, or confusing to you?
- What does this remind you of in your life or in the lives of people around you?
- How is this story different from what you expected? Why do you think these differences exist?

Instructional Activities for Second-Language or Dialectically Different Students

Students from second-language or dialectically different home backgrounds can profit from instruction about how to make required inferences, how to give attention to salient details, how to interpret figurative language, and how to draw on evidence from disparate parts of the text as well as on their personal experiences of the social world represented in the texts. Several instructional methods specifically address these difficulties.

TEACHING HISTORICAL PARTICULARS. Teaching historical background is important because reading and interpreting complex literature involves at least two domains: (1) knowledge of the social world represented in the texts as well as of the customs, values, motivation, and personality traits of typical and atypical characters; and (2) knowledge of the rules of significance operating within particular literary genres and particular literary traditions. Social customs, values, and personality traits of the characters, for example, are never simply broadly human; they are specific to unique cultures and the products of particular historical moments. Thus, culture, ethnicity, and historical place are variables influencing the knowledge base implicit in the act of interpreting literature. Students can be asked in whole-class and small group discussions to interpret what each speaker in a text or classroom conversation actually intended, to decide whether the words printed or said conveyed all that was implied, and to justify their answers.

PICTURE STORY FRAMES. Instruction by means of picture story frames occurs best in small groups. To begin the lesson, Xerox pictures from a book and place them randomly on a chart. Ask students to look at the pictures and think about what the author may have written to tell the story. Younger students then volunteer to tell the story orally in their own dialect; older students can write their dialectical version. When all who desire to share have had the opportunity, you can read the original story as the author wrote it. Students enjoy comparing each section or oral description of their stories to the author's. By ending the lesson with this comparison, students can deduce the differences between their dialect and Standard English; they can also read new words that can be used synonymously with those they normally use.

One of the reasons this activity produces rapid growth in Standard English dialect was determined by Norris (1991). He discovered that written texts are the best tools in oral/written language instruction for students who experience dialectical differences. Through written texts these students encounter the elements of language that are especially troublesome for them—including abstract vocabulary, complex syntactic and semantic structures, inflectional morphological forms, cohesion differences, inferences, temporal relationship markers, and types of discourse structures that are not common in their out-of-school oral or written language experiences (Hedrick & Cunningham, 1995; Norris, 1991).

After several sessions, many students enjoy tape-recording their stories and translating them into written Standard English whenever they replay the text. Also, using story frames (story maps), as shown in Table 10.1, Chapter 10, not only increases students' awareness of their dialectical differences but also builds traditional story structure knowledge that can be used to create oral and written stories in the future.

THE VILLAGE ENGLISH ACTIVITY. Because of the rich diversity found in the homes of students from different social, cultural, and dialectical backgrounds, it is becoming increasingly important to ensure that students understand the meanings of words they will frequently encounter in both printed and oral Standard English. This teaches students about the richness of their home language while displaying reciprocal word choices in Standard English.

To begin, you write OUR LANGUAGE HERITAGE at the left side of a poster board and STANDARD AMERICAN ENGLISH at the right side. After explaining to students that their dialect or language contains many expressions and vocabulary words that vary from those used in Standard English, you can ask them to share some of the most cherished expressions in their families. As each is volunteered, other members of the group describe synonyms they use at home or have read in books. If the synonym suggested is a home language derivative, you list it in parentheses after the word on the left side of the poster board; if it is a version of Standard English, you list it on the right side of the board. You can conclude this activity by listing the most advanced Standard English vocabulary from a book students are to read next. As you list and define each term on the right side of the poster board, you can also ask students to suggest synonyms for this word that they use when they talk, or similar words they have read. Then they write these on the poster board as you hold up pictures from the book that illustrate individual vocabulary words.

The Village English Activity is particularly beneficial in that it portrays the value of having many different dialects in a country. Students can see how a varied vocabulary enables them to select the most specific word to communicate most accurately. Students can also better understand why a Standard English exists—people often want to speak in a conventional manner so that they can be understood by people from many varied language heritages. Students often add to this chart in the months that follow, when they hear or read a particularly vivid word or phrase at home or school. An important concept that this activity and the others in this section convey is that when students from different home language backgrounds do not understand a word or phrase as they read, it could be that the language used is different from their own. Pausing to reflect on expressions they would typically use in the situation described could be an effective strategy to employ at these points in their reading so that meaning-making is not interrupted.

"I" MEMOIRS. "Tell me a story about when I was little" is a strategy developed by Burke (1991) to increase dialectically different students' knowledge of the richness of their home language. She discovered that students who come to appreciate the communication capacity of their own language significantly increase their desire to learn and understand Standard English. "I" memoirs appeal to students because as parents and caregivers recount past family adventures, they provide a snapshot of the students' own behavior and personality as well as evidences of how they used their language to connect with other members of their family. Significant moments in their own development are vicariously recaptured. Moreover, through this oral sharing, more bonds are created between the adult who tells the tale and the child who shares the intimacy of the moment conveyed through the story.

You begin this lesson by asking students to think of events in their lives they would like to learn more about. Instruct them to ask adult family members questions like these:

"Tell me about something I did when I was little."

"Tell me about a time when I got lost or lost something."

"Tell me about the neighborhood where we lived when I was born."

"Tell me about the neighborhood where you lived when you were little."

"Tell me about someone who used to come and visit at your house when you were growing up and why you liked them so much."

"Tell me about my favorite things to do when I was little."

After the adult has recounted a family story, recommend that the child practice retelling it. You can ask the parent to write it for younger students, or ask older students to write their favorite aspects of the story. Alternatively, you can record students' stories on tape to keep as evidence of their oral language development. Burke (1991) also recommends that you send the tape home so that it can become a treasured documentation of the family's history.

This lesson can begin or culminate with students' reading books that offer varied views of family life and that explain how different activities become "I" memoirs for families from varied cultures and dialectic backgrounds. Resource Card 19 lists books in this genre that are recommended by Burke (1991).

USING MINIMAL PAIR CONTRASTS TO TEACH ABSTRACT WORDS. As you know, teaching pictorial nouns to dialectically distinct and second-language learners is relatively easy when compared to teaching abstract, nonpictorial words. One method of teaching abstract words, however, is to compare minimal contrasts between their spellings and the spelling of a pictorial word.

For example, to teach the words *the* and *three*, compare their spellings to the pictorial word *tree*. To do so, draw a tree on a sheet of paper and write TREE below it. Ask second-language learners to repeat the word orally, then to read it. Then write THREE and THE beneath TREE. Ask second-language learners to repeat these words and then to read them. Last, write THE and THREE on another sheet of paper and ask students to picture the

RESOURCE CARD 19

Books That Can Help Build Oral Language Abilities in Dialectically Different Learners

Flournoy, V. (1985). *The patchwork quilt.* New York: Dial. (Memories of a family are conveyed in a homemade coverlet. This book assists students to reflect on heirlooms in their own lives.)

Houston, G. (1992). My *great aunt Arizona.* New York: HarperCollins. (A description of the author's great aunt, who influenced generations of schoolchildren.)

Johnson, A. (1989). *Tell me a story, Mama.* New York: Orchard. (An African American child asks his mother to tell stories about her childhood but supplies the events from the story by heart before the mother can recite them.)

MacLachlan, P. (1985). *Sarah, plain and tall.* New York: HarperCollins. (The author obtained the inspiration for this book from the family stories her mother used to tell when she was a young girl.)

MacLachlan, P. (1994). *Skylark.* New York: HarperCollins. (A sequel to *Sarah, plain and tall.*)

Martin, B., & Archambault, J. (1987). *Knots on a counting rope.* New York: Holt. (A Native American boy and his grandfather sit at a campfire as the grandfather recounts the boy's favorite tale about his childhood.)

Polacco, P. (1988). *The keeping quilt.* New York: Simon & Schuster. (A companion to *The patchwork quilt* in that methods of recording family memoirs are described.)

Say, A. (1993). *Grandfather's journey.* New York: Houghton Mifflin. (A young boy reminisces about his grandfather's love for his homeland and America.)

outline of the word by drawing a box to contain the word. Some will also enjoy creating their own abstract picture to convey meaning of the word. For example, one student outlined the word *the* like this:

Last, repeat the words and ask students to tell the minimal contrasts between them. Then remove the visual images and ask each student, individually, to come to the board and read each word and use it in a sentence.

DEMONSTRATING FIRST LANGUAGES OF YOUR STUDENTS. If you do not know how to read or speak Spanish or another first language of your students, attempting to read a book in that language to the class enables these students to become class heroes. As they assist you to pronounce words, you can also demonstrate how persistent attention to words increases competence. Second-language speakers will also see that by the end of the book you are able to read the frequently repeated words unaided.

This modeling builds their confidence and models a process they can follow to learn English. Fournier (1993) reports another value of this method:

> The discussion [as I read the book] was a manifestation of everything I had always hoped could happen in a truly bilingual classroom, where both languages and all cultures were valued and where great literature lived within its walls. No one dictated the format, just as no one dictated the content of this discussion. It occurred naturally because the conditions were right and because the book was really good. The implications were significant because this was the first time I had experienced monolingual English children working for meaning from a Spanish-language text. Spanish-speaking children helped me with the pronunciation of words I stumbled on. They also helped the monolingual English children with ideas they could not pick up through the illustrations. (p. 178)

LABELING CLASSROOM OBJECTS IN TWO LANGUAGES OR DIALECTS. Labeling or having directions in two languages communicates the high value you place on bilingualism and on your students' culture. Key phrases in Spanish you can use in your classroom include these:

sí = yes

muchas gracias = thank you

buenos días = good morning

adiós = good-bye

hola = hello

¿cómo está usted? = how are you?

me gusta = I like

quiero = I want

me llamo = my name is

¿qué? = what?

¿por qué? = why?

¿dónde está? = where is he/she/it?

la mesa = the table

la puerta = the door

la silla = the chair

la ventana = the window

los libros = the books

uno = one

dos = two

tres = three

cuatro = four

cinco = five

seis = six

siete = seven

ocho = eight

nueve = nine

diez = ten

Labeling increases vocabulary, as does wide reading (Nagy, Herman, & Anderson, 1985). As demonstrated in Figure 13.3, Kristina, a fourth grade Russian student, learned English in less than 6 weeks with a reader in the fifth grade who created a new English–Russian sheet (with the help of a Russian–English dictionary). They worked together for 45 minutes daily. After studying the words together, Kristina turned her paper over and wrote the English words from memory as Lisa dictated them to her.

USING MODIFIED JOURNAL WRITINGS. Journal writing assists bilingual and dialectically different students with their oral language abilities as well as with their written language skills. As discussed in Chapter 11, in journal writing the format is not as formal as required for other types of writing, and the language used for journal entries approximates that of spoken English. And journal entries should be read orally. This oral reading can be completed by the student or by a friend as this student reads along orally or silently.

Journal writing can begin with rebus writings in which single sentences are composed. Such writing can also begin with conversational prompts that you write on the

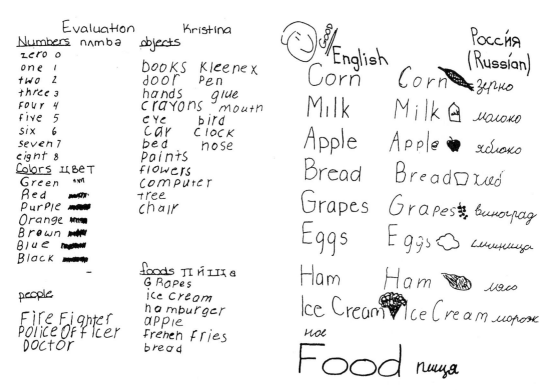

FIGURE 13.3 Labeling Activity to Teach English Equivalents: A Russian Example

board; this way, students can create a full story with single sentences without having to create a plot—which would require story grammar knowledge that they may not have mastered. This activity will be the first that you can use to lead students into a stronger ability to use vivid verbs and write better descriptions of explicit details.

Second-language users are now ready to write their own autobiographies as the first step into creating story grammar. They also profit from dialogue journals between you and themselves. As Shuy (1987) found, students who write in dialogue journals more than double the number of written and oral questions they ask their teacher. Also, through such student-centered instruction and journal writing, Cazden (1986) reported that migrant children moved 1.5 to 4.2 grade levels in reading ability in only one year. Hayes (1991) reported similar growth.

When individual students are ready, you can also introduce basic sentence structures in English, including the placement of adjectives and adverbs and the agreement of nouns and verbs. An effective method is to present several concepts orally, using familiar objects as props. For example, bilingual students could hear, say, and then write the words *under, up, on, beside, table, chair, book, in, over,* and *behind* in sentences to describe the location of a book, which they would place in different spots relative to a chair and table.

Increasing Oral Reading Fluency

Related to oral language problems is reading fluency. Nonfluent reading is the greatest impediment to meaning-making for speakers and readers (Smith, 1985; Stiles, 1991). Most nonfluent readers find it difficult to focus on meaning when they are struggling to sound out letters, moving their lips, subvocalizing, pointing to individual words, losing their place, and feeling frustrated by their line-by-line decoding failures. Therefore, because fluency is necessary for comprehension, this section of the chapter describes several methods of building fluency for students with oral language difficulties. Most do not realize that increased speed enables greater oral and written comprehension—an anomaly they never expected, as this student reported (Stiles, 1991, p. 19):

> I tried reading faster and it worked really good. I read about 25 pages today. I didn't talk and didn't move my lips. I understood everything. I didn't think it would work, but it did!

Another reason fluency is important is that slowness decreases the number of words read in a year. Specifically, as Stanovich (1986) reported, the three most fluent students in a sixth grade class will read more words in a 10-month period outside of school than the three least fluent readers would in 46 years! At this rate, most fluent readers will read more in a year and a half than the least fluent readers in their lifetime.

Unfortunately, in past years oral reading practices significantly hindered oral language fluency for less accomplished readers (Allington, 1980). Improper patterns of correcting oral reading errors can cause many of these students to stop reading, lose their train of thought, interrupt the rhythm of English language clues, and frequently lose their place. Although some teachers correct fewer than a third of more proficient readers' oral reading errors, they generally interrupt less accomplished students constantly and immediately, at the point of all errors, rather than waiting until the end of the sentence or dismissing some errors. When such interruptions occur, these students are reluctant to talk before their peers, and they rapidly fall into the habit of slow, staccato, word-by-word reading. To help you judge normal rates, average rates of speed for readers are shown in Table 13.4.

Another benefit of oral reading fluency for students with oral language needs is that listening to their voices while reading often enhances their self-concepts and decoding abilities. The rhythm clues of English assist in meaning-making, especially for communication apprehension students. This is particularly apparent among such students in grades 4 and above, as they are frequently required to decode words that are not common in their everyday lives and school-based experiences. Furthermore, without fluency, slow reading and hesitations result in greater difficulty with silent reading comprehension.

Whenever possible, do not ask students with oral language difficulties to read orally if listeners are reading the text along silently. Such reading practices are particularly embarrassing for these students. A more effective strategy, when a student reads haltingly, is to ask, "Can you read this quickly?" or say, "Put the words all together so it sounds like talking" (Clay, 1993, p. 52).

The most frequent reason for an absence of fluency is that students are continually asked to read text that is too difficult. Because of the decoding challenge, they rarely experience the pleasure of problem-free reading or the beauty of the flow of English words. Most fluency work should occur with materials that the students consider easy and interesting and that present no decoding or comprehension challenges.

To reduce the difficulty of reading material, **choral reading**—an interpretation of text by a group of voices—can be used (Rhodes & Dudley-Manning, 1988). The benefits and

TABLE 13.4 Average and Slow Oral Reading Rates

Grade Level	Average Rate (wpm)	Slow Rate (wpm)
2	70–100	
3	95–130	
4	120–170	120
5	160–210	160
6	180–230	180
7	180–240	180
8	195–240	198
9	215–260	215
12	225–260	225

Source: R. Richek, A. List, & J. Lerner (1983) "Reading Problems: Diagnosis and Remediation," *The Reading Teacher, 23*(4), p. 133; adapted from A. J. Harris & E. R. Sipay (eds.) (1990), *How to Increase Reading Ability: A Guide to Developmental & Remedial Methods,* 9th ed. New York: Longman. Copyright © 1990 by Longman. Reprinted by permission of Addison Wesley Educational Publishers Inc.

procedures for implementing this method appear in Table 13.5. Once students are adept at reading chorally, they also enjoy reading lyrics of their favorite songs and rap songs they create. Figure 13.4 is a sample of such a creative rap composition.

In another method for developing fluency, you begin a discovery discussion with a book the student considers easy and interesting. Place an acetate over the first page of this text, and on the acetate have the student draw a continuous underline until he or she reaches a place where a pause would occur if the student were reading the text orally. Then the student begins a new underline, again stopping where a pause would occur. When finished, you use a different color marker to demonstrate how, when reading orally, one can read to the end of phrases and sentences without pausing. You draw continuously beneath the words as you read them orally without pausing between individual words. Then ask the student to read the words that are continuously underlined

---

TABLE 13.5 Choral Reading

Choral reading is also called choral speaking, verse speaking, and unison speaking. Choral reading is the interpretation of poetry or prose by many voices speaking as one. It is best to allow developing readers to arrange the text into the type of speaking parts they desire.

Benefits of Choral Reading

- Develops an appreciation for reading and speaking as well as for good literature
- Adds beauty and enjoyment to a speech and reading improvement program
- Encourages group participation and cooperation
- Reduces students' inhibitions about speaking before a group
- Increases developing readers' fluency

Types of Choral Reading

1. *Unison Reading:* All voices speak as one.
   > Stop! Look! Listen!
   > Before you cross the street.
   > Use your eyes; use your ears;
   > *Then* use your feet!
   > > —Anonymous

2. *Line-a-Child or Sequence Reading:* Each child reads at least one line. Readers must come in on time to prevent missing a beat.

   This Little Cow

1st Child:	This little cow eats grass.
2nd Child:	This little cow eats hay.
3rd Child:	This little cow drinks water.
4th Child:	This little cow runs away.
5th Child:	This little cow does nothing
All:	But just lies down all day.

   > —Mother Goose

TABLE 13.5 *(continued)*

3. *Antiphonal Reading:* The group is divided into two sections (girls/boys, etc.). Each group takes half the selection. A question–answer format or dialogue poetry is well suited to this arrangement.

Baa, Baa, Black Sheep

Group I: Baa, baa, black sheep,
                Have you any wool?
Group II: Yes, sir; yes, sir.
                Three bags full.
                            —Mother Goose

4. *Refrain Reading:* Students have the responsibility of coming in on time and responding rhythmically with the repetition of a word or phrase.

A Farmer Went Trotting

Teacher: A farmer went trotting upon his grey mare;
   Class: Bumpety, bumpety, bump!
Teacher: With his daughter behind him so rosy and fair;
   Class: Lumpety, lumpety, lump!
                            —Traditional

5. *Three- or Four-Part Reading:* Better suited for upper elementary grades in which voices can be classed as light or dark or as high, middle, and low. Each group is given a stanza. Shel Silverstein's poem, "Sick," works well. In this type of Choral Reading, Group 1 reads the first stanza, and Groups 2–4 read the second through the fourth, respectively. Group 1 reads stanza 5, and the cycle is repeated.

Sources of Choral Reading Literature

- *Sounds of Language Series* (1972) by Bill Martin and Margaret Brogan
- Shel Silverstein's *Where the Sidewalk Ends* (1974) and *A Light in the Attic* (1981)

---

without pausing. In the next session you can use the same procedure to increase this reader's ability to continue oral reading until the end of each sentence.

A third method to increase oral reading fluency uses **repeated readings.** Repeated readings occur when you read a page and then a student rereads that page, using the same speed and intonations that you voiced. Then ask the student to reread that page a second time and ask what improvements the student noticed in his or her own reading. For example, as Lecretia, a third grade student, noticed:

> One important thing I did was to put more emphasis on punctuation. I caught on to how my teacher read the page and I was able to read it better than last week. When I first read, it sounded boring [monotone], but I can change that and I did, quickly! (Michel, 1994, p. 114)

Pretend that a space traveler has come to visit you. He is friendly and loves to rap. Help him compose a rap song about his visit to Earth that you will perform to introduce him to the people of Earth.

The following lines will get you started. Good luck!

> This is a story about a dude who was good,
> Traveled 'round planets . . . stopped at my neighborhood.

> He traveled 'round the stars, a-rockin' through the land,
> Rappin' to the cool beat of his space-time band.

> He came to my house and jumped onto my bed.
> Wiggled his ears . . . said, "Hey man, I'm Fred."

Now continue the rap song with your own lyrics! Here are a few beginnings for suggested stanzas:

His ears . . . _____

_____

His skin . . . _____

_____

He sang . . . _____

_____

He saw . . . _____

_____

He said . . . _____

_____

He ate . . . _____

_____

He left . . . _____

_____

> So that's how it went with my kookie space friend,
> The story's all finished and this is the end!!!!

FIGURE 13.4 Using Rap Music to Develop Listening, Speaking, and Reading Vocabulary

Figure 13.5 is a repeated readings chart in which you can plot the progress of individual students' reading speed and decreased number of errors. Many readers enjoy keeping their own records on this chart as a visual representation of their increased oral reading power.

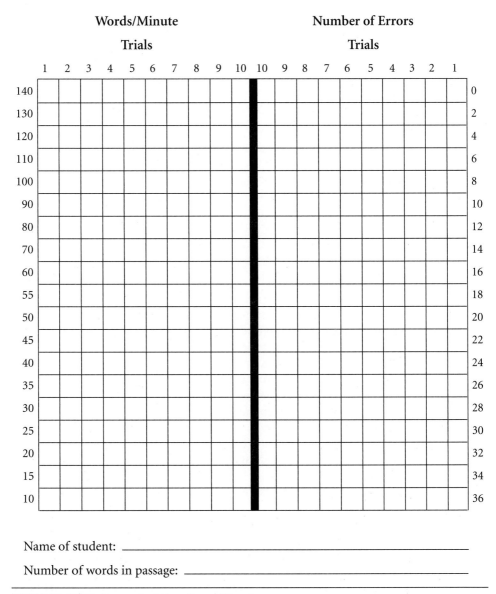

FIGURE 13.5 Repeated Readings Chart

Source: Adapted from E. E. Ekwall & J. L. Shanker (1989), *Locating and Correcting Reading Difficulties,* 5th ed., p. 383. New York: Merrill. Used with permission.

Repeated reading also enables students to hear the variety of printed language patterns that do not occur in everyday speech. In addition, it assists students to establish an expectation for how stories are constructed, fosters their listening abilities, and builds background vocabulary. As two less accomplished readers stated:

> When my teacher reads to us. That's what I'm learning to read for. Like sometimes during the story I pretend I'm the one. Like the person in the book. Then something good happens to me, or I'm the hero. That's why I'm reading. When I can read the book, I can be in the story.

> Our library teacher makes stories like a game. She talks to you about them before she reads. Then, when you get to the part she talked about, you almost know what happened. But not always. Sometimes she fools us. Then we think it's funny and laugh. With her reading is like watching TV and pretending it's real. I like this kind of reading. You don't have to worry about the words or the questions. (Michel, 1994, p. 71)

Many readers profit from having you read the book orally a second time. That is when the glow of enthusiasm for the beauty of language subsides and they can more directly focus on learning new words and their meanings. With these activities, you can diagnose and instruct language-delayed and second-language users whose comprehension is impaired by halting reading.

Assessing Oral Language Growth

There are three types of assessments for oral language growth of literacy users. The first comprises informal observations; in it, you make anecdotal records using the criteria and forms in Chapter 8 to document individual achievements. When these observations are shared with the student, unique speaking talents emerge. You begin by recording evidence of each literacy user's ability to collaborate, draw more frequently on peer information, verify information during oral exchanges, participate in longer group discussions, and make more challenging insights with more specific vocabulary. You can also note improvements in adapting dialect and phrasing to meet audience needs.

A second valuable assessment is made by the students themselves. When you ask students to self-assess their oral language growth and to follow this self-evaluation with a new goal, students rapidly eliminate weaknesses (Phelan, 1989). Sample self-assessments that you can use appear in Chapter 8.

Third, you and your students can establish four or five oral language goals as well as four or five activities through which you will interpret their achievement toward these goals. This assessment provides a profile of learning and pace of growth. This is important information for students as they set new goals. One such form developed by Daly (1991) appears in Figure 13.6. Similarly, students can set criteria for a specific oral presentation, such as giving a speech to the class. A form you can use or modify in such situations was created by Block and Mangieri (1995) and appears in Figure 13.7.

Name _____

Goals	Discussing, Planning, Problem Solving	Reporting, Summarizing, Interviewing	Persuading, Arguing	Describing, Narrating	Informing, Instructing
Activity					
Activity					
Activity					
Activity					

Criteria

Listens to others					
Takes an active part					
Contributes interesting ideas					
Evaluates information					
Chooses relevant information					
Organizes well					
Presents well					
Aware of audience					
Teams effectively					

GENERAL COMMENTS:

FIGURE 13.6 Speaking and Listening Record

Source: Adapted from E. Daly (1991), *Monitoring children's language development: Holistic assessment in the classroom,* p. 121. Portsmouth, NH: Heinemann. Used by permission.

★★★★★★★★★★★★★★★★★★★★★

Name of speaker _____ Date of speech _____

Place a check in each blank that describes the speech.

_____ Spoke loud enough

_____ Spoke slowly enough

_____ Looked at audience

_____ Related enough details to keep interest but not too many

_____ Appeared to be relaxed

_____ Appeared to have confidence and to know the subject

_____ Gave good introduction that made you want to listen

_____ Had good closing that helped you remember the main points

_____ Did not read note cards

_____ Had practiced the speech enough; good expression

_____ Tone of voice was good; not too nasal

_____ Voice was easy to listen to

_____ No nervous gestures, such as using hands in distracting ways or using a word or phrase over and over ("uh," "OK," "Know what I'm saying?" etc.)

_____ Speech met its purpose of informing, persuading, or entertaining

_____ Seemed to have a special style or talent for giving speeches, and that special talent was:

_____

_____ Speech was just the right length

_____ Speech was well organized and the speaker stuck to the important points

_____ Pitch was good; voice was not too high or too low

Strengths and special qualities of the speaker: _____

_____

Improvements you suggest: _____

_____

Methods to improve that you suggest: _____

_____

Rater's signature _____

★★★★★★★★★★★★★★★★★★★★★

FIGURE 13.7 Form to Grade Speeches

Source: Adapted from C. C. Block & J. N. Mangieri (1995), *Reason to Read: Thinking Strategies for Life, Volume 2,* p. 232. Palo Alto, CA: Addison-Wesley. Used with permission.

Chapter Summary

There are four types of oral language difficulties: developmental delays, pathological problems, second-language interferences, and dialect differences. Oral language difficulties can be overcome when cultural, socioeconomic, and self-esteem factors that accompany students' speaking abilities are respected and addressed as part of the instructional process. Among the activities that have increased speaking abilities of literacy users are using Spanish–English books, peer tutors, captioned TV, shared readings, labeling objects in the classroom in two languages, and writing and producing original dramas. Second-language learners and students with dialectical differences can benefit from activities such as picture story frames, the Village English Activity, "I" memoirs, minimal contrasts, and journal writing.

In this and the previous chapters, methods of improving oral literacy abilities were discussed. Chapter 14 presents programs and instructional activities for those who have not become proficient through the special strategies presented up to this point in the book.

Key Terminology

The following terms were defined in this chapter. Place a check mark in the blank that precedes each term you learned on your first reading of the chapter. Compare the percentage you learned this time to the percentage you learned in previous chapters. If your percentage is more than in previous chapters, does this tell you anything about how your literacy users learn new terms? If you decreased in the number of terms you learned this time, what method of vocabulary development in this chapter or previous chapters will you use for students who have difficulty extending their vocabularies through unassisted silent reading?

____ **developmentally related** (page 419)
____ **communication apprehension (CA)** (page 420)
____ **Readers' Theater** (page 423)
____ **shared readings** (page 425)

____ **language acquisition** (page 428)
____ **dialectically different** (page 434)
____ **choral reading** (page 443)
____ **repeated readings** (page 445)

 ## Case Study

Making Professional Decisions

Juanita has been in your classroom for 3 weeks. Although she talks in English and Spanish frequently in class, her messages are not always clear when she speaks in English. It seems as if she changes topics in midsentence. For instance, describing to you what she did over the weekend, she said: "I woke up and then Marquerita is my aunt. She was . . . um . . . call my Mother too." By contrast, when she speaks in Spanish or writes in English, her short sentences are sequential and contain complete ideas. What would you do to improve Juanita's oral literacy? Why?

Compare your answer to what Ms. Solomon, Juanita's third grade teacher, did, as described in the Answer Key at the end of the book. The instructional activity chosen by Ms. Solomon enabled Juanita to be understood by all people in the classroom.

Thinking and Writing about What You Have Learned

1. Recall a student you know who had speaking problems when you were in school or in a class that you taught. What would you diagnose to be the cause of this student's difficulty? Did the student receive help through any of the special methods described in this chapter? If so, what were the effects of that instruction? If not, which activities would you implement and why?

2. Hugo, a Spanish-speaking second-language learner, could not speak English when he was placed in Ms. Pearson's fifth grade class. Ms. Pearson modified her journal writing assignment from the first day Hugo arrived. She also paired Hugo with Marcus, a bilingual student whom she judged to have a compatible personality and who could translate her instructions, oral readings, and so forth. Marcus and Hugo became fast friends. For the first time Marcus had someone at school with whom he could speak Spanish fluently!

   On the first day Ms. Pearson read a story about Obadiah and used the modified journal entry method for Hugo while the rest of the class participated in a writing workshop. She allowed Hugo to write in Spanish. As you can see from the translation Marcus provided, however, Hugo was unable to write his thoughts in either Spanish or English. What would be the first two activities from this chapter you would use to increase Hugo's literacy abilities, and why?

   Hugo   April 15, 2002

   If I was Obadiah and nobody believed me, _____tú dices la verdad_____.

   (*Translation:* If I was Obadiah and nobody believed me, _____you tell the truth_____.
   Correct Spanish: If I was Obadiah and nobody believed me, _____diría la verdad_____.
   [I would still tell the truth.])

3. Reread the section on Stages of Literacy Achievement in Chapter 1. If you are currently teaching and have either language-delayed or second-language students in your class, analyze where they would appear along the continuum according to their present level of literacy achievement. When you have identified objectives that your students have mastered, present them with the next set of goals and ask them to select the goal they would like to achieve. Which activity in this chapter would you use to assist these students to reach these new goals?

4. Select the assessment or student self-assessment tool in this chapter that you judge to be most appropriate for the grade level you teach or plan to teach. Describe how and when you will use this assessment tool with students and how you will use the information you receive to further their abilities.

5. Margaret rarely read aloud before the class because she skipped many words, mispronounced others, and failed to acknowledge punctuation. However, whether she read silently or orally, her answers to comprehension questions and her spontaneous retellings clearly demonstrated that she comprehended what she read. She used the facts in the material to express her opinions articulately. Which of the activities cited in this chapter do you think would best have advanced Margaret's oral reading fluency, and why?

   You can compare your answer and explanation to that of Mr. Gomez, Margaret's teacher, by turning to the Answer Key at the back of the book. His choice of support removed the fractured elements in Margaret's oral and silent reading.

For Further Reference

To receive more information about captioned television decoders, contact the following:

The National Captioning Institute
5203 Leesburg Pike
Falls Church, VA 22041
Telephone 1-800-533-WORD

c h a p t e r 14

Reluctant readers/writers benefit from innovative technology. Here, students are viewing their video-enhanced yearbook that they created.

Support for Special Problems

Let me tell you about my eleven-year-old son. Billy started kindergarten, had done average work, went on to first grade. They waited till spring to tell me he was just immature; by now he was seven. I let them hold him back. I then started to watch more closely; halfway through the second year of first grade, he still couldn't read! They tested him (at my request); they said he had attention disorder. They assigned him to special education; he went through second grade with a class of seven students in his room that were disabled. Our doctor said they had made a mistake and would not order Ritalin. I put him in one year of vision therapy, three years of expensive tutors, and two more years in a reading study group at the university which is also expensive and wears us all out running back and forth. Now we wouldn't mind any of the above if some improvement had been made. At age eleven he's a normal all-boy child in every way but, even at half-way through the fourth grade, Billy still isn't reading.

—Anonymous parent
(Pinnell, Fried, & Estice, 1991, p. 11)

Chapter Overview: Key Points

The purpose of this chapter is to ensure that none of your students experience Billy's problem. The chapter describes diagnostic processes and instructional programs for the approximately 2 to 4 percent of students who have special problems—and who will be blocked from full literacy unless alternative services are provided. The first step in providing appropriate instruction for these students is to identify their specific learning needs so they can be supported with personalized instruction.

Key concepts in this chapter are:

- Diagnosing special literacy needs
- Recognizing special problems
- Using multiple intelligences theory to overcome literacy barriers
- Overcoming emotional and attentional barriers to pleasure-filled reading and writing
- Overcoming literacy barriers due to mental dysfunction
- Addressing dyslexia and neurologically correctible reading and writing difficulties

- Effective early intervention programs
- Special tutorial programs to meet special needs

By the end of the chapter, you will learn about the following:

1. How to include students in the diagnosis of special needs
2. How to refer students to alternative literacy programs
3. How to select between various early intervention programs
4. How to incorporate aspects of effective early interventions into regular classroom programs
5. How to coordinate extra support curriculum, such as the VAKT approach and Spalding Method, with daily classroom literacy instruction

Diagnosing Special Literacy Needs

When we diagnose special literacy needs, it is important that we take several precautions to ensure that students are not placed in inappropriate alternative programs. First, be sure to get input from the students themselves. Do not underestimate the value of their self-perceptions. Students should be asked to explain what they are thinking as they read and to describe what they judge to be their greatest barriers to literacy. Many students are not asked such questions and are not allowed to participate in their own diagnosis. They are simply referred to special programs because they scored significantly lower than classmates on one or more standardized tests. Extensive examination and documentation of individual literacy performances and developing strengths will eliminate much of this inappropriate placement.

A second precaution involves labels. Many educators believe that up to 15 percent of their student populations should be placed in special alternative literacy programs, but research has demonstrated that only 3 percent require specialized education (Allington, 1994; Pikulski, 1994). Because of inaccurate perceptions many educators are misdiagnosing far too many underachieving students. By attaching a label early in students' careers, some classroom teachers place blame for these students' limitations within the child or the home environment. They seek to remove "literacy problems" and "remedial readers" from their classrooms. However, our role as educators should be less like that of a screening lab technician and more like that of a doctor. Instead of trying to move "labeled" readers out of the classroom, the first step should be to build enabling literacy supports. Every child has the right to discover the joy that literacy can bring. We have the responsibility to ensure that this right is extended to readers with special needs. Instead of labeling students, therefore, we should describe their literacy performances. To reach this end, the most important diagnostic tool becomes our informed professional judgment of individuals as they are engaged in literacy.

A third diagnostic action is to evaluate and then encourage students' levels of self-expectations concerning literacy tasks. Many students with special needs must be convinced that it will be worth the effort to work hard if they are referred to an alternative program. They need your encouragement, because they initially believe full literacy to be impossible. Some teachers have raised students' aspirations by sharing examples of people they know who needed special instructional supports before they attained literacy. Through such discovery discussions you can convey the high value you place on each student as an individual. You also communicate the desire to become an important person in their lives and a positive force in their literacy development. Students will realize that you believe in them and will never give up on them. These two factors have been shown to advance significantly the literacy abilities of students with special needs (Allington, 1994; Block, 2001; Block & Pressley, 2002).

A fourth action that is central to a truly informed diagnosis is to document literacy performance. As you observe and record individual students' literacy performances, ask the following questions:

1. Does this reader have the ability and desire to achieve literacy in your classroom if additional time and support are provided? If the answer is yes, which of the programs described later in this chapter could most capture the student's learning strength?
2. Does this student have needs that cannot be addressed without an additional educator's assistance? If the answer is yes, how can a specialist and you spend time developing literacy for this student so that instructional time is doubled?
3. Is this student unable to prosper even with the instructional modifications you can make and with the help of outside supports? If the answer is yes, a case study should be undertaken to describe the student's present literacy accomplishments and confusions.

A case study referral form is presented in Box 14.1.

As described in Chapter 6, another diagnostic action is referral. You can refer students for highly specialized standardized tests as well as for informal tests to identify specific literacy needs. These tests are administered by reading specialists who assess specific causes for literacy differences; they are one step in the **referral process.** The purpose of this process is to provide in-depth information to outside personnel who place students in appropriate instructional programs in addition to the regular classroom program. Referrals will be most successful if they include interview data concerning what the student thinks as he or she is reading, as mentioned at the beginning of this section. They should also use at least five diagnostic tools. Once a case study referral form such as that shown in Box 14.1 is complete, it is given to the appropriate educational psychologist, clinic, or resource support person. Forms like this are designed to provide effective communication among educational personnel.

The sixth key diagnostic consideration is establishing the degree of discrepancy between the student's literacy potential and achievement. This discrepancy index helps you determine whether a student is reading less well than should be expected, even considering factors described in Chapters 3 through 5, or if the individual is using literacy as well as possible given his or her personal cognitive functioning abilities but still needs to learn special strategies before literacy can be attained.

14.1   READING SPECIALISTS

Case Study Referral Form: Indicators of Need for Special Instructional Placement

I. Student Information

Student's name: _____

Date of birth: _____ Sex: _____ Age: _____

Rank in family: _____ Members present in home: _____

School attending: _____

Grade: _____

Present classroom teacher: _____

II. Background Data

Family history and information received from family: _____

_____

_____

Social and personality factors: _____

_____

_____

Educational history: _____

_____

Characteristics of effective instructional situations for this student, including size of group in which student performs best: _____

_____

Physical factors influencing academic performance, including incipient illnesses and effect of instruction before and after meals: _____

_____

Responses to instruction and assessment experiences: _____

_____

III. Tests and Evaluations

Standardized tests administered (include dates): _____

_____

Student's general performance during testing as to the amount of effort, attention, ability, and interest placed into each assessment: _____

_____

14.1 READING SPECIALISTS

Case Study Referral Form: Indicators of Need for Special Instructional Placement *(continued)*

Information evaluations (include dates): _____
_____

a. Student's individual strengths: _____
_____

b. Time of day most problems occur: _____
_____

c. Day of the week most problems occur: _____
_____

d. Time of day when student's strengths are most evident: _____
_____

e. Maturational factors influencing performances: _____
_____

f. Motivational factors influencing performances: _____
_____

g. Cognitive factors influencing performances: _____
_____

h. Cultural factors influencing performances, including any counseling or outside-of-school diagnostic evaluative information: _____
_____

i. Student's reading, writing, and speaking/listening competencies (attach samples if available):
_____

j. Student interview information, including what he/she thinks about when reading and what the student judges to be barriers to his/her literacy: _____
_____

IV. Diagnosis

Level of placement recommended: _____
_____

Type of program requested and rationale for request: _____
_____

Summary and conclusions: _____
_____

continued

14.1 READING SPECIALISTS

Case Study Referral Form: Indicators of Need for Special Instructional Placement *(continued)*

V. Letter to Parents

(Should include the following information)

Appreciation of the child's strengths, including a positive anecdote

Description of what you learned, as well as your conclusions as stated in Part IV above

Student's present status

What you recommend and why

Suggested time for meeting to discuss the referral

Before the 1970s, schools administered intelligence tests to determine the discrepancy index. Based on these test scores, educators computed a Reading Expectancy Age (R Exp Age) as follows:

$$R \text{ Exp Age} = \frac{2 \text{ (mental age score on IQ test)} + \text{chronological age}}{3}$$

As shown in this formula, only a single IQ test score was used to determine if a student needed special instruction. Using a single score is not advisable, however, because of the probability of error. For example, research indicates that high intelligence will not necessarily guarantee that a student will be a good reader (Bell, 1995). Nor can the conclusion be drawn that a student with a low IQ score will *not* become a good reader. Moreover, the correlation between mental ability and reading success for very young students is only .35, which is at chance level (Bell, 1994). This evidence confirms that factors other than mental age (IQ) influence a child's success in reading.

In summary, students can overcome large obstacles to literacy when we (1) include their perspective in the diagnostic process, (2) describe students' performances instead of labeling possible causes, (3) assess and bolster their self-expectations for literacy success, (4) document their literacy performances with a case study report if necessary, (5) refer students for testing when appropriate, and (6) determine the discrepancy between students' literacy potential and their achievement, using more than one test score. Through these actions we can create an individual literacy portrait for each student. We can also eliminate the need to pigeonhole students into a labeled category. Such labels deemphasize special strengths of individuals that could be used to move them toward internally guided reading and writing.

The next section presents ways to sharpen your diagnosis of the special literacy needs that call for alternative instructional programs.

Recognizing Special Problems

In 1993, the Council for Exceptional Children adopted its policy on inclusive schools and community settings:

> The Council for Exceptional Children (CEC) believes all children, youth, and young adults with disabilities are entitled to a free and appropriate education and/or services that lead to an adult life characterized by satisfying relations with others, independent living, productive engagement in the community, and participation in society at large. To achieve such outcomes, there must exist for all children, youth, and young adults a rich variety of early intervention, educational, and vocational program options and experiences. Access to these programs and experiences should be based on individual educational need and desired outcomes. Furthermore, students and their families or guardians, as members of the planning team, may recommend the placement, curriculum option, and the exit document to be pursued.
>
> CEC believes that a continuum of services must be available for all children, youth, and young adults. CEC also believes that the concept of inclusion is a meaningful goal to be pursued in our schools and communities. In addition, CEC believes children, youth, and young adults with disabilities should be served whenever possible in general education classrooms in inclusive neighborhood schools and community settings. Such settings should be strengthened and supported by an infusion of specially trained personnel and other appropriate supportive practices according to the individual needs of the child. (1993, supplement)

Several definitions of specific literacy diversities have been proposed, but the definition created by the National Advisory Committee on Handicapped Children in 1994 is the most widely accepted and follows the criteria in Public Law 94-142 (the Education for All Handicapped Children Act of 1975), which provided guidelines for instruction for all students who have specific divergent learning needs. The definition reads:

> Children with special (specific) learning disabilities exhibit a disorder in one or more of the basic psychological processes involved in understanding or in using spoken or written language. These may be manifested in disorders of listening, thinking, talking, reading, writing, spelling, or arithmetic. (Bell, 1995, p. 3)

Learning Disabilities

A student with a strong discrepancy between intellectual potential and achievement will profit from one of the special programs discussed in this chapter if the discrepancy cannot be explained by environmental, emotional, instructional, cultural, or physical factors at home or school. The Slingerland Screen Test for Identifying Children with Specific Language Disability (Educators Publishing Services, 1984) can also be administered. Record results in the student's case study (see Box 14.1) as a part of his or her literacy portrait.

One immediate sign that learning disabilities may be present is the finding that a student does not misspell a word the same way twice. Other students may not be able to repeat a sentence in order although they repeat single words. Such students profit from tactile–kinesthetic instructional adaptations, as described later in this chapter. Other students with learning differences may use more global, image-producing thought processes than the normal population. Yet whereas diagrams and pictures will help these children comprehend verbal explanations, the same tools will only confuse others with less global neurological functions.

Whatever the circumstances, labeling a student as "learning disabled" should *not* occur, because every student's learning diversity is unique, as suggested in the few examples just mentioned. Literacy differences can begin in the motor, sensory, or cranial regions of the peripheral nervous system. The fact that an individual's literacy develops through uncommon learning processes does not necessarily mean that it cannot culminate in abilities just as powerful and valuable as those of students whose literacy develops through traditional instructional approaches.

The easiest and most effective modification in the classroom for students with disabilities is to allow extra time. One way to do so is by using computers, which can obviate the need for letter construction during writing. However, the computer does not help these readers/writers to organize their thoughts into coherent form. Therefore, pairing two students at a computer enables the student with learning differences to brainstorm orally with a partner before beginning to write. Another benefit of the computer is the tactile experience. When students type ideas, the motor and sensory avenues in their cognitive processing unite more rapidly. In this way, their words more easily attach to their ideas. When their brainstorming segment is printed out, students with learning differences have something tangible they can use to group common ideas together. Some find it easier to organize their ideas using different colored highlighters to group commonalties instead of rewriting them into an outline (Lee & Jackson, 1992).

Similarly, readers with organizational literacy difficulties may take hours to respond to one essay question. If necessary, this extra time should be allowed. Others benefit from writing ideas on individual index cards. By laying the cards in front of them, these readers can find the most logical organization of their thoughts. Unless they can manipulate information with their hands, their writing will only reflect a small portion of their knowledge.

Some readers with visual processing problems benefit from working on reading materials and tests apart from the rest of their class. In this way they can read the material out loud or to themselves without feeling self-conscious. In this separate setting they can also read questions to a tutor, who can verify that they read each word in the question correctly (Lee & Jackson, 1992).

Readers with learning differences can also develop word analysis abilities through tutorial programs that make daily use of the Elkonin Method, the Williams ABD Program, or the Lindamood-Bell Auditory Discrimination Program (Bell, 1991; Lindamood, Bell, & Lindamood, 1992).

Auditory Functions

Clinical study has identified an underlying problem in many reading disorders: incompletely developed *auditory conceptual function.* This auditory ability to register and compare the sequence of sounds within spoken words is also called *phoneme segmen-*

tation or *phonological awareness.* The primary cause of deficits in this function is neurophysiological—and it appears throughout the population, without apparent linkage to race, gender, cultural factors such as education and socioeconomic status, or even intelligence.

Secondary symptoms are adding, omitting, substituting, and reversing sounds and letters in reading and spelling; the same kinds of errors can also occur in speech. It is often (incorrectly) thought that students are just not paying attention when they mispronounce words or that they see letters inverted or scrambled when they spell "gril" for *girl* and "cret" for *correct,* or read "steam" for *stream,* "litter" for *letter,* "saw" for *was,* or "dad" for *bad.* These errors, however, are symptoms of an underlying problem. Persons who cannot judge the sequence of phonemes (sounds) within spoken words cannot grasp how our alphabet code represents words. They cannot judge how what they say matches what they see.

The evidence is increasingly clear. Basic research, clinical results, and classroom findings are now substantial. Auditory conceptual function/phonological awareness is directly related to literacy skills.

A published test, the Lindamood Auditory Conceptualization (LAC) Test, is available for evaluating phoneme segmentation ability. A lack of cognitive development in this area prevents a person from using phonics. A severe lack is usually evidenced in reading and spelling errors that are grossly unphonetic or in students' remaining nonreaders and nonspellers. Even a minor lack of development has an effect by interfering with a person's ability to recognize and self-correct reading and spelling errors. As already mentioned, this is not a problem just for those of below-average intelligence—even gifted individuals with this cognitive dysfunction will perform below their literacy potential.

One reason this factor has escaped detection until recently is that a person can say a word without being conscious of its component sounds. It had been thought that if you could say a word, you would be able to discriminate its sequence of sounds. This is not true for a significant percentage of the population. Whereas only 4 percent of the population is color-blind and cannot discriminate among colors, 30 percent have auditory conceptual difficulty from a moderate to a severe degree.

The problem can be resolved with specific treatment that yields significant improvement in reading and spelling—both for children with dyslexia and for those with less severe reading and spelling problems. The solution is conscious input to the brain from another sense modality: *feeling.* Feeling the action of tongue, lips, and mouth as they produce speech sounds gives the sounds an additional dimension. The sequence of sounds and letters involved in reading and spelling can be verified through this additional feedback to the brain. Through the integration of auditory, visual, and motor information, these students can become self-correcting readers and spellers because they can think more specifically about how to read and spell.

One widely used program to teach phonological awareness is the Lindamood-Bell Auditory Discrimination Program mentioned earlier. In this program, students are taught to *feel* various mouth positions for English sounds. Because these positions and feelings are given catchy labels—"lip poppers," "tip tappers," "nose sounds," "skinny sounds," "scrapers," "lip coolers"—students find them easy to learn. Some of the positions taught in this program are illustrated in Figure 14.1. As students duplicate their teacher's mouth positions, they learn to feel and make the sounds of individual words

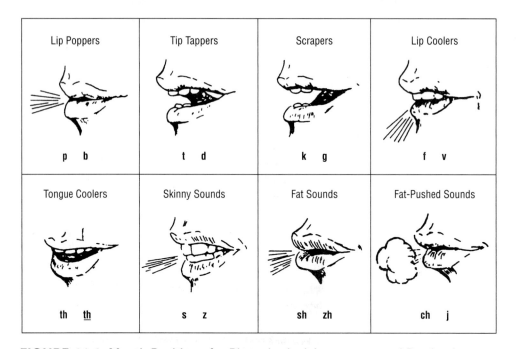

FIGURE 14.1 Mouth Positions for Phonological Awareness and Production

Source: C. H. Lindamood and P. C. Lindamood (1977), *Letter Sound Labels,* p. 4. Newark, DE: International Reading Association. Brochure. Reprinted by permission of the author and the International Reading Association.

and letters that they would not be able to pronounce or recognize auditorially (and retain visually) without this special instruction. The program also uses colored blocks or felt to represent the sounds; students are asked to arrange the blocks in the order in which the sounds occur in the words, adding a tactile dimension to the learning process. This program assists readers with learning differences because it ties letter-to-sound matches to consistent concrete, sensory, and visual stimuli (Howard, 1986; Vickery, Reynolds, & Cochran, 1987).

Two other programs are the Williams ABD Program, which uses textured letters, and the Elkonin Method, which uses picture associations to reduce this complexity.

Learning Style Differences

Another type of literacy difference that requires alternate instructional programs is learning style preference, also called aptitude–treatment interaction (Curry, 1990; Dunn & Dunn, 1991). **Learning styles** are defined as personal preferences for the way a student likes to learn. As illustrated in Figure 14.2, these personal preferences encompass physical conditions, environmental factors, emotional stimuli, and sociological supports that increase a student's value for and benefits from instruction. Research indicates that proficient readers easily adapt and continue to increase their literacy abilities even when their less preferred learning styles are called on in instruction (Curry, 1990;

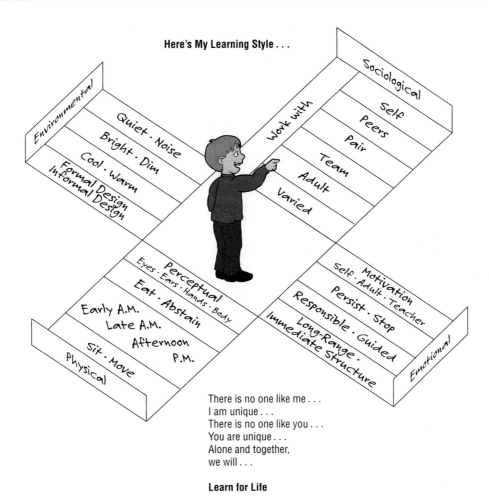

Here's My Learning Style . . .

There is no one like me . . .
I am unique . . .
There is no one like you . . .
You are unique . . .
Alone and together,
we will . . .

Learn for Life

FIGURE 14.2 Learning Style Components

Source: "My Learning Style Profile," Chart 2, designed by M. Dupler, 1989, Worthington Middle School, Worthington, OH. Used with permission.

Snow & Lohman, 1984; Snow & Ninio, 1986). Alternatively, many readers/writers with special needs require that their strongest learning modality (visual, auditory, tactile, kinesthetic, or a combination of these) be matched to instructional demands before they can achieve significant progress.

The diagnosis of learning modalities began in 1965 when the Learning Methods Test was first written by Robert Mills. His work as well as the research of Carbo (1984) and Dunn and Dunn (1991) has increased the number of programs designed to match students' learning style preferences to the form of literacy instruction they receive. Because most students develop full and productive literacy abilities without modality support and because insufficient evidence exists that testing and matching for all students is necessary, instruction matched to learning styles is best reserved for those students who need additional **intraphysic support** (defined as midcranial region stimulation).

For students who continue to be extremely limited in their integration and synthesis of decoding and comprehension abilities, optimal literacy is likely to be achieved when the individual student's learning style is identified. Several tests of learning styles have been written, including the Learning Style Inventory (Dunn, 1976) and the Mills Test (Mills, 1965). Students can also indicate their preferences by completing informal tests such as "What Would Help Me Read Better" (Box 14.2) and "My Learning Style Preference List" (Box 14.3). Parents can also assist in the diagnostic process by completing a parent report such as the one shown in Box 14.4.

Diagnosis of Learning Styles: "What Would Help Me Read Better?"

Name Sonia Sanchez   Date 8-2-2002

Directions: Number the following items in the order that they would help you become a better reader, with 1 being the most helpful and 10 being the least helpful. Teacher will read and describe each item. Teacher will assist students in determining their rankings.

_____10_____ Having more time to practice reading in class

_____2_____ If directions were given orally

_____6_____ If I worked one-on-one with the teacher

_____9_____ If I learned more strategies to help me understand what I read

_____1_____ If I helped teach someone else to be a better reader

_____4_____ If I knew I could receive awards for improvement and good work

_____3_____ Being able to work at my own speed through a packet of material

_____8_____ If assignments were more challenging

_____7_____ If more assignments were given where I could work in groups

_____5_____ If assignments were more interesting

Please add anything else that you think would help you become a better reader.

_____read each day_____

_____

_____

14.3 DIAGNOSIS AND ASSESSMENT

Diagnosis of Learning Styles: "My Learning Style Preference List"

Directions: Teacher reads each item and explains each by giving an example. Students check items that best describe them.

Constructive Learning Environment	Preferential seating: (specify) <u>Cooperative Group</u>
	Group size: ____ 1–1 w/teacher ____ 1–1 w/peer ✓ small group ____ large group
	Need for movement: ✓ Little ____ Average ____ High
	Distraction management: ____ Carrels ____ Headsets ____ Seating ____ Other
	Noise: ____ None ____ Quiet ____ Moderate
	Lighting: ____ Dim ____ Average ____ Bright
	Temperature: ____ Warm ____ Average ____ Cool
	Other: (specify) _____

Productive Learning Schedule	Peak learning time: ____ Early morning ____ Late morning ✓ Midday ____ Afternoon
	Best lesson length: ____ 5–10 min. ____ 15–20 min. ✓ 25–30 min. ____ 30+ min.
	Need for variation: ____ Little ✓ Some ____ Average ____ Much
	Other: (specify) _____

Best Stimulus/ Response Format	*Stimulus Format* *Response Format*
	Visual: ____ Observe ✓ Read Choose: ____ Point ✓ Mark
	Auditory: ____ Oral ✓ Discuss Tell: ____ Restate ✓ Explain
	Touch: ____ Hold ✓ Feel Write: ____ Word ✓ Essay
	____ Keyboard ____ Short answer
	____ Word process
	Model: ____ Demonstrate ____ Make/construct
	____ Guide performance ____ Demonstrate
	Other: (specify) _____ Other: (specify) _____

Useful Material Adjustments	____ Vary stimulus/response format ✓ Vary instructions ____ Vary sequence
	____ Highlight essential content ____ Use partial content ✓ Add steps
	____ Expand practice ____ Add self-checking ✓ Add facilitative learning aids
	Other: (specify) _____

continued

Diagnosis of Learning Styles: "My Learning Style Preference List" (continued)

Facilitative Learning
Aids

____ Advance organizers	✓ Paraphrasing
✓ Audiotapes of text	____ Partial outlines
____ Calculator	✓ Peer notetaker
____ Captioned films	✓ Peer prompter
____ Charted progress	✓ Peer tutor
____ Checklists of steps	____ Question guides
____ Completed activities	____ Self-questioning
____ Computer activities	____ Simplified directions
____ Contracts	____ Strategy posters
✓ Cooperative-learning group	____ Structured notes
____ Evaluation checklist	✓ Study buddy
____ Games for practice	____ Study guides
____ Highlighted text	____ Summaries
____ Interactive videodisk	____ Tape recorder
____ Manipulatives	____ Think alouds
____ Math number charts	____ Timed practice
____ Mnemonic guides	____ Verbal rehearsal
____ Organization charts	____ Visual imagery
____ Outlined tasks	____ Volunteer tutor
Other: ____ _____	____ _____

Source: Adapted from J. Choate (1993), "Inventory: My Learning Style Preference List" in *Teacher Training Notebook Number 3.* New York: Millbrook. Reprinted by permission of the Millbrook Press Inc.

Once students' learning preferences are identified, you can meet with them to design special small group centers that contain literacy materials supporting their learning style. For instance, one center might utilize movable words and letters on magnetic boards for students with a tactile learning preference. Some students may also profit from additional interactive learning-style instruction in programs outside of the classroom. Information about these special programs can be obtained from the Dunn & Dunn Learning Center or the Center for Success in Learning, all of whose addresses can be found at the end of the chapter.

The Center for Success in Learning has also created a multisensory planning guide (Figure 14.3) that can be used in several ways. First, you can write individual students' names in each quadrant to reflect these students' learning style preferences; then you can use this to plan whole-class literacy lessons that include activities

14.4 DIAGNOSIS AND ASSESSMENT

Diagnosis of Learning Styles: Parent Report of Student Learning Style Preferences

To the Parents of ——————————————:

The apple below is divided into sections that represent elements of learning styles. Becoming aware of your child's learning style preferences helps me to address his or her needs more effectively. None of the elements are "good" or "bad." There are, however, some areas that may need attention or improvement so that your child can make the most of every school day.

Would you please circle each of the icons in the apple that best describes your child?

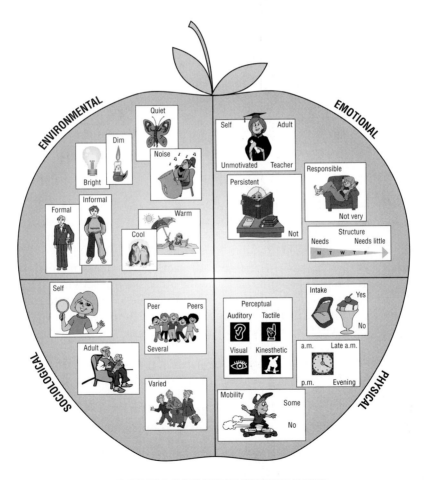

HINTS FOR IMPROVING PERFORMANCE

Assessment (other than paper-and-pencil):

Teacher-observed performance: *Suzanna prefers auditory stimuli and working*
with one to three peers

Student's goal and standard to be achieved: *Being able to work alone and read*
silently for 30 minutes

Auditory	Tactile
Monday: Listen to tape of book of choice alone as you read along silently for 30 minutes. Retell the story by taping it on the tape.	*Wednesday: For 20 minutes work alone. Build a model of what the house would be like if it were in our city.*
Visual	Kinesthetic
Tuesday: Read silently alone for 15 minutes, then write for 15 minutes and draw what you think will come next in story.	*Thursday & Friday: Work alone reading the ending of your book for 30 minutes, and prepare the script to be rehearsed & delivered to the class on Friday. On Friday, we'll evaluate which support best enabled you to reach your goal: auditory, visual, tactile, or kinesthetic.*

FIGURE 14.3 Multisensory Planning Guide

matched to each learning modality Alternatively, as used in Figure 14.3, a separate copy of the guide can be filled out for each student who is receiving instruction matched to his or her learning style preference. Daily classroom activities can be written on the form and assessed each day. Third, the form can be used as a communication memo between classroom and special resource teachers. In this instance, the student's classroom teacher would describe the objective and activity used during the regular reading lesson for that child. Then the resource teacher would reinforce that same objective in the special teaching segment of that student's day and record the results on the guide, which would be returned to the classroom teacher by the student. The cycle could repeat each day.

Before we conclude our discussion of learning styles, it is important to note that some educators believe students can become too dependent on instruction matched to their learning style preferences (see Witkin, Moore, Goodenough, & Cox, 1977). Others believe that students need to be taught how to adjust when their preferred method of learning is not present (Curry, 1990; Snow & Lohman, 1984). Taking this position into consideration, you can evaluate the effects of learning-style matching on literacy growth of individual students. For some, such an approach is all they need to reach literacy proficiency.

For example, one student had been misdiagnosed and labeled as having attention deficit disorder (ADD). When her learning style needs were identified and met, however, she went from making F's in the first 6 weeks of sixth grade to the A–B honor roll by the end of the semester. Another student, an eighth grade at-risk reader who felt he was going nowhere in life, was provided instruction to meet his exceptionally high need for mobility. His teacher assigned him two desks and told him to be at one or the other or on the way between them. This instructional adaptation settled the student to a point where he could learn to read using small group techniques (see Chapters 9 and 10) and individual tactile kinesthetic materials at home (Johns, 1993).

Using Multiple Intelligence Theory to Overcome Literacy Barriers

Howard Gardner (1983) proposed seven distinct types of intelligence, as follows:

1. Linguistic intelligence
2. Logical–mathematical intelligence
3. Spatial intelligence
4. Bodily–kinesthetic intelligence
5. Musical intelligence
6. Interpersonal intelligence
7. Intrapersonal intelligence

Although Gardner's theory is still being revised and researched, educators across the United States are designing instruction so readers can use intelligences other than linguistic to support their literacy development. To determine if students will profit from using another type of intelligence, you can implement an activity designed to stimulate a specific intelligence, such as one of the instructional activities based on Gardner's theory that are presented in *Seven Ways of Knowing: Teaching for Multiple Intelligence,* by David Lazear (1991). If students increase their literacy achievement while in that type of activity, you can design more activities in that intellectual domain. Modifications you can make for readers who display aptitude in these other areas of intelligence follow.

Logical–Mathematical Intelligence

Students who are highly logical and mathematical will make objective observations, draw conclusions, make judgments, and formulate hypotheses easily. The following activities utilize this type of intelligence to support reading comprehension:

- Making outlines of key points with at least two levels of detail
- Comparing/contrasting two books on the same subject
- Convincing others of hypotheses about upcoming chapters

Spatial Intelligence

Students who are highly visual and spatial will enjoy painting, sculpting, navigating, map making, architecture, and daydreaming. The following activities support their reading comprehension:

- Forming images and pictures in their mind
- Pretending they can do magical things to move objects and create dynamic events in story plots
- Describing heroic actions in adventure stories
- Working with artistic media to express their responses to reading
- Creating poster-size expressions of ideas and making games

Bodily–Kinesthetic Intelligence

Students who are highly kinesthetic will use their body to express their ideas. They learn best by doing things with what they read or enacting what they comprehend. These students can use the following activities to support their reading comprehension:

- Performing dramatic enactments of the responses, ideas, opinions, or feelings that reading aroused
- Learning vocabulary and concepts through physical gestures or moving
- Acting out the sequel to a book before they are asked to write what that sequel should be
- Using mime to portray the content read

Musical Intelligence

If readers are highly musical and rhythmical, they will be sensitive to sounds from the environment, human voices, and musical instruments. (Most of us relied on this type of intelligence to learn the order of the alphabet through the "ABC" song.) These students can use the following activities to support their reading comprehension:

- Listening to music as they read
- Singing about items to be memorized
- Humming as they read to create vibrations inside the brain
- Identifying rhythms and patterns in nature to understand changes that occur in story plots

Interpersonal Intelligence

If readers' strengths are in interpersonal intelligence, they will have exceptional abilities to work cooperatively in groups and communicate verbally and nonverbally. These students notice distinctions among people that go unnoticed by less interpersonally intelligent people. These students recognize moods, temperaments, motivations, intentions, fears, anticipations, and beliefs. The following activities can support these students' reading abilities:

- Discussing in pairs and groups after reading
- Listening to someone else's interpretation of a story before being asked to give theirs
- Setting purposes before reading that involve understanding something very specific about the main characters, such as trying to understand why they perform certain actions or what they likely feel, fear, or believe
- Engaging in team games in which joint answers have to be negotiated

Intrapersonal Intelligence

Readers who are highly gifted in intrapersonal intelligence will have a deeper understanding of their own feelings, ranges of emotional responses, metacognitions, self-reflections, and sense of intuition and spiritual reality. These students can use the following activities to support their reading comprehension:

- Dreaming of, and writing/enacting, the possible ramifications of something they have read in relation to their own life or the lives of others
- Reporting the pattern of connections a reading selection demonstrated to a larger order of things
- Comparing themselves to main characters
- Reporting the metacognitions they had as they read
- Describing how they related personally to a reading

Overcoming Emotional and Attentional Barriers to Pleasure-Filled Reading and Writing

Some students' emotional difficulties interfere with literacy development. The U.S. Department of Education (2002) designates such difficulties as "Emotional or Behavioral Disorders" and describes these conditions as

> (i) characterized by behavioral or emotional responses in school programs so different from appropriate age, cultural, or ethnic norms that the responses adversely affect educational performance, including academic, social, vocational or personal skills;
> (ii) more than a temporary, expected response to stressful events in the environment;
> (iii) consistently exhibited in two different settings, at least one of which is school-related; and
> (iv) unresponsive to direct intervention applied in general education, or the condition of a child is such that general education interventions would be insufficient (p. 13).

The term *emotional or behavioral disorders* includes a disability that coexists with other disabilities. It also includes a schizophrenic disorder, affective disorder, anxiety disorder, or other sustained disorder of conduct or adjustment that affects a child, if the disorder impairs educational performance as described in sentence (i).

Students within this category are not those who are socially maladjusted or temporarily distraught. Diagnosis must include evidence that a student's dysfunctional behaviors and emotions occur at a significantly greater rate and/or intensity than seen in the student's peer group and that these dysfunctions occur across different learning settings as well as in environments outside of school.

Readers with emotional difficulties should be referred for special programs if they are unable to progress in a classroom program based on the principles in this book. Before a teacher makes such a referral, at least three of five characteristics need to be documented on the referral report in Box 14.1. First, the student must demonstrate an inability to learn that cannot be explained by cognitive, sensory, physical, instructional, economic, cultural, or health factors. Second, the student must demonstrate an inability to build and maintain satisfactory interpersonal relationships with peers or teachers. Third, the student must display inappropriate behaviors and feelings (such as withdrawal, confused verbalizations, fantasizing, or preoccupation with emotional conflicts) in normal circumstances, as evidenced in artwork, writings, and acting-out behaviors. Fourth, emotionally disturbed students will have a general pervasive mood of unhappiness or depression. Last, students with emotional differences have a tendency to develop physical symptoms or fears associated with their personal problems (Price, 1988).

The most common misdiagnosis is to confuse emotional disturbances with **ADD or ADHD** (attention deficit hyperactivity disorder), or vice versa. A child who has ADD or ADHD will usually respond positively to medication and/or an appropriate instructional structure in the classroom. Licensed psychologists and psychiatrists will be required before discriminations between ADD, ADHD, and emotional difficulties can be made. The most effective instructional adaptation for readers with emotional disturbances is to provide tutoring before school each day. By providing this consistent time at which you are available, you can address many dysfunctional behavioral needs before peers arrive. For instance, one teacher reported: "I like to be in class half an hour before school starts. I find it is a good time to talk personally with Leigh—she often comes in if she's upset about something." And another: "Jenny knows that I am going to conference with her before playtime. It helps her manage her learning time."

In-class interventions that can be used simultaneously with out-of-school instructional programs include these:

1. Strengthen positive behaviors by providing feedback relative to objectives the student is trying to achieve. Turn negatives into positives. Instead of saying "Don't shout," say "That's right, we use quiet voices inside our classroom."
2. Work with the student to devise an individualized, personalized system of cues to alert the student when his or her behavior is not acceptable. For instance, one cue might be to place your hand on his or her right shoulder when you want the student to know that his or her voice needs to be lowered.
3. For some readers with emotional disturbances, consider scheduling weekly visits with the school counselor.

Overcoming Literacy Barriers Due to Mental Dysfunction

Some students have **mental dysfunctions,** which are outlined in Table 14.1. These differences can be diagnosed by (1) measured intelligence that is below normal, and (2) behavior that significantly deviates from typical cultural and age-appropriate social standards. Slow-learning students are an example of the mildest form of cerebral hemispheric difference. When these differences reach levels depicted in Table 14.1, students should receive special education supports for their literacy development. As shown in the table, by age 6 mild, moderate, severe, and profound levels of difference can be diagnosed through parent–teacher observations and administration of a standardized intelligence test.

TABLE 14.1 Types of Mental Dysfunction That Qualify for Special Education

	Developmental Characteristics		
Degree	*Preschool (0–5 years)*	*School Age (6–20 years)*	*Adult (21 and over)*
Mild (educable)	May not be diagnosed	Learns basic academic and prevocational skills with special help	Lives and works in community; may not be identified as retarded
Moderate (trainable)	Likely to have clinical diagnosis (e.g., Down syndrome) and fair motor skills	Learns self-help and functional academic skills; independent in familiar surroundings	Performs semiskilled work with supervision; may achieve competitive employment
Severe	Slow motor development; some communication; may have physical handicaps	May care for personal needs; may learn to communicate	Can contribute to self-maintenance with supervision in work and living situations
Profound	Minimal responsiveness; often has multiple disabilities	Slow motor development; learns basic self-care skills	May acquire some communication skills; cares for basic needs; may perform highly structured work activities

Source: Adapted from J. B. Schultz & C. D. Carpenter (1995), *Mainstreaming Exceptional Students,* 4th ed., p. 232. Boston: Allyn & Bacon. Copyright © 1995 by Allyn & Bacon. Adapted with permission.

Students with intelligences below the average range have been traditionally classified as (1) slow learning, (2) mildly mentally retarded, (3) moderately mentally retarded, (4) severely mentally retarded, and (5) profoundly mentally retarded. Students diagnosed as mildly or moderately mentally retarded can learn to read on a word-by-word basis through intensive instruction and massive reviews. These students typically are taught to read in special education classes and can achieve reading grade equivalent levels of 6 to 7.5 readability by the age of 16 (Schultz & Carpenter, 1995).

Students who have lower cognitive abilities differ from other readers in many ways. First, they typically learn at a slower pace. Without special support, they also become discouraged in mainstream classrooms because they experience continued failure. In addition, because slow learners typically enter first grade with a mental age between 5 and 6 years and with fewer readiness abilities, they profit from an emergent reading program that is more intense and prolonged than usual. They need a slower introduction of vocabulary—and the teacher or specialist should present phonetic associations by saying the sound, writing the letter, and then blending the sounds with sounds in other words that they recognize in environmental print.

At every grade level, learning will occur fastest for slower-learning readers when materials are presented at the concrete, pictorial, and abstract levels. When materials are presented in all three ways, large amounts of knowledge and new words can become a permanent part of these readers' sight vocabulary. For example, these students can learn to read the words *palm, fir, elm, maple,* and *pine* more rapidly if they hold a leaf from each, then see a picture of each, and then say the words as they read them.

Students who learn more slowly than their peers also need more review and step-by-step instructions. The directions on most standard reading materials (designed for independent practice) are often too complex for these readers to understand. Of paramount concern is to ensure that they can describe what they are to do before they begin an assignment. Such personalized expressions of learning tasks enable learning style strengths and depth of understanding to be applied to each reading assignment. Similarly, reading goals will be most successful if they are short-term. Most of these students lack the depth of understanding required to profit maximally from projects and goals that are not evaluated within 3 weeks or less. Most also enjoy rereading, because they realize a deeper and more complete understanding of material through extended exposure to the content. For example, when they can read a book or story in their special out-of-the classroom program on the day before they will use that same book in their regular classroom reading program, these readers' decoding and comprehension abilities increase. Some also benefit from retelling their comprehension of a reading before they respond to questions about it or write their ideas.

Through supports such as those presented here, you can assist students who learn more slowly to understand the nature of their disability, reassure them of their self-worth (e.g., by assigning them leadership responsibilities for activities in which they excel), and build their self-esteem by demonstrating that you care about them as people. They can become proficient readers and writers with your help and encouragement.

Addressing Dyslexia and Neurologically Correctable Reading/Writing Difficulties

Dyslexia is "a disorder manifested by difficulty in learning to read despite conventional instruction, adequate intelligence, and socio-cultural opportunity. It results from fundamental cognitive disabilities which are frequently of constitutional origin" (U.S. Dept. of Education, 2002, p. 317). Each fall nearly 3 million new students will begin kindergarten, and by the end of their school career 250,000 of them (1 in 12) will be misdiagnosed with some form of dyslexia. This condiiton is one of the most misunderstood, misdiagnosed, and underestimated of literacy differences. Fortunately, however, your students may not have to bear the unjust and inaccurate stigma that has scarred students with dyslexia in the past.

The causes of dyslexia are often erroneously attributed to "everything from emotional problems to brain damage to inner-ear dysfunction" (Levinson, 1985, p. 34). In addition, dyslexia is commonly perceived as a disease in which students merely have trouble putting written letters and words in proper order. Unfortunately, reality goes far beyond this simplistic perception, as the following self-reports illustrate:

> When I look at a word, my eye goes from the end of the word to the front, and then my mind will translate it from the front to the end. When I look at a word, I look at it from back to front, and then I mentally tell myself to flop it back the other way.
>
> —Heather, college student

> If someone put the words "pound," "proud, "and "pruned" on a line and asked me to pick out "proud" I have serious doubts as to whether I could accurately perform the task because the words look the same to me.
>
> —Anonymous adult who has dyslexia

> For me, printed symbols were not stationary, but three-dimensional and freely floating on the page. Letters appeared as three-dimensional entities and would revolve independently. Therefore, I could not discern a "b" or "d" from a "p." I could not fathom how to tell the difference between these three letters. In addition, the order of the letters was not stationary. To this day, I type "eht," and I still do not recognize that it should be "the."
>
> —Thomas Fleming, Director of Department of Commerce Law Library (Cody, 1985, p. 24)

Although dyslexia manifests itself differently in individual students, the characteristics of the disorder are relatively easy to recognize. Specifically, readers with dyslexia frequently exhibit delayed spoken language, errors in letter naming, difficulty in learning and remembering printed words, reversal of letters in words, repeated spelling errors, cramped and illegible handwriting, difficulty in finding the right word when speaking or writing, slow writing speed, reduced oral and written language comprehension, and directional spatial confusion. Also, these readers experience the added burden of being incorrectly judged lazy or retarded by many uninformed peers and adults.

Readers with dyslexia also have various language processing difficulties. For example, in addition to phonological processing differences, some students with dyslexia may have auditory perception problems that make it difficult for them to follow oral directions, visual perception problems that impair their memory for written words, poor fine-motor skills that inhibit their handwriting, or speech articulation difficulties that interfere with their being understood (Hyde, 1992). On the other hand, many have remarkable abilities in areas other than language, such as exceptional visual–spatial or artistic abilities. Unfortunately, as a result of their dyslexia, most also have mild to severe difficulties interacting with others. They may also have a poor self-image or attitudes of defeatism, depression, denial, or inappropriate bravado that can interfere with good peer relationships.

Readers with dyslexia also have difficulty acquiring metalinguistic knowledge—knowledge to how to translate spoken language into written symbols and vice versa. This inability interferes most when they decode unfamiliar words. Although they can learn many words by sight, their word recognition is slower and less accurate than that of more able readers. The most persistent indicator of dyslexia is the prevalence of writing problems. Contrary to popular perception, creative readers/writers with dyslexia do not reverse and transpose letters and words in any greater proportion to their overall reading and writing errors than do other children. At the same time, however, a small percentage do have severe, specific visual–spatial difficulties and make multiple letter/word reversals (Aaron, Joshi, & Williams, 1999; Hynds, 1994).

To date, research has not established whether dyslexia stems from multiple causes or has a single antecedent. Moreover, we do not know whether variations in the manifestations of dyslexia represent differences in causes or different types. In other words, we do not know if there are one or many dyslexias. Although several theories have been posited to explain the cause(s) of dyslexia, further research is crucial so more accurate diagnoses and corrective programs can be developed. In the meantime, educators are successful in mitigating many of the effects of dyslexia.

There are several theories as to its cause. Dyslexia could be the result of misconnections between cranial nerve centers, lesions in specific sections of the brain, inappropriate brain growth so that both cranial hemispheres are of equal size, developmental delays in specific sections of the brain, or variations of electrical activity within the language-controlling sections of the brain. Others even speculate that none of these deficits are causal; rather, they merely reflect subtle neurological deficits (Aaron, Joshi, & Williams, 1999; Hynds, 1994). Until specific causation can be established and corrected, we have the responsibility of correctly diagnosing and providing effective alternative literacy programs for a quarter of a million students in our schools today. Individual school districts have different screening tests for dyslexia; one example is shown in Table 14.2.

Effective Early Intervention Programs

Research demonstrates that the effects of reading failure compound as students progress through the grades (Stanovich, 1986). Five intensive early intervention programs, however, have been demonstrated to move students who were functioning on the lowest end

TABLE 14.2 Checklist for Possible High-Risk Dyslexia Candidates

If a student demonstrates 10 or more of the following characteristics, he or she should be referred for further assessment.

1. Is your child late or irregular in speech development?
2. Does your child have trouble keeping attention focused on one thing?
3. Does your child have trouble controlling a crayon or scissors?
4. Does your child have difficulty jumping rope, skipping, swimming, or doing other things that require repeated rhythmic movements?
5. Is your child clumsy?
6. Have your child's language difficulties persisted into adolescence?
7. Does learning to speak a foreign language seem to be an impossibility for your child?
8. Does your child reverse words, reading "was" instead of "saw," or make internal word mistakes, such as reading "want" for "went" or "house" for "horse"?
9. Is your child's handwriting difficult to decipher? Do letters look different each time your child writes them?
10. Is your child a poor speller?
11. Does your child have trouble finishing tests in the allotted time period?
12. Does your child have difficulties singing in tune?
13. Does your child seem slow in sports?
14. Is reading aloud painful for your child?
15. Does your child reverse numbers?
16. Does your child have to hold a book out farther than a normal 14 inches in order to read?
17. Are word problems (the ones that begin "If Johnny has 6 apples . . . ") difficult for your child?
18. Are reading skills far behind peers for no explanation?
19. Does your child confuse left and right?
20. Have other family members been poor readers?
21. Is your child immature when compared to peers?
22. In infancy, were there reversals in speech?
23. Was your child confused by concepts such as *up* and *down,* or *yesterday* and *tomorrow?*
24. Does your child have serious difficulty in learning and remembering printed words or symbols?
25. Does your child have difficulty following simple instructions?

Source: Adapted from D. Kaercher (1995, May), "Diagnosing and Treating Dyslexia," *Health,* pp. 10–11; and C. Drak (1994), *Symptoms Indicating Dyslexia.* Chicago, IL: The Orton Society. (Drak is a national expert on the subject and a dyslexic himself.)

of the continuum to literacy proficiency. As you read the program descriptions that follow, keep in mind three considerations. First, these programs are not necessarily designed for students with emotional barriers, mental dysfunction, or dyslexia. Second, if you are now teaching, think about whether you might want to use one of these programs. Third, try to identify characteristics common to all the programs. After all have been described, common characteristics that distinguish them from their less effective counterparts will be summarized.

Success for All

The Success for All program began at Johns Hopkins University's Center for Research on Effective Schooling for Disadvantaged Students. Its distinguishing features are that it is a total school program that coordinates regular classroom instruction and supplementary support; it extends from first through third grade; and it assigns 20 minutes of required homework each night. It contains five carefully designed literacy experiences for the 10 to 15 percent of students whose literacy development is "not on a time line similar to their peers who have had more extensive school-like home literacy experiences" (Slavin, Madden, Karweit, Dolan, & Wasik, 1991, p. 404).

The program provides extensive participation in reading and writing with continual guidance from teachers and at-home interactions. Daily instruction extends for 90 minutes in large group, direct instructional settings (no more than 15 to 20 students at a time) and in individual tutoring sessions. Group instruction lasts for 70 minutes; tutoring occurs for 20 minutes.

Large group instruction begins with the development of basic oral/listening/reading/writing knowledge concerning story structure through teachers' oral reading of a book, followed by students' retellings and storytelling activities. Word identification strategies are taught in conjunction with vocabulary development activities through basal readers, big books, and Peabody language development kits. Then students move into Cooperative Integrated Reading and Composition (CIRC) teams (Stevens, Madden, Slavin, & Farnish, 1987), in which cooperative learning activities are built around story structure, prediction, summarization, vocabulary building, decoding practice, and story-related writing. Students also work in CIRC teams to partner read, to conduct discussions of basal stories, to master vocabulary and content of the story, to create story-related writings, and to develop comprehension strategies.

The tutoring sessions emphasize the strategies introduced during group instruction. Tutors are certified teachers with experience teaching special education, primary grades, and/or classes receiving Title I funding. Tutoring normally occurs during the social studies period. In addition to providing support and practice for the strategy introduced that day, tutors teach alternative strategies (such as those found in Chapters 9–13 of this book) to target individual student needs.

A homework component is required. Twenty-minute home readings occur each night. Home readings comprise oral reading with parents or silent reading of student-selected books. Twice a week, home readings are shared through written summaries and presentations or puppet shows given during "book club" sessions.

To date, struggling readers/writers have experienced significant and cumulative gains from this program. Program developers continue to do evaluations but their first reports have shown promising outcomes:

> Making certain that students get off to a good start in reading in first grade is a key concern. . . . If students begin to receive effective instruction, tutoring, and other supports in first grade, they can develop the skills and confidence on which effective instruction in the later grades can build. (*CDS Report,* October 1991, p. 6)

The Winston-Salem Project

The Winston-Salem Project is designed for first grade students from lower- to middle-class socioeconomic backgrounds. Its distinguishing features are that it provides more time for self-selected silent reading than other effective programs and also provides a variable scale for the number of minutes individual students engage in reading-related activities. The basic program contains four 30-minute blocks of heterogeneously grouped instruction. The program can extend to 3¼ hours if developing readers need extended time to learn a literacy-related concept. When students need additional time, Chapter 1 and special education teachers work with them for 45 minutes in small homogeneous groups. These groups practice the concept introduced earlier in the day.

The first 30-minute block is the Basal Block. During this time, students read stories from a basal anthology and accompanying paperback books. This block is followed by the Writing Block, in which 5- to 10-minute minilessons are followed by composition activities. Third, the Working With Words Block consists of word identification activities in which students use activities (such as those in Chapter 9 of this book) to form words from letters. Last, the Self-Selected Reading Block enables students to read fiction and self-selected trade books related to science or social studies topics under study.

Early Intervention in Reading

The Early Intervention in Reading program began in Minnesota. Like many other programs, it is a first grade intervention program designed for students of lower- to middle-class socioeconomic status. It is distinctive in that the entire program is implemented by regular classroom teachers.

This program is designed for the five to seven readers per first grade class who have the least literacy proficiency. Early Intervention in Reading is a 25-minute daily addition to whatever basic reading program is followed in individual first grade classrooms. During the first 20 minutes, the regular classroom teacher focuses on the repeated reading of picture books (or on reading summaries of these books) and on strengthening students' phonemic segmentation, blending abilities, and other word recognition strategies. This instruction occurs in small groups. The last 5 minutes is spent in tutorials with an aide, parent volunteer, or the teacher. In these tutorials each student rereads the materials used during the 20-minute small group instructional lesson.

The Boulder Project

The Boulder Project is distinctive in that Chapter 1 teachers implement the curriculum. The program reorganizes and modifies Chapter 1 instruction for at-risk and disadvantaged students. The reorganization creates small groups of only three children. These students meet with a Chapter 1 teacher for 30 minutes each day while the Chapter 1 aide instructs a second group, following the Chapter 1 teacher's lesson plan. After one half year, groups are rotated.

Like the Early Intervention in Reading program, the Boulder Project focuses on the repeated reading of predictable trade books and on the instruction of word identification strategies. Like the Winston-Salem Project, it uses analogy or word patterns to build reading vocabularies, and students write about topics of choice.

Reading Recovery

Reading Recovery is a one-on-one tutorial intervention that increases emerging literacy abilities. Reading Recovery was created by Marie Clay in New Zealand and has been successful for students from diverse populations in the lowest 10 percent of their class as ranked by reading abilities (Clay, 1985; Pinnell, Lyons, DeFord, Bryk, & Seltzer, 1994).

During Reading Recovery lessons students read many short books whose writing style closely matches oral language. Most of these books also use predictable sentence patterns and repeat the same content words. In addition, the success of this program is attributed to several other features that distinguish it from less effective interventions.

For one, many early interventions require readers to complete worksheets that contain only one or two sentences (Allington & McGill-Franzen, 1989a). In contrast, Reading Recovery has a "bias toward text" (Clay, 1985). Instruction occurs during the real-world activity of reading to gain information or receive enjoyment. Therefore, students do not have to make the difficult, abstract conceptual transfer required to comprehend that words they circled on worksheets have meaning when they appear in sentences and stories.

Another effective feature of the Reading Recovery program is that skill practice does not follow a predetermined sequence. Instead, each reader receives instruction about strategies when an individual text requires it and the student is ready to understand it. Thus, the sequence of instruction is based on the specific responses and transfers of knowledge that occur in single instructional sessions with individual students. For example, some students in a discovery discussion may need only a single prompt (e.g., "Show me which part was hardest for you to read or understand") to report what they want to learn. Alternatively, other students may not know what was difficult for them. Thus, the Reading Recovery teacher performs an instant individualized diagnosis and begins instruction with a difficult sentence in the text, perhaps doing a think aloud about how that student can combine information from pictures and words in the sentence whenever many unknown words appear in a single sentence. During every session, teachers alter their approach if the initial instruction for a particular reader was unsuccessful. Instruction focuses on exactly what is needed at a specific point in time.

Another effective feature involves teacher training. Teachers in the Reading Recovery program are committed to working with less accomplished readers and must have at least a year of training before they are qualified to implement Reading Recovery. This training occurs at authorized universities and involves viewing, analyzing, and discussing lessons seen through a one-way viewing window. Teachers learn to engage struggling readers in intense targeted instruction, which is necessary if these students are to make the transition into beginning reading.

Because instruction in Reading Recovery is based on books, from the very beginning less accomplished readers are supported in their decoding and comprehension by the concept of story, which they are developing. The stories provide sense to support decoding. Moreover, because Reading Recovery books are divided into 15 levels of difficulty, vocabulary demands increase only slightly from book to book. Students thus have the support of knowing most of the vocabulary in each book and are therefore able to attend to the relatively few new concepts in a new book without losing the semantic clues available through context. In addition, all books can be read in one day—so story structure, plot completion, and story patterning can also assist comprehension. For older readers (grades 3–12), teachers use single chapters from easy-to-read books such as those in the Scholastic Action Series, Champion Series, Movie Star Series, and Sports Heroes Series; in general, the books in the original Reading Recovery program have interest levels for students aged 4 to 9 only.

Teachers introduce books in a prereading discussion by asking the student to anticipate the story through picture questioning. Then teachers discuss and write the difficult language and concepts that will be read. Teacher and student also examine the turning event (climax) of the story and special qualities of the author's writing style. Each day, immediately following the prereading discussion, the student reads the new book for the first time, with teacher prompting and minimal interrupting. Then the teacher points out and corrects errors so that on the second day, when the child reads the book again, more fluid reading will occur. In this second reading the teacher makes a running record (see Chapter 6) and provides more specific instruction related to error patterns. On subsequent days, rereading continues until the student achieves 90 percent accuracy and comprehension for this book. Figures 14.4 and 14.5 depict the lesson format.

Hi! Welcome to My Reading Recovery Lesson

Fluent Writing Practice

Before my 30-minute lesson begins, I get to write some words on the chalkboard. I'm learning to write little important words as fast as I can, so I write them in my stories. It's fun to write on the chalkboard!

Rereading Familiar Books

In every lesson every day I get to read lots of little books. I get to pick some of my favorite stories that I have read before. This is easy for me. I try to read a book like a story and make it sound like people are talking. My teacher says, "That's good reading—that's how good readers read!"

Taking a Running Record

Now I have to read a book all by myself! My teacher will check on me and won't help me unless I have a hard problem. If I can't figure out a word or get all mixed up, my teacher will tell me the word or say, "Try that again." I read this book yesterday. My teacher helped me work hard to figure out the tricky parts. Now I think I can read it pretty good all by myself!

FIGURE 14.4 Student's Conceptualization of a Reading Recovery Lesson

Letter Identification or Word Analysis (optional)

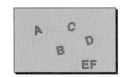

Sometimes I need to do work on learning about letters or important "chunks" of words. My teacher knows all about the things I need to learn. I like to move the magnetic letters around on the chalkboard—they help me understand what I am learning.

Writing a Story

Every day I get to think up my own story to write in my writing book. I can write lots of the little words all by myself. My teacher likes my stories and helps me work to figure out how to write some of the words. We use boxes and I say the word I want to write slowly so I can hear the sounds and then I write the letters in the boxes all by myself. I like to read my story when I'm done.

Cut-Up Sentence

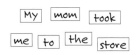

I read the story and my teacher writes it on a long strip of paper. My teacher cuts up my story so I can put it back together. I have to think real hard to get it all back together, then I have to check myself to see if I got it right. Most of the time I do!

New Book Introduced

I like this part of the lesson the best! My teacher picks out a new story just for me and tells what the story is all about. We look at the pictures and think about what the people and animals say in this book. My teacher also helps me think about some new, important words in my story. Isn't it fun to hear about the story and look at the beautiful pictures before you read it? I think it helps me read the story too!

New Book Attempted

Now it's my turn to work hard again, but I like this story and I know my lesson is almost over. When I come to a hard part my teacher will ask me questions to help me think or might show me what I should try to think about or do. My teacher is trying to teach me to do all the things that good readers do. If I have to work real hard on this story we will probably read it again together so I can just think about the story, but I'm not sure there is enough time.

Didn't I do lots of work in my lesson today? I hope you learned something too. Bye!

FIGURE 14.4 *(continued)*

Source: Adapted from a conceptualization by Ms. Jamie Mulleneix, teacher, Fort Worth Independent School District, Fort Worth, TX.

(10 minutes)

1. FAMILIAR READING
   Reread two or more familiar books.

2. RUNNING RECORD
   Reread yesterday's new book and take a running record.

(10 minutes)

3. LETTER ID
   Practice letter recognition (using magnetic board, salt box, and/or chalkboard).

4. WRITING
   Write a story (hearing sounds in the story).

5. CUT-UP STORY
   Cut up story for rearranging.

(10 minutes)

6. NEW BOOK
   Teacher introduces a new book, providing scaffolding.

7. REREAD NEW BOOK
   Student attempts to read new book, with the teacher providing assistance as needed.

FIGURE 14.5 Format for a Reading Recovery Lesson

Another feature of Reading Recovery is that the number of real, textual, nonisolated, authentic reading experiences are maximized in this 30-minute Tier 3 discovery discussion. Typically, every student's 30-minute lesson consists of reading three to five little books as well as writing and analyzing several sentences and words. As Maria Montessori believed 100 years ago, a child should never be allowed to fail until he or she has had a reasonable chance for success. Because children in this program select one from a set of 20 familiar books to start each discovery discussion, their first reading each day is almost guaranteed to be successful. As Henry Ford stated: "Failures are opportunities to begin again more intelligently." Therefore, teachers teach new information to overcome each mistake so students understand why each mistake was made and how to avoid it in the future.

When reading instruction is complete, there is a writing exercise in which the student writes stories, sentences, and/or words that he or she chooses. The teacher explains the letter-to-sound correspondences the student will need to spell words correctly after asking how the student thinks the words would be spelled. If the student makes errors in letter-to-sound correspondences, the teacher explains that sounds can be represented by many different letters. The teacher then demonstrates several words with that sound but different spelling patterns. If a word is too difficult for the student to spell, the teacher writes it. Because writing forces students to focus on visual clues, they learn early not to rely solely on pictorial clues and background experiences to decode. Samples of sentences one reader wrote after being able to read the words *like* and *to* independently from a book for the first time are shown in Figure 14.6.

It is important to note that Reading Recovery is not a "remedial" reading program. It provides intensive personalized intervention when the gap in the developmental ladder is still small, during the first emergence of literacy concepts. Because this intervention is provided while students are engaging in their first attempts to read, incorrect learning patterns have not become habitual and do not need to be unlearned.

Reading Recovery builds on students' strengths, using what they already know in their zone of proximal development to help them understand and apply more powerful strategies. This approach increases emerging developing readers' self-confidence. They are told about the things they already know and do that have value in their reading and writing (DeFord, Lyons, & Pinnell, 1994). They also learn specific strategies for applying knowledge about reading/writing that they deduce independently.

FIGURE 14.6 Samples of an Emerging Reader's Writing during a Reading Recovery Lesson

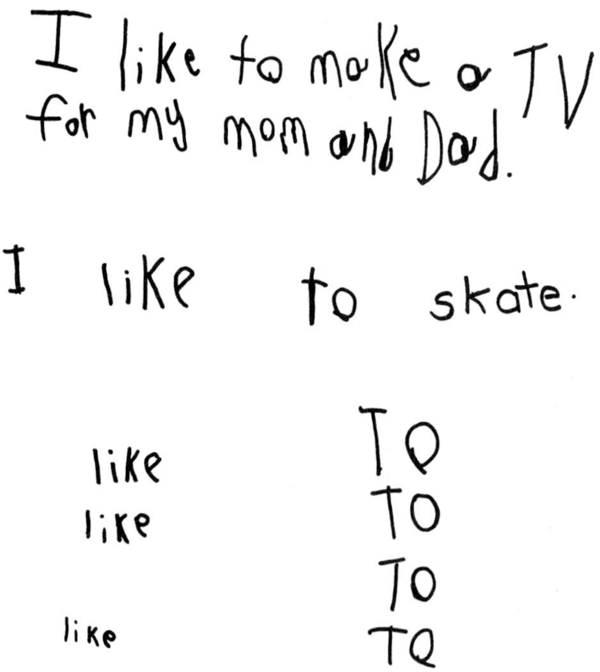

Students in the Reading Recovery program can increase their independent reading abilities because they are taught how to solve individual problems using specific metacognitive strategies (such as self-monitoring, cross-checking, predicting, and confirming). In turn, they orchestrate these strategies as their individual learning style dictates, rather than memorizing and following arbitrary rules. In other words, they are not given an out-of-context list of strategies to learn, but rather are brought to recognize when a specific strategy will help them decode or comprehend a specific text. Also, teachers describe internal processes students can use to create visible reading and writing behaviors. As they analyze these internal thoughts, students can more rapidly self-apply literacy strategies.

Reading Recovery instruction involves visual, auditory, kinesthetic, and tactile education in a setting in which the child takes action and leads. Based on these principles, research demonstrates that after as few as 20 weeks in the program, most students who began at the emergent literacy level typically perform at average reading level for their age.

Common Characteristics of Effective Early Intervention Programs

The following features have been identified as successful components of the five foregoing early intervention programs (DeFord, Lyons, & Pinnell, 1994; Pikulski, 1994).

1. One-to-one tutoring is demonstrated to be the most effective form of instruction (Slavin, Karweit, & Madden, 1989; Wasik & Slavin, 1990). In these five programs, classroom teachers, Chapter 1 teachers, special education teachers, teacher aides, parents, parent volunteers at school, and student peers are employed as tutors. In most cases, these sessions occur daily. Most important, tutoring sessions are based on two principles: First, the strategies taught are those introduced during regular reading instruction. Second, each tutor bases instruction on individual student needs rather than on unindividualized curriculum directives.

2. In each program, struggling readers/writers receive at least 90 minutes of daily instruction in literacy-related topics. Merely devoting extra time to reading instruction appears to be insufficient to advance struggling readers. As a matter of fact, time spent in pull-out compensatory programs that did not contain the features of these five programs was actually *detrimental* to struggling readers' progress (Hiebert, Colt, Catts, & Gury, 1992; Lyons, Place, & Rinehart, 1990). In contrast, the additional quality time for reading provided through these five programs enables highly targeted, intensive individualized instruction. This intensity proves to be more crucial for literacy development than the curriculum used or the slight differences in philosophy on which specific programs are based. Moreover, this instruction does not segment reading or slow the pace of reading instruction. Any intensive preventive measure that reduces the time students spend reading and solving individual problems will place less accomplished readers farther behind their more proficient peers (Allington, 1994).

3. All five of these programs integrate reading, writing, speaking, and listening in order to advance literacy. In three of the programs, students may choose what they read; in two programs, students write about topics of their choice. One program enables students to enact what they read; another teaches grammatical principles through

student-created sentences. As Clay (1985) stated: "A case can be made for the theory that learning to write letters, words, and sentences actually helps the child to make the visual discriminations of detailed print that he will use in his reading" (p. 54). Thus, in most effective programs, writing occurs daily, for brief periods, and focuses students' attention on features of letters and words in an interesting context.

4. All of the five programs discussed here emphasize word recognition strategies, with most focusing on word pattern instruction.

5. In most of the programs, students reread familiar text.

6. Four of these programs coordinate instruction with regular reading curriculum. As Pikulski (1994) states: "All programs [for readers in special programs] should try to ensure that students are receiving excellent and coordinated instruction both in their classrooms and in the special intervention program" (p. 38).

7. All five programs begin in first grade.

8. Predictable, easy-to-read texts and authentic trade books are the most productive and popular reading material. Moreover, all of these effective projects use some texts that students can read with 100 percent success: texts that are easier (even wordless in one program) than other materials introduced later in the lesson. These latter materials provide small but steady literacy challenges to readers. Further, it seems that young less accomplished readers benefit from predictable texts that are interesting and use natural language patterns. Also beneficial are texts that encourage students' successful application of word identification strategies (Pikulski, 1994).

9. None of these successful programs use traditional skill-and-drill workbooks or isolated skill practice sheets. Rather, skills are taught in the context of attaining meaning from books. All of the programs conceptualize reading as a meaning-making process and teach word identification strategies to build independence in decoding.

10. All of these programs use books that contain natural, noncontrolled vocabulary. Reading Recovery uses such books exclusively; the other four approaches employ some control over the time at which vocabulary and phonetic principles are taught. The Boulder Project uses curriculum designed specifically for that program. In all of these programs, most instruction is directed to developing word recognition ability (Pikulski, 1994).

11. The most common instructional activity is the repeated reading of books that students and teachers have selected. Research documents that this instructional activity is powerful for young struggling readers (Dowhower, 1987; Herman, 1985; Samuels, 1979).

12. All programs include regular, frequent, and ongoing assessment. The frequency of evaluation ranges from daily (Reading Recovery) to once every 8 weeks (Success for All).

13. All programs contain specific at-home activities and involve parents.

14. All programs hire consultants for teachers at least during the first year of implementation. Teachers receive education before beginning each program, although this training varies from a year's coursework to 30-hour workshops to a single day of instruction.

In summary, specific preventive actions can produce significant advancements for readers with literacy differences. For these reasons, it is important that as often as possible, preventive programs should begin in first grade. If such intervention occurs, a substantial portion of the money spent in compensatory, Chapter 1, and special education programs for older students can be redirected toward the goal of advancing all readers to deeper levels of understanding and appreciation of literacy.

Special Tutorial Programs to Meet Special Needs

Because no two students' literacy portraits are alike, instructional programs should be individually tailored. Most of the tutorial programs presented here do contain common elements, however. Each of the following Tier 3 and Tier 4 programs draws on the skill of experts from many fields. Each develops literacy through strategies that are multidisciplinary, and each contains diagnostic information derived from educational pedagogy, medicine, psychology, social work, and language theory. In addition, each of these tutorial programs is multisensory in its approach, with instruction designed to stimulate learning pathways related to seeing, hearing, touching, and awareness of motion. For example, in one activity students learn letters by feeling their shape (cut out of sandpaper), make cookies in the shape of words, trace words in sandboxes, eat alphabet cereal, mold words from play dough, or finger-paint words with pudding and whipped cream. In general, these programs teach letters through the alphabetic phonic system—emphasizing that words, which carry meaning, are made up of individual sounds that can be written down. Further, each program presented here has material organized and taught in a way that logically follows the nature of spoken and written language. Finally, each program helps learners to move, step by step, from simple, well-learned material to selections that are more complex. Descriptions of the most widely used tutorial programs follow.

The Slingerland Program, Spalding Method, and Writing Skills for the Adolescent

Three effective tutorials are the Slingerland Program, the Spalding Method, and Writing Skills for the Adolescent. These programs are based on Orton-Gillingham principles and are intended to interface with VAKT (visual–auditory–kinesthetic–tactile) procedures, as follows:

1. Students look at a word and study it carefully.
2. Students discuss the word to learn its pronunciation and meaning.
3. Students close their eyes and mentally visualize the word, then write it in the air.
4. Students write the word on their paper without looking at it.
5. Students trace the letters with their fingers.
6. Students write the word in a sentence and read the sentence.

The *Slingerland Program* follows the VAKT procedure, with an adaptation to be used with whole classes of students. It is also designed as a preventive program for students with learning disabilities. It is based on the premise that literacy for special needs students depends on intersensory functioning. Essentially, teachers say each letter sound in a word separately and ask individual children to name the letter while forming it in the air, then to name its keyword and give its sound. Teachers then hold up an alphabet card and ask the class to repeat the process again in unison. The 26 letters of the alphabet and 44 combinations of two, three, or four letters that make a single sound (e.g., /ai/, /igh/, /ough/) are spelled first and then written by students (Clark, 1988). Students are taught to spell and write 150 of the 1,700 most frequently used words using manuscript and cursive writing. Reading instruction does not begin until students have mastered 150 words—until they can spell them aloud, write them from dictation, and read them (Farnham-Diggory, 1992).

The *Spalding Method* teaches writing before reading and introduces the most commonly used English words first. This program also introduces students to children's literature and encourages them to write their own stories.

Writing Skills for the Adolescent (King, 1985) is probably the most comprehensive writing program for reluctant writers with special needs. It helps students improve their handwriting, spelling, and letter formations. It is essentially a tutorial program for college-bound adolescents who were not diagnosed with a literacy difference until high school. The tutor begins writing instruction in conjunction with spelling instruction by having students compose simple sentences from lists of spelling words. Once this activity can be accomplished with some facility, formal grammar instruction begins—first with parts of speech, and then moving on to clauses, participles, gerunds, and infinitives. Case studies have been conducted to validate the program. "Before" and "after" writing samples show significant improvements (King, 1985).

Alphabet Phonics

The *Alphabet Phonics* program is an adaptation of the VAKT approach that is designed for use in small groups as well as in one-to-one tutorials. It began at the Scottish Rite Hospital in Dallas, Texas, and emerged from a collaboration among Sally Childs, who was a colleague of Anna Gillingham; Lucius Waites, a neuro-pediatrician; and Aylett Cox, the teacher who wrote the curriculum. In addition to using a VAKT multisensory basis, Alphabet Phonics employs a discovery approach to learning (Attention Deficit Disorder, 2000; Lundbert & Tonnessen, 1999).

The daily structured lessons in this program take approximately an hour to complete. A typical lesson contains the following elements (Cox, 1985):

1. An alphabetic phonics activity emphasizes sequence and directionality of print.
2. Students discover a new element of language using multisensory techniques.
3. Students receive training in automatic recognition of letter names through flash cards called Reading Decks.
4. Students are trained to recognize letter sounds by pronouncing the sounds of letters in the Reading Decks and then writing these letters.
5. Students practice reading and spelling until they reach 95 percent mastery.
6. Students practice handwriting.
7. Students practice expression—first oral and later written—focusing on sequencing ideas, creative expression, vocabulary, and syntax.
8. Students listen to good literature and build comprehension skills.

The Stevenson Language Skills Method

The *Stevenson Language Skills Method* is the most comprehensive tutorial program, as it addresses 20 comprehension skills (see Table 14.3) in addition to teaching VAKT skills. In this program students are also taught through visual image association. For instance, students are taught common word patterns by being asked to think of such things as peanut butter and jelly sandwiches and layer cakes: Teachers might teach a two-vowel element such as /oa/ by relating it to the experience of making a peanut butter and jelly sandwich. Students know that they first take a slice of bread (the consonant) to which they add crunchy peanut butter (the vowel that makes a loud sound in the medial position). Then they add a smooth layer of jelly (the silent medial vowel). The final piece of the sandwich is the last slice of bread (the ending consonant). Teachers explain that the loud peanut butter covers up the sound of the silent jelly. To illustrate, if students were given the word boat, they would know that the /o/ is the loud sound because it is the layer of peanut butter, and the /a/ is silent because it corresponds to the layer of jelly.

TABLE 14.3 Stevenson Language Skills Program: 20 Comprehension Skills

Students need to work on the following comprehension skills so that they will be able to express themselves clearly when they speak or write.

1. Increasing attention span
2. Decoding
3. Spelling (encoding) at the cognitive rather than rote level
4. Increasing closure skill
5. Imaging
6. Categorizing and learning word functions (grammar)
7. Learning formal English usage versus creative writing sentence structures
8. Phrase building, orally and in writing
9. Sentence building (using the phrases), orally and in writing
10. Defining (using three types of syntactical structures)
11. Creating lead sentences
12. Illustrating meanings of new vocabulary words
13. Illustrating meanings of specific types of sentences
14. Answering particular types of questions in complete sentences
15. Answering questions that require the student to generate complex sentences (formal English)
16. Notebook organizing for the purpose of collecting information concerning each new vocabulary word (mapping)
17. Practicing dictionary work (defining)
18. Practicing grammar work specific to writing
19. Practicing inference work within a specific hierarchy
20. Organizing and sequencing for paragraph building

RESOURCE CARD 20

Books about Learning Problems

Betancourt, J. (1993). *My name is Brian.* New York: Scholastic.

Booth, Z. (1987). *Finding a friend.* Mount Desert, ME: Windswept House.

Byars, B. (1970). *Summer of the Swans.* New York: Viking.

Crary, E. (1983). *My name is not dummy.* Seattle, WA: Parenting Press.

Greenwald, S. (1985). *Will the real Gertrude Hollings please stand up?* New York: Dell.

Lasker, J. (1973). *He's my brother.* Chicago: A. Whitman.

Little, J. (1968). *Take wing.* Boston: Little, Brown.

Smith, L. B. (1979). *A special kind of sister.* New York: Holt, Rinehart & Winston.

Chapter Summary

Some students' barriers to literacy are so challenging that they require special supports and other adaptations, both inside the classroom and outside of school. This chapter presented information to assist you in recognizing the existence of special problems, diagnosing them properly, and planning the special supports needed for these students to become better readers and writers.

The chapter offered multiple intelligence theory as a way to stimulate students' linguistic abilities through their other types of intelligence—logical, spatial, kinesthetic, musical, interpersonal, and intrapersonal. It explored techniques you can use to overcome emotional and attentional barriers, as well as barriers due to mental dysfunction and dyslexia. It identified the most successful early intervention programs and their common characteristics. And finally, it presented several effective tutorial programs for readers with severe literacy differences.

As you implement these and all the techniques and programs discussed throughout this book, there is one overarching concern: When you describe readers/writers with learning differences, always *describe their behaviors* rather than assigning a label to the child. We must teach to remove the "remedial reader" label, thus ensuring every student the opportunity to reach his or her full literacy potential.

Key Terminology

Now that you have completed this chapter, do you know the meanings of the following terms? If you do, place a check mark in the blank that precedes each term. If you are not certain, review the term's meaning by turning to the page number that follows it. If you have learned four of these on your initial reading of this chapter, you can use this as an indication that you understood the chapter's intent.

_____ **referral process** (page 457)
_____ **learning styles** (page 464)
_____ **intraphysic support** (page 466)

_____ **ADD or ADHD** (page 474)
_____ **mental dysfunctions** (page 475)
_____ **dyslexia** (page 477)

 ## Case Study

Making Professional Decisions

This case study describes a first grade student, Jessica. This case study does not include all of the sources of evidence that will inform the referral process, as described in Box 14.1. Take the information that is given and complete the referral form in Box 14.1, noting the types of additional information you would want to obtain if you were to make a diagnosis to begin Jessica's instruction.

January 27, 2003

Jessica is a very bright, well behaved 6½-year-old child. She tries very hard and desperately seeks approval from myself as well as from the other students in my class. The other children look up to Jessica and tend to view her as a leader of the group.

Jessica has one sister, Tiji, who is 2 years older than Jessica. Tiji was retained in first grade and at this time is having a very difficult time in second grade.

Both girls have lived with their maternal grandparents since Jessica was born in July of 1987. Their father lives across the street, and they see him several times a week. Jessica speaks very highly of her father and his girlfriend. She seems well adjusted and readily accepts her living arrangements.

Jessica sees her mother only once a month. Several times during the year, Jessica has expressed displeasure toward her mother. It seems that sometimes she forgets to pick the girls up.

As I stated earlier, Jessica seems to be very well adjusted with her living arrangements. She speaks often of her grandparents, especially about her relationship with her grandfather. They seem to be very close.

Jessica's grandparents take an active role in her education. We have had numerous formal conferences and many more informal ones. I know that Jessica is read to every night and that she has a seemingly endless supply of paper, pencils, and markers for writing and drawing at home. I know this because several times a week she brings me a paper that she has written or drawn on. Compared with the other children in my class, Jessica has an almost perfect home situation. She has adults in her life who care and who work with her.

Based on scores from the Developing Skills Checklist and the Vane Kindergarten Test, as well as on parent and teacher observations, it was decided that Jessica would benefit from a year in my class. She was immature and developmentally not at a level where she could function successfully in first grade. The areas I focus on in my program are reading and writing. I try to provide an environment where my students feel safe to experiment with their own reading. Because "grades" are not assigned, I feel like the kids are able to take risks without fearing they may fail. My students also benefit from being in an environment that is full of rich literature. They are actively participating in choral readings, collaborative writing groups, individual reading and writing, and many opportunities to share.

Why am I concerned about Jessica? Jessica is not taking as many risks in her writing as I would like. Her work is filled with very short sentences that consist mainly of sight words. Although her oral vocabulary is very good, she will expand her written vocabulary only if someone is working with her. In her reading, Jessica is not reading for meaning. She loves to go through the motions of reading (she rarely does not have a book close to her), but it seems that she is not where she needs to be. This is the reason I chose Jessica for this case study.

I believe that reading and writing are developmental processes and that children will progress naturally across a continuum. I realize that children develop at different rates and that they may skip and sometimes regress as they grow. Jessica is a normal child, I do not feel that she will ever wear a negative label as a student. However, I must work out a plan to get her over this hump.

I am especially concerned because Jessica does live in an environment that appears to be highly conducive to learning. I believe that Jessica has the potential to be a very successful reader.

Thinking and Writing about What You Have Learned

1. Return to the opening vignette about 11-year-old Billy, the student who was misdiagnosed. Based on the information in the vignette, describe the misdiagnoses he was given. What would you have done to diagnose his needs?

2. Refer to Resource Card 20, a list of books that enable students to identify with the struggles of main characters and to establish new strategies for overcoming their literacy differences. Select and read a book of your choice. Then design a lesson that could be used to address many students' needs, based on the experiences in that book.

3. Students can write to obtain information on specific literacy difficulties about which they are curious—or on difficulties that they themselves experience. Provide the addresses listed under "For Further Reference" below for their letters of inquiry. Assist them to read and report on the information received.

For Further Reference

If you or your students desire more information about any of the programs described in this chapter, it can be obtained free of charge from the following sources:

LEARNING STYLE DIFFERENCES

Center for Success in Learning, 1700 Preston Rd., Suite 400, Dallas, TX 75202
Dunn & Dunn Learning Center, 1276 10th Avenue, New York, NY 10036

ALPHABETIC PHONICS

The Aylett Royal Cox Institute, 4111 North Central Expressway, Suite 201, Dallas, TX 75204-2197
Child Development Division, Dyslexia Laboratory, Scottish Rite Hospital for Crippled Children, 2222 Welborn St., Dallas TX 75219

SUPPORT FOR PARENTS OF STUDENTS WITH LEARNING DISABILITIES

Learning Disabilities Association, 4156 Library Rd., Pittsburgh, PA 15234

OTHER PROGRAMS

HOTS Program, Dr. Stanley Pogrow, School of Education, University of Arizona, Tucson, AZ 61790

Slingerland Multisensory Approach to Language Arts, The Slingerland Institute, 1 Bellevue Center, 411 198th Avenue N.E., Bellevue, WA 98004

Lindamood-Bell Learning Processes, Corporate Headquarters, 416 Higuera St., San Luis Obispo, CA 93401 (branch offices in Sacramento, Boston, San Diego, Chicago, and Sydney, Australia)

PRIVATE SCHOOLS FOR STUDENTS WITH SPECIAL NEEDS

Benchmark School, 2694 Hillcrest, Media, PA 15219

Landmark School, 193 Main Street, Prides Crossing, MA 02336

Riverview School (residential); Richard Lavoic, Executive Director; East Sandwich, MA 02563

Starpoint School of Learning Disabilities, Texas Christian University, 2829 Stadium Dr., Fort Worth, TX 76129; Kathy Williams, Principal, Barbara Trice, Administrative Assistant

ANSWER KEY

Chapter 1

The teacher in this classroom performed several exemplary actions for these struggling readers/writers. She began the day by listening to these readers' ideas and tied these ideas to the next day's activities by having them write a question relative to their ideas on the board to begin the class each morning. This teacher also removed the physical distance between herself and readers. She also enabled these students to become respected and fully participatory leaders in their class.

What would you do next? What would you add to this lesson? This teacher used a think aloud and modeling to assist the first student (Marco). She asked the second student (Tiffany) to engage in conversations with a peer who sat beside her. She asked this student to voice any associations she identified between the characters in her book and her own life. She scaffolded, or assisted Tiffany to begin the conversation, by asking her to describe what part of the material that she read was most pleasing to her. Once both students identified the topics and concepts that were most intriguing to them, she provided three books from the concept books on Resource Card 1 so they could extend their interests and vocabularies in those areas. Both students wrote about the information they learned and read their works to the class at the end of the week.

Chapter 2

1. *Environmental Factors*

   Home: Frequent family moves and possible lack of attention from parents due to pressures of jobs, recent marriage and move of sister, not being read to, age differences between siblings, early school start despite teacher recommendations, lack of kindergarten experience.

   School: Young entrance, lack of kindergarten, attendance in three different school systems with three different approaches, negative teacher comments.

   Social: Loss of friends.

   Cultural: Nonapparent.

   Individual Factors

   Emotional: Shy, withdrawn behavior reported by mother, school records, and reading teacher; lack of friends; response to test; difficulty discussing reading problems and reading orally.

2. Notice and praise Caroline's school success, plan for family trips with Caroline, keep in touch with teacher.

3. Use Caroline's interest in music. Read books about music and musicians, pursue her interest in the piano, listen to records to stimulate conversation and interest in reading or writing, dictate stories about music.

Chapter 3

Ms. Krieger diagnosed Sam as having a different cognitive learning style. Sam was a kinesthetic learner who preferred to read at home so he could move around freely and be comfortable as he read.

Chapter 4

Brian lacked an interest in reading or writing. His teacher, Mr. Cockran, used a choice of materials and tasks, as well as an attitude/interest survey (see Chapter 5). In doing so, Mr. Cockran discovered Brian's enjoyment of hearing stories about others' lives. Knowing this, Mr. Cockran introduced Brian to autobiographies and biographies. Brian began to enjoy reading for the first time. He wanted to read to learn strategies people used to overcome obstacles and improve their lives. And he wanted to use these strategies himself to improve his literacy and life.

After uncovering this interest, Mr. Cockran brought several books from the Scholastic series *Heroes, Great Leaders,* and *Sports Legends.* He recommended that Brian select a few books about people he admired and list what each person did to overcome difficulties. As Brian made his list he also kept a tally of which strategies were used most frequently. At the end of the month, Brian began his next discovery discussion with overflowing exuberance, eager to share all he had learned about becoming more successful. At this discovery discussion he made the statement cited in Chapter 4 and requested that Mr. Cockran show him the section of the library where he could find biographies about nine people he wanted to learn more about.

Chapter 5

ANSWERS TO CASE STUDY:

1. Severe. Reid has had problems since beginning school. He functions 3 years below his classmates. Also, he has an average potential as indicated by the Listening Task.

2. *Environmental Factors*

   Home, social, and cultural problems are not apparent.

   School: Early reading phonics methods inappropriate; possibly teachers' attribution of problems to carelessness may denote negative attitude toward Reid.

   Individual Factors

   Physical factors: Vision and general health good. Hearing: Middle ear infections, failure on school auditory screening tests; allergy cloggy ears; trouble with phonics, difficulty attending to auditory tasks, not responding when called; repetition of questions; possible speech problems; possibly below-average language development.

Language development: Saw a speech therapist, talked late, not verbally expressive.

Cognitive factors: None apparent.

3. Instruction should begin at the Primer Level. When word recognition, oral comprehension and word accuracy, and silent comprehension are considered, the highest level at which Reid meets all of the critical is Primer. Also, Reid's listening comprehension level is at the Primer Level. This indicates that this is the level at which Reid understands language.

ANSWER TO QUESTION 4 ON PAGES 139–140:

Ms. Beardon, the teacher, was describing the use of small group instruction for African American students at Stages 2 and 3 of literacy development. The small group task was designing lessons about decoding strategies that the students valued. They were going to teach these lessons to schoolmates who hadn't learned them.

Chapter 6

1. Meisong is a nonreader; it seems she may also lack some emergent concepts. She needs to reinforce these concepts and learn sight words. Possible strategies include echo reading and pointing, as well as using easy predictable books in shared reading, counting words, jumbled sentences, and "being the words."
2. Initial phonics and phonemic awareness could be taught through "acting beginning sounds," segmentation, and letter-sound manipulation. Nursery rhymes and rhyming books, identifying beginning sounds, rhymes and riddles, counting sounds, acting beginning sounds, letter-sound manipulation, and spelling.
3. Meisong needs opportunities to hear rich language by being read to, in peer-paired groups, or through guided discussion focused on books that have been read to students. Shared book experiences and language experience activities would also help, as would supplying words to wordless text.

Chapter 7

ANSWERS TO CASE STUDY:

1. *Environmental Factors*

   Home, social, and cultural problems are not apparent.

   School: Possible entrance at a young age.

   Individual Factors

   Physical: Referral from vision screening test; findings of vision test by professional; possible problem with seeing balls etc., in sports; selection of large-print books; losing place while reading; history of "cross-eyed" condition. Note: Snellen chart tests only for myopia—other problems could be unnoticed. No general health, hearing, or neurological problems suggested.

Potential: On-grade listening level suggests adequate potential.

Emotional: Dislike of reading evidenced in reluctance to read in general and to co-operate at Reading Center. However, note that dislike appears to have developed after problems were evident.

2. Yes, David is a struggling reader. He functions 2 years below most classmates and has had problems since grade 2, despite normal potential as evidenced by listening task.

3. Word recognition. David broke down in the grade 3 oral reading because of word recognition problems, which then caused a lack of comprehension. Strong comprehension is also indicated by his listening level. Better silent than oral reading suggests good use of context clues, but problems pronouncing words.

4. Second grade is suggested by the instructional level on the IRI and by performance in school.

ANSWER TO QUESTION 7 ON PAGE 227:

Paired grouping

Chapter 8

ANSWERS TO CASE STUDY:

1. *Environmental Factors*

   Home and social problems are not apparent.

   School: Lack of schooling in native country; lack of support with English after coming to United States.

   Cultural: Nonuse of English outside of school; despite parents' lack of formal education, they support Ramón's schooling and encourage him to continue.

   Motivational: Low self-esteem centering on reading problems; somewhat withdrawn from teachers, but this could be cultural; becomes very uncomfortable when faced with difficulty.

2. Comprehension is an instructional need apparent in all areas. Word recognition and fluency does not seem to be a problem. Comprehension difficulties were noted by teachers and were apparent on the IRI and standardized test. When Ramón was asked to read high school text, he demonstrated comprehension problems.

3. Begin with individual instruction in Tier 3 support settings until Ramón feels somewhat better about his reading achievement and is more willing to cope with difficulty.

4. Instruction should begin at sixth grade level so Ramón will not encounter too many difficulties during the early phases of instruction.

5. Ramón needs to learn strategies for comprehension. Ramón should work extensively with the think-aloud strategy. He would also benefit from reciprocal teaching when he enters group instruction. Combining this with the Buddy Reading strategy for expository text would also be recommended for Ramón, as would self-responsibility charts and serial books.

ANSWER TO QUESTION 4 ON PAGE 261:

To assess how well you diagnosed and can plan instruction for emergent readers, compare the answers you wrote to the following diagnosis and instruction that was prescribed for each of the following students.

Student 1 (Figure 8.11): This boy is attempting to print. Because he is writing letters with downstrokes, curves, slants, and vertical as well as horizontal lines, it is evident that he knows the recurring principles of our language. Because he can now decipher and manipulate print, he is at the stage of his development at which he wants to know how to consistently replicate his newfound pleasure of making images called letters. He seeks to learn more about letters and their sounds. For this reason, his teacher began reading the trade books that repeat phonic elements and teach letter names from them.

Student 2 (Figure 8.12): This girl demonstrates knowledge of the sign principle. She is writing with the intention of having it read by others. Her teacher began creating rebus stories, using sentences and logos the student brought to school.

Student 3 (Figure 8.13): This boy is in the process of developing the concept of words. His teacher asked him to assist her to label items around the room. This student said the words and wrote them with his teacher's help.

Chapter 9

ANSWERS TO CASE STUDY:

1. Areas of word recognition needing instructional support:
   a. Use of context clues. Mary does not use them in any task.
   b. Structural analysis. Mary missed word endings and syllabication on Word Recognition List and in Spelling Test.
   c. Phonics skills on *r*-controlled vowels and less frequent vowel patterns, such *ou, ow, all.* Mary had problems on Word Recognition List and Spelling Test.

   Sight words are relatively strong.

2. Because Mary needs instruction in both use of context clues and structural analysis, begin with words in context; identify unknown words and use analogy, building on Mary's strong sight vocabulary.

3. Focus on immediate instructional needs. Vocalization may be helping Mary identify unknown words at this point. Wait until she has developed some strategic approaches to identifying unfamiliar words before trying to wean her from vocalizing.

4. Focus on word recognition strategies with no special attention to reversals at this time. The reason: Mary's reversals are only occasional. They are not unusual at her reading level.

ANSWER TO QUESTION 3 ON PAGE 315:

Phonics activities should be used because the boy is relying on whole word clues. "Writing for Phonics," "Comparing and Contrasting Vowel Patterns," "Making Phonics Tactile and Kinesthetic," "Blending Made Easy," and Lesson 5 would be valuable activities to teach.

Chapter 10

ANSWER TO TABLE 10.3:

"puppy"

ANSWERS TO CASE STUDY:

1. All areas except literal comprehension. Identifying main thoughts is in special need. Marcus's instruction should also focus on identifying appropriate background knowledge and connecting this knowledge to reading.

2. Focus on expository text would best help Marcus address immediate school demands. Strategies to help him activate background knowledge include semantic maps and K-W-L.

3. For reading teacher: Help Marcus with specialized vocabulary and develop advanced organizers; model various note-taking strategies.

4. Marcus seems to have little enthusiasm for reading, He needs to have opportunities to select his own books. The teacher might present him with several books from his culture from which to choose. Books about baseball or baseball players would be a good place to start.

   Strategies that will help Marcus make a personal investment in reading and help him focus on the organizational patterns of text are recommended, especially activities in Chapters 3 and 10.

ANSWERS TO QUESTION 7 ON PAGE 357:

Ms. Guitterez began developing Loretta's metacognition by using reverse think alouds and reciprocal thinking because she profited so much from discovery discussions. After these activities, Loretta was told to make a check mark, a ?, or an X in the left margin of pages at locations where she was monitoring her comprehension: a check mark at each point where she knew she was understanding what she read; a ? at points where she knew she was confused; and an X at points where she was not certain if she was comprehending or not.

Chapter 11

ANSWER TO CASE STUDY:

Juan was using the activity of modeling his writing after one of his favorite authors. In Juan's case, the author was the writer of comic books. After reading Juan's second writing, his teacher gave the following feedback: "I can tell that you are enjoying writing because you are using more exclamation points to show the emotion you have placed in your stories. Your readers want to read on and on because every one of your sentences is filled with descriptions and actions that you have never stated before. Your spelling is also improving. Is it because you want to ensure that your readers understand your message? What is the most important improvement you notice and value in your writing, and why?"

The clues in Juan's second writing sample that indicate he is developing his voice are: (1) He is lending his name to the hero in the story; (2) he is using the word "I" and first-person narratives, which require self-disclosure; and (3) he is using the active rather than the passive voice.

ANSWER TO QUESTION 4 ON PAGE 391:

Robert's teacher diagnosed a need to develop creativity more fully. The first instruction was how to use more vivid, unusual, and inventive words. Robert was also taught how to combine sentences with the same subject, because he tended to write choppy sentences. He was also taught to reorganize paragraphs so that the most important main idea was stated first or last; he usually chose to write the main idea as the first sentence.

Chapter 13

ANSWER TO CASE STUDY:

Ms. Solomon, Juanita's teacher, would have liked to have placed her in an ESL program, but there were no openings in that program. She also diagnosed that Juanita was not yet fluent enough in reading Spanish or English to benefit from silent or oral reading of books printed in both Spanish and English. Therefore, Ms. Solomon held discovery discussions every afternoon in which she wrote one or more sentences that Juanita wanted to learn to say and write. In addition, she used captioned television. For 30 minutes each day Juanita viewed captioned television and wrote her responses to the show. After 3 weeks of this activity, Ms. Solomon taught the story frame approach. Juanita read her completed frame to the class frequently, until she could tell the story she had viewed each day without reading from her story frames. Because of this sequence of activities, Juanita's oral language improved. Soon Juanita was speaking confidently.

ANSWER TO QUESTION 5 ON PAGE 453:

Choral Readings and Readers' Theater would be the best choices for Margaret because both build correct pronunciation and oral reading fluency/phrasing.

REFERENCES

Aaron, P. G., Joshi, R. M., Mahboobeh, A., Elsberry, A., Henderson, J., Alvermann, D., & Phelps, S. (1998). *Content reading literacy: Succeeding in today's diverse classrooms.* Boston: Allyn & Bacon.

Aaron, P. G., Joshi, M., & Williams, K. (1999). Not all reading disabilities are alike. *Journal of Learning Disabilities, 32,* 120–137.

Adams, M. J. (1993). *Beginning to read: Thinking and learning about print.* Cambridge: MIT Press.

Adams, M. J. (1993, December). *Differences in decoding in whole language and traditional classrooms.* Paper presented at the National Reading Conference, San Antonio, TX.

Adams, P. (1995). Teaching Romeo and Juliet in the nontracked English classroom. *Journal of Reading, 38*(6), 424.

Allington, R. (1980). Teacher interruption in behaviors during primary grade oral reading. *Journal of Educational Psychology, 72,* 371–377.

Allington, R. (1983). The reading instruction provided readers of differing reading abilities. *Elementary School Journal, 83,* 548–559.

Allington, R. (1993). Michael doesn't go down the hall anymore. *Reading Teacher, 46,* 602–605.

Allington, R. (1994). The schools we have, the schools we need. *Reading Teacher, 48*(1), 14–27.

Allington, R. (1995). *Inclusion: What we know and don't know.* Paper presented at the International Reading Association annual meeting, Anaheim, CA.

Allington, R., & McGill-Franzen, A. (1989b). School response to reading failure: Instruction for Chapter 1 and special education students in grades two, four, and eight. *Elementary School Journal, 89,* 529–542.

Anderson, J. (1992/1993). Journal writing: The promise and the reality. *Journal of Reading, 36*(4), 304–308.

Anderson, L., Brubaker, N., Alleman-Brooks, J., & Duffy, G. (1984). A qualitative study of seatwork in first grade classrooms. *Elementary School Journal, 86,* 123–140.

Anderson, R. C., Hiebert, E. H., Scott, J. A., & Wilkerson, I. A. G. (1985). *Becoming a nation of readers: The report of the Commission on Reading.* Washington, DC: National Institute of Education.

Anderson, R. C., & Pearson, P. D. (1984). A schema-theoretic view of basis process in reading comprehension. In P. D. Pearson (Ed.), *Handbook of reading research* (Vol. 2, pp. 255–292). New York: Longman.

Anderson, R., Wilson, P., & Fielding, L. (1988). Growth in reading and how children spend their time outside of school. *Reading Research Quarterly, 23*(3), 285–303.

Annual Review of Psychology, 32. (1981). Palo Alto, CA: Annual Reviews, Inc.

Applebee, A. N. (1988). *A study of book-length works taught in high school English courses.* (Report Series 1.2). Albany, NY: Center for the Learning and Teaching of Literature.

Applebee, A. N. (1993). Lower track students spend relatively little time with literature and an inordinate amount of time with skill worksheets. *Literature in the Secondary School.* Urbana, IL: NCTE.

Applebee, A. N., Langer, J. S., Jenkins, L. B., & Mullis, L. (1990). The writing report card, 1984–1988: Findings from the nation's report card. Princeton, NJ: Educational Testing Service.

Ardizzone, P. M. (1992). The journal—a tool in the ESL classroom. *Writing Teacher, 6*(2), 31.

Armbruster, B., Anderson, T., & Meyer, L. (1991). A microanalysis of the small-group, guided reading lesson. *Reading Research Quarterly, 26*(4), 417–442.

Askov, E. N., & Peck, M. (1982). Handwriting. In H. E. Mitzel, B. Hardin, & W. Rabinowitz (Eds.), *Encyclopedia of Educational Research* (5th ed.). New York: Free Press.

"Attention Deficit Disorder—Part 1." (2000, August). *Harvard Mental Health Letter, 17,* p. 24.

Atwell, N. (1984). Writing and reading literature from the inside out. *Language Arts, 61,* 240–252.

Au, K. (1991). Constructing the theme of a story. *Language Arts, 69,* 106–111.

Au, K. (1994). *Literacy instruction in multicultural settings.* San Diego, CA: Harcourt Brace College Publishers.

Avery, C. (1993). *And with a light touch.* Portsmouth, NH: Heinemann.

Baker, A., & Greene, E. (1987). *Storytelling art and technique.* New York: Bowker.

Baker, E. (2001). Technology and values: Connecting with classroom literacy learning. In P. Schmidt & A. Pailliotet (Eds.), *Exploring values through literature, multimedia & literacy events* (pp. 102–112). Newark, DE: International Reading Association.

Baker, J., & Zigmond, N. (1990). Are regular education classes equipped to accommodate students with learning disabilities? *Exceptional Children, 56,* 515–526.

Baker, L., & Brown, A. (1983). Metacognitive skills and reading. In P. D. Pearson (Ed.), *Handbook of reading research* (pp. 491–572). New York: Longman.

Baker, L., & Brown, A. (1984). The role of metacognition in reading and studying. In J. Orasonu (Ed.), *Reading Comprehension.* Hillsdale, NJ: Erlbaum.

Bakhtin, M. M. (1986). *Speech genres and other late essays* (C. Emerson & M. Holquist, Eds.; V. McGee, Trans.). Austin: University of Texas Press.

Bandura, A. (1990, April). *Self-efficacy and motivation.* Paper presented at the annual meeting of the American Educational Research Association, San Francisco, CA.

Bandura, A. (1994). *Discussion of self-efficacy.* Invited presentation at Stanford University, Palo Alto, CA.

Banks, J., & Banks, C. (Eds.). (1993). *Multicultural education: Issues and perspectives.* Boston: Allyn & Bacon.

Banks, J., & Banks, C. (1995). *Handbook of research on multicultural education.* New York: Macmillan.

Banks, J., & McGee, C. (1993). Social studies teacher education, ethnic diversity, and academic achievement. *International Journal of Social Education, 7*(3), 24–38.

Banks, J. A. (1989). *Multiethnic education: Theory and practice* (2nd ed.). Boston: Allyn & Bacon.

Banks, J. A. (1991). *Teaching strategies for ethnic studies* (5th ed.). Boston: Allyn & Bacon.

Barger, R. (1991). *Evaluating multicultural education.* Charleston: Eastern Illinois University.

Barillas, M. (2000). Literacy at home: Honoring parent voices. *The Reading Teacher, 54,* 302–308.

Barr, R., Kamil, M. L., Mosenthal, P., & Pearson, P. D. (Eds.). (1991). *Handbook of reading research.* New York: Longman.

Baumann, J. F., & Bergeron, B. S. (1993). Story map instruction using children's literature: Effects on first graders' comprehension of central narrative elements. *Journal of Reading Behavior, 25*(4), 407–437.

Beach, R., & Hynds, S. (1991). Research on response to literature. In R. Barr, M. Kamil, P. Mosenthal, & P. Pearson (Eds.), *Handbook of reading research* (Vol. 1, pp. 453–489). White Plains, NY: Longman.

Beal, C. R. (1990). Development of knowledge about the roles of inference in text comprehension. *Child Development, 61*(3), 1011.

Bean, R., Cooley, W., Eichelberger, R., Lazar, M., & Zigmond, N. (1991). In class or pullout. *Journal of Reading Behavior, 23*(4), 445–464.

Bean, R. M., & Hamilton, R. (1992). *Collaboration: Key to implementing process teaching in a remedial reading program.* Harrisburg, PA: Pennsylvania Department of Education.

Beck, I. L., & McKeown, M. (1991). Conditions of vocabulary acquisition. In R. Barr, M. Kamil, P. Mosenthal, & P. D. Pearson (Eds.), *Handbook of reading research* (Vol. 2, pp. 789–814). New York: Longman.

Beck, I. L., McKeown, M. G., McCaslin, E. S., & Burkes, A. M. (1979). Instructional dimensions that may affect reading comprehension: Examples from two commercial reading programs. Pittsburgh: Learning Research and Development Center, University of Pittsburgh. (ERIC Document No. Ed. 197322)

Beck, I., & Dole, J. (1992). Reading and thinking with history and science text. In C. Collins & J. Mangieri (Eds.), *Thinking development: An agenda for the twenty-first century.* Hillsdale, NJ: Erlbaum.

Bell, A. (1995). Language and the media. *Annual Review of Applied Linguistics, 15,* 23–41.

Bell, J. (1994). The challenge of multicultural classes. *Mosaic, 2*(1), 1–5.

Bell, N. (1991). Gestalt imagery: A critical factor in language comprehension. *Annuals of Dyslexia, 41,* 246–260.

Bellanca, A., & Fogarty, R. (1990). *Blueprints for thinking in the cooperative classroom.* Palatine, IL: Skylight.

Bereiter, C., & Scardamalia, M. (1987). An attainable version of high literacy: Approaches to teaching higher order skills in reading and writing. *Journal of Curriculum, 17,* 9–30.

Berghoff, B., & Egawa, K. (1991). No more "rocks": Grouping to give students control of their learning. *Reading Teacher, 44*(8), 536–542.

Berliner, D. (1992). International comparisons of student achievement. *Phi Kappa Phi Journal, 73*(4), 25–29.

Berlinger, D. (1994). Increasing thinking abilities. In C. C. Block & J. N. Mangieri (Eds.), *Creating more powerful thinking in teachers and students.* Fort Worth, TX: Harcourt Brace.

Beyersdorfer, J. M., & Shauer, D. K. (1993, September). All work and no play? Add play production to literacy learning. *Journal of Reading, 37*(1), 4–10.

Biemiller, A. (1970). The development of the use of graphic and contextual information as children learn to read. *Reading Research Quarterly, 6,* 75–96.

Biemiller, A. (1993). *Bringing language and basic reading skills together: Some observations on acquiring and using reading skills in elementary schools.* Paper presented at the annual meeting of the National Reading Conference, Charleston, SC.

Blanton, W., & Moorman, G. (1990). The presentation of reading lessons. *Reading Research and Instruction, 29*(3), 35–55.

Block, C. (1992, May). *Increasing students' motivation through strategy instruction.* Paper presented at the International Reading Association annual convention, New Orleans, LA.

Block, C. (1993a). Strategic instruction in a literature-based reading program. *Elementary School Journal, 94,* 139–151.

Block, C. (1993b). *Teaching the language arts: Expanding thinking through student centered instruction.* Boston: Allyn & Bacon.

Block, C. (1994). Developing problem-solving abilities. In J. Mangieri & C. Block (Eds.), *Creating powerful thinking in teachers and students.* Fort Worth, TX: Harcourt Brace.

Block, C. (1996, May). *Resources and teacher actions that increase students' engagement.* Paper presented at the International Reading Association annual meeting, New Orleans, LA.

Block, C. C. (2001). Case for exemplary reading instruction: Effects on students who begin school without the precursors for reading success. *National Reading Conference Yearbook, 50,* 71–89.

Block, C. C., & Dellamura, R. (2000/2001). Better book buddies. *The Reading Teacher, 54*(4), 364–370.

Block, C. C., & Pressley, M. (2002). *Comprehension instruction: Research-based best practices.* New York: Guilford.

Block, C. C. (2002a). The expertise of literacy teachers: A continuum from preschool to grade 5. *Reading Research Quarterly, 37*(2), 178–208.

Block, C. C. (2002b). Teaching nonfiction: What we do well, what we need to do, and what we need to learn in the future. *California Reader, 35*(2), 3–11.

Block, C., & Graham, M. (1994). *Elementary students as co-teachers and co-researchers.* Paper presented at annual meeting of the National Reading Conference, Charleston, SC.

Block, C., & Mangieri, J. N. (1994). *Creating powerful thinking in teachers and students.* Fort Worth, TX: Harcourt Brace.

Block, C., & Mangieri, J. N. (1995). *Reason to read* (Vols. 1 & 2). Menlo Park, CA: Addison-Wesley.

Boggiano, A. K. (1992). Helplessness deficits in students: The role of motivational orientation. *Motivation and Emotion, 16,* 278–280.

Bohline, D. (1985). Intellectual and affective characteristics of attention deficit disordered children. *Journal of Learning Disabilities, 18*(10), 604–608.

Bond, G., Wasson, B., Tinker, M., & Wasson, J. (1994). *Reading Difficulties.* Boston: Allyn & Bacon.

Booth, D. (1989). *Keynote address.* Child-centered experience based on learning conference, Winnipeg, Manitoba.

Borkowski, J. G., Carr, M., & Pressley, M. (1987). Spontaneous strategy use: Perspectives from metacognitive theory. *Intelligence, 11,* 61–75.

Bosch, K., Bon, W., & Schreider, R. (1995). Poor readers' decoding skills. *Reading Research Quarterly, 30*(1), 110–125.

Bradley, J. M., & King, P. (1992). Effects of proofreading on spelling: How reading misspelled and correctly spelled words affects spelling accuracy. *Journal of Reading Behavior, 24*(4), 413–432.

Bransford, J. D. & Stein, B. S. (1993). *The IDEAL problem solver* (2nd ed.). New York: Freeman.

Bratcher, S. (1994). *Evaluating children's writing: A handbook of communication choices for classroom teachers.* New York: St. Martin's Press.

Bridwell, N. (1988). *Clifford's birthday party.* New York: Scholastic.

Brody, G., Stoneman, Z., & McCoy, J. (1995/1996). How caretakers support the literacy development of Head Start graduates in a rural setting. *Reading Teacher, 49*(4), 340–342.

Brookhart, S., & Rusnak, R. (1993). A pedagogy of enrichment, not poverty. *Journal of Teacher Education, 44*(1), 17–26.

Brophy, J. (1986). Classroom management techniques. *Education and Urban Society, 18*(2), 195–210.

Brophy, J. (1994). Trends in research on teaching. *Midwestern Educational Researcher, 7*(1), 29–39.

Brophy, J., & Alleman, J. (1991). A caveat: Curriculum integration isn't always a good idea. *Educational Leadership, 49*(2), 66.

Brophy, J., & Good, T. (1974). *Teacher-student relationships: Causes and consequences.* New York: Holt, Rinehart & Winston.

Broudy, H. S. (1987). *The role of imagery in learning; part 1.* Los Angeles: The Getty Center for Education and the Arts, paper 1.

Brown, A., & Campione, J. (1986). Interactive learning environment and the teaching of science and mathematics. In M. Gardner, J. Greens, F. Reif, A. Schoenfeld, A. diSessa, & E. Stage (Eds.), *Toward a scientific practice of science education.*

Brown, A. L. (1980). Metacognitive development and reading. In R. J. Spiro, B. C. Bruce, & W. F. Brewer (Eds.), *Theoretical issues in reading comprehension* (pp. 453–481). Hillsdale, NJ: Erlbaum.

Brown, A. L., Palinscar, A. S., & Purcell, S. E. (1986). Cognitive-based classroom instruction. In B. Smey-Richman (Ed.), *Involvement in learning for low-achieving students* (pp. 34–66). Philadelphia: Research for Better Schools.

Brown, H., & Cambourne, B. (1989). Evaluation in a whole language classroom. In E. Daly (Ed.), *Monitoring children's language development.* Carlton, South Victoria: Australia Reading Association.

Browning, N., & McClintic, S. (1995). Acting, talking and thinking like writers: Sixth graders become authors. *Language Arts, 72*(2), 105–112.

Bruen, M., & Treiman, R. (1992). Learning to pronounce words. *Reading Research Quarterly, 27*(4), 374–388.

Burke, J. (1991). Teaching clothes and gang violence. *Educational Leadership, 40*(1), 13.

Calkins, L. (1991). *Living between the lines.* Portsmouth, NH: Heinemann.

Canfield, J., & Wells, H. (1994). *100 ways to enhance self-esteem in the classroom.* Boston: Allyn & Bacon.

Carbo, M. (1987). Deprogramming reading failure. *Phi Delta Kappan, 69*(3), 197–202.

Carlson, T. (1993). *Carlson Analytical Originality Scale.* San Antonio, TX: Psychological Corporation.

Carr, E., & Ogle, D. (1987). K-W-L Plus: A strategy for comprehension and summarization. *Journal of Reading, 30,* 626–631.

Carr, K. S., Buchanan, D. L., Wentz, J. B., Weiss, M. L., & Brant, K. J. (2002). Not just for the primary grades: A bibliography of picture books for secondary content teachers. *Journal of Adolescent and Adult Literacy, 42*(2), 145–153.

Carr, W. (1960, January). Action—not talk. *National Education Association Journal, 7.*

Carver, R. (1992). Commentary: Effect of prediction activities, prior knowledge, and text type upon amount comprehended: Using Rauding theory to critique schema theory research. *Reading Research Quarterly, 27,* 164–174.

Carver, R. (1994). Percentage of unknown vocabulary words in text as a function of the relative difficulty of the text. *Journal of Reading Behavior, 26*(4), 413–437.

Carver, R. (1995). The effects of reading library books at different levels of difficulty upon gain in reading ability. *Reading Research Quarterly, 30*(1), 26–48.

Cazden, C. (1986). ESL teachers as language advocates for children. *Dialogue* (Center for Applied Linguistics), *3*(2), 2–3.

Cazden, C. (1992). *Classroom discourse: The language of teaching and learning.* Portsmouth, NH: Heinemann.

Cazden, C. (1993). *Whole language plus.* Portsmouth, NH: Heinemann.

Cazden, C. (1994). *The art of teaching writing* (2nd ed.). Portsmouth, NH: Heinemann.

Cazden, C. (1995, May). *A new look at Reading Recovery.* Paper presented at the annual meeting of the American Educational Research Association, San Francisco, CA.

CDS Report. (1991, October). Washington, DC: Child Development Society.

Chall, J. (1983). *Stages of reading development.* New York: McGraw-Hill.

Chall, J. (1989). Learning to read: The great debate 20 years later—a response to "Debunking the great phonics myth." *Phi Delta Kappan,* 521–538.

Chall, J. (1993). *Stages of reading development* (2nd ed.). New York: McGraw-Hill.

Chance, P. (1986). *Thinking in the classroom.* New York: Teachers College Press.

Children Today. (1988, November). P. 201.

Chipman, S., & Segal, J. (1985). Thinking and learning skills: The contributions of NIE. *Educational Leadership, 42*(1), 85–89.

Chomsky, N. (1975). *Reflections on language.* New York: Random House.

Clark, D. B. (1988). *Dyslexia: Theory and practice of remedial instruction.* Parkton, MD: York Press.

Clark, R. (1985). Evidence for confounding in computer-based instruction studies. *Educational Communications and Technology Journal, 33,* 249–262.

Clay, M. (1975). *What did I write?: Beginning writing behavior.* Aukland, New Zealand: Heinemann.

Clay, M. (1985). *The early detection of reading difficulties.* Portsmouth, NH: Heinemann.

Clay, M. (1990). What is and what might be in evaluation (research currents). *Language Arts, 67*(3), 288–298.

Clay, M. (1991). *Becoming literate: The construction of inner central.* Portsmouth, NH: Heinemann.

Clay, M. (1993). *Reading Recovery. A guidebook for teachers in training.* Portsmouth, NH: Heinemann.

Cleary, B. (1983). *Dear Mr. Henshaw.* New York: Morrow.

Cobb, L. (1840). *The North American reader.* New York: Collins & Brother.

Cody, D. (1985, October). Dealing with dyslexia. *Sky,* p. 24.

Coleman, S. (1992). *Bibliotherapic section in the library.* Unpublished manuscript. Fort Worth: Texas Christian University.

Collins, C. (1987). *Time management for teachers.* Englewood Cliffs, NJ: Prentice-Hall.

Collins, C. (1988). Principals: Taking the lead in thinking skills development. *Reach* (Vol. 3). Austin: Texas Education Agency.

Collins, C. (1989). *Increasing thinking ability through middle school reading instruction.* Paper presented at the annual meeting of the National Reading Conference, New Orleans, LA.

Collins, C. (1990). *Strategies for active engagement in reasoning: Vignettes that build a questioning mind.* Paper presented at the annual meeting of the International Reading Association, Atlanta, GA.

Collins, C. (1991a). Audiotaped transcript of Tracy Boyd's tutoring session. Fort Worth: Texas Christian University.

Collins, C. (1991b). *Diary of daily events in a nonsegregated African-American school.* Unpublished manuscript. Fort Worth: Texas Christian University.

Collins, C. (1992a). Improving reading and thinking: From teaching or not teaching skills to interactive interventions. In M. Pressley, K. Harris, & I. Guthrie (Eds.), *Promoting academic competence and literacy in schools.* San Diego, CA: Academic Press.

Collins, C. (1992b). *126 strategies that build the language arts.* Boston: Allyn & Bacon.

Collins, C. (1992c). Thinking development through intervention: Middle school students come of age. In C. Collins & J. Mangieri (Eds.), *Thinking development: An agenda for the twenty-first century.* Hillsdale, NJ: Erlbaum.

Collins, C., & Mangieri, J. (Eds.). (1992). *Thinking development: An agenda for the twenty-first century.* Hillsdale, NJ: Erlbaum.

Commission on Reading's Report. (1985). Washington, DC: Commission on Reading.

Cooper, P. (1993). *When stories come to school.* New York: Teachers and Writers Collaborative.

Corno, L. (1993). The best-laid plans: Modern conceptions of volition and educational research. *Educational Researcher, 22*(2), 14–22.

Corno, L. (1994, April). *Implicit teaching and self-regulated learning.* Paper presented at the annual meeting of the American Educational Research Association, New Orleans, LA.

Council for Exceptional Children. (1993). *Policy statement concerning optimal educational opportunities for students with special needs.* Washington, DC: CEC.

Cox, C. (1985). Filmmaking as a composing process. *Language Arts, 62,* 60–69.

Craven, R., Marsh, H., & Debus, R. (1991). Effects of internally focused feedback and attributional feedback on enhancement of academic self-concept. *Journal of Educational Psychology, 83,* 17–27.

Crawford, S. D., & Bentley, R. H. (1990). An inner-city IQ test. *Reading Research Quarterly, 26*(4), 390.

Cullinan, B. (Ed.). (1992). *Invitation to read: More children's literature in the reading program.* Newark, NJ: International Reading Association.

Culp, M. (1985). Literature's influence on young adult attitudes, values, and behavior, 1975 and 1984. *English Journal, 74*(8), 31–35.

Cummins, J. (1979). Cognitive–academic language proficiency, linguistic interdependence, optimal age and some other matters. *Working Papers in Bilingualism, 19,* 197–205.

Cummins, J. (1986). Empowering minority students: A framework for intervention. *Harvard Educational Review, 56,* 18–36.

Cunningham, P. (1990). The Name Test: A quick assessment of decoding ability. *Reading Teacher, 44*(2), 124–130.

Cunningham, P. M. (1995). *Phonics they use: Words for reading and writing* (2nd ed.). New York: HarperCollins.

Curry, L. (1990). Learning styles in secondary schools: A review of instruments and implication for their use. Madison: Wisconsin Center for Educational Research.

Dahl, R. (1961). *James and the giant peach.* New York: Puffin.

Dallas Morning News. (1993, November 14). P. 27B.

Daly, C., & Stern, J. (Eds.). (1989). *Rural education: A changing landscape.* Washington, DC: Office of Educational Research and Improvement (ED).

Daly, E. (1989). *Holistic assessment in the classroom.* Portsmouth, NH: Heinemann.

Daly, E. (1991). *Monitoring children's language development: Holistic assessment in the classroom.* Portsmouth, NH: Heinemann.

D'Andrade, R. G. (1984). Cultural meaning systems. In R. W. Schweder & R. A. LeVine (Eds.), *Cultural theory: Essays on mind, self and emotion* (pp. 88–118). New York: Cambridge University Press.

Darling-Hammond, L., & Wise, A. (1985). Beyond standardization: State standards and school improvement. *Elementary School Journal, 85*(3), 315–336.

Deci, E. L., & Ryan, R. M. (1987). *Intrinsic motivation and self-determination in human behavior.* New York: Plenum.

DeFord, D. (1993). *Theory building in Reading Recovery: Teachers in transition.* Paper presented at the annual meeting of the National Reading Conference, Charleston, SC.

DeFord, D. E., Lyons, C. A., & Pinnell, G. S. (1991). *Bridges to literacy: Learning from Reading Recovery.* Portsmouth, NH: Heinemann.

DeFord, D. E., Lyons, C. A., & Pinnell, G. S. (1994). Evaluation of Reading Recovery. *Reading Research Quarterly, 24,* 173–199.

Dewey, J. (1899). *School & society.* Chicago: University of Chicago Press.

Dewey, J. (1963). *Experience and education.* New York: Collier. (Original work published in 1938.)

Dewitz, P., & Palm, K. (1993). *The benefits of portfolio assessment to remedial readers.* Paper presented at the American Educational Research Association annual meeting, Atlanta, GA.

De Young, A. J., & Lawrence, B. K. (1995). On Hoosiers, Yankees and mountaineers. *Phi Delta Kappan, 27*(2), 104–109.

Diederich, P. (1991). *Writing inservice guide for English language arts and TAAS.* Austin: Texas Education Agency.

Dole, J. A., Buffy G. G., Roehler, L. R., & Pearson, P. D. (1991). Moving from the old to the new: Research on reading comprehension instruction. *Review of Educational Research, 61,* 239–264.

Dowhower, S. L. (1987). Effects of repeated reading on second-grade transitional readers' fluency and comprehension. *Reading Research Quarterly, 22,* 389–406.

Downing, S. (1995). Teaching writing for today's demands. *Language Arts, 72,* 200–205.

Duin, J. A., & Graves, M. F. (1987). Teaching vocabulary as a writing prompt. *Journal of Reading, 22,* 204–212.

Dunn, R. (1976). *Learning style inventory.* Reston, VA: Reston.

Dunn, R. (1993). *Learning styles.* Paper presented at seminar for the staff of ASCD, Reston, VA.

Dunn, R., & Dunn, K. (1991). Footloose and free to learn. *Principal, 70*(3), 34–37.

Durkin, D. (1978/1979). What classroom observations reveal about reading comprehension. *Reading Research Quarterly, 14,* 481–533.

Durkin, D. (1984). Is there a match between what elementary teachers do and what basal reader manuals recommend? *Reading Teacher, 37,* 734–744.

Durkin, D. (1987). Influences on basal reader programs. *Elementary School Journal, 87*(3), 331–341.

Durkin, D. (1988). *Teaching them to read* (5th ed.). Boston: Allyn & Bacon.

Durrell, D. (1937). *Improvement of basic reading abilities.* Yonkers, NY: World Book Company.

Duvall, B. (1986). Kindergarten performance for reading and matching four styles of handwriting. [1984] Government document No. CS 209 466. RIEJun86.

Duvall, J. (1983). Writing for reading: Will resistant readers teach each other? Classroom research study No. 7. California University–Berkeley, School of Education, RIEMay85.

Dymock, S. (1993, October). Reading but not understanding. *Journal of Reading, 37*(2), 86–91.

Edelman, M. (1991). Kids first! *Mother Jones, 16*(3), 31–32.

Eeds, M., & Wells, D. (1989). Grand conversations: An exploration of meaning construction in literature study groups. *Research in the Teaching of English, 23,* 4–29.

Ehri, L. (1980). The development of orthographic images. In U. Frith (Ed.), *Cognitive processes in spelling* (pp. 311–338). London: Academic.

Ehri, L. (1993). *Effects of phonological awareness on young children's pre-spelling knowledge.* Paper presented at the annual meeting of the National Reading Conference, San Diego, CA.

Ehri, L., & Robbins, C. (1994). Reading storybooks to kindergartners helps them learn new vocabulary words. *Journal of Educational Psychology, 86*(1), 54–64.

Ehri, L. C., & Wilce, L. S. (1987). Does learning to spell help beginners learn to read words? *Reading Research Quarterly, 22*(1), 47–65.

Ehri, L., & Sweet, J. (1991). Finger-point reading of memorized text: What enables beginners to process the print? *Reading Research Quarterly, 26,* 442–462.

Ekwall, E. E. (1983). *Locating and correcting reading difficulties* (3rd ed.). New York: Merrill.

Ekwall, E. E., & Shanker, J. L. (1993). *Locating and correcting reading difficulties* (6th ed.). New York: Merrill.

Elementary and Secondary Education Act (ESEA). (1965).

Elias, M. J., & Tobias, S. E. (1990). *Problem solving/decision making for social and academic success.* Washington, DC: NEA.

Elster, C. (1994). Patterns within preschoolers' emergent reading. *Reading Research Quarterly, 29*(4), 403–418.

Englert, C., & Raphael, T. (1988). Constructing well-formed prose: Process structure and metacognitive knowledge. *Exceptional Children, 54*(6), 513–520.

Fader, D., Duggins, J., Finn, T., & McNeil, E. (1976). *The new hooked on books.* New York: Berkley.

Farnham-Diggory, S. (1992). *The learning-disabled child.* Cambridge, MA: Harvard University Press.

Farr, M. (1993). Essayist literacy and other verbal performances. *Written Communication, 10*(1), 4–38.

Federal Register. (1993). Washington, DC: U.S. Government Printing Office.

Fernald, G. M. (1943). *Remedial techniques in basic school subjects.* New York: World Book.

Feitler, F., & Hellekson, L. (1993). Active verbalization plus metacognitive awareness yields positive achievement gains in at-risk first graders. *Reading Research and Instruction, 33*(1), 7.

Field, M., & Aebersold, J. (1990). Cultural attitudes toward reading. *Journal of Reading, 33*(6), 406–410.

Fielding, L., & Roller, C. (1992). Making difficult books accessible and easy books acceptable. *Reading Teacher, 45,* 678–685.

Fillmore, C., & Kay, P. (1981). *Text semantic analysis of reading comprehension tests* (Progress Report No. 79-0511). Washington, DC: National Institute of Education.

Fine, M. (1995). *Habits of mind.* San Francisco, CA: Jossey-Bass Education Series.

Fitzgerald, J. (1993). Literacy and students who are learning English as a second language. *Reading Teacher, 46*(8), 638–647.

Fitzgerald, J. (1995). How literacy emerges. *Language Learning Journal, 9,* 32–35.

Fitzgerald, J., & Markham, L. (1987). Teaching children about revision in writing. *Cognition and Instruction, 4,* 3–24.

Flavell, J. H. (1976). Metacognitive aspects of problem solving. In L. B. Resnick (Ed.), *The nature of intelligence* (pp. 231–235). Hillsdale, NJ: Erlbaum.

Fleckenstein, K. S. (1991, October). *Inner sight: Imagery and emotion in writing engagement.* Washington, DC: TETYC.

Flickinger, G., & Long, E. (1990). Beyond the basal. *Reading Improvement, 27*(2), 149–154.

Ford, P. (1897). *The New England primer.* New York: Dodd, Mead.

Fournier, J. M. (1993, March). Seeing with new eyes: Becoming a better teacher of bilingual children. *Language Arts, 70,* 178.

Freppon, P. S., & Dahl, K. L. (1991). Learning about phonics in a whole language classroom. *Language Arts, 68*(3), 190–198.

Fresch, M. (1995). Self-selection of early literacy learners. *Reading Teacher, 49*(3), 220–227.

Fry, E. B., Fountoukidis, D. L., & Polk, J. (1985). *The new reading teacher's book of lists.* Englewood Cliffs, NJ: Prentice-Hall.

Frymier, J. (1992). Children who hurt, children who fail. *Phi Delta Kappan, 74*(3), 257–259.

Fu, D. (1995). *My trouble is my English.* Portsmouth, NH: Heinemann.

Gambrell, L. B., & Bales, R. J. (1986). Mental imagery and the comprehension monitoring performance of fourth and fifth grade poor readers. *Reading Research Quarterly, 21*(1), 460–462.

Gambrell, L. B., & Jawitz, P. B. (1993). Mental imagery, text illustrations, and children's story comprehension and recall. *Reading Research Quarterly, 28,* 3.

Gambrell, L. B., & Koskinen, P. (1982). *Mental imagery and the reading comprehension of below average.* Paper presented March 19–23 at the annual meeting of the American Educational Research Association, New York.

Garcia, E. (1991). *Factors influencing the English reading test performances of Spanish-speaking Hispanic children.* (Technical Report 539). Washington, DC: National Clearinghouse for Bilingual Education.

Garcia, G., & Pearson, P. (1993). The role of assessment in a diverse society. In E. H. Hiebert (Ed.), *Literacy for a diverse society* (pp. 253–278). New York: Teachers College Press.

Garcia, V., & Pearson, P. D. (1994). *Present cultural and social influences on literacy achievement.* Paper presented at the annual meeting of the National Reading Conference, Austin, TX.

Gardner, H. (1983). *Frames of mind: The theory of multiple intelligences.* New York: Basic Books.

Gardner, H. (1993). *Multiple intelligences: The theory in practice.* New York: Basic Books.

Gardner, R., Alexander, P., Gillingham, M., Kulikowich, J., & Brown, R. (1991). Interest and learning from text. *American Educational Research Journal, 28*(3), 643–659.

Garmston, R., & Wellman, B. (1994). Insights from constructivist learning theory. *Educational Leadership, 51*(7), 84–85.

Garner, R. (1987). *Metacognition and reading comprehension.* Norwood, NJ: Ablex.

Gaskins, R. W., Gaskins, J. C., & Gaskins, I. W. (1991). A decoding program for poor readers—and the rest of the class too! *Language Arts, 68*(3) 213–225.

Gay, G. (1995). At the essence of learning: Multicultural education. *Kappa Delta Pi, 36*(2), 51–59.

Gee, J. (1992). What is literacy? In P. Shannon (Ed.), *Becoming political: Readings and writings in the politics of literacy education.* Portsmouth, NH: Heinemann.

Genishi, C. (1992). Developing the foundation. In C. Seefeldt (Ed.), *The early childhood curriculum: Review research* (pp. 85–117). New York: Teachers College Press.

Gentry, J. (2000). A retrospective on invented spelling and a look forward. *The Reading Teacher 54*(6) 318–332.

Gergen, K. (1985). *The saturated self: Dilemmas of identity in contemporary life.* New York: Basic Books.

Getsie, R., Langer, J., & Glass, G. (1985). Meta-analysis of the effects of type and combination of feedback on children's discrimination learning. *Review of Education Research, 55,* 9–22.

Giorgis, C., & Johnson, N. (2001). Creativity. *The Reading Teacher, 54,* 632–640.

Glazer, S. M. (1989). Oral language and literacy development. In D. S. Strickland & L. M. Morrow (Eds.), *Emerging literacy: Young children learn to read and write* (pp. 16–26). Newark, DE: International Reading Association.

Glenn, H. S., & Nelson, J. (1994). *Raising self-reliant children in a self-indulgent world.* New York: Simon & Schuster.

Glover, M., & Pfeiffer, J. (1993). Living the legend of the Indian paintbrush. *Reading Teacher, 46*(8), 718–720.

Golden, J. M. (1986). Children's concept of story in reading and writing. *Reading Teacher, 37,* 578–584.

Gonzales, N., Moll, L. C., Floyd-Tenery, M., Rivera, A., Rendon, P., Gonzales, R., & Amanti, C. (1993). *Teaching research on funds of knowledge: Learning from households.* San

Diego, CA: National Center for Research on Cultural Diversity and Second Language Learning.

Goodlad, J. I. (1984). *A place called school: Prospects for the future.* New York: McGraw-Hill.

Goodman, K. (1967). Reading: A psycholinguistic guessing game. *Journal of the Reading Specialist, 126*–135.

Goodman, K. (1973). *Miscue analysis: Application of reading instruction.* Urbana, IL: National Council of Teachers of English.

Goodman, K. (1986). *What's whole in whole language?* Portsmouth, NH: Heinemann.

Goodman, Y., Watson, A., & Burke, C. (1987). *Reading miscue inventories* (revised). Portsmouth, NH: Heinemann.

Goodman, Y. M. (1989). Roots of the whole-language movement. *Elementary School Journal, 90*(2), 113–127.

Gordon, C., & Mac Ginnis, D. (1993). Using journals as a window on students' thinking in mathematics. *Language Arts, 70,* 37–43.

Gough, P. B., Alford, J. A., & Holly-Wilcox, P. (1981). Words and contexts. In O. L. Tzeng & H. Singer (Eds.), *Perception of print: Reading research in experimental psychology.* Hillsdale, NJ: Erlbaum.

Grace, L., & Buser, R. (1987). Motivation. *The Practitioner: Newsletter of the National Association of Secondary School Principals, 14*(1), 1–12.

Graesser, A. C., & Person, N. K. (1994). Question asking during tutoring. *American Educational Research Journal, 31*(1), 104–137.

Graham, S., & Barker, G. (1990). The downside of help. *Journal of Educational Psychology, 82,* 7–14.

Graves, B. (1995). Desktop presentation software. In N. Groneman & K. Kaser (Eds.), *Technology in the classroom.* Reston, VA: National Business Education Yearbook, No. 33.

Graves, D. (1994). *A fresh look at writing.* Portsmouth, NH: Heinemann.

Graves, D. H. (1991). *Build a literate classroom.* Portsmouth, NH: Heinemann.

Graves, M., Cooke, C., & Laberge, M. (1983). Effects of previewing difficult short stories on low-ability junior high school students' comprehension, recall and attitudes. *Reading Research Quarterly, 18,* 262–275.

Green, J., & Weade, R. (1987). In search of meaning: A sociolinguistic perspective on lesson construction and reading. In D. Bloome (Ed.), *Literacy and schooling* (pp. 3–34). Norwood, NJ: Ablex.

Griffith, P. L., & Olson, M. W. (1992, March). Phonemic awareness helps beginning readers break the code. *Reading Teacher, 45*(7).

Guthrie, J., Martuza, V., & Seifert, M. (1979). Impacts of instructional time in reading. In L. Resnick & P. Weaver (Eds.), *Theory and practice of early reading* (pp. 153–178). Hillsdale, NJ: Erlbaum.

Guthrie, J., Schafer, W., Wang, Y., & Afflerbach, P. (1995). Relationships of instruction to amount of reading: An exploration of social, cognitive, and instructional connections. *Reading Research Quarterly, 30*(1), 8–25.

Haas, T., & Lambert, R. (1995). To establish the bonds of common purpose and mutual enjoyment. *Phi Delta Kappan, 77*(2), 136–140.

Haberman, M. (1991). *The Haberman urban teacher selection interview.* Milwaukee: University of Wisconsin–Milwaukee.

Haladyna, T., Nolen, S., & Hass, N. (1991). Raising standardized achievement test scores and the origins of test score pollution. *Educational Researcher, 20*(5), 2–7.

Halliday, M. A. K. (1973). *Exploration in the functions of language.* London: Edward Arnold.

Halliday, M. A. K. (1975). *Learning how to mean: Explorations in development of language.* London: Edward Arnold.

Hanna, J. L. (1992). Connections: Arts, academics, and productive citizens. *Phi Delta Kappan, 73*(8), 601–607.

Harp, B. (1993). *Bringing children to literacy: Classrooms at work.* Norwood, MA: Christopher-Gordon.

Harris, J. (1994). Impersonations. *Journal of computing in childhood education, 5*(3–4), 241–255.

Harris, K., & Graham, S. (1992). Fifth invited response. *Remedial and Special Education (RASE), 14*(4), 30–34.

Harris, L. A., Pearson, P. D., & Garcia, G. (1995). *Reading difficulties: Instruction and assessment.* (2nd ed.). New York: McGraw Hill.

Harris, V. (1993). *Multiculturalism and children's literature.* Paper presented at the NRC annual meeting, Charleston, SC.

Harste, J. (1986). *Composition and composition instruction as projected code: Understanding semistic universals and practical theory.* Paper presented at New Directions in Composition Scholarship conference, University of New Hampshire, Durham.

Hartle-Schutte, D. (1993). Literacy development in Navajo homes. *Language Arts, 70*(8), 642–654.

Hayden, R. (1995/1996). Training parents as reading facilitators. *Reading Teacher, 44*(4), 334–336.

Hayes, C. W. (1991). *Peeking out from under the blinders: Some factors we shouldn't forget in studying writing.* Washington, DC: Office of Educational Research and Improvements.

Heath, S. B. (1983). Questioning at home and at school. In G. Spindler (Ed.), *Doing the ethnography of schooling: Educational anthropology in action* (pp. 102–131). New York: Holt, Rinehart & Winston.

Heath, S. B. (1983). *Ways with words.* London: Cambridge University Press.

Heath, S. B. (1988, November 19). *Will the schools survive?* Speech at the National Council of Teachers of English convention, St. Louis, MO.

Hedrick, W. B., & Cunningham, P. (1995). The relationship between wide reading and listening comprehension of written language. *Journal of Reading Behavior, 27*(3), 425–438.

Helgers, T. L. (1984, February). Toward a taxonomy of beginning writer's evaluative statements on written composition. *Research in the teaching of English, 20*(1), 35–55.

Henderson, E. H. (1990). *Teaching spelling.* (2nd ed.). Boston: Houghton Mifflin.

Hennings, D. (2000). Contextually relevant word study: Adolescent vocabulary development across the curriculum. *Journal of Adolescent & Adult Literacy, 44*(3), 268–279.

Henning-Stout, M. (1994). *A framework for responsive assessment.* San Francisco: Jossey-Bass.

Herman, P. A. (1985). The effects of repeated readings on reading rate, speech, pauses, and word recognition accuracy. *Reading Research Quarterly, 29,* 553–564.

Hicks, D. (1995). Discourse, learning, and teaching. *Review of Research in Education, 21,* 48–95.

Hicks, P. (1991). Cooperative learning motivates reluctant readers. *Journal of Reading, 35*(2), 148.

Hiebert, E. H. (Ed.). (1991). *Literacy for a diverse society.* New York: Teachers College Press.

Hiebert, E. H., Colt, J. M., Catts, S. L., & Gury, E. C. (1992). Reading and writing of first-grade students in a restructured Chapter 1 program. *American Educational Research Journal, 29*(3), 545–572.

Hiebert, J., Hutchison, B., & Raines, S. (1991). Fourth graders' gradual construction of decimal fractions during instruction using different physical representations. *Elementary School Journal, 91*(4), 321–341.

Hill, B. C., & Ruptic, C. A. (1994). *Practical aspects of authentic assessment: Putting the pieces together.* Norwood, MA: Christopher-Gordon.

Hillard, A. G. (1989). Teaching and cultural styles in a pluralistic society. *National Education Association, 7*(6), 65–69.

Hillerich, R. L. (1985). *Teaching children to write, K–8: A complete guide to developing writing skills.* Englewood Cliffs, NJ: Prentice-Hall.

Hilliard, A. (1992). Behavior style, culture and teaching and learning. *The journal of Negro Education, 61,* 370–377.

Hilliard, A. (1993). Thinking skills and students placed at greatest risk in the educational system. Washington, DC: Restructuring Learning.

Hilliker, J. (1986). Labelling to beginning narrative. In N. Thomas & N. Atwell (Eds.), *Understanding writing.* Portsmouth, NH: Heinemann.

Holdaway, D. (1979). *The foundations of literacy.* Portsmouth, NH: Heinemann.

Holmes, B. C. (1987). Children's inferences with print and pictures. *Journal of Educational Psychology, 79*(5), 14.

Howard, M. (1986). *Effects of pre-reading training in auditory conceptualization on subsequent reading achievement.* Doctoral dissertation, Brigham Young University, Provo, UT.

Huck, C. (1990). *Children's literature in the elementary school.* (10th ed.). New York: Macmillan.

Huck, C. (1994). Literacy and literature. *Language Arts, 69,* 520–526.

Hunt, C., & Vipond, L. (1985). Crash-testing a transactional model of literacy learning. *Reader, 14,* 23–39.

Hyde, D. (1992). *Evaluating student learning in language arts in the primary grades through whole language assessment techniques.* Dissertation from Nova University.

Hynds, S. (1994). *Making connections: Language and learning in the classroom.* Norwood: MA: Christopher-Gordon.

Ingersol, B., & Goldstein, S. (1993). *Attention deficit disorder and learning disabilities.* New York: Doubleday.

Irwin, R., & Mitchell, J. (1983). A procedure for assessing the richness of retelling. *Journal of Reading, 26,* 391–396.

Jackson, F. (1993–1994). Seven strategies to support a culturally responsive pedagogy. *Journal of Reading, 37*(4), 298.

Jacobs, J., & Paris, S. (1987). Children's metacognition about reading. *Educational Psychologist, 22,* 255–278.

Jensema, C. (1983). *Captioning improves comprehension.* Baltimore: Maryland School for the Deaf.

Jensen, E. (1992). *101 at-risk student strategies and solutions.* Delmay, CA: Turning Point for Teachers.

Jensen, E. (2000). Moving with the brain in mind. *Educational Leadership, 58,* 34–37.

Johns, K. (1993). *Learning differences into learning strengths.* Dallas, TX: Center for Success in Learning.

Johnson, D., & Johnson, R. (1982). *A meta-analysis of cooperative, competitive, and individualistic goal structure.* Hillsdale, NJ: Erlbaum.

Johnson, D., & Johnson, R. (1995). *Learning together and alone.* Englewood Cliffs, NJ: Prentice-Hall.

Johnson, L. (1965, January 11). The president's message to congress. *New York Times,* pp. 1, 20.

Johnston, P. (1985). Understanding reading disability: A case study approach. *Harvard Educational Review, 55,* 153–177.

Johnston, P. (1992). *Constructive evaluation of literate activity.* New York: Longman.

Johnston, P., Allington, R., & Afferbach, P. (1985). The congruence of classroom and remedial instruction. *Elementary School Journal, 85,* 465–477.

Johnston, P., & Winograd, P. (1985). Passive failure in reading. *Journal of Reading Behavior, 17,* 279–301.

Jongsma, K. (2000). Developing the magic and wonder of words. *The Reading Teacher, 54,* 80–82.

Jordan, G., Snow, C., & Porche, M. (2000). Project ease: The effect of a family literacy project on kindergarten students' early literacy skills. *Reading Research Quarterly, 35,* 524–546.

Joshi, R. M., & Aaron, P. G. (2000). The component model of reading: Simple view of reading made a little more complex. *Reading Psychology, 21,* 81–97.

Juel, C. (1988). Learning to read and write. *Journal of Educational Psychology, 80,* 437–447.

Juel, C., Griffith, P., & Gough, P. (1986). Acquisition of literacy: A longitudinal study of children in first and second grade. *Journal of Educational Psychology, 78,* 243–255.

Kang, Y. (1993). *Teachers' strategy use and its effect on self-efficacy beliefs of elementary and middle school children.* Presented at the AERA (American Educational Research Association) annual meeting, Atlanta, GA.

Kimmel, S., & MacGinitie, W. (1985). Helping students revise hypotheses while reading. *Reading Teacher, 38*(8), 768–771.

King, A. (1994). Guiding knowledge construction in the classroom: Effects of teaching children how to question and how to explain. *American Educational Research Journal, 51*(2), 338–368.

King, D. (1985). Writing skills for the adolescent. Writing program based on Orton-Gillingham. Dallas, TX: Scottish Rite Hospital.

Kintgen, E., Kroll, B., & Rose, M. (Eds.). (1988). *Perspectives on literacy.* Carbondale: Southern Illinois University Press.

KIRIS Descriptors. (1994). (Kentucky Department of Education). Lexington: Kentucky University.

Klenk, L., & Palinscar, A. (1994). Dynamic classroom observations: An alternative assessment in the referral and evaluation of young children referred to special education. Dynamic Observation: Paper presented at the annual meeting of the National Reading Conference. San Diego, CA.

Kletzien, L. (1991). Strategy use by good and poor comprehenders. *Reading Research Quarterly, 26*(1), 70–94.

Kobrin, D., et al. (1993). Learning history by doing history. *Educational Leadership, 50*(7), 39–41.

Kos, R. (1991). Persistence of reading disabilities: The voices of four middle school students. *American Educational Research Journal, 28*, 875–895.

Krampen, G. (1987). Differential effects of teacher comments. *Journal of Educational Psychology, 79*, 137–146.

Krashen, S. (1985). *The input hypothesis: Issues and implications.* New York: Longman.

Krashen, S. (1989). We acquire vocabulary and spelling by reading: Additional evidence for the input hypothesis. *The Modern Language Journal, 73*, 440–464.

Kucera, C. (1995). Detours and destinations: One teacher's journey into an environmental writing workshop. *Language Arts, 72*(3), 179–187.

Labbo, L., & Teale, W. (1990). Cross-age reading: A strategy for helping poor readers. *Reading Teacher, 43*, 362–369.

Labur, M. (1994). *Columbus.* New York: Macmillan.

Ladson-Billings, G. (1995). Toward a theory of culturally relevant pedagogy. *American Educational Research Journal, 32*(3), 465–491.

Lazear, D. (1991). *Seven ways of knowing. Teaching for multiple intelligence* (2nd ed.). Palatine, IL: Skyline.

Lazear, D. (1994). *Seven pathways of learning.* Tucson, AZ: Zephyr Press.

Lee, C., & Jackson, R. (1992). *Faking it: A look into the mind of a creative learner.* Portsmouth, NH: Heinemann.

Lee, C. D. (1995). A culturally based cognitive apprenticeship: Teaching African American high school students skills in literary interpretation. *Reading Research Quarterly, 30*(4), 608–631.

Lee, N., & Neal, J. (1993). Reading Rescue: Intervention for a student. *Journal of Reading, 36*(4), 276–282.

Lehr, J. (1988). *The child's developing sense of theme: Responses to literature.* New York: Teacher's College Press.

Lehr, J., & Harris, H. (1988). *At-risk, low-achieving students in the classroom.* Washington, DC: NEA Professional Library.

Leibert, R. (1991). *The child at-risk: Strategies of intervention.* Englewood Cliffs, NJ: Prentice-Hall.

Leinhardt, G., & Bickel, W. (1989). Instruction's the thing wherein to catch the mind that falls behind. In R. Slavin (Ed.), *School and classroom organization.* Hillsdale, NJ: Erlbaum.

Lesgold, A., & Resnick, L. (1982). How reading difficulties develop: Perspectives from a longitudinal study. In J. Das, R. Mukahey, & A. Wall (Eds.), *Theory and research in learning disabilities* (pp. 155–187). New York: Plenum.

Leu, D. (2001). Exploring literacy on the internet: Internet project: Preparing students for new literacies in a global village. *The Reading Teacher, 54*, 568–572.

Levin, A. (1985). 'Look—Jane!' Perception skills in the English classroom. *English Journal, 74*(7), 46–48.

Levinson, R. (1985). *Watch the stars come out.* N.Y.E.P. New York: Dutton.

Lindamood Auditory Conceptualization Test (LAC). San Antonio, TX: The Psychological Corporation.

Lindamood, P., Bell, N., & Lindamood, P. (1992). Issues in phonological awareness assessment. *Annals of Dyslexia, 42,* 177–200.

Linden, M. J., & Whimbey, A. (1990). *Why Johnny can't write.* Hillsdale, NJ: Erlbaum.

Lindsey, K. (1999). Decoding and sight-word naming: Are they independent components of word recognition skill? *Reading and Writing: An Interdisciplinary Journal, 11,* 89–127.

Lipson, M. (1986). *Making sense of prior knowledge research.* Remarks presented at the meeting of the National Reading Conference, San Antonio, TX.

Literacy Assessment Corporation. (1992). *Hunter/Grundin literacy profiles: Reading for meaning: Level three.* Clearwater, FL: Literacy Assessment Corporation.

Loxterman, J. A., Beck, I. L., & McKeoon, M. G. (1994). The effects of thinking aloud during reading on students' comprehension of more or less coherent text. *Reading Research Quarterly, 29*(4), 353–366.

Luke, A. (1995). Critical discourse analysis. *Review of Research in Education, 21,* 3–48.

Lundberg, I. (1987). Phonological awareness facilitates reading and spelling acquisition. In W. Ellis (Ed.), *Intimacy with language* (pp. 56–63). Baltimore: Orton Dyslexia Society.

Lundbert, I., & Tonnessen, T. (Eds.). (1999). *Dyslexia: Advances in theory and practice: A diagnostic procedure based on reading component model.* New York: McGraw-Hill.

Lyman, F. (1990). *Think–pair–share: A cooperative learning strategy.* Southern Teacher Education Center in Howard County.

Lyons, C., Place, W., & Rinehart, J. (1990). *Factors related to teaching success in the literacy education of young at-risk children* (Tech. Rep. No. 10). Columbus: Ohio State University.

Mac Iver, D. (1992). *The Incentives for Improvement Program teacher's manual.* Baltimore: Johns Hopkins University, Center for Research on Effective Schooling for Disadvantaged Students.

Madden, N., Slavin, R., Karweit, N., Livermon, B., & Dolan, L. (1989). *Success for all.* Baltimore: Johns Hopkins University, Center for Research on Elementary and Middle Schools.

Mandler, J. (1978). Representation. In P. H. Mussen (Ed.), *Handbook of child psychology.* New York: Wiley.

Manzo, A., & Manzo, C. (1990). *Content area reading: A heuristic approach.* Columbus, OH: Merrill.

Manzo, A., & Manzo, C. (1993). *Literacy disorders: Holistic diagnosis and remediation.* Fort Worth, TX: Harcourt Brace College Publishers.

Manzo, A., & Manzo, C. (1995). *Teaching children to be literate.* Orlando, FL: Harcourt Brace.

Marrou, H. (1982/1948). *A history of education in antiquity.* Madison: University of Wisconsin Press.

Marshall, N. (1985). The effects of prior knowledge and instruction on memory for expository text. In H. Niles & R. Lalik (Eds.), *Issues in literacy: A research perspective* (pp. 89–96). Rochester, NY: National Reading Association.

Marzano, R. (1992). *A different kind of classroom: Teaching with dimensions of learning.* Alexandria, VA: ASCD.

Maslow, A. (1956). Self-actualizing people: A study of psychological health. In C. E. Moristakas (Ed.), *The self: Explorations in personal growth* (pp. 190–191). New York: Harper & Row.

Mason, J. (1984). An examination of reading instruction in third and fourth grades. *Reading Teacher, 36,* 906–913.

Matthews, M. (1992). Gifted students talk about cooperative learning. *Educational Leadership, 50*(2), 48–50.

Matute-Bianchi, M. (1986). Ethnic identities and pattern of school success and failure among Mexican descent and Japanese American students in California high schools. *American Journal of Education, 95*(1), 233–255.

Maynard, J., Tyler, L., & Arnold, M. (2000). Co-occurrence of attention deficit disorder and learning disability: An overview of research. *Journal of Instructional Psychology 26, 3,* 5.

McCarthey, S. (1992). The teacher, the author, and the text: Variations in form and content of writing conferences. *Journal of Reading Behavior, 24*(1), 51–82.

McCarty, T. (1993). Language, literacy and the image of the child in American Indian classrooms. *Language Arts, 70*(3), 183–192.

McCombs, B. (1991). Unraveling motivation. *Journal of Experimental Education, 60*(l), 3–38.

McCombs, B. (1995, May). *Exploring components of motivation.* Paper presented at the annual meeting of the American Educational Research Association, San Francisco, CA.

McConnell, S. (1989). From who's who to how-to. In D. Norton (Ed.), *The effective teaching of language arts* (4th ed., pp. 645–692). New York: Merrill.

McGee, L., & Reigns, D. (1990). *Literacy's beginnings: Supporting young readers and writers.* Boston: Allyn & Bacon.

McGinn, M., Winne, P., & Butler, D. (1993, May). *Interactions of feedback and motivation in classroom learning.* Presented at the annual meeting of the American Educational Research Association, New Orleans, LA.

McKenna, M. (1983). Informal reading inventories: A review of the issues. *The Reading Teacher, 36,* 674.

McKenna, M., Robinson, R., & Miller, J. (1993). Whole language and research. In D. Lew & C. Kinder (Eds.), *Examining central issues in literacy research, theory & practice. Forty-third yearbook of the National Reading Conference.* (pp. 141–152). Chicago: NRC.

McKeown, M. (1993). Creating effective definitions for young word learners. *Reading Research Quarterly, 28*(1), 17.

McLaughlin, M., & Aubrey, S. (1995). A new look at the benefits of community agencies for today's youth. *Phi Delta Kappan, 76*(8), 535–547.

McNeil, L. (1986). *Contradictions of control: School structure and school knowledge.* New York: Routledge & Kegan Paul.

Means, B., & Knapp, M. (1991). Introduction: Rethinking teaching for disadvantage students. In B. Mean, C. Chaiemer, & M. Knapp (Eds.), *Teaching advance skills to at-risk students.* San Francisco: Jossey-Bass.

Meek, M. (1982). What counts as evidence in theories of children's literature? *Theory in Practice, 21*(4), 284–292.

Meichenbaum, D. (1985). *Cognitive behavior modifications: An integrative approach.* New York: Plenum.

Meier, T., & Caskey, C. (1982). Research update. *Language Arts, 49*(5), 504–512.

Meltzer, L., & Solomon, B. (1988). *Educational prescriptions for the classroom for students with learning problems.* Cambridge, MA: Educators Publishing Service.

Menke, D. J., & Pressley, M. (1994). Elaborative interrogation: Using 'why' questions to enhance the learning from text. *Journal of Reading, 37*(8), 642.

Mezynski, K. (1983). Issues concerning the acquisition of knowledge: Effects of vocabulary training on reading comprehension. *Review of Educational Research, 53*(2), 253–274.

Michel, P. A. (1994). *The child's view of reading.* Boston: Allyn & Bacon.

Miller, W. H. (1993). *Reading teacher's complete diagnosis: Correction manual.* Englewood Cliffs, NJ: Center for Applied Research in Education.

Mills, R. (1965). *The Mills test: Learning methods test.* San Antonio, TX: Psychological Corporation.

Morocco, C., & Neuman, S. (1986). Word processors and the acquisition of writing strategies. *Journal of Learning Disabilities, 19*(4), 243–247.

Morphett, M., & Washburne, C. (1931). When should children begin to read? *Elementary School Journal, 31,* 496–503.

Morris, R. (1981). Concept or word: A development phenomenon in the beginning reading and writing processes. *Language Arts, 58,* 659–668.

Morrow, L. (1987). Promoting inner city children's recreational reading. *Reading Teacher, 24,* 266–276.

Morrow, L. (1993). The impact of independent reading and writing periods on literacy achievement, use of literature and attitude. *Reading Teacher, 47*(3), 160–167.

Nagy, W., & Herman, P. (1987). Depth and breadth of vocabulary knowledge: Implications for acquisition and instruction. In M. G. McKeown & M. E. Curtis (Eds.), *The nature of vocabulary acquisition* (pp. 19–35). Hillsdale, NJ: Erlbaum.

Nagy, W. E., Herman, P., & Anderson, R. C. (1985). Learning words from context. *Reading Research Quarterly, 20,* 233–253.

Nakamura, J. (Ed.). (1989). *Something about the author.* Detroit: Gayle Research.

National Captioning Institute. (1990). Information regarding TV captioning (pamphlet). Falls Church, VA: The Institute.

National Clearinghouse for Bilingual Education. (1991). *School based management* (Program Info Guide #5). Washington, DC: NCBE.

National Society for the Study of Education. (1948). *The forty-seventh yearbook: Part II.* Chicago: National Society for the Study of Education.

Neilsen, D. (1993). The effects of four models of group interaction with storybooks on the literacy growth of low-achieving kindergarten children. *Examining Central Issues in Literacy Research, Theory & Practice 33*(4), 209–219.

Nell, V. (1988). *Lost in a book.* New Haven, CT: Yale University Press.

Neuman, S. (1990). *Captions improve language and literacy skills in students learning English as a second language.* Lowell, MA: NCI.

Neuman, S., & Gallagher, P. (1994). *Joining together in literacy learning: Teenage mothers and children.* Newark, DE: International Reading Association.

Neuman, S., & Roskos, K. (1993). *Language and literacy learning in the early years.* Fort Worth, TX: Harcourt Brace College Publishers.

Newmann, F. M. (1991, February). Linking restructuring to authentic student achievement. *Phi Delta Kappan, 72*(6), 458–464.

Norris, J. A. (1991). From frog to prince: Using written language as a context for language. *Topics in Language Disorders, 12,* 66–81.

Norton, D. (1993). *The effective teaching of language arts* (4th ed.). New York: Merrill.

Norton, R. (1995). *Maintaining DACUM quality.* Cleveland, OH: Ohio Regional Educational Service Center.

Numbers and needs: Ethnic and linguistic minorities in the United States. (1991, January). *Wall Street Journal,* p. 2.

Oakes, J. (1986). Tracking inequality and the rhetoric of school reform: Why schools don't change. *Journal of Education, 186,* 61–80.

Ogle, D. (1986). K-W-L: A teaching model that develops active reading of expository text. *Reading Teacher, 39*(7), 564–567.

Olson, D. (1994). Aboriginal literacy: Critical notice. *Interchange, 25*(4), 389–394.

O'Neil, J. (1991). A generation adrift? *Educational Leadership, 49*(1), 4–9.

O'Rourke, J. (1974). *Toward a science of vocabulary development.* The Hague, The Netherlands: Mouton.

Orton, S. T. (1928). Special reading disability—Strephosymbolia. *Journal of American Medical Association, 90,* 1095–1099.

Osborn, J., & Chard, D. (2001). *Guidelines for examining phonics and decoding instruction in early reading programs.* Texas Center for Reading and Language Arts, Texas Education Agency. Austin, TX.

Ostosis, J. (2000). Reading strategies for students with ADD and ADHD in the inclusive classroom. *Preventing School Failure, 43*(3) pp. 7–10.

Palinscar, A. S., & Brown, A. L. (1984). Reciprocal teaching of comprehension-fastening and comprehension-monitoring activities. *Cognition and Instruction, 1*(2), 117–175.

Palinscar, A. S., & Brown, A. L. (1989). Instruction for self-regulated reading. In L. B. Resnick & L. E. Klopfer (Eds.), *Toward the thinking curriculum: Current cognitive research* (pp. 19–39). Alexandria, VA: Association for Supervision & Curriculum Development.

Paradis, E. E., Chatton, B., Boswell, A., Smith, M., & Yovich, S. (1991). Accountability: Assessing comprehension during literature discussion. *Reading Teacher, 45*(1), 8–18.

Paris, S., Calfee, R., Filby, N., Hiebert, E., Pearson, P., Valencia, S., & Wolf, K. (1992). A framework for authentic literacy assessment. *Reading Teacher, 46*(2), 88–99.

Paznik, J. (1976). *The artistic dimension of Black English: A disclosure model and its implications for curriculum and instruction.* Unpublished doctoral dissertation, Columbia University Teachers College, New York, NY.

Pearson, P. D., Barr, R., Kamil, M. L., Mosenthal, P. (Eds.). (1994). *Handbook of reading research.* New York: Longman.

Peck, M., Askov, E. N., & Fairchild, S. H. (1980). Another decade of research in handwriting: Progress and prospect in the 1970s. *Journal of Educational Research, 73,* 283–98.

Peregory, S., & Owen, E. (1993). *Reading, writing and learning in ESL.* New York: Longman.

Perkinson, H. (1991). *The imperfect panacea: American faith in education, 1865–1990.* New York: Random House.

Peterson, M., & Haines, L. (1992). Orthographic analogy training with kindergarten children: Effects on analogy use, phonemic segmentation, and letter-sound knowledge. *Journal of Reading Behavior, 24*(1), 19–29.

Peterson, R. (1992). *Life in a crowded place: Making a learning community.* Portsmouth, NH: Heinemann.

Phelan, P. (1989). *Talking to learn.* Urbana, IL: National Council of Teachers of English.

Phelan, P., Yu, H., & Davidson, A. (1994). Navigating the psychosocial pressures of adolescence: The voices and experiences of high school youth. *American Educational Research Journal, 31*(1), 414–447.

Phinney, M. (1988). *Reading with the troubled reader.* Portsmouth, NH: Heinemann.

Piaget, J. (1967). Language and thought from the genetic point of view. In D. Elkind (Ed.), *Six psychological studies* (p. 154). New York: Random House.

Pierce, K., & Gibbs, C. (1992). *Cycles of meaning.* Portsmouth, NH: Heinemann.

Pikulski, J. (1994, September). Preventing reading failure. *Reading Teacher, 48*(1), 7–12.

Pinnell, G., Lyons, C., DeFord, D., Bryk, A., & Seltzer, M. (1994). Comparing instructional models for the literacy education of high-risk first graders. *Reading Research Quarterly,* 291.

Pinnell, G. S., Fried, M. D., & Estice, R. M. (1991). Reading Recovery: Learning how to make a difference. *Reading Teacher, 43*(4), 282–295.

Pipho, C. (1992). *The impact of a national test at the state level.* Paper presented at AERA annual meeting, San Francisco, CA.

Place, N. (1993). *The effects of literacy portfolios on students, teachers, and parents.* Paper presented at IRA annual meeting, Orlando, FL.

Platt, N. (1994). Grandparents who parent their grandchildren. *Gerontologist, 34*(2), 206–216.

Poole, C. (1997). Maximizing learning: A conversation with Renate Numella Caine. *Educational Leadership, 54,* 13.

Portfolio News. (1990). Newsletter of the UWLM. Santa Monica, CA: UWLM.

Powell, W. (1968). Reappraising the criteria for interpreting informal reading inventories. In D. DeBoer (Ed.), *Reading diagnosis and evaluation.* Newark, DE: IRA.

Powell, W. R., & Dunkeld, C. (1971). Validity of the IRI reading levels. *Elementary English, 48,* 637–642.

Presseisen, B. (1987). *Teaching thinking and at-risk students.* Paper presented at Cross-Laboratory National Conference, Research for Better Schools, Philadelphia.

Pressley, M. (1977). *Mastropieri advances in learning and behavioral disabilities.* Greenwich, CT: JAI Press.

Pressley, M., Allington, R., Wharton-McDonlak, R., Block, C. C., & Morrow, L. (2001). *Learning to read: Lessons from exemplary first grade classrooms.* New York: Guilford.

Pressley, M., & Harris, K. (1990). What we really know about strategy instruction. *Educational Leadership, 48*(1), 319–370.

Pressley, M., Johnson, C. J., Symons, S., McGoldrick, J. A., & Brown, R. (1989). Strategies that improve children's memory and comprehension of text. *Elementary School Journal, 90,* 3–32.

Price, J. (1988, Fall). Diagnosis: Severely emotionally disturbed student. *Insights,* CPC Millwood Hospital, Arlington, TX.

Purcell-Gates, V. (1988). *Can early reading achievement be predicted with traditional learning disabilities tests? A case study.* Reports—Descriptive (141). Cleveland, OH: Ohio State Publicational Center.

Purcell-Gates, V., McIntyre, E., & Freppan, P. (1995). Learning written storybook languages in school: A comparison of Law—SES children in skills-based and whole languages classroom. *American Education Research Journal, 32*(3), 659–685.

Putnam, J., & Markovchick, K. (1989). *Cooperative learning and cooperative staff development to promote social integration.* Augusta: Maine State Department of Education & Cultural Services.

Quintero, E., & Rummel, M. (1993). *Voice unaltered: Marginalized young writers speak.* Duluth: University of Minnesota.

Raetkin, J., Simpson, M., Alvermann, D., & Dishner, E. (1985). Why teachers resist content reading instruction. *Journal of Reading, 28,* 432–437.

Raphael, T., McMahon, S., Goatlez, V., Bentley, J., Boyd, E., Pardo, L., & Woodman, D. (1992). Research directions: Literature and discussion in the reading program. *Language Arts, 69.*

Raphael, T. (1984). Teaching learners about sources of information for answering comprehension questions. *Journal of Reading, 27,* 303–311.

Raphael, T., Florio-Ruane, S., Kehus, M., George, M., Hasty, N., & Highfield, K. (2001). Thinking for ourselves: Literacy learning in a diverse teacher inquiry network. *The Reading Teacher, 54,* 596–607.

Raphael, T. E., & McKinney, J. (1983). An examination of fifth and eighth grade children's question-answering behavior: An instructional study in metacognition. *Journal of Reading Behavior, 15*(3), 67–86.

Rasinski, T., & Padak, N. (1990). Multicultural learning through children's literature. *Language Arts, 67,* 576–580.

Reimer, K. (1992, January). Multicultural literature: Holding fast to dreams. *Language Arts, 69*(1), 14–21.

Reese, L., Garnier, H., Gallimore, R., & Goldenberg, C. (2000). Longitudinal analysis of the antecedents of emergent Spanish literacy and middle school English reading achievement of Spanish-speaking students. *American Educational Research Journal, 37*(3), 633–662.

Reutzel, D., Oda, L., & Moore, B. (1989). Developing print awareness, reading readiness and word reading. *Journal of Reading Behavior, 21,* 197–217.

Reyes, M., Laliberty E., & Orbanosky, J. (1993, December). Emerging biliteracy and cross-cultural sensitivity in a language arts classroom. *Language Arts, 70,* 221–229.

Reyhner, J., & Garcia, R. (1989). Helping minorities read better. *Reading Research & Instruction, 28*(3), 84–91.

Rhodes, L., & Dudley-Manning, C. (1988). *Reading and writing with a difference.* Portsmouth, NH: Heinemann.

Rhodes, L., & Natenson-Mejia, S. (1990). Anecdotal records: A powerful tool for ongoing literacy assessment. *Reading Teacher, 45*(7), 44–48.

Rhodes, L., & Shanklin, N. (1994). *Windows into literacy: Assessing learners K–8.* Portsmouth, NH: Heinemann.

Richards, J., & Gipe, J. (1992). Activating background knowledge. *Reading Teacher, 45*(1), 475.

Rief, L. (1994, February). Writing for life: Language arts in the middle. *Language Arts, 71,* 491–499.

Robinson, H., Faraone, V., Hittleman, D., & Unruh, E. (1990). In J. Fitzgerald (Ed.), *Reading comprehension instruction 1783–1987: A review of trends and research.* Newark, DE: International Reading Association.

Rogers, T. (1991). Students as literary critics: The interpretative experiences, beliefs and processes of elementary grade students. *Journal of Reading Behavior, 23,* 391–423.

Roller, C. (1994). An in-depth comparative analysis of one study from two perspectives. *Reading Research Quarterly, 29*(1), 7–12.

Rose, L. (1992). *The writing cycle.* Unpublished manuscript, Mississippi State University.

Rosenbaum, L. (2001). *Word map approach to vocabulary development.* Boston: Allyn & Bacon.

Rosenblatt, L. (1985). *Literature as exploration* (3rd ed.). New York: Modern Language Association.

Rosenblatt, L. (1988). *Writing and reading: The transactional theory* (Technical Report No. 416). Urbana: University of Illinois Center for the Study of Reading.

Rosenshine, B., & Stevens, R. (1984). Teaching functions. In M. C. Wittrock (Ed.), *Handbook of research on teaching* (3rd ed., pp. 376–391). New York: Macmillan.

Roskos, K. (1992). *Free response with a sketch.* Unpublished manuscript. University Heights, OH: John Carroll University.

Routman, R. (1991). *Invitations: Changing as teachers and learners K–12.* Portsmouth, NH: Heinemann.

Robert, H. (1994). *The impact of a parent involvement program designed to support a first-grade reading intervention program.* Chicago, IL: National Reading Conference Yearbook.

Ruddell, R. (1995). Those influential literacy teachers. *Reading Teacher, 48*(6), 454–463.

Ruddell, R., & Ruddell, M. (1994). *Teaching children to read and write.* Des Moines, IA: Allyn & Bacon.

Ruddell, R. B., & Ruddell, M. R. (1995). Language acquisition and literacy processes. In R. B. Ruddell, M. R. Ruddell, & H. Singer, (Eds.), *Theoretical models and processes of reading* (4th ed., pp. 83–104). Newark, DE: International Reading Association.

Rueda, R., & Garcia, E. (1992). *A comparative study of teachers' beliefs about reading assessment with Latino language minority students.* Santa Cruz: National Center for Cultural Diversity and Second Language Learning, University of California in Santa Cruz.

Ruiz, R. (1993). *The effect of homogenous groupings in mathematics.* Washington, DC: Office of Educational Research and Improvement.

Rumelhart, T. (1976, April). *The interactive model of comprehension.* Paper presented at the annual convention of the American Educational Research Association, New Orleans, LA.

Russell, D., Ousby, O., Wolfing, G., & Haynes, G. (1948–1951). *The Ginn basic readers.* Boston: Ginn.

Sadoski, M., Goetz, E. T., Olivarez, A., Lee, S., & Roberts, N. M. (1990). Imagination in story reading: The role of imagery, verbal recall, story analysis, and processing levels. *Journal of Reading Behavior, 22*(1), 55–70.

Sakiey, E., & Fry, E. (1984). 3,000 *instant words* (2nd ed.). Providence, RI: Jamestown Publications.

Salinger, T. (1992). In C. Collins & J. Mangieri (Eds.), *Teaching thinking.* Hillsdale, NJ: Erlbaum.

Samuels, J. (1979). The method of repeated readings. *Reading Teacher, 32,* 403–408.

Sargent, B. (1991, October). Writing 'Choose Your Own Adventure' stories. *Reading Teacher, 45*(2), 158.

Sawyer, W. (1989). Whole language in context: Insights into the current debate. *Topics in Language Disorders, 11,* 1–13.

Scardamalia, M., & Bereiter, C. (1984). Development of strategies in text processing. In H. Mandl, N. Stein, & T. Trabasso (Eds.), *Learning and comprehension of text* (pp. 379–406). Hillsdale, NJ: Erlbaum.

Scardamalia, M., & Bereiter, C. (1986). Research on written composition. In M. C. Wittrock (Ed.), *Handbook of research on teaching* (3rd ed., pp. 778–803). New York: Macmillan.

Scheid, K. (1991). *Effective writing instruction for students with learning problems.* Washington, DC: Office of Special Education and Rehabilitative Services.

Schloss, P., Smith, M., & Schloss, C. (1995). *Instructional methods for adolescents with learning and behavior problems* (2nd ed.). Boston: Allyn & Bacon.

Schlozman, S., & Schlozman, V. (2000). Chaos in the classroom: Looking at ADHD. *Educational Leadership, 58,* 28–33.

Schneider, B., & Yongsook, L. (1991). School and home environment of East Asian students. *Anthropology and Educational Quarterly, 16*(2) 117–128.

Schultz, J., & Carpenter, C. (1995). *Mainstreaming exceptional students* (3rd ed.). Boston: Allyn & Bacon.

Schunk, D., & Cox, P. (1986). Strategy training and attributional feedback with learning disabled students. *Journal of Educational Psychology, 78,* 201–209.

Schunk, D., & Rice, J. (1991). Learning goals and progress feedback during reading comprehension instruction. *Journal of Reading Behavior, 23*(3).

Scruggs, T., & Mastropieri, M. (1994). The case for mnemonic instruction: From laboratory research to classroom applications. *Journal of Special Education, 24*(1), 7–32.

Shands, E., Deines, S., & Zuckerman, M. (1994). *Creative dramatics as a remedial reading technique.* Unpublished research paper. Minneapolis, MN: University of Minnesota.

Shannon, D. (1991). *Teacher evaluation: A functional approach.* Paper presented at the 14th annual meeting of Eastern Educational Research Association, Boston, MA.

Shapiro, J., Ogden, M., & Lind-Blad, A. (1990). Auditory perceptual processing in reading disabled children. *Journal of Research in Reading, 13*(2), 123–132.

Shaughnessey, M. (1994, March). Educating for understanding: An interview with H. Gardner, J. Siegel, & M. Siegel. *Phi Delta Kappan, 75*(7), 81–89.

Shefelbine, J. (1990). Student factors related to variability in learning word meanings from context. *Journal of Reading Behavior, 22,* 71–97.

Shepard, L. (1991). Will national tests improve students' learning? *Phi Delta Kappan, 73,* 232–238.

Shepard, L. (1992). Negative policies for dealing with diversity. In E. Hiebert (Ed.), *Literacy for a diverse society* (pp. 279–299). New York: Teachers College Press.

Short, K., & Armstrong, J. (1993, Summer). Moving toward inquiry: Integrating literature into the science curriculum. *The New Advocate, 6*(3).

Short, R., Kane, M., & Peeling, T. (2000). Retooling the reading lesson: Matching the right tools to the job. *The Reading Teacher, 54,* 284–295.

Shuy, R. (1987). Dialogue as the heart of learning. *Language Arts, 64,* 890–897.

Slavin, R. (1990). Point–counterpoint: Ability grouping, cooperative learning and the gifted. *Journal for the Education of the Gifted, 14,* 3–8.

Slavin, R., Karweit, N., & Madden, N. (Eds.). (1989). *Effective programs for students at risk.* Boston: Allyn & Bacon.

Slavin, R., Madden, N., Karweit, N., Dolan, L., & Wasik, B. (1991). Research directions: Success for all: Ending reading failure from the beginning. *Language Arts, 68,* 404–409.

Smey-Richman, B. (1988). *Involvement in learning for low-achieving students.* Philadelphia: Research for Better Schools.

Smith, D. (1987). Talking with young children about their reading. *Australian Journal of Reading, 10*(2), 120–123.

Smith, F. (1971). *Understanding reading.* New York: Holt, Rinehart & Winston.

Smith, E. (1977). Making sense out of reading instruction. *Harvard Educational Review, 47,* 386–395.

Smith, F. (1984). Myth of writing. *Language Arts, 58*(8), 792–798.

Smith, F. (1985). *Reading without nonsense.* New York: Teachers College Press.

Smith, M. (1989). *The role of external testing in elementary schools.* Los Angeles: Center for Research on Evaluations, Standards and Student Testing, UCLA.

Smitherman, G. (1977). *Talking and testifying.* Boston: Houghton Mifflin.

Smitherman-Donaldson, G., Daniel, J., & Jeremiah, M. (1987). 'Makin a way outa no way': The proverb tradition in the Black experience. *Journal of Black Studies, 17*(3), 14–26.

Snow, C., & Ninio, A. (1986). The contracts of literacy: What children learn from learning to read books. In W. Teale & E. Sulzby (Eds.), *Emergent literacy, writing and reading* (pp. 116–138). Norwood, NJ: Ablex.

Snow, R., & Lohman, D. (1984). Toward a theory of cognitive aptitude for learning from instruction. *Journal of Educational Psychology, 76,* 347–376.

Sottle, J. (1987, July/August). Developing students' interest. *Learning,* 345–350.

Stahl, S. (1994). Saying the "p" word: Nine guidelines for exemplary phonics instruction. *Reading Teacher, 45,* 618–625.

Stahl, S. A., & Fairbanks, M. M. (1986). The effects of vocabulary instruction: A model-based meta-analysis. *Review of Educational Research, 56,* 72–110.

Standards and Assessment Development and Implementation Council of the State of Colorado. (1995).

Stanovich, K. (1980). Toward an interactive compensatory model of individual differences in development of reading fluency. *Reading Research Quarterly, 16,* 32–71.

Stanovich, K. (1985). Cognitive determinants of reading in mentally retarded individuals. In N. R. Ellis & N. W. Bray (Eds.), *International review of research in mental retardation* (pp. 181–214). New York: Academic Press.

Stanovich, K. (1986). Matthew effects in reading: Some consequences of individual differences in the acquisition of literacy. *Reading Research Quarterly, 21,* 360–407.

Stanovich, K. (1991). Word recognition: Changing perspectives. In R. Barr, M. Kamil, P. Mosenthal, & P. Pearson (Eds.), *Handbook of reading research* (pp. 418–452). White Plains, NY: Longman.

Stanovich, K. (1993). It's practical to be rational. *Journal of Learning Disabilities, 26*(8), 524–532.

Staton, J. (1982). Writing and counseling: Using a dialogue journal. *Language Arts, 57,* 514–518.

Stauffer, R. (1969). *Direct reading and thinking approach.* Urbana, IL: National Council of Teachers of English.

Stein, B., & Kirby, J. (1992). The effects of text-absent and text-present conditions on summarization and recall of text. *Journal of Reading Behavior, 24*(2).

Stern, J. (Ed.). (1994). *The condition of education in rural schools.* Washington, DC: U.S. Department of Education.

Sternberg, R., & Lubert, T. (1991). Creativity reconsidered. *Educational Researcher, 20*(8), 4–14.

Stetson, E. (1985). A perspective on evaluating spelling programs. *Guides for the Classroom Teacher,* (52). Austin: Texas Education Agency.

Stevens, R. J., Madden, N. A., Slavin, R. W., & Farnish, A. M. (1987). Cooperative integrated reading and composition: Two field experiments. *Reading Research Quarterly, 22*(4), 433–454.

Stevens, R. R., & Slavin, R. E. (1995). The cooperative elementary school: Effects on students' achievement, attitudes, and social relations. *American Educational Research Journal, 32*(2), 321–351.

Stevenson Learning Skills. (2000). *Clearing up your students' confusion about* b *and* d. Retrieved December 10, 2000, from www.stevensonsemple.com.

Stiles, G. (1991). *With promise: Redefining reading and writing for special students.* Portsmouth, NH: Heinemann.

Stipek, D. (1982). *Motivation to learn: From theory to practice.* Englewood Cliffs, NJ: Prentice-Hall.

Stotsky, S. L. (1989). *Differences in search process between high school and college seniors, and a comparison with search process of students who have difficulty writing.* Paper presented at the American Educational Research Association annual meeting, New Orleans, LA.

Strommen, E. (1994). *Interactive technology research report.* New York: International Business Machines.

Sulzby, E., Branz, C., & Buhle, R. (1993). Repeated readings of literature and low socioeconomic status black kindergartners and first graders. *Reading and Writing Quarterly, 9,* 183–196.

Surace, E. (1992). Everyone wants to join the chorus. *Phi Delta Kappan,* 608.

Svotlovskaya, N. (1992, May 18). *Children who do not read well.* Moscow, Russia: University of Moscow. Paper presented to U.S. Citizen Ambassadors Reading Delegation.

Swain, S. (1994). *How portfolios empower process teaching and learning.* Portsmouth, NH: Heinemann.

Taylor, B., Harris, L. A., Pearson, P. D., & Garcia, G. (1995). *Reading difficulties: Instruction and assessment* (2nd ed.). New York: McGraw-Hill.

Taylor, D., & Dorsey-Gaines, C. (1988). *Growing up literate: Learning from inner-city families.* Portsmouth, NH: Heinemann.

Teale, W. (1986). Home background and young children's literacy development. In W. H. Teale & E. Sulzby (Eds.), *Emergent literacy: Writing and reading* (pp. 173–206). Norwood, NJ: Ablex.

Teale, W., & Sulzby, E. (1986). *Emergent literacy. Writing and reading.* Norwood, NJ: Ablex.

Teale, W., & Sulzby, E. (1987). Literacy acquisition in early childhood: The roles of access and mediation in storybook reading. In D. A. Wagner (Ed.), *The future of literacy in a changing world.* New York: Pergamon.

Templeton, S. (1992, October). New trends in an historical perspective: Old story, new resolution—sound and meaning in spelling. *Language Arts, 69,* 263–280.

Texas Education Agency. (1994). *Characteristics of at-risk youth.* Austin: Texas Education Agency Practitioner's Guide Series Number One.

Texas Education Agency. (2000). *Beginning reading instruction: Texas reading initiative.* Austin: Texas Education Agency.

Thirteen Mental Measurement Yearbook. (2002). Lincoln: Buros Institute of Mental Measurements, University of Nebraska.

Thomas, B. (1993). *Program created by the center for slower learning students.* Dallas, TX: Center for Slower Learning Students.

Thomas, S., & Oldfather, P. (1995). Enhancing student and teacher engagement in literacy learning. *Reading Teacher, 49*(3), 192–202.

Tiedt, P., & Tiedt, I. (1995). *Multicultural teaching: A handbook of activities, information and resources* (4th ed.). Boston: Allyn & Bacon.

Tonnessen, F. E. (1995). Literacy in Norway. *Journal of Adolescent & Adult Literacy, 39*(3), 244–246.

Toomey, D. (1993). Parents hearing their children read. *Educational Research, 35,* 223–236.

Topping, K., & Whiteley, M. (1990). Participation evaluation of parent tutored and peer tutored projects in reading. *Educational Research, 32,* 14–27.

Travers, R. (1982). *Essentials of learning: The new cognitive learning of students in education.* New York: Macmillan.

Treiman, R. (1988). The role of intrasyllabic units in learning to read and spell. In P. Gough (Ed.), *Learning to read.* Hillsdale, NJ: Erlbaum.

Trueba, H. (1987). *Success or failure.* Cambridge, MA: Newbury.

Trueba, H. (1989). *Raising silent voice: Educating the linguistic minorities for the twenty-first century.* New York: Harper & Row.

Turner, A., & Paris, S. (1995). How literacy tasks influence children's motivation for literacy. *Reading Teacher, 48*(8), 662–673.

Turner, J. (1995). A motivational perspective on literacy instruction. In D. Lew and C. Kinzer (Eds.), *Examining central issues in literacy research, theory & practice.* Forty-fifth yearbook of the NRC. Chicago: National Research Conference.

Uhry, J., & Sheperd, M. (1993). Segmentation/spelling instruction as part of a first-grade reading program. *Reading Research Quarterly, 28*(3), 219–233.

U.S. Census Bureau. (2000). *Data concerning education in the United States.* Washington, DC: U.S. Department of Education.

U.S. Department of Education. (2002). *No child left behind.* Washington, DC: U.S. Department of Education.

U.S. Department of Labor. (1994). *Wager earnings to related to education levels. Report 173.* Washington, DC: U.S. Department of Labor.

Valencia, S. (1990). A portfolio approach to classroom reading assessment: The whys, whats, and hows. *Reading Teacher, 43,* 338–342.

Valencia, S., Hiebert, E., & Afflerbach, P. (1994). *Authentic reading assessment.* Newark, DE: International Reading Association.

Venezky, M. (1994). *Getting to know the world's greatest artists.* Chicago: Children's Press.

Vickery, K., Reynolds, C., & Cochran, J. (1987). Multisensory teaching approach for reading, spelling, and handwriting: Orton-Gillingham based curriculum. *Annuals of Dyslexia, 37,* 189–200.

Villaume, S. (1994). Developing literate voices: The challenges of whole languages. *Language Arts,* 460–468.

Voss, M. (1993). "I Just Watched": Family influences on one child's learning. *Language Arts, 70,* 639.

Vukelich, C. (1993, September). Play: A contest for exploring the functions, features, and meaning of writing with peers. *Language Arts, 70,* 111–120.

Vygotsky, L. (1962). *Thought and language.* Cambridge, MA: MIT Press.

Vygotsky, L. (1978). *Mind and society.* Cambridge, MA: MIT Press.

Vygotsky, L. (1986). *Thought and language* (rev. ed.). Translated by Alex Kozulin. Cambridge, MA: MIT Press.

Wagner, B. (1994). *Drama as a learning medium.* Washington, DC: National Education Association.

Walberg, H., & Tsai, S. (1983). Matthew effects in education. *American Educational Research Journal, 20,* 359–373.

Walker, B. (1992). *Supporting struggling readers.* Markham, Ontario: Pippin.

Walmsley, S. (1992). State of elementary literature instruction. *Language Arts, 69*(7), 508–514.

Walmsley, S., & Walp, T. (1990). Integrating literature and composing into language arts curriculum. *Elementary School Journal, 90,* 251–274.

Walsh, D. (1988). Critical thinking to reduce prejudice. *Social Education, 52*(4), 280–282.

Walvoord, B., & Singer, D. (1984). *Process-oriented writing instruction in a case-method class.* Paper presented at the annual meeting of the American Management Association, Boston, MA.

Walz, G., & Bleuer, J. (1992). *Students' self-esteem: A vital element of school success.* Ann Arbor, MI: Counseling and Personnel Services.

Wasik, B. A., & Slavin, R. E. (1990). *Preventing early reading failure with one-to-one tutoring: A best evidence synthesis.* Baltimore: Johns Hopkins University, Center for Research on Effective Schooling for Disadvantaged Students.

Watkins, E. (1922). *How to teach silent reading to beginners.* Chicago: Lippincott.

Wattenberg, W., & Clifford, C. (1966). *Relationship of self-concept to beginning achievement in reading.* (U.S. Office of Education, Cooperative Research Project No. 377). Detroit: Wayne State University.

Weaver, C., & Kintsch, W. (1991). Expository text. In R. Barr, M. Kamil, P. Mosenthal, & P. Pearson (Eds.), *Handbook of reading research* (Vol. 2, pp. 230–245). New York: Longman.

Weiner, B. (1980). Attribution principles. In J. Leving & M. Wong (Eds.), *Teachers and student perceptions.* Hillsdale, NJ: Erlbaum.

Weiner, B. (1983). *Human motivation.* New York: Holt, Rinehart & Winston.

Weiner, B. (1986). *An attributional theory of motivation and emotion.* New York: Springer Verlag.

West, J., & Oldfeather, P. (1993, September). On working together: An imaginary dialogue among real children. *Language Arts, 70,* 54.

Whimbey, A. (1984). The key to higher order-thinking is precise processing. *Educational Leadership, 42*(1), 66–70.

White, E. (1952). *Charlotte's Web.* New York: Harper & Row.

White, S. (1989). *Teaching and assessing writing* (2nd ed.). San Francisco: Jossey-Bass.

White, S. (1990). *Teachers' Forum.* New York: Scholastic.

Wilde, J. (1993). *A door opens: Writing in the fifth grade.* Portsmouth, NH: Heinemann.

Wilde, S. (1992). *You Kan Red This! Spelling and punctuation for whole language classrooms, K–6.* Portsmouth, NH: Heinemann.

Willinsky, J. (1990). *The new literacy.* New York: Routledge.

Winograd, P. (1994). Developing alternative assessments: Six problems worth solving. *Reading Teacher, 47*(5), 420–424.

Witkin, H., Moore, C., Goodenough, D., & Cox, P. (1977). Field-dependent and field-independent cognitive styles and their educational implications. *Review of Educational Research, 47,* 1–64.

Wittrock, M., & Alesandrini, K. (1990). Generation of summaries and analogies and analytic and holistic abilities. *American Educational Research Journal, 27,* 489–502.

Wlodkowski, R. (1986). *Motivation and teaching: A practical guide.* Washington, DC: National Education Association.

Wong, B. (1987). How do the results of metacognitive research impact on the learning disabled individual? *Learning Disability Quarterly, 10,* 189–195.

Worcester, S. (1828). *Primer of the English language.* Boston: J. T. and E. B. Buckingham.

Worthy, J. (1996). A matter of interest: Literature that hooks reluctant readers and keeps them reading. *The Reading Teacher, 50,* 204–212.

Worthy, J. (2000). Conducting research on topics of student interest. *The Reading Teacher, 54,* 298–299.

Yaden, D., Smolkin, L., & Conlon, A. (1989). Preschoolers' questions about pictures, print conventions and story text during read alouds at home. *Reading Research Quarterly, 24,* 188–214.

Yao, E. (1991). Adjustment needs of Asian immigrant children. *Elementary School Guidance and Counseling, 19*(1), 222–227.

Yolen, P. (1994). The story between. *Language Arts, 62*(6), 590–592.

Zane, N., Li-tze Hu, W., & Jung-Hye, K. (1991). Asian-American assertion. *Journal of Counseling Psychology, 38*(1), 63–70.

Zarnowski, M. (1991). An interview with author Nicholas Mohr. *Reading Teacher, 45*(2), 100–106.

Zieme, N. (2000). *Stevenson and sample learning programs.* Fort Worth: Texas Christian University, Paper presented at the Green Honor's Chair Conference, November 17, 2000.

Zimmerman, W. (1994). Teaching immigrants English. *Migration World Magazine, 22*(2–3), 13–16.

NAME INDEX

Readers *(continued)*
  levels of affect in, 83–84
  remedial, 1–27
  social and cultural richness in,
    104–135
Reader-selected miscues, 309–310
Readers' Theater, 423
Reading. *See also* Choral reading
  addressing dyslexia and
    neurologically correctable
    difficulties in, 477–478
  aesthetic, 48
  antiphonal, 445
  assisted, 218
  buddy system for, 204, 213–214
  comprehension in, 46–47,
    319–355
  early intervention programs in,
    478–489
  efferent, 48
  increasing fluency in oral,
    442–448
  with interrupted meaning-
    making, 4
  overcoming emotional and
    attentional barriers to,
    pleasure-filled, 473–474
  proficiency in, 4
  recognizing disabilities in, 36–37
  refrain, 445
  remedial, 5
  repeated, 25, 218, 445, 447, 448
  resources for alternative
    programs to improve, 58
  round-robin, 202
  self-selected, 190, 202
  three- or four-part, 445
  unison, 444
  word-by word, 4
Reading consultants, 6
Reading Continuum Checklist,
  187–189
Reading diagnosticians, 6
Reading Expectancy Age (R Exp
  Age), 460
Reading failure, response to, 83
Reading instruction. *See also*
    Instruction; Literacy
    instruction
  resources for alternative
    programs in, 58
  for struggling readers, 41–43
Reading Is Fundamental (RIF)
  program, 372
Reading levels, determining, from
  an IRI, 165–167
Reading miscue inventories (RMIs),
  168–169

Reading readiness, emergent literacy
  versus, 231–233
Reading Recovery, 482–487
Reading response groups, 209–211
  assessing reluctant reader's
    participation in discussions,
    212
Reading workshops, 209
REAL Enterprises (Rural
    Entrepreneurship through
    Action Learning), 125–126
Rebus stories, 239, 241–242
Reciprocal teaching, 25, 345–346
Recurring principle, 234–235
Referral process, 457
Reflecting questions, 21
Reflective, expert reading and
    distinguished writing, 4–5
Refrain reading, 445
Reliability, 143, 151
Reluctant readers. *See also* Emergent
    readers; Struggling readers
  assessing participation of, in
    reading response group
    discussions, 212
  strategies for, in class discussions,
    13
Reluctant writers, 359–388. *See also*
    Emergent writers
  diagnosing and assessing,
    381–384
  encouraging creativity in,
    380–381
  first-draft writing for, 367–376
  prewriting stage for, 364–367
  revising stage for, 377–380
  tier 1–4 supports for, 360–364
Remedial readers, 1–27. *See also*
    Reluctant readers; Struggling
    readers
Remedial reading, 5
Repeated readings, 25, 218, 445, 447,
  448
  chart for, 447
Research groups, 214–215
Resources, providing, for home,
  246–250
Resource teachers, 6
Response groups, 40
Retellings, 171–174
Reverse think alouds, 348
Revising, 377–380
  connections and transitions in,
    379
  feedback in, 379–380
  self-questioning in, 378–379
  stages in, 377–378
Rhymes, 291

Round-robin reading, 202
Running records, 169–171
Rural cultures, students from,
  124–126

Scaffolding, 18–19, 21, 84
Schema, 14, 71
  differences in, 71–75
  innate intelligence and, 73–75
Schizophrenic disorder, 473
School, bringing home to, 250–252
School-day scheduling, 40
Scribble/doodle boards, 369–370
Scribble stage of writing, 395
Secondary school readers, different
    versions of fairy tales for, 23
Second-language learners
  instructional activities for for,
    436–442
  program models for, 427
  speaking difficulties for, 426–433
  speaking needs of, diagnosing,
    428–429
  using graduated books with,
    21–23
Self-appraisal, 181
Self-assessments, 181, 183–184
  procedures for, 183
Self-concept of student, 83
Self-corrections, 164–165
Self-efficacy, 82
Self-esteem, building literacy,
  85–87
Self-initiated, value-filled meaning-
  making, 321
Self-monitoring, explaining
    metacognitions and, 347–348
Self-questioning, 378–379
Self-regulation, 181
Self-selected reading, 190
Self-selected silent reading times,
  scheduling, 202
Semantic context clues, 276–282
Semantic maps, 326–327, 365
Semantics, 45
Semiphonetic stage of spelling, 395
Sentences
  concept of, 237
  transformation of, 408
  transforming, 281–282
  writing richer, 376
Sequence reading, 444
Serial books, 72–73
Shared readings, modified, 425–426
Sheltered English, 427
Sight word knowledge, diagnosis
    and instructional interventions
    to build, 268